MW00716873

ACAPULCO
IXTAPA & ZIHUATANEJO

BRUCE WHIPPERMAN

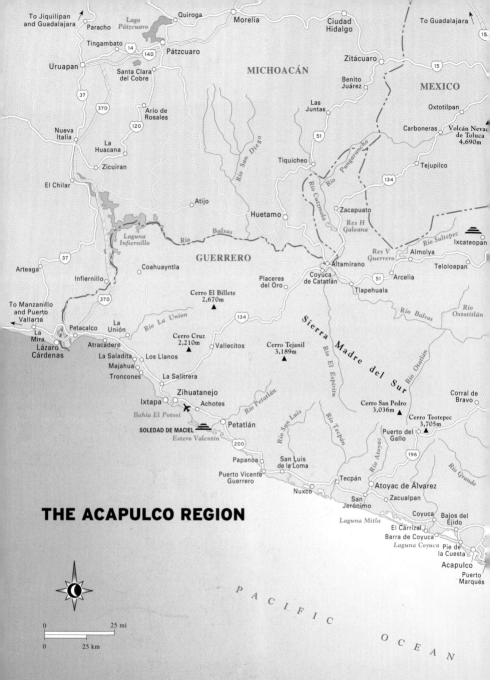

To Jiquilpan and Guadalajara

Paracho

Lago Pátzcuaro

Quiroga

Morelia

Ciudad Hidalgo

To Guadalajara

15

Tingambato

14

Pátzcuaro

Zitácuaro

15

Uruapan

14D

MICHOACÁN

Benito Juárez

MEXICO

Santa Clara del Cobre

Oxtotilpan

37

37D

Ario de Rosales

Las Juntas

51

Tiquicheo

Carboneras

Volcán Nevado de Toluca 4,690m

Nueva Italia

120

La Huacana

Tejupilco

134

Zicuiran

Río San Diego

Atijo

Huetamo

Zacapuato

Río Panigaranche

Río Cutzmala

Res H Galeana

El Chilar

Río Balsas

Laguna Infiernillo

GUERRERO

Ixcateopan

37

Arteaga

Coahuayntla

Placeres del Oro

Altamirano

Res V Guerrero

Río Sultepec

Almolya

Teloloapan

Infiernillo

Cerro El Billete 2,670m

Coyuca de Catatlán

51

Arcelia

37D

To Manzanillo and Puerto Vallarta

Petacalco

La Unión

Río La Unión

134

Tlapehuala

Río Balsas

Río Oxtotitlán

La Mira

Lázaro Cárdenas

Atracadero

Cerro Cruz 2,210m

Vallecitos

Cerro Tejanil 3,189m

Sierra Madre del Sur

Río El Espíritu

Río Otatlán

La Saladita

Los Llanos

Majahua

Troncones

La Salitrera

Zihuatanejo

Achotes

Río Petatlán

Cerro San Pedro 3,036m

Corral de Bravo

Ixtapa

Bahía El Potosí

Petatlán

Cerro Teotepec 3,705m

SOLEDAD DE MACIEL

Estero Valentín

200

Río San Luis

Río Tecpán

Río Atoyac

Puerto del Gallo

196

Papanoa

San Luis de la Loma

Río Grande

Puerto Vicente Guerrero

Nuxco

Tecpán

San Jerónimo

Zacualpan

Atoyac de Álvarez

Coyuca

Bajos del Éjido

THE ACAPULCO REGION

Laguna Mitla

El Carrizal

Barra de Coyuca

Laguna Coyuca

Pie de la Cuesta

Acapulco

Puerto Marqués

25 mi

25 km

P A C I F I C   O C E A N

DISCOVER ACAPULCO, IXTAPA & ZIHUATANEJO

The worldwide renown of Acapulco, Ixtapa and Zihuatanejo, Mexico's south-seas resort trio, less than four hours by direct air south of the border, is more deserved now than ever. Acapulco, associated worldwide with visions of good food, gala parties, and palm-shaded beaches, and the plumy petite resort pair of Ixtapa and Zihuatanejo are simply irresistible for both a legion of Mexican vacationers and a fresh international generation of lovers of Mexico.

Acapulco, the planet's original world-class tropical resort, still shines as much as it always has: by day, beside its emerald-green, half-moon bay, and by night, with a gleaming galaxy of twinkling city lights. Along the same shoreline, less than half a day northwest by car or bus, lie Ixtapa and Zihuatanejo. Ixtapa is fashionably modern and brilliant white at sunrise on its creamy golden sands; neighboring Zihuatanejo still resembles the old-Mexico fishing village that once

Decorations hang outside the Mochitlán church.

slumbered (and sometimes still does) beside its diminutive crescent-shaped bay.

The appeal of Acapulco, Ixtapa, and Zihuatanejo has expanded beyond their city limits, overflowing into the region that encompasses virtually the entire state of Guerrero. On the northwest coast, around Ixtapa and Zihuatanejo, visitors are discovering the delights of relaxing getaways, including lots of reading, snoozing in hammocks, wildlife-viewing, and beachcombing in small resorts such as Troncones, Barra de Potosí, and Playa Escondida. On the region's southeastern side, around Acapulco and beyond, the same is true at the small, refreshingly downscale beach resorts of El Carrizal, Pie de la Cuesta, and Playa Ventura.

Farther southeast, including towns bordering the state of Oaxaca, travelers who enjoy tracing paths less traveled can explore Guerrero's indigenous and African-Mexican heartlands. At colorful village markets, where Spanish is a foreign tongue, travelers can enjoy a bit of

On the beach in Troncones, any time seems like hammock time. © BRUCE WHIPPERMAN person-to-person bargaining with indigenous Mixtec- and Amusgo-speaking villagers in the towns of Ometepec and Xochistlahuaca. Similarly, in the nearby municipality of Cuajinicuilapa, visitors can stroll the bustling town market and visit Guerrero's African-Mexican museum and community center.

Although most visitors come for the beach diversions, comfortable hotels, and tasty food, Acapulco, Ixtapa, and Zihuatanejo offer much more, including a treasury of fetching for-sale handicrafts, an inviting menu of outdoor diversions, and a number of fascinating ancient archaeological sites. To name a few, travelers can explore a park of petroglyphs within sight of downtown Acapulco itself, the 3000-year old lost Olmec city of Teopantecuantlán, ancient Olmec cave paintings, and a submarine rock wall that is speculated to have been built around A.D. 1400 by Zihuatanejo's king as part of his royal bathing resort.

As for colonial history, Acapulco ranks as one of Mexico's earliest colonial cities, whose founding predates the Pilgrims at Plymouth Rock by nearly a century. The past blooms in old Acapulco at the

a remarkable bas relief on the Pyramid of Quetzalcoatl at Xochicalco historic banyan-shaded old town plaza and peaks at the bastion of colonial Acapulco, Fuerte San Diego. The fort still stands, like a sentinel of old, proudly overlooking Acapulco's inner harbor shore where it guarded the Chinese gold, silk, and porcelain treasures of the fabled Manila Galleon against a dozen generations of English, Dutch, and French pirates.

Visitors seeking natural diversions can explore the region's hidden beaches (some right within the city limits of Acapulco, Ixtapa, and Zihuatanejo); enjoy brilliant sunsets to their heart's delight; camp, surf, beachcomb, and fish on wild, open-ocean strands; and view grand flocks of seabirds, either on the beach or by boat or kayak on broad mangrove lagoons.

The shoreline alone would be enough for adventure-seeking travelers, but within a half-day's highway travel lay the oak- and pine-tufted highland valleys. Here the museums and monuments of historic colonial-revolutionary towns of Chilpancingo and Iguala, not unlike Philadelphia and Boston to Americans, stand as virtual shrines to Mexican independence. Not far from these centers a host

the colorful and delicate hand embroidery of San Pedro Amusgos
© BRUCE WHIPPERMAN

of active diversions reward travelers willing to spend a few days venturing north of Acapulco, which offers the possibility of exploring the monumental limestone caverns of Cacahuamilpa and Juxtlahuaca, basking in the crystalline springs of the Río Azul, rafting the rapids of the Río Papagayo, exploring ancient lost cities, and selecting from a treasury of handicrafts.

Finally, all visitors' trails seem to lead to Taxco, the celebrated silver-rich colonial gem of the Sierra, set on the slope of a towering mountain. Here, join the many, mostly Mexican folks, who love strolling Taxco's narrow winding lanes, decorated with the baroque monuments of its opulent past. Along the way, you can select from handcrafted silver jewelry and fascinating masks, assortments of flowers, baskets, pottery, and much more.

As you can see, the road to enjoying the manifold delights of Acapulco, Ixtapa and Zihuatanejo, and the surrounding regions is open and easy to follow. Whichever you prefer, be it glamour and luxury, the offbeat and rustic, or a little bit of both, this book will show the way.

Patience is sometimes necessary on Acapulco backcountry roads.

Contents

MAP CONTENTS

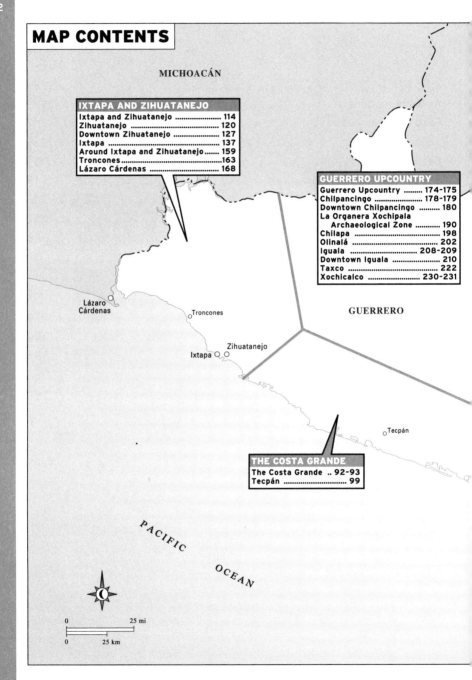

MICHOACÁN

Lázaro
Cárdenas

Troncones

GUERRERO

Zihuatanejo

Ixtapa

Tecpán

PACIFIC

OCEAN

| 0 | | 25 mi |
| 0 | | 25 km |

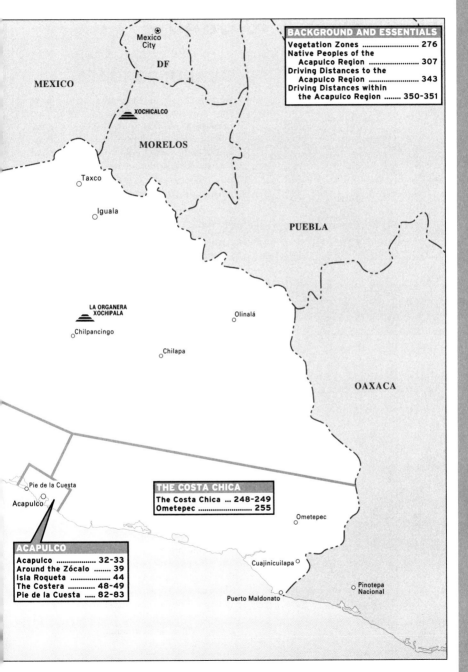

MEXICO

Mexico City ⊛

DF

XOCHICALCO

MORELOS

Taxco ○

Iguala ○

PUEBLA

LA ORGANERA
XOCHIPALA

Olinalá ○

○ Chilpancingo

Chilapa ○

OAXACA

○ Pie de la Cuesta

Acapulco ○

Ometepec ○

Cuajinicuilapa ○

○ Pinotepa
Nacional

Puerto Maldonato ○

The Lay of the Land

ACAPULCO

Acapulco has been reinventing itself for more than a decade. Many of Acapulco's original hostelries, renowned for their perches on the palmy, golden beachfront, have been refurbished and now welcome a new generation of lovers of Acapulco. Moreover, Acapulco's most precious resource, its azure offshore waters, once less than pristine, are once again clean and clear. A glittering line-up of new restaurants, clubs, and shopping plazas now decorate the newest, east, side of the Acapulco Bay beachfront.

But that's only part of the story; old Acapulco, the intimate colonial-era neighborhood that nestles around Acapulco's historic westside cove, is now being discovered by a fresh host of tropical travelers.

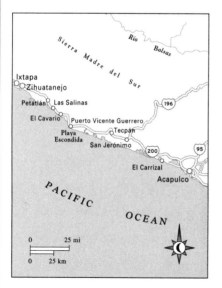

THE COSTA GRANDE

The Costa Grande, the state of Guerrero's "Big Coast," extends northwest along the 150-mile (242 km) stretch of Highway 200 from Acapulco to Ixtapa and Zihuatanejo. Here you can enjoy tropical country Mexico at its purest, with groves of swaying coconut palms; wildlife-rich mangrove lagoons, seemingly endless beaches, market towns, and a sprinkling of mini-resorts.

Moving northwest from Acapulco, Highway 200 crosses the many creeks and rivers that flow southward from the Sierra Madre. These streams, often muddy torrents in the wet summer, shrink to clear trickles in the dry late fall and winter, when they fill a host of coastal lagoons with clear fresh water.

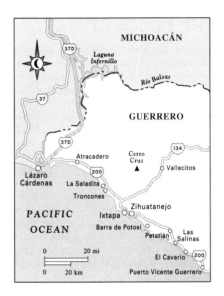

IXTAPA AND ZIHUATANEJO

Despite its gradual upscale shift, Zihuatanejo, with its plumy, *lancha*-lined beachfront and pedestrian-friendly downtown, still resembles the original fishing village, while Ixtapa, its highrise cousin-resort five miles to the northwest, appeals to those who prefer something fashionably up-to-date.

The popularity of Ixtapa and Zihuatanejo has led to the discovery of country charms outside the town limits, such as Troncones, about 20 miles (32 km) northwest of Ixtapa, and, on the opposite, southeast side, about 15 miles (24 km) from Zihuatanejo, a growing number of visitors seek heaven on earth in Barra de Potosí village.

GUERRERO UPCOUNTRY

Visitors who travel north of Acapulco, away from the tropical coast enter an older, more traditional domain where, in towns such as Chilpancingo (the Guerrero state capital) and Iguala (the former state capital), a big piece of the rich tapestry of Mexican history was woven.

Traveling from south to north, you first arrive at River Country. Farther north is the valley of the crystalline blue Río Azul, the town of Chilapa and Taxco, Mexico's celebrated, charmingly picturesque silver capital. Out of town must-sees include the monumental duo of the Grutas de Cacahuamilpa limestone cavern complex and the legendary Xochicalco archaeological site.

THE COSTA CHICA

Highway 200, which heads out of Acapulco virtually due east (note that the ocean lies on the south side), traverses the so-called Costa Chica (Little Coast) along 200 miles, into the far southern state of Oaxaca.

The town of Ometepec, about 110 miles east of Acapulco, is where you'll begin to brush shoulders with lots of Costa Chica indigenous people, most of whom will be speaking the Amusgo language. Southeast of Ometepec, you'll begin to meet a majority of African-Mexican people in the lively main market town of Cuajinicuilapa.

From Cuajinicuilapa, a country road heads south to the laid-back coastal fishing hamlet of Puerto Maldonado. Another hour east you enter the mixed Amusgo and Mixtec country of Oaxaca and the mid-sized town of Pinotepa Nacional.

Planning Your Trip

Clearly it would take at least two busy months to enjoy all the highlights that Acapulco, Ixtapa, Zihuatanejo, and their environs offer. Best save something for your next trip and plan a strategy that fits your time available, such as pairing the itineraries 10-Day Best of Acapulco and Guerrero Upcountry and 10-Day Best of Ixtapa, Zihuatanejo, and the Costa Grande.

WHEN TO GO

Although temperatures and rainfall are crucial in deciding when to visit Acapulco, Ixtapa, and Zihuatanejo, they don't tell the whole story. Crowds, high-priced high seasons, and low-priced low seasons are also factors. The first thing to consider is that the Acapulco region has two sharply defined seasons: wet summer-fall and dry winter-spring. For folks arriving from the U.S. West Coast, the summer contrast is sharp. The change from dust-dry California in August to the tropical-moist Acapulco region can be exotically refreshing.

Some people say that the Acapulco region is too hot in the summer. This, however, isn't necessarily the case. In fact, increased summer cloud cover and showers can actually push average daily July, August, and September temperatures lower than bright and clear April, May, and June. And being near the coast, Acapulco nights never get warmer than balmy, even during the summer.

The other advantage to visiting in summer is the vegetation. If you like lush, green landscapes, the summer–fall may be your season. This is true everywhere, but especially in the highlands, where myriads of multicolored wildflowers decorate the roadsides, and the clouds seem to billow into a 1,000-mile-high blue sky.

By contrast, during the admittedly sunnier and more temperate winter, by February it hasn't rained for months. In natural areas trees are bare of leaves, grass is brown, and cacti seem to be the only green plants. The landscape continues to be dry and dusty during February through April, turning hot in April and May, until the rains arrive and green breaks out again by late June.

Crowding and high prices are another factor. If you want to avoid both, don't go to the Acapulco region resorts during the high Christmas to New Year's rush (Dec. 20–Jan. 3) or the Semana Santa pre-Easter week up through and including Easter Sunday.

Well, then when should you go? If you shun crowds but like the sunny, temperate winter, January, a low-occupancy mini-season, is a good bet, especially on the beach. The landscape still retains some green and hotels often offer discounts.

October through mid-December is also a good time to go. Hotel prices are cheapest, the landscape is lush and green, beaches are beautifully uncrowded, and it's cooler and not as rainy as July, August, and September. Although the first two weeks in October may still be a little too empty for folks who enjoy lots of company, the pace picks up by mid-October and continues through mid-December, when moderate temperatures, blue skies, low prices, and enough company create the best of all possible worlds in the Acapulco region.

HOW TO GO

Most Acapulco-, Ixtapa-, and Zihuatanejo-bound travelers go by regularly scheduled airlines (in approximate four-hour flights, some seasonal) from certain U.S. and Canadian gateways. At this writing, the major Acapulco-direct gateways are Phoenix (America West Airlines), Tijuana (Aviacsa), Dallas (American), Houston (Continental), and Chicago (Mexicana). For Ixtapa-Zihuatanejo direct, the gateways are Phoenix (America West), San Francisco and Los Angeles (Alaska), and Calgary (Air Canada). Travelers can also go by regularly scheduled flights to either

Acapulco or Ixtapa-Zihuatanejo from several U.S. and Canada gateways, using a plane change in Mexico City. These gateways include San Jose (Mexicana), San Diego (Aeromexico), Las Vegas (Mexicana), Portland (Alaska), Vancouver (Mexicana), Denver (Mexicana), Atlanta (Delta), Miami (Mexicana), New York (Delta), and Toronto and Montreal (Air Canada).

Moreover, travelers can also go by seasonal charter flights from many Northern U.S. and Canadian gateways. These usually include Seattle, San Francisco, Vancouver, Winnipeg, Minneapolis, Chicago, Cleveland, New York, and Toronto.

For cost-conscious travelers, express **buses** provide a safe and sure route to the Acapulco region. Hundreds of buses head south daily from central bus stations (*camioneras centrales*) in the south-of-the-border towns of Tijuana, Mexicali, Nogales, Ciudad Juárez, Nuevo Laredo, Reynosa, and Matamoros. By all means, for comfort and speed, go luxury-class (about $80–100, 20–30 hours).

Although it isn't a route for everyone, some travelers drive their **cars or RVs** to the Acapulco region. Driving time runs 3–5 south-of-the-border days at the wheel, and costs around $80–120 in (very worthwhile) expressway tolls for passenger cars and light trucks (about triple that for motor homes).

WHAT TO TAKE

"Men wear pants, ladies be beautiful" was once the dress code of one of the Mexican Pacific Coast's classiest hotels. Men in casual Acapulco, Ixtapa, and Zihuatanejo can get by easily without a jacket, women with simple skirts, pants, and blouses.

Loose-fitting, hand-washable, easy-to-dry clothes make for trouble-free tropical vacationing. Synthetic or cotton-synthetic-blend shirts, blouses, pants, socks, and underwear will fit the bill everywhere in the coastal Acapulco region. For breezy nights on the coast, bring a lightweight windbreaker. If you're going to the highlands (Chilpancingo, Chilapa, Olinalá, and Taxco), add a medium-weight jacket.

In all cases, leave showy, expensive clothes and jewelry at home. Stow items that you cannot lose in your hotel safe or carry them with you in a sturdy zipped purse or a waist pouch on your front side.

What you pack depends on how mobile you want to be. If you're staying the whole time at a self-contained resort, you can take the two suitcases and one carry-on allowed by airlines. If, on the other hand, you're going to be moving around a lot, you'd do better to condense everything to one easily carried bag with wheels that doubles as luggage and soft backpack. Experienced travelers accomplish this by packing prudently and tightly, choosing items that will do double or triple duty (such as a Swiss army knife with scissors).

Campers will have to be super careful to accomplish one-bag packing. Fortunately, camping along the tropical coast generally requires no sleeping bag. Simply use a hammock (buy it in Mexico) or a sleeping pad and a sheet for cover. In the winter, you may, at most, have to buy a light blanket. A compact tent that you and your companion can share is a must against bugs, as is mosquito repellent. A first-aid kit is absolutely necessary.

Explore Acapulco, Ixtapa and Zihuatanejo

10-DAY BEST OF ACAPULCO AND GUERRERO UPCOUNTRY

Although its golden beaches are the stuff of legend, Acapulco offers much more, both in and out of town. In town, discover Acapulco's shady old-town plaza, its world-class museums, a fascinating park of petroglyphs, a secluded offshore island preserve, and its rich dining and exciting nightlife. Out of town, scarcely an hour north of the city, explore historic city-shrines to Mexico's independence, rivers for rafting and kayaking, forests for hiking, crystalline springs for swimming and inner-tubing, and magnificent limestone caves for exploring. Farther along the trail, visit vibrant handicrafts markets and villages and the mysterious ruins of ancient forgotten kingdoms. Finally, at Guerrero's pine-scented Sierra summit, explore jewel-like Taxco, decorated with the baroque monuments of its silver-rich past and a glittering legion of shops offering treasuries of irresistible handcrafted jewelry.

DAYS 1-2

Arrive in Acapulco, rest up for a few hours, then enjoy sunset cocktails at the Hotel Los Flamingos clifftop *mirador* and dinner in the adjacent restaurant. The next day spend the morning around the *zócalo* (old-town plaza), the colonial-era Fuerte San Diego and museum, and the nearby Casa de la Máscara (House of Masks). Take the afternoon off, relaxing by the pool or on the beach. In the evening, join the crowd viewing the cliff divers at La Quebrada.

DAYS 3-4

In the morning, ride a tour boat from Playa Caleta to offshore Isla Roqueta. Walk the island trail (two hours), and snorkel/swim and sun at hidden Playa las Palmitas. Enjoy a late lunch or dinner at Restaurant Palao on the island before returning to the mainland. The next day you might do some browsing for handicrafts mementos at Bonita handicrafts store and Mercado de Parrazal handicrafts market, both near the old town plaza. Alternatively, taxi up to Palma Sola Archaeological Site for a stroll and a picnic among the petrolgyphs. Spend the rest of the day relaxing by your hotel pool or strolling, sunning, or swimming at the beach. Enjoy a splurge dinner at Kookaburra (or if on a budget, at either Taco Tumbra, 100% Natural, or El Zorrito restaurants). Continue for an evening walk to sample the nightclub scene and (maybe even risk a bungee jump) on the Costera Miguel Alemán (also called the Costera) just east of the Diana Circle.

DAYS 5-6

Head upcountry for either rafting at Bravo Town on the Río Papagayo, or exploring the Juxtlahuaca cave near Colotlipa. Continue to Chilpancingo for an overnight. After dinner at either Nutrilite restaurant or Café Vivaldy, enjoy a stroll around the Chilpancingo plaza. If Day 6 happens to be a Sunday (or you planned it to be), spend it in Chilapa at the intense Sunday crafts market, an hour by car or bus east of Chilpancingo. Otherwise, if you have kids in tow, show them a good time in Chilpancingo at the Museo La Avispa. If not, consider heading north an hour to the intriguing and scenic La Organera Xochipala Archaeological Zone. In any case, continue north by car or bus to Iguala for an overnight.

DAYS 7-8

After breakfast in Iguala at La Parroquia, stroll the shady Iguala plaza, take a look around inside the gold market a block away, then spend an hour in the Museo y Santuario a la Bandera (Museum and Sanctuary of the Flag). Make the highlight of your Iguala visit a trip uphill to gaze in wonder at the giant Mexican flag on the C.N.O.P. hilltop south of town.

Continue north to Taxco. In the evening, after dinner at Café Sasha or Del Ángel Inn stroll the Taxco *zócalo* (main plaza) and browse through some silver and handicrafts shops.

The next day, after breakfast at La Parroquia on the *zócalo*, see the sights, such as Santa Prisca church, Museo Guillermo Spratling, the town market, and maybe ride the cableway to the top of Monte Taxco and visit more of Taxco's excellent silver and handicrafts shops.

DAYS 9-10

On Day 9, be sure to at least visit Grutas de Cacahuamilpa limestone cave national park. If you arrange a tour, start early enough with your own wheels, or hire a taxi ($40) from Cacahuamilpa by early afternoon, you'll have time to also visit the legendary must-see Xochicalco UNESCO. World Heritage archaeological site and museum 25 miles (40 km) farther, past Cacahuamilpa. On the last day, return to Acapulco and head home (or continue to the Ixtapa, Zihuatanejo, and the Costa Grande itinerary below).

10-DAY BEST OF IXTAPA, ZIHUATANEJO, AND THE COSTA GRANDE

The twin resorts of Ixtapa and Zihuatanejo crown the Guerrero Costa Grande, an alluring land of perpetual summer, where the palms always seem to be swaying in the breeze, the frigate birds soaring overhead, and the billows washing the crystalline sand. Here choices for relaxation seem endless, from the comfortable luxury of Ixtapa, to the old-Mexico village ambience of Zihuatanejo, and the tranquil seclusion of a diadem of nearby mini-paradises, such as Troncones, Barra de Potosi, and Playa Escondida, where the fishing is good and the living easy.

DAYS 1-2

Arrive in Ixtapa or Zihuatanejo. Rest up a few hours, then stroll around downtown Zihuatanejo and along the beachfront Paseo del Pescador. Browse some of the handicrafts shops and enjoy dinner downtown at Tamales y Atoles "Any" or Mi Chayita Chinese restaurant.

The next morning, after breakfast in Zihuatanejo at Restaurant Margarita, visit the Museo Arqueología de la Costa Grande, then ride a water taxi from the pier to Playa Las Gatas for sunning on the beach, and snorkeling or maybe a scuba lesson. In the mid-afternoon, return and freshen up at your hotel, then enjoy the sunset and a splurge dinner at Il Mare or Kau Kan (or, if on a budget, Restaurant La Perla on Playa La Ropa).

DAYS 3-4

On Day 3, after breakfast at outdoor Cafe Toko Tucán or Restaurant Mama Norma and Deborah in Ixtapa, browse the handicrafts at the Ixtapa handicrafts market and perhaps some of the Ixtapa shops in the Los Patios shopping complex. Then, either take a taxi, drive, or ride the minibus to Playa Linda to see the crocodiles. Later, take the ferry across to Isla Ixtapa for sunning, strolling, swimming and/or snorkeling and a seafood lunch at a beachfront *palapa*.

On Day 4 you could kick back and simply relax, or follow your own interests. A few options include: unwinding on the beach or by the pool, renting a bike and following the Ixtapa *ciclopista* (bike path) for a few hours, going horseback riding at Playa Linda, taking a fishing trip, or taking the Zihuatanejo handicrafts shopping tour.

DAYS 5-6

On Day 5, head northwest an hour for a getaway in Troncones. Get an early start and check in at a comfortable beachfront inn, such as Casa Ki, the Inn at Manzanillo

Bay, or Eden Beach Hacienda. After whiling away the afternoon, strolling the beach, lazing in a hammock, or swimming beyond the breakers, enjoy dinner at either El Burro Borracho or the Cocina del Sol restaurant at the Eden Beach Hacienda.

Day 6 you might want to spend more actively, maybe taking a surfing lesson, or going on a jungle canopy ride and exploring the local limestone cavern. Or, whether you have your own wheels or get an early start by bus, you could explore the coast northwest, checking out the beach hamlets of La Saladita and Atracadero, and maybe even going all the way to the grand Río Balsas dam, where Highway 200 crosses the border into the state of Michoacán.

DAYS 7-8

Return southeast past Ixtapa and Zihuatanejo for a day around the village of Barra de Potosí, perhaps combined with a wildlife-viewing tour, such as Zoe Kayak Tours, on the grand mangrove lagoon, Laguna de Potosí. Stay overnight at either of the Barra de Potosí bed-and-breakfasts, Casa Frida or Casa del Encanto, or return to your hotel in Ixtapa or Zihuatanejo.

Day 8 you could simply relax, according to your own interests, in either Ixtapa, Zihuatanejo, or Barra de Potosí. If you want more activity, in Zihuatanejo you might visit the lively town market, go on a fishing trip, do either the Zihuatanejo or Ixtapa beach walk, or check out Zihuatanejo's excellent tourist handicrafts market and shops. Alternatively, from either Barra de Potosí, Ixtapa, or Zihuatanejo, you could go on an excursion south to Petatlán and visit the plaza-front gold market shops and pay your respects to Petatlán's beloved patron, Padre Jesús. Enjoy a late lunch or early dinner at Petatlán's Restaurant Mi Pueblito on the plaza.

DAYS 9-10

Finally, do some genuine relaxing and let your body rest and your mind wander, whether you're spending Day 9 in Ixtapa, Zihuatanejo, or Barra de Potosí. (If, however, you crave more activity and beautiful places, you might go for an excursion south to one or both of the lovely Playa Ojo de Agua and Playa Escondida.)

Day 10, head back home, or continue traveling with the previous Acapulco and Guerrero Upcountry itinerary.

BEST BEACHES

These are many of the Acapulco region's loveliest, creamiest stretches of sand. Nearly all are good for most beach delights, such as surf fishing, camping, beachcombing, swimming, snorkeling, and surfing. Beaches, however, are often good for particular reasons. Here are some of the very best in each region.

ACAPULCO

Most Pristine: Playa Larga, on Acapulco's far southeast shore, is breezy, wave-tossed, and rich with seabirds, nesting sea turtles (summer and fall), seasonal shells, and driftwood.

Best Snorkeling: At sheltered Playa Roqueta on Isla Roqueta, simply pull on your mask and snorkel and step into the water, and get up close and personal with squadrons of colorful tropical fish.

Best Surfing: The open-ocean rolling breakers at Playa Revolcadero (with lifeguards) are Acapulco's most reliable for intermediate-to-advanced surfing.

Best Surf Fishing: With its powerful close-in breakers, Playa Pie de la Cuesta is a fine spot for fishing the waves.

Most Child-Friendly: The waves at Playa Caleta are blue ripples, gentle and safe for the little ones.

Most Intimate: Tidepool-studded Playa Las Palmitas, on Isla Roqueta, is small and hidden, with clear water, crystalline sand, an unobstructed sunset horizon, and only occasional visitors.

Best Sunsets: Playa Angosta is Acapulco's only beach with a clear sunset horizon. (Alternatively, the clifftop spots above the waves at the Sinfonia del Sol sunset amphitheater and the sunset *mirador* at the Hotel Los Flamingos are also super for sunsets.)

Best Camping: Playa Luces, near Pie de la Cuesta, with its fine RV and camping park, nesting sea turtles, even a big blue swimming pool, is tops for formal camping in the Acapulco region.

THE COSTA GRANDE

Most Beautiful: Powerful rolling waves, breaking around a mountainous sea-rock and over a forest of bird-decorated tidepool rocks makes Playa Piedra Tlalcoyunque a Costa Grande must-see.

Most Pristine: The remote barrier beach of Laguna de Mitla is a seemingly endless beachcomber's heaven of rolling breakers, delicate seasonal shells, and skittering crabs and sandpipers.

Best for Everything: Playa Escondida, in an intimate hidden cove, with surfable rolling breakers, mild undertow, a good hotel and restaurant, and fishing and camping opportunities, is a favorite with local folks and savvy travelers.

Best Surf Fishing: Several beaches are good, especially near the Costa Grande's Acapulco end, such as at El Carrizal, where the waves roll and crash on the sand, close-in.

Most Child-Friendly: Both kids and their parents love the gorgeous palm-shaded beach on the lagoon side of barrier beach El Carrizal, near Hotel Paraíso Playa Azul.

Most Intimate: A small strip of sand, sprinkled with a few restaurants, nestled against forested coastal bluffs, and with a freshwater spring, makes Playa Ojo de Agua a local family favorite.

Best Sunsets: Visitors to the clifftop overlook above Playa El Calvario (where the sun sets not out to sea, but in a direction nearly parallel to the coast) are often blessed with spectacular sunsets.

Best Camping: Breezy, golden Playa La Barrita, with a good, friendly restaurant beside a small freshwater lagoon and tree-shaded space for tents or a small RV, seems perfect for a day or season of camping.

IXTAPA AND ZIHUATANEJO

Most Beautiful: True to its name, Playa Hermosa (accessible through the Hotel Brisas Ixtapa) is a lovely, open-ocean strand of yellow sand and clear water that nestles picturesquely beneath a green forested hillside and between tidepool-decorated headlands.

Most Pristine: Playa Coral, on Isla Ixtapa, is a bright coral-strewn open-ocean nook, perching on a petite, rocky cove.

Best for Everything: Beachfront restaurants with shade *palapas,* crystalline sand, gentle child-friendly waves, and mild undertow make Playa la Ropa Zihuatanejo's favorite resort beach.

Best Snorkeling and Surfing: Calm, clear waters and a good beachfront scuba shop make Playa Las Gatas in Zihuatanejo both a snorkeling and scuba diving haven, right from the beach.

Best Surf Fishing: Turbulent, close-in surf and super-clean water produce ideal fishing conditions at Playa Las Pozas, south of Zihuatanejo.

Most Child-Friendly: Playa Cuachalatate (koo-ah-chah-lah-TAH-tay), on Isla Ixtapa's sheltered inner shore, is a children's tropical playground of crystal sand, clear water, and gentle ripples.

Most Intimate: Isla Ixtapa's Playa Carey, an open-ocean dab of sand nestling between petite, rocky headlands, is easily accessible by boat, but not frequently visited.

Best Sunsets: Zihuatanejo's mile-long Playa La Ropa, with its broad airy western horizon and *palapa* restaurants is a favorite spot to watch the sun go down.

THE COSTA CHICA

Best for Everything: Playa Ventura, a seemingly endless stretch of yellow sand, sprinkled with modest hotels, *palapa* restaurants, and friendly folks, offers surfable rollers, turtles who nest in the summer and fall, and lots of open space for tents and RVs.

Best Surfing: Surfing is a regular pastime at Puerto Maldonado, where waves swell inshore past a picturesque rocky point and break diagonally along the beach line.

Most Child-Friendly: Playa las Peñitas, with a family of sandstone shoreline rocks, provides a happy playground for kids to scamper and splash in the gentle waves and sheltered tidepools.

Best Camping: The downscale beach village of Barra Tecoanapa, with stores, water, lots of good fishing, and a long, level beachcomber-friendly strand could be heaven for visitors equipped to enjoy informal beachfront tent or RV camping.

OUTDOOR ADVENTURES

The Acapulco region abounds with beaches for strolling; hills and mountains for hiking and climbing; rivers for kayaking and rafting; caves for exploring; coasts and offshore islands for boating and kayaking; mangrove lagoons for kayaking, boating, and bird-watching; and even a jungle canopy for touring. Moreover, the region is a veritable wildlife treasury, with everything from iguanas and crocodiles to dolphins, whales, and white herons for watching and photographing. Here are the Acapulco region's best of all of the above, by activity.

WALKING, HIKING, AND BICYCLING

Many beaches offer good walking options, beginning right at the resorts on Acapulco and Zihuatanejo Bays, Ixtapa, and both Barra de Potosí and Troncones. Other good walking beaches are at El Carrizal, Laguna Mitla, and El Calvario, on the Costa Grande; and on the Costa Chica at Playa Ventura, Playa Las Peñitas, and Puerto Maldonado.

Hiking can also start right in Acapulco for visitors who follow the forested trails on Isla Roqueta and also at the fascinating park and petroglyph-sprinkled Palma Sola Archaeological Site. Adventurers who enjoy the challenge of scrambling to hidden beaches can do their thing on Isla Ixtapa.

In Guerrero Upcountry, Bravo Town ecotourism center offers guided hiking, rapelling, climbing, and camping tours from their base on the Río Papagayo.

Furthermore, bicycling is easy and healthful on the Ixtapa and Zihuatanejo *ciclopista* (bike path). Either bring your own or rent a bike in Ixtapa.

SURFING

A number of Acapulco region beaches offer good surfing opportunities: Start at the resorts, at Playa Revolcadero near Acapulco, Playa Las Gatas in a corner in Zihuatanejo Bay, and Manzanillo Bay in Troncones. Farther afield, good surf is often up on the Costa Grande, at Playa Escondida,

El Calvario, Playa Ojo de Agua, and Playa Cayaquitos (the last two both near Papanoa); and on the Costa Chica at Playa Ventura and Puerto Maldonado.

Moreover, for those who want to learn to surf, an enterprising Californian couple offers both surfing travel packages and on-the-spot lessons at Troncones, north of Ixtapa and Zihuatanejo.

SNORKELING AND SCUBA DIVING

Few beaches afford good snorkeling and scuba diving right from the sand, except for these: Playas Las Gatas at Zihuatanejo, Playa Cuachalatate on Isla Ixtapa, and Playa Roqueta on Isla Roqueta (Acapulco).

Professional scuba dive shops both instruct beginners and guide experienced scuba divers (bring your certificate) on a variety of excursions in Acapulco, Ixtapa, and Zihuatanejo.

RIVER KAYAKING, RAFTING, AND INNER-TUBING

Although many of Acapulco region's rivers, such as the Ríos Coyuca, Tecpán, and Petatlán on the Costa Grande; the Ríos Copala, Marquelia, Quetzala, and Arenas on the Costa Chica; and Ríos Balsas and Papagayo in Guerrero Upcountry, are easily navigable by experienced adventurers with their own equipment. The Río Papagayo adds the convenience of guided rafting tours from the Bravo Town ecotourism center about an hour north of Acapulco by highway.

The best of all possible inner-tubing rivers is the crystalline Río Azul, an upper tributary of the Río Papagayo system. It rises year-round from springs at El Borbollón and meanders, about two feet deep, gently downhill, past a number of rustic bathing resorts, notably Balneario Santa Fe.

KAYAKING AND BOATING

Near the resorts, tour boats offer mangrove lagoon excursions for enjoying the breeze, the scenery, and seeing squadrons of herons, ducks, geese, cormorants, anghingas, lily walkers, gulls, sometimes even crocodiles, and much more. Find them at Laguna Coyuca at Pie de la Cuesta north of Acapulco, Laguna Tres Palos south of Acapulco, and at Laguna Barra de Potosí near Zihuatanejo.

If you want a thrilling, fast-lane version of the above, go on a Jet-Boat tour through Shotover Jet outfitters in Acapulco.

On the other hand, if you bring your own kayak and/or boat you can put it in the water at all of the above, in addition to at least a dozen scenic Acapulco region locations. For starters, sheltered ocean kayaking is easy right from the beaches at Isla Ixtapa near Ixtapa and Zihuatanejo and Isla Roqueta near Acapulco.

Other more remote but inviting mangrove lagoons ripe for kayaking, boating, and camping are on the Costa Chica, at El Carrizal, Laguna de Mitla, and Camalote; and on the Costa Grande at Laguna Chautengo.

CAVE EXPLORING

The Acapulco region abounds with limestone caverns (called grutas in Spanish). The grandmother of all Mexican caves is the Grutas de Cacahuamilpa, near Taxco. Less well-known, yet equally worthy, is the smaller but exquisitely pristine Grutas de Juxtlahuaca, an hour by road east of Chilpancingo.

BIRD-WATCHING AND WILDLIFE-VIEWING

Although you can be on the lookout for birds and wildlife on any Acapulco-region beach or in any forest at any time, some places are consistently alive with throngs of birds and wildlife. Easiest to access are the tropical mangrove lagoons of Laguna Coyuca and Laguna Tres Palos near Acapulco. Operating out of Ixtapa, Zoe Kayak Tours offers professional wildlife-viewing tours at Laguna de Potosí, south of Zihuatanejo.

JUNGLE CANOPY RIDE

Enjoy a short but thrill-packed tour, suspended from a cable, downhill through the tropical forest canopy at Troncones, north of Zihuatanejo.

RV-ING AND CAMPING

Two well-equipped formal RV and tent-camping parks, the Acapulco Trailer Park and the super Trailer Park and Campground Playa Luces, operate in the Acapulco region, at Pie de la Cuesta. Two smaller spots operate at Zihuatanejo Playa La Ropa and Playa Ventura in the Costa Chica.

However, many informal, but customary, spots welcome campers. These are usually on the beach, at or near *palapa* restaurants, whose owners allow you to set up beneath their *ramada* in exchange for selling you some meals. The best spots have lovely, pristine locations, the local people are welcoming, the sites are secure, and nearby grocery stores and *palapa* restaurants are available for food and supplies.

The best spots that I've seen are El Carrizal, Laguna de Mitla, and La Barrita, in the Costa Grande; and Playa Ventura, Barra de Tecoanapa, and Puerto Maldonado, in the Costa Chica.

CULTURAL, HISTORICAL, AND ARCHAEOLOGICAL TREASURES

The Acapulco region preserves a wealth of tradition in its museums, handicrafts galleries, cathedrals, pilgrimage shrines, native markets, and archaeological sites.

ACAPULCO

In Acapulco's old town, first explore the world-class Fuerte San Diego and museum. Nearby, continue to the Casa de la Máscara, an amazing museum of masks. Back at the Acapulco old-town *zócalo*, step inside to admire (especially the ceiling of) the art deco-style cathedral.

Later, be sure to see the Casa de Dolores Olmedo and its monumental street-front mosaic of Mexican mythology by celebrated artist Diego Rivera.

Finally, on a hillside overlooking the city's west-end old town, enjoy a picnic and a stroll through the leafy Palma Sola Archaeological Site, dotted with a treasury of fascinating petroglyphs.

COSTA GRANDE

Moving up the coast from Acapulco, if you take the side trip to the Laguna de Mitla, be sure to stop by and see the ancient pottery remains preserved in the tiny Santa Cruz de Mitla Museo Comunitario (Community Museum) in the hamlet's municipal *kiosco* (kiosk).

Farther north, at Petatlán, step inside the pilgrimage church, Parroquia de Padre Jesús and pay your respects to the town's fabulously beloved patron, Padre Jesús. Nearby, check out the ancient monoliths by the main plaza bandstand and the monumental stone ball-game rings (*anillos de piedra*), mounted beside the highway in town, a few blocks from the plaza.

A few miles north of town, investigate the source of Petatlán's antiquities, the Soledad de Maciel Archaeological Zone. Start by viewing the amazing life-death motif monolith, the "King of Chole," in front of the village-center church. Continue to the adjacent small museum, where you can contact a guide.

IXTAPA AND ZIHUATANEJO

First on your list should be the regional

museum, Museo Arqueología de la Costa Grande, with its treasury of ancient Costa Grande artifacts.

To see a storied on-site artifact of Zihuatanejo's past, take the water taxi over to Playa Las Gatas for a beachfront (or underwater snorkel or scuba) look at what remains of the protective "wall" that, legend says, the local preconquest Tarascan king built offshore.

GUERRERO UPCOUNTRY

Begin at Chilpancingo, the Guerrero state capital, to see the heroic statue of José María Morelos and the revered meeting hall of the Mexican Independence Congress of Anahuac. Then see it all colorfully illustrated by the grand historical mural in the Museo Regional de Chilpancingo next door to the Templo de Santa María de la Asunción.

On the way north to Iguala, the important and very ancient, partly reconstructed, ruined city at the La Organera Xochipala Archaeological Zone is worth at least a two-hour stop.

An hour farther north, visit the Iguala plaza-front Museo y Santuario a la Bandera, and culminate your Iguala visit at the hilltop south of town, with a close-up view of the wondrous, fantastically large, quarterton Mexican flag.

Those who like ruins can have a good day exploring a pair of important archaeological sites in a side trip east of Iguala: Cuetlajuchitlán (kooay-tlah-hoo-chee-TLAHN), and another hour and a half farther east, ancient (circa 1000 B.C.) Olmec-era Teopantecuantlán (tay-oh-pahn-tay-kooan-TLAHN).

In Taxco, less than an hour north of Iguala, trace the town's colorfully rich history via a self-guided walking tour of the spectacularly baroque Santa Prisca Church, the Museo Guillermo Spratling, the Casa Humboldt colonial religious art museum, and the Museo Platería (Silver Museum).

About an hour and a half outside of Taxco, you must visit the legendary Xochicalco archaeological site and museum. On another day, history enthusiasts would enjoy a half-day excursion from Taxco to Ixtcateopan village to visit the museum and shrine honoring the Aztecs' gritty last emperor, Cuauhtémoc, and his (now controversial) remains.

THE COSTA CHICA

The eastern Costa Chica, beginning about a hundred miles east of Acapulco and extending into Oaxaca, is a rich repository of the cultural traditions of both the indigenous (mostly Mixtec- and Amusgo-speaking) people, and a large (perhaps 50,000 strong) rural farm community of African Mexicans (known officially as *Afromestizos,* but popularly called *costeños* because their isolated settlements are near the coast).

The eastern Guerrero market towns north of Highway 200, especially Ometepec (ohmay-tay-PEK) and Xochistlahuaca (sohchees-tlah-WAH-kah), are the big indigenous centers, where thousands of folks in colorful *traje* (traditional dress) arrive for big Sunday *tianguis* (native markets, tee-AHN-geese).

By contrast, the African Mexicans, nearly all of whom live south of Highway 200, often arrive in majority numbers at the busy market town of Cuajinicuilapa (kwah-hee-nee-kwee-LAH-pah). Here, the Museo de las Culturas Afromestizos should be your priority stop.

Farther east, on the Oaxaca side of the Costa Chica, the town of Pinotepa Nacional is the big market hub for the mostly Mixtec-speaking nearby villages. The Pinotepa Nacional native market, big every day and even bigger on Wednesdays and Sundays, is where the indigenous action is.

From Pinotepa Nacional, good roads fan north and east to more remote indigenous villages: north to Mixtec-speaking Pinotepa Don Luis (for *pozahuancos* and masks), and Amusgo-speaking San Pedro Amusgos (for lovely hand-embroidered *huipiles*); and east along Highway 200 to Mixtec-speaking Huazolotitlán (for masks), and Jamiltepec, the coastal Mixtec capital, with a large and fascinating daily native market.

ONE DAY IN...

If you're arriving on a cruise ship, or hurrying through, and all you have is a day, you can still enjoy yourself strolling and taxiing around the Acapulco region's prime destinations.

ACAPULCO

Morning

Start out early with breakfast at homey Cafe Los Amigos by the *zócalo*. Next, stroll east, past the cruise-ship dock and over the Costera, to Fuerte San Diego. Explore the fort and museum for at least an hour. Afterward, walk a block west, along the fort's level hilltop, past the bus parking lot, to the Casa de la Máscara. Continue west a few blocks back to the *zócalo*, and have a look inside the art deco plaza-front church. Cross over the Costera to the sportfishing dock to see what the catch has been so far. Enjoy an early lunch at Cafe Los Amigos or Restaurant La Flor de Acapulco on the *zócalo*. Then taxi five minutes to La Quebrada for the cliff-diver show at 1 P.M.

Afternoon

After the cliff-diver show, hire a taxi to take you to the Casa de Dolores Olmedo for a look at the monumental Diego Rivera mosaic out front. Continue to Playa Caleta and ride a tour boat over to Isla Roqueta. Take a seat at one of the inner-shore (Playa Roqueta) restaurants and relax, maybe do some sunning or snorkeling on the sand or walking on the excellent Isla Roqueta trail network. Around 5 P.M., ride the boat back to Caleta, and taxi uphill to Hotel Los Flamingos to enjoy sunset cocktails at the hotel's panoramic viewpoint gazebo.

IXTAPA AND ZIHUATANEJO

Morning

Start out early strolling around downtown Zihuatanejo and along the beachfront Paseo del Pescador. Then browse the Zihuatanejo tourist handicrafts market stalls and some of the handicrafts shops on the Zihuatanjeo Handicrafts Tour, and visit the Museo Arqueología de la Costa Grande. Enjoy lunch downtown at Tamales y Atoles "Any" or Mi Chayita Chinese restaurant (nevertheless beneath a Mexican *palapa* roof).

Afternoon

After lunch, ride a water taxi from the Zihuatanejo pier to Playa Las Gatas for an hour of sunning, swimming, or snorkeling on the beach. Return to Zihuatanejo, taxi over to Ixtapa, continuing past the hotels along the main Ixtapa beach boulevard, Paseo Ixtapa, to outer Playa Linda and have a look at the crocodiles. By around 3 P.M., ride a ferry from the Playa Linda pier out to Isla Ixtapa and enjoy an hour's stroll to the island's hidden Playa Coral and Playa Varadero. Return by ferry, then taxi back to Zihuatanejo by 5 P.M. to enjoy sunset cocktails and maybe early dinner at Restaurant Il Mare.

ACAPULCO

Acapulco (pop. 1.5 million), the "Queen of Mexican Beach Resorts," is still Mexico's favorite and as sunny and breezy as ever. By day, viewed either from the shore or an airy hilltop, Acapulco's golden strand curves around its picture-perfect half-moon bay. At night, myriad twinkling city lights decorate the same space, bordered below by the bay's ebony darkness and above by the starry firmament.

In Acapulco as in its latter-day metropolitan cousins, Hollywood and Las Vegas, the new, the brash, the loud, and the bright far outshine the quiet, charming side of Acapulco that few visitors know.

But despite the hullabaloo you can easily enjoy Acapulco's hidden feast of old-Mexico diversions: intimate neighborhoods around the *zócalo*, with their upcountry traditional food restaurants, fascinating museums, and the fetching trove of handicrafts at Mercado de Parrazal.

Of course, modern Acapulco was built for people who like to party, and if you're so inclined you can sample Acapulco's best, at a legion of bars, clubs, and discotheques; a shoreline nighttime bungee jump; nightclub extravaganza shows; and with the rich and famous at choice restaurants, where both the cuisine and the view—of a seeming galaxy of twinkling city lights—are equally stunning.

What's more, Acapulco offers manifold outdoor diversions, such as acquainting yourself with tropical fish either through the floor of a glass-bottomed boat or via a snorkeling or scuba diving adventure. On another day, explore the forested corners and hidden

HIGHLIGHTS

The Zócalo: Here, at the charming heart of old Acapulco, join the folks who stroll in the shade beneath the ancient *higuera* trees, people-watch from park benches, or take a look inside the art-deco *zócalo*-front church (page 40).

Fuerte San Diego: Just a few blocks from the *zócalo*, spend an interesting afternoon at the grand colonial-era fort that protected Acapulco from marauders for more than 300 years (page 40).

Casa de la Máscara: A treasury of masks, from a tradition that still comprises an important part of ritual in indigenous Mexico, is the major attraction of this fascinating small museum (page 41).

Isla Roqueta: This pristine forested island that beckons across the blue channel from Playa Caleta is easily reachable by glass-bottomed boat tour. Easy trails lead uphill to the lighthouse and continue above panoramic cliff-top ocean views to hidden beach Playa las Palmitas and relaxing Restaurant Palao, fine for lunch or an early supper (page 44).

Hotel Los Flamingos: Its spectacular sunset-view perch would be attraction enough, but this old-Acapulco jewel offers much more. Linger to enjoy a lobby gallery of old Hollywood–Acapulco connection photos, a precious cliff-top gazebo for sunset cocktails, and an airy view *palapa* restaurant for dinner (page 46).

Laguna Coyuca Boat Tour: Pie de la Cuesta, the beach village just northwest of Acapulco, is the jumping off point for this relaxing day excursion. En route, as you enjoy the cooling breeze, your boat threads through mangrove-laced channels and passes islands festooned with nesting herons, cormorants, and pelicans (page 81).

LOOK FOR **[** TO FIND RECOMMENDED SIGHTS, ACTIVITIES, DINING, AND LODGING.

beach-nooks of offshore Isla Roqueta, and maybe hike through a sylvan mountainside park, decorated by a trove of ancient petroglyphs, and finally, at day's end, soak up the sunset vista at Hotel Los Flamingos.

With more time, you can adventure beyond the edges of the Acapulco metropolis and discover more hidden Acapulcos: such as the grand, glassy Laguna Tres Palos via either a breezy jet-boat ride or your own kayak, or by strolling the driftwood-strewn strands of Playa Larga, or by tour boat to south-seas islands, such as Isla Montosa, in wildlife-rich mangrove Laguna Coyuca; and if Acapulco has persuaded you to linger, stay a night or two at the palmy, charmingly out-of-date downscale resort village of Pie de la Cuesta.

PLANNING YOUR TIME

Of course even in a month of Sundays you won't be able to do everything that Acapulco offers, so you might as well save something for your next visit. But spend at least a day around the old-town **zócalo** neighborhood. Start out with breakfast at Café Los Amigos, and sit down and do some people-watching from a bench beneath the shady trees. Wander south a few blocks to **Fuerte San Diego** and spend a couple of hours perusing its fascinating displays, climbing to its crenallated battlements to enjoy the airy bay view. On your way back be sure to stop for a half hour at the **Casa de la Máscara.** By late afternoon, it will be time to enjoy the sunset, so taxi over to **Hotel Los Flamingos** for drinks at their sunset gazebo and perhaps supper in their adjacent restaurant. Later continue by taxi on to La Quebrada to ooh and ahh at the divers' amazingly scary exhibition.

Having hit some of the highlights, you might concentrate on your own interests. For example, from Playa Caleta, lovers of the outdoors could take a glass-bottomed boat tour, and spend the day hiking the forested paths of **Isla Roqueta** and doing some sunning and snorkeling (bring your own gear) from the island's hidden beaches. On another day, you might taxi uphill to Palma Sola Archaeological Site for a picnic and a shady mountainside stroll among the petroglyphs. On a third day, take a scuba diving lesson from the Acapulco Scuba Center or go on a fishing trip with Fish-R-Us.

On the other hand, handicrafts shoppers could spend at least an hour at the Bonita handicrafts shop near the *zócalo,* and at least another hour at the nearby Mercado de Parrazal handicrafts market. After lunch (maybe at Sanborn's near the *zócalo*), you could taxi to Acapulco town market to see the piñatas, then continue east for a couple hours, browsing the handicrafts arcades and stores in mid-town.

If you want a party you can always do that right in Acapulco. A good place to start out would be Restaurant El Olvido for dinner (or if you're on a budget, Restaurant El Zorrito or Taco Tumbra) and continue to the lineup of clubs (Barbarossa, Crazy Lobster, Beto) and the bungee jump just east of the Diana Circle, which will probably occupy you until at least midnight. With time to spare, continue on to more clubs, such as Baby O and Nina's on the Costera, east end.

© BRUCE WHIPPERMAN

Petroglyphs decorate the forested pathways at Palma Sola Archaeological Site.

ACAPULCO

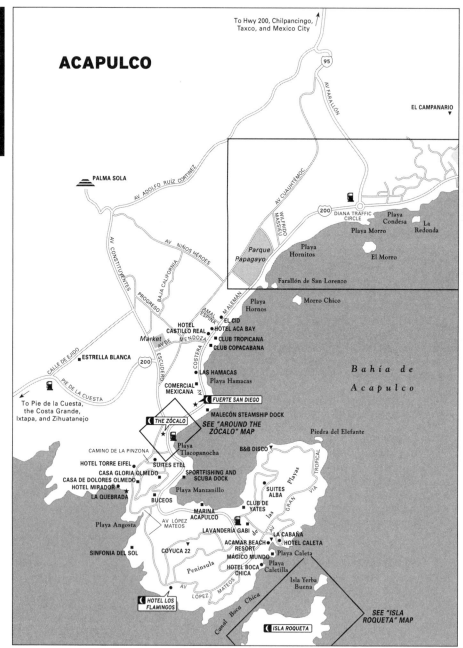

ACAPULCO

To Hwy 200, Chilpancingo,
Taxco, and Mexico City

95

AV FARALLON

EL CAMPANARIO

PALMA SOLA

AV. ADOLFO RUIZ CORTINEZ

AV. CUAUHTEMOC

WILFRIDO MASSIEU

200

DIANA TRAFFIC CIRCLE

Playa Condesa

La Redonda

Playa Morro

Playa Hornitos

AV NIÑOS HEROES

AV. CONSTITUYENTES

BAJA CALIFORNIA

PROGRESO

Parque Papagayo

El Morro

Farallón de San Lorenzo

AV DE MENDOZA

Market

CALLE DE EJIDO

ESTRELLA BLANCA

200

ESCUDERO

PIE DE LA CUESTA

To Pie de la Cuesta,
the Costa Grande,
Ixtapa, and Zihuatanejo

AMAL ESPINA

M ALEMAN

Playa Hornos

Morro Chico

HOTEL CASTILLO REAL

EL CID

HOTEL ACA BAY

CLUB TROPICANA

CLUB COPACABANA

COSTERA

Bahía de Acapulco

LAS HAMACAS

Playa Hamacas

COMERCIAL MEXICANA

FUERTE SAN DIEGO

THE ZÓCALO

MALECÓN STEAMSHIP DOCK

SEE "AROUND THE ZÓCALO" MAP

Playa Tlacopanocha

B&B DISCO

Piedra del Elefante

CAMINO DE LA PINZONA

HOTEL TORRE EIFEL

SUITES ETEL

CASA GLORIA OLMEDO

SPORTFISHING AND SCUBA DOCK

AV GRAN VIA TROPICAL

CASA DE DOLORES OLMEDO

HOTEL MIRADOR

Playa Manzanillo

SUITES ALBA

Playas

LA QUEBRADA

BUCEOS

CLUB DE YATES

MARINA ACAPULCO

LAVANDERÍA GABI

las AV de

LA CABAÑA

AV LÓPEZ MATEOS

Playa Angosta

ACAMAR BEACH RESORT

HOTEL CALETA

SINFONIA DEL SOL

COYUCA 22

MÁGICO MUNDO

Playa Caleta

Peninsula

HOTEL BOCA CHICA

Playa Caletilla

Isla Yerba Buena

AV LÓPEZ MATEOS

HOTEL LOS FLAMINGOS

Canal Boca Chica

ISLA ROQUETA

SEE "ISLA ROQUETA" MAP

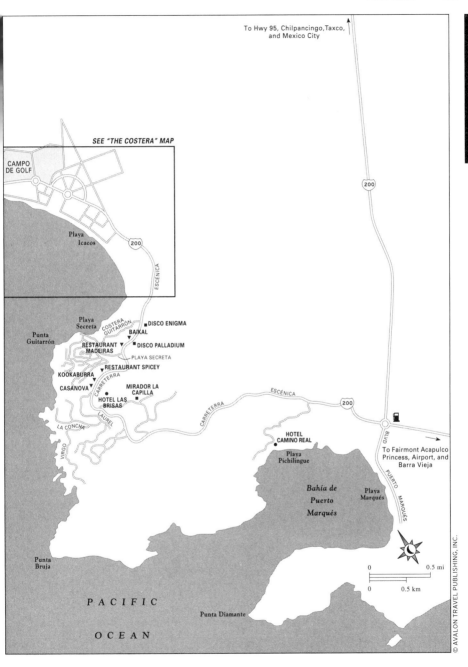

To Hwy 95, Chilpancingo, Taxco, and Mexico City

200

SEE "THE COSTERA" MAP

CAMPO DE GOLF

Playa Icacos

200

ESCÉNICA

Playa Secreta

COSTERA GUITARRÓN

DISCO ENIGMA

BAIKAL

Punta Guitarrón

RESTAURANT MADEIRAS

DISCO PALLADIUM

PLAYA SECRETA

RESTAURANT SPICEY

KOOKABURRA

CARRETERRA

CASANOVA

MIRADOR LA CAPILLA

HOTEL LAS BRISAS

LAUREL

ESCÉNICA

CARRETERRA

200

LA CONCHA

VIRGO

HOTEL CAMINO REAL

Playa Pichilingue

To Fairmont Acapulco Princess, Airport, and Barra Vieja

BLVD

Bahía de Puerto Marqués

Playa Marqués

PUERTO MARQUÉS

Punta Bruja

0   0.5 mi

0   0.5 km

PACIFIC

OCEAN

Punta Diamante

And finally if the night is still young, continue to the super-disco Palladium on the far east-side Las Brisas hillside.

Beyond the Town Limits

With another day or two you could explore some of Acapulco's country corners. For example, head northwest to Pie de la Cuesta for a boat tour of the wildlife-rich mangrove-laced **Laguna Coyuca** and its delightfully rustic south-seas island mini-paradise Isla Montosa. You might linger for a day or two more in a comfortable Pie de la Cuesta beachfront hotel, such as Villa Nirvana or upscale Hotel Vaymas.

Alternatively, head southeast of town for a few hours of beachcombing and a picnic on breezy Playa Larga Or, continue to the palm-shaded end-of-the-road village Barra Vieja for lunch in a rustic beachfront *palapa* restaurant and a tour and some bird-watching (or a jet-boat ride) on the grand, mangrove Laguna Tres Palos.

Yet another out-of-town option would be to head north for river rafting on the Río Papagayo from October through March.

History

IN THE BEGINNING

Experts believe that Acapulco Bay, with its trove of seafood ripe for the picking, was home to bands of hunter-gatherers beginning at least 4,000 years ago. They left mute testimony, rock paintings of their gods at Puerto Marqués, Pie de la Cuesta, and the newly opened site at Palma Sola, uphill from present-day Acapulco town. Moreover, these earliest inhabitants left direct evidence of their daily life at seaside sites: stone metates and pottery utensils that experts have dated to around 2500 B.C.

Acapulco's bounty eventually led to more leisure and more sophistication. At Las Sabanas, at the northern edge of the Acapulco suburb, archaeologists unearthed a trove of fetching female statuettes, reminiscent of early Polynesian and Asian artifacts. Such discoveries have added credence to widespread legends of early Chinese influences on the Mexican Pacific coast long before Columbus.

Highland Influences

Evidence of far-flung influences is equally intriguing. Among the most fascinating of finds are the ancient paintings at the caves of Juxtlahuaca, not far from Chilpancingo, in the mountains north of Acapulco. Here, deep in a regal limestone-draped grotto, captivating multicolored Olmec-origin paintings decorate the cavern walls. Although a trove of similar finds all over the state of Guerrero led historians to the conclusion that Acapulco's early inhabitants were undoubtedly influenced by Mexico's high civilizations—Olmec, Mixtec, Zapotec, and Aztec—and frequented by their traders, the same experts believe that Acapulco never came under their direct control but instead remained the domain of a fiercely tenacious tribe, known as the Yopes, until the Spanish conquest.

CONQUEST AND COLONIZATION

Enter Hernán Cortés, who in 1519 sailed in command of a small fleet west from Cuba. He didn't find the elusive passage to China, but, hearing of a grand kingdom in the mountains to the west, marched overland and boldly took the Aztec Emperor Moctezuma captive. Nearly immediately, Cortés asked Moctezuma about Mexico's southern coast and dispatched expeditions west and south, founding villages and shipbuilding ports in Oaxaca, at Huatulco and Tehuántepec, and in the Acapulco region, at Zacatula and Acapulco.

One of the earliest of those expeditions, commanded by Juan Rodríguez de Villafuerte, landed at Acapulco Bay on the feast day of

THE LEGEND OF ACAPULCO

The *Codex Mendoza* records that, in 1499, en route south from their capital of Tenochtitlán, Aztec commanders and their armies first gazed downward at the blue sweep of Acapulco Bay. Motivated by their need for tropical treasures, such as exotic bird feathers and cacao – so valuable that cacao seeds served as the Aztecs' currency – Aztec forces tried but failed to subdue the fierce Yope tribes that ruled the Acapulco coast.

Nevertheless, the Aztec-origin name, Acapulco, from *acatl*, the Náhuatl (Aztec-language) word for reed, remained. Although translations of Acapulco vary, the meaning "place where the reeds are destroyed" appears most credible. First of all, the Aztec hieroglyph for Acapulco shows a pair of hands, one of which is shown breaking a reed. Moreover, there is the Yope legend of Acapulco that tells the story of Acatl, the son of the Aztec commander. It seems that Acatl fell hopelessly in love with Quiahuitl, comely daughter of the Yope chieftain. When his father forbade him to marry Quiahuitl, Acatl screamed with sorrow. His tears flowed so profusely that they melted him, transforming Acatl into a pond bordered by a reed thicket. Meanwhile, Quiahuitl, vaporized by her all-consuming grief, rose to the heavens as a cloud, condemned to float aimlessly over land and sea. But the lovers nevertheless received fulfillment every year during the summer rains, when Quiahuitl would float over Acapulco and rain upon Acatl's pond, uniting the lovers with so much ardor that the downpour flattened and drowned the reeds lining the pond.

Santa Lucia in 1523. Following Spanish custom, Villafuerte christened his discovery the Bahía de Santa Lucia, a name it retained for years. A safe anchorage, good fresh water, and an abundance of big trees led Villafuerte to establish an outpost and shipbuilding port by the latter 1520s. Word got back to the authorities, and by royal decree, in 1528, "Acapulco and her land… where the ships of the south will be built…" passed directly into the hands of the Spanish Crown.

Voyages of discovery set sail from Acapulco for Peru, the Gulf of California, and Asia. None returned from across the Pacific, however, until navigator-priest Father Andrés de Urdaneta discovered the northern Pacific tradewinds, which propelled him and his ship, loaded with Chinese treasure, to Acapulco in October 1565.

The Manila Galleon

From then on, for more than 250 years, a special yearly trading ship, renowned in Mexico as the Nao de China and in England as the Manila galleon, set sail exclusively from Acapulco for Asia. Tensely anticipating the Manila galleon's return, Acapulco authorities sent ships to scan the northwestern horizon. Runners and signal fires brought the news to Acapulco and Mexico City, setting in motion a long line of Acapulco-bound traders.

The galleon's arrival sparked an annual trade fair, swelling Acapulco's population with merchants from not only all of Mexico, but from as far as Spain and Peru. Loaded down with gold-filled purses, the traders jostled to bargain for the Manila galleon's shiny trove of silks, satins, damasks, porcelain, gold, ivory, and lacquerware. Fortunes were not only exchanged at trading; they were also gained and lost gambling at raucous cockfights and exciting horse races, in which African Mexicans soon became the star riders.

Pirates and Forts

Acapulco's yearly treasure soon attracted marauders. In 1579, Francis Drake, during his circumnavigation of the globe, and blessed by England's Queen Elizabeth, threatened the Spanish Pacific coast from Chile to California. One of his most notorious raids was at Huatulco, on April 13, 1579, when he even stole the church bell. Drake waited fruitlessly for the

THE EPIC VOYAGE OF AMBASSADOR HASEKURA TSUNENAGA

By 1600, competition with the Portuguese and Dutch for missionary and trade concessions in east Asia pushed Spanish authorities toward closer ties with Japan. In 1602, Rodrigo de Vivero, acting governor of the Philippines, initiated contact with Shogun Tokugawa Ieyasu (of *Shogun* movie and novel fame).

Vivero's efforts were successful, but literally by accident. During his return to Acapulco in 1609, Vivero's ship, the galleon *San Francisco*, was wrecked on the Japanese coast near Edo (now Tokyo). Fortunately for the Spanish this incident coincided with a serious deterioration in relations between the Tokugawa government and the Dutch trade mission. To their own detriment, the Dutch had issued impossibly stiff rules for buying Japanese silk and added insult to injury by trying to hog all Japanese foreign trade for themselves.

Vivero must have impressed the shogun, for Tokugawa ended up giving him an entire new ship (built by English samurai William Adams, also of *Shogun* movie fame), a small fortune in gold to fit out and operate the ship, a Spanish-Japanese trade treaty, and a request to the king of Spain for an exchange of ambassadors. Vivero, in his new ship, christened the *San Buenaventura*, sailed on August 1, 1610, and landed safely in Acapulco three months later.

This set the stage for one of history's most remarkable odysseys. In reciprocation for the requested Spanish ambassador, explorer Sebastián Vizcaíno, who arrived from Acapulco on June 10, 1610, the Japanese authorities designated nobleman Hasekura Tsunenaga as ambassador-elect to the Spanish court in Madrid.

How Hasekura accomplished his task is one of history's great little-known but epic adventures. First, he needed an oceangoing ship (few if any of which were available in Japan) to carry him across the entire Pacific and return. With the enthusiastic backing of the *daimyo* (baron) of Sendai in northwest Japan, a sturdy vessel christened the *San Sebastián* was built by 7,000 workers in a mere six months, and it sailed from Sendai (where, to this day, a monument marks the event) on October 27, 1613.

Hasekura's reception in Acapulco three months later was a celebration long remembered. To the multiple booms of cannon salutes, an array of blasting harquebuses, and the rhythm of drums, fifes, and trumpets, port authorities escorted Tsunenaga's

Manila galleon as far north as Cape Mendocino, before continuing west across the Pacific.

Later, corsair Thomas Cavendish managed similar mischief, burning Huatulco in 1586. He continued northwest, where, off Cabo San Lucas, Cavendish was the first to capture the Manila galleon, the *Santa Ana.* The cash booty alone, 1.2 million gold pesos, severely depressed the London gold market.

On October 11, 1614, a five-ship Dutch fleet, consisting of the *Sun, Moon, Pechelinga, Jager* and *Meeuve,* attacked the unfortified village of Acapulco. Already weakened by scurvy and hunger, the Dutch sailors called off the attack and, for food and water, traded two dozen hostages they had captured in Peru.

Such attacks pushed Viceroy Diego Fernandez de Córdoba to build a fort overlooking Acapulco Bay. In 1615, he commissioned, ironically, Dutch architect Adrian Bott, who completed the citadel, called Fuerte San Diego, with five sturdy crenellated ramparts, arranged in a formidable pentagonal array. Although the fort was mostly symbolic, it limited subsequent attacks on Acapulco throughout the 16th and 17th centuries to a few unsuccessful attempts. In reality, sun, termites, and earthquakes posed the fort's most serious hazards. Repairs seemed to be constantly necessary until a terrible earthquake in 1776 finished the old fort off.

It was resurrected in grand style by

entourage of 78 (including his entire family) to "lodgings that were ordered to be as luxurious as possible."

After a short Acapulco stay, Hasekura pushed ahead. His entire entourage, which had swollen to hundreds, continued to Mexico City, where they were likewise received with due tumult and honor and where all of the Japanese accepted baptism.

They continued to Veracruz, pushed eastward to Cuba, and finally arrived in Spain on October 5, 1614. After being feted at a number of towns, notably Seville, along the way, Hasekura continued to Madrid and presented his credentials to King Phillip III on January 30, 1615. He accepted a second baptism, this time taking the name of Felipe Francisco (in honor of both the Spanish king and the Franciscan order), on February 17. Continuing to Rome, via Barcelona and Genoa, Hasekura was declared a Roman citizen by the city fathers and received by Pope Paul V on November 3, 1615.

Despite all of the honors, pageantry, and polite talk, Hasekura's mission accomplished virtually nothing. He received no promises of trade from the Spanish authorities nor support from the pope. The reason was a feisty combination of economics and politics. Many, including rich Christian merchants in India, Macao, and the Philippines, were opposed to Spanish-Japanese trade. The Spanish Jesuits, who already had a bishop in Japan, were opposed to Hasekura because his Christian support came from the rival Franciscans. Perhaps most devastating were the machinations of the shogun, who suspected that Spanish incursion into Japan might lead to domination. He was persecuting Japanese Christians and expelling a crowd of Spanish priests from Japan at the very moment Hasekura was conducting negotiations in Spain.

Disheartened, ill with fever, and nearly broke, Hasekura left Rome and returned quickly west. Without even stopping in Madrid, he and his entourage left Spain in July 1617, continuing via their reverse route through Mexico. They departed from Acapulco in late 1617 in the *San Sebastián* and arrived in Manila in February 1618. In the Philippines, Hasekura renewed efforts on behalf of Japanese-Spanish trade and diplomatic contacts, but to no avail. He returned in August 1620, to a Japan increasingly hostile to any foreign trade or Christian missions. During the next dozen years, thousands of Japanese Christian converts were burned at the stake and all external trade, except for a trickle limited to the Dutch, was forbidden. Thus Japan remained a hermit empire, with virtually all foreign contact punishable by death, for 230 years.

military engineers Miguel Costanzo, who drew the plans, and Ramón Panón, who supervised the construction. The entire job, completed in July 1783, cost about 600,000 gold pesos, which would amount to many tens of millions of U.S. dollars today. Now serving as a distinguished museum, the Fuerte San Diego, austere and grand, still proudly stands guard over Acapulco Bay.

INDEPENDENCE AND MODERN ACAPULCO

Scarcely a month after Miguel Hidalgo's impassioned *grito* that inspired revolt against Spain, Hidalgo's *insurgente* compatriot, José María Morelos, was leading a rebel regiment against the royalist garrison in Acapulco. Attracted by the Manila galleon wealth he assumed was hidden there, Morelos besieged the Fuerte San Diego. Although he squeezed down on the fort, eventually surrounding it after a several-month siege, the royalist garrison broke out and scattered Morelos's soldiers. Consequently, the Manila galleon was able to land more or less annually until 1820, when rebel forces cut off all support from Mexico City, stopping the Manila galleon forever.

At the end of the war for independence, in 1821, Acapulco was almost completely in ruins. Most of its 3,000 inhabitants, the majority poor African Mexicans, were hungry and ill-clothed. Housing consisted nearly entirely of grass huts, except for the 30 or 40 stone or adobe homes of Acapulco's business and professional gentry.

By the mid-1800s, Acapulco's fine natural harbor began to turn its fortunes around. After 1850, Acapulco became a stopover for a flotilla of steamships filled with San Francisco–bound gold-rush adventurers. Subsequently Acapulco also served as a coaling station for British, American, and French navy steamers that were plying the Pacific in increasing numbers.

Modern Acapulco

On November 11, 1927, the Mexican government blasted through the first Mexico City–Acapulco automobile road; the first cars shortly began arriving (after a six-day trip, however). The first luxury hotel, the Mirador, at La Quebrada, went up in 1933; soon airplanes began arriving.

During the late 1940s, Mexican President Miguel Alemán fell in love with Acapulco and thought everyone else should have the same opportunity. He built new boulevards, power plants, and modern Highway 95, which cut the Mexico City driving time to six hours. Investors responded with a lineup of high-rise hotels. Finally, in 1959, U.S. president Dwight Eisenhower and Mexican president Adolfo

López Mateos convened their summit conference in a grand Acapulco hostelry.

Movie stars such as Elvis Presley and Lana Turner began coming, staying for weeks, and buying homes. Elizabeth Taylor married movie magnate Michael Todd in the posh Hotel Villa Vera overlooking the new Acapulco. International jet service began in 1964.

Thousands of Mexicans flocked to fill jobs in the shiny hotels and restaurants. They built shantytowns, which climbed the hills and spilled over into previously sleepy communities nearby. The government responded with streets, drainage, power, housing, and schools.

However, by the 1980s overdevelopment was beginning to tarnish Acapulco's luster. Hotels had aged; some had become run-down. Untreated sewage was beginning to pollute Acapulco's once-pristine bay.

Fortunately, the government acted to reverse Acapulco's decline. New sewage works were built, clearing up the pollution. New streets and parks were constructed, and dozens of middle-aged hotels were returned to their former grandeur.

By the year 2000 Acapulco had been largely restored and was attracting new investments. Its sky was again blue, its azure waters were again clean, and it is now a magnet for millions of yearly visitors, foreign and domestic.

Sights

GETTING ORIENTED

In one tremendous sweep, Acapulco curves around its dazzling half-moon bay. Face the open ocean and you are looking due south. West will be on your right hand, east on your left. (The Pacific Ocean lies to the south, not the west? Unexpected but true. Remember that everywhere on earth, the sun sets in the west, and then notice where the sun sets in Acapulco: not out to sea, as in San Francisco or Seattle, but in a direction approximately parallel to the shoreline.)

One continuous beachfront boulevard, appropriately named the Costera Miguel Alemán (the "Costera," for short), unites old (pre-1950) Acapulco, west of the Parque Papagayo amusement zone, with new Acapulco, the lineup of big beach hotels that stretches around the bay to the Las Brisas condo headland. There, during the night, a big cross glows, marking the hilltop lookout, Mirador La Capilla, above the bay's east end.

On the opposite, old-town side of Parque Papagayo, the Costera curves along the palmy,

ACAPULCO

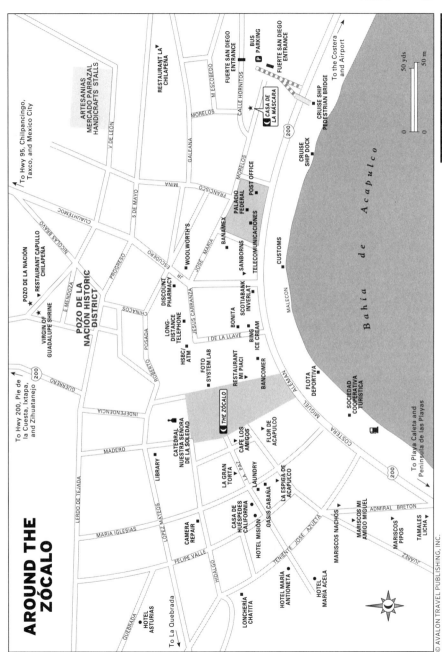

AROUND THE ZÓCALO

To Hwy 95, Chilpancingo,
Taxco, and Mexico City

ARTESANIAS
MERCADO PARRAZAL
HANDICRAFTS STALLS

RESTAURANT LA
CHILAPEÑA

M ESCOBEDO

FUERTE SAN DIEGO
ENTRANCE

BUS
PARKING

FUERTE SAN DIEGO
ENTRANCE

To the Costera
and Airport

MORELOS

CALLE HORNITOS

CASA DE
LA MÁSCARA

CRUISE SHIP
PEDESTRIAN BRIDGE

200

CRUISE
SHIP DOCK

50 yds

50 m

GALEANA

V DE LEON

MINA

MORELOS

POST OFFICE

CUSTOMS

CUAHTEMOC

NICOLAS BRAVO

POZO DE LA NACION

RESTAURANT CAPULLO
CHILAPEÑA

VIRGIN OF
GUADALUPE SHRINE

POZO DE LA
NACIÓN HISTORIC
DISTRICT

5 DE MAYO

ESCUDERO

PROGRESO

JR. JOSÉ MARIA

FRANCISCO

PALACIO
FEDERAL

BANAMEX

WOOLWORTH'S

SANBORNS

TELECOMUNICACIONES

Bahía de Acapulco

E MENDOZA

CHINACOS

POSADA

ROBERTO

DISCOUNT
PHARMACY

LONG-
DISTANCE
TELEPHONE

JESUS CARRANZA

I DE LA LLAVE

BONITA

SCOTIABANK
INVERLAT

BING
ICE CREAM

MALECON

GUERRERO

200

INDEPENDENCIA

HSBC/
ATM

FOTO
SYSTEM LAB

RESTAURANT
MI PIACI

BANCOMER

MIGUEL ALEMAN

FLOTA
DEPORTIVA

SOCIEDAD
COOPERATIVA
TURISTICA

To Hwy 200, Pie de
la Cuesta, Ixtapa,
and Zihuatanejo

THE ZÓCALO

To Playa Caleta and
Peninsula de las Playas

LERDO DE TEJADA

CATEDRAL
NUESTRA SEÑORA
DE LA SOLEDAD

MADERO

LIBRARY

LA PAZ

CAFE LOS
AMIGOS

FLOR DE
ACAPULCO

COSTERA

200

LOPEZ MATEOS

MARIA IGLESIAS

CAMERA
REPAIR

CASA DE
HUÉSPEDES
CALIFORNIA

LA GRAN
TORTA

LAUNDRY

LA ESPIGA DE
ACAPULCO

HOTEL MISIÓN

OASIS CABAÑA

MARISCOS NACHOS

MARISCOS MI
AMIGO MIGUEL

ADMIRAL BRETON

FELIPE VALLE

HIDALGO

TENIENTE JOSE AZUETA

MARISCOS
PIPOS

TAMALES
LICHA

JUAREZ

HOTEL
ASTURIAS

LONCHERIA
CHATITA

HOTEL MARIA
ANTONIETA

HOTEL
MARIA ACELA

QUEBRADA

To La Quebrada

© AVALON TRAVEL PUBLISHING, INC.

uncluttered Playas Hornos and Hamacas to the steamship dock. Here the Costera, called the *malecón* as it passes the *zócalo* (town plaza), continues to the mansion-dotted hilly jumble of Peninsula de las Playas.

GETTING AROUND

Buses run nearly continuously along the Costera. Fare averages the equivalent of about $0.40. Bus routes—indicated by such labels as Base (BAH-say, the naval base on the east end), Centro (*zócalo*), Caleta (the beach, at the far west end), Cine (movie theater near the beach before the *zócalo*), and Hornos (the beach near Parque Papagayo)—run along the Costera.

Taxis, on the other hand, cost between $2 and $6 for any in-town destination. They are not metered, so agree upon the price *before* you get in. If the driver demands too much, hailing another taxi often solves the problem.

A WALK AROUND OLD ACAPULCO

In old Acapulco, traffic slows and people return to traditional ways. Couples promenade along the *malecón* dockfront, fishing boats leave and return, while in the adjacent *zócalo,* families stroll past the church, musicians play, and tourists and businesspeople sip coffee in the shade of huge banyan trees.

🔲 The Zócalo

Start your walk beneath those *zócalo* trees. Under their pendulous air roots, browse the bookstalls, relax in one of the cafés; at night, watch the clowns perform, listen to a band concert, or join in a pitch-penny game. Take a look inside the mod-style **cathedral** dedicated to Our Lady of Solitude. Admire its angel-filled sky-blue ceiling and visit the Virgin to the right of the altar.

Outside, cross the boulevard to the *malecón* dockside; in midafternoon, you may see huge marlin and swordfish being hauled up from the boats.

🔲 Fuerte San Diego

Head out of the *zócalo* and left along the Costera and continue for about three blocks be-

a neo-colonial-style kiosk at the Acapulco old-town *zócalo*

© BRUCE WHIPPERMAN

neath the big pedestrian bridge to the uphill entrance stairway on the left. (Or, alternately, at the big signalled Costera intersection, at Sanborn's, head inland a block, and turn right at Jesús Carranza, at Woolworth's. Continue uphill about three blocks to the parking lot entrance, on the right.) Continue ahead over the great moat and enter the grand Fuerte San Diego (tel. 744/482-1114, fuertedesandiego@ prodigy.net.mx, 9:30 A.M.–6:30 P.M. daily except Mon.), a pentagonal maze of massive walls, all topped by bristling battlements, completed by engineer Miguel Costanzo in 1783.

Inside, galleries within the original fort storerooms, barracks, chapel, and kitchen illustrate local pre-Columbian, conquest, and colonial history. The excellent, unusually graphic displays include much about pirates (such as Francis Drake, Thomas Cavendish, and John Hawkins, known as "admirals" to the English-speaking world); Spanish galleons, their history and construction; and famous visitors. One notable visitor was Japanese ambassador Hasekura Tsunenaga, who in 1613 built a ship and sailed all handcrafted for the myriad traditional fiestas celebrated in towns and villages all over the state of Guerrero.

Besides the well-known examples, such as the clownish Viejitos (old ones), grinning red devils, scary jaguars, and angelic cherubs, be sure to see the masks that poke fun at the Spanish colonials, with features such as three eyes, double noses, bald heads, and big ears.

Although in modern society masks serve merely theatrical and celebratory functions, in parts of rural Mexico certain masks retain their pre-Columbian function and significance: By donning a mask, a person soaks up the supernatural power of the god that the mask depicts. Jaguar masks, for example, are a remnant of the jaguar cult, common in Mesoamerican tradition. Many ancient Mexican and Central American stone glyphs and paper or bark codices show half human, half jaguar personages, which anthropologists commonly interpret as depictions of priests in jaguar mask and costume, thus elevated to the powerful realm of the gods.

Cannons at Fuerte San Diego protected Acapulco from raiders for more than 300 years.

from Sendai, Japan, to Acapulco; he continued overland to Mexico City, by sea to Spain, to the pope in Rome, and back again through Acapulco to Japan. Before you leave, be sure to visit the museum's excellent bookstore, on the right after you pass the ticket booth.

Fuerte San Diego puts on an *espectáculo* (sound and light show), using symphonic melodies and dramatic projection upon curtains of water and the old fortress walls themselves to recount Acapulco's remarkable history. Showtimes, customarily at around 7 P.M., depend on season. Confirm the schedule (*horario*) at the museum or at the tourist information office, tel. 744/484-4416 or 744/484-4583.

◖ Casa de la Máscara

As you exit the Fuerte San Diego, continue along the lane that begins just west of the museum parking lot. In half a block, you'll arrive at Casa de la Máscara (no phone, pedriola240@hotmail.com, 10 A.M.–4 P.M. Tues.–Sun., admission free). Inside, enjoy six rooms decorated with a trove of fascinating indigenous masks,

ceremonial jaguar mask

Before leaving, be sure to visit the room of masks exotically reminiscent of West Africa, made by the *costeños,* or African Mexicans, most of whom now live along the Guerrero–Oaxaca coast east of Acapulco.

Pozo de la Nación Historic District

Pozo de la Nación, Acapulco's oldest permanent neighborhood, where the merchants that prospered from the Manila galleon trade built their homes, spreads uphill, behind the cathedral, north from the *zócalo.* The heart of the several-square-block district is the small intersection-square, at the corner of Calles Allende and Alarcón. A monument at the square's north, uphill, corner marks the *pozo* (well) for which the district is named. In 1850, governor Juan Álvarez ordered the well dug to furnish a clean water source and alleviate the devastating local cholera epidemic.

Acapulco people remember that wise and kindly act, especially around January 12, when droves of folks arrive to pay homage at the illuminated shrine to the Virgin of Guadalupe across the square from the *pozo.*

Behind the Guadalupe shrine, pause (especially if it's a warm day) in the cool shade beneath the great **Árbol del Fraile** (Tree of the Friar), brought from Peru as a seedling centuries ago. Locals enjoy the sweet yellow fruit that it drops from its spreading branches during the month of June.

Another good place to pause, especially if you're hungry, is at the clean *comedor*-style Restaurant El Nuevo Capullo Chilapeño, behind and to the right of the *pozo* monument.

La Quebrada

Head back to the *zócalo* and continue west from the front of the cathedral. After three short blocks to Avenida López Mateos, continue uphill to the La Quebrada diver's point, marked by the big parking lot at the hillcrest. There, Acapulco's energy focuses five times a day (at 1 P.M. and hourly 7–10 P.M.) as tense crowds watch the divers plummet more than 100 feet to the waves below. Admission is about

Celebrated artist Diego Rivera's monumental mosaic of Mexican myth embellishes the front wall of the Casa de Dolores Olmedo.

$2, collected by the divers' cooperative. Performers average less than $100 per dive from the proceeds. The adjacent Hotel Mirador charges about $5 cover to view the dives from its terrace.

Casa de Dolores Olmedo

Celebrated muralist and painter Diego Rivera (1886–1957), whose renown has received a boost from the latter-day fame of his second wife, Frida Kahlo, spent the last years of his life with his friend Dolores Olmedo, grand dame of Acapulco. Señora Olmedo, who herself died in July 2002, was perhaps the world's foremost collector of Rivera works. One of the most visible decorates the front wall of Olmedo's former home compound, on a quiet side street in the upscale Peninsula de las Playas neighborhood, not far from La Quebrada.

The work is a rainbow-hued mosaic, dynamically depicting some of Rivera's favorite prime actors of Mexican mythology. Foremost is the feathered serpent god Quetzalcoatl, who writhes along more than half of the 100-foot length of the mosaic. Also present is the beloved Mexican hairless dog, Xoloitzciutle.

Rivera, weakened by age, toiled for a year and a half during 1956 and 1957 to complete the mosaic. Loyal to his own communist ideology, he included a red hammer and sickle; in response to a government request, Rivera removed it before he died.

Rising behind the mural is Dolores Olmedo's former house, where Rivera stayed and worked, covering the inside chamber walls with a treasury of stunning murals. It's to be hoped that Señora Olmedo's heirs will continue her practice of allowing public viewing tours of some of the inside rooms. For more information, contact Guerrero Turismo at tel. 744/484-4583 or 744/484-4416.

Get there most easily by taxi. If you don't mind (or would welcome) a short but steep hike (best in morning or late afternoon), go from La Quebrada. Cross busy Avenida López Mateos and continue south, heading up steep, winding Camino de la Pinzona. Turn right at the first street (after about a quarter mile), Camino de la Inalambrica, and continue another quarter mile to the Olmedo house, and mosaic, on the right at Inalambrica 6.

Palma Sola Archaeological Site

On a high hillside above Acapulco's west-side neighborhood, a trove of petroglyphs has been excavated for public viewing (approximately 9 A.M.–5 P.M. daily, admission $2). The site, at an elevation of about 1,200 feet, adjacent to ridgetop El Veladero ecological park, displays a number of big (3–20 feet) geometric-, animal-, and human-form petroglyphs. Created by an ancient people, known generically as "Los Yopes," the stone carvings date from between 200 B.C. and A.D. 600. Get there most easily by tour or taxi, up Avenida Palma Sola to road's end before the hilltop, where a path leads you the last few hundred yards. Take a hat, water, and walking shoes. Local guides will most likely be available on-site. You may also want to arrange a tour through a travel agent, such as American Express, at the west end of the Hotel

Palma Sola Archaeological Site preserves a treasury of ancient petroglyphs.

© BRUCE WHIPPERMAN

ACAPULCO

Continental Emporio, tel. 744/435-2200. For more information, contact the tourist information office, tel. 744/484-4416.

BEACHES
Old Town Beaches
These start not far from the *zócalo*. At the foot of the Fuerte San Diego, the sand of **Playa Hamacas** (hammocks) begins, changing to **Playa de Los Hornos** (ovens) and curving northeasterly a mile to a rocky shoal-line called Farallón de San Lorenzo. Hornos is the Sunday favorite of Mexican families; boats buzz beyond the very tranquil waves and retirees stroll the wide, yellow sand while vendors work the sunbathing crowd.

Moving south past the *zócalo* and the fishing boats, you'll find **Playa Tlacopanocha,** a petite strip of sand beneath some spreading trees. Here, bay-tour launches wait for passengers, and kids play in the glassy water, which would be great for swimming if it weren't for the refuse from nearby fishing boats.

Playas Caleta and Caletilla
From the inland side of the Costera, hop onto one of the parade of buses marked Caleta to gemlike Playa Caleta and its twin Playa Caletilla on the far side of the hilly peninsula (named, appropriately, Peninsula de las Playas). With medium-coarse yellow sand and blue ripples for waves, Caleta and Caletilla are for people who want company. They are often crowded, sometimes nearly packed solid on Sundays and holidays. Boats offer banana-tube rides, and snorkel gear is rentable from beach concessionaires. Dozens of stalls and restaurants serve food and refreshments. Prominent among them is the stall of Arturo "Chocolate" Castro and his oyster divers, who serve their own catch-of-the-day mussels, oysters, and octopus right on the west end of the beach.

Mágico Mundo water park (tel. 744/483-1215, 9 A.M.–6 P.M. daily, $4 adult, $2 child) perches on the little peninsula between the beaches. You'll find an aquarium, restaurant, water slides, swimming pool, and sea lion, piranha, and turtle shows.

◖ Isla Roqueta
An Isla Roqueta ticket tout will often try to snare you as you get off the Caleta bus. The round-trip, which runs around $3, is usually in a boat with a glass bottom, through which you

© BRUCE WHIPPERMAN

Isla Roqueta's trails lead to some of Acapulco's quiet, hidden places.

can peer at the fish as they peer back from their aqua underwater world. On the other side, you can relax on sunny little Playa Roqueta and have lunch at one of several beachside *palapas.*

Later, you might visit the small hillside **zoo,** in the forest above the beach. Animals include some of the endangered local species, such as spider monkey, jaguar, mountain lion, coatimundi, *javelín* (peccary), crocodile, and ocelot.

Other Isla Roqueta options include hiking the mid-island trail uphill from Playa Roqueta a few hundred yards through the shady tropical deciduous forest to the **faro** (lighthouse) at the island summit. The few marines who guard the place are lonely and welcome company. Say hello through the gate and they may let you in for a look around.

Afterward, you could cool off with a swimming, snorkeling, and sunning excursion at one of the island's intimate hidden beaches. For example, from the lighthouse, continue uphill a few hundred yards, then fork right at the clifftop trail and stroll downhill about a mile, where you can cool off, paddling in the tidepools at Playa Las Palmitas, at Roqueta's secluded western tip. (Bring your snorkel, mask, and sunscreen.)

Alternatively, on the island's east side past the zoo, a trail climbs to the hillcrest and leads steeply downhill to tiny, secluded **Playa Marin,** where you can loll to your heart's content in the waves that funnel into the narrow channel.

A **boat tour** from Playa Caleta (from the Mágico Mundo island) is another way to get to Isla Roqueta. Glass-bottomed boats leave several times an hour during mid-day, for 90-minute tours (about $5 per person, last boat back around 5 P.M.). Trips include viewing underwater life, shoreline vistas, 1940s movie stars' (Pedro Infante, John Wayne, Johnny Weismuller) homes, the Virgen Submarina (a holy image of the Virgin of Guadalupe submerged in the Isla Roqueta channel), a stop on the island, and snorkeling. Beer and soft drinks are customarily sold onboard.

An especially nice spot to linger and kick back after your Isla Roqueta exertions is Polynesian-mode **Restaurant Palao** (noon–6 P.M.

daily), perched invitingly above the island's west side channel-front. If you've got an appetite, satisfy it with their melt-in-your mouth Hawaiian-style pork ribs.

◖ Hotel Los Flamingos

After a spell exploring the delights of Playa Caleta and Isla Roqueta, be sure to stop nearby (take a taxi west, uphill, along clifftop Av. López Mateos) at gorgeously out-of-date Hotel Los Flamingos for a meal, a refreshment in their airy view gazebo (*mirador*), or just a look around. Former home of Johnny Weismuller, the most famous Tarzan of them all, the Hotel Los Flamingos blooms with delights, from a breathtaking clifftop ocean vista and a lusciously leafy hilltop mango garden-jungle, to a precious blue designer pool. Before you leave, be sure to take in the fascinating gallery of 1940s and '50s photos of luminaries who used to call the Hotel Los Flamingos home, such as John Wayne, Frank Sinatra, Peter Lawford, and Rory Calhoun. The place is so lovely you may be tempted to check in for a week's stay.

Playa Angosta

Back on the mainland, you can visit another hidden beach nearby, Playa Angosta (Narrow Beach), the only Acapulco strand with an unobstructed sunset horizon. A breezy dab of a beach, sandwiched between a pair of sandstone cliffs, Angosta's ocean waves roll in, swishing upon the sand. A food *palapa* occupies one side of the beach and a few fishing launches and nets are on the other. With caution, swimming, bodysurfing, and boogie boarding are sometimes possible here; otherwise, Angosta is best for scenery and picnics.

Just uphill, a few hundred yards along the southbound cliffside Avenida López Mateos, is **Sinfonia del Sol** sunset amphitheater. Here, local folks begin gathering around 5 P.M. daily during the winter (6:30 P.M. in the summer) to enjoy the sun's oft-spectacular twilight performance.

Costera Beaches

These are the hotel-lined golden shores where affluent Mexicans and foreign visitors stay and

Evening is balmy and uncrowded on Acapulco bay beaches.

© BRUCE WHIPPERMAN

The Sinfonia del Sol amphitheater is a great place to watch the sunset.

play in the sun. They are variations on one continuous curve of sand. Beginning at the west end with **Playa Hornitos** (also known as Playa Papagayo), it continues, changing names from **Playa Morro** to **Playa Condesa** and finally **Playa Icacos,** which curves and stretches to its sheltered east end past the naval base. All of the same semicoarse golden silica sand, the beaches begin with fairly broad 200-foot-wide Playas Papagayo and Morro. They narrow sharply to under 100 feet at Playa Condesa, then broaden again to more than 200 feet along Playa Icacos.

The surf is mostly gentle, breaking in one- or two-foot waves near the beach and receding with moderate undertow. This makes for safe swimming within float-enclosed beachside areas, but waves generally break too near the beach for bodysurfing, boogie boarding, or surfing. Beyond the swimming floats, motorboats hurry along, pulling parasailers and banana-tube riders, while personal watercraft cavort and careen over the swells.

Such motorized hubbub lessens the safety and enjoyment of quieter sports off most new-town beaches. Sailboaters and sailboarders with their own equipment might try the remote, more tranquil east end of Playa Icacos, however.

Water-skiing, officially restricted to certain parts of Acapulco Bay, has largely moved to Laguna Coyuca northwest of the city. Laguna Coyuca also has enough space for many good motorboat-free spots for sailboaters and sailboarders.

Rocky outcroppings along Playas Papagayo, Morro, and Condesa add interest and intimacy to an already beautiful shoreline. The rocks are good for tidepooling and fishing by pole-casting (or by net, as locals do) above the waves.

Beaches Southeast of Town
Drive, taxi ($10), or ride a Puerto Marqués- or Lomas-marked bus along the Costera eastward. Past the naval base entrance on the right, the road climbs the hill, passing a number of panoramic bay viewpoints. After the Las Brisas condo-hotel complex, the road curves around the hill shoulder and heads downward past picture-perfect vistas of **Bahía de Puerto Marqués.** At the bottom-of-the-hill intersection and overpass, a road branches right to Puerto Marqués.

The little bayside town is mainly a Sunday seafood and picnicking retreat for Acapulco families. Dozens of *palapa* restaurants line its motorboat-dotted sandy beach. One ramshackle hotel, at the far south end of the single main beachfront street, offers lodgings.

If you're driving, mark your odometer at the hill-bottom intersection and head east toward the airport. If traveling by bus, continue via one of the Lomas buses, which head east from Acapulco about once an hour. About a mile farther, a turn-off road goes right to the Fairmont Acapulco Princess and the Pierre Marques hotels and golf course on Playa Revolcadero.

Beach access is by side roads or by walking directly through the hotel lobbies. If you come by bus, hail a taxi from the highway to the Hotel Princess door for the sake of a good entrance.

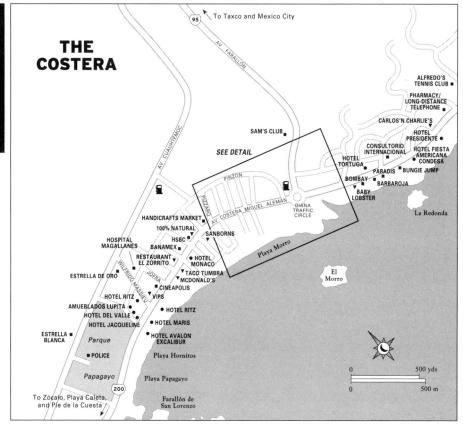

Playa Revolcadero, a broad, miles-long, yellow-white strand, has the rolling open-ocean billows that Acapulco Bay doesn't. The sometimes-rough waves are generally good for boogie boarding, bodysurfing, and even surfing, especially near the shoals on the northwest end. Because of the waves and sometimes hazardous currents, the hotel provides lifeguards. The Playa Revolcadero breeze is also brisk enough for sailing and sailboarding with your own boat or board. Some rentals may be available from the hotel beach concession.

Playa Larga

About seven miles (11 km) from the Puerto Marqués traffic intersection, the Barra Vieja road forks right and heads along breezy, wild Playa Larga. If you're in the mood for some exercise, bring a bike and take advantage of the new *ciclopista* (bike path) that begins at the Barra Vieja (Km 11) road fork and parallels the road all the way to Barra Vieja. Although I didn't see them on my last trip, my taxi driver said that concessionaires at both ends of the *ciclopista* rent bicycles on weekends.

About two miles from the fork, you will pass the lovely retreat Villas San Vicente, a collection of several small villas and two studio cottages, all nestled in their own palmy, private beachside park.

A rustic campground and trailer park has opened up for business on Playa Larga. Watch

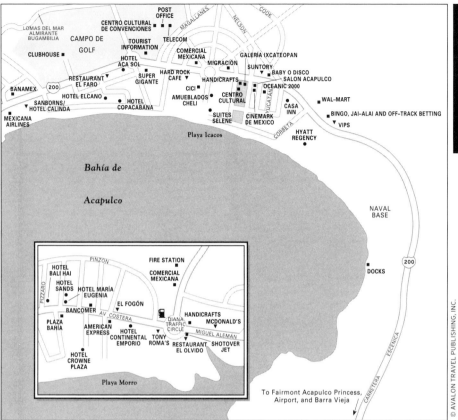

© AVALON TRAVEL PUBLISHING, INC.

for their sign about four miles from the fork. If you do camp on Playa Larga, you'll be able to share in enjoying the wide, breezy strand, whose rolling waves, with ordinary precautions, appear to be good for boogie boarding, bodysurfing, and possibly surfing. The sun sets on an unobstructed horizon, and the crab-rich beach is good for surf fishing (or by boat if you launch during morning calm). Additionally, the firm, level sand is excellent for jogging, walking, and beachcombing.

For the past several years a hardy group of eco-volunteers has patrolled Playa Larga (Long Beach). In times past, they've been camping for the summer–fall turtle season about 10 miles (16 km) from the fork at their Campamento Tortuguero Playa Larga. If you see them, stop and say a word of encouragement and perhaps donate some food or money to help them sustain their lonely vigil. Even better, set up your own tent nearby and volunteer your help recovering, incubating, and finally releasing the turtle hatchlings.

Barra Vieja and Laguna Tres Palos

About a mile farther on, the stores (groceries and long-distance phone) and modest houses of fishing village Barra Vieja dot the roadside. Many seafood *palapas* line the beach side. The better among them include Don Beto's and Gloria del Mar, both with pools.

(Prices, however, are very steep. Expect to pay $2.50 for a beer or orangeade and $12–15 for a fish plate, although buying lunch entitles you to occupy your table for the rest of the day.)

In addition to the beach, Barra Vieja visitors enjoy access to the vast Laguna Tres Palos mangrove wetland from the *estero* at the east end of town before the bridge. From there, boatmen (ask for José Organes, Beto Godoy, or Felipe or Pedro Sala) take parties on fishing and wildlife-viewing excursions for about $35 for six people. Horseback rides are also available for about $20 per person.

The road (which maps routinely show going through to Highway 200) crosses a lagoon bridge and ends about two miles farther east at scruffy Lomas de Chapultepec village.

Accommodations

Location largely determines the price and style of Acapulco hotels. Most of the budget hotels are in old Acapulco, near the *zócalo*. None of them are near a beach, and with only one deluxe exception, none of them have wheelchair access. Nevertheless, their doors lead directly to a nearby feast of old-Mexico sights and sounds, and their prices are certainly right.

Old Acapulco does offer beachfront hotel options, however. A number of good, moderately priced beachfront hotels are available in the Peninsula de las Playas on Playas Caleta and Caletilla and east of the *zócalo* on Playa de Los Hornos. Here, guests enjoy semideluxe resort amenities and luscious ocean vistas.

New Acapulco hotels, by contrast, lie in new Acapulco, along the Costera Miguel Alemán either right on the beach or within a block or two of it. Guests at the fancier beachfront hostelries enjoy a wealth of resort amenities and luxury view rooms at correspondingly luxurious prices. Most have wheelchair access.

Many Acapulco lodgings, however, defy categorization. Acapulco offers numerous choices to suit individual tastes and pocketbooks. Moreover, *Acapulco occupancy is highly seasonal.* In the new-town luxury hotels, Americans and Canadians crowd in during the winter. In old Acapulco, popular with middle- and working-class Mexican families, high season is during holidays and July and August. All hotels are full during the major Christmas–New Year's and Semana Santa pre-Easter week holidays. During the low seasons, you can usually save money by requesting a package (*paquete*) and four-night, weekly, or monthly discounts (*descuentos*). For high-season lodgings, always call, email, fax, or write (use global priority mail) early for reservations. More information about the hotels listed here is available at their websites.

(*Note:* Addresses along Acapulco's main boulevard, Av. Costera Miguel Alemán, do not correspond with location. Instead, numbers seem to have been mostly assigned chronologically.)

HOTELS NEAR THE ZÓCALO

A number of clean, budget-to-moderately priced hotels cluster in the colorful working-class neighborhood between the *zócalo* and La Quebrada divers' point.

Under $25

Three blocks west of the *zócalo* on the quiet cul-de-sac end of Avenida La Paz stands the spartan three-story **Hotel María Acela** (Av. La Paz 19, Acapulco, Guerrero 39300, tel. 744/482-0661, $8 s, $12 d). Its family management lends a homey atmosphere more like a guesthouse than a hotel. The 21 austerely furnished fan rooms, although clean enough (but not immaculate), lack hot water. Guests enjoy a small lobby library of paperback books.

Also on quiet side street La Paz stands good budget buy **Casa de Huéspedes California** (Av. La Paz 12, Acapulco, Guerrero 39300, tel. 744/482-2893, $10 s, $20 d low season, $12 s and $24 d high). Guests enjoy about 20 plainly decorated but clean rooms, in two stories surrounding a quiet, tropical inner patio.

One block farther away from the *zócalo,* the aging 1960s-vintage **Hotel María Antioneta** (Teniente Azueta 17, Acapulco, Guerrero 39300, tel. 744/482-5024, $8 s, $17 d year-round except for Christmas and Easter) fronts the busy store- and restaurant-lined Avenida Azueta. The 34 plainly furnished, somewhat worn rooms are nevertheless light, especially on the upper floor, and have fans, air-conditioning, and hot water. Bathrooms could use a good scrubbing, however. Most rooms are fortunately recessed along the leafy inner courtyard, away from street noise. Guests have the use of a handy communal kitchen and an unfurnished but potentially attractive upstairs terrace (that I suggested to the manager would be greatly improved with some tables and chairs). Credit cards are not accepted.

Uphill above and south of the La Quebrada parking lot is 🄲 **Hotel Torre Eifel** (Inalambrica 110, Acapulco, Guerrero 39300, tel. 744/482-1683, fax 744/483-5727, hoteltorreeifel@hotmail.com; $10 s, $15 d, $20 t low season; $15 s, $30 d, $45 t holidays) with fans, hot water, and parking. Above a hillside garden overlooking the La Quebrada divers' point tourist mecca, guests enjoy 25 simply but comfortably furnished rooms overlooking an inviting pool and patio. Guests in the uppermost rooms enjoy breezy sea views and a sunset horizon. (*Note:* The hotel's Inalambrica address is misleading: you'll find it at the corner of Avenida Pinzona, one block uphill, on the right from the La Quebrada parking lot.)

$25-50

The **Hotel Asturias** (Quebrada 45, Acapulco, Guerrero 39300, tel./fax 744/483-6548, cerardoancera@aol.com; $15 s, $25 d, $40 t year-round with fans; $25 s, $40 d, with a/c and TV), on Avenida Quebrada a few blocks uphill from the *zócalo,* offers a relaxing atmosphere at budget rates. Its two stories hold 15 plain but tidy rooms surround a plant-decorated pool and patio with chairs for sunning. Get an upper room for more light and privacy. Find

it four short blocks west of the cathedral, between Ramírez and Ortiz.

Arguably the most charming of *zócalo*-area hotels is the authentically colonial-era 🄲 **Hotel Misión** (Felipe Valle 12, Acapulco, Guerrero 39300, tel. 744/482-3643, fax 744/482-2076, hotelmision@hotmail.com, $14 s, $28 d low season, $18 s, $36 d high), at the corner of La Paz, two blocks west of the *zócalo.* The owner, María Elena Sayago, relates the history of her hotel-home. From 1930 to 1966, it was a school, the Colegio Acapulco. When she began repairs several years ago, her workers uncovered broken antique Chinese porcelain, most likely brought from Asia by the colonial-era Manila galleons. Before the 1910–1917 Revolution, she says, the place housed army offices, and before that, it was a banklike *estango* (depository) for valuables. The front-section walls and rooms were preserved in the original adobe, and the columns in the original stone. Most of the guest rooms, however, she had rebuilt, in two stories around a plant-decorated patio shaded by a spreading mango tree. When the mangoes ripen in April guests get their fill of the fragrant fruit. Rates for her 24 attractively decorated rooms include fans, hot water, and parking in an adjacent lot.

Five blocks west of the *zócalo,* up winding Avenida Pinzona, the 🄲 **Hotel Etel Suites** (Av. Pinzona 92, Acapulco, Guerrero 39390, tel. 744/482-2240 or 744/482-2241, etelsuites@terra.com.mx) perches on the view hillside above old Acapulco. Well managed by friendly owner Etel Sutter Álvarez (great-granddaughter of renowned California-Swiss pioneer Johann A. Sutter) and her daughter, the three-building complex stair-steps downhill to a luxurious view garden and pool. Its airy hillside perch lends the Etel Suites a tranquil, luxurious ambience unusual in a moderately priced lodging. Chairs and sofas in a small street-level lobby invite relaxed conversation with fellow guests. The primly but thoughtfully furnished and well-maintained rooms vary from singles to multibedroom view apartments. The dozens of rooms and suites rent from about $30 s or d low season,

OWNING PARADISE

Droves of repeat visitors have fled their northern winters and bought or permanently rented a part of their favorite Mexican Pacific paradises. They happily live all or part of the year in beachside developments that have mushroomed, especially around Acapulco, Ixtapa, Zihuatanejo, Manzanillo, and Puerto Vallarta. Deluxe vacation homes, which foreigners can own through special trusts, run upward from $100,000; condos begin at about half that. Time-shares, a type of rental, start at about $5,000.

TRUSTS

In the past, Mexicans have feared, with some justification, that foreigners were out to buy their country. As a consequence, present laws prohibit foreigners from holding direct title to property within 30 miles (50 km) of a beachfront or within 60 miles (100 km) of a national border.

However, Mexican law does permit *fideicomisos* (trusts), which substitute for outright foreign ownership. Trusts allow you, as the beneficiary, all the usual rights to the property, such as use, sale, improvement, and transfer, in exchange for paying an annual fee to a Mexican bank, the trustee, which holds nominal title to the property. Trust ownership has been compared to owning all the shares of a corporation, which in turn owns a factory. While not owning the factory in name, you have legal control over it.

Although some folks have been bilked into buying south-of-the-border equivalents of the Brooklyn Bridge, Mexican trust ownership is a happy reality for growing numbers of American, Canadian, and European beneficiaries who simply love Mexico. Take note, however, that *the great majority of Mexican real estate sales are cash only.* Real estate mortgage loans in Mexico, while not unheard of, are definitely the exception.

Bienes raíces (bee-AY-nays rah-EE-says, real estate) in Mexico works a lot like it does in the United States and Canada. Agents handle multiple listings, show properties, assist negotiations, track paperwork, and earn commissions for sales completed. If you're interested in buying a Mexican property, work with one of the many honest and hardworking agents in Mexico, preferably recommended through a reliable firm back home or trustworthy, property-savvy friends in Mexico.

$50 high, with fans, air-conditioning, and hot water. Completely furnished view apartments with kitchens go for about $50 low season, $70 high, with discounts negotiable for monthly rentals. There is some parking, and credit cards are accepted. (*Note:* If you arrive in Acapulco on a crowded high-season weekend without a reservation, the Etel Suites will probably be the last decent place in town likely to have a room.)

Over $100

At the cliff end of Calle Quebrada stands the *zócalo* area's only upscale hostelry, the **Hotel El Mirador Acapulco** (Plazoleta La Quebrada 74, Acapulco, Guerrero, 39300, tel. 744/483-1155, toll-free Mex. tel. 800/021-7557 or U.S./Can. tel. 866/765-0608, fax 744/482-4564, mirador@hotelelmiradoracapulco.com.mx, www.hotelelmiradoracapulco.com.mx, $110 d standard, $130 deluxe, $210 d large suite with private view balcony and kitchenette). Acapulco's first deluxe hotel, El Mirador was built in the early 1930s. El Mirador appropriately uses the La Quebrada diver in its logo. Directly below the hotel restaurant-bar, the divers accomplish their feat to the acclaim of hundreds of spectators five times daily. The hotel has much more to recommend than spectacle, however. Guests choose from a collection of about 50 semidetached picturesquely perched hillside lodgings. Inside, they are attractively furnished in dark masculine tones, shiny rustic floor tiles, decorator reading lamps, and deluxe bathrooms. Two airy, sunset-view restaurants, bars, and three swim-

Once you find a good property and have a written sales agreement in hand, your agent should recommend a *notaria pública* (notary) who, unlike a U.S. notary public, is an attorney skilled and licensed in property transactions.

A Mexican notary, functioning much as a title company does in the United States, is the most important person in completing your transaction. The notary traces the title, ensuring that your bank-trustee legally receives it, and makes sure the agreed-upon amounts of money get transferred between you, seller, bank, agent, and notary.

You and your agent should meet jointly with the notary early on to discuss the deal and get the notary's computation of the closing costs. For a typical trust-sale, closing costs (covering permit, filing, bank, notary, and registry fees) are considerable, typically 8-10 percent of the sale amount. After that, you will continue to owe property taxes and an approximately 1 percent annual fee to your bank-trustee.

TIME-SHARING

Started in Europe, time-sharing has spread all over the globe. A time-share is a prepaid rental of a condo for a specified time period per year. Agreements usually allow you to temporarily exchange your time-share rental for similar lodgings throughout the world.

Your first contact with time-sharing will often be someone on a resort street corner who offers you a half-price tour for "an hour of your time." Soon you'll be attending a hard-sell session offering you tempting inducements in exchange for a check written on the spot. The basic appeal is your investment – say $10,000 cash for a two-week annual stay in a deluxe beach condo – which will earn you a handsome profit if you decide to sell your rights sometime in the future. What isn't mentioned is that time-shares have become increasingly difficult to sell and the interest or dividends you could get for your $10,000 cash would go far toward renting an equally luxurious vacation condo every year without entailing as much risk.

And risk there is, because you would be handing over your cash for a promise only. Read the fine print. Shop around, and don't give away anything until you inspect the condo you would be getting and talk to others who have invested in the same time-share. It may be a good deal, but don't let anyone rush you into paradise.

ming pools complete the attractive picture. All rooms have cable TV, air-conditioning, some rooms have wheelchair access, and parking.

PENINSULA DE LAS PLAYAS HOTELS

Many of old Acapulco's mid- to high-end lodgings are spread along one continuous boulevard that winds through the plush Peninsula de las Playas neighborhood. The boulevard starts as the Costera Miguel Alemán as it heads past the *zócalo*. A couple of miles farther southwest, the boulevard curves left as the Gran Via Tropical, rounding the Peninsula de las Playas clockwise. Passing Playas Caleta and Caletilla, the boulevard changes to Avenida López Mateos and continues along the peninsula's sunset (southwest) side past Playa Angosta and La Quebrada

divers' point before ending back in the *zócalo* neighborhood.

(*Note:* Playas Caleta and Caletilla are customarily crowded with local picnickers and vacationers all holidays and most weekends, especially Sunday. If noise is a problem for you, you had better stay at the Acamar Beach Resort or the Hotel Boca Chica weekdays only; or alternatively stay at the Hotels Los Flamingos or Caleta, both with more spacious grounds and removed from the beachfront hubbub.)

A quartet of highly recommendable semi-deluxe hotels decorates the peninsula's luscious south-side oceanfront. Least expensive is the **Hotel Caleta** (Cerro San Martin 225, Playa Caleta, Acapulco, Guerrero 39300, tel. 744/483-9334, 744/483-9234, or 744/483-9140, toll-free Mex. tel. 800/716-2159 or

800/700-0979, fax 744/485-1810, meigaca@ prodigy.net.mx, www.meigashoteles.com, $60 per person, $85 per person holidays and July–Aug.), formerly Grand Meigas Acapulco, on the east headland bordering Playa Caleta. Hotel guests enjoy a big blue pool and view sundeck, an intimately private (but sometimes jetsam-strewn) rock-enfolded open-ocean beach, lush green garden, and comfortable rooms, with private panoramic view balconies. Although renovated in the mid-1990s, the hotel is now showing a bit of wear around the edges. The all-inclusive rates cover all meals, drinks, and in-house sports and entertainment. All rooms have air-conditioning, phones, cable TV, some rooms have wheelchair access, and parking; credit cards are accepted.

A block farther east, right on the beach, stands the ◖ **Acamar Beach Resort** (Av. Costera M. Alemán 26, Fracc. Las Playas, Acapulco, Guerrero 39390, tel. 744/482-0570, 744/482-0571, or 744/482-0572, toll-free Mex. tel. outside Acapulco 800/719-3684, fax 744/482-2119, rentas@acamaracapulco.com,

www.acamaracapulco.com), formerly Hotel Playa Caleta. The hotel's popularity among middle-class Mexican vacationers flows from its semideluxe amenities and lovely beachfront location, all at moderate prices. Above the 1950s-style but attractively renovated lobby-restaurant-bar rise six floors of 136 rooms, invitingly decorated in white stucco, with shiny marble floors, cheery tropical-bright bedspreads, polished rattan furniture, and modern-standard shower baths. Reserve an upper (floors 4, 5, or 6) for more quiet, light, and a gorgeous ocean view. Rentals ordinarily run about $55 d, $65 t, street view only, or $72 d, $85 t with ocean view. Add $15 for kitchenette (stove, sink, dishes, and utensils, but no refrigerator). Rates rise approximately double during pre-Easter week and Christmas–New Year's holidays. For a splurge, treat yourself to a corner suite, with panoramic 270-degree view, about $150 d. Amenities include cable TV, air-conditioning, beachfront pool-patio, some rooms have wheelchair access, parking ($3/day), and credit cards accepted.

© BRUCE WHIPPERMAN

Playa Caleta, at the west end of Acapulco's Peninsula de las Playas, is an Acapulco family favorite, for its soft sand and good, moderately priced hotels.

Two blocks farther west along the beach, guests of the 🄲 **Hotel Boca Chica** (Playa Caletilla s/n, Acapulco, Guerrero 39300, tel./fax 744/483-6601 or 744/483-6741, bocach@acabtu.com.mx, $80 d) enjoy an enviable beach vantage and semideluxe amenities. Here, views of Playa Caletilla on one hand and the green Isla Roqueta beyond an azure channel on the other are stunning. The hotel perches on a rocky point, invitingly close to the sand and clear aqua water from the pool deck and surrounding garden paths. The light, comfortably furnished rooms vary; if you have the option, look at two or three before you choose. Early reservations year-round are strongly recommended. Rates for the 45 rooms with phones and air-conditioning stay the same year-round, with breakfast, some rooms have wheelchair access; credit cards are accepted, and parking is available.

Half a mile farther west uphill, a different but equally attractive option is available at the 🄲 **Hotel Los Flamingos** (P.O. Box 70, Acapulco, Guerrero 39300, tel. 744/482-0690, 744/482-0691, or 744/482-0692, fax 744/483-9806, flamingoo@prodigy.net.mx, www.flamingosacapulco.com). Los Flamingos is the place where oldsters reminisce and youngsters find out who John Wayne, Johnny Weissmuller, and Rory Calhoun were. Personable owner-manager and musician Adolfo Santiago González enjoys playing his guitar and relating his experiences with his famous guests of yesteryear. Vintage Hollywood photos decorate the open-air lobby walls, while pathways lead through a hilltop jungle of palm, hibiscus, and spreading mangoes. The 40-odd rooms, several with private, ocean-view balconies, perch on a cliffside that plummets into foaming breakers hundreds of feet below. Soft evening guitar music in an open-air sunset-view restaurant and a luxurious clifftop pool and patio complete the lovely picture. The rooms, in standard, superior, and junior suite grades, ordinarily run about $70, $82, and $93 d, and $80, $100, and $112 holidays. Add about $30 for an extra person. The hotel also offers **Casa Redonda,** a secluded clifftop ocean-view house,

the former Acapulco home-away-from-home of Johnny Weissmuller (the most famous Tarzan), who died in 1984. All with parking, some air-conditioning; credit cards are accepted.

On the peninsula's east side, apartment-style **Suites Alba** (Gran Via Tropical 35, Acapulco, Guerrero 39390, tel. 744/483-0073, fax 744/483-8378, alba@suitesalba.com.mx, www.suitesalba.com.mx, $85 d low season, $105 d high) rambles through its well-kept hilltop garden of palms and pools. The mostly Canadian and American middle-class guests enjoy many facilities, including a pair of pools, a whirlpool tub, a restaurant, a mini-mart, some rooms have wheelchair access, and a bayside beach club with its own saltwater pool. The 292 comfortably furnished apartments have kitchenettes, air-conditioning, and private garden-view balconies. Discounts are available for monthly rentals, credit cards are accepted, and parking is available.

PLAYA DE LOS HORNOS HOTELS

As Acapulco development moved eastward around the bay during the 1940s and '50s, a row of comfortable, multifloored hotels were built across the Costera from the long, plumy Playa de Los Hornos beachfront grove, now midway between the *zócalo* and new Acapulco. Many of these hotels, recently renovated, remain popular, especially with Mexican weekenders and savvy budget-conscious foreign vacationers, who enjoy airy, uncluttered panoramic bay views from upper-floor rooms.

One of the best is the very worthy **Hotel Castillo Real** (Av. Costera M. Alemán 265, Fracc. Hornos, Acapulco, Guerrero 39350, tel./fax 744/486-2300, toll-free Mex. tel. 800/711-4609, hotelcastilloreal@yahoo.com.mx). This middle-aged but well-maintained, locally owned hostelry offers 135 rooms on 10 floors; about half the rooms have panoramic ocean views. Rooms are all the same high standard: immaculate and comfortably furnished with two double beds, modern wood furniture, a wall-mounted reading lamp, and a smallish but attractively tiled modern shower bath. Other amenities include a spare but sunny top-floor pool-patio, fine for lap swimming. Monday–Thursday, rooms go for about $60 s or d, $67 t, $75 q; weekends, holidays, and July–August they're $66, $76, and $86. With either fans or air-conditioning, cable TV, parking, and credit cards accepted. (*Note:* At this writing, the Hotel Castillo Real was closed down by employees picketing for back wages. Hopefully by the time you read this the hotel will have re-opened.)

Meanwhile, next door, find another excellent choice, **Hotel Aca Bay** (Av. Costera M. Alemán 266, Fracc. Hornos, Acapulco, Guerrero 39350, tel. 744/485-8228, toll-free Mex. tel. 800/714-2762 or U.S./Can. tel. 877/400-9302, fax 744/485-0774, acabay@prodigy.net.mx, www.hotel-acabay.com.mx). This modest, 1960s-modern resort-style hotel offers 118 rooms in 20 floors. Four room grades are available: standard for one or two people; double for up to four; junior suite, with more room for up to six; and larger, choicer master suites, all immaculate and comfortably furnished, with attractive wood furniture, reading lamps, marble floors, shiny shower baths, and most with panoramic bay views. Normal (other than holidays and July–Aug.) walk-in asking prices run, respectively, about $75, $90, $110, and $120. Get a discount (to about $55, $75, $90, or $110) by reserving directly through the hotel (instead of through an agent). Rooms vary; look at more than one. Add about 25 percent to these rates during Easter and Christmas–New Year's holidays. Get an upper-floor room (above the 10th story) for more quiet and a better view. All with cable TV, telephones, restaurant, bar, ocean-view pool-patio, kiddie pool, some rooms have wheelchair access, and parking. Credit cards accepted.

Other Los Hornos longtime beachfront hotels that might be worth checking out include **Las Hamacas** (tel. 744/482-2861, fax 744/483-0575, hamas@hamacas.com.mx, www.hamacas.com.mx, about $60 d), on the Costera a couple of blocks east of the Fuerte de San Diego; and **El Cid** (tel. 744/485-1312, fax 744/485-1312 or 744/485-1387, www.elcida-

capulco.com, about $50 d), about five blocks farther east, just east of the corner of Capitán Mal Espina.

COSTERA HOTELS: WEST SIDE

With few exceptions, these hostelries line both beach and inland sides of the busy Costera Miguel Alemán, east of Papagayo amusement park. Hotels are nearly all either right on or just a short walk from the beach.

Under $50

Among the most economical is the modest **Hotel del Valle** (G. Gomez Espinosa 8, Acapulco, Guerrero 39670, tel. 744/485-8336 or 744/485-8388, www.travelbymexico.com/guer/hoteldelvalle), on the side street that borders the east end of the Papagayo amusement park. Two motel-style floors of clean, comfortable rooms border a small but inviting pool-patio. On a side street away from the noisy boulevard, the del Valle is a tranquil winter headquarters for retirees and youthful budget travelers. The 20 rooms ordinarily rent for about $30 s, $40 d, with fan only; $40 s, $50 d holidays, all with hot-water shower baths; add about $10 for a more deluxe air-conditioning-equipped room.

If the Hotel del Valle is full, you might try its similarly budget-priced (but without pools) petite next-door neighbors, **Hotel Jacqueline** (tel./fax 744/485-9338, $45 s or d) and **Amueblados Lupita** (tel. 744/485-9412, $35 s or d).

On the beach side of the Costera, a block or two east of McDonald's, the small, three-story **Hotel Monaco** (Av. Costera M. Alemán 137, Acapulco, Guerrero 39670, tel./fax 744/485-6467, 485-6415, or 485-6518, monac_otel@hotmail.com, $46 d low season, $63 d holidays) offers a tropical mini-retreat from the Costera noise and bustle. Past the small lobby, a big, round blue pool, decorated with shade umbrellas and edged by palms and leafy greenery, invites relaxation. (The patio's attractiveness, however, leads to its drawback: for peace and quiet, spend your time here on the beach during the weekends, when families love to frolic in the pool. Weekdays by the pool are usually more tranquil.) Upstairs, the rooms are plain but clean, with the basics: hot showers and two double beds. Rooms include air-conditioning, phone, TV, and parking. Hotel Monaco is close to everything, just a block from the beach.

$50-100

A few blocks farther east, check out best-buy ◖ **Hotel Sands** (Av. Costera M. Alemán 178, P.O. Box 256, Acapulco, Guerrero 39670, tel. 744/484-2261, 744/484-2262, 744/484-2263, or 744/484-2264, toll-free Mex. tel. 800/710-9800, fax 744/484-1053, sands@ sands.com.mx, www.sands.com.mx, $50 d). In addition to a pool-patio and restaurant next to the main 1960s-modern building, the hotel's spacious grounds encompass a shady green park in the rear that leads to an attractive hidden cluster of garden cabanas. Of the main building rooms, the uppers are best; many have been redecorated with light, comfortable furnishings. Cabana guests, on the other hand, enjoy tasteful browns, tile decor, and big windows looking out into a leafy garden. Cabanas 1–8 are the most secluded. The 59 rooms and 34 cabanas ordinarily cost about 50 percent more during Christmas–New Year's and Easter holidays. Low-season discounts on weekdays and for longer stays may be available; be sure to ask. All with air-conditioning, cable TV, and phones. Parking and use of squash courts are included; credit cards are accepted.

Just east of the Hotel Sands stands the compact but nevertheless worthy and kid-friendly **Hotel Hacienda María Eugenia** (Av. Costera M. Alemán 176, Acapulco, Guerrero 39670, tel. 744/481-2989 or 744/481-2990, toll-free Mex. tel. 800/712-6628, fax 744/481-0071, haciendamariaeugenia@prodigy.net.mx, www.haciendamariaeugenia.com.mx, $65 d except holidays). Only a block and a half from the beach, the hotel has about 50 rooms in three stories, around a petite, leafy pool-patio, embellished with a meandering kiddie pool, small water slide, and playground equipment. A modest but well-managed boulevard-front restaurant offers a hearty, economical breakfast buffet. Upstairs, rooms are invitingly furnished, with two double beds, attractive rustic wooden furniture and floor tiles and modern-standard shower baths. Light, however, usually must be artificial, since rooms face exterior corridors, where curtains must be drawn for privacy. (However, a number of kitchenette-equipped rooms have doors opening to private side balconies, and thus more light.) Two kids stay free with parents; rooms have cable TV, air-conditioning. Parking costs $6, and credit cards accepted. The customary promotion runs about $270 for three nights, fourth night free, including daily breakfast buffet.

The renovated, longtime **Auto-Hotel Ritz** (corner of Av. Costera M. Alemán and Wilfrido Massieu, Acapulco, Guerrero 39670, tel. 744/486-2081, toll-free Mex. tel. 800/715-2159, fax 744/484-0984, reservaciones@ hotelesposeidon.com.mx, www.hotelesposei-don.com.mx, $62 d low season, $90 high), near the west end, stands just a block from the beach. The downstairs, with its chandeliered but dowdy lobby, leads nevertheless to an invitingly tropical pool and patio, climaxed by plumy, exotic fan palms. The rooms (get an upstairs one for more privacy) are likewise attractive: light and clean, with big double beds, marble baths, and airy, private patio-view balconies. Rates include air-conditioning, cable TV, and parking.

Just a block from Papagayo amusement park and right on the beach stands the mid-rise **Hotel Maris** (Av. Costera M. Alemán 59, Acapulco, Guerrero 39670, tel. 744/485-8440, fax 744/485-3934, $82 d, $140 holidays). Here, guests enjoy spacious rooms with private view balconies for surprisingly reasonable rates. Lobby-level amenities include a small pool above the beach club *palapas,* with bar and restaurant. (You may want to ask someone to turn down the TV volume.) Rates for the 85 rooms include air-conditioning, TV, and phones. Street parking only.

Several blocks farther east on the inland side, the lovely, low-rise ◖ **Hotel Bali-Hai** (Av. Costera M. Alemán 186, Acapulco, Guerrero

© BRUCE WHIPPERMAN

Although on the inland side of the busy Costera, the patio of the moderately priced Hotel Bali-Hai provides a tranquil haven from the Acapulco hubbub.

39670, tel. 744/485-6622 or 744/485-6336, fax 744/485-7972, balihai@balihai.com.mx, www.balihai.com.mx, $100 d) offers a bit of class at reasonable rates. The superbly maintained hotel offers 108 motel-style rooms in two floors, all enfolding a palmy interior parking-pool-patio. A pair of designer pools (one of them shallow and kid-friendly) furnished with a collection of chaise lounges set the relaxing tone. Furthermore, the hotel layout, set far back from the boulevard, produces a surprisingly tranquil ambience, shielded from the Costera traffic hubbub. Inside the rooms themselves, spotless marble and tile, handsome Polynesian-mode wood furniture, and modern standard baths complete the inviting picture. The only blot on this lovely portrait is that rooms often must be artificially lit, since they face outward on to the corridor and drapes must be drawn for privacy. Reserve an upper room in the rear for more quiet and privacy. Rooms come in two grades: standard is large and deluxe, sleeping up to four. Superior is larger and more deluxe, sleeping up to six. Rates decrease to $75

d for the second, third, and fourth nights. Add about 20 percent for superior rooms, and about 50 percent for holidays. All with air-conditioning, cable TV, refrigerator, parking, bar, and quiet air-conditioned restaurant out front.

Beachside, the **Hotel Maralisa** (Alemania s/n, Acapulco, Guerrero 39670, tel. 744/485-6677, fax 744/485-9228, www.bestday.com/acapulco/hotels/maralisa, $60 d low season, about $200 holidays) nestles among its towering beachfront condo neighbors. The Maralisa is a luxuriously simple retreat, where guests, after their fill of sunning beside the palm-lined pool-patio, can step down onto the sand for a jog or stroll along the beach. Later, they might enjoy a light meal in the hotel's beachside café and go out dancing in nearby resort hotels. Several of the Maralisa's 90 comfortable rooms, tastefully decorated in whites and warm pastels, have private balconies. Up to two kids younger than 12 stay free; be sure to ask for a discount or package. Rates include air-conditioning, cable TV, phones, and parking; credit cards are accepted.

Over $100

Long-time lovers of Acapulco are welcoming the return of the landmark ◖ **Hotel Ritz** (corner of Wilfrido Massieu and the Costera, tel. 744/485-8958, toll-free Mex. tel. 800/503-5757 or U.S./Can. tel. 866/765-0608, inform@acapulco.com, www.acapulco.com/es/hotels/ritz, $130 d low season), one of Acapulco's long-time best hotels. The Ritz's beachfront pool, restaurant, and refined festive atmosphere were a magnet for a legion of both foreign and Mexican middle-class vacationers during the 1970s and '80s. After a hiatus as an all-inclusive Qualton Club during the 1990s, the Ritz, with its superb beachfront and graceful beachfront tower of marble-embellished deluxe rooms, has returned. Add about 25 percent to rates during holiday periods.

A mile farther east, the super-popular long-time luxury ◖ **Hotel Fiesta Americana Condesa** (Av. Costera M. Alemán 1220, Acapulco, Guerrero 39690, tel. 744/484-2828, toll-free Mex. tel. 800/503-7080 or U.S./Can. tel. 800/FIESTA-1 (800/343-7821), fax 744/484-1828, rinternet@posadas.com, www.fiestamericana.com, $130 d low season, $150 d high) presides atop its rocky shoreline perch smack in the middle of the Costera action. Boulevard traffic roars nonstop past the front door and nearby nightclubs rock (on the west side; ask for an east-side room for peace and quiet). On winter days, ranks of middle-class American and Canadian vacationers sun on the hotel's spacious pool deck and downstairs at its *palapa*-shaded beach club. Resort facilities include multiple restaurants and bars, nightly live music, shops, auto rental, golf nearby, and all aquatic sports. Rooms, most with private bay-view balconies, are furnished in luscious pastels, rattan, and designer lamps. Rates include air-conditioning, cable TV, phones, parking, and full wheelchair access; credit cards are accepted. Low-season promotions or discounts may be available.

COSTERA HOTELS: EAST SIDE

East of the golf course stretches the newest, shiniest part of Acapulco, where seemingly every enterprise, including Wal-Mart and McDonalds, Hooters and Hyatt Regency, has strained to locate during the recent past. Despite the hubbub, corners of tranquillity do exist, especially among many of the high-rise hostelries and condominiums that occupy the golden beachfront.

Under $50

A few vintage east-side remnants of Acapulco "the way it used to be" live on, seemingly oblivious to the fast-lane world around them. At the CICI water park corner, walk straight toward the beach, along Calle Cristobal Colón. Just before the beach, on the left, you'll find ◖ **Suites Selene** (Cristobal Colón 175, Acapulco, Guerrero 39860, tel./fax 744/484-2977 or 744/484-3643, suitesselene@hotmail.com, $47 per day, $58 with kitchenette). Here, just half a block from the beach, by a shady street's-end park, stands a complex of 24 modest apartments. Exterior amenities include a leafy garden, a blue pool and patio, and parking sensitively situated in the rear, away from the garden and apartments. Most of the somewhat worn but clean units have one bedroom with two double beds, a living-dining room, bathroom, and a kitchenette, with stove, refrigerator, utensils and dishes, and purified water in a five-gallon *garafón* (demijohn) for cooking. The remaining six units have everything but the kitchenette. Rates are higher for holidays, but discounts are customarily available for weekly or monthly rentals.

Walk away from the beach two doors and find neighboring complex **Amueblados Cheli** (Cristobal Colón 155, Acapulco, Guerrero, tel. 744/484-3160 or 744/484-2019), also scarcely a block from the beach. The complex (amueblados literally means furnished) consists of about 20 apartments in two floors, set around a lovingly tended tropical garden and parking patio. On the south, beach side of the apartments is an inviting pool-patio for guest use. The whole place is set behind a sturdy security fence, probably mostly to keep beachgoers from wandering in at all hours. The only possible drawback here might be the music and noise from the CICI water park (open 10 A.M.–6 P.M. daily) across the street. Although the owner told me that she rents most apartments by the month, vacant rentals are often rented by the day, for about $50, depending on season. (Although the manager wasn't available to show me individual apartments, judging from the well-tended look of the place, Amueblados Cheli is certainly worth checking out.) Contact the owner via telephone (in Spanish).

$50-100

Moving several blocks farther east along the Costera, find the **Casa Inn** (Av. Costera M. Alemán 2310, Acapulco, Guerrero 39860, tel. 744/435-2000 or 744/435-2037, reserva@ casainnacapulco.com.mx, www.casainna-capulco.com.mx, $60, $150 holidays), a less refined but still best-buy hostelry, especially during low season. The youngish, mostly single clientele also like the lively late-night bar and the big pool deck where they can rest and recover during the day. The 279 light and comfortable rooms come with air-conditioning, TV, views, and phones. Most have kitchenettes, and sleep one–four people. Be sure to ask for a discount or a package. Parking is available, and credit cards are accepted.

For a very worthy moderately priced alternative, return west a few blocks to check out the classy small **Hotel Aca Sol** (Av. Costera M. Alemán 53B, Acapulco, Guerrero 39690, tel. 744/484-3091 or 744/484-2782, fax 744/484-0977, reservaciones@turismointersol.com, www.hotelacasol.com or www.turismointersol.com, $70 s or d), just a block and a half from the beach. Enter the petite but invitingly chic lobby and continue to an airy, palm-decorated rear pool-patio. To one side, an attractive small restaurant, shielded from street noise, serves guests. Upstairs, the 35 rooms in four floors enfold the patio. Inside, rooms are white, marbled, and squeaky clean. Guests in most rooms enjoy exterior balconies. Get a room overlooking Almendro, the adjacent quiet side street. Rates are higher for Easter, Christmas, and July and August. Stay three nights and the fourth night is free; rates include air-condition-

ing, parking, cable TV, and telephone. Credit cards are accepted.

Over $100

Those who hanker for a party can have it, right on the beach, at **Hotel Copacabana** (Tabachines 2, Fracc. Club Deportivo, Acapulco, Guerrero 39690, tel. 744/484-3260 or tel./fax 744/484-6268, toll-free Mex. tel. 800/710-9888 or U.S. tel. 800/562-0197, acapulco@ hotelcopacabana.com, www.hotelcopacabana.com, $120 d). Past the midsize inviting lobby, guests enjoy a live music restaurant-bar, a beach-view pool deck, and a squadron of private beachfront *palapas*. Everywhere inside, the marble, brass, and rattan are polished; the guests are youngish; and the mood is upbeat. Upstairs, the 18 floors of 400-plus rooms are deluxe, comfortable, marble-floored, and cheerily decorated in yellows and whites, with bamboo furniture and bedsteads. Third and fourth guests stay free; rates are higher holidays and July and August, but always include air-conditioning, cable TV, and parking. Boogie boards, kayaks, water polo, aerobics, and volleyball available at no extra cost. Other downstairs amenities include shops, travel agent, and business center. Credit cards accepted.

On the other hand, lovers of peace and quiet often choose the grand, dignified **Hotel Elcano** (Av. Costera M. Alemán 75, Acapulco, Guerrero 39690, tel./fax 744/435-1500 or fax 744/484-2230, toll-free U.S. tel. 877/260-1765 or Can. tel. 800/917-4901, elcano@hotel-elcano.com.mx, www.hotel-elcano.com.mx, $135 d, $300 holidays), two blocks removed—and with rooms facing away from the Costera traffic. The hotel was named after Ferdinand Magellan's navigator, Sebastián Elcano (who actually was the one who first circumnavigated the globe; Magellan died en route but got the credit). Hotel Elcano is austerely luxurious, hued in shades of nautical blue, from the breezy, gracefully columned lobby and the spacious turquoise beachside pool to the 180 immaculate, marble-tiled view rooms. Unlike some of Acapulco's beachfront hostelries, the Elcano has plenty of space for guests to enjoy its load of extras, which includes two restaurants, three bars, poolside hot tub, beach club, kiddie pool, gym, nine-hole golf course three blocks away, and video games center. Rooms all have private ocean-view balconies. Be sure to ask for possible promotional packages, or midweek or weekly rates.

Towering over the Costera's east end is the 20-story, high-rise ◖ **Hyatt Regency Acapulco** (Av. Costera M. Alemán 1, Acapulco, Guerrero 39869, tel. 744/469-1234, toll-free Mex. tel. 800/005-0000 or U.S./Can. tel. 800/223-1234, fax 744/484-3087, reservehyatt@prodigy.net.mx or hyatt-reserv@acabtu.com.mx, www.acapulco.regency.hyatt.com). Its lavish beachfront facilities include spacious gardens, blue lagoon swimming pool, a Tarzan jungle waterfall, a squadron of personal beach *palapas,* restaurants, bars, frequent live music, shops, all aquatic sports, tennis, and golf nearby. The 690 rooms, all with private view balconies, are large and luxurious. Standard rooms rent from as little as $135 low season promotional rate up to about $245 holidays, with air-conditioning, cable TV, phones, parking, and full wheelchair access; credit cards are accepted.

OUT-OF-TOWN HOTELS
Pie de la Cuesta

For many more budget beachfront lodgings, check out the sleepy Pie de la Cuesta downscale beach resort village on placid Laguna Coyuca (about six miles by the oceanfront Highway 200 northwest from the Acapulco *zócalo*). There, you'll find plenty of inexpensive palm-shaded shoreline hotels and bungalows. Drive, taxi (about $10), or ride a bus marked Pie de la Cuesta from Avenida Escudero in front of Sanborn's and Woolworth's near the *zócalo*. For details, see the *Pie de la Cuesta* section at the end of this chapter.

Hotels East of Town

A number of luxury hostelries spread along the Playa Revolcadero oceanfront, on the beach side of the airport road.

One of the most heavenly choices is the ◖ **Villas San Vicente** (tel. 744/462-0149 or 744/462-0120, www.villassanvicente.com.mx), a mini-paradise with plenty of space, sweeping green lawns, swaying palms, and a long gorgeous strand. Seekers of peace and quiet can have it all: afternoons in splendid isolation, reading by the pool, long walks on the beach, savoring the tropical breeze, and watching the sun go down. Guests in the five spacious, super-deluxe mini-villas enjoy two bedrooms with king-size beds, two baths, designer living-dining room, completely equipped kitchen, hot tub, air-conditioning, and a small private pool. The two smaller units are more modest but still comfortable studios, with bath, kitchenette, and air-conditioning, set at the upper edge of the property, a bit farther from the beach. All residents share a lusciously inviting main pool and patio, with bar, tennis courts, and parking, all on about 10 palm-shaded beachfront acres. Low season rentals run about $105 for the studios, upward from $300 for the mini-villas, depending on location and amenities. High-season rates are about 30 percent more. Reservations (mandatory high season, strongly recommended low) are available by contacting the Villas' Acapulco office (tel. 744/486-4037, fax 744/485-6846, sanvicentevillas@aol.com). Get to Villas San Vicente by following the airport road eastbound about seven miles (11 km) past the hill-bottom Puerto Marqués traffic interchange. Instead of heading straight ahead to the airport, fork right, toward Barra Vieja. After a mile or two, you'll reach the Villas San Vicente gate, on the right.

Closer in (only about a mile east of the Puerto Marqués interchange) along the airport road, the showplace **Hotel Fairmont Acapulco Princess** (Playa Revolcadero, P.O. Box 1351, Acapulco, Guerrero 39300, tel. 744/469-1000, toll-free Mex. tel. 800/257-7544 or U.S./Can. tel. 800/866-5577, fax 744/469-1012, aca.reservations@fairmont.com, www.fairmont.com/acapulco, $200 d low season, $400 d including breakfast and dinner high season) provides an abundance of resort facilities (including an entire 18-hole golf course), spreading from luscious beachfront garden grounds. Although the hotel centers on a pair of hulking neo-pyramids (with a total of 1,019 rooms), the impression from the rooms themselves is of super luxury; from the garden it is of Edenlike jungle tranquillity—meandering pools, gurgling cascades, strutting flamingos, swaying palms—that guests seem to soak up with no trouble at all. All rooms are deluxe with a plethora of up-to-date amenities; guests also enjoy a host of facilities, all sports, and full wheelchair access. Credit cards are accepted.

For another super-deluxe option, consider the **Vidafel Mayan Palace** (Av. de las Palmas, Fracc. Playa Diamante, Acapulco, Guerrero 39300, tel./fax 744/469-6000; toll-free Mex. tel. 800/366-6600, U.S. tel. 800/292-9446 or 800/996-2926, Can. tel. 800/421-4161; reservations@mayanresorts.com, www.mayanresorts.com.mx, $300 d low season, $450 d high), about a mile farther east along the beach from the Fairmont Acapulco Princess. Here, in a palace like the Mayan kings never had, you'll find an 18-hole golf course, 12 clay tennis courts, a kilometer-long swimming pool (no kidding), five bars, three restaurants, fountains, waterfalls, and an entire blue lagoon, all overlooking a gorgeous, breezy beach. Hotel rates vary for a luxurious and spacious marble and pastel room with everything; promotional packages might include breakfast.

LONG-TERM RENTALS

Probably the best source of Acapulco long-term rentals is the website **www.acabtu.com.mx,** an electronic, Spanish-only descendant of the former community newspaper *Acapulco Heat.* (Curiously, "btu" refers to British thermal unit, commonly used to measure heat energy.) Go directly to the real estate (*bienes raices*) page, www.acabtu.com.mx/acaweb/bienesraices.html, for information on individual villa, condo, and house rentals by owner as well as agencies that maintain their own rental listings.

Another potentially useful Internet site is the English-language **www.mexonline.com,** which links to some individual Acapulco rentals by owner and several agencies.

For folks less familiar with the Internet,

some of the more useful rental sources can also be contacted easily by telephone. For example, in Acapulco, check out **Bachur Real Estate** (Av. Costera M. Alemán 20, Hotel Tropicana, Fracc. Costa Azul, Acapulco, Guerrero 39300, tel./fax 744/484-1333, bachur@bachur.com.mx, www.bachur.com.mx), specializing in condos and villas. Others that you might try are: **Monica Quevedo Real Estate** (Av. Comandante Carreon 175, Fracc. Costa Azul, Acapulco, Guerrero 39300, tel./fax 744/484-2764) or **M and M Real Estate** ("M y M" in Spanish, tel. 744/481-0057, mymbr@acabtu.com.mx, www.mymrealestate.com.mx), office of agent Martha Blunt Pérez.

Furthermore, some U.S. and Canadian real estate networks have Acapulco branches. One of the most active is the local branch of Century 21, **Century 21 Realty Mex** (Calle Alonso Martín 43, Fracc. Magellanes, Acapulco, Guerrero 39670, tel. 744/485-9090 or 744/486-6110, fax 744/486-4187) in the eastern Costera neighborhood. Although it specializes in condominiums, with a listing of about two dozen, the staff also may be able to get you a house or villa rental (or suggest someone who can).

Finally, don't forget the three moderately priced apartment complexes recommended in this chapter: ◖ **Hotel Etel Suites,** in *Hotels near the Zócalo,* and the **Amueblados Cheli** and ◖ **Suites Selene** in *Costera—East End.*

TRAILER PARKS AND CAMPING

Although condos and hotels have crowded out virtually all of Acapulco's in-town trailer parks, good prospects exist nearby. The best are the **Acapulco Trailer Park** and the ◖ **Playa Luces RV Park and Campground,** right on the beach in Pie de la Cuesta, six miles by the coast highway northwest of the Acapulco *zócalo.* For details, see the *Pie de la Cuesta* section at the end of this chapter.

And although development and urbanization have likewise squeezed out in-town camping, possibilities exist in the trailer parks in Pie de la Cuesta and on Playa Larga near Barra Vieja, east of town.

Food

SNACKS AND BREAKFAST
Near the Zócalo

Eat well for under $3 at 🕻 **Lonchería Chatita** (Avenida Azueta, corner of Hidalgo, 8 A.M.–10 P.M. daily), where a friendly female kitchen squad serves mounds of wholesome, local-style specialties. On a typical day, these may include savory *chiles rellenos,* rich *puerco mole de Uruapan, pozole* (savory hominy soup), or potato pancakes.

Something fancier is available at **La Flor de Acapulco** (formerly Restaurant La Parroquia), on the upstairs balcony overlooking the *zócalo,* good for a snack or a light lunch as you soak in the scene below.

For something creamy and cool, go to **Bing** ice cream (9 A.M.–11 P.M. daily), one block from the *zócalo* toward the steamship dock.

Continue another block to **Sanborn's** (on the Costera corner of Escudero, tel. 744/482-4095, 7:30 A.M.–11 P.M. daily, $4–10). Here, you can enjoy the cool air-conditioning and a home-style selection, including ham and eggs, hamburgers, roast beef, and apple pie.

Alternatively, **Woolworth's** (tel. 744/480-0072, 9:30 A.M.–8:30 P.M. daily), one block from the Costera, behind Sanborn's, also offers air-conditioned ambience and similar fare at cheaper prices.

Finally, for dessert, head back over to the opposite side of the *zócalo* to **La Espiga de Acapulco** (on Juárez, tel. 744/482-2699, 7 A.M.–10 P.M. daily), a bakery a block west of the *zócalo* with tasty tarts and pieces of cake (about $1).

On the Costera

Snack food concentrates in Acapulco, as in many places, around **McDonald's,** with at least two branches: the original one, at the corner of Esclavo and Costera M. Alemán, a few blocks east of the landmark Hotel Ritz, and another farther east, on the Costera east of the Diana fountain and traffic circle. Here, you have it all, from breakfast Egg McMuffins to Chicken McNuggets and the Big Mac, priced about a third higher than back home. Open daily 8 A.M.–11 P.M.

For an interesting contrast, visit 🕻 **Taco Tumbra** (tel. 744/485-7261, 6:30 P.M.–2 A.M. Sun.–Thurs., 6:30 P.M.–4 A.M. Fri.–Sat.), across the adjacent street from the original McDonald's. Here, piquant aromas of barbecued chicken, pork, and beef and strains of Latin music fill the air. For a treat, order three of the delectable tacos ($2) along with a refreshing *jugo* (fruit juice, $1.50) or fruit-flavored *agua* ($1).

A few blocks east of McDonald's and across the street, 🕻 **Restaurant El Zorrito** (The Little Fox, 24 hours daily, except 6 A.M.–1 P.M. Tues.) packs in the crowds with just about the tastiest Mexican food in town. If you're in the mood for some serious eating, fill up with a Filete Tampiqueña (beef fillet Tampico style, $11), a *chiles rellenos* plate (enough for two, $7), or *lomo* (roast pork loin, $6).

A block farther east, on the beach side of the boulevard, **Sanborn's** (formerly Denny's, tel. 744/485-5360, 7 A.M.–1 A.M. daily) provides a blessedly cool, refined, and thoroughly modern Mexican refuge from the street hustle. Here, almost around the clock daily, you can sample an international menu of either North American favorites (eggs, pancakes, bacon, and bottomless coffee), or hearty Mexican specialties ($4–10). Sanborn's also offers a rack of American magazines, such as *Time, Glamour,* and *National Geographic.*

On the other hand, **100% Natural** (tel. 744/485-3982, 7 A.M.–11 P.M. daily), in competition directly across the Costera from Sanborn's, offers appropriately contrasting fare: many veggie and fruit drinks (try the Conga, made of papaya, guava, watermelon, pineapple, lime, and spinach), several egg breakfasts, breads, sandwiches, tacos, and enchiladas ($3–6). You can also find 100% Natural branches in at least two more locations: mid-Costera (tel. 744/484-6447), next door to Carlos'n Charlie's across from Hotel Presidente; and on the east side (tel. 744/484-8440), next to Baby O disco.

Two miles farther along the Costera, at Hotel Calinda, the **Sanborn's** central Costera branch (tel. 744/481-2426, 7 A.M.–1 A.M. daily) offers the same Sanborn's refined atmosphere, good food, and a big book and gift store.

ZÓCALO AND PENINSULA DE LAS PLAYAS RESTAURANTS

Even though Acapulco has seemingly zillions of restaurants, only a fraction may suit your expectations. Local restaurants come and go like the Acapulco breeze, though a handful of solid longtime eateries continue, depending on a steady flow of repeat customers.

For plain good eating and homey sidewalk atmosphere morning and night, try outdoor ◖ **Cafe Los Amigos** (Calle La Paz, tel. 744/483-8732, 8:30 A.M.–10 P.M. daily, $3–6), a few steps off the *zócalo*. Shady umbrellas beneath a spreading green tree and many familiar favorites, from tuna salad and chili to waffles, T-bone steak, and breaded shrimp, attract a friendly club of Acapulco Canadian and American longtimers during the winter, and mostly local clientele in the summer, when the menu shifts to Mexican favorites, including a bountiful afternoon *comida corrida.*

Meanwhile, on the *zócalo*'s opposite, east side, **Mi Piace** (tel. 744/482-5555, 9 A.M.–1 A.M. daily) pizza and Italian restaurant (pronounced mee pee-AH-chay; the name means My Piece) profits from the abundant *zócalo* foot traffic. Here, you can choose between cool inside seating and umbrella-shaded outdoor tables. Select from several styles of pizza (veggie to seafood, $4–10), four salad choices ($3–5), many pastas ($4–6), and more.

La Gran Torta (La Paz 6, tel. 744/483-8476, 7 A.M.–midnight daily), one block west from the *zócalo*, is an old town headquarters for hearty local-style food at local-style prices. Specialties here are bountiful breakfasts ($3), a four-course afternoon *comida corrida* ($4), and *tortas* (hearty sandwiches, $2–4) of *pierna* (roast pork), *chorizo* (spicy sausage), or *pollo*

(chicken), all with tomato and avocado stuffed in a *bolillo* bun. An additional favorite is hearty *pozole* Thursday and Friday afternoons and evenings ($3–4).

Although the very clean, strictly local-style **Restaurant La Chilapeña** (Cinco de Mayo 36, tel. 744/482-0498, 10 A.M.–11 P.M. daily) requires walking a few blocks east from the *zócalo,* it's worth it. Friendly owner Consuela Araiz de Rosario welcomes everyone to sample her Guerrero-style *antojitos* cooked the way she learned from her mother years ago in upcountry Chilapa. It's best to organize a party so you can sample everything. Besides the tostadas, tacos, enchiladas, and *chalupas* ($2–4), be sure to order the house specialty, *pozole* ($3–4)—which Señora Consuela claims was invented in Chilapa; see the *Origin of Pozole* wall painting—complete with its bountiful vegetable plate. Additionally, Señora Consuela is very proud of her *pata* (leg of pork vinaigrette, $2) with *zanahorias* (carrots). Get to La Chilapeña from the *zócalo* by walking east two blocks to the Avenida Escudero corner (at Sanborn's). Turn left and walk along the east side of the street (passing Woolworth's) three blocks north to Cinco de Mayo. Turn right and walk a block and a half to Restaurant La Chilapeña on the right.

For more good local eating, Señora Consuela recommends nearby **Restaurant La Chilapeña III** (at Calle Petaquillas 3). To get there from the first Restaurant La Chilapeña, continue west along Cinco de Mayo, turn right at the next corner, Calle Galeana, and walk a few steps to Calle Petaquillas and the restaurant.

Similar and also highly recommended is the **Restaurant El Nuevo Capullo Chilapeño** (Alarcón 16, tel. 744/482-4311, 7:30 A.M.–midnight daily), in the Pozo de la Nación district. Afternoons are good for enjoying the four-course *comida corrida* set lunch ($3–4); evenings, go for the upcountry Guerrero specialties, Chilapa-style *antojitos* such as *chalupas* (or, on Thursdays only, pork or chicken *pozole verde*).

For another very popular variation on local-

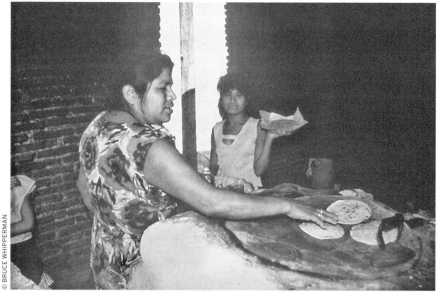

© BRUCE WHIPPERMAN

The foundation of Mexican food is corn, usually consumed via the tortilla, shown being grilled on a traditional mud-brick oven griddle.

style cooking go to **◖ Tamales Licha** (Av. Costera M. Alemán 322, corner of Almirante Breton, tel. 744/482-2021, 6–11 P.M. nightly except Wednesdays, $2–4), two blocks west of the *zócalo*. Here, appetizing south-of-the-border specialties—succulent tamales, savory *pozole,* crunchy tostadas, and tangy enchiladas—reign supreme. Portions are generous, ambience is relaxed, and hygiene standards are impeccable.

Good, reasonably priced **seafood** restaurants are unexpectedly hard to come by in Acapulco. An important exception is the lineup of local-style seafood eateries along Avenida Azueta three blocks west from the *zócalo*. Situated right where the boats come in, they get the freshest morsels first. Local longtimers swear by the excellence of seafood served at **◖ El Amigo Miguel** (corner of Juárez and Azueta, tel. 744/483-6981, 10 A.M.–9 P.M. daily), where continuous patronage assures daily fresh shrimp; prawns; half a dozen kinds of fish, including house specialties *pescado empapelado* and *filete miguel* ($5–12); and lobster (big,

$25, smaller, $15). Similarly successful is rival **Mariscos Nachos,** across the street, open the same hours.

If you prefer something a bit fancier, head a block farther from the *zócalo* to tourist favorite **Mariscos Pipos** (Almirante Breton 3, tel. 744/482-2237, around 11 A.M.–8 P.M. daily). The freshest of everything, cooked and served to please, runs $6–14.

Continue west to the Peninsula de las Playas for rave-review seafood at **La Cabaña** (tel. 744/482-5007 or 744/483-7121, 9:30 A.M.–9 P.M. daily)on Playa Caleta, next to landmark white beachfront Acamar Beach Resort. Part of the fun here is the luscious view (arrive while it's still light) location, where you can choose from a number of delicious specialties. Favorites are the thick *dorado* (mahimahi) fillet ($10), *cazuela de mariscos* (seafood stew, $8), or whole fish (red snapper recommended, $8).

Many visitors' Acapulco vacations wouldn't be complete without a dinner at the luxuriously scenic clifftop *palapa* restaurant at the **◖ Hotel Los Flamingos** (Av. López Mateos s/n, tel. 744/482-0690, 8 A.M.–10:30 P.M. daily), about a mile uphill to the west from Playa Caleta. Here all the ingredients for a memorable evening—attentive service, tasty seafood, chicken, and meat entrées ($7–15), airy sunset view, and soothing instrumental melodies—come together. Credit cards are accepted. Coat not necessary (but on breezy winter evenings a windbreaker might feel cozy).

COSTERA RESTAURANTS

Moving east, first find 🌓 **VIPs** (Av. Costera M. Alemán, a block past Papagayo Amusement Park, tel. 744/486-8574, 8 A.M.–10:30 P.M. daily), where you can glimpse the Mexico of the future. Here, Mexican middle-class families flock to a south-of-the-border-style Denny's that beats Denny's at its own game. Inside, the air is as fresh as a spring breeze; the windows, water glasses, and utensils shine like silver; the food is tasty and reasonably priced ($4–10); and the staff is both amiable and professional. Credit cards are accepted. (Also, visit VIPs' newer Costera locations: beachside near the Hotel Calinda, and at the far east side across the boulevard from the Hyatt Regency.)

Although these days sometimes overlooked, enduring open-air terrace 🌓 **Restaurant El Olvido** (tel. 744/481-0214, 744/481-0236 or 744/481-0203, 6 P.M.–2 A.M. daily) remains one of Acapulco's best. The Forgotten One, as its name translates, is on the mid-Costera, rear of Plaza Marbella, beach side of the Diana Circle, and it seems the model by which some of Acapulco's now-trendy eateries were created. What's remarkable is that such a tranquil tropical mini-island could exist so close to the smoggy roar of the Costera traffic. By day, guests enjoy a palm-tufted airy bay view and by night an ebony star-studded sky bordered below by myriad twinkling city lights. The excellent cuisine, however, provides the main attraction. Choose from a very recognizable menu of lots of pasta ($6–9), meat ($8–18), and fish ($10–20), including a number of nouveau international specialties. For example,

start off with Boston lettuce with watercress and strawberries ($7), continue with black fettuccine with smoked Norwegian salmon ($15) or quail with honey and pineapple ($16), and finish off with tiramisu ($5). Reservations recommended, especially on weekends.

No tour of Acapulco restaurants would be complete without a stop at **Carlos'n Charlie's** (Av. Costera M. Alemán, tel. 744/484-0039, 6 A.M.–midnight daily, $6–18), across from and a block east of Hotel Fiesta Americana Condesa. Like all locations of the late Carlos Anderson's worldwide chain, it specializes in the zany. The fun begins with the screwy decor; continues via the good-natured, tongue-in-cheek antics of the staff; and climaxes with the very tasty food and drink, which is organized on the menu by categories such as "Slurp," "Munch," "Peep," "Moo," and "Zurts." Credit cards are accepted.

Another successful culinary experiment is the Acapulco branch of the worldwide 🌓 **Suntory** (tel. 744/484-8088, 2–11 P.M. daily, $8–20) Japanese restaurant chain, across from the Oceanic 2000 building, at the east end of the Costera. Although a Japanese restaurant in Mexico is as difficult to create as a Mexican restaurant in Japan, Suntory, the giant beer, whiskey, and wine manufacturer, carries it off with aplomb. From the outside, the clean-lined wooden structure appears authentically classic Japanese, seemingly lifted right out of 18th-century Kyoto. The impression continues in the cool interior, where patrons enjoy a picture-perfect tropical Zen garden, complete with moss, a stony brook, sago palm, and feathery festoons of bamboo. Finally comes the food, from a host of choices—vegetables, rice, fish, and meat—that chefs (who, although Mexican, soon begin to look Japanese) individually prepare for you on the grill built into your table. Credit cards are accepted.

SPLURGE RESTAURANTS

Acapulco visitors and well-to-do residents enjoy a number of fashionable, top-of-the-line restaurants, renowned for their super-scenic locations, fine cuisine, or both. Here's a sampling of the worthy, west to east.

Longtime favorite **Coyuca 22** (Calle Coyuca 22, tel. 744/483-5030, 7–11:30 P.M. daily Nov. 1–Apr. 30) is both the name and the address of the restaurant so exclusive and popular it manages to close half the year. (Coyuca is a side-street off Av. López Mateos on the Peninsula de las Playas.) The setting is a spacious hilltop garden, where tables spread down an open-air bay- and city-view terrace. Arrive early (around 5:30 P.M. winter, 7 P.M. late spring–early summer) to enjoy the sunset sky lighting up and painting the city ever-changing colors, ending in a deep rose as finally the myriad lights shimmer and stars twinkle overhead. After that, the food (specialties such as prime rib and lobster tails, $20–30) and wines seem like dessert. Credit cards are accepted and reservations are required.

Another super-romantic cocktail-dinner spot is the showplace **El Campanario** (tel. 744/484-8830, 7 P.M.–midnight daily, closed May–December, $15–30), commanding a second-to-none view of all of Acapulco. Here, owners have converted a former mansion into a regal bar and restaurant, leading through a princely, arched stone hall to airy vista terraces and a luxuriously inviting pool and patio outside. House specialties are red snapper Azteca with *cuitlacoche* sauce, rolled fillet of beef with spinach, and Chambertine chicken in mushroom sauce. Reservations recommended.

El Campanario has no precise address. It's a landmark mansion atop the hill only accessible by car or taxi. The only address given is Calle Paraiso s/n ("sin numero" without number). The best way to go is by taxi from the costera ($3). By car, turn from uphill from the costera at Av. Deportes (at the Pizza Hut, adjacent to the west side of the golf course). Continue uphill at each intersection until you reach the top of the hill. Ask for directions to El Campanario; everyone will know it.

C Restaurant El Faro (The Lighthouse, at Hotel Elcano, noon–11 P.M. daily) has raised Acapulco to new heights of culinary fantasy, at least equal to that of its rotating beacon high above the Costera. The cool subdued interior is reminiscent of a 1940s Hollywood supper club, tinted in suave greens and blues; the numerous nautical accents climax in an overhead stained glass submarine mural. The total impression is as if you and your fellow diners are inhabitants of a grand aquarium, visible only to the poor exterior denizens through the street-level porthole windows. The cuisine is no less than you'd expect: mostly seafood, some exotic, such as *koktoxas* of grouper (fish cheeks, $20); or more recognizable, such as cod a la Vasque ($22) or grilled shrimp with vegetables and wild rice sauteed in sesame oil ($20). Meat lovers, nevertheless, will do quite well, with entrées such as lusciously tender rib-eye steak ($25) or lamb ribs in their own juice ($18), marinated in oils of wild grass, apple puree, and shallots. High-season reservations recommended; call the Hotel Elcano, tel. 744/235-1500, and ask for Restaurant El Faro.

The east-end bayview Las Brisas district has acquired an exclusive sprinkling of stylish restaurants. Among them, one of the places to be seen is **C Kookaburra** (tel. 744/446-6020 or 744/446-6039, 6 P.M.–midnight daily), where, among the beautiful people, you can gaze out on yet another view of Acapulco. In the cool of the evening, from afar, the heat, fumes, and congestion of the Costera give way to a curtain of twinkling lights, like a galaxy, sliced by the curving ebony line of the bay. The food (for example, start with crab cakes, $10, continue with roast duck with mandarin sauce, $25, finish with almond cake, $6) simply embellishes the effect. Reservations are mandatory.

Kookaburra is on east side boulevard Carretera Escenica, between the restaurants Spicey and Casanova and across the highway from the Hotel Las Brisas. Best take a taxi ($4) from the costera, a *lomas* or Puerto Marques bus ($0.40).

Acapulco's hottest "must do" restaurant among the rich and famous is **Baikal** (Carretera Escenica 22, tel. 744/446-6867, 6 P.M.–midnight daily except Monday), right in the middle of the Las Brisas bayview strip, across from landmark Palladium disco. Join the well-heeled mostly Mexico City crowd and soak in the relaxed elegance—massive white columns, draped windows looking out on the gleaming galaxy of the Acapulco night—all to the soothing strains of live jazz. Start off with a fine overview of the entire scene, accompanied by appetizers, at the upper bar, then take a main-floor table for your entrée and dessert. After such an introduction, the food may seem like an afterthought. For example, for an appetizer, try fresh mussels, $16; for salad, arugula with pear, $13; and entrée, salmon in honey and balsamic vinaigrette, $25. Reservations strongly recommended any time.

Nearby, at Italian-style **Casanova** (Carretera Escenica Las Brisas 5236, tel. 744/446-6237, 744/446-6238, or 744/446-6239, 7 P.M.–2 A.M. daily except Monday), you can enjoy either a cool inside section or the same starry, panoramic view outside, while sampling from a long list of tasty salads, pastas, meats, chicken, and seafood specialties ($15–30). The house especially recommends its super-fresh shrimp fettuccine ($22). Reservations mandatory.

Entertainment and Events

STROLLING AND SIDEWALK CAFÉS

The old *zócalo* is the best place for strolling and people-watching. Bookstalls, vendors, band concerts, and, on weekend nights especially, pitch-penny games, mimes, and clowns are constant sources of entertainment. When you're tired of walking, take a seat at a sidewalk café, such as La Flor de Acapulco (upstairs balcony) or Cafe Los Amigos, and let the scene pass *you* by for a change.

MOVIES

The best cinemas are the Costera multiplexes. As you move eastward, past Papagayo Park, first comes **Cineapolis** (tel. 744/485-3178), in the shopping plaza next to VIPs restaurant, at the corner of the Costera and Wilfrido Massieu.

Next comes **Cinema 5** (tel. 744/485-5124, admission $3), on the third floor of the Plaza Bahía shopping center, next to the Hotel Crowne Plaza. Screenings include first-run American dramas and comedies.

Finally, at the east end, three blocks before the Hotel Hyatt Regency, is **Cinemark de Mexico** (tel. 744/481-0656), in the Oceanic 2000 plaza across from Baby O disco.

TOURIST SHOWS

The **Salon Acapulco** (tel. 744/484-3252 or 744/484-0114), Acapulco's nightclub *espectáculo* performance, goes on two, three, or four days a week, beginning around midnight, depending on the season. Performances generally include a little bit of everything, from folkloric dance and rope twirling, to jugglers and glittering chorus lines. Tariff runs about $25, including open bar. For information and reservations contact a travel agent, such as American Express, tel. 744/435-2200, or call Salon Acapulco directly. Find it on the Costera, east-end, next to the Oceanic 2000 shopping center, across from Baby O disco.

SUNSETS

West-side hills block Acapulco Bay's sunset horizon. Sunset connoisseurs remedy the problem by gathering at ocean-view points on the west-side Peninsula de las Playas, such as the Sinfonia del Sol sunset amphitheater, La Quebrada, Playa Angosta, and especially the cliff-side restaurant and gazebo/bar of the Hotel Los Flamingos before sunset.

Far east-side beach locations around the Hotel Hyatt Regency and hilltop viewpoints, such as restaurant-bar El Campanario and the east-end Las Brisas Scenic Highway (Carretera Escenica) restaurants, also provide unobstructed sunset-viewing horizons.

BAY CRUISE PARTIES

One popular way to enjoy the sunset and a party at the same time is via a cruise aboard the steel excursion ship **Bonanza** (tel. 744/483-1803). It leaves from its bayside dock on the Costera half a mile (toward the Peninsula de las Playas) from the *zócalo*. Although cruise schedules vary seasonally, offerings can include midday (11 A.M.–2 P.M.), sunset (4:30–7 P.M.), and moonlight (10:30 P.M.–1 A.M.) cruises. Tickets are available from hotels, travel agents, or at the dock. Tickets run about $20 per person, kids 1.4 meters (about four feet, nine inches) tall and under go for half price.

BULLFIGHTS

Bullfights are staged every Sunday at 5:30 P.M. seasonally, usually January through March, at the arena (here called a *frontón*) near Playa Caletilla. Avoid congestion and parking hassles by taking a taxi. Get tickets (about $25) through a travel agent or the ticket office, tel. 744/483-9561.

JAI-ALAI, BINGO, AND OFFTRACK BETTING

About $10 gains you entrance to Acapulco's big jai-alai *frontón* (Av. Costera M. Alemán, tel. 744/484-378, 9 P.M.–1 A.M. Tues.–Sun.), an indoor stadium—look for the Bingo sign—on the east end of the Costera, across from the Hyatt Regency. Here, it's hard not to ooh and aah at the skill of players competing in the ancient Basque game of jai-alai (Fri. and Sat. beginning at 9 P.M.). With a long, narrow, curved basket tied to one arm, players fling a hard rubber ball, at lethal speeds, to the far end of the court, where it rebounds like a pistol shot and must be returned by an opposing player. You can place wagers on your favorite player, or join the home-town crowd of local folks playing bingo in the adjacent room, or head downstairs to bet on horse races and other sports events taking place far away.

MUSIC AND DANCING

Acapulco's hottest new dance nightclub is the class-act **B&B** disco (9 P.M.–3 A.M. daily, no phone, $5 cover) in the upscale Peninsula de las Playas residential neighborhood. In contrast with other clubs, B&B has two separate dance floors. If you like the electronic thump-thump and flashing lights, start off downstairs. Later, for soothingly romantic soft lights and recorded oldies but goodies, go upstairs.

Several of the Costera hotels have live or recorded music for dancing at their lobby bars. As you move east along the Costera, the better possibilities are the **Hotel Crowne Plaza** (tel. 744/440-5555, beginning around 9 P.M. Tues.–Sun.), the **Hotel Fiesta Americana Condesa** (tel. 744/484-2828), and the **Hyatt Regency** (tel. 744/469-1234). Call to verify programs.

A number of restaurant/bars along the Costera have nightly dance music, both recorded and live. A pair of favorites of both long-time Mexican tourists and local people are the **Tropicana** (tel. 744/485-3050, live from around 9 P.M., Thurs.–Sat., recorded Sun.–Wed., $3), and the neighboring **Copa Cabana** (on the beach side, near the corner of Amal Espina, same hours and cover charge as Tropicana). Both have cocktails and live or recorded Latin (sometimes called "tropical") music for dancing till around 3 A.M.

A lively band also plays nightly during the high season at the restaurant/club **Paradise** (tel. 744/484-5988, across from the Hotel Romano, during low season Fri.–Sun. 4–9 P.M., closed Mon.), on the Costera beachside entertainment strip west of the Hotel Fiesta Americana Condesa. Zany waiters, a lively and varied musical repertoire, and good-enough food all spell happy times at the Paradise.

On the other hand, lovers of quieter music enjoy the piano bar evenings at the Hotel Tortuga's **Restaurant Pacífico** (on the mid-Costera, between the Diana Circle and the Hotel

Fiesta Americana Condesatel, tel. 744/484-8889, beginning at 6:30 P.M.).

The same is approximately true at the posh **Escala** view piano bar, across the east-side highway from Hotel Las Brisas.

DISCOS AND HANGOUTS

Discotheques usually monitor their entrances carefully and are consequently safe and pleasant places for a night's entertainment (provided you are either immune to the noise or bring earplugs). They open their doors around 10 P.M. and play relatively low-volume music and videos for starters until around 11 P.M., when fogs descend, lights flash, and the thumping begins, continuing sometimes till dawn. Admission runs about $7 to $15 or more for the tonier joints.

Acapulco's discos and dance hangouts concentrate in two major east-side spots. As you move east, between the Diana Circle and the Hotel Fiesta Americana Condesa, a solid lineup of clubs, hangouts, and discos occupies the Costera's beach side. During peak seasons, the dancing crowds spill onto the street. Stroll along and pick out the style and volume that you like.

Of the bunch, **O'Beach** disco is the loudest, brashest, and among the most popular. For the entrance fee of $5, the music and the lights go till dawn. Other neighboring discos, such as Ole Mammy's, Barbarossa, Crazy Lobster, and Beto, while sometimes loud, are nevertheless subdued in comparison.

Another mile east, Planet Hollywood and Hard Rock Cafe, both of which actually serve food, signal the beginning of a second lineup on both sides of the street of about a dozen live-music or disco clubs. The energy they put out daily trying to outdo each other with brighter lights, louder music, and larger and flashier facades is exceeded only by the frequency at which they seem to go in and out of business. More or less permanently fixed are **Planet Hollywood** (tel. 744/484-0717, noon–midnight, no cover), with recorded music and videos; **Hard Rock Cafe** (tel. 744/484-0047, 10:30 P.M.–1 A.M., no cover), live music; **Baby O** disco and concert hall

(tel. 744/484-7474, 10 P.M.–4 A.M., $12 cover), "There's only one Acapulco and only one Baby O"; and **Nina's** night club (tel. 744/484-2400, 10 P.M.–4 A.M., cover $25, including open bar), with "guaranteed fun."

Reigning above all of these lesser centers of discomania is **Palladium** (tel. 744/446-5490), visible everywhere around the bay as the pink neon glow on the east-side Las Brisas hill. Go there, if only to look, though call for a reservation beforehand, or you might not be let in. Inside, the impression is of ultramodern fantasy—a giant spaceship window facing outward on a galactic star carpet—while the music explodes, propelling you, the dancing traveler, through inner space. A mere $35 cover (women $20) gets you through the door; inside, cocktails are around $10, while French champagne runs upward of $300 a bottle. Open 10 P.M.–6 A.M. Monday–Saturday high season and Tuesday, Thursday, Friday, and Saturday low season. Ladies' nights ($10 admission for women) Tuesday and Thursday.

CHILD'S PLAY

CICI (east end of Costera between golf course and Hyatt Regency, tel. 744/484-8210, 10 A.M.–6 P.M. daily, $10 adult, $7 child), short for Centro Internacional de Convivencia Infantil, is the biggest of Acapulco's water parks. An aquatic paradise for families, CICI has acres of liquid games, where you can swish along a slippery toboggan run, plummet down a towering kamikaze slide, or loll in a gentle wave pool. Other pools contain performing whales, dolphins, and sea lions. Sea mammal performances during the low season are customarily only at 2 P.M., except 2 and 4 P.M. Saturday. High-season performances are customarily at 12:30, 3:30, and 5:30 P.M. Call to verify schedule. Patrons also enjoy a restaurant, a beach club, and much more.

Mágico Mundo (tel. 744/483-1215, 9 A.M.–6 P.M. daily, $4 adult, $2 child), Acapulco's other water park, is on the opposite side of town at Playa Caleta. It includes an aquarium, museum, restaurant, water slides, cascades, and more.

Sports and Recreation

WALKING AND JOGGING

The most interesting beach walking in Acapulco is along the two-mile stretch of beach between the Hotel Fiesta Americana Condesa and the rocky point at Parque Papagayo. Avoid the midday heat by starting early for breakfast along the Costera (a good choice is Sanborn's, tel. 744/481-2426, at the Hotel Calinda) and walking west along the beach with the sun to your back. Besides the beach itself, you'll pass rocky outcroppings to climb on, tidepools to poke through, plenty of fruit vendors, and *palapas* to rest in from the sun. Bring a hat, shirt, and sunscreen and allow two or three hours. If you get tired, ride a taxi or bus back. You can do the reverse walk just as easily in the afternoon after about 3 P.M. from Playa Hamacas just past the steamship dock after lunch on the *zócalo* (try the Cafe Los Amigos).

Soft sand and steep slopes spoil most jogging prospects on Acapulco Bay beaches. However, the green open spaces surrounding the Centro Cultural de Convenciones, just east of the golf course, provide a good in-town substitute.

TENNIS AND GOLF

Acapulco's tennis courts are all private and mostly at the hotels. Try the Hotel Crowne Plaza (tel. 744/444-5555, $8/hr days, $15 nights) or Acapulco Park (tel. 744/485-5437, $7/hr days, $13/hr nights), on the Costera near the Hotel Crowne Plaza. Lessons by in-house teaching pros customarily run $20–30 an hour. The Acapulco Campo de Golf also rents tennis courts.

One of the coziest places for tennis in town is **Alfredo's Tennis Club** (Av. Prado 29, tel. 744/484-0004, call ahead of time), the home of the late former tennis champion Alfredo Millet. His family continues the tradition, renting their two night-lit courts for $8 per hour by day, $12 per hour at night, including towel, refreshment, and use of their swimming pool. Lessons run about $5 extra per hour; get there via Avenida Deportes, next to the Pizza

Hut. Go uphill one block, then left another to Alfredo's, at the corner of Prado.

The Acapulco **Campo de Golf** (tel. 744/484-0781 or 744/484-0782, 6:30 A.M.–10 P.M. daily), right on the mid-Costera, is open to the public on a first-come, first-served basis. Greens fee is about $45 for nine holes and $70 for 18 holes. Caddy costs $17, club rentals are $10.

Much more exclusive are the fairways at the **Club de Golf** (tel. 744/469-1000) of hotels Fairmont Acapulco Princess and Pierre Marques, about five miles past the southeast edge of town. Here, the 18-hole greens fee runs about $120, including shared caddy.

The **Vidafel Mayan Palace** (tel. 744/469-6000), farther east past the Fairmont Acapulco Princess, also has a luxury beachfront golf course.

SWIMMING, SURFING, AND BOOGIE BOARDING

Acapulco Bay's oft-tranquil and invitingly clear green waters usually allow safe swimming from hotel-front beaches. The water is often too calm for surf sports, however. Strong waves off open-ocean Playa Revolcadero southeast of the city often give good rides. Be aware; the waves can be dangerous. The Fairmont Acapulco Princess on the beach provides lifeguards. Check with them before venturing in. Bring your own equipment; rentals may not be available.

SNORKELING AND SCUBA DIVING

The best local snorkeling is off **Isla Roqueta.** Closest access point is by boat from the docks at Playa Caleta and Playa Tlacopanocha. Such trips usually run about $20 per person for two hours, equipment included. Snorkel trips can also be arranged through beachfront aquatics shops at hotels such as the Ritz, Hotel Crowne Plaza, Hotel Fiesta Americana Condesa, Hyatt Regency, and the scuba shops below.

Although local water clarity is often not ideal, especially during the summer–fall rainy season, Acapulco does have a few professional dive shops. Contact instructor José Vasquez's **Acapulco Scuba Center** (tel. 744/482-9474, www.acapulcoscuba.com), near the Bonanza tour boat dock, about half a mile west, past the old-town *zócalo*. They have PADI and NAUI-licensed instructors. A resort course and one dive runs about $70; open-water certification runs abut four days and $350.

Another option, near the same old-town dockfront location, is the very professional, safety-conscious **Divers de Mexico** (tel. 744/482-1398 or 744/483-6020), offering a resort course for $65 and snorkeling and scuba tours by yacht for $70 per hour.

SAILING AND SAILBOARDING

Close-in Acapulco Bay waters (except off west-end Playa Icacos) are generally too congested with motorboats for tranquil sailing or sailboarding. Nevertheless, some beach concessionaires at the big hotels, such as the Hotel Crowne Pacific and Hyatt Regency, do rent (or take people sailing in) simple sailboats from $15 per hour.

Outside of town, tranquil **Laguna Coyuca,** on the coast about 20 minutes' drive northwest of the *zócalo,* offers good sailboarding and sailing prospects.

PERSONAL WATERCRAFT RIDING, WATERSKIING, AND PARASAILING

Power sports are very popular on Costera hotel beaches. Concessionaires—recognized by their lineup of beached mini-motorboats—operate from most big hotel beaches, notably around the Hotel Ritz, Hotel Crowne Plaza, Hotel Fiesta Americana Condesa, and the Hyatt Regency. Prices run about $60 per hour for personal watercraft, $50 per hour for water-skiing, and $20 for a 10-minute parasailing ride.

ECOADVENTURING

Shotover Jet (tel. 744/484-1155, fax 744/484-2648, www.shotoverjet-acapulco.com), a jet-boat excursion company that originated in New Zealand, offers breezy, spray-laced jet-boat excursions on the big wildlife-rich Tres Palos mangrove lagoon at Barra Vieja, an hour drive west of Acapulco. The tariff runs about $60, including transportation, from their office at the Plaza Marbella (beach side of the Diana Circle) in mid-Costera.

They also offer a menu of ecoadventures from their upcounty Río Papagayo canyon base, which they call "Bravo Town," 40 miles (66 km) north of Acapulco, off Highway 95 near Tierra Colorada. From Bravo Town they also offer rafting, hiking, camping, caving, rappelling, and climbing.

Like the Shotover Jet, the rafting excursions (Aug.–Jan.) take off from their Plaza Marbella headquarters. The cost is about $50 per adult, $20 kids, including transportation to and from Acapulco.

SPORTFISHING

Fishing boats line the *malecón* dockside across the boulevard from the *zócalo*. Activity centers on the dockside office of the 20-boat blue and white fleet of fishing boat cooperative **Sociedad Cooperativa Servicios Turístico** (tel. 744/482-1099, 8 A.M.–3 P.M. daily), whose dozens of licensed captains regularly take visitors for big-game fishing trips. Although some travel agents may book you individually during high season, the Sociedad's office rents only entire, captained boats, including equipment and bait.

Rental prices and catches depend on the season. Drop by the dock after 2 P.M. to see what the boats are bringing in. During good times, boats might average one big marlin or sailfish apiece. Best months for sailfish (*pez vela*) are said to be November, December, and January; for marlin, February and March.

Big 40-foot boats with five or six fishing lines rent from $250 per day. Smaller boats, with three or four lines and holding five or six passengers, rent from around $200. All of the Cooperativa boats are radio-equipped, and have toilet, life preservers, tackle, bait, and ice. Customers usually supply their own food and drinks. Although the Cooperativa is generally competent, look over the boat and check its equipment before putting your money down.

You can also arrange fishing trips through a travel agent or your hotel lobby tour desk.

Sailfish and marlin are neither the only nor necessarily the most desirable fish in the sea. Competently captained *pangas* can typically haul in three or four large 15- or 20-pound excellent-eating *robalo* (snook), *huachinango* (snapper), or *atún* (tuna) in two hours just outside Acapulco Bay.

Such lighter boats are rentable from the cooperative for about $20 per hour or from individual fishermen on Playa Las Hamacas (past the steamship dock at the foot of Fort San Diego).

A number of independent sportfishing captains operate from the excursion ship *Bonanza* dock about a mile west of the *zócalo*. One of the best organized and English savvy is **Fish-R-Us** (tel. 744/482-8282 or 744/487-8787, toll-free Mex. tel. 800/FISHRUS or 800/347-4787, toll-free U.S. tel./fax 877/3FISHRUS or 877/334-7478, reservation@fish-r-us.com, www.fish-r-us.com), which offers fully equipped fishing yachts (40-foot, five lines, $450, or $75 per person if individual reservations are available) and scuba diving for all levels from beginner to advanced.

MARINA AND BOAT DOCKING

A safe place to dock your boat is the **Club de Yates** (Av. Costera M. Alemán 215, Fracc. Las Playas, Acapulco, Guerrero 39300, tel. 744/482-3859, fax 744/483-7436, cyates@acabtu.com.mx or gg@clubdeyatesaca.com.mx, www.clubdeyatesaca.com.mx), on the Peninsula de las Playas's sheltered inner shoreline. The slip rate is around $1 per foot per day, use of the ramp for launching runs about $75. Services include 110/220-volt power, pump-out, toilets, showers, restaurant, repair facilities, access to the swimming pool, and more.

The Club de Yates is accessible from the Gran Via Tropical on the inner, bay side of the Peninsula de las Playas. Get there via the Costera west of the *zócalo*. About 2.5 miles west of the *zócalo*, where the boulevard splits at the gas station, fork left along Gran Via Tropical. Continue straight ahead about 300 yards, to the Club de Yates entrance gate on the left.

Shopping

MARKET

Acapulco, despite its modern glitz, has a very colorful traditional market, which is fun for strolling through even without buying anything. It is open daily, dawn to dusk. Vendors arrive here with grand intentions: mounds of neon-red tomatoes, buckets of *nopales* (cactus leaves), towers of toilet paper, and mountains of soap bars. As you wander through the sunlight-dappled aisles, past big gaping fish, bulging rounds of cheese, and festoons of huaraches, don't miss **Piñatas Uva,** one of the market's friendliest shops. You may even end up buying one of Uva's charming paper Donald Ducks, Snow Whites, or Porky Pigs. The market is at the corner of Mendoza and Constituyentes, a quarter mile inland from Hornos Beach. Ride a Mercado-marked bus or take a taxi.

SUPERMARKETS AND DEPARTMENT STORES

In the *zócalo* area behind Sanborn's, **Woolworth's** (on Escudero, corner of Morelos, tel. 744/480-0072, 9:30 A.M.–8:30 P.M. daily) is a good source of a little bit of everything at reasonable prices. Its lunch counter, furthermore, provides a welcome refuge from the midday heat.

Comercial Mexicana, with three Acapulco branches, is a big Mexican Kmart, which, besides the expected film, medicines, cosmetics, and housewares, also includes groceries and a bakery. Its locations are: on the Costera at Cinco de Mayo (tel. 744/854-4924, 9 A.M.–11 P.M. daily), just east of the Fuerte San Diego; on Farallones, a couple of blocks uphill from the Costera's Diana Circle (tel. 744/484-3412, same hours as above); and two miles farther, across from CICI water park (tel. 744/484-3373, open 24 hours).

If you can't find what you want at Comercial Mexicana, try the huge **Sam's Club** (tel. 744/469-0202), just uphill from the Farallones Comercial Mexicana; and the giant **Wal-Mart** (tel. 744/485-3462), at the far east end across from the Hyatt Regency.

PHOTOGRAPHY

Acapulco visitors enjoy the services of a number of photo stores. One of the best is the very professional **Foto y Mechanica** (corner of Iglesia and Hidalgo, tel. 744/483-1603, 10 A.M.–2 P.M. and 4–7 P.M. Mon.–Fri., 10 A.M.–2 P.M. Sat.), one block west of the *zócalo.* Goods and services include film and development; cameras, both film and digital; a number of digital services; and expert camera repair.

For more basic photo needs (and Internet access) go to **Foto System Lab** (tel. 744/482-2112, 9 A.M.–10 P.M. daily), right on the *zócalo,* supplying photofinishing, a few cameras and accessories, and some popular film varieties. On the corner of J. Carranza, right side as you enter the *zócalo* from the Costera.

On the east end of the Costera, among the several photo stores, try **Foto Imagen** (tel. 744/484-5770, 9 A.M.–9 P.M. daily), in the basement of Gigante supermarket, across the Costera from the Acapulco Convention Center.

HANDICRAFTS

Despite much competition, asking prices for Acapulco handicrafts are relatively high. Bargaining is usually necessary to bring them down to size. **Sanborn's** (Av. Costera M. Alemán and Escudero, tel. 744/482-4095, 8 A.M.–11 P.M. daily), two blocks from the *zócalo,* has a bookstore and restaurant. The all-Mexico selection includes, notably, black

Oaxaca *barra* pottery, painted gourds from Uruapan, Guadalajara leather, Taxco silver jewelry, colorful plates from Puebla, and Tlaquepaque pottery and glass.

Keeping the prices at Sanborn's in mind, head one block toward the *zócalo* to **Bonita** handicrafts store (I. de la Llave and Av. Costera M. Alemán, local 1, tel. 744/482-0590 or 744/482-5240, 9 A.M.–7 P.M. Mon.–Sat., 9 A.M.–3 P.M. Sun. during holidays), where, in the basement of the big old Edificio Oviedo, glitters an eclectic fiesta of Mexican jewelry. Never mind if the place is empty; cruise-line passengers regularly fill the aisles. Here you'll be able to see artisans adding to the acre of gleaming silver, gold, copper, brass, fine carving, and lacquerware around you. Don't forget to get your free margarita (or soft drink) before you leave.

Another bountiful handicrafts source near the *zócalo* is the artisans' market **Mercado de Parrazal.** From Sanborn's, head away from the Costera a few short blocks to Vasquez de León

Piñatas seem to come alive at Acapulco markets.

and turn right one block. There, a big plaza of semipermanent stalls offers a galaxy of Mexican handicrafts: Tonalá and Tlaquepaque papier-mâché, brass, and pottery animals; Bustamante-replica eggs, masks, and humanoids; Oaxaca wooden animals and black pottery; Guerrero masks; and Taxco jewelry. Although most of the store assortments aren't particularly unusual, a fortunate exception is **Yazmin,** in the middle of the complex, open 9 A.M.–6 P.M. daily. They have an unusual collection of one-of-a-kind jewelry, ceramics, and woodwork examples. Sharp bargaining is necessary, however, to lower the excessive asking prices.

A number of handicrafts shopping centers line the new-town Costera. Check out the pair of handicrafts arcades, **Dalia** and **Pueblito,** across the Costera from the Plaza Bahía shopping mall (just west of the Hotel Crowne Pacific). Stalls along shady interior walkways display a host of moderately priced leather, silver, hand-embroidered dresses, *huipiles,* bedspreads, napkins, ceramics, glass, stoneware, and much more.

For a grand selection of largely inexpensive, but still attractive, native-made handicrafts, go to the large indigenous **mercado de artesanías** warren of stalls, on the mid-Costera, just east of the Diana Circle, inland side.

Not far from the Costera's eastern end, the state of Guerrero operates **Casa Artesanal Guerrerense** (10 A.M.–8 P.M. daily), in the shady mango grove-now-park a couple of blocks east of the CICI water park. Step inside and peruse the modest all-Guerrero handicrafts selection, which usually includes Taxco bright silver, fierce jaguar masks from Chilapa, shiny lacquerware from Olinalá, and fetching *huipiles* from Xochistlahuaca.

In the same park, about half a block farther east, visit the **Galería Ixcateopan** (9 A.M.–9 P.M. daily), which exhibits and sells paintings and sculpture of prominent local artists.

The above-mentioned handicrafts store and gallery are part of the **Centro Cultural Guerrerense** that encompasses the entire park. Additional facilities, hidden in the shady rear section, away from the boulevard, are the student library, open 9 A.M.–9 P.M. daily, and the auditorium, venue for a cultural program of dance, plays, music, and more every Saturday at 7 P.M.

A final long-time handicrafts source that displays a moderately priced all-Mexico selection is the streetfront stall a block east of Galería Ixcateopan, in front of the El Embarcadero restaurant, which is closed but a good landmark. It's open approximately noon until 10 P.M.

Information and Services

TOURIST INFORMATION AND TRAVEL AGENTS

An easily accessible local tourist information office is the *modulo* (tel. 744/484-4416 or 744/484-4583, 9 A.M.–9 P.M. daily), in front of the convention center, two blocks east of the golf course. Here, workers staff a small crafts shop and money exchange office.

Acapulco is stuffed with travel agents. Probably it's best to start at your hotel travel desk. Alternatively, some of the most experienced local travel agents include **Acuario Tours** (Av. Costera Miguel Alemán 48, tel. 744/485-6100, 8 A.M.–9 P.M. Mon.–Sat.), in mid-Costera; **American Express** (tel. 744/435-2200) offers full-service travel services and the customary financial services, such as cashing of travelers checks, and, for American Express cardholders, personal checks. Find them in the Hotel Continental Emporio, at the west side of the hotel's Costera-front shopping plaza.

PUBLICATIONS

The best new-book sources in town are the three branches of **Sanborn's.** As you move west to east, you'll find the *zócalo* branch (tel. 744/482-4095, 7 A.M.–11 P.M. daily), on the Costera across from the steamship dock; the mid-Costera branch (tel. 744/482-2426) at the Hotel Calinda; and the east-Costera branch (tel. 744/484-2035, 7:30 A.M.–1 A.M. daily) on the ground floor of the Oceanic 2000 shopping plaza, beach side of the Costera, a few blocks from the east end.

English-language international newspapers, such as the *Miami Herald,* the *Los Angeles Times,* and *USA Today,* are often available in the large hotel bookshops, especially at the Hotel Fiesta Americana Condesa and the Hyatt Regency. In old town, newsstands around the *zócalo* regularly sell the *Miami Herald.*

Pick up the commercial but handy and widely available American Express–sponsored tourist booklet *Acapulco Passport* free at a hotel, store, or travel agency.

Acapulco's former expatriate and tourist English-language newspaper *Acapulco Heat* has gone completely electronic as the Spanish-only website, www.acabtu.com.mx. It provides a number of useful links to mostly midscale hotels, restaurants, community events and organizations, travel activities, and entertainments.

PUBLIC LIBRARY

The small, friendly Acapulco *biblioteca* (Madero 5, corner of Quebrada, tel. 744/482-0388, 9 A.M.–9 P.M. Mon.–Fri.) is near the *zócalo* adjacent to the cathedral. Its collection, used mostly by college and high school students in the airy reading room, is nearly all in Spanish.

LANGUAGE INSTRUCTION

Get Spanish-language instruction at the reputable private **Universidad Americana** (Av. Costera M. Alemán 1756, Fracc. Magellanes, Acapulco 39670, tel. 744/486-5618 or 744/486-5619, info_uda@uaa.edu.mx, www.uaa.edu.mx) on the Costera, approximately across from the Hotel Crowne Pacific. For more information, contact coordinator Elba Molina at ext. 122.

MONEY EXCHANGE

In the *zócalo* neighborhood, long-hours **HSBC Bank** (Jesús Carranza 8, tel. 744/483-5722, 8 A.M.–7 P.M. Mon.–Sat.) is the best bet, on the one-block side street tucked near the *zócalo's* northeast corner. Alternatively, go to **Bancomer** (tel. 744/484-8055, 9 A.M.–4 P.M. Mon.–Fri., 10 A.M.–2 P.M. Sat.), fronting the Costera, to change U.S. cash or travelers checks only. Although the lines at nearby **Banamex** (tel. 744/483-6425, 9 A.M.–4 P.M. Mon.–Fri.), two blocks from the *zócalo* next to Sanborn's, are usually longer, it exchanges major currencies. You can avoid the lines by using the bank ATMs, which are routinely connected with international networks.

On the new side of town, also change money at **HSBC** (tel. 744/485-5309, 8 A.M.–7 P.M. Mon.–Sat.), across from McDonald's; or at **Bancomer** (tel. 744/484-7245, 9 A.M.–4 P.M. Mon.–Fri., 9 A.M.–2 P.M. Sat.), a few blocks west of the Diana Circle, for U.S. and Canadian currency and travelers checks.

After normal bank hours on the Costera, the **Consultorio International** (tel. 744/484-3108, 9 A.M.–6 P.M. Mon.–Fri., 9 A.M.–1 P.M. Sat.), in Galería Picuda shopping center, across the street and a block west from the Hotel Fiesta Americana Condesa, exchanges currency and travelers checks.

AMERICAN EXPRESS OFFICE

The Acapulco American Express branch (tel. 744/435-2200, 9 A.M.–6 P.M. Mon.–Fri., 9 A.M.–1 P.M. Sat.) is in the Costera-front commercial plaza of the Hotel Continental Emporio, a block west of the Diana Circle. Besides full travel services, they provide member financial services, including cashing travelers checks and personal checks. Check-cashing hours may be shorter than regular office hours.

COMMUNICATIONS

Acapulco has at least three neighboring pairs of government post and telecommunications offices. The main Acapulco **correo** (post office) (8 A.M.–8 P.M. Mon.–Sat.) is in the Palacio Federal across the Costera from the steamer dock three blocks from the *zócalo*. It provides Mexpost—fast, secure mail similar to U.S. Express Mail—and philatelic services. **Telecomunicaciones** (tel. 744/482-2622 or 744/482-2621, 8 A.M.–8 P.M. Mon.–Fri., 9 A.M.–noon Sat.–Sun.), next to the main post office, provides money order, telegram, and fax services.

Another **correo** and telecommunications office is at the Estrella de Oro bus terminal (Cuauhtémoc and Massieu, 9 A.M.–8 P.M. Mon.–Fri., 9 A.M.–1 P.M. Sat.). The neighboring **Telecomunicaciones** (telephone, fax, and money orders) is open 8 A.M.–7:30 P.M. Monday–Friday, 9 A.M.–12:30 P.M. Saturday and Sunday. Find them both on the outside upstairs walkway, at the west end of the terminal building.

In mid-Costera, you can conveniently go to the small branch **correo** (tel. 744/484-8029, 8 A.M.–4 P.M. Mon.–Fri.), and next-door **Telecom** (tel. 744/484-6976, 9 A.M.–3 P.M. Mon.–Fri.), at the Centro de Convenciones (convention center).

For lowest phone rates, use the widely available Ladatel cards in the many public street telephones; first dial 001 for long distance to the United States or Canada and 01 for Mexico. Otherwise, near the *zócalo* you can call *larga distancia* (long distance) 8 A.M.–10 P.M. daily from either the small office on J. Carranza at Calle de la Llave, or on the *zócalo*'s other side, next to Restaurant Los Amigos, 9 A.M.–9 P.M. Monday–Friday, 9 A.M.–2 P.M. and 4–9 P.M. Saturday–Sunday.

HEALTH AND EMERGENCIES

If you get sick, ask your hotel to call a doctor for you or contact the **Hospital Magellanes** (W. Massieu 2, corner of Colón, tel. 744/485-6544 or 744/485-6597, ext. 119 for the pharmacy), one of Acapulco's most respected private hospitals, for both office visits and round-the-clock emergencies. One block from the Costera and the Hotel Qualton Club, facilities include a lab, 24-hour

pharmacy, and an emergency room with many specialists on call.

A group of American-trained IAMAT physicians (International Association for Medical Assistance to Travelers) offers medical consultations in English. Contact them at the medical department of the Hotel Fairmont Acapulco Princess (tel. 744/469-1000, ext. 1309).

For routine medications near the *zócalo* go to one of many pharmacies, such as at **Sanborn's** (corner of Escudero and the Costera, tel. 744/482-6167) or the big **discount pharmacy** (at Escudero and Carranza, tel. 744/482-0804, 8 A.M.–10 P.M. daily), across the street from Woolworth's.

For police emergencies, contact one of the many tourist police (on the Costera, in safari pith helmets, tel. 744/485-0650 or 744/486-8220), or call the officers at the municipal police Papagayo station (tel. 744/485-0490), at the end of Avenida Camino Sonora, on the inland side of Papagayo Park.

In case of fire, call the **bomberos** (tel. 744/484-4122), on Avenida Farallón, behind Comercial Mexicana two blocks off the Costera from the Diana Circle.

IMMIGRATION AND CUSTOMS

If you lose your tourist card go to **Migración** at the airport (sufficiently early on your day of departure) or on the Costera (tel. 744/484-9022, 9 A.M.–1 P.M. Mon.–Fri.), across the traffic circle from Comercial Mexicana, same side of the Costera. Bring proof of your identity and some proof (such as your stamped passport, airline ticket, or a copy of your lost tourist card) of your arrival date in Mexico. If you try to leave Mexico without your tourist card, you may face trouble and a fine. Also report to Migración if you arrive in Acapulco by yacht.

The **Aduana** (customs) office (tel. 744/466-9005, 8 A.M.–3 P.M. Mon.–Fri.) is on the Costera, *zócalo* area, at the dock across from Sanborn's. If you have to temporarily leave your car in Mexico, check to see what paperwork, if any, must be completed.

CONSULATES

Acapulco has several consular agents and officers. The offices of the U.S. consular officer, Alexander Richards (tel. 744/481-1699, 744/484-0300, or 744/481-0100, fax 744/484-0300, consular@ prodigy.net.mx, 10 A.M.–2 P.M. Mon.–Fri.), are in the Hotel Continental Emporio. He's a busy man, and he asks that you kindly have your problem written down, together with a specific request for information or action. In emergencies only, contact him at tel. 744/431-0094.

The Canadian consul, Diane McLean de Huerta (tel. 744/484-1305, fax 744/484-1306 or 744/481-1349) holds office hours 9 A.M.–5:30 P.M. Monday–Friday at the Centro Comercial Marbella, suite 23. After hours, in an emergency, call toll-free Mex. tel. 800/706-2900.

For the British consul, Lorraine Bajas, call 744/484-1735. Contact the German consul, Mario Wichtendahl, at Antone de Alamino 26, tel. 744/484-1860. The Netherlands consul, Ángel Díaz, can be reached at tel. 744/486-6179.

For additional information and assistance, the consulates maintain a joint **Consular Corps** office (tel. 744/481-2533, 9 A.M.–2 P.M. Mon.–Fri.) in the Centro de Convenciones just east of the golf course.

LAUNDRY

Near the *zócalo,* get your laundry done at **Lavandería Laradin** (8 A.M.–10 P.M. Mon.–Sat.), at the corner of Iglesias and La Paz, one block west of the *zócalo.* Alternatively, near Playa Caleta, try **Lavandería Gabi** (Av. Lopez Mateos 12A, 9 A.M.–7 P.M. Mon.–Sat.), two blocks inland from the beach.

Getting There and Away

BY AIR

Several airlines connect the Acapulco airport (code-designated ACA, officially the Juan N. Álvarez International Airport) with U.S. and Mexican destinations.

Aeroméxico (reservations tel. 744/485-1625 or 744/485-1600, toll-free Mex. tel. 800/021-4000; flight information tel. 744/466-9296 or 744/466-9109) flights connect directly with Mexico City, Tijuana, and Guadalajara.

Mexicana Airlines (reservations tel. 744/486-7586, 744/486-7587, or 744/466-9121, toll-free Mex. tel. 800/502-2000; flight information tel. 744/466-9136) flights connect five times daily with Mexico City and once daily with Guadalajara via associated Aerolitoral airline.

America West Airlines (tel. 744/466-9121, toll-free U.S. tel. 800/235-9292) flights connect with Phoenix.

Continental Airlines (reservations toll-free Mex. tel. 800/900-5000; flight information

tel. 744/466-9063) flights connect with Houston (Mon.–Sat.) and Newark (Sat. only).

American Airlines (reservations toll-free Mex. tel. 800/904-6000; flight information tel. 744/466-9227) flights connect with Dallas during the winter season.

Aviacsa Airlines (reservations tel. 744/481-3240 or 744/481-3242; flight information tel. 744/466-9209 or 744/466-9205) flights connect with Tijuana, Guadalajara, Mexico City, and Cuernavaca.

Delta Air Lines (toll-free Mex. tel. 800/902-2100), an Aeroméxico affiliate, charters flights connect with Los Angeles, Portland, and Dallas during the winter season.

AIR ARRIVAL AND DEPARTURE

After the usually quick immigration and customs checks, Acapulco arrivees can find airport car rentals, efficient transportation for the 15-mile trip to town, a *buzon* (mailbox), and ATMs.

Local car rental agents often available for arriving flights include **Hertz** (tel. 744/485-8947 or 744/485-6889); **Avis** (tel. 744/466-0075); **Alamo** (tel. 744/466-9444 or 744/484-3305, fax 744/484-3652); **Budget** (tel. 744/481-2433 or 744/466-9003); **Thrifty** (tel. 744/486-1940, fax 744/486-4219); and **SAAD Jeep and Car Rentals** (tel. 744/484-3445, 744/484-5325, or 744/466-9179). You can ensure availability and often save money by bargaining for a reservation with agencies via their U.S. national toll-free numbers.

Tickets for ground transport to town are sold by agents near the terminal exit. Options include a *colectivo* GMC Suburban (about $8), which deposits passengers at individual hotels. *Taxis especiales* run about $20 to $45, depending on distance.

On your departure day, save money by sharing a taxi with fellow departees. Don't get into the taxi until you settle the fare. Having already arrived, you know what the airport ride should cost. If the driver insists on greed, hail another taxi.

If you lost your tourist permit (which immigration stamped upon your arrival) either go to Migración (tel. 744/484-9022) before your departure date, or arrive early enough at the airport to iron out the problem with airport Migración officials (tel. 744/446-9025) before departure. Bring some proof of your date of arrival, either a stamped passport, airline ticket copy, or a copy of your lost tourist permit.

The Acapulco air terminal building has a number of shops upstairs for last-minute handicrafts purchases, a *buzón* (mailbox), stamp vending machine, long-distance telephones (be sure to ask the operator for the price before completing a call), and a restaurant.

BY BUS
Major competitors Estrella Blanca and Estrella de Oro operate three separate long-distance *centrales de autobús* (central bus terminals), one (Estrella Blanca only—the Ejido) on the west side and two (both Estrella Blanca and Estrella de Oro) stations on Avenida Cuauhtémoc, on the east side of town.

Estrella Blanca (tel. 744/469-2028, 744/469-2029, or 744/469-2030) coordinates the service of its subsidiary lines Elite, Flecha Roja, Autotransportes Cuauhtémoc, Turistar, Futura, and Gacela at two separate terminals. Credit cards are accepted. Most first- or luxury-class departures use the big west-side Ejido terminal at Avenida Ejido 47. The airy station is so clean you could sleep on the polished onyx floor and not get dirty; bring an air mattress and blanket. Other conveniences include left-luggage lockers, food stores across the street, Sendatur deluxe and midscale hotel booking agency, and Sendatel 24-hour *larga distancia* and fax office open daily 6 A.M.–10 P.M.

Also from the Ejido station, scores of Estrella Blanca *salidas locales* (local departures) connect with destinations in three directions: northern interior, Costa Grande (northwest), and Costa Chica (southeast) coastal destinations. Most of the departures are first-class Estrella Blanca, Elite, Turistar, and Futura. Specific northern interior connections include dozens daily to Toluca or Cuernavaca (via Chilpancingo), Altamirano (six daily), Guadalajara (three daily), and dozens to Mexico City (to either terminals Sur or Norte, some via Taxco).

Many first-class (about 10 per day) and second-class (hourly) departures connect northwest with Costa Grande destinations of Zihuatanejo and Lázaro Cárdenas and many intermediate points. Southeast Costa Chica connections with Puerto Escondido, some continuing to Huatulco and Salina Cruz, include four first-class daily (one via Ometepec) and several second-class connections per day.

Also from the Ejido Estrella Blanca terminal, a few daily first-class departures connect with the U.S. border (Mexicali and Tijuana) via the entire Pacific coast route, through Zihuatanejo, Manzanillo, Puerto Vallarta, and Mazatlán. Other departures connect with the U.S. border at Ciudad Juárez, via San Luis Potosí, Zacatecas, Torreón, and Chihuahua.

Many additional first- and luxury-class buses

depart from Estrella Blanca's separate east-side big Papagayo terminal (tel. 744/469-2081), on Avenida Cuauhtémoc about five blocks west of the Estrella de Oro Terminal. Facilities and services include an air-conditioned waiting room, left-luggage service, fax service (744/485-8331), a snack bar, and hotel reservations. From the Papagayo terminal, luxury-class and first-class buses connect with northeast Mexico and the U.S. border, via Querétaro, San Luis Potosí, Monterrey, and Reynosa, at the U.S. border. Other departures connect northwest, with Cuernavaca, Morelia, Guadalajara, Leon, Celaya, and Irapuato; and north with Puebla and Mexico City bus stations Norte and Sur; and northwest, with Zihuatanejo.

The busy, modern **Estrella de Oro** bus terminal (at Cuauhtémoc and W. Massieu, tel. 744/485-8758, 744/485-8705, or 744/485-9360) on the east side of town provides connections with the Mexico City corridor (Chilpancingo, Iguala, Taxco, Cuernavaca, Mexico City) and northwest Costa Grande destinations via Zihuatanejo with Lázaro Cárdenas. Departures include dozens of first- and luxury-class to Mexico City and intermediate points. Several connect directly through Taxco and Iguala. Four departures connect daily with the Costa Grande, three with Zihuatanejo, one only with Lázaro Cárdenas. Estrella de Oro offers no Costa Chica (Ometepec–Oaxaca) connections southeast.

Services in the terminal are spare, including only toilets, left-luggage lockers, an Auto Turismo hotel reservation service downstairs, and no food except sweets, chips, and drinks. Outside, at the terminal's west end, are the post and telecommunications offices: For telephone, fax, and money orders, **Telecomunicaciones** (tel. 744/485-5177) is open 8 A.M.–7:30 P.M. Monday–Friday and 9 A.M.–12:30 P.M. Saturday and Sunday; the *correo* is open 8 A.M.–9 P.M. Monday–Friday.

BY CAR OR RV

Good highways connect Acapulco north with Mexico City, northwest with the Costa Grande and Michoacán, and southeast with the Costa Chica and Oaxaca.

The Mexico City Highway 95 *cuota autopista* (toll superhighway) would make the initial leg connection via Chilpancingo (73 miles, 117 km, about two hours) easy if it weren't for the Acapulco congestion. (Go by the tunnel, if you can afford the steep $6 toll.) The uncluttered superhighway *cuota* extension (125 miles, 201 km, $30 for a car, about double that for motorhome) to Cuernavaca is a breeze in 2.5 hours. For Iguala and Taxco, leave the superhighway at the Chilpancingo north end and follow the winding but scenic Highway 95 northwest *libre* (nontoll) cutoff 75 miles (120 km) to Iguala, continuing 22 miles (35 km) to Taxco. Continuing from Cuernavaca, the over-the-mountain leg to Mexico City (53 miles, 85 km) would be simple except for possible Mexico City gridlock, which might lengthen it to two hours. Better allow a minimum of around 5 driving hours for the entire 247-mile (398-km) Acapulco–Mexico City trip. Make sure you arrive on a day permitted by the last digit of your license plate.

The Costa Grande section of Highway 200 northwest toward Zihuatanejo is generally uncluttered and smooth (except for occasional bumps and potholes). Allow about four hours for the 150-mile (242-km) trip.

The same is true for the Costa Chica stretch of Highway 200 southeast to Ometepec (122 miles, 197 km), Pinotepa Nacional (157 miles, 253 km), and Puerto Escondido (247 miles, 398 km). Allow about three driving hours to Ometepec, four to Pinotepa, and about 6.5 hours total to Puerto Escondido.

Acapulco's most congested ingress-egress bottleneck used to be the over-the-hill leg of Highway 95 from the middle of town. Although this route has been speeded up by an expensive (about $6) one-mile toll tunnel, the scenery is much prettier if you drive east along the Costera past uphill Hotel Las Brisas as if you were heading to the airport. Continue about three miles past the big cloverleaf intersection at the bottom of the hill. After another mile or so, pass the Hotel Fairmont, on the right, and continue to the *cuota autopista* entrance on the left. Enter, pass the toll gate (about $5), and breeze north an easy 10 minutes to either the Highway 200 exit (where you should turn off right, east, for the Costa Chica), or continue north along the *autopista* straight ahead for Highway 95 and northern upcountry Guerrero points of Chilpancingo, Iguala, and Taxco.

Pie de la Cuesta

The translation of the name Pie (pee-YAY) de la Cuesta, Foot of the Hill, aptly describes this downscale resort village. Tucked around the bend a few miles northwest of Acapulco, between a wide open-ocean beach and placid Laguna Coyuca, Pie de la Cuesta appeals to those who want the excitement the big town offers and the peace and quiet that it doesn't.

Although tranquil, Pie de la Cuesta offers plenty of outdoor fun, such as mangrove-jungle boat tours, horseback riding, beach sunset-watching, hammock snoozing, water-skiing, beachcombing, boat and kayak launching, and swimming and fishing, in the adjacent palm-tufted freshwater Laguna Coyuca.

Laguna Coyuca, kept full by the sweet waters of the Río Coyuca, has long been known for its fish, birdlife, and tranquil, plumy shoreline. During the early 1400s, the Purépecha kings (who ruled from the Michoacán highlands) established a provincial capital near the town of Coyuca. After the Aztecs drove out the Purépecha a century later (and the Aztecs in turn were defeated by the Spanish), Pie de la Cuesta and its beautiful Laguna Coyuca slumbered in the shadow of Acapulco.

SIGHTS

Laguna Coyuca is a large sandy-bottomed lake, lined by palms and laced by mangrove channels. It stretches 10 miles along the shoreline west from Pie de la Cuesta, which occupies the southeast (Acapulco) side. The barrier sandbar, wide Playa Pie de la Cuesta, separates the lagoon from the ocean. It extends a dozen miles west to the river outlet, which is open to the sea only during the rainy season. A road runs along the beach west the length of Laguna Coyuca to the tourist hamlet of Barra de Coyuca. There, *palapas* line the beach and serve seafood to busloads of Sunday visitors.

Playa Pie de la Cuesta, a seemingly endless, 100-yard-wide stretch of yellow sand, is fine for surf fishing, beachcombing, jogging, and long sunset walks. However, its powerful (mostly March through October) open-ocean waves are unsuited for surfing and hazardous for swimming. They often break thunderously near the sand and recede with strong, turbulent undertow. Fortunately Pie de la Cuesta waves settle down to pleasantly tranquil during invitingly balmy December through February.

On the inland side, however, the tranquil Acapulco (east) end of Laguna Coyuca is an embarkation point for lagoon tours and the center for water-skiing and personal watercraft riding. Among the best equipped of the shoreline clubs that offer powerboat services is the **Restaurant and Club de Skis Tres Marias** (tel. 744/460-0013). Besides a pleasant lake-view shoreline *palapa* restaurant (good breakfasts: open daily 8 A.M.–8 P.M.) it offers water-skiing at about $45/hour and personal watercraft riding for about $75/hour.

If you want to launch your own boat, you can do so easily at Club de Skis Tres Marias and others for about $28. The boat traffic, which confines itself mostly to mid-lagoon, does not deter swimming in the lagoon's clear waters. Slip on your bathing suit and jump in anywhere along the sandy shoreline.

◖ Laguna Coyuca Boat Tour

Lagoon tours begin from several landings

dotting the Pie de la Cuesta end of the lagoon. Half-day regular excursions (maximum 10 people, about $8 per person) push off daily around 11 A.M., noon, and 1:30 P.M. Along the way, they pass islands with trees loaded with nesting cormorants, herons, and pelicans. In midlake, gulls dip and sway in the breeze behind your boat while a host of storks, ducks, avocets, and a dozen other varieties paddle, preen, and forage in the water nearby. Other times, your boat passes through winding channels hung with vines and lined with curtains of great mangrove roots.

At midpoint, boat tours usually stop for a bite to eat at **Isla Montosa.** (Ask ahead of time, because you shouldn't miss it.) While ashore, be sure to allow time for a stroll to restful **Restaurant Polin,** on the island's palm-shadowed south side, where you'll probably meet some descendants of the pioneer settler, known simply as Esteves. As the legend goes, he arrived during the 1930s with six women with whom he founded the present colony, which now numbers about a hundred residents, all related to their illustrious ancestor. For this reason, Isla Montosa is sometimes known as the

"La Isla del Hombre Con Seis Mujeres" (The Island of the Man with Six Women).

Judging from the happily bucolic ambience of Isla Montosa, Esteves was thoroughly successful. Here, roosters crow, pigs root, bougainvillea blooms, and a settlement of fishing families live, unencumbered by 21st-century conveniences, beneath their majestic shoreline palm grove.

Barra de Coyuca

On another day, drive your car or ride one of the frequent buses that head from Pie de la Cuesta to Barra de Coyuca village at the west end of the lagoon. Along the way, you will pass several scruffy hamlets and a parade of fenced lots, some still-open meadows where horses graze while others are filled with shady gardens and big houses. Lack of potable water, local residents complain, is a continuing problem on this dry sandbar.

At road's end, 10 miles west from Pie de la Cuesta, a few tourist stores and a colony of hammock-equipped beach *palapa* restaurants serve holiday crowds. Boats head for tours from lagoonside, where patrons at the **Restaurant**

To Acapulco Bypass,
Hwy 95, Ixtapa, and Zihuatanejo

200

0   200 yds
0   200 m

DOCKS

DOCKS

LAGUNA COYUCA
BOAT TOUR

DOCKS DOCKS

1ST-CLASS
BUS STOP

COPIES

DOCTOR/
PHARMACY

GROCERY AND
VEGETABLES

POLICE
STATION

200

To Acapulco

LONG-DISTANCE
TELEPHONE

INTERNET

VILLA ROXANA

VILLA NIRVANA

© AVALON TRAVEL PUBLISHING, INC.

Dos Vistas enjoy a double view of both beach and lagoon.

(Mobile travelers without a lot of luggage can also continue west from here, by cross-lagoon launch to La Barra, thence to Costa Grande points west.)

ACCOMMODATIONS
Hotels and Bungalows

Approximately 20 mostly basic accommodations line Pie de la Cuesta's single beachside road, officially Avenida de la Fuerza Aerea (Air Force), but often called Avenida Pie de la Cuesta. Competiton keeps rooms clean, management sharp, and prices low. Nearly all lodgings cluster along a mile-long roadfront, enjoying highly visible locations right on the beach. Telephone, fax, or email for reservations, especially for the winter season and holidays. Many have only tepid, room-temperature bath water and do not accept credit cards; exceptions are noted.

Note: Some unscrupulous Acapulco taxi drivers are trying to squeeze commissions from Pie de la Cuesta lodgings in return for bringing customers to their doorsteps. Typical tactics include outright refusing to take customers to places that don't pay commissions, or telling customers that the hotel they request *"no sirve"* ("is not running"). You can combat this on the spot by making sure, before you get into the taxi, that the driver agrees to take you to the hotel of your choice, and, once in Pie de la Cuesta, insisting that he follows through, or don't pay. Daytime taxi fares from Acapulco shouldn't run more than about $5 from old town, $7 from the Costera; nighttime tariffs should be no more than double those amounts. Plenty of daytime buses run there for less than half a dollar.

Under $50: The enduringly lovely ◖ **Villa Nirvana** (Av. de la Fuerza Aerea 302, P.O. Box 950, Acapulco, Guerrero 39300, tel. 744/460-1631, fax 744/460-3573, nirvana@ acabtu.com.mx, www.lavillanirvana.com) attracts a steady stream of repeat guests. Look around and the reason becomes clear: clean, comfortable accommodations in an attractive garden beachfront compound, with an invitingly blue pool and patio, restaurant, and parking thoughtfully moved to an adjacent lot. Friendly owners Daniel Reams and Pamela Fox offer rates from about $20 d low season, $30 high, for the smallest room to about $90 for their deluxe four-person kitchenette suite. Most rooms, spacious and invitingly decorated, rent for about $45 d low season, $55 high. All accommodations have fans only and hot-water shower baths. Discounts (about 30 percent) for long-term rentals may be available.

Very popular with a loyal cadre of Canadian winter returnees is **Casa de Huéspedes Playa Leonor** (Carretera Pie de la Cuesta 63, Pie de la Cuesta, Guerrero 39900, tel. 744/460-0348, $25 d low season, $30 high). Guests enjoy camaraderie around the tables of the *palapa* restaurant that occupies the beachside end of a large parking-lot garden. The several breezy, more private, upper-floor, plain but clean units are most popular. All 10 accommodations have two beds, showers, and fans, and a discount of approximately 20 percent is available for monthly rentals.

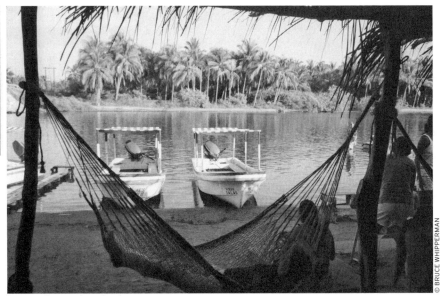

Laguna Coyuca tour boats

The **Villa Roxana** (Av. de la Fuerza Aerea 320, Pie de la Cuesta, tel. 744/460-3252, $30 low season, $40 high), on the inland side of the Villa Nirvana, is managed by owner Roxana and her daughter Alexis and also offers attractive choices. There are a dozen-odd clean, comfortable fan-only rooms, in two stories around a flowery pool-garden. (Beach access from the Villa Roxana is not direct, however. You must walk out the front gate and circle around to the beach.)

Also attractive nearby are the **Bungalows María Cristina** (Av. De La Fuerza Aerea 351, Pie De La Cuesta 39900, near the east end of the lagoon beach, side, between the doctors' office and the Hotel Ukae Kim, mailing address: P.O. Box 607, Acapulco, Guerrero 39300, tel. 744/460-0262), with eight units (four rooms, four kitchen-equipped bungalows) set between a streetside parking lot and a palmy beachside restaurant/garden. The clean, fixed-up and painted rooms with toilets and hot-water showers rent for about $35 d low season, $50 d

Christmas–New Year's. The kitchenettes, most of which face the ocean, run about $70 low season, $100 holidays, for up to four people. Negotiate for long-term discounts.

Guests at the **Hotel and Restaurant Casa Blanca** (Av. de la Fuerza Aerea 370, Pie de la Cuesta, Guerrero 39900, tel. 744/460-0324 or 744/460-4028, fax 744/460-4027, casablanca@prodigy.net.mx), enjoy a tranquil, car-free tropical garden, small blue beachfront pool and restaurant, and savvy French-Argentine management. Rents for the approximately 15 very clean and comfortable rooms, all with toilets and tepid (not hot) water showers and air-conditioning, run around $35 for one to four people, $50 weekends, around $100 Easter and Christmas–New Year's holidays. Discounts may be available for monthly or low season (May–Oct.) rentals. Credit cards are accepted.

Solid comfort, an airy beachfront view, a big blue pool, and a good restaurant draw a steady stream of vacationers to **Hotel Tres Marias** (378 Av. de la Fuerza Aerea, tel. 744/460-0178, tresmariasacapulco@yahoo.com). The eight comfortably furnished rooms are arranged in two double-story wings, one at beachfront and the other behind. Guests in the beachfront wing enjoy ocean-view porches, with the two upstairs rooms especially scenic and desirable. Inside, onyx marble floors, white rustic-chic stucco walls, large windows affording plenty of light and air, and shiny, modern standard shower baths (but tepid, not hot, water only) complete the attractive picture. Rentals, all with fans only and TV, run $40 d in one bed, $60 for up to four in two beds. Owner-manager Maria del Carmen adds about $5 weekends.

$50-100: Ten comfortable rooms, a lagoon-front view location, coupled with a invitingly palmy pool-patio, and airy *palapa* restaurant are the prime offerings of **Hotel Veranda I** (Av. de la Fuerza Aerea 41, Pie de la Cuesta, Guerrero 39900, tel. 744/460-3624, lorena_hava@ hotmail.com, www.hotelveranda.com.mx). Rooms are tiled and white stucco throughout, and simply but comfortably furnished with double or king-size beds. Two rooms have hot water; others have tepid water only. Upstairs rooms away from the highway (numbers 1, 2, 3, 4 and 5) have tranquillity and especially scenic lagoon views. Rentals run about $60 d during the winter season, drop to around $45 d during low fall season, and rise to around $90 during the Easter and Christmas–New Year's holidays.

Trying hard to be deluxe is the **Hotel Ukae Kim** (Av. de la Fuerza Aerea 356, Pie de la Cuesta, Guerrero 39900, tel./fax 744/460-2187 or 744/460-7159, roberto_calles_aragon@hotmail.com). Here, the builder packed 21 rooms into a small, albeit palmy space, rendering the rooms private but small and generally dark. Amenities include a petite but inviting pool-patio and *palapa* restaurant at the hotel's beach-view end. The clean, tastefully decorated rooms with hot water and air-conditioning go, low season, for about $40 s or d, $60 for ocean view, $100 with ocean view and hot tub. Corresponding high season rates

are about $60, $80, and $120. Credit cards are accepted.

Pie de la Cuesta's class-act upscale lodging is the innovative boutique **✦ Hotel Vaymas** (Av. de la Fuerza Aerea 378, Pie de la Cuesta, Guerrero 39900, tel. 744/460-2882 or 744/460-5260, fax 744/460-0697, vayma@ vayma.com.mx, www.vayma.com.mx). Here, guests enjoy the best of all possible rustic chic, including a grandly intimate blue pool, romantically illuminated at night with flickering torches, and 20 individually designed super-deluxe rooms, with names such as Ravel, Berlioz, Debussy, and Pause I and Pause II. Charming Afghan-born owner-manager Parwin Kojani has decorated her rooms richly, with soft, roomy beds, exotic dark brown hardwood accents, designer lamps, and richly tiled bathrooms. Rentals, which are often occupied by Parwin's friends—diplomats, entertainers, politicos and business executives—from all over Mexico and

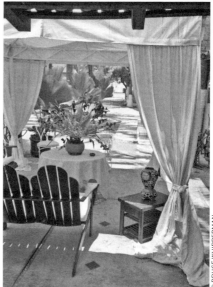

shady restaurant tables at the Hotel Vaymas at Pie de la Cuesta the world, rent from around $60 upwards to about $200 for the largest suites. Get your holiday reservations in early.

Trailer Parks and Camping

RV-equipped Pie de la Cuesta vacationers have two recommendable trailer park choices. First to consider is the homey and popular **Acapulco Trailer Park** (P.O. Box 1, Acapulco, Guerrero 39300, tel. 744/460-6086, fax 744/460-2457, acatrailerpark@yahoo.com), with about 60 densely packed palm-shaded spaces at beachfront and roomier choice lagoonside spaces, all with hookups. It's located near the west end of town, about a block before the road jogs, at the air force base gate. A congenial atmosphere, attentive on-site management, and many extras, including a mini-mart with wine and oven-roasted chickens, and a secure fence and gate, keep the place full most of the winter. Facilities include a boat ramp, blue pool, a security guard, and clean restrooms and showers. Their oceanfront spaces rent for about $23 daily, non-oceanfront $18, electric power for air-conditioning included. Long-term rates run $330 per month. Tent spaces go for $14. Get your winter reservation in early.

The security guard at the Acapulco Trailer Park is a reminder of former times, when muggings and theft were occurring with some frequency on Playa Pie de la Cuesta. Although bright new night lights on the beach (which soldiers patrol while locals walk the streets) have greatly reduced the problem, some (but not all) local folks still warn against camping or walking on the beach at night.

About two miles farther west, on the Barra de Coyuca road, right on the the beach, spreads the █ **Trailer Park and Campground Playa Luces** (tel./fax 744/444-4277, playaluces@ hotmail.com), formerly a KOA Kampground. Lavishly-equipped Playa Luces offers many spaces right on the beach, plus a plethora of extras. Every space, however, whether beachfront or not, is a stone's throw from the long, silky strand, fine for sunsets, shells, strolling, and surf fishing. The owners even help maintain a **turtle-saving program** and invite residents to pitch in to rescue and help incubate turtle

eggs during the summer–fall season when the turtles come ashore. The reward, in the early fall, is the excitement of watching dozens upon dozens of turtle hatchlings return safely to the sea. Facilities include a snack restaurant, mini-store, security fence, laundry, playground, big blue pool, and kiddie pool. Roomy RV spaces with all hookups run $30 by the beach, $22 away from beach, tent spaces go for $16; all get a 20 percent discount for monthly rentals. Tents themselves rent for $15.

FOOD

Most Pie de la Cuesta restaurants are beach-front *palapas* that line Pie de la Cuesta road. One of the most reliable, especially for breakfast on the lagoon, is the lake-view *palapa* of the █ **Restaurant and Club de Skis Tres Marias** (Av. de la Fuerza Aerea 375, tel. 744/460-0013, 8 A.M.–8 P.M. daily). Here, you can start the day off right with an omelette, pancakes, or eggs over easy with ham ($4–6). In the afternoon kick back and pick your favorite from their long list of super-fresh seafood entrées ($5–10).

If instead you prefer an oceanfront location, you can have it, right across the street at **Hotel and Restaurant Tres Marias** (tel. 744/460-0178, 8 A.M.–8 P.M. daily), which offers similar attentive service, good breakfasts, and seafood and Mexican plates.

Gourmet cuisine has arrived in Pie de la Cuesta, at upscale █ **Restaurant Vayma** (tel. 744/460-5260 or 744/460-2882, 8 A.M.–11 P.M. daily), where you can enjoy all the best of food, while being soothed by the murmur of the waves and the romantic flicker of tiki torches at night. A big menu lays out the finest. For example, start with Nicoise salad ($6), continue with super-fresh oysters Rockefeller ($10), and either a tasty broccoli-zucchini-to-mato-mozzarella pizza ($10), or a fine rib-eye steak ($15). Finish off with tiramisu ($5) accompanied by a savory-smooth Graham's 10 year-old Portuguese port.

On the other hand, a few steps down the economic scale, but equally choice, especially for enjoying the cooling afternoon offshore

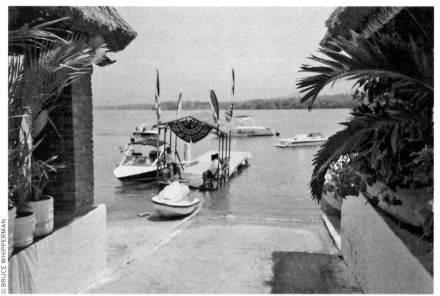

© BRUCE WHIPPERMAN

The Club de Skis Tres Marias offers waterskiing and a ramp to launch your boat.

breeze or watching the sunset, try local favorite **Coyuca 2000** (8 A.M.–10 P.M. daily). Here, hearty snack food is the specialty, such as chicken fajitas, rich guacamole ($3) and a load of tropical margaritas (strawberry, guava, pineapple, $4) to choose from.

ENTERTAINMENT AND EVENTS

Pie de la Cuesta's big fiesta honors the local patron, the **Virgin of Guadalupe,** with Masses, processions, fireworks, and dances on December 10, 11, and 12. The fiesta's climax, de rigueur for visitors, is the mass pilgrimage around the lake by boat.

A few local discotheques, such as **Hawaii 5-0,** fire up seasonally and occasionally on weekends. Brightly painted signs on the roadside at mid-village make them impossible to miss.

The deluxe **Parador del Sol** (tel./fax 744/444-4050 or 744/444-4125, fax 744/444-4125, parador@acabtu.com.mx, toll-free Mex. tel. 800/111-3210, www.paradordelsol.com.mx)

all-inclusive resort (about a mile west of Pie de la Cuesta village—turn right at the Barra de Coyuca fork before the air base) invites visitors to buy day and/or evening guest memberships for about $40 per adult (kids 4–11 half price) per eight-hour day session (10 A.M.–6 P.M.) and evening session (7 P.M.–2 A.M.). Day guests enjoy breakfast (10–11 A.M.), lunch (1–2 P.M.), open bar, and free use of the pools, beach club, kiddie playground, exercise gym, and basketball, volleyball, mini-golf course, and tennis courts. The evening program kicks off at 7, with sports (including night-lit tennis) and swimming, continuing with supper (8:30–9:30 P.M.), open bar, and dancing at the discotheque until after midnight. If after a day you haven't had your fill, you might want to accept the resort's invitation to stay overnight for about $80 per person low season, double occupancy, $100 high.

SERVICES

Although most services are concentrated half an hour away in Acapulco, Pie de la Cuesta nevertheless provides a few essentials. For medical consultations, see either Dr. Patricia Villalobos or her husband, Dr. Luis Amados Rios (tel. 744/460-0923), at their pharmacy where the lagoon begins, right in the middle of the village. Between them, they understand both English and French.

A scattering of mini-markets supply food. Two public long-distance phones are available, one in front of the Acapulco Trailer Park and the other on the highway by the doctors' pharmacy. In emergencies, go to the **policía,** at the small station near the intersection of the Pie de la Cuesta road and the highway to Acapulco.

GETTING THERE AND AWAY

Pie de la Cuesta is accessible via the fork from Highway 200 near Km 10, six miles (10 km) northwest of the Acapulco old town *zócalo* by car, taxi ($5), or local bus. The same road fork is also 144 miles (232 km) southwest of Zihuatanejo. First-class buses drop passengers at the roadside, where they can continue either on foot, by taxi, or one of the very frequent local *colectivos.*

Alternatively, mobile travelers can travel west toward the Costa Grande via local bus from Pie de la Cuesta west to Barra de Coyuca, thence by launch northwest across the Laguna Coyuca to La Barra and points west.

THE COSTA GRANDE

The Costa Grande, the "Big Coast" of the state of Guerrero, stretches 150 miles northwest from Acapulco to Zihuatanejo. Before the highway came during the 1960s, this was a land of corn, coconuts, fish, and fruit. Although it's still that, the road added a new ingredient: a trickle of visitors seeking paradise in Zihuatanejo, a sleepy fishing village on a beautiful bay.

Now, however, that trickle of visitors is increasingly enjoying the host of country delights along the way. These include historic market towns, such as Coyuca and Tecpán de Galeana; a beloved pilgrimage shrine at Petatlán; the fascinating archaeological zone of Soledad de Maciel; breezy beaches for camping, beachcombing, and surf fishing, such as Laguna de Mitla, Playa Paraíso, Piedra Tlalcoyunque, Arroyo Seco, La Barrita, Playa Ojo de Agua,

and petite resort hideaways such as El Carrizal, Hotel Resort Villas San Luis, Playa Escondida, and Papanoa.

PLANNING YOUR TIME

Although the temptation is to drive or bus the entire Costa Grande from Acapulco to Zihuatanejo in one quick day, that would be a pity. Better, take the scenic route and linger at some of the Costa Grande's plumy paradises enroute.

For example, spend a day or two at **El Carrizal,** at its top-pick Hotel Paraíso Playa Azul where you can enjoy both the breezy beach on one side and the hotel's lusciously relaxing lagoonside setting on the other. Farther up the coast, you could enjoy different, but equally inviting delights at the Hotel Los Arcos on invitingly petite **Playa Escondida.**

© BRUCE WHIPPERMAN

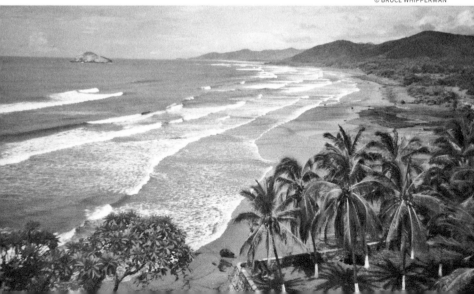

HIGHLIGHTS

◖ **El Carrizal:** The word "charming" barely begins to describe this south-seas mini-Eden, with the advantage of a pristine open-ocean beach on one side and a rustically lovely palm-tufted lagoon on the other (page 94).

◖ **Laguna de Mitla:** This pristine wildlife-rich beach and lagoon might be heaven for adventurers who hanker for a day or a week soaking up the natural delights of sun, sea, and sand. Be sure to continue to hamlet Santa Cruz de Mitla for a look at the collection of artifacts in the village community museum (page 95).

◖ **Playa Paraíso:** This hidden, family-friendly nook offers a palmy lagoon-front setting for a breezy afternoon boat ride for lunch on the beach across the lagoon, or some restful days of camping and playing in the swimming pools at the picturesque Florentine's Garden Balneario (page 97).

◖ **Playa Escondida:** The fine hotel and restaurant Los Arcos is just the beginning of enjoying this intimate, best-for-everything jewel of a beach (page 103).

◖ **Playa Ojo de Agua:** The beach nestles beneath forested headlands and is popular partly for its unique spring that provides a cooling freshwater bath for washing away the sand and saltwater after a dip in the ocean (page 105).

◖ **Playa El Calvario:** Stop for at least a drink or lunch at one of the sprinkling of cliff-top restaurants and enjoy the airy panorama of waves, sun, and sand. More vigorous adventurers continue downhill to the beach for an afternoon of shells, surfing, boogie boarding and fishing (page 106).

◖ **Las Salinas:** This village of salt harvesters combines age-old technology with ingenuity to harvest salt from nothing more than sun and seawater (page 107).

◖ **Soledad de Maciel Archaeological Zone:** The first stop in this large, ancient, but unexcavated village archaeological zone should be the village church. Later, visit the small village museum where you can contact a guide for a tour (page 110).

LOOK FOR ◖ TO FIND RECOMMENDED SIGHTS, ACTIVITIES, DINING, AND LODGING.

On the other hand, equipped lovers of the outdoors could be equally content with a few days camping, surf fishing, beachcombing, and maybe even surfing, on the beach at secluded **Laguna de Mitla,** or spectacular and breezy Piedra Tlalcoyunque, and the delightfully intimate beach hideaways, Playa La Barrita and **Playa Ojo de Agua.**

Moreover, if you're into fishing, boating, canoeing, or kayaking, you might also, besides Laguna de Mitla, consider spending an overnight or more at lagoon-front informal campgrounds at Camalote and **Playa Paraíso.**

Up the coast, not far from Zihuatanejo, the area around Petatlán offers enough for a few relaxing days, starting with shopping at Petatlán's plaza-front gold jewelry market stalls, then paying your respects to Petatlán's miraculous patron Padre Jesùs, enjoying some wildlife viewing and kayaking at nearby Estero Valentín, and relaxing with a tour of the **Soledad de Maciel Archaeological Zone.**

History

Long before Zihuatanejo's latter-day popularity, people had been attracted to the Costa Grande. Their oldest remains, pottery dating from around 3000 B.C., decorates the displays at the Zihuatanejo archaeological museum. Later, around 1000 B.C., the Olmecs (famous for their monumental Gulf coast sculptures) left their unmistakable mark on regional pottery.

After them came waves of settlers, including the barbaric Chichimecs (Drinkers of Blood), the agricultural Cuitlatecs, and an early invasion of Aztecs, perhaps wandering in search of their eventual homeland in the Valley of Mexico.

None of those peoples were a match for the armies of Tarascan emperor Hiripan, who during the late 14th century A.D. invaded the Costa Grande from his Michoacán highland capital and established a coastal province, headquartered at the present town of Coyuca de Benítez, less than an hour's drive west of Acapulco.

Three generations later the star of the Aztec emperor Tízoc was rising over Mexico. His armies invaded the Costa Grande and pushed out the Tarascans. By 1500 the Aztecs ruled the coast from their provincial town capital at Cihuatlán, the "Place of Women" not far from present-day Zihuatanejo.

THE COSTA GRANDE

The Road Along the Costa Grande

By bus, go by first- or second-class (whose drivers, if asked, will let you off most anywhere) from the Estrella Blanca west-side Avenida Ejido terminal in Acapulco.

Drivers, follow Avenida Ejido from Acapulco, bear right at the Avenida Pie de la Cuesta T intersection and continue northwest along the coastal Highway 200. Let the many highway signs and kilometer markers (both at roadside and painted on the highway asphalt highway itself, all measured from the Acapulco old-town *zócalo*) be your guide to the many palmy paradises along the way.

COYUCA DE BENÍTEZ

Coyuca de Benítez (pop. about 20,000), 20 miles (32 km) from Acapulco, is the market and service center of the southwest Costa Grande. Besides being a trading center for the produce of upcountry *fincas cafelatera* (coffee farms) and the *copra* of coastal coconut plantations, Coyuca is famous for its Easter celebration, when folks from all over the Costa Chica crowd in for the fun. Locally known as the **Fiesta de la Palmera,** the festival climaxes the few days before Easter Sunday, with pageants of the Passion of Jesus, and a carnival of food, rides, games, fireworks, bull-roping and riding (*jaripeo*), and cockfights (*peleas de gallos*).

Traffic slows to a crawl at the stall-crowded heart of town, marked by the corner bus station.

Accommodations and Food

The most comfortable nearby hotel accommodations are at beach resort El Carrizal. In town, the best hotel is the **Posada Coyuca** (Las Palmeras 6, tel. 781/452-0569), right on the highway, north side, a block east of the town center. The dozen-odd rooms are plainly decorated but very clean and reasonably priced, at $15 s or d in one double bed, $25 d, t, q in two double beds, all with fans, TV, and attractive open-air restaurant downstairs. Add $10 for air-conditioning. For more quiet and privacy, get an upstairs rear room, away from the highway. In an emergency, check out the very basic but clean **Hotel Imperio** (tel. 781/452-1661, $15 d) and **Hotel Provinciano** (tel. 781/452-0243, $20 d), near the south side of the town plaza.

As for **camping,** go either to the Laguna Coyuca at La Barra or the beach at El Carrizal (see the *La Barra* and *El Carrizal* sections of this chapter for details).

Coyuca is well-known for its good seafood. Three restaurants are especially recommended. Try either **La Brasa,** on the east, Acapulco side of the town center, or the airy ◖ **Bella Vista** view *palapa,* perched above the riverfront at the west end of town, or local favorite **Coyuca 33** across the street from Bella Vista.

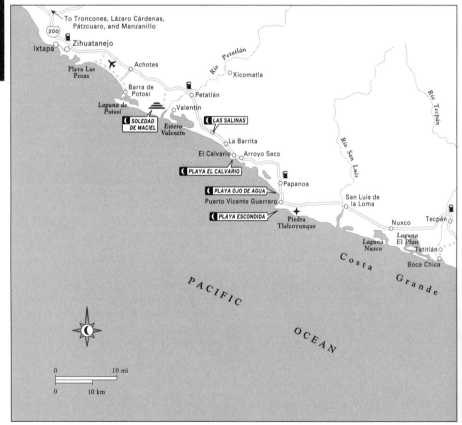

Get your groceries and fruits and vegetables at the **market,** big every day, that sprawls over several town blocks north and south of the highway.

Services

Beyond the market stalls, on the north side, find the town plaza, with the *presidencia municipal* (tel. 781/452-1164), *telégrafos* (telegraph office) and *correo.*

Back on the main street, services include a **Banamex** bank (tel. 781/452-0021, 9 A.M.–4 P.M. Mon.–Fri.), on the Acapulco side of the highway, with 24-hour ATM; *abarrotes* (groceries), *farmacias* (pharmacies), and Ladatel card-operated street telephones. Alternatively, go to the *caseta larga distancia* (long-distance telephone office), in the center of town by the highway, south side, across from the Farmacia Padre Jesús.

Also nearby, find an *agencia de viajes* (on Guerrero, corner of Reforma, tel. 781/452-0034, 9 A.M.–8 P.M. Mon.–Sat.), and a *centro de salud* (Domínguez 36, north of the plaza uphill, tel. 781/452-0515). The **bus station** (tel. 781/452-0238) is in the center of town on the north side of the street. For police and information, visit the small but well-marked roadside office (tel. 781/452-1164), a couple blocks east of the town center.

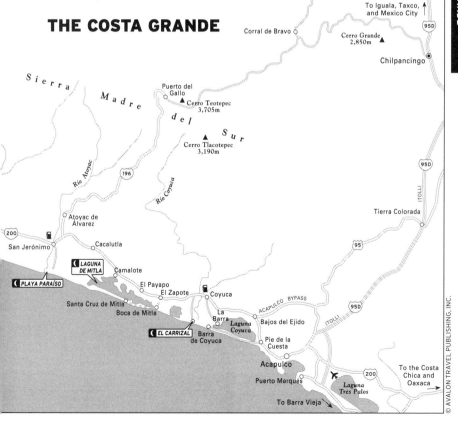

THE COSTA GRANDE

To Iguala, Taxco, and Mexico City

Corral de Bravo

Cerro Grande 2,850m

Chilpancingo

Sierra *Madre* *del* *Sur*

Puerto del Gallo

Cerro Teotepec 3,705m

Cerro Tlacotepec 3,190m

Tierra Colorada

Río Atoyac

Río Coyuca

Atoyac de Álvarez

San Jerónimo

Cacalutla

LAGUNA DE MITLA

Camalote

PLAYA PARAÍSO

El Payapo

El Zapote

Coyuca

Santa Cruz de Mitla

Boca de Mitla

EL CARRIZAL

Barra de Coyuca

La Barra

Laguna Coyuca

Bajos del Ejido

ACAPULCO BYPASS

Pie de la Cuesta

Acapulco

To the Costa Chica and Oaxaca

Puerto Marqués

Laguna Tres Palos

To Barra Vieja

© AVALON TRAVEL PUBLISHING, INC.

LA BARRA

This breezy lakefront boating, kayaking, fishing, and wildlife-viewing haven is reachable directly by car, taxi, or *colectivo,* via the paved road south from the Coyuca town-center corner of Highway 200 and Calle Guadencia Parra.

If driving, mark your odometer. At Mile 1.7 (Km 2.7) pass through Las Lomas village (stores, pharmacy); at Mile 3.8 (Km 6.1), pass palmy, riverfront *palapa* La Palma (open seasonally only). Arrive at the breezy boat jetty and local-style waterfront *palapa* restaurants at Mile 4.1 (Km 6.6).

From La Barra, the broad mangrove-fringed freshwater Laguna Coyuca spreads both a mile south across the river estuary to Barra de Coyuca ocean beach and east 10 miles to downscale Pie de la Cuesta resort village, on the edge of Acapulco.

The most popular La Barra activity is the boat ride, roaring directly across the lagoon ($1 per person in collective boat; $5 per boatload one way by private boat) a mile to the Barra de Coyuca tourist village restaurants and beach. Alternatively, and with more tranquillity, try fishing (with your own equipment) and/or viewing (bargain for about $50 per boat per day) the trove of birds and other wildlife that prowl, perch, and preen among the lake's lacy channels and palmy islets. Bring your binoculars, bird book, hat, repellent, and sunscreen. Along the way, you might visit an island or two, especially the drowsy south-sea haven Isla Montosa (for details, see the *Pie de la Cuesta* section at the end of the *Acapulco* chapter) and restaurants, in the lagoon, about four miles east of La Barra.

On the other hand, adventurers might do much the same with their own boat or kayak. It's best to hire a guide; offer $10–20 for a half day.

Camping or RV parking is a fertile possibility nearby. The best two or three spots appear to be on the shady Río Coyuca estuary-front, near the Restaurant Las Palmas, by the road, a quarter-mile back toward Coyuca.

◖ EL CARRIZAL

You know you may be in for something special when you see the Zona Ecoturística sign near the Km 37 marker three miles west of Barra de Coyuca. At the end of the road, you can have all the pleasures of easy country beach living.

If you're on foot, hire a taxi or ride a *colectivo* from the highway. If by car, mark your odometer at the highway just before turning south. At Mile 4.1 (Km 6.6) pass through Epinarillo village, with a sprinkling of stores and a pharmacy or two.

At Mile 4.6 (Km 7.4), arrive at the beach, a gorgeous miles-long medium-steep golden-yellow fine-sand shoreline with powerful, close-in breaks. Flocks of seabirds skitter along the sand, glide over the billows, and dive for fish offshore. Waves seasonally deposit shells and driftwood. The surf, although unsuitable for surfing and generally too rough for swimming, appears excellent for wading and surf fishing. Boat launching, although not impossible, appears difficult at best.

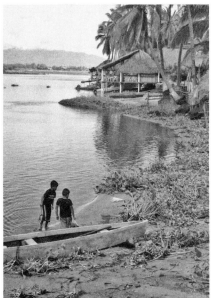

© BRUCE WHIPPERMAN

children playing on the beach at El Carrizal

At the beach, you can either go right or left. Go right for a miles-long breezy strand, ripe for tenting or RV camping. Go left for a long lineup of permanent, family-friendly *palapa* restaurants and *cabaña* lodgings.

A few of the beachfront establishments stand out. Immediately on the right, find inviting **Restaurant Dunas** and adjacent, away from the beach, **Bungalows El Carrizal** (tel. 781/452-1869). Owned and operated by personable Virginia Díaz, the five small, spartan but clean rooms rent for about $20 s or d, $30 weekends and holidays, with hot-water showers, TV, fans, and shaded parking. Señora Díaz also runs a snack restaurant (separate from neighbor Restaurant Dunas) whose menu features plenty of fruit, vegetables, yogurt, and granola.

Continue east along the beachfront road a few hundred yards, passing a number of *palapas,* to the inviting and popular family-friendly beach **Resort and Restaurant Nautilus** (tel. 781/452-1933). Managers rent about five plain but clean cabañas, two with private bath, $20; three with shared bath, $15, next to their large, beachview *palapa* restaurant and blue pool. Although weekdays (except Christmas, Easter, July, and August) would generally be quiet here, seekers of peace and quiet on a weekend better stay elsewhere. Nevertheless, tent camping is customary, for a nominal fee, in the shade on the beach, right in front of the restaurant.

The Nautilus's friendly owner, Amado Fajardo Colixto, takes parties of up to eight people on lagoon tours in the adjacent Laguna Coyuca for about $20 per hour. He also sells lots for homes along the beach. (In all property transactions, work through a well-established real estate agent; see the sidebar "Owning Paradise" in the Acapulco chapter.)

Continue east to the palmy, picturesque road's end, at Mile 6.3 (Km 10.1), where boats line docks, ready to whisk visitors on lagoon wildlife-viewing and restaurant excursions.

Here, lagoon-front **⟨** **Hotel Paraíso Playa Azul** (tel. 781/452-2051 or 781/452-2052, $40 weekdays, $50 d weekends and holidays) offers the only deluxe local accommodations, in a cluster of about a dozen attractively decorated rooms around an invitingly grassy pool-patio. Rooms, however, are unfortunately dark (without turning on the lights) and make little use of the beautiful lagoonside setting. Nevertheless, accommodations are comfortable, each with a pair of soft double beds, hot-water shower bath, and small refrigerator. They include air-conditioning, cable TV, a lovely shaded *palapa* sitting area and restaurant overlooking the leafy lagoon; massages are available at extra cost. The gorgeous beach is only a few steps away across the road. More relaxing ocean- and lagoon-view *palapa* restaurants are also nearby.

⟨ LAGUNA DE MITLA

Curiosity alone might drive adventurous lovers of tropical Mexico to explore the reaches of the grand, freshwater Laguna de Mitla. Its 25-mile (40-km) high-water length makes it the longest natural lake in Guerrero, so big that it has enough room for three separate bays along its north shoreline. The rewards along the road are a lush, freshwater swimming lagoon; beachfront seafood *palapa* restaurants; local fisherfolk willing to guide parties on fishing and wildlife-viewing trips; and a long, pristine, breeze-swept wild beach (but largely shadeless, except for many palm-frond beachfront *ramadas*), ready for camping or RV parking, surf-fishing, and beachcombing. At the end of the road, you'll even find a small community museum and a rancho with a freshwater well.

Get there from Highway 200, at El Zapote, 30 miles (48 km) from Acapulco. Drivers, mark your odometer. Hikers, hire a taxi, thumb a ride, or simply walk the 1.2 miles (2 km) to **Boca de Mitla.** There, cross the bridge over the channel that connects the east and west branches of the Laguna de Mitla.

You may not need to go any farther. Mangroves decorate the river; a few *lanchas* and *canoas* rest on the bank; men, waist-deep in the water, cast nets; and kids splash downstream nearby. You might either hire a *lancha* and guide, or launch your own boat or kayak for your private fishing or bird-watching expedition. Be equipped, however, with a hat, binoculars, repellent, bottled water, and fishing tackle.

Continue about a quarter mile to (closed at this writing) Restaurant Mitla at Mile 1.5 (Km 2.4). Turn right and continue past the military post on the left, at Mile 1.9 (Km 3.1). Ahead, follow along the unpaved airstrip; at Mile 2.4 (Km 3.9) fork left. At the beach, turn right (west), and arrive at attractively rustic beachfront *palapa* **(Restaurant Yenifer** at Mile 3.1 (Km 5.0), with drinks, fresh seafood, and plenty of breezy space for nearly all beach delights except surfing. A fine golden-sand beach seems to stretch endlessly both west and east. Powerful waves break suddenly along long fronts and recede with strong undertow. Tiny crabs, sandpipers, and plovers scurry along the sand, sunbleached driftwood lies for the taking, and several unused temporary palm-frond *ramadas* await new occupants. With the restaurant nearby and plenty of room to spread out, beach tenting or RV parking could hardly be better here.

Farther along, at Mile 3.4 (Km 5.5), pass the ponds of a local aquaculture cooperative where workers cultivate fish (tilapia), prawns, and shrimp, and net wild fish in the lagoon when they're not working. The gravel road continues, bumping along, paralleling the beach, through miles of short scrub and cactus. Occasional houses, remnants of a moribund Acapulco Pacifico second-home development, dot the flat, sandy landscape. Finally, at Mile 8.1 (Km 13), head inland, away from the beach, to the Santa Cruz de Mitla village plaza, store, and kiosk, labeled **Santa Cruz de Mitla Museo Comunitario.** Inside, the village exhibits ancient, locally discovered pottery artifacts. Nearby, beneath some trees, stands the rancho of friendly pioneer Eleuterio Diego Flores, who welcomes visitors and offers fresh sweet water from his well. You may have to ask someone to open it up for you.

A caravan of two wagons delivers fresh water to some of Laguna de Mitla's residents.

The church at Santa Cruz de Mitla, even while unfinished, is in service.

CAMALOTE, PLAYA PARAÍSO, AND SAN JERÓNIMO

Visit each of these little places and fill entirely different needs: Camalote for seafood, boating, and camping; Playa Paraíso for a picnic and a cooling swim and snooze in the shade; and San Jerónimo for groceries and essential services.

Camalote

Reach this lagoon-shore refuge by turning left (westbound) 36 miles (58 km) northwest of Acapulco. Follow the signed dirt access road about a half mile to the pair of permanent country-style restaurants perched on the airy east shoreline of the freshwater Laguna de Mitla.

This pretty spot offers easy boating, fishing, and kayaking on the broad lagoon. Some shady sites beneath lakefront trees also invite tenting and RV parking. However, you may have to start by cleaning a bit of trash from your site.

Never mind the trash: A pair of nearby private picnic-campgrounds offer cleaner choices. At the end of the lakefront Camalote road, on the left, find **Restaurant La Bolua,** with space for picnicking, tenting, RV parking, and boat and kayak launching. Even better is the more

secluded ◖ **Cabaña Galapagos** (follow the signed dirt road that forks left from the main Camalote ingress road near the highway) with all of the above, and the additional plus of much more space to spread out, beneath shady lakefront trees. Camping charge will run about $5 per day per car during weekends and holidays, free other times when they're empty.

◖ Playa Paraíso

Formerly known as Playa Paraíso Perdido (Paradise Lost Beach), this place has now been found, and for good reason. Local folks love it for its gorgeous swimming-picnicking-camping ground and the breezy boat rides across the Río Atoyac lagoon to good seafood restaurants and a long open-ocean beach.

Get there via the Highway 200 turnoff signed Hacienda de Cabaña, near the Km 81 highway marker, 50 miles northwest of Acapulco (and two miles before San Jerónimo).

Along the Road to Playa Paraíso

After about five miles (8 km) along a good paved road, arrive at family-friendly **Florentine's Garden Balneario** mini-resort.

Cross over on its picturesque hanging bridge and enjoy a swim in the pool, a picnic, or an overnight in the walk-in palm-shaded campground. Like virtually all places in the country, Florentine's Garden Balneario has no telephone and operates only on a drop-in basis.

Continue to the adjacent estuary-front boat landing that, on weekends and holidays, buzzes with motorboats that whisk families ($1 per person) to the restaurants and long open-ocean beach on the other side. Alternatively, rent a launch for fishing tilapia, *robalo* (snook), or *pez gallo* (roosterfish), or launch your own boat or kayak.

If you decide to linger, tent camping space is available at the road's boat landing, on the left, beneath the palms.

If you want to stay overnight, but lack camping gear, Playa Paraíso now has small **Hotel Mary** (tel. 742/424-2259, $15 d), oddly crowded next to the road, across the lagoon from Florentine's Garden Balneario. (This odd placement, however, allows guests to enjoy a spacious, grassy lagoon-front back yard in the extra space.) Hotel Mary, designed to be a "love" hotel for couples who lack a private place to sleep together, offers two stories of about 10 tiny but clean rooms with air-conditioning. Get an upper room for more light and privacy.

San Jerónimo

The small market town of San Jerónimo (pop. 10,000), on Highway 200 52 miles (84 km) east of Acapulco, offers a modicum of services and lodging.

At the highway-center of town, find the bus station. On the town plaza nearby is **Telecomunicaciones** with public telephone, money orders, and fax. Nearby, also find a post office, a pharmacy, *centro de salud,* and a pair of modest hotels if you're desperate, the Posada San Francisco and the Hotel and Restaurant Villa del Mar.

BOCA CHICA AND TETITLÁN

For the fun and adventure of it, visit Boca Chica, a beach village accessible sometimes by boat only. Here, camping is de rigueur, since even permanent residents are doing it. It makes no sense to pour concrete on a sandbar where palm fronds are free and the next wave may wash everything away anyway.

The jumping-off spot is near Km 98 (88 miles, 142 km southeast of Zihuatanejo and 61 miles, 98 km northwest of Acapulco), where a sign marks the road to Tetitlán (pop. 2,000). In about three miles, turn left at the T intersection at the town plaza (with long-distance phone, pharmacy, groceries) and continue a couple of miles along a bumpy, but negotiable when dry, road to the Laguna Tecpán, which, during the dry season, may have narrowed to a river or dried completely. Here, launches will ferry you (or you can walk) the mile across to the village on the sandbar. Bargain the *viaje redondo* (return-trip) price with your boatman before you depart.

On the other side, the waves thunder upon the beach and sand crabs guard their holes, while the village's four separate societies—people, dogs, pigs, and chickens—each go about their distinct business. Shells and driftwood decorate the sand, and surf fishing with bait from the lagoon couldn't be better.

Most visitors come for the eating only: super-fresh seafood charcoal-broiled in one of the dozen *palapas* along the beach. If, however, you plan to camp overnight, bring drinking water, a valuable Boca Chica commodity.

During the summer rainy season, the Río Tecpán, which feeds the lagoon, breaks through the bar. Ocean fish enter the lagoon, and the river current sometimes washes Boca Chica, *palapas* and all, out to sea.

TECPÁN

The major service center of the central Costa Grande, Tecpán de Galeana (pop. 25,000), commonly shortened to Tecpán, is the birthplace of celebrated independence hero Hermanegildo (air-mah-nay-HEEL-doh) Galeana (1762–1814). Galeana, son of a prominent farming family, successfully operated his family's hacienda until he joined the *insurgente* cause in 1811, at the age of 49.

TECPÁN

To Ixtapa and Zihuatanejo

HOTEL RAMOS
FOTO STUDIO ALBARRÁN
CHURCH
To Río Tecpán
TELEPHONE OFFICE
BANCOMER   PHARMACY
MONUMENT
HERMANEGILDO   GALEANA
POST OFFICE
Park
BANCO SANTANDER SERFIN
HSBC
200
CALLE PARROQUIA
CALLE
REFORMA
0   100 yds
0   100 m
To Acapulco
HOTEL VIRREY

© AVALON TRAVEL PUBLISHING, INC.

THE COSTA GRANDE

According to scholars, the town's name has two interpretations, both from the Náhuatl (Aztec language): either from *tetl* (stone) and *pan* (atop or on), meaning "atop the stone"; or from *tecutli* (lord) and *pan* (place of), meaning "place of the lord."

Orientation and Sights

Tecpán spreads along the west bank of the broad south-flowing Río Tecpán. Highway 200, approaching westerly from Acapulco, bends north and continues for two miles through the town before turning west again and crossing the river.

A modern abstract stone monument on the highway's west side marks the center of town. It also marks Tecpán's main east–west street, appropriately named Hermanegildo Galeana. If from that point you head west, away from the highway, you pass the church on your right (north side) at Calle Parroquia, which continues south as Calle Reforma. After another block, you arrive at the red and pink-adorned town *parque* that harmonizes cheerily with its bougainvillea floral decor.

Accommodations and Food

Tecpán has four or five simple hotels, at least two of which are recommendable. The best is the homey, family-run █ **Hotel Ramos** (Ana Acostada de Ramos 3, Tecpán de Galeana, Guerrero 40911, tel. 742/425-3012 or 742/425-1515, $16 d fan only, $30 d with a/c). The hotel offers 32 clean, simply but comfortably decorated rooms, built in two stories around a shady parking patio, on a quiet side street one block north of the town plaza. All with TV, private hot-water baths, and parking.

Also recommendable is the compact **Hotel Virrey** (Reforma 22, Tecpán de Galeana, Guerrero 40911, tel. 742/425-1342, $16 d with fan, $23 with a/c), a block south of the HSBC bank. It offers 18 very clean, sparely but comfortably furnished rooms, all with private hot water bathrooms, TV, and parking. (This hotel is very popular with business travelers; if you're arriving late, call ahead for a reservation.)

Tecpán's most highly recommended restaurant is the refined Mexican-style family █ **Restaurant Fogata** (tel. 742/425-0033, 7 A.M.–11 P.M. daily). The restaurant, whose name means campfire, is on the through-town highway, about four blocks north of Galeana.

Services

Several service establishments are handily within a block or two of the plaza: the *correo* (post office), one block west; Farmacia del Centro (tel. 742/425-2858, 9 A.M.–9 P.M. daily), across Galeana from the plaza; long-distance telephone, across Galeana from the plaza and half a block east; HSBC bank (on Reforma, 8 A.M.–7 P.M. Mon.–Sat.), east of the plaza and around the corner, or Banco Santander Serfén (9 A.M.–4 P.M. Mon.–Fri.), across the street, both with ATMs; and photo and film at Foto Studio Albarrán (on Calle Parroquia, tel. 742/425-2323, 8 A.M.–8 P.M. daily), across from the church.

A number of doctors—gynecologist, internist, pediatrician, and traumatologist—are available at the Centro de Especialidades medical offices (tel. 742/425-0258), a few blocks south on the highway downtown. After medical office hours, go to the town Centro de Salud (tel. 742/425-0030).

HERMANEGILDO GALEANA: GENTLEMAN REBEL

Hermanegildo Galeana (1762–1814) wasted little time in rallying to Father Miguel Hidalgo's cry for Mexican independence. A well-to-do Mexican-born *hacendado*, Galeana resented having to bow to the arrogant *peninsulares* who were elevated to Mexico's ruling upper crust by the sole virtue of having been born in Spain.

Galeana was born in Tecpán on April 13, 1762, of a criollo mother and an English sea captain father who established a successful farm in the fertile Río Tecpán valley. As a youth, Hermanegildo benefited from the modicum of advantages that his landed criollo class enjoyed.

During most of his adult years, Galeana enjoyed the life of a country gentleman, successfully managing his family estate, Hacienda El Zanjón, while fathering a brood of children by a succession of six wives.

All that changed drastically when rebel priest José María Morelos, under direct orders from Hidalgo, marched into Tecpán in front of his newly recruited rebel brigade. Drawn by Morelos's charismatic determination, Galeana and his two brothers joined Morelos's force, bringing with them dozens of their workers and a swarm of their Tecpán friends and followers. Thus, at the late age of 49, Hermanegildo Galeana launched the final heroic chapter of his life.

Soon the Galeanas rose to field command rank, joining Morelos's circle of most trusted adjutants. The Spanish challenged them right away, with little success. On January 4, 1811, the Galeanas fought bravely, achieving a rebel victory at El Veledero, which won them 800 prisoners and a trove of captured arms and ammunition.

From then on, Hermanegildo Galeana fought side by side with Morelos, bravely orchestrating a series of signal victories, including the triumph at Tixtla, Vicente Guerrero's hometown.

HOTEL RESORT VILLAS SAN LUIS

Little was spared to embellish the pretty hacienda-like corner of a big mango, papaya, and coconut grove that's occupied by ◖ Hotel Resort Villas San Luis (Carretera Zihuatanejo-Acapulco, Km 143, Buenavista de Juárez, Guerrero 40906, tel./fax 742/427-0282 or 742/427-0235, $45 s or d, $70 holidays). It appears as if the owner, tiring of all work and no play, built a park to entertain his friends. Now, his project blooms with lovely swimming and kiddie pools, a big *palapa* restaurant, a smooth *palapa*-housed dance floor, a small zoo, basketball and volleyball courts, and an immaculate hotel.

Ideal for a lunch/swim break or an overnight rest, the 40 immaculate and attractively furnished hotel rooms include air-conditioning and hot water. Credit cards are not accepted. If you'll be arriving on a weekend or holiday, be sure to make a reservation. Find it on the eastbound (south) side of the road near Km 142, 61 miles (98 km) southeast of Zihuatanejo, 89 miles (143 km) northwest of Acapulco.

SAN LUIS DE LA LOMA

Nearby, two miles east of the resort, the picturesque little market town of San Luis de la Loma (pop. 5,000) perches along its hilltop main street that angles off Highway 200 near Km 140. Besides a number of groceries, fruit stalls, and pharmacies, San Luis has a clean, comfortable guesthouse, **Hotel Hermanos Ruiz** (tel. 742/427-0512, $10 s, $15 d with a/c) and recommendable **Hotel Anita** (tel. 742/427-0288, similar prices). There is also a post office, a health center, a *larga distancia,* a dentist, and doctors (gynecologist Leonarda Z. Pacheco and general practitioner Reynaldo Soria, both at tel. 742/427-0473). First-class buses also stop and pick up passengers where the main street intersects with the highway.

PIEDRA TLALCOYUNQUE

At Km 150 (94 miles, 151 km from Acapulco or 56 miles, 90 km from Zihuatanejo) a

Buoyed by success, Morelos led his triumphant army north, quickly capturing Cuautla, in the present state of Morelos. However, Galeana's severest challenge came when Spanish forces counterattacked and laid a 73-day siege upon the rebels. The siege climaxed when the Spanish attackers penetrated the rebels' perimeter, flanking Morelos and Galeana. A royalist colonel got near Morelos and fired his pistol but missed. Galeana returned fire with his rifle at point-blank range, saving Morelos's life.

Galeana fought on, commanding a victorious battalion in Huajuapan, Oaxaca, in July 1812. In 1813, back south on the coast, Galeana and his men surprised a Spanish force entrenched on Isla Roqueta, an action that led to the rebel capture of Acapulco.

By mid-1814, Galeana was riding a wave of victories. He had won the admiration of his men, who called him, affectionately, "Tata" (Daddy) Gildo, for his selfless, heroic devotion to them and the *insurgente* cause.

But his days were numbered. On June 27, 1814, royalist General Calleja's soldiers ambushed and killed Galeana at Salitral, near Tecpán. Aviles, the royalist commander, ordered Galeana's head cut off, placed on the point of a lance, and exhibited in the Tecpán town plaza. But, because of the riot that such barbarous action ignited, Aviles had Galeana's head taken down and buried with his body inside the Tecpán church. Later, a pair of Galeana's soldiers buried his remains in a secret location to avoid further mutilation.

The independence cause for which Galeana had fought finally prevailed. The new republican government of an independent Mexico elevated beloved Tata Gildo to the revered national rank of Benemérito de la Patria on July 19, 1823.

© BRUCE WHIPPERMAN

Pelicans rest atop rocks and foaming tidepools at Piedra Tlalcoyunque.

SAVING TURTLES

Sea turtles were once common on the beaches of the Acapulco region. Times have changed, however. Now a determined corps of volunteers literally camps out on isolated beaches, trying to save the turtles from extinction.

This is a tricky business because their poacher opponents are invariably poor, determined, and often armed. Since turtle tracks lead right to the eggs, the trick is to get there before the poachers. The turtle-savers dig up the eggs and hatch them themselves, or bury them in secret locations where they hope the eggs will hatch unmolested. The reward – the sight of hundreds of new hatchlings returning to the sea – is worth the pain for this new generation of Mexican ecoactivists.

Once featured on dozens of Acapulco restaurant menus, turtle meat, soup, and eggs are now illegal commodities. Though not extinct, the Mexican Pacific's main sea turtle species – including the green, olive ridley, hawksbill, and leatherback – have dwindled to a small fraction of their previous numbers.

Turtle activists point out that poaching is only one of the hazards that have driven sea turtles to the edge of extinction. Beach habitat loss; ingestion of floating debris, such as plastic bags and tar balls; disease; and accidental capture by trawler nets continue to take deadly tolls.

The **green turtle** (*Chelonia mydas*), the second-largest sea turtle species, is named for the color of its fat (although in Mexico it's called the *tortuga negra* or *caguama*). Officially endangered, the prolific green turtle nevertheless remains relatively numerous. Female green turtles can return to shore up to eight times during the year, depositing 500 eggs in a single season. When not mating or migrating, the vegetarian greens can be spotted often in lagoons and bays, nipping at seaweed with their beaks. Adults, usually three or four feet long and weighing 200-300 pounds, are easily identified out of water by the four big plates on either side of their shells. Green turtle meat was once prized as the main ingredient of turtle soup.

The **olive ridley** (*Lepidochelys olivacea*), or

green turtle

BOB RACE

---

signed side road heads seaward to Piedra Tlalcoyunque and the **Carabelas Restaurant.** About a mile down the paved road, the restaurant appears, perching on a bluff overlooking a monumental sandstone rock, Piedra Tlalcoyunque. Below, a wave-tossed strand, ripe for beachcombing and surf fishing, stretches for miles. Powerful breakers with fine right-hand surfing angles roll in and swish up the steep beach.

For fishing, buy some bait from the net fishermen on the beach and try some casts beyond the billows crashing into the south side of the Piedra. Later, stroll through the garden of eroded-rock sea stacks on the north side. There you can poke among the snails and seaweeds in a big sheltered tidepool, under the watchful guard of the squads of pelicans roosting on the surrounding pinnacles.

The house on the beach, now nearly a ruin, is the former headquarters of the **Campamento Playa Piedra de Tlalcoyunque,** whose mission was to rescue, incubate, and hatch as many turtle eggs as possible. Several staff members still patrol the beach during the summer–fall hatching (and egg-poaching) season. Although they are dedicated to their task, their vigil is a lonely one, and they welcome visitors and contributions of drinks and food.

At the Carabelas Restaurant on the bluff

locally, *golfina*, turtle population, thanks to persistent government and local volunteer efforts, seems to be stabilizing at several hundred thousand worldwide. Olive ridleys (so-named for their dull green shells) nest in significant numbers at isolated Acapulco-region beaches, notably Playa Revolcadero, east of Acapulco, and Playa Piedra Tlalcoyunque, west on the Costa Grande. Among the smaller of sea turtles, olive ridleys (80-100 pounds, with two-foot-long shells at maturity) come ashore to nest, customarily during summer. They lay clutches of around 80-100 eggs, which they bury with their flippers, and quickly return to the sea. They hunt most of the year near shorelines for shellfish, crabs, fish, and squid.

By contrast, the severely endangered **hawksbill** (*Eretmochelys imbricata*) has vanished from many Mexican Pacific beaches. Known locally as the *tortuga carey* (kah-RAY), it was the source of both meat and the lovely translucent tortoiseshell that has been supplanted largely by plastic. Adult *careys*, among the smaller of sea turtles, run two to three feet in length and weigh 30-100 pounds. Their usually brown shells are readily identified by shinglelike overlapping scales. During late summer and fall, females come ashore to lay clutches of eggs (around 100) in the sand. *Careys*, although preferring fish, mollusks, and shellfish, will eat almost anything, including seaweed. When attacked, *careys* can be plucky fighters, inflicting bites with their eagle-sharp hawksbills.

hawksbill turtle

You'll be fortunate indeed if you glimpse the rare **leatherback** (*Dermochelys coriacea*), the world's largest turtle. Experts have learned much about the leatherback (*laut* or *tortuga de cuero*) in recent years. About 100,000 female leatherbacks are thought to nest on their favorite breeding ground, the Mexican Pacific coast. Tales of the leatherback — of fisherfolk catching seven- or eight-foot individuals weighing nearly a ton — are legend. If you see even a small one you'll recognize it immediately by its back of leathery skin, creased with several lengthwise ridges.

above, you can take in the whole breezy scene while enjoying the recommended catch of the day. The name Carabelas (caravels) comes from the owner's admiration of Christopher Columbus. He christened his restaurant's three petite ocean-view gazebos after Columbus's three famous caravels: the *Niña*, the *Pinta*, and the *Santa María*.

For an overnight or a short stay, ask the restaurant owners if it's okay to set up your tent or park your (self-contained) RV in the restaurant lot or by the beach below the restaurant. For shower and dishwashing water, drop your bucket down into their well, at the bottom of the rise before the restaurant.

◖ PLAYA ESCONDIDA

Puerto Vicente Guerrero, a small workaday fishing port and naval training center, 97 miles (156 km) from Acapulco and 52 miles (84 km) from Zihuatanejo, hides a pearl of a beach, appropriately known as Playa Escondida (Hidden Beach), beyond its southeast headland.

Two miles from the signed highway turnoff, continue through the port village, bearing uphill to the left (east) at the village-center road fork overlooking the harbor. Pass the naval training center at the road's summit, and continue ahead a few blocks downhill to the Hotel Los Arcos at Playa Escondida.

THE COSTA GRANDE

Beyond the several permanent *palapa* restaurants that populate the beachfront spreads a wide yellow-sand beach, sheltered on both sides by rocky headlands. Strong waves break and roll in along a nearly level shoreline, receding with only mild undertow.

Playa Escondida (also known locally as Playa Secreta) appears ideal for every kind of beach entertainment, from kiddie play and beachcombing, to intermediate surfing and scuba diving. The beach even has ample room for tent camping, especially on the east side.

New lodgings are receiving a growing number of visitors. Most prominent is 【 **Hotel and Restaurant Los Arcos** (tel. 742/427-0252 or 742/424-0556, $35 s, $40 d, $50 t). Its dozen-odd modern, light, and comfortably furnished rooms encircle an inviting pool and parking patio. On the beach side, guests also enjoy an airy beach-view restaurant. Room rentals include hot-water shower baths and air-conditioning.

Folks interested in sportfishing and other water sports might want to stay at the **Bahía la Tortuga Fishing Lodge** (U.S. tel. 956/455-6931, www.escapeixtapa.com), which has been receiving guests (by reservation only) at Playa Escondida for several years. Owner-operators John and Angélica Lorenz advertise a number of packages, such as a three-night, four-day package that starts at $745 for two, including two days of sportfishing, one meal daily, and airport pickup. They also offer kayaking, snorkeling, scuba diving, surfing lessons, and whale- and turtle-watching, in season.

One or two bed-and-breakfasts and local homeowners also rent rooms during the winter season. Follow their signs, posted along the street above Hotel Los Arcos.

One especially recommended local scuba diving site is El Morro, the big rock island visible off the coast northwest around Papanoa town. Although no dive shop is operating locally, experienced divers might get there with John Lorenz of the Bahía la Tortuga Fishing Lodge or **Nautilus Divers** (tel. 755/554-9191, nautilusdivers@hotmail.com) in Zihuatanejo.

PLAYA BRISAS DEL MAR

Scarcely more than a mile on the Acapulco side from Puerto Vicente Guerrero, this breezy gem of a beach spreads west from the point where Highway 200 skirts the oceanfront, at Km 154.

A dirt side road leads 100 yards past very rustic *palapa* restaurants and houses that line the near (west) end of the beach. The dirt road forks left and continues east along the beach, a pristine 200-foot-wide golden strand with rollers that break gradually about 100 yards out. All beach diversions, including surfing, boogie boarding, kiddie play, beachcombing, surf fishing, and boat launching (provided you can negotiate the soft sand) appear promising here. Although no shade is available, at least one abandoned beach *palapa* appears ready for new occupants. Tenting and RV parking also appear customary. Out of courtesy, ask locally if it's okay to camp on the beach.

PAPANOA

The small town of Papanoa (pop. 3,000) straddles the highway 103 miles (165 km) northwest of Acapulco and 47 miles (75 km) south of Zihuatanejo. Local folks tell the tongue-in-cheek story of its Hawaiian-sounding name. It seems that there was a flood, and the son of the local headman had to talk fast to save his life by escaping in a *canoa*. Instead of saying "Papa… canoa," the swift-talking boy shortened his plea to "Papa… noa."

At least two recommendable hotels offer rooms. At the center of town, a block north of the highway, on Calle Telecino Moreno, stands the spiffy, family-run 【 **Hotel La Sirena** (Papanoa, Guerrero 40907, tel. 742/422-2029, $20 d, $35 with a/c). Here you'll get a very spacious, clean, and comfortable room with hot-water shower bath and ceiling fan, with parking in the patio.

Alternatively, stay at the resort-style **Hotel Club Papanoa** (Papanoa, Guerrero 40907, tel. 742/422-0150, $50 s or d low season, $60 high). Near the beach about a mile southeast of town, the hotel offers about 30 large rooms, a restaurant, and a big pool set in spacious ocean-view garden grounds. Built to be luxurious but now aging, the hotel is full during holidays and nearly empty most other times. Rooms have air-conditioning. Ask for a discount.

The hotel grounds adjoin the beach, **Playa Cayaquitos.** The wide, breezy, yellow-gray strand stretches for two miles, washed by powerful open-ocean rollers with good left and right surfing breaks. Additional attractions include surf fishing beyond the breakers and driftwood along the sand. Beach access is via the off-highway driveway just north of the hotel. At the beach, a parking lot borders a seafood restaurant. Farther on, the road narrows (but is still motorhome accessible) through a defunct beachside home development, past several brush-bordered informal RV parking or tent camping spots.

A pair of clean restaurants, the **Annel** and the **Cabaña,** in the town center on the south side of the highway, serve passable country-style food.

As for services, Papanoa offers friendly doctor Salvador Zarate (tel. 742/422-0046), with pharmacy; a photo shop, Universo (tel. 742/422-0150); a *gasolinera;* first-class bus stops; a long-distance telephone; and Ladatel card-operated public phones.

◖ PLAYA OJO DE AGUA

Nestled in the little nook between a pair of headlands, about half a mile southeast of the Hotel Club Papanoa, is the petite half-moon beach, named Playa Ojo de Agua for its cooling and cleansing fresh-water spring. Local families flock here on weekend afternoons to play in the surf, eat fresh seafood at the beachfront *palapas,* and rinse themselves in the community spring (*ojo de agua,* literally eye of water) that trickles from a hillside spot, marked by a concrete arch, above the beach. (*Note:* If you use the spring, remember it's only a trickle, so kindly conserve water by dipping a bucket, bottle, or can in the collection basin for water to pour over yourself.)

Playa Ojo de Agua is a lovely place, wide and level, with very surfable waves from about 200 yards out, and a number of shady possible tent-

An arch and a stream of fresh water marks the spring behind the trees.

ing spots. There is little or no convenient space for RV parking on the beach, however.

PLAYAS ARROYO SECO, EL CALVARIO, AND CAYACAL

Between Km 178 and Km 183, Highway 200 veers spectacularly close to the ocean. Here, three long beaches, Arroyo Seco, Calvario, and Cayacal, join in one continuously scenic sweep of sand, sea, and sky. From the Acapulco end, first comes long, wild Playa Arroyo Seco; then Playa El Calvario, stunningly viewable from any one of several clifftop *palapa* restaurants; and finally golden Playa Cayacal, seemingly extending forever west.

Along this entire stretch, conditions seem perfect for a day or a week of beach diversions. Waves, fine for boogie boarding or surfing, roll in gradually with little undertow. Seasonal storms deposit a few shells and a bit of driftwood. Rock outcroppings provide resting spots for resident gulls, pelicans, boobies, and cormorants, while a sprinkling of visitors stroll the sand and play in the surf.

THE COSTA GRANDE

Playa Arroyo Seco

Get the best view of this breezy, palm-lined strand at headland Mirador El Calvario by cliff-top Restaurant El Mirador, near Km 181. The restaurant is open from around 7 A.M. to 7 P.M., and the menu includes Mexican-style breakfasts (such as huevos mexicanas, omelets, and chilaquiles) until noon, and and fish (whole pan fried, filet with garlic or breaded, or in tacos) the rest of the day. Below the restaurant, look along the long Playa Arroyo Seco below to the petite palm grove and abandoned *palapa* restaurant at the bottom of the cliff. It currently appears ripe for RV parking or tenting. (With no one around, though, security might be questionable. Check at the restaurant to be sure.) You could also set up your tent or park your RV in the parking lot by the restaurant.

Check out Playa Arroyo Seco close-up via at least two access roads. Either try the dirt road (easy by high-clearance truck or SUV, difficult by ordinary car) at the bottom of the bluff, at Km 180.5; or more easily, reach Playa Arroyo Seco via the dirt road, on the west, Zihuatanejo side of the Río Arroyo Seco, at around Km 183. Pass through the village of the same name to the palm-lined beach after about a mile.

◖ Playa El Calvario

In contrast to secluded Playa Arroyo Seco, Playa El Calvario is well-frequented, especially by the dozens of daily visitors who stop at one of its several clifftop restaurants perched above the beach. Playa Calvario, although especially fine for surfing and nearly everything else (except maybe surf fishing because of the flat shallows), isn't good for camping because it's only about 100 feet wide and vulnerable to flooding at high tide. Instead, camp on Playa Arroyo Seco or Playa Cayacal at either end (or stay at the hotels in Papanoa or Puerto Vicente Guerrero).

Nevertheless, Playa Calvario is an irresistible spot to stop and take in the gorgeous scene. Gulls soar, pelicans dive, waves carry surfers shoreward, and cormorants preen and cackle on the Piedras Calvarios, visible at the Acapulco end, and Piedra Fierre, in the middle.

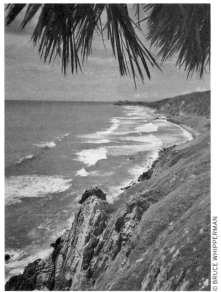

© BRUCE WHIPPERMAN

At Playa El Calvario, waves, cliff, and blue sky seem to stretch endlessly to the blue horizon.

Furthermore, at the Playa Calvario clifftop, the sun, at dawn and sunset, graphically demonstrates why the Spanish explorers called the Pacific Ocean the Mar del Sur, the Southern Sea. Here, from the clifftop in late afternoon, you can see the sun (which everywhere rises in the east and sets in the west), shining along a line parallel to the beach line. Thus, south, perpendicular to the east–west beach line, is straight out toward the ocean.

PLAYA LA BARRITA AND LAS SALINAS

These two little roadside spots are interesting for completely different reasons. Playa La Barrita is a lovely beachside mini-paradise, while at Las Salinas, people continue to make their living from technology whose origin is lost in time.

Playa La Barrita

Of the several small *palapa* restaurants that decorate Playa La Barrita, around Km 188, none has such an attractive setting as **◖** **Restaurant Paraíso Escondido** (Hidden

Paradise). Although the food (shrimp, octopus, fish, prawns) is good enough, the site is stunning. The fine, yellow-sand beach stretches for about a mile in both directions, and waves wash in from about 100 yards out with little undertow. Surfing, boogie boarding, and surf fishing and boat launching appear distinctly possible. For tots, the restaurant even has a blue kiddie pool out front.

Best of all, however, are the luscious camping prospects by the restaurant's shady, forested lagoon (which also makes a fine swimming hole). What's more, the owner welcomes campers, for no more than the price of a meal or two in his restaurant. (The only drawback is the popularity of this place, especially on weekends and holidays, when, if you must have tranquillity, you had better stay in a hotel or camp down the beach a way.)

◖ Las Salinas

Families of Las Salinas (pop. 500) village of salt harvesters use the inner flats of the neighboring arm of the ocean, Estero El Cuajo, to make their living. Pause by the highway around Km 193 or 194 to see how they do it. With long-handled wooden trowels, workers fashion diked ponds, about 10 feet (three meters) square, from the dried mud of the lagoon. They surface the ponds' bottoms with lime, which soon hardens into an impervious basin.

The salt workers channel the seawater into the ponds. The sun evaporates the water and the salt crystallizes on the edges. The workers scoop the salt crystals to small piles outside the ponds, where they are dried by the sun; the salt is then taken to the warehouse and bagged.

Along Highway 200 in the village, around Km 192, you can see the results of all this. Instead of waiting by the roadside for customers, villagers let their salt bags do the waiting, perched on posts, like roadside mailboxes, for someone to stop and leave a dollar for a one-kilo sack. They don't mind doing this; the loss of an occasional dollar is small compared to long hours of waiting. And besides, every dollar they make this way is one they didn't have in the first place.

THE COSTA GRANDE

© BRUCE WHIPPERMAN

Playa La Barrita seems the perfect spot for a season of relaxing beach diversions.

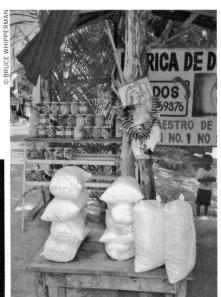

© BRUCE WHIPPERMAN

THE COSTA GRANDE

Las Salinas folks simply place their bags of salt by the roadside, for motorists to buy.

Other Las Salinas families around Km 195 sell both salt and "colorines," yummy pastel-colored candied coconut. They're fresh, sweet, delicious, and healthy, to boot.

PETATLÁN

The town of Petatlán (pop. about 25,000), only 22 miles (35 km) east of Zihuatanejo, besides being Guerrero's most cherished pilgrimage site, has a distinguished pre-Columbian heritage that has only recently begun to be appreciated.

Sights

All roads seem to lead to Petatlán's inviting central *parque municipal,* a fraction of a mile south of Highway 200, around Km 207. Here, near the bright pink *kiosko* bandstand, stand a pair of intriguing **monoliths,** excavated and brought from Soledad de Maciel (see *Soledad de Maciel Archaeological Zone* later in this chapter) to save them from looters. One is a circular stone ring, undoubtedly used in the pre-Columbian ceremonial ball game. The other, pro-

tected beneath a covered structure nearby, is a carved disk-shaped monolith, said to represent the god Tlaltecutli.

While in the *parque,* be sure to step inside the adjacent **Parroquia de Padre Jesús,** hallowed ground for the many thousands of pilgrims who arrive yearly from all over Guerrero and Mexico. Inside the innovative parabolic-arched nave, the faithful pay their respects to the venerated wooden image, known affectionately as "Papa Chuy," that arrived under miraculous circumstances as the gift of a mysterious but grateful "Christian Pirate" around 1600. The Petatlán townsfolk fete their beloved Papa Chuy at least twice a year, during the pre-Easter Semana Santa celebration and the August 6–7 Fiesta del Padre Jesús. During both occasions the *parque* is awash with merrymakers watching folkloric dances, eating traditional sweets, and thrilling to the boom and flash of fireworks overhead.

During your downtown stroll, be sure to visit the **Mercado de Oro** (Gold Market) lineup of plaza-front stalls offering a trove of bright solid-gold necklaces, amulets, chains, bracelets, and much more.

Practicalities

A dozen-odd modest downtown hotels accommodate overnight guests. Ordinarily they're not crowded, but if you're going to stay in Petatlán during the Padre Jesús festival (around Aug. 6 and 7), the week before Easter, or Christmas–New Year's, be sure to get reservations far ahead of time.

One of the best is **Hotel Mi Pueblito III** (Independencia 108, no phone, $20 d with fan, $30 d with a/c), next to Telmex. They offer about 10 comfortable, spacious, light and airy rooms with hot-water shower baths, TV, and parking.

Another good hotel choice is posada-style **Hotel-Restaurant La Flor de Petatlán** (Calle N. Bravo 168, corner of Independencia, no telephone, about $30 d). Friendly owner Aralino Chávez offers eight basic but clean, spacious and comfortable rooms, all with two beds and

THE LEGEND OF PADRE JESÚS

Sometime during the late 1500s, a priest was assigned to minister to the people of Petatlán. Upon arrival, the priest sympathized with the people's sorry state. For years they had endured both the terrible ravages of smallpox and the greed and cruelty of the Spanish soldiers and colonists. The priest taught them and helped heal them, and, after a few years he had gained their confidence.

During the yearly Semana Santa celebration the priest saw that the people had been carrying an old rickety image of San Antonio for the reenactment of the Stations of the Cross. In a church meeting, he convinced his congregation to take up a collection to obtain a true image of Jesus for the upcoming Semana Santa celebration.

Although the collection amounted to only a few small coins, the priest prepared to journey somewhere to get an appropriate new image of Jesus.

Meanwhile, a great storm had been blowing off the coast. Unknown to the priest and the people of Petatlán, a pirate ship, dismasted and waterlogged, was in danger of sinking. On the ship was an image of Jesus, to which the pirate sailors prayed to save their ship. The pirate captain vowed that, if they were saved, he would take the image to the nearest town and donate it to the local people.

The pirates were saved: The storm drove them aground on the Bahía de Potosí's sandy shoreline. The pirate captain, true to his vow, took the image ashore with two of his crew.

The priest, meanwhile, had been in a quandary; he did not know where he could find a suitable image of Jesus for the few coins that he had collected. Late one night, as he was praying for guidance, the priest was startled by a hard knock on his door. It was the pirate captain, who told the priest that he had the image of Jesus that the priest was looking for. Then, without further explanation, the pirate disappeared into the night.

Barely able to believe the mysterious man who became known as the "Christian Pirate," the priest nevertheless delayed his trek to find a new image.

Easter Sunday came, and the promised image had not appeared. The priest was relating the story of Jesus's death and resurrection to his congregation when a poor woodcutter pushed himself through the assembly and cried out that Jesus with a cross had appeared to him nearby.

The people followed the woodcutter to a clear stream where, under a great tree, was the sculpture of Padre Jesús. The people joyfully carried Padre Jesús back to their church, where he remains in Petatlán to this day.

This is a synopsis of the story of Padre Jesús as researched and written by Petatlán's official historian, Señor Agapito Galeana.

religious goods outside the Church of Padre Jesús in Petatlán fans. A plus here is the hotel's airy view veranda, overlooking the town's main plaza.

Petatlá's most highly recommended restaurant is the refined airy *palapa* 【 **Restaurant Mi Pueblito** (tel. 758/538-3104, 9 A.M.–1 A.M. daily), on the *parque*'s south side, serving a long menu of Mexican country-style favorites.

While downtown, you can avail yourself of a number of services. These include **Bancomer** (tel. 758/538-2977, 9 A.M.–4 P.M. Mon.–Fri.); a *correo;* Ladatel card-operated street telephones; **Agencia de Viajes Mayte** (Guerrero 4, tel. 758/538-2047); the police (at the *presidencia municipal,* tel. 758/538-4040); and a doctor, **Saul Enríquez Garcia** (Bravo 42, tel. 758/538-2321).

Excursions from Petatlán

Adventurers might go for an upcountry side trip to **Ximalcota** (shee-mahl-KOH-tah), about eight miles (12 km) via the country road from Petatlán's north side, to enjoy picnicking, hiking, and other diversions possible on the bank of the cascading mountain Río Petatlán. Activity options include cooling off in a cascade or paddling in a swimming hole decorated with friendly rocks, smoothed through eons of the river's flow. Nearby, visit a tree so old and large that it requires a dozen people holding hands to encircle its base. Get there by car, taxi, or guide (contact the travel agent in town). (*Note:* This trip is best enjoyed during the drier months from October through May, when the river runs clear, in contrast to the rainy months of June, July, August, and September, when the river turns an unappealing brown.)

In the opposite, southerly direction, consider an excursion to the freshwater mangrove lake **Estero Valentín** for fresh seafood, wildlife-watching, turtle rescuing, pristine beach camping, fishing, and more. Drive or taxi the country road south from Highway 200 in mid-Petatlán. The three families in charge offer seafood dinners at their palm-shadowed lagoon-front *palapa.* Nearby, from their rustic dockfront, they take visitors on wildlife-watching tours on the mangrove-fringed expanse of Estero Valentín. During the turtle season, be sure to visit their government-sponsored **turtle sanctuary,** and, if you're equipped, camp on the pristine, boat-accessible-only barrier beach that separates the estuary from the ocean.

For a good eco-adventure tour of Estero Valentín, contact very experienced 【 **Zoe Kayak Tours** (tel. 755/553-0496, zoe5@aol. com, www.zoekayaktours.com), which operates out of Ixtapa. Call manager-owner Brian for reservations.

【 SOLEDAD DE MACIEL ARCHAEOLOGICAL ZONE

Find this important archaeological site five miles (8 km) south of Highway 200, via the good signed side road at Km 214, about three miles (5 km) east of Petatlán or nineteen miles (31 km) east of Zihuatanejo. It was first explored by INAH (National Institute of Archaeology and History) investigators around 1925. From time to time excavations have continued, although

© BRUCE WHIPPERMAN

an ancient ball ring, found at the nearby Soledad de Maciel Archaeological Zone

none of the structures has yet been restored. It is only recently that local folks (who call their site El Chole) have begun to benefit from it. They now welcome visitors to their small artifact museum, introduce them to the monumental "King of Chole" monolith, and offer tours.

Investigators identify a classic-era (circa A.D. 300) habitation and ceremonial zone that extends over at least a square mile (2 or 3 square km) around the present Soledad de Maciel village. Identified structures (but completely unreconstructed rubble) include three pyramids, ceremonial mounds and courtyards, a ball court, and extensive former habitation zones. Many artifacts have been uncovered; examples include pottery, on display at the Zihuatanejo archaeological museum, the two monoliths at the Petatlán downtown *parque,* and two ball rings beside Highway 200 in town.

King of Chole Monolith and Touring the Archaeological Zone

Artifacts are on display at the modest village museum, also the point of departure for the local tour (in Spanish, of course). Find the museum on the right at the first intersection in the village. The major village artifact is the "King of Chole" monolith, in front of the village church, adjacent to the museum. It represents a personage with two faces, looking in opposite right and left directions. One face, representing death, is emaciated, the other, representing life, is vital.

Guides offer their services for a one- or two-hour tour of the environs. Highlight of the tour is the 200-foot, forested **Cerro de las Peñas,** or Hill of the Rocks. On the way up, ask your guide to point out the plants along the way. These include the wild, plumlike *ciruela;* the *cuachalalope* tree, with buds on the trunk that are boiled for a rejuvenating tonic; the *cacahuanache* tree, whose boiled bark makes a good shampoo; and the *paniko* tree, which makes a sedative tonic.

At the breezy summit, the broad hinterland of corn and tobacco (for locally made cigars) fields and communal coconut groves spreads to the ocean, visible on the southern horizon. Also uphill, you will find a monumental *órgano* (organ cactus), some petroglyphs (of the Lord of the Hill), and a small cave, complete with bats and more petroglyphs. Bring a flashlight. Among the best qualified of the local guides is Adan Belez Romero, available at the museum or local cell 044-755/551-4851. Offer $10–20 for a two-hour tour.

IXTAPA AND ZIHUATANEJO

The resort pair of Ixtapa and Zihuatanejo present an irresistible opportunity for a season of relaxed vacationing. The choices seem nearly endless. You can sun to your heart's content on luscious beaches, choose from a feast of delicious food, and shop from a trove of fine, Mexican handicrafts. Furthermore, outdoor lovers can enjoy their fill of unhurried beachwalking and snorkeling, bicycling, horseback riding, kayaking, swimming, surfing, scuba diving, and caving.

Whether you stay in Ixtapa or Zihuatanejo depends on your inclinations. Zihuatanejo still resembles the small fishing village it once was, with many reminders of old Mexico, and a mix of small to medium-size hotels. Ixtapa, on the other hand, is for modern travelers who prefer

the fashionable glitter of a luxuriously comfortable facility-rich hotel on a crystalline strand. (On the other hand, where you stay may not really matter, because Ixtapa and Zihuatanejo are only five miles apart.)

PLANNING YOUR TIME

There's hardly a better place for balmy winter vacation than the Ixtapa and Zihuatanejo coast, whether it be for simply a four- or five-day-long weekend or a month of Sundays.

If your stay is limited to four or five days, you'll still have time for some sunning and snoozing on the beach or by the pool, sampling some of the excellent Zihuatanejo restaurants, visiting the **Museo Arqueología de la Costa Grande,** browsing Zihuatanejo's

HIGHLIGHTS

◖ **Museo Arqueología de la Costa Grande:** Zihuatanejo's first stop for history aficionados illustrates the prehistory of the Costa Grande with a treasury of dioramas, paintings, and precious locally discovered and donated artifacts (page 119).

◖ **Playa La Ropa:** Enjoy this best of all possible resort beaches, tucked along a golden mile of Zihuatanejo Bay's sheltered eastern flank (page 121).

◖ **Playa Las Gatas:** Only boat accessible, Playa Las Gatas seems like a remote south-seas island, a place where sun, sea, and sand and the rustle of the palms invite relaxation. When you get hungry, a lineup of *palapa* restaurants provide fresh seafood; for exercise, beach stalls rent snorkel gear, which you can use to acquaint yourself with squadrons of tropical fish a few steps offshore (page 122).

◖ *Teleférico* **and Playa del Palmar:** Late afternoon, stroll along Ixtapa's creamy resort beach, Playa del Palmar, to the south end where the *teleférico* will whisk you uphill for a panoramic sunset view and cocktails and dinner at the El Faro view restaurant (page 123).

◖ **Isla Ixtapa:** Visitors to this petite, pristine island-jewel can enjoy three different beaches, Playa Cuachalatate, Playa Varadero, and Playa Coral, tucked on the island's three sheltered corners. A fourth beach, for romantics only, Playa Carey, is a petite sandy nook accessible by boat only on the island's wild open-ocean shore (page 124).

◖ **Barra de Potosí:** This rustic palm-shadowed village, with a grand, mangrove-laced,

wildlife-rich lagoon on one side and a luscious beach on the other, seems perfect for a spell of relaxed living (page 160).

◖ **Troncones:** Once an isolated fishing village on a coral-decorated shoreline, Troncones has become a winter refuge for a loyal cadre of sun-starved Americans and Canadians (page 162).

LOOK FOR ◖ TO FIND RECOMMENDED SIGHTS, ACTIVITIES, DINING, AND LODGING.

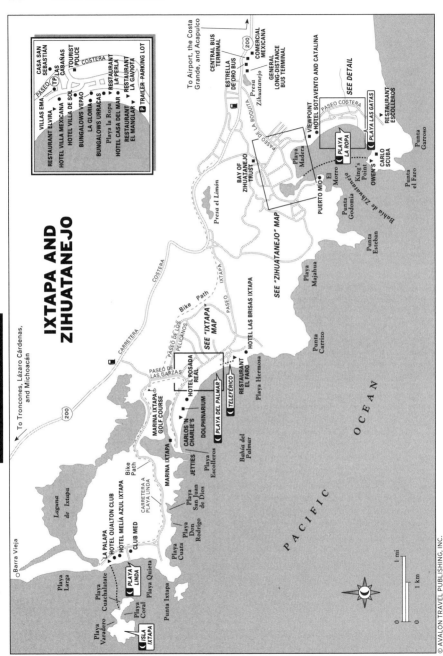

IXTAPA AND ZIHUATANEJO

To Troncones, Lázaro Cárdenas, and Michoacán

IXTAPA AND ZIHUATANEJO

VILLAS EMA
RESTAURANT ELVIRA
CASA SAN SEBASTIAN
HOTEL VILLA MEXICANA
HOTEL VILLA DE SOL
LAS CABAÑAS
TOURIST POLICE
BUNGALOWS VEPAO
LA GLORIA
RESTAURANT LA PERLA
BUNGALOWS URRACAS
Playa la Ropa
HOTEL CASA DEL MAR
RESTAURANT LA GAVIOTA
RESTAURANT EL MANGLAR
TRAILER-PARKING LOT

Barra Vieja

Laguna de Ixtapa

Playa Larga

Playa Varadero
Playa Coral
ISLA IXTAPA
Playa Cuachalalate
Playa Quieta
PLAYA LINDA
Punta Ixtapa

Playa Cuata
Playa Don Rodrigo
Playa San Juan de Dios

LA PALAPA
HOTEL QUALTON CLUB
HOTEL MELIA AZUL IXTAPA
CLUB MED

Bike Path
CARRETERA A PLAYA LINDA

MARINA IXTAPA
JETTIES
Playa Escolleros

MARINA IXTAPA GOLF COURSE
PASEO DE LAS GARZAS
PASEO DE LOS PELICANOS
Bike Path

CARRETERA

COSTERA

SEE "IXTAPA" MAP
HOTEL POSADA REAL

CARLOS 'N CHARLIE'S
DOLPHINARIUM
PLAYA DEL PALMAR
TELEFÉRICO
RESTAURANT EL FARO

Bahía del Palmar

Playa Hermosa

HOTEL LAS BRISAS IXTAPA

PACIFIC   OCEAN

Presa el Limón

PASEO DE LA BOQUITA

To Airport, the Costa Grande, and Acapulco

CENTRAL BUS TERMINAL
COMMERCIAL MEXICANA
ESTRELLA DE ORO BUS
GENERAL LONG-DISTANCE BUS TERMINAL

Presa Zihuatanejo
Presa

BAY OF ZIHUATANEJO TRUST

Playa Madera

SEE "ZIHUATANEJO" MAP

SEE DETAIL

VIEWPOINT
HOTEL SOTAVENTO AND CATALINA
PASEO COSTERA
PLAYA LAS GATAS
RESTAURANT ESCOLLEROS

PLAYA LA ROPA

PUERTO MÍO
El Morro
King's Point
OWEN'S
CARLO SCUBA

Punta Garroso
Punta el Faro

Bahía de Zihuatanejo

Punta Godomia
Punta Esteban

Playa Majahua

Punta Carrizo

200

N

0   1 mi
0   1 km

© AVALON TRAVEL PUBLISHING, INC.

irresistible trove of handicrafts, and spending an afternoon at either secluded **Playa Las Gatas** or **Isla Ixtapa.**

With more time, you can concentrate more on your individual interests. Handicrafts, for example, are a major Zihuatanejo specialty. Start with an hour or two at the tourist market on the west side of town, with many stalls stuffed with tempting treasures from all over Guerrero and Mexico. Then spend the rest of the day browsing the top-pick private handicrafts shops, such as Casa Marina, Artesanías Olinalá, Cerámicas Tonalá, and Galería Maya.

On the other hand, active vacationers will want to get into Ixtapa and Zihuatanejo's great outdoors. You might start off with a day sunning, hiking, and snorkeling off the beaches of Isla Ixtapa. If you want more, you could try the same at Playa Las Gatas with a scuba-diving lesson thrown in. For still more outdoor adventures, do some bicycling on Ixtapa's new *ciclopista,* or head southeast to **Barra de Potosí** or northwest to **Troncones.**

Everyone can partake of Zihuatanejo's fine cuisine, whether local country-style or gourmet nouvelle Mexican. Simply follow the icons of the top-pick restaurants, covering the whole range: strictly Mexican at Tamales y Atoles "Any" and Cocina Economica Doña Licha; simply good food at Mama Norma and Deborah, Da Baffone, Coconuts, and Capricio; and gourmet splurges at Il Mare, Kau Kan, and La Gula.

With more days, head out of town south to Barra de Potosí for wildlife-viewing on the Laguna de Potosí or north to Troncones for sunning, swimming and surfing, and lingering a few nights at a comfortable bed-and-breakfast.

Out of Town Getaways

With a week or more, you'll have time to rent a car or take a taxi or bus northwest for an overnight or two in a comfortable **Troncones** beachfront bed-and-breakfast, or do the same by traveling southeast to **Barra de Potosí.** While in Troncones, adventurers will want to explore the limestone cave, do the forest canopy cable ride, maybe take a surfing lesson,

or hire a boat for fishing. At the village resort of Barra de Potosí, you can easily spend a couple of days sunning and beachcombing; dining on super-fresh seafood at rustic, palm-shaded *palapa* restaurants; and exploring, by boat or kayak, the grand, wildlife-rich Laguna de Potosí.

HISTORY
In the Beginning

The Purépecha people who lived in the area around A.D. 1400 were relative latecomers, preceded by waves of immigrants to Zihuatanejo. The local archaeological museum displays ancient pottery made by Zihuatanejo artisans as many as 5,000 years ago. Later, more sophisticated artists, influenced by the renowned Olmec mother-culture of the Gulf of Mexico coast, left their indisputable mark on local pottery styles.

By the beginning of the Christian era, local people had developed more sophisticated lifestyles. Instead of wandering and hunting and gathering their food, they were living in permanent towns and villages, surrounded by fields where they grew most of what they needed. Besides their staple corn, beans, and squash, these farmers, called Cuitlatecs by the Aztecs, were also cultivating tobacco, cotton for clothes, and cacao for chocolate. Attracted by the Cuitlatecs' rich produce, the highland Aztecs, led by their emperor Tizoc, invaded the coast during the late 1400s and extracted a small mountain of tribute yearly from the Cuitlatecs.

Conquest and Colonization

Scarcely months after Hernán Cortés conquered the Aztecs, he sent an expedition to explore the "Southern Sea" and find the long-sought route to China. In November 1522 Captain Juan Álvarez Chico set sail with boats built on the Isthmus of Tehuántepec and reconnoitered the Zihuatanejo coast all the way northeast to at least the Río Balsas, planting crosses on beaches and claiming the land for Spain.

Cortés, encouraged by the samples of pearls and gold that Chico brought back, built more ships and outfitted more expeditions. At a personal cost of 60,000 gold pesos (probably equivalent to several million dollars today) Cortés had three ships built at Zacatula, at the mouth of the Río Balsas. He commissioned Captain Alvaro Saavedra Cerón to command the first expedition to find the route to Asia. Saavedra Cerón set off from Zihuatanejo Bay on October 31, 1527. He commanded a modest force of about 110 men, with 30 cannons, in three small caravels, the flagship *Florida,* the *Espíritu Santo* and the *Santiago.* The *Florida,* Saavedra Cerón's sole vessel to survive the fierce Pacific typhoons, reached present-day Guam on December 29, 1527, and the Philippines on February 1, 1528. As he did not know any details of the Pacific Ocean and its winds and currents, it is not surprising that Saavedra Cerón failed to return to Mexico. He died at sea in October 1529 in search of a return route to Mexico.

No fewer than seven more attempts were needed (from Acapulco in 1532, 1539, and 1540; Tehuántepec in 1535; and Barra de Navidad, two in 1542 and one in 1564) until finally, in 1565, navigator-priest Andrés de Urdaneta coaxed Pacific winds and currents to give up their secret and returned triumphantly to Acapulco from Asia.

The Manila Galleon

Thereafter, the trading ship called the Manila galleon sailed yearly from Acapulco for Asia. For more than 250 years, it returned to Acapulco within a year, laden with a fortune in spices, silks, gold, and porcelain. Although Acapulco's prominence all but shut down all other Mexican Pacific ports, the Manila galleon would from time to time stop off at Zihuatanejo. The same was true for the occasional pirate ship (or fleet) that lurked along the coast, hungry to capture the galleon's riches.

The most famous corsair was Francis Drake, who landed in Zihuatanejo in 1579. Later came the Dutch fleet of Hugo Schapenham in 1624. English Captain William Dampier entered Zihuatanejo Bay in 1704, recording that the shoreline village had about 40 grass huts, inhabited by about 100 unfriendly people who vigorously discouraged his disembarkation. The luckiest of all the corsairs was Cap-

tain George Anson, who, in 1715, captured the Manila galleon and returned to England with booty then worth 800,000 pounds sterling—upwards of $50 million today.

On one occasion, no one knows when exactly, a galleon evidently lost some of its precious silk cargo, which washed ashore on one of Zihuatanejo's beaches, now known as Playa La Ropa (Clothes Beach).

Independence

In 1821, Mexico became independent, stopping the Manila galleon forever. Deprived even of an occasional galleon or pirate, Zihuatanejo went to sleep and didn't wake up for more than half a century. The occasion was the arrival of ex-President Lerdo de Tejada, who, during the 1870s, embarked from Zihuatanejo for exile in the United States.

By the 20th century, some of the maritime prosperity of Acapulco, which benefited from the stream of California-bound steamers, spilled over to Zihuatanejo. During the 1920s, nearby resources were exploited, and what is now known as Playa Madera (Wood Beach) earned its label as a loading point for fine hardwood timber exports.

Modern Zihuatanejo

Recognition of Zihuatanejo's growing importance came on November 30, 1953, when the Guerrero state legislature decreed the formation of the Zihuatanejo *municipio,* whose governmental center was established at the budding town on the bay of the same name.

In the 1960s, a new airport suitable for propeller passenger airplanes, and the paved highway, which arrived from Acapulco around the same time, jolted Zihuatanejo from its final slumber. No longer isolated, Zihuatanejo's headland-rimmed aqua bay began to attract a small colony of people seeking paradise on earth.

Tourism grew steadily. Small hotels and restaurants were built to accommodate visitors. Zihuatanejo had a population of perhaps 5,000 by the late 1970s when Fonatur, the government tourism-development agency, decided to develop Zihuatanejo Bay. Local folks, however,

PIRATES OF ZIHUATANEJO

For 10 generations, from the late 1500s to independence in 1821, corsairs menaced the Mexican Pacific coast. They often used Zihuatanejo Bay for repair and resupply.

The earliest was the renowned and feared English privateer Sir Francis Drake (see the sidebar "Sir Francis Drake: The Pirate El Draque" in the *Background* chapter). During his circumnavigation of 1577-1580, Drake raided a number of Spanish Pacific ports.

The biggest prize, however, was the Manila galleon, for which he searched the Mexican coast for months. Finally, low on water and food, he dropped anchor and resupplied briefly at Zihuatanejo Bay before continuing northwest.

ENTER THE DUTCH

Dutch corsairs also scoured the seas for the Manila galleon. In October 1624, a Dutch squadron commanded by Captain Hugo Schapenham grouped in a semicircle outside Acapulco Bay to intercept the departing galleon. Port authorities, however, delayed the sailing, and the Dutch began running out of food and water. They tried to trade captives for supplies, but the Spanish refused, offering only inedible gold for the captives. In desperation, Schapenham tried to attack the Acapulco fort directly, but his vessels were damaged and driven off by the fort's effective artillery fire.

The starving Dutch sailors retreated up the coast to Zihuatanejo Bay where, after a few weeks, rested and resupplied, they set sail for Asia on November 29, 1624.

Although most of them arrived in the Moluccas Islands in the East Indies, they disbanded. Most of them, including Schapenham, who was dead by the end of 1625, never returned to Europe.

DAMPIER AND ANSON

A much more persistent and fortunate galleon hunter was English captain William Dampier (1652-1715), who, besides accumulating a fortune in booty, was renowned as a navigator and mapmaker. Lying in wait for the Manila galleon, Dampier anchored in Zihuatanejo Bay in 1704. On December 7, Dampier came upon the Manila galleon *Nuestra Señora del Rosario*. However, a ferocious Spanish defense forced Dampier's squadron to retreat.

Six years later, commanding another squadron jointly with Captain Woodes Rogers, Dampier captured both the galleon *Encarnación* and the *Nuestra Señora de Begoña* between January 1 and January 5, 1710. Rogers and Dampier returned triumphantly to England in the *Encarnación*, which they had rechristened the *Batchelor*.

Luckiest of all Manila galleon treasure hunters was George Anson (1697-1762), who volunteered for the English navy at the age of 15 and rose rapidly, attaining the rank of captain at the age of 25.

In command of a small fleet of ships and many hundreds of sailors, he arrived off Acapulco on March 1, 1742. After waiting three weeks for the galleon to sail, and running low on food and water, Anson sailed northwest, resupplied at Zihuatanejo, and then departed west across the Pacific. On July 1, 1743, off Guam, Anson's forces caught up with and captured the galleon *Nuestra Señora de Covdonga*, with 1.3 million pieces of eight, 35,000 ounces of silver, and a trove of jewels. (A "piece of eight" is an old label for a famous Spanish coin, coveted by pirates the world over.)

Although suffering from the loss of 90 percent of his men, Anson finally returned to England in command of his last remaining ship, carrying booty worth 800,000 pounds sterling, a fortune worth many tens of millions of dollars today.

Sheltered, blue Zihuatanejo Bay is the place to shed your winter worries.

objecting that the proposed lineup of high-rise hotels would block the view of their beautiful bay, squelched the plan.

Fonatur regrouped and alternatively proposed Ixtapa (often translated as White Place, but it more likely means White Top, for the several guano-topped offshore islets) five miles north of Zihuatanejo as a perfect site for a world-class resort. Investors agreed, and the infrastructure—drainage, roads, and utilities—was installed. The jet airport was built, hotels rose, and by 2000, the distinct but inseparable twin resorts of Ixtapa and Zihuatanejo (combined pop. 80,000) were attracting a steady stream of Mexican and foreign vacationers.

Sights

GETTING ORIENTED

Both Ixtapa and Zihuatanejo are small and easy to know. Zihuatanejo's little Plaza de Armas town square overlooks the main beach, Playa Municipal, that fronts the palm-lined pedestrian walkway, Paseo del Pescador. From the plaza looking out toward the bay, you are facing south. On your right is the pier (*muelle,* moo-AY-yay), and on the left the bay curves along the outer beaches Playas La Ropa, Madera, and finally Las Gatas beneath the far Punta El Faro (Lighthouse Point).

Turning around and facing inland (north), you see a narrow but busy waterfront street, Juan Álvarez, running parallel to the beach past the plaza, crossing the main business streets (actually tranquil shady lanes) Cuauhtémoc and Guerrero. A third street, bustling Benito Juárez, one block to the right of Guerrero, conducts traffic several blocks to and from the shore, passing the market and intersecting a second main street, Avenida Morelos, about 10 blocks inland from the beach. There, a right turn will soon bring you to Highway 200 and, within five miles, Ixtapa.

Most everything in Ixtapa lies along one three-mile-long boulevard, Paseo Ixtapa, which parallels the main beach, hotel-lined Playa del Palmar. Heading westerly, arriving from Zihuatanejo, you first pass the Club de Golf Ixtapa, then the big Hotel Barceló on the left, followed by a succession of other high-rise hotels. Soon comes the Zona Comercial shopping malls and the Paseo de las Garzas corner on the right. Turn right for either Highway 200 or the outer Playas Cuata, Quieta, Linda, and Larga. At Playa Linda, boats continue to heavenly Isla Ixtapa.

If, instead, you continued straight ahead from the Paseo de las Garzas corner, you would soon reach the Marina Ixtapa condo development and yacht harbor.

GETTING AROUND

In downtown Zihuatanejo, shops and restaurants are within a few blocks of the plaza. For the beaches, walk along the beachfront *andador* (walkway) to Playa Madera, take a taxi ($3) to Playa La Ropa, and a launch from the pier ($5) to Playa Las Gatas.

For Ixtapa or the outer beaches, take a taxi (about $5) or ride one of the very frequent minibuses, labeled by destination, which leave from both Juárez, across from the market, and the northeast downtown corner of Juárez and Morelos, a few blocks farther north from the beach. In Ixtapa, walk or ride the minibuses that run along Paseo Ixtapa.

◖ MUSEO ARQUEOLOGÍA DE LA COSTA GRANDE

Zihuatanejo's smallish but interesting archaeological museum (east end of Álvarez, beachside, tel. 755/554-7552, 10 a.m.–6 p.m. Tues.–Sun., admission $3 per person) authoritatively details the prehistory of the Costa Grande. Professionally prepared maps, paintings, dioramas, and artifacts—many donated by local resident and innkeeper Anita Rellstab—illustrate the development of local cultures, from early hunting and gathering to agriculture and, finally, urbanization by the time of the conquest. The museum, on the east side of the Zihuatanejo main beachfront, has an official address: Plaza Olaf Palme, Paseo del Pescador, Zihuatanejo, Guerrero.

IXTAPA AND ZIHUATANEJO

© BRUCE WHIPPERMAN

Rock outcroppings decorate Playa Madera (Wood Beach) on Zihuatanejo Bay.

IXTAPA AND ZIHUATANEJO

ZIHUATANEJO

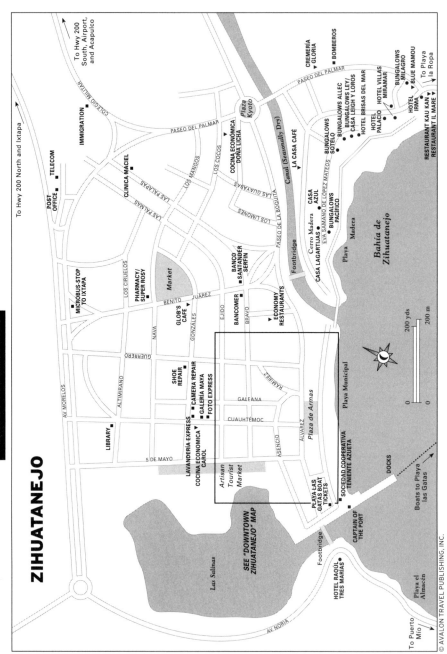

To Hwy 200 North and Ixtapa

To Hwy 200 South, Airport, and Acapulco

COLEGIO MILITAR

IMMIGRATION

TELECOM

POST OFFICE

CLINICA MACIEL

LAS PALMAS

LOS MANGOS

LOS COCOS

PASEO DEL PALMAR

PASEO DEL PALMAR

Plaza Kyoto

CREMERÍA GLORIA

BOMBEROS

BUNGALOWS MILAGRO

To Playa la Ropa

HOTEL VILLAS MIRAMAR

BUNGALOWS ALLEC

BUNGALOWS LEY/ CASA LEIGH Y LOROS

HOTEL BRISAS DEL MAR

HOTEL PALACIO

HOTEL IRMA

BLUE MAMOU

RESTAURANT KAU KAN
RESTAURANT IL MARE

Canal (Seasonally Dry)

LA CASA CAFÉ

BUNGALOWS SOTELO

MICROBUS STOP TO IXTAPA

PHARMACY/ SUPER ROSY

LOS CIRUELOS

Market

COCINA ECONÓMICA DOÑA LICHA

LAS GUAYABAS

LOS LIMONES

PASEO DE LA BOQUITA

Footbridge

Cerro Madera

CASA LAGARTIJAS

CASA AZUL

EVA SAMANO DE LÓPEZ MATEOS

BUNGALOWS PACÍFICO

Playa Madera

Bahía de Zihuatanejo

GLOB'S CAFÉ

BENITO JUÁREZ

BANCO SANTANDER SERFIN

GONZÁLES

EJIDO

BANCOMER

BRAVO

ECONOMY RESTAURANTS

NAVA

GUERRERO

ALTAMIRANO

AV. MORELOS

SHOE REPAIR

CAMERA REPAIR

GALERIA MAYA

FOTO EXPRESS

RAMÍREZ

GALEANA

CUAUHTÉMOC

Plaza de Armas

Playa Municipal

LIBRARY

LAVANDERÍA EXPRESS

COCINA ECONÓMICA CAROL

5 DE MAYO

Artisan Tourist Market

ALVAREZ

ASENCIO

SEE "DOWNTOWN ZIHUATANEJO" MAP

PLAYA LAS GATAS BOAT TICKETS

SOCIEDAD COOPERATIVA TENIENTE AZUETA

DOCKS

Boats to Playa las Gatas

CAPTAIN OF THE PORT

Footbridge

Las Salinas

HOTEL RAÚL TRES MARÍAS

Playa el Almacén

To Puerto Mío

AV. NORIA

To Playa la Ropa

200 yds

200 m

0

0

© AVALON TRAVEL PUBLISHING, INC.

BEACHES AROUND ZIHUATANEJO BAY

Ringed by forested hills, edged by steep cliffs, and laced by rocky shoals, Zihuatanejo Bay would be beautiful even without its beaches. Five of them line the bay.

Playas El Almacén, Municipal, and Madera

Zihuatanejo Bay's west side shelters narrow, tranquil Playa El Almacén (Warehouse Beach), mostly good for fishing from its nearby rocks. Moving east past the pier toward town brings you to the colorful, bustling Playa Municipal. Its sheltered waters are fine for wading, swimming, and boat launching (which anglers, their motors buzzing, regularly do) near the pier end. For maximum sun and serenity, continue walking east away from the pier along Playa Municipal. Cross the pedestrian bridge over the usually dry Agua de Correa creek, which marks the east end of Playa Municipal. Continue along the concrete *andador* that winds about 200 yards along the beachfront rocks that run along the west end of Playa Madera. (If you prefer, you can also hire a taxi to take you to Playa Madera, about $3.)

Playa Madera (Wood Beach), once a loading point for lumber, stretches about 300 yards, decorated with rocky nooks and outcroppings and backed by the lush hotel-dotted hill **Cerro Madera.** The beach sand is fine and gray-white. Swells enter the facing bay entrance, breaking suddenly in two- or three-foot waves that roll in gently and recede with little undertow. Madera's usually calm billows are good for child's play and easy swimming. Bring your mask and snorkel for glimpses of fish in the clear waters. Beachside restaurant/bars at the Hotel Brisas del Mar and the Hotel Irma, above the far east end, serve drinks and snacks.

◖ Playa La Ropa

Zihuatanejo Bay's favorite resort beach is Playa La Ropa (Clothes Beach), a mile-long crescent of yellow-white sand washed by oft-gentle surf.

© BRUCE WHIPPERMAN

Playa Municipal, the main Zihuatanejo town beach, is relaxed, shady, and decorated with fishing *lanchas*.

The beach got its name centuries ago from the apparel that once floated in from a galleon wrecked offshore. From the bay's best *mira-dor* (viewpoint) at the summit of the approach road, **Paseo Costera,** the beach sand, relentlessly scooped and redeposited by the waves, appears as an endless line of half moons.

On the 100-foot-wide beach, vacationers bask in the sun, personal watercraft buzz beyond the breakers, rental sailboats ply the waves, and sailboards rest on the sand. The waves, generally too gentle and quick-breaking for surf sports, break close-in and recede with only mild undertow. Joggers come out mornings and evenings. Restaurants at the several beachfront hotels provide food and drinks.

❰ Playa Las Gatas

Secluded Playa Las Gatas, reachable by very rough shoreline rock-hopping or easily by launch from the town pier, lies sheltered beneath the south-end Punta El Faro headland. Legend has it that the apparent line of rock rubble visible 200 feet off the beach are the remains of a walled-in royal bathing pool that the emperor of the Purépecha people (who still inhabit the highlands of Michoacán) had built to protect his family and friends from the small cat-whiskered nurse sharks that frequent the shoreline. Although the emperor is long gone, the sharks continue to swim off Playa Las Gatas (Cats Beach), named for the sharks' whiskers. (The nurse sharks, however, are harmless; moreover, Las Gatas scuba instructors Thierry and Jean-Claude Duran told me that authoritative archaeological investigators have shown that the rocks are a natural formation.)

Generally calm and quiet, often with super-clear offshore waters, Playa Las Gatas is both a snorkeling haven and a jumping-off spot for dive trips to prime scuba sites. Beach booths rent gear for beach snorkelers, and a professional dive shop right on the beach, Carlo Scuba, instructs and guides both beginner and experienced scuba divers. (For many more diving details, see *Sports and Recreation.*)

For a treat (high season only, however), pass the beach restaurant lineup and continue to

Secluded Playa Las Gatas seems like a beach on some faraway south-seas island.

Owen's *palapa* restaurant (tel. 755/554-8307, 8 A.M.–7 P.M. daily, closed Sept. and Oct.), visible on King's Point, the palm-shaded outcropping past the far curve of the beach. There, enjoy some refreshment, watch the surfers glide around the point, and feast on the luscious beach, bay, and hill views.

IXTAPA INNER BEACHES

Ixtapa's 10 distinct beaches lie scattered like pearls along a dozen miles of creamy, azure coastline. As you move from the Zihuatanejo end, **Playa Hermosa** comes first. The elevators of the super-luxurious clifftop Hotel Brisas Ixtapa make access to the beach very convenient. At the bottom you'll find a few hundred yards of seasonally broad white sand, with open-ocean (but often gentle) waves usually good for most water sports except surfing. Good beach-accessible snorkeling is possible off the shoals at either end of the beach. Extensive rentals are available at the beachfront aquatics shop. A poolside restaurant serves food and drinks. Hotel access is only by car or taxi.

◖ *Teleférico* and Playa del Palmar

For a sweeping vista of Ixtapa's beaches, bay, and blue waters, ride the *teleférico* (cableway, 7 A.M.–11 P.M. daily except Sat. low season) to **El Faro** view restaurant (tel. 755/555-2525 or 755/555-2510, 8 A.M.–10 P.M. daily in high season, 5–10 P.M. daily in low season, breakfast $5–10, lunch $8–15, dinner entrees $14–25) at the south end of Ixtapa's main beach, Playa del Palmar.

Long, broad, and yellow-white, Playa del Palmar could be called the Billion-Dollar Beach for the investment money it attracted to Ixtapa. The confidence seems justified. The broad strand stretches for three gently curving miles. Even though it fronts the open ocean, protective offshore rocks, islands, and shoals keep the surf gentle most of the time. Here, most sports are of the high-powered variety—parasailing ($20), personal watercraft riding and water-skiing ($40), and banana-tubing ($10)—although boogie boards can be rented for $5 an hour on the beach.

Challenging surfing breaks roll in consistently off the jetty at **Playa Escolleros,** at Playa del Palmar's far west end. Bring your own board.

IXTAPA OUTER BEACHES

Ixtapa's outer beaches spread among the coves and inlets a few miles northwest of the Hotel Zone. Drive, bicycle (rentals near HSBC bank, in front of the Hotel Emporio), taxi, take a minibus marked Playa Linda along the Paseo de las Garzas (drivers, turn right just past the shopping mall), then fork left again after less than a mile. After the Marina Golf Course (watch out for crocodiles crossing the road, no joke), the road turns toward the shoreline, winding past a trio of beach gems: Playa San Juan de Dios, Playa Don Rodrigo, and Playa Cuata. Sadly, illegal development has now blocked access to the beaches.

Although Mexican law theoretically allows free public oceanfront access, guards might try to shoo you away from any one of these beaches on the open-ocean side, even if you arrive by boat. If somehow you manage to get there, you will discover a cream-yellow strip of sand, nestled between rocky outcroppings, with oft-gentle waves and correspondingly moderate undertow for good swimming, body-surfing, and boogie boarding. Snorkeling and fishing are equally good around nearby rocks and shoals.

On the peninsula's sheltered northern flank, **Playa Quieta** (Quiet Beach) is a place that lives up to its name. A ribbon of fine yellow sand arcs around a smooth inlet dotted by a regatta of Club Med kayaks and sailboats plying the water. Get there via the north-end access stairway from the parking lot, signed Playa Quieta Acceso Público. Stop by the beachfront restaurant for refreshment or a fresh seafood lunch.

PLAYA LINDA

Playa Linda, the open-ocean yellow-sand beach at road's end, stretches for miles northwest, where it's known as Playa Larga (Long Beach). Flocks of sandpipers and plovers skitter at the surf's edge and pelicans and

© BRUCE WHIPPERMAN

A family of wild crocodiles attracts visitors at Playa Linda.

cormorants dive offshore while gulls, terns, and boobies skim the wavetops. Driftwood and shells decorate the sand beside a green-tufted palm grove that seems to stretch endlessly to the north.

In addition to the beach, mangrove-fringed **Laguna de Ixtapa,** an arm of which extends south to the bridge before the Playa Linda parking lot, is becoming an attraction. The lagoon's star actors are crocodiles that often sun and doze in the water and along the bank beneath the bridge.

Officially, the bicycle path ends at the bridge, but you can continue on foot or by bicycle about 1.5 miles to Barrio Viejo village. Take a hat, water, insect repellent, your binoculars, and your bird-identification book. (For more bicycling information, see the *Sports and Recreation* section.)

The friendly downscale **La Palapa** beach restaurant, at pavement's end, offers beer, sodas, and seafood, plus showers, toilets, and free parking. Neighboring stable **Rancho Playa Linda** (11 A.M.–6 P.M. daily), managed

by friendly "Spiderman" Margarito, provides horseback rides for about $20 per hour.

The flat, wide Playa Linda has powerful rollers often good for surfing. Boogie boarding and bodysurfing—with caution, don't try it alone—are also possible. Surf fishing yields catches, especially of *lisa* (mullet), which locals have much more success netting than hooking.

◖ ISLA IXTAPA

Every few minutes a boat heads from the Playa Linda embarcadero to mile-long Ixtapa Island (9 A.M.–5 P.M. daily; $4 round-trip). Upon arrival, you soon discover the secret to the preservation of the island's pristine beaches, forests, and natural underwater gardens: "No trash here," the *palapa* proprietors say. "We bag it up and send it back to the mainland." And the effort shows. Great fleshy green orchids and bromeliads hang from forest branches, multicolored fish dart among offshore rocks, shady native acacias hang lazily over the shell-decorated sands of the island's little beaches.

Boats from Playa Linda arrive at **Playa Cuachalatate** (koo-ah-chah-lah-TAH-tay), the island's most popular beach, named for a local tree whose bark is said to relieve liver ailments. Many visitors stay all day, splashing, swimming, and eating fresh fish, shrimp, and clams cooked at any one of a dozen beachfront *palapas*. Visitors also enjoy the many sports and equipment on offer: water skis ($50/half hour), banana-tube rides ($5), fishing-boat rentals ($60/half day), aquatic bicycles ($6/hr), snorkel gear ($3/hr), and kayaks ($5/hr).

For a change of scene, follow the short concrete walkway over the west-side (to the right as you arrive) forested knoll to **Playa Varadero** and **Playa Coral** on opposite flanks of an intimate little isthmus. Varadero's yellow-white sand is narrow and tree-shaded, and its waters are calm and clear. Behind it lies Playa Coral, a steep coral-sand beach fronting a rocky blue bay. Playa Coral is a magnet for beach lovers, snorkelers, and the scuba divers who often arrive by boat to explore the waters around the offshore coral reef.

Scuba diving is so rewarding here that a dive

Ixtapa's Playa Linda and Isla Ixtapa (in horizon silhouette) are too lovely not to visit.

© BRUCE WHIPPERMAN

shop, **Oliverio,** is operated by the sons of the late founder, near the west end of Playa Cuachalatate. Other shops in Zihuatanejo (see *Sports and Recreation*) are better equipped to provide the same services, however.

Isla Ixtapa's fourth and smallest beach, secluded **Playa Carey,** is named for the sea-turtle species (see the sidebar "Saving Turtles" in the *Costa Grande* chapter). For access, hire a boat from Playa Cuachalatate.

Accommodations

The Ixtapa and Zihuatanejo area is one of the Mexican Pacific Coast's loveliest but also most highly seasonal resorts. Hotels and restaurants are most likely to be full during the sunny winter–spring high season, customarily beginning about December 20 and running through Easter week. Low season begins during the oft-hot dry months of May and June and continues until early December. Some restaurants even shut down during September and October. Nevertheless, for those who crave peace and quiet, bargain hotel prices, just-right balmy weather, and lush verdure, late fall—mid-October through

mid-December—is an excellent time to visit. Hotel rates listed here as "low season" are the prices you're most likely to encounter most of the year. Prices listed as "high season" are generally the steeper rates that you will encounter during the Christmas–New Year's and Easter holidays. Hotels are grouped by location—Zihuatanejo Downtown, Zihuatanejo Playa La Madera, Zihuatanejo Playa La Ropa, Ixtapa, and Ixtapa Playa Linda—and listed in ascending order of low-season price in each section.

Zihuatanejo and Ixtapa hotels divide themselves by location (and largely by price) between

IXTAPA OR ZIHUATANEJO?

Your choice of local lodging sharply determines the tone of your stay. Zihuatanejo still resembles the colorful seaside village that visitors have enjoyed for years. Fishing *pangas* decorate its beach side, while *panaderías*, *taquerías*, and *papelerías* line its narrow shady lanes. Many of its hotels – budget to moderate, with spartan but clean fan-only rooms – reflect the tastes of the bargain-conscious travelers who "discovered" Zihuatanejo during the 1960s.

Ixtapa, on the other hand, mirrors the fashionwise preferences of new-generation Mexican and international vacationers. A broad boulevard fronts your Ixtapa hotel, while on the beach side thatch-shaded chairs on a wide strand, a palmy garden, blue pool, and serene outdoor restaurant are yours to enjoy. Upstairs, your air-conditioned room – typically in plush pastels, with private sea-view balcony, marble bath, room service, and your favorite TV shows by satellite – brings maximum convenience and comfort to a lush tropical setting.

Actually, you needn't be forced to choose. Split your hotel time between Ixtapa and Zihuatanejo and enjoy both worlds.

the budget-to-moderate downtown and more expensive Playa Madera, Playa La Ropa, and Ixtapa. For more information on most Zihuatanejo and Ixtapa lodgings, visit the excellent websites www.zihuatanejo.net and www.ixtapa-zihuatanejo.com, or individual hotel websites listed. Although Zihuatanejo hotels (with the few exceptions noted) provide little or no wheelchair access, all accommodations described in the *Ixtapa Hotels* section do.

ZIHUATANEJO DOWNTOWN HOTELS
Under $50

Right in the middle of the downtown beachfront action is **Casa de Huéspedes Elvira** (Paseo del Pescador 9, Zihuatanejo, Guerrero 40880, tel. 755/554-2061), operated since 1956 by its founder, Elvira R. Campos. Every day, Elvira looks after her little garden of flowering plants, feeds rice to her birds—both wild and caged—and passes the time with friends and guests. She tells of the "way it used to be" when all passengers and supplies arrived from Acapulco by boat, local *almejas* (clams) were as big as cabbages, and you could pluck fish right out of the bay with your hands. Her petite eight-room lodging divides into an upstairs section, with more light and privacy, and a lower, with private baths. The leafy, intimate lower patio leads to the airy upper level via a pair of quaint plant-decorated spiral staircases. The rooms themselves are small, authentically rustic, and clean. The four upper rooms share a bathroom and toilet. Rates run about $10 s or d, $15 t low season and $11 s, $15 d, $22 high. If nighttime noise bothers you, bring earplugs; TV and music from Elvira's adjoining restaurant continues until about 11 P.M. most evenings during the winter high season.

On the west side, across the lagoon-mouth by footbridge from the end of Paseo del Pescador, is the **Hotel Raoúl Tres Marias** (Noria 4, Colonia Lázaro Cárdenas, Zihuatanejo, Guerrero 40880, tel. 755/554-2191). Its longtime popularity derives from its (formerly) low prices and the colorful lagoon-front boat scene, visible from porches outside some of its 25 rooms. Otherwise, facilities are strictly bare-bones, with only room-temperature water. Rooms rent for a modest $10 s, $20 d, $25 t low season and $28 s, $38 d, $48 t high season, with fans and most with private baths.

A few blocks north and west, find unpretentious guesthouse (**Casa de Huéspedes Idalia** (Guerrero 9, Zihuatanejo, Guerrero 40880, tel. 755/554-2062). The grandmotherly owner offers two floors of about a dozen plain but clean rooms, with room-temperature-only shower baths. Idalia's guests enjoy an airy upstairs corridor-view porch, furnished with hammocks, rocking chairs, and shelves of thick paperback books. Rentals go for $15 s, $20 d,

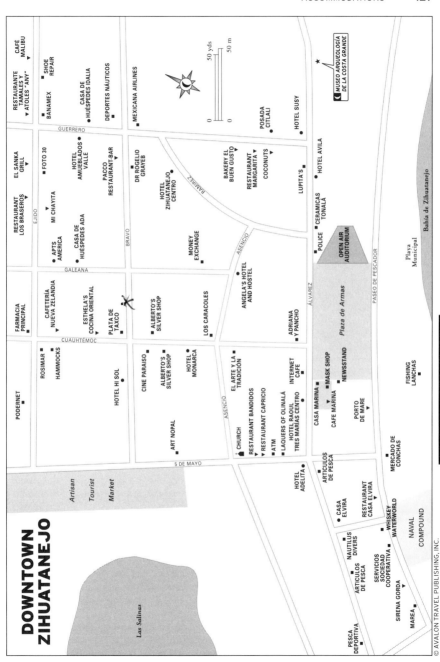

DOWNTOWN ZIHUATANEJO

IXTAPA AND ZIHUATANEJO

50 yds
50 m

Bahía de Zihuatanejo

MUSEO ARQUEOLOGÍA DE LA COSTA GRANDE

CAFÉ MALIBU
RESTAURANTE TAMALES Y ATOLES "ANY"
SHOE REPAIR
BANAMEX
CASA DE HUÉSPEDES IDALIA
DEPORTES NÁUTICOS
MEXICANA AIRLINES
POSADA CITLALI
HOTEL SUSY

GUERRERO

EL SANKA GRILL
FOTO 30
HOTEL AMUEBLADOS VALLE
PACCO RESTAURANT-BAR
DR ROGELIO GRAYEB
BAKERY EL BUEN GUSTO
RESTAURANT MARGARITA
COCONUTS
LUPITA'S
HOTEL AVILA

EJIDO

RESTAURANT LOS BRASEROS
MI CHAYITA
APTS AMERICA
CASA DE HUÉSPEDES ADA
HOTEL ZIHUATANEJO CENTRO
MONEY EXCHANGE
RAMÍREZ
BRAVO
ASENCIO

CERAMICAS TONALÁ
POLICE

GALEANA

FARMACIA PRINCIPAL
CAFETERÍA NUEVA ZELANDIA
ESTHELA'S COCINA ORIENTAL
PLATA DE TAXCO
ALBERTO'S SILVER SHOP
LOS CARACOLES
ANGELA'S HOTEL AND HOSTEL
ADRIANA Y PANCHO
ALVAREZ
OPEN AIR AUDITORIUM
Playa Municipal

CUAUHTÉMOC

ROSIMAR
HAMMOCKS
PODERNET
HOTEL HI SOL
CINE PARAISO
ALBERTO'S SILVER SHOP
HOTEL MONARCA
EL ARTE Y LA TRADICIÓN
INTERNET CAFE
MASK SHOP
NEWSSTAND
Plaza de Armas
PASEO DE PESCADOR

ART NOPAL
ASENCIO
CHURCH
RESTAURANT BANDIDOS
RESTAURANT CAPRICIO
ATM
LAQUERS OF OLINALÁ
HOTEL RAOUL TRES MARÍAS CENTRO
CASA MARINA
CAFE MARINA
PORTO DE MARE
FISHING LANCHAS

5 DE MAYO

Artisan Tourist Market

HOTEL ADELITA
ARTICULOS DE PESCA
MERCADO DE CONCHAS

CASA ELVIRA
RESTAURANT CASA ELVIRA
WHISKEY WATERWORLD
NAVAL COMPOUND

NAUTILUS DIVERS
ARTICULOS DE PESCA
SERVICIOS SOCIEDAD COOPERATIVA
SIRENA GORDA
MAREA
PESCA DEPORTIVA

Las Salinas

with fans only, or $35 s or d, with air-conditioning and TV.

Downhill, a block from the beach, budget-conscious travelers will appreciate the attractive 🄲 **Angela's Hotel and Hostel** (Ascencio 10, Zihuatanejo, Guerrero 40880, tel. 755/554-5084, angelashostel@hotmail.com, www.zihuatanejo.com.mx/angelas), competently managed by friendly Angela Villalobos and Gregg Thompson. They offer a range of clean, invitingly rustic fan-only accommodations, including private rooms with beds for kids ($22 d, $27 t) and dormitories (male, female, and mixed, $9 per person).

In the same neighborhood a block east, **Hotel Susy** (corner of Guerrero and Álvarez, Zihuatanejo, Guerrero 40880, tel./fax 755/554-2339) offers three floors of rooms around a shady inner patio. The seven upper-floor bayside rooms have private view balconies. Inside corridors unfortunately run past room windows, necessitating closing curtains for privacy, a drawback in these fan-only rooms. Avoid traffic noise by requesting an upper-floor room away from the street. The 20 clean but plain rooms go for $20 s, $25 d (in one bed), $35 d or t (in two beds) low season, and $25 s, $30 d, $40 t high, including fans and hot water.

Next door, another good moderately priced choice, if you don't mind a bit of morning noise from the adjacent school, is the popular 🄲 **Posada Citlali** (Guerrero 3, Zihuatanejo, Guerrero 40880, tel./fax 755/554-2043). The hotel (Citlali means star in Náhuatl) rises in a pair of three-story tiers around a shady, plant-decorated inner courtyard. The 20 plain, rather small, but clean rooms are all thankfully removed from direct street-traffic hubbub. Guests on the upper floors experience less corridor traffic and consequently enjoy more privacy. Reservations are mandatory during the high season and strongly recommended at other times. Rates run about $30 s, $40 d, $45 t low season and $40 s, $50 d, $55 t high, with hot water and fans.

Its location near the pier draws many fishing enthusiasts to the **Hotel Raoúl Tres Marias**

Centro (Juan Álvarez and Cinco de Mayo, Zihuatanejo, Guerrero 40880, tel./fax 755/554-6706, garroboscrew@prodigy.net.mx). Some of the 18 rooms have private balconies looking out on the street below. Newcomers might pick up some local fishing pointers after dinner at the hotel's restaurant, Los Garrobos. Rooms go for about $35 s or d, $55 t low season and $70 and $80 high season, with hot water and air-conditioning.

On a quiet midtown east-side lane, find the big **Hotel Zihuatanejo Centro** (Ramírez 2, Zihuatanejo, Guerrero 40880, tel. 755/554-2669, 755/554-5330, or 755/554-5340, fax 755/554-6897, zihuacentro@prodigy.net.mx, www.ixtapa-zihuatanejo.net/zihuacenter, $40 d low season, $60 d high), a favorite of Mexican families. Hotel guests are sheltered from the town hubbub by rooms that face inward on to an inviting pool-courtyard. The approximately 75 rooms rising in four floors are clean and simply but comfortably furnished in pastels and vinyl floor tile. Some rooms have two double beds, others have one king- or queen-size bed. For more air and light, ask for a room with a balcony. Rooms have air-conditioning, fans, TV, and hot-water showers; parking and a restaurant are on-site. Credit cards are accepted.

A block north stands **Hotel Amueblados Valle** (Guerrero 33, Zihuatanejo, Guerrero 40880, tel. 755/554-2084, fax 755/554-3220). Inside the front door, find eight units in three floors around an inviting inner patio. The apartments themselves, all with kitchenettes and either one or two bedrooms and shower baths, are clean, spacious, and comfortably furnished. Upper units are breezier and lighter. One-bedroom units go for about $40 s or d; two bedrooms about $60 for up to five persons. Discounts are possible for monthly rentals. All with TV and fans, but no parking facilities.

A block east, guests at **Apartments America** (Galeana 16, Zihuatanejo, Guerrero 40880, tel. 755/554-4337, zihuatanejoamerica7@hotmail .com) enjoy a choice, shady, traffic-free location. The 10 one- and two-bedroom kitchenette apartments, stacked in two floors around an inner patio-corridor, are plainly but comfortably furnished with tile floors, bedspreads, curtains, and well-maintained shower baths. Choose an upstairs apartment for more light and air. The one-bedroom apartments, sleeping one or two adults, rent for about $30/day, $500/month. The two-bedroom units, sleeping up to six, go for about $40/day, $600/month. Add $10/day for air-conditioning and 20 percent during the winter. All come with TV and fans.

Next door, sharing the same tranquil street-front as Apartments America, stands Ada Aburto Pineda's modest guesthouse, **⬛ Casa de Huéspedes Ada** (Galeana 14, Zihuatanejo, Guerrero 40880, tel. 755/554-2186, nos@prodigy.net.mx). Her seven rentals differ markedly. Downstairs, she offers three plain, dark, small but clean rooms, two with fans, one with air-conditioning. Her four upstairs accommodations are much larger and lighter and much more recommendable. Two are airy, multiroom kitchenette apartments with fans, accommodating up to four or five people. They open to a spacious, leafy front porch overlooking the shady street scene below. The two remaining upstairs units are in the rear and are smaller but still comfortable and clean, with fans and double beds. The larger of the two has a kitchenette. The big upstairs apartments rent for $50 d low season, $60 d high, or $500/month in low season, $1,200 high. The smaller upstairs kitchenette goes for $30 d low, $40 d high, or $300/month low, $700 high; the nonkitchenette, $20 d low, $25 d high. All units come with private baths and TV, but no parking.

$50-100

Right in the middle of downtown, overlooking the hubbub, is compact **Hotel Monarca** (Cuauhtémoc 13, Zihuatanejo, Guerrero 40880, tel./fax 755/554-2030 or 744/553-2922). Choose from six attractive kitchenette (microwave only) studios in three floors. Units are clean, airy, and comfortable; two have private view balconies. They accommodate two to four people with combinations of double and single beds. Rentals run a reasonable $50 d per day, $1,200 per month, all with TV, refrigerator, fans, and coffeemaker.

Fishing parties are steady customers at the **Hotel Hi-Sol** (Bravo 120, Zihuatanejo, Guerrero 40880, tel./fax 755/554-0595), three blocks from the beach. The hotel offers two floors of around a dozen spacious, clean, semideluxe rooms. All have shiny shower baths and are invitingly decorated with tile and cheery yellow and blue motif bedspreads and curtains. All rooms open to airy, private street-view balconies. Rates run about $50 s or d, $60 t, and $70 q low season and $80 s or d, $90 t, and $100 q high; with TV, fans, and telephone.

Hotel Ávila (Juan Álvarez 8, Zihuatanejo, Guerrero 40880, tel./fax 755/554-2010), downtown Zihuatanejo's only beachfront hostelry, is popular for its location. Rooms, although simply decorated, are comfortable. Guests in the hotel's several beachfront rooms enjoy luxurious private-patio bay and beach views. If possible avoid taking a room on the noisy streetfront side. The 27 rooms rent for about $60 s or d with view and $50 without in the low season. Corresponding high-season rates are about $70 s or d with view, $60 without. All rooms have fans, TV, air-conditioning, phones, and hot water. Credit cards are accepted.

ZIHUATANEJO PLAYA MADERA HOTELS

Another sizable fraction of Zihuatanejo's lodgings spreads along and above Playa Madera on the east side of the bay, easily reachable in a few blocks on foot from the town plaza, via the scenic beachfront *andador* (walkway). Many of the lodgings are picturesquely perched along leafy Calle Eva Samano de López Mateos, that runs atop Cerro Madera, the bayfront hill just east of town, while others dot Avenida Adelita at the foot of Cerro Madera. Guests in all of the Playa Madera lodgings described below enjoy direct beach access by simply strolling a block or less downhill to luscious Playa Madera.

Note: Because of Zihuatanejo's one-way streets (which fortunately direct most noisy traffic away from downtown), getting to Cerro Madera by car is a bit tricky. The key is Plaza Kyoto, the traffic-circle intersection of Paseo de la Boquita and Paseo del Palmar a quarter mile east of downtown. Keep a sharp eye out and follow the small Zona Hotelera signs. At Plaza Kyoto, marked by a big Japanese *torii* gate, bear right across the canal bridge and turn right at the first street, Señora de los Remedios. Continue for another block to Avenida Adelita, address of several Playa Madera hotels, which runs along the base of Cerro Madera. At Adelita, continue straight uphill to the lane that runs atop Cerro Madera, Calle Eva Samano de López Mateos.

Under $50

Playa Madera's only beachfront low-end lodging is the circa-1960s **Bungalows Allec** (Calle Eva Samano de López Mateos, Cerro Madera, Zihuatanejo, Guerrero 40880, tel./fax 755/554-2002, buallec@hotmail.com, www.ixtapa-zihuatanejo.net/bun_allec). Comfortable, light, and spacious although worn, the 12 clean, fan-only apartments have breezy bay views from private balconies. Six of the units are very large, sleeping up to six, with kitchenettes. The others are smaller doubles without kitchenette. No pool, but Playa Madera is a few steps downhill. The kitchenette apartments go for about $80 low season, $140 high; the smaller doubles are about $45 low, $80 high. Long-term discounts may be available.

A couple of blocks inland from the beach find the downscale but homey **Bungalows El Milagro** (Av. Marina Nacional s/n, Playa Madera, P.O. Box 71, Zihuatanejo, Guerrero 40880, tel. 755/554-3045, klausbuhrer@hotmail.com), the project of Dr. Niklaus Bührer and his wife, Lucina Gomes. A haciendalike walled compound of cottages and apartments clustering around a shady pool, Bungalows El Milagro is winter headquarters for a cordial group of German longtime returnees. The friendly atmosphere and the inviting pool and garden account for the El Milagro's success, rather than the plain but clean kitchenette lodgings, which vary in style from rustic to 1940s motel. Look at several before you choose. The 17 units rent (excepting Christmas–New Year's, and Easter holidays) for about $50 d ($700/month) for the smaller rooms to about $80 ($1,100/month) for the larger, six-person suites. All come with kitchenettes, hot water, fans, pool, and parking.

$50-100

On Avenida Adelita, right above the beach, stands the longtime Mexican family-run **Hotel Palacio** (Av. Adelita, Playa Madera, P.O. Box 57, Zihuatanejo, Guerrero 40880, tel./fax 755/554-2055, hotelpalacio@prodigy.net.mx), a beachfront maze of rooms connected by meandering, multilevel walkways. Room windows along the two main tiers face corridor walkways, where curtains must be drawn for privacy. Upper units fronting the quiet street avoid this drawback. The rooms themselves are clean, renovated, brightly decorated, and comfortable, with fans or air-conditioning and hot water. Guests enjoy a small but very pleasant bay-view pool, kiddie pool, and sundeck, which perches above the waves at the hotel beachfront. Low season rentals run about $45 s, $55 d with fan, $50 s and $60 d with air-conditioning, all with TV and hot water, but street parking only. Add about 20 percent during holidays.

Back uphill on Cerro Madera, consider a pair of home-in-a-home style lodgings. First, find **Casa Lagartija** (Calle Eva Samano de López Mateos 43, Zihuatanejo, Guerrero 40880, tel. 755/554-9391, larbym41@bigplanet.com, www.casa-lagartija.com), named for the *lagartijas* (geckos) that benignly inhabit tropical area houses such as this one. Personable owner Joan Rubaloff rents two clean, spacious, and comfortable two-bedroom fan-only apartments for two to six people, with kitchen, living-dining room, and full bath. Rentals go for about $60 d low season, $75 d high. Add $10 for each additional person.

A few doors away, 🌙 **Casa Azul** (tel. 755/554-3534, marsha_gould@msn.com, www.mexonline.com/sucasita.htm) offers similar good value and restful ambience. Owner Marsha Gould likewise rents two apartments, an upper and a lower. The upper is a tropical hideaway for two or three, with a luxurious *palapa* roof, kitchenette, loft bedroom with king-size bed, and an airy bay view from both the shower and the private balcony. The larger apartment, downstairs, is equally comfortable, but darker, with two bedrooms sleeping up to six, with bath, living-dining room, and a back garden town-view patio. The upper unit rents for $85 d, the lower for $70 d; add $5 for each extra person, and $20 for holidays. All are nonsmoking. Marsha closes down from about May 1 until mid-October, when you can contact her in Denver, Colorado, at U.S. tel. 303/458-8630. (She also rents a deluxe view condo, Buena Vista del Mar, for about $85 d, $105 d Christmas–New Year's, on the same quiet street. Visit www.mexonline.com/vistadelmar.htm or contact the owner, Linda Schanfein, directly at U.S. tel. 415/332-6929, zihuaview@hotmail.com.)

Several apartment bungalow–style complexes cluster along the same scenic Cerro Madera hilltop street. Although their details differ, their basic layouts—which stair-step artfully downhill to private beachfront gardens—are similar. Typical among them is **Bungalows Sotelo** (Calle Eva Samano de López Mateos 13, Zihuatanejo, Guerrero 40880, tel./fax 755/554-6307). Guests in a number of the clean stucco-and-tile apartments enjoy spacious private or semiprivate terraces with deck lounges and bay views. Rents for the few smaller units without kitchenette run about $45 d low season, $70 high; larger kitchenette suites rent for about $75 d low season, $120 high (for one bedroom) and $120 low season, $150 high (for two bedrooms). Some readers have commented that the loose Bungalows Sotelo management leaves something to be desired. Rentals vary; look at more than one before deciding. No pool, street parking only, but with air-conditioning; get your winter reservations in early.

Also atop Cerro Madera, consider the spiffy **(** **Bungalows Ley** (Calle Eva Samano de López Mateos s/n, Playa Madera, P.O. Box 466, Zihuatanejo, Guerrero 40880, tel. 755/554-4087, fax 755/554-1365, bungalowsley@prodigy.net.mx). Here, several white-stucco studio apartments stair-step directly

downhill to heavenly Playa Madera. Their recent decorations show nicely. Bathrooms shine with flowery Mexican tile, hammocks hang in spacious, rustic-chic *palapa*-roofed view patios, and bedrooms glow with wall art, native wood details, and soothing pastel bedspreads. Except for a two-bedroom kitchenette unit at the top, all are kitchenette studios. No pool, but the beach is straight down the steps from your door. The fan-only studios run about $60 d low season, $92 high. The beautiful two-bedroom unit with air-conditioning runs $110 low season, $170 high. Long-term low-season discounts (of 15–30 percent for 6- to 21-night stays) are available.

Back downhill, the **(** **Hotel Villas Miramar** (Av. Adelita, Playa Madera, P.O. Box 211, Zihuatanejo, Guerrero 40880, tel. 755/554-2106, fax 755/554-2149, villasm@prodigy.net.mx) clusters artfully around gardens of pools, palms, and leafy potted plants. The gorgeous, manicured layout makes maximum use of space, creating both privacy and intimacy in a small setting. The designer rooms have high ceilings, split levels, built-in sofas, and large, comfortable beds. The street divides the hotel into two different but lovely sections, each with its own pool. The restaurant, especially convenient for breakfast, is in the shoreside section but still serves guests who sun and snooze around the luxurious, beach-view pool-patio on the other side of the street. The garden rooms rent for about $65 d low season, $75 high; the ocean-view apartments about $75 d low, $85 high; all have phones and air-conditioning, some have wheelchair access. Credit cards are accepted. Additional discounts may be available during May–Dec. 15 low season. Reservations strongly recommended during the high season.

Half a block east, overlooking the beach, **(** **Hotel Irma** (Av. Adelita, Playa Madera, Zihuatanejo, Guerrero 40880, tel./fax 755/554-8003 or 755/554-8472, fax 755/554-3738, www.mexicocondores.com/zihuatanejo/hotelirma) remains a favorite of longtime lovers of Zihuatanejo, if for no reason other than its location. Guests enjoy very comfortable renovated deluxe rooms, a passable sunset-view terrace restaurant and bar, and a pair of blue pools perched above the bay. A short walk downhill and you're at creamy Madera beach. Best of all, many of the front-tier rooms have private balconies with just about the loveliest view on Playa Madera. The 70 rooms rent for about $70 s or d low season, $90 high, with view ($60 low and $65 high without view), all with air-conditioning, TV, and hot water. Low-season packages and discounts may be available May–June and September–November. Rooms can be reserved directly with the hotel or through the agency Mexico Condo Reservations (toll-free U.S./Can. tel. 800/262-4500, info@mcrx.com, www.mcrx.com).

Over $100

One of the fanciest Cerro Madera options is the **Hotel Brisas del Mar** (Calle Eva Samano de López Mateos s/n, Cerro Madera, Zihuatanejo, Guerrero 40880, tel. 755/554-8332 or 755/554-2142, fax 755/544-6710, info@hotel.brisasdel-mar.com, www.brisasdelmar.com). Owners have completely renovated the original complex and have added a big new wing of a dozen spacious, rustic-chic view suites with native Mexico decor to the original 20 apartments. The brightest spot of this entire complex, besides its sweeping bay views, is the hotel's lovely beach club, with its shady *palapas,* lounge chairs, and big blue pool. For such amenities, Brisas del Mar asks premium prices. Its original (but upgraded) fan-only apartments rent for about $100 d low season, $150 high, with cable TV. For the spacious new-wing junior suites, expect to pay about $120 low season, $200 high, all with air-conditioning and cable TV.

Next door, perched atop Bungalows Ley, with the same address but completely separate, is upscale **Casa Leigh y Loros** (Calle Eva Samano de López Mateos s/n, Playa Madera, Zihuatanejo, Guerrero 40880) the lovely life project of personable Californian Leigh Roth and her pet parrot, Loros. Casa Leigh y Loros, which Leigh rents when she's away, is a multi-tilevel, art-decorated, white-stucco-and-tile, two-bedroom, two-bath villa with roof gar-

den, airy bay-view balconies, and up-to-date kitchen appliances. High winter season (except Christmas) rent runs about $195/day, with fans only, $230 with air-conditioning, $1,500/week; during low season, Leigh asks $175/day fan only, $180 with air-conditioning, $1,150/week. With TV and daily maid service; cooking is available at an extra charge. Leigh also rents a number of smaller but similarly luxurious apartments in villa **Casa San Sebastián** on the hillside, a mile away, above Playa La Ropa. For a more economical option, ask Leigh (or Lila, as she's known locally) about **Bamboo Bungalow** which she also rents, across the street from Casa Leigh y Loros. Contact her or her agent at tel. 755/554-3755 or 755/554-7405, zihua01@earthlink.net, www.zihuatanejo-rentals.com. She also acts as agent for a number of small luxury hotels, bed-and-breakfasts, and villas, mostly along Playa Madera and Playa Ropa.

A few hundred yards farther east along cliffside Paseo Costera toward Playa La Ropa, find ☪ **La Casa Que Canta** (Camino Escénico a Playa La Ropa, Zihuatanejo, Guerrero 40880, tel. 755/555-7030 or 755/555-7000, toll-free Mex. tel. 800/710-9345 or U.S. tel. 888/523-5050, fax 755/554-7900, info@lacasaquecanta, www.lacasaquecanta.com), which is as much a work of art as a hotel. The pageant begins at the lobby, a luxurious soaring *palapa* that angles gracefully down the cliffside to an intimate open-air view dining-room. Suite-clusters of natural adobe sheltered by thick *palapa* roofs cling artfully to the craggy precipice decorated with riots of bougainvillea and gardens of cactus. From petite pool terraces perched above foamy shoals, guests enjoy a radiant aqua bay panorama in the morning and brilliant ridge-silhouetted sunsets in the evening. The 18 art-bedecked, rustic-chic suites, all with private view balconies, come in three grades: super deluxe "terrace" rooms, more spacious "grand suites," and even more spacious and luxurious "master suites," the latter two options with their own small pools. Low-season rentals run about $470, $540, and $780 respectively; high season $530, $620, and $880. Low-season discounts may be available. All come with air-conditioning, fans, and phone, but no TV; no kids under 16 allowed. Make winter reservations very early.

(*Note:* Casa Que Canta now offers the best of all possible upscale worlds within its present grounds: the El Murmullo super-private 10,000-square-foot four-villa inner sanctum compound, built for a maharaja, with complete all-exclusive staff, from gardener, chambermaids, and butler, to waiters, kitchen staff, and gourmet chefs, all for only $3,500 daily.)

ZIHUATANEJO PLAYA LA ROPA HOTELS $50-100

For Playa La Ropa's most moderately priced lodging, go nearly all the way to the end of the road to the **Hotel Casa del Mar** (Playa La Ropa, Zihuatanejo, Guerrero, 40880, tel./fax 755/554-3873, email reserv@zihua-casadelmar.com, www.zihua-casadelmar or www.zihuatanejo-rentals.com/casadelmar/.htm), founded by scuba master Juan Barnard Avila and his wife, Margo. In the mid-1990s, Juan and Margo renovated an old hotel, cleaned up the adjacent mangrove lagoon and nurtured its wildlife (dozens of bird species and a number of crocodiles) back to health. They added 14 units around a rear jungle-garden and pool-patio. Now, new owners carry on Juan and Margo's ecological mission, with a restful hotel and beachfront restaurant where guests may stay and relax for a week or a season, enjoy wholesome food and friendly people, and sample the good snorkeling, scuba diving, kayaking, turtle hatching, and fishing available right from the beach. Choose your room from one of two sections: beach view in front, or garden view in back. All rooms are immaculate and simply but comfortably furnished with handsomely handcrafted wooden beds, lamps, and cabinets. Low-season rentals run about $60 fan only, $75 air-conditioning; $105 and $120 high; all with hot water, parking, and small tank pool. Reservations are mandatory in winter.

Back at the Zihuatanejo end of the beach, where luscious Playa La Ropa begins, is

Hotel Sotavento (P.O. Box 2, Zihuatanejo, Guerrero 40880, tel. 755/554-2032 or 755/554-2024, fax 755/554-2975, info@beachresortsotavento.com.mx, www.beachresortsotavento.com.mx). Good hands-on owner-management keeps the rambling complex, which perches on a leafy bayview hillside, healthy. The Sotavento is a big 70-room mod-style stucco warren-on-pillars that stair-steps five floors down a verdant tropical forest slope. Each floor of rooms opens to a broad, hammock-hung communal terrace overlooking the beach and bay. Inside, the rooms are spartan 1960s-style, clean, comfortable, and spacious, most opening onto the view terrace, with king- or queen-size beds and ceiling fans. Low-season rates begin at about $65 d for a nonview room, $75 d for view, rising to about $110 for the largest deluxe family-sized bungalows. Prices often double during the Christmas–New Year's and Easter holidays. (*Note:* Views, light, and shade depend on your room's vertical position in the layout. Guests in upper-level rooms enjoy expansive bay and sunset vistas, while guests in less-pricey, lower-level rooms nevertheless enjoy intimate tropical verdure-framed sunset vistas of the bay beyond. Look at both kinds of rooms before choosing.) The Hotel Sotavento's amenities include a beachside pool, room fans, parking, restaurants, and a beach aquatics shop; credit cards are accepted.

Among the dozen-odd hotels, bungalow complexes, and restaurants that sprinkle the La Ropa beachfront is a trio of comfortable housekeeping bungalow-type complexes that share the same choice shoreline as the renowned Hotel Villa del Sol (see below), but offer lodging at much more modest prices.

One of these is ◖ **Bungalows Urracas** (Playa La Ropa, Zihuatanejo, Guerrero 40880, tel. 755/554-2053 (Spanish), fax 755/554-2049), about 15 petite brick cottages, like proper rubber planter's bungalows out of Somerset Maugham's *Malaysian Stories,* nestling in a shady jungle of leafy plants, trees, and vines. Inside, the illusion continues: dark, masculine wood furniture, spacious bedrooms, shiny tiled kitchenettes and baths, and rustic beamed ceilings overhead. From the bungalows, short "jungle" paths lead to the brilliant La Ropa beachfront. About eight additional bungalows occupy beachfront view locations in front. Amenities include private, shady front porches (use insect repellent in the evenings), hot water, and fans. Rentals run a bargain $70 d low season, $80 high. Ask for a long-term discount. Get your winter reservations in early.

In contrast nearby, is **Bungalows Vepao** (Playa La Ropa, Zihuatanejo, Guerrero 40880, www.vepao.com). Here, owner Gonzalo Ramírez offers a clean, pleasantly tranquil beach lodging, simply but architecturally designed, with floor-to ceiling drapes, modern-standard kitchenettes, tiled floors, shower baths, white stucco walls, and pastel bedspreads and shaded lamps. Guests in each of the six side-by side apartments enjoy front patios (upper ones have some bay view) that lead right to the hotel's private row of beachfront *palapas* a few steps away. Rates run about $75 d low season, $85 high, with parking, fans, and long-term discounts possible. Reserve through the owner, tel. 755/554-3619 (in Spanish), vepaozg@prodigy.net.mx; or friendly manager Margarita Castro, tel. 755/554-2631 (in Spanish), at her house at the back (by the entrance gate) of the property.

On the same property, also find **☾ Casa Gloria Maria** (755/554-2055, www.zihuatanejo.net/casagloriamaria, casagloriamaria@hotmail.com), a designer white stucco beachfront house of four apartments. Each of the deluxe units (two upstairs and two down) is attractively decorated with native rustic tile floors, bright floral tile baths, and whimsical hand-painted wall designs at the head of the two queen-sized beds. Each unit has its own kitchenette in an outdoor beachview patio. For more breeze and privacy, ask for one of the top-floor units. Rentals run about $90 low season, $110 high, with air-conditioning, hot water baths, and parking. For reservations, go through the Bungalows Vepao contacts, or call or email the owner. For more information, visit www.zihuatanejo.net/casagloriamaria, or agent

Leigh Roth at zihua01@earthlink.net, www.zihuatanejo-rentals.com

Back near the Zihuatanejo end, a block off the beach, **☾ Villas Ema** perches at the top of a flowery hillside garden. Here, the enterprising husband-and-wife owners of downtown Posada Citlali have built kitchenette apartments, beautifully furnished with white tile floors, matching floral drapes and bedspreads, modern-standard shower baths, plenty of windows for light, and sliding doors leading to private view porches for reading and relaxing. Amenities include air-conditioning or fans, hot water, a beautiful blue pool, and the murmur of the waves on Playa La Ropa nearby. Rates for the nine smaller units, with kitchen in common, run about $80 d low season, $110 high. The three top-level units, although sunnier (and consequently warmer), have the best views and most privacy. A pair of ground-level larger *villitas,* each with its own kitchen and patio and sleeping four, rent for about $100 d each in low season, $130 high. For reservations, highly recommended in winter, contact the owners through Posada Citlali (Av. Guerrero 3, Zihuatanejo, Guerrero 40880, tel./fax 755/554-2043 or at home (in Spanish) tel. 755/554-4880, villasema@zihuatanejo.com.mx). To avoid confusion, be sure to specify your reservation is for Villas Ema.

Next door (uphill), the 40-odd *cabañas,* rooms, and suites of the neighboring **Catalina Beach Resort** (tel. 755/554-9321, 755/554-9322, 755/554-9323, 755/554-9324, or 755/554-9325; toll-free Mex. tel. 800/640-1111, U.S. tel. 877/287-2411, or Can. tel. 866/485-4312; fax 755/554-2137, info@catalinabeachresort.com, www.catalinabeachresort.com) are scattered picturesquely beneath shady hillside trees all the way down to the beach. The Catalina's comfortably appointed tropical-rustic lodgings maximize privacy, being mostly semi-detached units with individual view terraces and hammocks, in four categories: small casitas, standard casitas, and standard bungalows (all with fan only) and deluxe bungalows (with a/c). Low-season rates run about $70, $80, $100, and

$120, respectively; high season, $120, $150, $180, and $190. Hotel amenities include a beachfront aquatics shop offering sailing, sailboarding, snorkeling, and other rentals. Those who simply want to rest can enjoy chairs beneath the shady boughs of a beachside grove. For food, guests may choose from a café-bar at beach level and an airy upper-terrace view restaurant.

Over $100

Back downhill on the beach, the **Hotel Villa Mexicana** (Playa La Ropa, Zihuatanejo, Guerrero 40880, tel./fax 755/554-3776, 755/554-3636, or 755/554-1331, vtasmexhotels@prodigy.net.mx) seems to be popular for nothing more than its stunning location right in the middle of the sunny beach hubbub. Its 75 rooms, comfortable and air-conditioned, are packed in low-rise stucco clusters around an inviting beachfront pool-patio-restaurant. This seems just perfect for the mostly North American winter package-vacation clientele, who ride personal watercraft, parasail, and boogie board from the beach, snooze around the pool, and socialize beneath the *palapa* of the beachside restaurant. Low-season rates begin at about $105, $190 high. Low-season three-night rates package run about $290 d, including breakfast. Some rooms have wheelchair access. Parking is available; credit cards are accepted. Rooms can be reserved directly through the hotel or with the agency Mexico Condo Reservations (toll-free U.S./Can. tel. 800/262-4500, info@mcrx.com or reservations@mcrx.com, www.mexicocondores.com/zihuatanejo).

German expatriate Helmut Leins left Munich and came to create paradise on Playa La Ropa in 1978. The result is Playa La Ropa's renowned (**Hotel Villa del Sol** (Playa La Ropa, P.O. Box 84, Zihuatanejo, Guerrero 40880, tel. 755/555-5500, 755/554-3239, or 755/554-4066, toll-free U.S. tel. 888/389-2645, fax 755/554-2758, info@hotelvilladelsol.com, www.hotelvilladelsol.com). Here, in Helmut's exquisite beachside mini-Eden, a corps of well-to-do North American, European, and Mexican clients return yearly to

enjoy tranquillity and the elegance of the Villa del Sol's crystal-blue pools, palm-draped patios, and gourmet, *palapa*-shaded restaurants. The lodgings vary, from luxuriously spacious at the high end to large at the low end; all have rustic-chic floor tile, handcrafted wall art, and big, soft beds. The plethora of extras includes restaurants, bars, pools, night tennis courts, a newsstand, art gallery boutique, beauty salon, and meeting room. The least expensive of the approximately 70 accommodations begin at $330 s or d low season, $600 high. Superplush room options include more bedrooms and baths, ocean views, and small private whirlpool tubs for around $800 and up. All lodgings come with cable TV, phone, air-conditioning, and parking; some have wheelchair access. Credit cards are accepted, but children are permitted in two-bedroom suites only. Make reservations directly with the hotel or through agent Mexico Boutique Hotels (toll-free U.S./Can. tel. 800/728-9098, villadelsol@mexicoboutiquehotels.com, www.mexicoboutiquehotels.com/villadelsol).

IXTAPA HOTELS

Ixtapa's dozen-odd hotels line up in a luxurious strip between the beach and boulevard Paseo Ixtapa. Guests in all of them enjoy deluxe resort-style facilities and wheelchair access. All are high-end (more than $100/day) accommodations.

Near the northwest end, consider the best-buy European-owned (**Hotel NH Krystal Ixtapa** (Paseo Ixtapa s/n, Ixtapa, Guerrero 40880, tel. 755/553-0333, toll-free U.S. tel. 888/726-0528 or Can. tel. 866/299-7096, fax 755/553-0216, nhkrystalixtapa@nh-hoteles.com.mx, www.nh-hoteles.com, $105 d low season, $175 high). The hotel, which towers over its spacious garden compound, has an innovative wedge design that ensures an ocean view from each room. Relaxation centers on the blue pool, where guests enjoy watching each other slip from the water slide and duck beneath the waterfall all day. Upstairs, the 260 tastefully appointed deluxe rooms and suites have private view balconies, satellite TV, air-conditioning, and phones. Check for

© BRUCE WHIPPERMAN

The Hotel NH Krystal is one of Ixtapa's best-buy luxury hotels.

additional discounts through extended-stay or other packages. Extras include tennis courts, racquetball, an exercise gym, and parking. Credit cards are accepted.

Another good-value choice is the Best Western **Hotel Posada Real** (Paseo Ixtapa s/n, Ixtapa, Guerrero 40880, tel. 755/553-1625 or 755/553-1745, Best Western toll-free U.S./Can. tel. 800/528-1234, fax 755/553-1805, ixtapa@posadareal.com.mx, www.bestwestern.com or www.posadareal.com.mx, $120 d low season, $165 high), at Paseo Ixtapa's northwest end. Get there via the street, beach side, just past the big corner restaurant on the left. With a large grassy soccer field instead of tennis courts, the hotel attracts a seasonal following of soccer enthusiasts. Other amenities include a large airy beachfront restaurant and two luscious pools. Although the 110 (rather small) rooms are clean and comfortable, many lack ocean views. Extended-stay or low-season discounts, such as a third night free, are often available. Kids under 12 with parents stay free. Amenities include air-conditioning,

satellite TV, phones, and parking; credit cards are accepted.

Right in the middle of the hotel zone stands the **Hotel Dorado Pacífico** (Paseo Ixtapa s/n, P.O. Box 15, Ixtapa, Guerrero 40880, tel. 755/553-2025, fax 755/553-0126, reserv@doradopacifico.com.mx, www.doradopacifico.com.mx, $160 d low season, $200 high). Here, three palm-shaded blue pools, water slides, a swim-up bar, and three restaurant/bars continue to satisfy a year-round crowd of vacationers. Upstairs, the rooms, all with sea-view balconies, are pleasingly decorated with sky-blue carpets and earth-tone designer bedspreads. The 285 rooms have air-conditioning, phones, and TV. Low-season and extended-stay discounts may be available. Other extras include tennis courts and parking; credit cards are accepted.

At the east end, **Hotel Barceló Ixtapa Beach** (Paseo Ixtapa s/n, Ixtapa, Guerrero 40880, tel. 755/555-2000, toll-free U.S. tel. 800/BARCELO or 800/227-2356, fax 755/553-2438, reservas@barceloixtapa.com

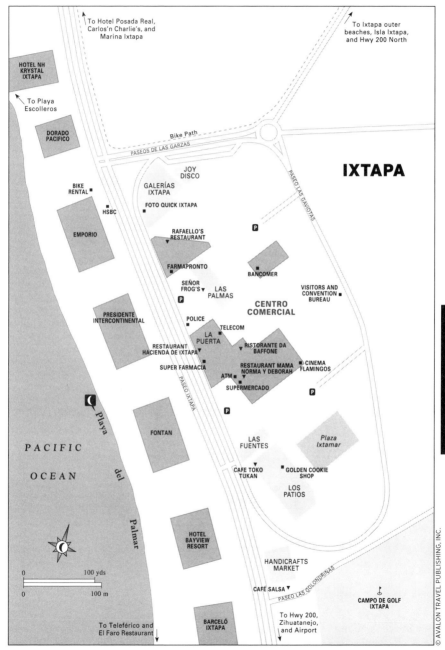

To Hotel Posada Real, Carlos'n Charlie's, and Marina Ixtapa

To Ixtapa outer beaches, Isla Ixtapa, and Hwy 200 North

HOTEL NH KRYSTAL IXTAPA

To Playa Escolleros

DORADO PACIFICO

Bike Path

PASEOS DE LAS GARZAS

JOY DISCO

IXTAPA

BIKE RENTAL

GALERÍAS IXTAPA

HSBC

FOTO QUICK IXTAPA

PASEO LAS GAVIOTAS

EMPORIO

RAFAELLO'S RESTAURANT

FARMAPRONTO

BANCOMER

SEÑOR FROG'S

LAS PALMAS

CENTRO COMERCIAL

VISITORS AND CONVENTION BUREAU

PRESIDENTE INTERCONTINENTAL

POLICE

TELECOM

LA PUERTA

RISTORANTE DA BAFFONE

RESTAURANT HACIENDA DE IXTAPA

SUPER FARMACIA

RESTAURANT MAMA NORMA Y DEBORAH

ATM

CINEMA FLAMINGOS

PASEO IXTAPA

SUPERMERCADO

PACIFIC OCEAN

Playa del Palmar

FONTAN

LAS FUENTES

Plaza Ixtamar

CAFE TOKO TUKAN

GOLDEN COOKIE SHOP

LOS PATIOS

0   100 yds

0   100 m

HOTEL BAYVIEW RESORT

HANDICRAFTS MARKET

CAFÉ SALSA

PASEO LAS GOLONDRINAS

CAMPO DE GOLF IXTAPA

To Teleférico and El Faro Restaurant

BARCELÓ IXTAPA

To Hwy 200, Zihuatanejo, and Airport

IXTAPA AND ZIHUATANEJO

or ixtapa@barcelo.com, www.mexonline.com/
barcelo-ixtapa.htm or www.barcelo.com),
across from the golf course at the east end of the
beach, rises around a soaring lobby/atrium. The
Barceló, formerly the Sheraton, offers a long list
of resort facilities, including pools, all sports,
an exercise gym, several restaurants and bars,
cooking and arts lessons, nightly dancing, and
a Fiesta Mexicana show-buffet. The 330-odd
rooms in standard (which include inland-view
balconies only), ocean view, and junior suite
grades, are spacious and tastefully furnished in
designer pastels and include air-conditioning,
phones, and satellite TV. The Barceló operates
both room-only and all-inclusive programs.
Room-only tariffs run about $175 d low season,
$220 high, including breakfast, kids under 12
free. All-inclusive (all drinks, food, and entertainment included) rates are $240 d low, $300
d high, kids under 6 free, 6–12 $35.

From its east-end jungly hilltop perch, the
queen of Ixtapa hotels, the █ **Hotel Las
Brisas Ixtapa** (Paseo de la Roca, P.O. Box
97, Ixtapa, Guerrero 40880, tel. 755/553-2121,

toll-free Mex. tel. 800/227-4727 or U.S./Can.
tel. 866/559-4329, fax 755/553-1038, ixtapa@
brisas.com.mx, www.brisas.com.mx) slopes
downhill to the shore like a latter-day Aztec
pyramid. The monumentally stark hilltop
lobby, open and unadorned except for a clutch
of huge stone balls, contrasts sharply with its
surroundings. The hotel's severe lines immediately shift the focus to the adjacent jungle.
The fecund forest aroma wafts into the lobby
and the terrace restaurant, where, at breakfast
during the winter and early spring, guests sit
watching iguanas munch hibiscus blossoms
in the nearby treetops. The hotel entertains
guests with a wealth of luxurious resort facilities, including pools, four tennis courts,
a gym, aerobics, an intimate shoal-enfolded
beach, restaurants, bars, and nightly piano-
bar music. The standard rooms, each with its
own spacious view patio, are luxuriously spartan, floored with big designer tiles, furnished
in earth tones, and equipped with big TVs,
small refrigerators, phones, and air-conditioning. More luxurious options include suites with
individual pools and hot tubs. The 427 rooms
begin at about $185 for a standard low-season
double, $210 high, and run about twice that
for super-luxury suites. June–October, bargain
packages can take prices even lower.

IXTAPA PLAYA LINDA HOTELS

A trio of all-inclusive resort hotels decorate
the luscious, tranquil Playa Linda shoreline
about five miles northwest of the main Ixtapa
Hotel Zone.

The original of the three is the **Club Med
Ixtapa** (toll-free U.S. tel. 800/CLUBMED or
800/258-2633, www.clubmed.com) which, as
its long-time clients have acquired families, has
become kid friendly. Besides deluxe rooms, the
usual good Club Med food, and a plethora of
included activities, from sailboating and surfing to water aerobics and chess, children can
also enjoy a full supervised program of kid-
appropriate activities. At Club Med, the usual
lodging arrangement is for a minimum of one
week, paid in advance. Typical winter (non-
holiday) weekly rates run about $1,000 per

© BRUCE WHIPPERMAN

Hotel Las Brisas Ixtapa

adult, double occupancy, with discounts for kids. Travel agents and websites sometimes offer discount packages.

Alternatively, you might consider the Club Med's worthy neighbors, the **Hotel Melia Azul Ixtapa** (tel. 755/555-0000, toll-free U.S./Can. tel. 800/336-3542, fax 755/555-0092, www.meliaazulixtapa.solmelia.com) and the **Hotel Qualton Club** (tel. 755/552-0070, fax 755/486-8324, sales@qualton.com, www.qualton.com/ixtapa). They are both kid friendly and offer deluxe amenities, food, and activities comparable to Club Med, often at reduced prices.

TRAILER PARKS AND CAMPING

The Ixtapa and Zihuatanejo area has one small, very basic trailer park. At south-end **Trailer Park Las Cabañas** (a block from Playa La Ropa, P.O. Box 179, Zihuatanejo, Guerrero 40880, tel. 755/554-4718) you can find out what it's like to park or camp in someone's shady backyard. To make ends meet, friendly, retired owner-managers María Elena and Hernán Cabañas decided to rent out their front and back yards. The result is enough space for a dozen tents or four medium-sized RVs in back,

and one in front, with electricity, water, showers, and toilets. The price is certainly right—about $4 per person for tents, RVs $12—and it's only a block from one of the loveliest resort beaches on the Mexican Pacific coast.

HOUSE, APARTMENT, AND CONDO RENTALS

Zihuatanejo residents sometimes offer their condos and homes for temporary lease through agents. Among the most experienced and highly recommended is **Judith Whitehead** (tel. 755/554-6226, cell tel. 044-755/557-0078, fax 755/553-1212, jude@prodigy.net.mx, www .paradise-properties.com.mx).

Also, owner-agent **Francisco Ibarra** (tel. 755/554-4924, fax 755/554-0595, donfrancisco@zihua.net, www.donfranciscoproperties.com) rents several moderately priced condos and houses on Playa La Ropa.

For many more house, condo, and apartment rentals, visit the excellent websites www.zihuatanejo.net and www.zihuatanejo-rentals.com.

For modestly priced rentals, don't forget the **Hotel Monarca, Casa de Huéspedes Ada, Apartments America,** and **Hotel Amueblados Valle** in the *Zihuatanejo Downtown Hotels* section.

Food

ZIHUATANEJO
Snacks, Bakeries, and Breakfasts

For something cool in Zihuatanejo, stop by the **Paletería y Nevería Michoacana** (no phone, 9 A.M.–9 P.M.) ice shop across from the plaza. Besides ice cream, popcorn, and safe *nieves* (ices), it offers delicious *aguas* (fruit-flavored drinks, $0.50) that make nourishing, refreshing non-Pepsi alternatives.

All roads seem to lead to downtown Zihuatanejo bakery **Buen Gusto** (Guerrero 11, 8 A.M.–10 P.M. daily, about $0.20–0.50 apiece for the pastries), on the east side of the street a few doors up from the restaurant Coconuts. Choose from a simply delicious assortment of

fruit and nut tarts and cakes: pineapple, coconut, peach, strawberry, pecan, with coffee to go with them all.

For hot sandwiches and good pizza on the downtown beach, try the **Cafe Marina** (tel. 755/554-2462, 8 A.M.–10 P.M. Mon.–Sat., closed approx. June to mid-Sept.), on Paseo del Pescador just west of the plaza. The friendly, hardworking owner features aribs and potato salad ($8) on Wednesday night. The shelves of books for lending or exchange are nearly as popular as the food.

Playa Madera's prime breakfast spot is family-run **(La Casa** (Av. Adelita 7, tel. 755/554-3467, 8 A.M.–1 P.M. daily except

Mon., closed Sept. and Oct.), at the bottom of Cerro Madera, west end. Dad, mom, and the kids serve up a steady stream of bountiful omelettes, pancakes, breakfast burritos, fruit, tamales, sausage, ham, and fried potatoes ($3–6) to a legion of loyal customers.

A local vacation wouldn't be complete without dropping in to the **Sirena Gorda** (Fat Mermaid, tel. 755/554-2687, 9 A.M.–11 P.M. daily except Wed.), near the end of Paseo del Pescador across from the naval compound. Here the fishing crowd relaxes, trading stories after a tough day hauling in the lines. The other unique attractions, besides the well-endowed sea nymphs who decorate the walls, are tempting shrimp-bacon and fish tacos, juicy hamburgers, fish *mole,* and conch and *nopal* (cactus leaves, minus the spines) plates, ranging between $4 and $7.

On at least one Zihuatanejo day, be sure to enjoy breakfast at successful newcomer ◖ **Restaurant Margarita** (on Guerrero a block from the beach, tel. 755/554-8130, 8 A.M.–11 P.M. daily Nov. through Mar., 8 A.M.–5 P.M. daily April–Oct.), across the street from the restaurant Coconuts. Besides a pleasantly refined old-world ambience including rustic beamed ceilings and soft music, they offer tasty, light entrées and attentive service. For example, for breakfast, choose an omelette ($3) or simply scrumptious *panes dulces* (pastries, $2) along with your cappuccino ($2) and fresh-squeezed orange juice ($1.50). For lunch, go for a tuna salad ($6) or *chiles rellenos* ($6); for supper try one of their excellent seafood entrées ($7–10).

Restaurants

Local chefs and restaurateurs, long accustomed to foreign tastes, operate a number of good local restaurants, mostly in Zihuatanejo (where, in contrast to Ixtapa, most of the serious eating occurs *outside* of hotel dining rooms). Note, however, that a number of the best restaurants are closed during the low-season months of September and October. The listings here move across downtown, generally from east to west.

Local folks swear by ◖ **Cocina Economica Doña Licha** (on Calle Cocos, tel. 755/554-3933, 7 A.M.–11 P.M. daily) in downtown Zihuatanejo's northeast neighborhood. (From Plaza Kyoto, follow Palmera west one block, turn left on to Cocos and continue half a block.) The reason is clear: tasty local-style food, served promptly in an airy, spic-and-span setting. Here customers can have it all. For example, for breakfast try *huevos a la Mexicana* ($3) or pancakes ($3); for *lonche,* go for the four-course *comida corrida* set lunch ($3–7); for *cena* (supper), try one of their super-fresh fish fillets ($5–6) or a seafood brochette (shrimp, oysters, octopus, fish $9).

All expatriate trails seem to lead to **Restaurant Glob's** (corner of Juárez and Ejido, 755/554-5727, 8 A.M.–9 P.M. daily year-round), on the east side of downtown three blocks from the beach. Here the cool, coffee-shop atmosphere is refined but friendly, and the food is strictly for comfort—good American breakfasts, hamburgers, spaghetti, and salads. Most entrées $4–8.

Zihuatanejo has a pair of good, genuinely Mexican-style restaurants in the central downtown area. ◖ **Tamales y Atoles "Any"** (corner of Guerrero and Ejido, tel. 755/554-7373, 9 A.M.–11 P.M. daily), arguably Zihuatanejo's best, is the spot to find out if your favorite Mexican restaurant back home is serving the real thing. Tacos, tamales, quesadillas, enchiladas, *chiles rellenos* ($4–8) and such goodies are called *antojitos* in Mexico. At Tamales y Atoles "Any," they're savory enough to please even demanding Mexican palates. Incidentally, Any (AH-nee) is the co-owner, whose perch is behind the cash register, while her friendly husband cooks and tends the tables.

Restaurant Los Braseros (Ejido 21, tel. 755/554-8736, 4 P.M.–1 A.M. daily), half a block farther west along Ejido between Cuauhtémoc and Guerrero, is similarly authentic and popular. Waiters are often busy after midnight even during low season serving seven kinds of tacos ($3) and specialties such as Gringa, Porky, and Azteca ($3–5), from a menu it would take three months of dinners (followed by a six-month diet) to fully investigate.

Asian-food fanciers have a choice of two good options. First, consider the very tasty offerings of **Mi Chayita** Chinese restaurant beneath its shady *palapa* (on Ejido, south side, between Guerrero and Galeana, tel. 755/554-5799, 11 A.M.–9 P.M. daily except Sun.). Here, a California-trained chef satisfies vegetable-hungry appetites, starting with bountifully delicious plates of chow mein ($4) and chop suey ($4). On the other hand, meat eaters can choose from a list of many delicious favorites, such as sweet and sour pork ($6), breaded shrimp ($7), whole fish ($8), and much, much more.

For another Asian option, try **Esthela's Cocina and Express** (on Cuauhtémoc between Ejido and Bravo, tel. 755/554-0352, 2–9 P.M. daily except Mon.), where local chef and Phillipine-American resident Esthela Buenaventura has relocated her popular, long-time enterprise. She continues to offer her uniquely personal menu, but now in an over-the-counter format (plastic utensils and bowls only), for either take-out guests or a few sit-down diners. Her tasty entrées consist of variations of stir-fried vegetables, to which she can add meat or fish for an additional price at your choice. For starters, Esthela offers such goodies as *lumpia* (Philippine-style spring rolls, $5), cucumber salad ($3), Buddha's Delight ($5), and much more.

Up the street one block, families fill the tables at petite **Cocina Economica Carol** (on Cuauhtémoc between Ejido and Gonzales, 11 A.M.–9 P.M. daily except Sun.). Diners enjoy country-style breakfasts such as *chilaquiles* and *huevos a la Mexicana* ($2–3); *comida corrida* (set lunch of soup, rice, meat entrée, and dessert, $3–4); and supper of tacos, enchiladas, tostadas, and tamales ($2–3).

Down at the beach by the naval compound, longtime **Casa Elvira** (Paseo del Pescador, tel. 755/554-2061, 1–10 P.M. daily), founded long ago by now-octogenarian Elvira Campos, is as popular as ever, still satisfying the palates of a battalion of loyal Zihuatanejo longtimers. Elvira's continuing popularity is easy to explain: a palm-studded beachfront, strumming guitars, whirling ceiling fans, and a list of super-fresh salads and soups ($4–6), fish ($6–12), meat ($4–12), and Mexican specialties ($4–8), expertly prepared and professionally served. Reservations recommended during the high season.

If Elvira's is full, an excellent alternative would be **Porto de Mare** (tel. 755/554-5902, 3–11 P.M. daily except Sun.), also on the beach, half a block east. It's the labor of love of its Italian architect owner, who designed and crafted its elegant open-air interior himself. As would be expected, his specialties are Italian-style pastas blended with superbly fresh local seafood (entrées $8–18).

No guide to Zihuatanejo restaurants would be complete without mention of 🅒 **Coconuts** (on Guerrero a block from the beach, tel. 755/554-2518, noon–midnight daily in season, closed approx. July–Oct.), across from Posada Citlali. Here, the food, whether it be light (pasta primavera, $12) or hearty (rib-eye steak, $24), appears to be of importance equal to the airy garden setting and good cheer generated among the droves of longtimers who return year after year.

The owners of up-and-coming **Restaurant Capricio** (on Cinco de Mayo by the church, 11 A.M.–11 P.M. daily), on the southwest corner of downtown, have followed the successful Coconuts example. Soft background jazz, fairy lights, and a tropical greenery-festooned patio set the scene, while the cuisine of especially good seafood pastas, hamburgers, and steaks ($7–16) provides the main event.

Splurge Restaurants

Restaurant Kau Kan (tel. 755/554-8446, noon–6 P.M. and 7 P.M.–midnight daily), on the clifftop road east and above Playa Madera, continues to be popular for both its romantic view location and its excellent food and service. While music plays softly and bay breezes gently blow, waiters scurry, bringing savory appetizers ($5–12), Caesar salad ($7), and cooked-to-perfection *dorado,* lobster, steak, and shrimp ($12–30). High-season reservations mandatory.

Right next door and equally worthy is Mediterranean boutique ⟨ **Restaurant Il Mare** (tel. 755/554-9067, noon–midnight daily high season, 4 P.M.–midnight daily low season). Enter and let the luscious ambience—soothing Italian arias, waves crashing against the rocks far below, the golden setting sun—transport you somewhere to the southern Amalfi coast: *O! Sole mio!* The menu extends the impression: start with *bruschetta alla Romagna* ($4); follow with soup *brodetta di pesce* ($7); salad *pomodoro cipolla rossa con gorgonzola* ($6); and *scampi al vino bianco* ($20), accompanied by a bottle of good Chilean Sendero chardonnay ($19). Finish off with lemon liqueur *Sogna di Sorrento* ($5). Reservations strongly recommended in high season.

For a nouvelle variation, head downhill to Avenida Adelita (foot of Cerro Madera) and sample the "fusion" cuisine of **Restaurant La Gula** (tel. 755/554-8396, 5:30–11 P.M. daily except Sun., closed Sept.–Oct.). Here, chefs practice the art of small portions and artful presentations of seafood (clams, lobster, shrimp, scallops, $15–30) and pastas, steaks, and fowl ($12–25). Reservations strongly recommended.

IXTAPA
Bakeries and Breakfasts
The perfume wafting from freshly baked European-style yummies draws dozens of the faithful to the nearby **Golden Cookie Shop** (tel. 755/553-0310, 8 A.M.–3 P.M. Mon.–Fri., 8 A.M.–1 P.M. Sat., closed approx. July–Sept.), brainchild of local longtimers Helmut and his late wife, Esther Walter. On the inner patio, upper floor of Los Patios shopping complex, Helmut continues their mission of satisfying homesick palates with a continuous supply of scrumptious cinnamon rolls, pies, and hot buns, and hearty American-style breakfasts daily ($4–6). In recent years, Helmut has served an authentic German buffet ($10) every Friday; call to confirm.

For breakfast, the ⟨ **Cafe Toko Tucán** (tel. 755/553-0717, 8 A.M.–10 P.M. daily, closed Tues. and Wed. low season, call to confirm hours), on the west front corner of the Los Patios shopping complex, across the boulevard from Hotel Bayview Resort, offers a refreshing alternative to hotel breakfasts. White cockatoos and bright toucans in a leafy patio add an exotic touch as you enjoy the fare, which, besides the usual juices, eggs, hotcakes, and French toast, includes lots of salads, veggie burgers, and sandwiches, from about $4 to $7.

Restaurants
Restaurants in Ixtapa have to be exceptional to compete with the hotels. One such, the **Bella Vista** (tel. 755/553-2121, 7 A.M.–11 P.M. daily), *is* in a hotel, being the Las Brisas Ixtapa's view-terrace café. Breakfast is the favorite time to watch the antics of the iguanas in the adjacent jungle treetops. These black, green, and white miniature dinosaurs crawl up and down the trunks, munch flowers, and sunbathe on the branches. The food and service, incidentally, are quite good. Breakfast buffet runs about $12, à la carte lunch $6–12, dinner entrées $10–20. Call ahead to reserve a terrace-edge table; credit cards are accepted.

An Ixtapa restaurant that has customers when most others don't is ⟨ **Restaurant Mama Norma and Deborah** (tel. 755/553-0274, 7:30 A.M.–11 P.M. daily), in the rear of La Puerta shopping center near Da Baffone Italian restaurant. Canadian expatriate proprietor Deborah Thompson manages with aplomb, working from a menu of delicious specialties familiar to North American and European palates. Whatever your choice, be it Greek salad ($7), lobster ($25), steak ($15), or fettuccine Alfredo ($10), Deborah makes sure it pleases. Lately, she's been open for breakfast; call to confirm morning hours.

Folks hankering for Italian-style pastas and seafood walk next door to ⟨ **Ristorante Da Baffone** (tel. 755/553-1122, 4 P.M. until about midnight daily). The friendly owner, a native of the Italian isle of Sardinia, claims his restaurant is the oldest in Ixtapa. He's most likely right: he served his first meal here in 1978, simultaneously with the opening of Ixtapa's first hotel. While Mediterranean-Mex decor covers the walls, marinara-style shrimp

($12), calamari, clams with linguini ($10), ricotta- and spinach-stuffed cannelloni ($12), and glasses of Chianti and chardonnay ($5) load the tables. Call to confirm hours and for reservations.

If Da Baffone is full or closed, try the highly recommended Italian gourmet restaurant **Becco Fino** (tel. 755/553-1770, 9 A.M.–11 P.M. daily) in the Marina Ixtapa. Reservations are usually necessary. Figure spending at least $30 per person for dinner.

(Other Ixtapa restaurants, popular for their party atmosphere, are described under *Entertainment and Events*.)

Entertainment and Events

In Zihuatanejo, visitors and residents content themselves mostly with quiet pleasures. Afternoons, they stroll the beachfront or the downtown shady lanes and enjoy coffee or drinks with friends at small cafés and bars. As the sun goes down however, folks often head to Ixtapa for its sunset vistas, happy hours, shows, clubs, and dancing.

SUNSETS

Sunsets are tranquil and often magnificent from the **Restaurant/Bar El Faro** (tel. 755/555-2525 or 755/555-2510, 5:30–10 P.M. daily), which even has a cableway (7 A.M.–7 P.M. daily except Sat.) that rises from the south end of the Ixtapa beach. Restaurant reservations are recommended in high season and on weekends. High-season hours may be extended to include breakfast; call to confirm. Many visitors stay to enjoy sunset dinner and the relaxing piano bar. By car or taxi follow the uphill road toward the Hotel Las Brisas Ixtapa, east of the golf course; at the first fork, head right for El Faro.

For equally brilliant sunsets in a lively setting, try the lobby bar of the **Las Brisas Ixtapa.** Happy hour runs 6–7 P.M.; live music begins around 7:30 P.M. Drive or taxi, following the signs, along the uphill road at the golf course, following the signs to the crest of the hill just south of the Ixtapa beach.

The west-side headland blocks most Zihuatanejo sunset views, except for spots at the far end of Playa La Ropa. Here, guests relax at the longtime favorite **Restaurant La Perla** (tel. 755/554-8700, 8 A.M.–10 P.M.). Alternatively, follow the road past Playa La Ropa and continue uphill to enjoy the panoramic Zihuatanejo sunset bay vista from showplace **Restaurant Los Escolleros** (taxi $5), perched high on the Zihuatanejo south bay hillside.

Sunset and Sunshine Cruises

Those who want to experience a sunset party while at sea ride the trimaran *Tri Star,* which leaves from the Zihuatanejo pier daily around 5 P.M., returning around 7:30 P.M. The tariff runs about $50 per person, including open bar.

The *Tri Star* also heads out daily on a Sunshine Cruise around 10 A.M., returning around 2:30 P.M. Included are open bar, lunch, and snorkeling, for about $65 per person. Book tickets for both of these cruises, which customarily include transportation to and from your hotel, through a hotel travel agent, or directly through the *Tri Star* office (tel. 755/554-2694, ydelsol@prodigy.net.mx) at Puerto Mío, the small marina about half a mile across the bay from town. Get there via the road that curves around the western, right-hand shore of Zihuatanejo Bay. (*Note:* During the summer–fall low season, cruises go from Puerto Mío on the smaller, romantic windjammer sailing ship the *Vlatava*.)

MOVIES

Head over to the petite **Cine Paraíso** (on Cuauhtémoc, tel. 755/554-2318), three blocks from the beach in downtown Zihuatanejo, to escape into American pop, romantic comedy, and adventure. About the same is available daily from 4:30 P.M. at **Cine Flamingos** (tel. 755/553-2490), in the rear of the La Puerta shopping plaza across the boulevard from the Hotel Presidente Intercontinental, behind the Supermercado.

TOURIST SHOWS

Ixtapa hotels regularly stage **Fiesta Mexicana** extravaganzas, which begin with a sumptuous buffet and go on to a whirling skirt-and-sombrero folkloric ballet. After that, the audience becomes part of the act, with piñatas, games, cockfights, and dancing, while enjoying drinks from an open bar. In the finale, fireworks often boom over the beach, painting the night sky in festoons of reds, blues, and greens.

Entrance runs about $30–40 per person, with kids under 12 usually half price. The most reliable and popular shows are staged (often seasonally only) at the **Presidente Intercontinental** (tel. 755/553-0018); **Dorado Pacífico** (tel. 755/553-2025, Tuesday); and **Barceló** (tel. 755/555-2000, Wednesday). Usually open to the public; call ahead for schedule confirmation and reservations.

CLUBS AND HANGOUTS

Part restaurant and part wacky seasonal nightspot, **Carlos'n Charlie's** (tel. 755/553-0504, 5:30 P.M.–1 A.M. daily) is as wild and as much fun as all of the other Carlos Anderson restaurants from Puerto Vallarta to Paris. Here in Ixtapa you can have your picture taken on a surfboard in front of a big wave for $3, or have a fireman spray out the flames from the chili sauce on your plate. You can also enjoy the food, which, if not fancy, is innovative and tasty. Entrées run $8–16, and loud rock music ($10 minimum) customarily goes on 10 P.M.–4 A.M. during the winter season. Find it on the beachfront about half a block on the driveway road west of the Hotel Posada Real.

For more of the same, but even more loud and outrageous, go to **Señor Frog's** (tel. 755/553-2282, 6 P.M.–3 A.M. daily), in the shopping plaza across from the Hotel Presidente Intercontinental.

On the other hand, some folks prefer Zihuatanejo's quieter nightlife scene. For example, at

Paccolo bar (Bravo 38, tel. 755/554-9116), just west of the corner of Guerrero, a guitarist plays jazz melodies from about 7 P.M. Thurs.–Sat. in season. Furthermore, **Restaurant Bandidos** (Av. Cinco de Mayo, tel. 755/553-8072, 11 A.M–2 A.M. daily, Nov.–Apr.; closed Sundays May–Oct.), colorfully decorated in faux 1910 Revolution style, with plenty of old Pancho Villa and Emiliano Zapata *bandido* photos, welcomes guests to sing along to the music, both live and recorded, usually weekends low season until the wee hours. Call to confirm hours. The restaurant is located on the west side of Av. Cinco de Mayo, just south of the corner of ascencio, a block from the beach.

Zihuatanejo's hottest new club is **Blue Mamou** (Paseo Playa la Ropa s/n, tel. 755/544-8023, www.bluemamou.com, from 7 P.M. daily), "Zihuatanejo's Home of Jazz," unmissable on the right side along the road to Playa La Ropa. Here you can enjoy barbeque, snacks, and cocktails ($5–15) in a stylish blue-motif night club setting. For programs, check the website or see the local tourist newspapers.

DANCING AND DISCOTHEQUES

Many Ixtapa hotel lobbies blossom with dance music from around 7 P.M. during the winter high season. Year-round, however, good medium-volume groups usually play for dancing nightly from about 7 P.M. at the **Dorado Pacífico** (tel. 755/553-2025); the **Presidente Intercontinental** (tel. 755/553-0018); the **Barceló** (tel. 755/555-2000); and **Las Brisas** (tel. 755/553-2121). Programs change, so call ahead to confirm.

Christine (in the Hotel NH Krystal, tel. 755/553-0333, from 10 P.M. Wed.–Sat.), Ixtapa's big-league discotheque, offers fantasy for a $25 cover charge. The patrons warm up by listening to relatively low-volume rock, watching videos, and talking while they can still hear each other. That stops around 11:30 P.M., when the fogs descend, the lights begin flashing, and the speakers boom forth their 200-decibel equivalent of a fast freight train roaring at trackside. Hours may be extended during the winter high season. Call to verify times; cover customarily runs $25 for men, women go free.

Sports and Recreation

STROLLING, WALKING, AND JOGGING

Zihuatanejo Bay is strollable from Playa Madera all the way west to Puerto Mío. A relaxing half-day adventure could begin by taxiing to the Hotel Irma (Av. Adelita, on Playa Madera) for breakfast. Don your hats and follow the stairs down to Playa Madera and walk west toward town. After a few hundred yards on the Playa Madera sand, head along the *andador* (walkway) that twists along the rocks around the bend toward town. Continue over the creek bridge and along the downtown beachfront walkway, Paseo del Pescador; past the pier at the west end, across the lagoon bridge, then left along the bayside road to Puerto Mío for a drink at the **Hotel Villa Vera** restaurant (tel. 755/553-8165, 8 A.M.–10 P.M. daily) and perhaps a dip in the pool. Allow three hours, including breakfast, for this two-mile walk; do the reverse trip during late afternoon for sunset drinks or dinner at the Hotel Irma.

Playa del Palmar, Ixtapa's main beach, is good for similar strolls. Start in the morning with breakfast at the **Restaurant El Faro** (tel. 755/555-2510 or 755/555-2525), atop the hill at the south end of the beach. The restaurant is open 6–11 A.M. daily in high season, but during the low may only open in the late afternoon, in which case you can do the walk in reverse at sunset—see below. Call to confirm restaurant hours. Ride the cableway (adjacent to the restaurant, 7 A.M.–11 P.M. daily except Sat.) or walk downhill. With the sun at your back stroll the beach, stopping for refreshments at the hotel pool-patios en route. The entire beach stretches about three miles to the marina jetty, where you can often watch surfers challenging the waves and where taxis and buses return along beach boulevard Paseo Ixtapa. Allow about four hours, including breakfast. The reverse walk would be equally enjoyable during the afternoon. Time yourself to arrive at the El Faro cableway about half an hour before sundown or around 5:30 P.M. to enjoy the sunset at Restaurant El Faro over drinks or dinner. Or, get to Restaurant El Faro by driving or taxiing via Paseo de la Roca, which heads uphill off the Zihuatanejo road at the golf course. Follow the first right fork to El Faro.

Adventurers who enjoy ducking through underbrush and scrambling over rocks might enjoy exploring the acacia forest and pristine beaches of the uninhabited west side of **Isla Ixtapa.** Take water, lunch, and a good pair of walking shoes.

Joggers often practice their art either on the smooth, firm sands of Ixtapa's main beachfront or on Paseo Ixtapa's sidewalks. Avoid crowds and midday heat by jogging early mornings or late afternoons. For even better beach jogging, try the flat, firm sands of uncrowded Playa Quieta, about three miles by car or taxi northwest of Ixtapa. Additionally, mile-long Playa La Ropa can be enjoyed by early morning and late afternoon joggers.

GOLF AND TENNIS

Ixtapa's 18-hole, professionally designed **Campo de Golf** (tel. 755/553-1062, 7 A.M.–5 P.M. daily) is open to the public. In addition to its manicured, 6,898-yard course, patrons enjoy full facilities, including pool, restaurant, pro shop, lockers, and tennis courts. Greens fee runs $55, cart $30, club rental $22, 18 holes with caddy $16, and golf lessons $25 an hour. The clubhouse is off Paseo Ixtapa, across from the Hotel Barceló. No reservations are accepted; morning golfers, get in line early during high season.

The **Marina Golf Course** (tel. 755/553-1410 or 755/553-1424), offers similar services for higher prices: greens fee $57 per person including shared cart, club rental $25, caddy $20.

Ixtapa has virtually all of the local tennis courts, and all of them are private. The **Campo de Golf** (tel. 755/553-1062, 8 A.M.–10 P.M. daily) has some of the best. Rentals run about $6/hour during the day, $10/hour nights. Reservations may be seasonally necessary. A pro shop rents and sells equipment. A teaching professional offers lessons for about $25 per hour.

Several hotels also have tennis courts, rental equipment, and lessons. Contact **Barceló** (tel. 755/555-2000); **Dorado Pacífico** (tel. 755/553-2025); **NH Krystal** (tel. 755/553-0333); and **Las Brisas** (tel. 755/553-2121) for information.

HORSEBACK RIDING

Rancho Playa Linda on Playa Linda rents horses daily for beach riding for about $15/hour low season, $20/hour high. Travel agencies and hotels offer the same, though for higher prices.

BICYCLING

Ixtapa's hot new activity is bicycling along the 10-mile round-trip *ciclopista* northwest to Playa Linda. A new Zihuatanejo leg of the *ciclopista* splits off southeast from the original (Playa Linda) leg and continues about three miles (5 km), all the way to Zihuatanejo. The bike rental station is on Paseo Ixtapa, in front of the Hotel Emporio near HSBC bank. Bargain for a discount from the steep $10/hour asking rate.

The *ciclopista* takes off north, at the boulevard intersection across from the rental station, and parallels the north side of Paseo de las Garzas for a few hundred yards, soon dividing into two respective legs. One leg, the Playa Linda leg, turns west, toward Playa Linda, while the Zihuatanejo leg heads east, toward Zihuatanejo. Officially, the Playa Linda leg ends five miles northwest, at the bridge and crocodile-viewing point at the Playa Linda parking lot, but you can continue another 1.5 miles to Barrio Viejo village at the lagoon's edge. Be sure to take a hat, water, and insect repellent.

If, on your return approach to Ixtapa, you haven't enjoyed your fill of bicycling, you can rack up more mileage along the Zihuatanejo *ciclopista* leg: Heading back to Ixtapa, about 100 yards after the intersection that directs traffic left to Highway 200, bear left at Paseo de los Pelicanos and follow the Zihuatanejo leg past

the back (northwest) side of the golf course, another six miles (10 km) round trip, to Zihuatanejo and back.

SWIMMING AND SURFING

Calm Zihuatanejo Bay is fine for swimming and sometimes good for boogie boarding and bodysurfing at Playa Madera. On Playa La Ropa, however, waves generally break too near shore for either bodysurfing or boogie boarding. Intermediate surfing is generally good at Playa Las Gatas, where swells sweeping around the southern point give good rolling left-handed breaks.

Heading northwest to more open coast, waves improve for bodysurfing and boogie boarding along Ixtapa's main beach, Playa del Palmar, while usually remaining calm and undertow-free enough for swimming beyond the breakers. As for surfing, good breaks sometimes rise off the Playa Escolleros jetty at the west end of Playa del Palmar.

Along Ixtapa's outer beaches, swimming is great along very calm Playa Quieta; surfing, bodysurfing, and boogie boarding are correspondingly good at Playa Linda, but hazardous in the sometimes mountainous open-ocean surf of Playa Larga farther north.

SNORKELING AND SCUBA DIVING

Clear offshore waters (sometimes up to 100-foot visibility during the dry winter–spring season) have drawn a steady flow of divers and nurtured professionally staffed and equipped dive shops. Just offshore, good snorkeling and scuba spots, where swarms of multicolored fish graze and glide among rocks and corals, are accessible from Playa Las Gatas, Playa Hermosa, and Playa Carey (on Isla Ixtapa).

Many boat operators take parties for offshore snorkeling excursions. On Playa La Ropa, contact the aquatics shop at the foot of the hill beneath Hotels Sotavento and Catalina.

Playa Las Gatas, easily accessible by boat for $5 from the Zihuatanejo pier, also has snorkel equipment and excursion boat rent-

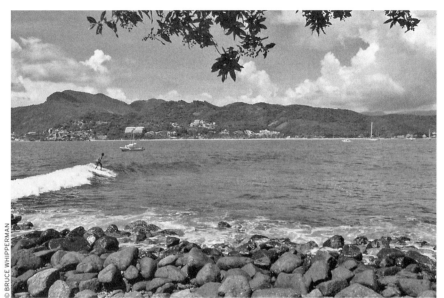

Surfing is fine on the rollers that curl around the eastern point of Zihuatanejo Bay at Playa Las Gatas.

als. In Ixtapa, similar services are available at beachside shops at the Hotels Las Brisas, Barceló, NH Krystal, and seasonally at other hotels.

Other even more spectacular offshore sites, such as Morros de Potosí, El Yunque, Bajo de Chato, Bajo de Torresillas, Piedra Soletaria, and Sacramento, are accessible with the help of professional guides and instructors.

A pair of local scuba dive shops stands out. In Zihuatanejo, licensed long-time instructors Carlos Bustamante and L. Ricardo Gutiérez carry on Zihuatanejo's professional scuba tradition with **Nautilus Divers** (Juan Ávarez 33, tel. 755/554-9191, nautilusdivers@hotmail.com, www.nautilus-divers.com), two blocks west of the Zihuatanejo beachfront plaza. They begin with the resort course, with two hours pool instruction and a guided dive, for $80. Open water NAUI certification takes three or four days and runs about $450. For certified divers (bring your certificate) they offer night, shipwreck, deep-water, and marine biology dives at more than three dozen coastal sites.

At **Carlo Scuba** (tel./fax 755/554-6003, carloscuba@yahoo.com, www.carloscuba.com), on Playa Las Gatas, friendly manager-owner Jean-Claude Duran (known locally as Jack Cousteau) and his son Thierry offer professional scuba services. The PADI-trained instructors offer a resort course, including one beach dive, for $60; a five-day open-water certification course, $400; and a two-tank dive trip for certified participants, $80, one-tank $55. They also conduct student referral courses and night dives.

SAILING, SAILBOARDING, AND BEACH KAYAKING

The tranquil waters of Zihuatanejo Bay, Ixtapa's Playa del Palmar, and the quiet strait off Playa Quieta are good for these low-power aquatic sports. Shops on Playa La Ropa (at Hotels Sotavento and Catalina) in Zihuatanejo Bay and in front of Ixtapa hotels, such as Las Brisas Ixtapa, Barceló, and NH Krystal, rent small sailboats, sailboards, and kayaks hourly.

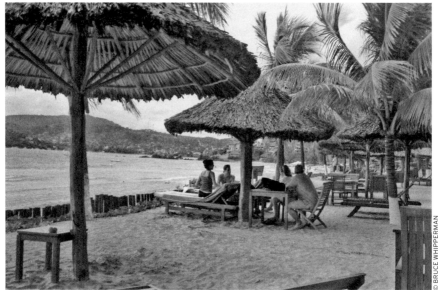

© BRUCE WHIPPERMAN

Zihuatanejo's Playa La Ropa rates as one of the loveliest best-for-everything beaches on the Mexican Pacific coast.

LAGOON KAYAKING AND BIRD-WATCHING

The grand Laguna de Potosí and the smaller, more remote Estero Valentín, about 10 and 20 miles (16 and 32 km) southeast of Zihuatanejo respectively, have become prime wildlife-viewing sites, due to the enterprise of Ixtapa-based **Zoe Kayak Tours** (tel. 755/553-0496, zoe5@ aol.com, www.zoekayaktours.com). The earnest, wildlife-sensitive operators conduct thoroughly professional excursions, designed to maximize the quality of participants' wildlife-viewing experience and appreciation. Itineraries vary from half-day outings to extended overnights and more.

FISHING

Surf or rock casting with bait or lures, depending on conditions, is generally successful in local waters. Have enough line to allow casting beyond the waves (about 50 feet out on Playa La Ropa, 100 feet on Playa del Palmar and Playa Linda).

The rocky ends of Playas La Ropa, La Madera, del Palmar, and Las Gatas on the mainland and Playa Carey on Isla Ixtapa are also good for casting.

For deep-sea fishing, you can launch your own boat or rent one. *Pangas* are available for rent from individual fishermen on the beach, the boat cooperative at Zihuatanejo pier, or aquatics shops of the Hotel Sotavento on Playa La Ropa or the Hotels Las Brisas Ixtapa, Barceló, NH Krystal, and others on the beach in Ixtapa. Rental for a seaworthy *panga,* including tackle and bait, should run about $20 per hour, depending upon the season and your bargaining skills. An experienced boatman can help you and your friends hook, typically, six or eight big fish in about four hours, which local restaurants are often willing to serve as a small banquet for you in return for your extra fish.

BIG-GAME SPORTFISHING

Zihuatanejo has long been a center for billfish (marlin, swordfish, and sailfish) hunting. Most local captains have organized themselves into cooperatives, which visitors can contact either directly or through town or hotel travel agents. Trips begin around 7 A.M. and return at 2 or 3 P.M. Fishing success depends on seasonal conditions. If you're not sure of your prospects, go down to the Zihuatanejo pier around 2:30 P.M. and see what the boats are bringing in. During good times they often return with one or more big marlin or swordfish per boat (although captains are increasingly asking that billfish be set free after the battle has been won). Fierce fighters, the sinewy billfish do not make the best eating and are often discarded after the pictures are taken. On average, boats bring in two or three other large fish, such as *dorado* (dolphinfish or mahi mahi), yellowfin tuna, and roosterfish, all more highly prized for the dinner table.

The biggest local sportfishing outfitter is the blue and white fleet of the **Sociedad Cooperativa Teniente José Azueta** (Muelle Municipal, Zihuatanejo, Guerrero 40880, tel./fax 755/554-2056, 6 A.M.–6 P.M. daily), named after the naval hero Lieutenant José Azueta. You can see many of its several dozen boats bobbing at anchor adjacent to the Zihuatanejo pier. Arrangements for fishing parties can be made through hotel travel desks or at its office at the foot of the pier. The largest 36-foot boats, with four or five lines, go out for a day's fishing for about $275 low season, $350 high. Twenty-five-foot boats with three lines run about $150 per day low season, $250 high. Smaller *pangas* go out for about $100 low season, $150 high.

The smaller (18-boat) **Servicios Sociedad Cooperativa Triangulo del Sol** (tel./fax 755/554-3758, 9 A.M.–7 P.M. daily) is trying harder. Its 36-foot boats for six start around $350; a 25-foot for four, about $150. Contact the office across from the naval compound, near the west end of Paseo del Pescador.

On the adjacent corner next door, newest and trying even harder, is **Whiskey Water World** (Paseo del Pescador 20, tel./fax 755/554-0147, local cell 044-755/556-6488, long-distance cell 01-755/556-6488, whiskey@

prodigy.net.mx, www.zihuatanejosportfishing.com), which claims to employ only sober captains. Its top-of-the-line-only boats run from 30 feet and $300, including license, bait, and drinks. Jack Daniel's is extra. Captains will take two people fishing, from 7 A.M. to 2 P.M., for $40 apiece (six-person minimum). Proud members of the IGFA (International Game Fishing Association), captains follow sailfish, tuna, and *dorado* catch-and-release policy. Alternatively, check out Ixtapa Sportfishing Charters (U.S. tel. 570/688-9466, www.ixtapasportfishing.com).

Prices quoted by providers often (but not necessarily) include fishing licenses, bait, tackle, and amenities such as beer, sodas, ice, and on-board toilets. Such details should be pinned down (ideally by inspecting the boat) before putting your money down.

Sportfishing Tournament

Twice a year, usually in May and January, Zihuatanejo fisherfolk sponsor the **Torneo de Pez Vela,** with prizes for the biggest catches of sailfish, swordfish, marlin, and other varieties. Entrance fee runs around $800, and the prizes usually include a new Dodge pickup, cars, and other goodies. For information, contact the local sportfishing cooperative, Sociedad Cooperativa Teniente José Azueta (tel. 755/554-2056); the fishing tournament coordinator, Crecencio Cortés (tel. 755/554-8423); or Whiskey Water World (tel./fax 755/554-0147).

MARINA AND BOAT LAUNCHING

Marina Ixtapa (tel./fax 755/553-2180, 755/553-0222 or 755/553-2365, info@marinaixtapa.com, www.marinaixtapa.com, 9 A.M.–2 P.M. and 4–7 P.M. daily) at the north end of Paseo Ixtapa, offers excellent boat facilities. The slip charge runs about $0.90 per foot per day for 1–6 days ($0.65 for 7–29 days), subject to a minimum charge per diem. This includes use of the boat ramp, showers, pump-out, electricity, trash collection, mailbox, phone, fax, and satellite TV. The harbormaster's office is in the marina-front white building on the right a block before the big white lighthouse.

Marina Ixtapa's smooth, gradual boat ramp, open to the public for a modest fee, is on the right-hand side street leading to the water, just past the big white lighthouse. Get your ticket beforehand from the harbormaster.

SPORTS EQUIPMENT SHOPS

Deportes Náuticos (corner of N. Bravo and Guerrero, tel. 755/554-4411, 10 A.M.–2 P.M. and 4–9 P.M. Mon.–Sat.) in downtown Zihuatanejo sells snorkel equipment, boogie boards, tennis racquets, balls, and a load of other general sporting goods.

A pair of shops on Álvarez, near the pier, sell fishing equipment and supplies. Check out **Pesca Deportiva** (tel. 755/554-3651, 9 A.M.–2 P.M. and 4–7 P.M. Mon.–Sat.), which specializes in fishing rods, reels, lines, weights, and lures. Find them at the far west end of Álvarez, corner of Armada de Mexico.

Alternatively, a block east and across the street, another shop offers a similar selection of heavy-duty fishing goods (Álvarez 35, tel. 755/554-6451, 9 A.M.–2 P.M. and 4–8 P.M. Mon.–Sat.).

Shopping

ZIHUATANEJO

Every day is market day at the Zihuatanejo *mercado* on Avenida Benito Juárez, four blocks from the beach. Behind the piles of leafy greens, round yellow papayas, and huge gaping sea bass, don't miss the sugar and spice stalls. There you will find big cones of raw *panela* (brown sugar); thick, homemade golden honey; mounds of fragrant *jamaica* petals; crimson dried *chiles;* and forest-gathered roots, barks, and grasses sold in the same pungent natural forms as they have been for centuries.

For more up-to-date merchandise, go to the big Kmart-style **Comercial Mexicana** (tel. 755/554-8321 or 755/554-8384, 8 A.M.– 11 P.M. daily), behind the bus terminals on Highway 200, about a mile east (Acapulco direction) of downtown. Its shelves are stacked with a plethora of quality goods, from bread and bananas to flashlights and film.

For convenience shopping downtown by the beach, go to the small grocery **Adriana y Pancho,** at the plaza-front corner of Álvarez and Cuauhtémoc.

Zihuatanejo Handicrafts Shopping Tour

Although some stores in the Ixtapa Centro Comercial shopping complexes and stalls at the adjacent Tourist Market (across from the Hotel Barceló) sell handicrafts, Zihuatanejo offers the best selection and prices.

A workable plan for your Zihuatanejo handicrafts tour would be to first stroll the stalls at the Zihuatanejo Tourist Market that line the downtown's west side street, Calle Cinco de Mayo, to see what's generally available and check out asking prices. Continue down to the beachfront and do the same at the Mercado de Conchas (Shell Market). Then, continue to the private shops, beginning with the Casa Marina at the beachfront just west of the plaza, then wind your way around the downtown, visiting several of the best shops along the main downtown shopping streets of Álvarez, Cinco de Mayo, and Cuauhtémoc.

Vendors at the Zihuatanejo **Tourist Market** display a flood of crafts brought by families who come from all parts of the Mexican Pacific coast mainland states. Their goods—delicate Michoacán lacquerware, bright Tonalá birds, gleaming Taxco silver, whimsical Guerrero masks, rich Guadalajara leather—although common here, often make treasured souvenirs and gifts back home. Compare prices; although bargaining here is customary, the glut of merchandise makes it a one-sided buyer's market, with many sell-

© BRUCE WHIPPERMAN

Zihuatanejo's many Tourist Market stalls

ers barely managing to scrape by. If you err in your bargaining, kindly do it on the generous side.

Continue to Zihuatanejo's other, smaller, tourist market, the **Mercado de Conchas** on the Zihuatanejo beachfront Paseo del Pescador, a block west of the plaza. The many fetching offerings include lovely seashells and shell jewelry, paintings, pottery, and much more.

Many private downtown Zihuatanejo shops offer an abundance of fine handicrafts. The best place to start is the **Casa Marina** shopping complex (tel. 755/554-2373, 10 A.M.– 2 P.M. and 4–8 P.M. Mon.–Sat.), a family project started by late community leader Helen Krebs Posse. Her adult children and spouses own and manage stores on the bottom floor of the two-story building, just west of the beachfront town plaza. The original store, **Embarcadero,** on the lower floor, streetside, has an unusually choice collection of woven and embroidered finery, mostly from Oaxaca. In addition to walls and racks of colorful, museum-quality traditional blankets, flower-

embroidered dresses, and elaborate crocheted *huipiles,* they also offer wooden folk figurines and a collection of intriguing masks. Other stores in the Casa Marina that you should visit include **La Zapoteca,** specializing in weavings from Teotitlán del Valle in Oaxaca. Also very worthwhile are **Metzli,** featuring all-Mexico crafts and a resort wear selection, **El Jumil** (lacquerware and masks), and **Costa Libre** (one-of-a-kind crafts and hammocks). Furthermore, Zapotec indigenous weavers from Oaxaca demonstrate their craft, often in the Embarcadero and La Zapoteca stores, mornings and afternoons November through April. Credit cards are generally accepted throughout the complex.

A block farther west, toward the pier, be sure to visit **Marea** (tel. 755/554-6733, 8 A.M.– 10 P.M. daily), a clothing shop on Paseo del Pescador across from the naval compound. It would be easy to pass because of its mounds of ho-hum T-shirts out front; but if you look inside, you'll find racks of many fetching hand-crocheted *huipiles* and blouses from backcountry Guerrero and Oaxaca.

Return west two blocks along Avenida Álvarez and turn inland at the corner of Cinco de Mayo, and find **Artesanías Olinalá** (Cinco de Mayo 2, tel. 755/554-6733, 9 A.M.–9 P.M. daily). Inside, you can enjoy a virtual museum of the venerable Guerrero lacquerware tradition, showcased by their seemingly endless trove of glossy boxes, trays, gourds, plates, and masks, all painstakingly crafted by age-old methods in the remote upcountry town of Olinalá.

Continue up Cinco de Mayo past the church to **Art Nopal** (tel./fax 755/554-7530, 9 A.M.– 9 P.M. Mon.–Sat. high season, 9 A.M.–3 P.M. and 4:30–9 P.M. Mon.–Sat. low season), whose owner loves things from Oaxaca, especially baskets. He fills his shop with an organized clutter, including unique woven goods and ceramics.

Next, head east on the next street, Bravo, one block to Cuauhtémoc, for a look through several more interesting shops. At the corner, turn left on Cuauhtémoc and continue a block, passing Ejido. A few doors farther, on the right, find

IXTAPA AND ZIHUATANEJO

Galería Maya (tel. 755/554-4606, 10 A.M.–2 P.M. and 5–9 P.M. Mon.–Sat.). Inside, owner Tania Scales displays a multitude of one-of-a-kind folk curios from many parts of Mexico. Her wide-ranging, carefully selected collection includes masks, necklaces, sculptures, purses, blouses, *huipiles,* ritual objects, and much more. Furthermore, be sure not to miss Tania's labor of love, several regal sculptures that represent a number of indigenous female deities: Ixta Bay, Maya jungle goddess; Coyolxauhqui, Aztec moon goddess; and Cihuateteo, representing all the women of Zihuatanejo.

Head back along Cuauhtémoc toward the beach. After half a block, on the right, step into **Rosimar,** the creation of Josefina and Manuel Martínez, at the corner of Ejido. Inside, they offer an eclectic, priced-to-sell collection of Tonalá and Tlaquepaque pottery, papier-mâché, and glassware.

Continue another block downhill, past Bravo, to **Alberto's** (tel. 755/554-2161, 9 A.M.–9 P.M. Mon.–Sat.) pair of shops, on opposite sides of the street and offering an extensive silver jewelry collection. As with gold and precious stones, silver prices can be reckoned approximately by weight, at between $1 and $1.25 per gram. The cases and cabinets of shiny earrings, chains, bracelets, rings, and much more, are products of a family of artists, taught by master craftsman Alberto, formerly of Puerto Vallarta, now deceased. Many of the designs are original, and, with bargaining, reasonably priced. Credit cards are accepted.

Continue another block downhill, past the corner of Ascencio, to **El Arte y Tradición** (tel. 755/554-4625, 9 A.M.–2 P.M. and 4–8 P.M. daily), where you can admire the lovely Talavera stoneware collection. This prized ceramic style, the finest of which is made by a few families in Puebla, comes in many shapes, from plates and vases to pitchers and tea cups. Talavera's colorful floral motifs originate from a fusion of traditions—notably Moorish, Italian, Turkish, and Persian—from the Mediterranean basin.

Now that you're again near the beachfront, head east along Avenida Álvarez half a block past the plaza to **Cerámicas Tonalá** (Av. Álvarez 12B, tel. 755/554-2161, 9 A.M.–2 P.M. and 4–8 P.M. Mon.–Sat.), on the beach side, to view one of the finest Tonalá ceramics collections outside of the renowned source itself. Here, friendly owner Eduardo López's graceful glazed vases and plates, decorated in traditional plant and animal designs, fill the cabinets, while a menagerie of lovable owls, ducks, fish, armadillos, and frogs, all seemingly poised to spring to life, crowd the shelves. Credit cards are accepted.

IXTAPA

Ixtapa's **Centro Comercial** mall complex stretches along the midsection of Paseo Ixtapa across from the hotels. It has four (of about 10 planned but still not functioning) viable subcomplexes fronting the boulevard. As you move east to west, first come the Los Patios and Los Fuentes subcomplexes, where mini-marts, T-shirt and trinket shops, and expensive designer stores occupy the choice boulevard frontages. Behind them, dozens of mostly small and ordinary crafts and jewelry shops languish along back lanes and inside patios. More of the same occupies the La Puerta subcomplex 100 yards farther on. Next comes the police station, and, after that, the Galerías Ixtapa subcomplex at the corner of Paseo de las Garzas.

For groceries, wines, and some fruits and vegetables, go to the mid-sized **Supermercado** (tel. 755/553-1514 or 755/553-1508, 8 A.M.–11 P.M. daily) at the front of the La Puerta subcomplex.

Information and Services

TOURIST INFORMATION OFFICE

Ixtapa and Zihuatanejo's main tourist information office is the **Visitors and Convention Bureau** (Paseo Las Gaviotas 12, Ixtapa, tel. 755/553-1570 or 755/553-0819, fax 755/553-1270, info@ixtapa-zihuatanejo.org, www.ixtapa-zihuatanejo.org, 9 A.M.–2 P.M. and 5–7 P.M. Mon.–Fri.), behind the La Puerta shopping center, past the movie theater. They answer questions and hand out maps and information folders.

An alternate information office in Zihuatanejo is FIBAZ, the **Fideocomiso de la Bahí de Zihuatanejo** (Bay of Zihuatanejo Trusteeship, Av. Morelos, tel. 755/544-8361 or 755/544-8350, 8 A.M.–4 P.M. Mon.–Fri.), on the northeast side of downtown, by the *deportivo* (sports field) swimming pool.

PUBLICATIONS

The best local English-language book and magazine selection fills the many shelves of the **Hotel Las Brisas** shop (tel. 755/553-1031, ext. 3483, 8 A.M.–11 P.M. daily). Besides dozens of new paperback novels and scores of popular U.S. magazines, it stocks *USA Today* and the *Miami Herald* Mexico edition and a small selection of Mexico coffee table books of cultural and historical interest.

The **newsstand** (8 A.M.–8 P.M. daily), on the west side of the Zihuatanejo plaza, is a handy source of popular U.S. magazines, such as *Vogue, Time,* and *Sports Illustrated,* plus the *Miami Herald* Mexico edition (around 1 P.M.) and maybe *USA Today.*

A small library of used paperbacks fill the bookshelf at friendly **Cafe Marina** (8 A.M.–10 P.M. Mon.–Sat., closed June to mid-Sept.), adjacent to the beach just west of the plaza.

The small Zihuatanejo *biblioteca* (public library, on Cuauhtémoc, 9 A.M.–8 P.M. Mon.–Fri., 9 A.M.–5 P.M. Sat.), five blocks from the beach, also has some shelves of English-language paperbacks.

ECOLOGICAL ASSOCIATION AND HUMANE SOCIETY

The grassroots organization **SOS BAHIA** (Paseo del Pescador 9, tel. 755/553-1853, www.sosbahia.org) sponsors local beach and lagoon cleanup, tree-planting, save-the-turtles, and other projects. For information, contact the organization's sparkplug president, architect Edgar Morales. Their headquarters shares space with the Animal Protection Society (see below) on the upper floor of Casa Marina, just west of the Zihuatanejo beachfront plaza.

The family members of the late Helen Krebs Posse are the guiding lights of the **Sociedad Protectora de Animales** (tel. 755/555-7227 or 755/555-6191, fax 755/555-3533, www.zihuatanejo.net/spaz/), which is working hard to educate people about animal issues. Contact one of the family members at the family's shop complex, Casa Marina (Paseo del Pescador 9, tel. 755/554-2373), just west of the Zihuatanejo plaza.

MONEY EXCHANGE

Several banks, all with ATMs, cluster on the east side of downtown Zihuatanejo. Most crowded is usually **Banamex** (corner of Guerrero and Ejido, tel. 755/554-7293 or 755/554-7294, 9 A.M.–5 P.M. Mon.–Fri., 9 A.M.–2 P.M. Sat.), two blocks from the beach. Alternatively, walk to the corner of Bravo and Juárez, where you'll find **Bancomer** (tel. 755/554-7492, 9 A.M.–4 P.M. Mon.–Fri., 10 A.M.–3 P.M. Sat.) and **Banco Santander Serfén** (tel. 755/554-3941, 9 A.M.–4 P.M. Mon.–Fri., 10 A.M.–2 P.M. Sat.).

After bank hours, go to the **Casa de Cambio Guibal** (at Galeana and Asencio, tel. 755/554-3522, fax 755/554-2800, 8 A.M.–9 P.M. daily), two blocks from the beach, with long-distance telephone and fax, to change U.S., Canadian, and European currencies and travelers checks. For the convenience, it offers you a few percent less for your money than the banks.

In Ixtapa, for long money-changing hours,

go to **HSBC** bank (on Paseo Ixtapa, tel. 755/553-0641, 755/553-0642, or 755/553-0646, 8 A.M.–7 P.M. Mon.–Fri., 8 A.M.–3 P.M. Sat.) in front of the Hotel Emporio. Alternatively, go to **Bancomer** (tel. 755/553-2112, 755/553-0535, or 755/553-0525, 8:30 A.M.–4 P.M. Mon.–Fri.), in the Los Portales complex behind the shops across the boulevard from the Hotel Presidente Intercontinental.

COMMUNICATIONS

The only *correo* serving both Zihuatanejo and Ixtapa is in Zihuatanejo at the **Centro Federal** (tel. 755/554-2192, 8 A.M.–3 P.M. Mon.–Fri., 9 A.M.–1 P.M. Sat.), in the northeast corner of downtown five blocks from the beach and about three blocks east of the Ixtapa minibus stop at Juárez and Morelos. Also in the post office is a suboffice of the very reliable government Mexpost (similar to U.S. Express Mail), which offers upgraded, secure mail service.

Next door is **Telecomunicaciones** (fax 755/554-2163, 8 A.M.–7 P.M. Mon.–Fri.), which offers long-distance telephone, public fax, telegrams, and money orders. Another similar telecommunications office serves Ixtapa, in the La Puerta shopping center (rear side), across Paseo Ixtapa from the Hotel Presidente Intercontinental.

Money-changer **Casa de Cambio Guibal** (tel./fax 755/554-3522, 8 A.M.–9 P.M. daily), on Galeana, the lane parallel to Cuauhtémoc, corner of Bravo, is also downtown Zihuatanejo's private *larga distancia* telephone and fax office.

In both Ixtapa and Zihuatanejo, many streetside public phone booths provide economical national and international long distance service, using Ladatel telephone cards (call the United States for about $1 per three minutes). Cards are readily available in grocery, drug, and liquor stores everywhere.

Note: Beware of certain private "To Call Long Distance to the U.S.A. Collect and Credit Card" telephones, commonly installed prominently in airports, tourist hotels, and shops. Tariffs on these phones can run as high as $30 for three minutes. Always ask the operator for the rate, and if it it's too high, get a Ladatel phone card (see above) and make the same three-minute call for a dollar.

Internet Access

Of Zihuatanejo's several Internet connections, one of the most convenient is the **Internet Café**, (9 A.M.–10 P.M. daily) across Òlvarez from the town plaza, just west of Av. Cuauhtémoc. Three blocks inland, also find **Podernet** on Ejido, between Cuauhtémoc and Cinco de Mayo, open approximately 9 A.M.–10 P.M. daily.

PHOTOGRAPHY

In Zihuatanejo, **Foto 30** (on Ejido, tel. 755/554-7610, 9 A.M.–8 P.M. Mon.–Sat., 10 A.M.–2 P.M. Sun.), between Galeana and Guerrero two blocks from the plaza, offers 30-minute develop-and-print service and stocks lots of film and accessories. These include a host of cameras, including SLRs, and film, including 120 print, 35mm slide, and sheet film, plus filters, tripods, and flashes.

In Ixtapa, **Foto Quick** (8:30 A.M.–8 P.M.Mon.–Sat., 10 A.M.–4 P.M. Sun.) offers approximately the same products and services. in shopping center Galerías Ixtapa, across the boulevard from Hotel Emporio, offers approximately the same products and services.

HEALTH AND EMERGENCIES

For medical consultations in English, contact U.S.-trained IAMAT associate **Dr. Rogelio Grayeb** (Bravo 71A, Zihuatanejo, tel. 755/554-3334, 755/553-1711, or 755/554-2040, fax 755/554-5041), beach side between Guerrero and Galeana.

Another Zihuatanejo medical option is the very professional **Clínica Maciel** (Palmas 12, tel. 755/554-2380 or 755/554-0517), which has a dentist, pediatrician, gynecologist, surgeon, and general practitioner on 24-hour call, two blocks east, one block north of the market.

Neither Ixtapa nor Zihuatanejo has any state-of-the art private hospitals. However, many local people recommend the state of Guerrero *hospital general* (on Avenida

Morelos, corner of Mar Egeo, tel. 755/554-3965, 755/554-3650, or 755/554-3436), just off Highway 200, for its generally competent, dedicated, and professional staff.

For medicines and drugs in Ixtapa, ask your hotel desk to put you in contact with a *farmacia*. Alternatively, call one of the many pharmacies in downtown Zihuatanejo, such as the **Farmacia La Principal** (corner of Cuauhtémoc and Ejido, tel. 755/554-4217, 9 A.M.–9 P.M. Mon.–Sat.), two blocks from the beachfront plaza.

For police emergencies in Ixtapa and Zihuatanejo, contact the **cabercera de policía headquarters** (on Calle Limón, near Highway 200, Zihuatanejo, tel. 755/554-2040). Usually more accessible are the police officers at the *caseta de policía* 24-hour police booth at the Zihuatanejo plaza-front, and in Ixtapa on Paseo Ixtapa, across from the Hotel Presidente Intercontinental. On Playa La Ropa, go to the small police station on the Paseo Costera, at the north-end intersection by the Hotel Villa del Sol.

IMMIGRATION AND CUSTOMS

If you lose your tourist permit, go to **Migración** (on Avenida Colegio Militar, tel. 755/554-2795, 9 A.M.–3 P.M. Mon.–Fri.), about five blocks north of Plaza Kyoto, on the northeast edge of downtown. Bring your passport and some proof of the date you arrived in Mexico, such as your airline ticket, stamped passport, or a copy of your lost tourist permit. Although it's not wise to let such a matter go until the last day, you may be able to accomplish the needed paperwork at the airport Migración office (tel. 755/554-8480, 8 A.M.–6 P.M. daily); call first.

The **Aduana** (Customs) office (tel. 755/554-3262, 9 A.M.–7 P.M. daily) is at the airport, off Highway 200 about seven miles south of Zihuatanejo. If you have to temporarily leave the country without your car, have someone fluent in Spanish call about the required paperwork, if any.

TOUR GUIDES

A number of reliable local agents arrange and/or guide local excursions. One of the most experienced all-around is **Turismo International del Pacífico** (corner of Álvarez and Benito Juárez, tel. 755/554-7510, fax 755/554-7509, tipzihua@prodigy.net.mx, www.ixtapa-zihuatanejo.net/tip, 9 A.M.–6 P.M. Mon.–Sat.) in downtown Zihuatanejo. They offer air and hotel reservations, transportation, sportfishing, and many tours, from a one-day Acapulco tour to horseback riding and a Playa Las Gatas beach party.

Off-the-beaten-track adventuring, including bicycling, kayaking, and snorkeling, is the specialty of **Adventours** (tel. 755/553-1069 or 755/553-1946, adventours@zihuatanejo.net, www.ixtapa-adventours.com).

Really get off the beaten track with very professional **Zoe Kayak Tours** (tel. 755/553-0496, zoe5@aol.com, www.zoekayaktours.com), which specializes in serious lagoon kayaking and bird-watching. For more information contact manager-owner Brian in Ixtapa.

LAUNDRY

In Zihuatanejo, take your laundry to **Lavanderia Express** (on Cuauhtémoc, 8 A.M.–8 P.M. daily), four blocks from the beach near the corner of Gonzales.

Getting There and Away

BY AIR

The Ixtapa-Zihuatanejo area has its own airport, and five major air carriers connect Ixtapa and Zihuatanejo directly with U.S. and Mexican destinations year-round; two more operate during the fall–winter season.

Many **Aeroméxico** (reservations tel. 755/554-2018 or 755/554-2019; flight information tel. 755/554-2237 or 755/554-2634) flights connect daily with Mexico City, and one with Guadalajara, where connections with U.S. destinations may be made.

Mexicana Airlines (reservations tel. 755/554-2208 or 755/554-2209; flight information tel. 755/554-2227) flights connect directly with Mexico City.

Alaska Airlines (toll-free Mex. or U.S. tel. 800/426-0333) connects with Los Angeles, San Francisco, and Seattle.

America West Airlines (toll-free Mex. or U.S. tel. 800/235-9292) connects with Phoenix.

Continental Airlines (toll-free Mex. tel. 800/900-5000) connects with Houston seasonally during the late fall, winter, and spring.

A number of seasonal and charter flights operated by airlines such as Air Canada, Frontier, American, and Northwest connect with northern U.S. and Canadian destinations during the winter. For more information, contact a travel agent or the airlines' respective websites.

AIR ARRIVAL AND DEPARTURE

Ixtapa and Zihuatanejo are quickly accessible: Zihuatanejo only seven miles (11 km) north of the airport via Highway 200. Ixtapa is four miles (7 km) farther north. Arrival is generally simple if you come with a day's worth of pesos and hotel reservations. Although the terminal does have an ATM (by the exit door near the car rentals), it has neither a tourist information booth nor hotel reservation service. Best arrive with a hotel reservation and not leave the choice up to your taxi driver, who will probably deposit you at the hotel that pays him a commission on your first night's lodging.

Transportation to town is usually by *taxi especial* (private taxi, $20–30 for three or four people) or *colectivo* ($7–10 per person depending on destination). Tickets are available at booths near the terminal exit. Taxis to Troncones run about $50. Mobile budget travelers can walk the few hundred yards to the highway and flag down one of the frequent daytime Zihuatanejo-bound buses (very few, if any, continue to Ixtapa, however). At night, spend the money for a *colectivo* or taxi.

Several major **car rental** companies staff airport arrival booths. Avoid problems and save money by negotiating your car rental through the agencies' toll-free numbers before departure. Agents include **Hertz** (tel. 755/554-2255 or 755/554-3050); **Budget** (tel. 755/554-4837 or 755/553-0397); and **Alamo** (tel. 755/553-0206).

Departure is quick and easy if you have your passport, tourist permit (which was stamped on arrival), and $20 cash (or the equivalent in pesos) international departure tax (if your air ticket doesn't already cover it). Departees who've lost their tourist permits can avoid trouble and a fine by either getting a duplicate at Zihuatanejo Immigration or (perhaps) by having a stamped passport, a copy of the lost permit, or at least some proof of their date of arrival, such as an airline ticket.

For last-minute postcards and shopping, the airport has a mailbox, several gift shops, and a pretty fair magazine stand.

BY CAR OR RV

Three routes, two easy and one longer and more difficult, connect Ixtapa and Zihuatanejo with Playa Azul and Michoacán to the northwest, Acapulco to the southeast, and Ciudad Altamirano and central Guerrero to the northeast.

Traffic sails smoothly along the 76 miles (122 km) of Highway 200, either way, between Zihuatanejo and Lázaro Cárdenas/Playa Azul;

allow about two hours. Several miles before Lázaro Cárdenas the new Highway 37 D *cuota* (toll) expressway allows easy access to highland central Michoacán (190 miles, 312 km, 4.5 hrs to Uruapan, add another hour to Pátzcuaro) from Zihuatanejo. The same is true of the 150-mile (242-km, allow four hrs) Highway 200 southern extension to Acapulco.

The story is much different, however, for the winding, sparsely populated, cross-sierra Highway 134 (intersecting with Highway 200 nine miles north) from Zihuatanejo to Ciudad Altamirano. Rising through vine-hung, jungly foothills, the paved but sometimes potholed road leads over cool, pine-clad heights and descends to the rich Altamirano oasis river valley after about 100 miles (160 km). The continuing leg to Iguala and the Acapulco–Mexico City highway is longer, about 112 miles (161 km), but equally winding and often busy. Allow about eight hours westbound and nine hours eastbound for the entire trip. Keep filled with gasoline, and be prepared for emergencies, especially along the Altamirano–Zihuatanejo leg, where no hotels and few services exist.

BY BUS

Zihuatanejo has three major bus terminals. They stand next to each other on the Acapulco-bound side of Highway 200 on the east side of town. The biggest and busiest is the big Estrella Blanca Central de Autobús station. Inside its shiny airline-style terminal, travelers have few services available, save a battery of Ladatel card-operated telephones, a left-luggage service, and only a small snack bar. If you're going need supplies for a long bus trip, prepare by stocking up with water and food goodies before you go to the station.

Estrella Blanca (tel. 755/554-3477), the only carrier, computer-coordinates the service of its subsidiaries first-class Elite, Estrella Blanca, Futura, and luxury-class Turistar. Tickets can be purchased with either cash or credit cards for all departures from computer-assisted agents.

Most buses run along the Highway 200 corridor, connecting with Lázaro Cárdenas/Playa Azul and northwestern points, and with Acapulco and points south and east.

Several luxury- and first-class buses and some second-class buses connect daily with Acapulco. Several of them continue to Mexico City, and at least one continues east along the Oaxaca coast all the way to Salina Cruz. In the opposite direction, many luxury-, first-, and second-class buses (at least one an hour) connect daily with Lázaro Cárdenas, Playa Azul junction, and northwest points.

Other departures connect north, via Michoacán. Among them, at least one daily departure connects north with points of Uruapan and Morelia via the new expressway. Another departure connects north via the expressway, via Uruapan, continuing northwest, passing through Guadalajara and Mazatlân, continuing all the way to the U.S. border at Mexicali and Tijuana.

Competing major bus carrier **Estrella de Oro** (tel. 755/554-2175) operates out of its separate station, just west of the Estrella Blanca station. It offers some long-distance first-class connections southeast along the coast via Acapulco, thence inland, via Chilpancingo, Iguala, and Taxco, to Mexico City.

Transportes Autobuses del Pacifico (TAP) (tel. 755/554-2175) departures, also operating out of the Estrella de Oro station, connect northwest, via Uruapan, Guadalajara, and Mazatlan, with Mexicali and Tijuana at the U.S. border.

A third major terminal, west of the Estrella de Oro station, offers mostly first- and luxury-class departures from a number of competent, well-equipped carriers, all of which are reservable via tel. 755/112-1002 or 755/544-8723: **La Linea Plus** luxury-class departures connect north with Guadalajara via Uruapan and also northwest, with Puerto Vallarta, via Lázaro Cárdenas and Manzanillo; **Autovias** first-class departures connect northeast, with Mexico City, via Morelia and Toluca; **Parhikuni** first-class departures connect northeast, with Morelia, via Uruapan; **Omnibus de Mexico** first-class departures connect north with Monterrey; and **Primera Plua** luxury-class departures connect northeast with Irapuato, Leon, and Aguascalientes.

South of Ixtapa and Zihuatanejo

Playa Las Pozas, Playa Blanca, and Barra de Potosí, the trio of pocket paradises not far southeast of Zihuatanejo and long known by local people, are now being discovered by a growing cadre of off-the-beaten-track seekers of heaven on earth. Taken together, they offer a feast of quiet south-seas delights: good fishing, beachcombing, camping, wildlife-viewing, and comfortable, reasonably priced lodgings.

Playa Las Pozas, a surf-fishing and seafood haven, is reachable via the Zihuatanejo airport road. A pair of palm-shaded bungalows offers comfortable accommodation. Playa Blanca, a mile farther southeast, is a long, lovely golden-sand beach, decorated by a lovely boutique hotel and restaurant. A few miles farther, Barra de Potosí village offers the ingredients of a heavenly one-day or one-week tropical excursion: palm-shaded seafood *palapas,* room for tent or RV camping, stores for supplies, a wildlife-rich mangrove lagoon, and a long beach, ripe for swimming, surfing, fishing, and beachcombing. A trio of petite bed-and-breakfast lodgings and a downscale beachfront hotel offer accommodation.

PLAYA LAS POZAS

Playa Las Pozas rewards visitors with a lagoon full of bait fish, space for RV or tent camping (be careful of soft sand), a wide beach, and friendly beachside *palapa* restaurants. The beach itself is 100 yards wide, of yellow-white sand, and extends for miles in both directions. It has driftwood but not many shells. Fish thrive in its thunderous, open-ocean waves. Consequently, casts from the beach can yield five-pound catches by either bait or lures. Local folks catch fish mostly by net, both in the surf and the nearby lagoon. During the June–September rainy season, the lagoon breaks through the bar. Big fish, gobbling prey at the outlet, can themselves be netted or hooked at the same spot.

Camping is popular here on weekends and holidays. Other times you may have the place to yourself. As a courtesy, ask at the friendly Neto family restaurant (on the west end by the lagoon), the best of the *palapa* restaurants, if it's okay to camp nearby.

Rustic accommodations have arrived at Playa Las Pozas through the ingenuity of builder Jeffry Meyers, who has erected the **Tree Tops Bungalows** (tel. 755/554-8278, treetopsbeach@hotmail.com, www.barra-potosi.com/treetops/) next to a beachside swimming pool and bar. There are only two bungalows, and rates are about $90 per night for two; discounts may be available for longer stays. If you're bringing kids under 15, you're asked to rent both bungalows. Closed approximately June–October.

Get to Playa Las Pozas by following the well-marked airport turnoff road at Km 230. After one mile, turn right before the cyclone wire fence just before entering the terminal complex and follow the bumpy but easily passable straight level road 1.1 miles (1.8 km) to the beach.

PLAYA BLANCA

In 2001, friendly but savvy and hardworking owner-builders from Phoenix, Arizona, decided to create heaven on lazy, lovely Playa Blanca. The result was **◖ Hotel Las Palmas** (cell 755/557-0634, locally dial 044-755/557-0634, hotellaspalmas@hotmail.com, www.hotellaspalmas.net), replete with precious architecture-as-art, including polished natural tree-trunk-beamed ceilings, elegant tropical hardwood shutters, and massive overhanging thatched *palapa* roofs. A recipe for paradise? Yes, but there's even more: a big blue pool, a good restaurant and bar, all set in cool green grassy grounds overlooking a long, creamy, yellow-white strand. Their six super-comfortable, hand-crafted rooms, four with air-conditioning, two with ceiling fans, rent for $150 d low season (June–Oct.), $225 d high, with breakfast, but without TV or phones. No credit cards accepted nor kids under 18; not wheelchair accessible. Get there by continuing about

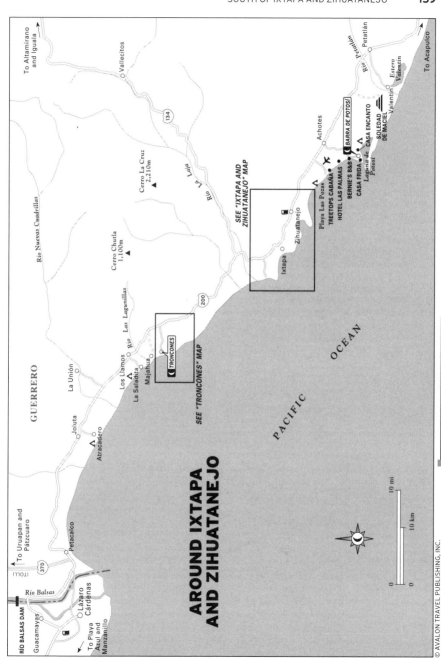

AROUND IXTAPA AND ZIHUATANEJO

IXTAPA AND ZIHUATANEJO

SEE "IXTAPA AND ZIHUATANEJO" MAP

SEE "TRONCONES" MAP

TRONCONES

GUERRERO

PACIFIC OCEAN

To Altamirano and Iguala

Vallecitos

Vallecillos

To Acapulco

Petatlán

Río Petatlán

Estero Valentín

Valentín

SOLEDAD DE MACIEL

CASA ENCANTO

Laguna de Potosí

CASA FRIDA

BARRA DE POTOSÍ

BERNIE'S B&B

HOTEL LAS PALMAS

TREETOPS CABAÑA

Playa Las Pozas

Achotes

Zihuatanejo

Ixtapa

134

Cerro La Cruz 2,210m

Río La Laja

Cerro Chutla 1,100m

Río Nuevas Cuadrillas

Las Lagunillas

Río

Los Llamos

La Saladita

Majahua

La Unión

Joluta

Atracadero

Petacalco

RÍO BALSAS DAM

Guacamayas

Lázaro Cárdenas

Río Balsas

To Uruapan and Pátzcuaro

To Playa Azul and Manzanillo

200

37D

(TOLL)

10 mi

10 km

© AVALON TRAVEL PUBLISHING, INC.

ZIHUATANEJO, "PLACE OF WOMEN"

An oft-told Costa Grande story says that when Captain Juan Álvarez Chico was exploring at Zihuatanejo in 1522, he looked down on the round tranquil little bay lined with flocks of seabirds and women washing clothes in a freshwater spring. His Aztec guide told him that this place was called Cihuatlán, the "Place of Women." When Chico described the little bay, Cortés tacked "nejo" (little) on the name, giving birth to "Zihuatlanejo," which later got shortened to the present Zihuatanejo.

Investigators have offered a pair of intriguing alternative explanations for the "Place of Women" name, a handle that evokes visions of a land of Amazons. They speculate that either Isla Ixtapa or the former royal bathing resort at Playa Las Gatas may have given rise to the name. The bathing resort, founded around 1400 by the Purépecha emperor, was most probably a carefully guarded preserve of the emperor's dozens of wives and female relatives. If not that, Isla Ixtapa may have been used as a refuge for the isolation and protection of women and children against the Aztec invaders who thus attached the label "Place of Women" to the locality.

1.5 miles (2.5 km) along the beach road from Playa Las Pozas to Playa Blanca and Hotel Las Palmas. Reservations can be made through the hotel or the owners' Arizona agent, Gold Coast Travel (335 W. Virginia Ave., Phoenix, AZ 85003-1020, fax 602/253-3487, goldcoast-travel@hotmail.com).

◖ BARRA DE POTOSÍ

At Achotes, on Highway 200, nine miles (15 km) south of Zihuatanejo, a Laguna de Potosí sign points right to Barra de Potosí, an idyllic fishing hamlet at the sheltered south end of the Bahía de Potosí. After a few miles through green, tufted groves, the paved road parallels

the bayside beach, a crescent of fine white sand, with a scattering of houses, a few comfortable bed-and-breakfasts, and one modest beachfront hotel.

The waves become even more tranquil at the beach's southeast end, where a sheltering headland rises beyond the village and the adjacent broad lagoon. Beneath its swaying palm grove, the hamlet of Barra de Potosí (pop. 1,000) has all the ingredients for tranquil living. Several broad, hammock-hung *palapa* restaurants (here called *enramadas*) front the bountiful lagoon.

Sights and Recreation

Home for flocks of birds and waterfowl and shoals of fish, the **Laguna de Potosí** stretches for miles to its far mangrove reaches. Adventure out with your own boat or kayak, or go with Orlando, who regularly takes parties out for fishing or wildlife-viewing tours. Bring water, a hat, and insect repellent.

If you want to do more but don't have your own kayak, Ixtapa-based **Zoe Kayak Tours** (tel. 755/553-0496, zoe5@aol.com, www.zoekayaktours.com) leads kayaking trips on Laguna de Potosí's pristine waters.

Bait fish, caught locally with nets, abound in the lagoon. Fishing is fine for bigger catches (jack, snapper, mullet) by boat or casts beyond the waves. Launch your boat easily in the lagoon, then head past the open sandbar like the local fishermen.

Accommodations and Food

In the village, a pair of bed-and-breakfast-style hotels offer lodging. First consider the charming flower-bedecked **Casa del Encanto** (House of Enchantment, tel. 755/556-8199, locally dial 044-755/556-8199, lauragecko2@hotmail.com, www.casadelencanto.com) on a village side street. Owner Laura Nolo rents her lovingly decorated rooms for about $65 d low season, $80 d high (Nov.–May), including private hot-water bath and full breakfast.

Beneath the plumy grove nearby, guests at ◖ **Casa Frida** (cell 755/556-3944, locally dial 044-755/556-3944, casa-frida@zihuatanejo.net, www.zihuatanejo.net/casafrida), life project of Mexican-French couple Anabella and François, enjoy fondly decorated rooms within a charmingly compact pool-patio garden. Room furnishings, based on a Frida Kahlo theme, include handcrafted art and furniture, mosquito curtains over the double beds, and bright Talavera-tiled hot-water bathrooms. Rates run about $80 d, including breakfast; adults only, no pets, closed May 1–November 1.

About a mile out of the village, back toward Zihuatanejo, the downscale **Hotel Resort Barra de Potosí** (tel. 755/554-8290) perches right on the beach. The surf is generally tranquil and safe for swimming near the hotel, although the waves, which do not roll but break rather quickly along long fronts, do not appear good for surfing. The hotel, once neglected, has been largely restored. Rooms have been renovated and the pool has been returned to a brilliant blue. The owner says that the restaurant will be open during the high winter season, but will close during the low summer and fall. The beach, nevertheless, remains inviting year-round. Kitchenette apartments rent for about $50 d, studios $40 d, but with only room-temperature water. All lamps are bare-bulb; bring your own lampshade or booklight.

About a mile farther from town on the same luscious beachfront, near the spot where the road from Achotes arrives at the beach, **Bernie's Bed and Breakfast** (cell 755/556-6333, locally dial 044-755/556-6333, playacalli@hotmail.com, www.barra-de-potosi.com/playacalli/) offers three comfortable rooms with "no TV, or piped-in-music" (says friendly owner Bernie Wittstock) and an oceanfront pool and patio. Rentals run about $70 s or d low season, $110 high, with breakfast. If you give him a day's notice, Bernie will cook a light meal for you.

Camping is common by RV or tent along the uncrowded edge of the lagoon. Village stores can provide basic supplies. Prepared food is available at about a dozen permanent

© BRUCE WHIPPERMAN

Barra de Potosí offers both comfortable lodgings and tropical country ambience.

lagoon-side *palapa* restaurants. **Restaurant Teresita** is especially recommended.

For more information about Barra de Potosí, visit www.barra-de-potosi.com.

Getting There and Away
Get to Barra de Potosí by following the signed turnoff road from Highway 200 at Km 225, nine miles (14 km) south of Zihuatanejo, just south of the Río Los Achotes bridge. Continue along the good, mostly paved road; pass the hotel at Mile 5 (Km 8) and continue to the village at Mile 5.5 (Km 8.9). Alternatively, get to Barra de Potosí by continuing east about three miles along the beach road from Hotel Las Palmas at Playa Blanca.

North of Ixtapa and Zihuatanejo

Visitors to Troncones and Majahua (mah-HAH-wah) can enjoy a long, pristine, coral-studded beach as well as the natural delights of a small kingdom of forested, wildlife-rich hinterland that stretches for miles above and behind the beach. While Troncones has acquired a modicum of modern travel amenities, including a number of restful bed-and-breakfast inns and gourmet restaurants, Majahua remains charmingly rustic.

(TRONCONES
Troncones (pop. 1,000) has a little bit of everything: shady seafood *ramadas,* cozy seaside inns and houses for rent, a sprinkling of good restaurants, and room to park your RV or set up a tent by the beach. Most folks get there from Ixtapa or Zihuatanejo via the side road off of Highway 200 about 20 miles north of Ixtapa.

But that's just the beginning. Troncones has acquired a growing colony of North Americans, some of whom operate small accommodations for lovers of peace, quiet, and the outdoors. Besides lazing in hammocks and sunning on the sand, guests at all Troncones lodgings share the same luscious shoreline. You can swim, surf, body-surf, and boogie board the waves, jog along the sand, explore a limestone cave, and thrill to a treetop-cable adventure in the adjacent jungle. Back by the shore, you can beachcomb to your heart's content while enjoying views of the wildlife trove—fish, whales (Dec.–Mar.), dolphins, turtles (Nov.–Jan.),

swarms of herons, boobies, egrets, and cormorants—that abounds in the ocean and in nearby lagoons.

Accommodations and Food
Many Troncones accommodations fall into the $50–100 category. As you move northwest (from the entrance road, turn right at the beach) after the bridge, first comes (**Casa Ki** (P.O. Box 405, Zihuatanejo, Guerrero 40880, tel. 755/553-2815, casaki@ yahoo.com, www.casa-ki.com), the life project of Ed and Ellen Weston, now tended by daughter Tina. Casa Ki (named after the Japanese word for energy and wholeness) offers four immaculate, charmingly rustic cottages tucked in a lovingly tended seaside garden compound. Each cottage sleeps approximately two adults and two children and comes with shower, toilet, fans, and a refrigerator. Guests share a shady outside cooking and dining *palapa.* High-season (Nov. 1–Apr. 30) rentals run $90 s, $110 d (approximately $65 s, $95 d low season) for the cottages, including full breakfast. Tina also rents a lovely two-bedroom, two-bath house that sleeps up to six, with full kitchen and daily maid service, for about $195 high, $140 low. Get your winter reservations in early.

After another quarter mile find **Casa de la Tortuga** (P.O. Box 37, Zihuatanejo, Guerrero 40880, tel./fax 755/553-2862, casadelatortuga@yahoo.com or casadetortuga@troncones.net), the original Troncones lodging, built by friendly pioneer Dewey McMillin during

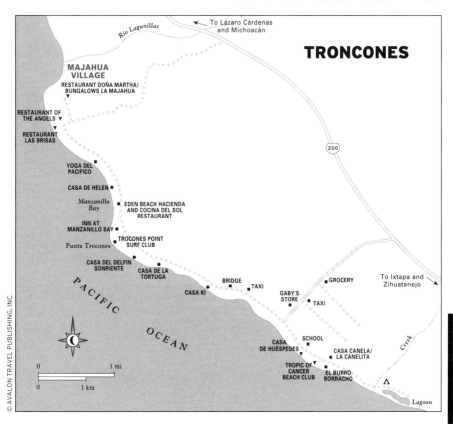

© AVALON TRAVEL PUBLISHING, INC.

the late 1980s. Although he used to rent individual rooms, Dewey has lately been renting the whole place (sleeping a dozen or more) for about $350/day, $2,000/week, $7,500/month during the high season, with staff; guests supply their own food. Reservations are mandatory during the winter. Rates during the low May–October season are discounted about 20 percent. If business is too slow, Casa de la Tortuga closes June, July, and August.

Continuing another half mile, you'll find one of Troncones' longstanding gems, the **Inn at Manzanillo Bay** (tel. 755/553-2884, fax 755/553-2883, manzanillobay@aol.com, www.manzanillobay.com). Here, owner-chef Michael Bensal has realized his dream of paradise: a plumy haven of eight rustic-style *palapa*-

roofed cabanas, comfortably furnished with deluxe amenities, set around a luscious blue swimming pool and leafy patio. Here you can have it all: a gently curving, wave-washed surfable shoreline, with the murmur of the billows at night and plenty of hammock time by day. There's a good restaurant and even TV if you want it. All this from about $117 d high season, $88 low.

Finally, 100 yards farther along the beach, you arrive at the six-room **Eden Beach Hacienda and La Cocina del Sol Restaurant** (tel. 755/553-2802, evaandjim@aol.com, www.edenmex.com), which shares the same luscious tropical forest oceanfront as all the other lodgings. The amenities include 14 immaculate lodgings—six comfortable fan-only

Troncones offers a number of restful bed-and-breakfast lodgings, such as the Inn at Manzanillo Bay, shown.

© BRUCE WHIPPERMAN

rooms in the original house and eight airy beachfront air-conditioned suites—all invitingly decorated in stucco and Talavera tile, with king-size beds and private hot-water bathrooms. High-season rates (Jan.–Oct.) run $85 d in the main house to $110 on the beachfront, including breakfast. Rates drop to $85 for all accommodations November 1–December 20. Make reservations with the hotel or via mail or fax in the United States (41 Riverview Dr., Oak Ridge, TN 37830, fax 801/340-9883). Credit cards are not accepted.

A star of the Eden show is chef Christian Shirmer, American graduate of the Baltimore culinary academy, whose menus feature traditional Mexican cuisine with a nouveau flair, focusing on fresh ingredients and seasonal foods. At least stop in for lunch or dinner and meet Christian and the builder-owners, Eva Robbins and Jim Garrity.

At the opposite, southeast end of the Troncones beach, **☎ El Burro Borracho** (The Drunken Burro, P.O. Box 37, Zihuatanejo, Guerrero 40880, tel./fax 755/553-2834, cell 044-755/553-0732) beachfront *palapa* restaurant and inn has become a favorite stopping place for the growing cadre of daytime visitors venturing out from Ixtapa and Zihuatanejo. Here, owner Dewey McMillin continues the standard set by former owner/chef Michael Bensal with spicy shrimp tacos, rum-glazed ribs, jumbo shrimp grilled with coconut-curry sauce, and broiled pork chops with mashed potatoes. Besides the shady ocean-view *palapa* restaurant, El Burro Borracho offers six "elegantly simple" airy rooms, each with bath, in three stone duplex beachfront cottages. Rooms include king-size bed, rustic-chic decor, hot water, and fans. Shared cooking facilities are also available. Sports and activities include swimming, surfing, and boogie boarding, plus kayaks, for use of guests. Room rentals run about $60 d high season, $35 low, with continental breakfast. Facilities also include five (shadeless) RV spaces, with all hookups, adjacent to the cottages for about $15 per night. Discounts are negotiable for long-term rentals. Reservations are mandatory in winter.

For more choices, consider some of the platoon of newer guesthouses, bed-and-breakfast inns, hotels, and vacation rental houses that have recently sprouted on the Troncones beachfront. For example, budget-conscious travelers might enjoy the Mexican (owned and operated by Amada Bueno Martínez) Casa de Huéspedes (tel. 755/553-2908), with four simple beachfront rooms for about $30 d, with private toilet and shower and a kitchen for guest use. Find them from the Zihuatanejo entrance road by heading left at the beach a couple of blocks.

Many more choices, most of them upscale, are available. They include a cluster of jointly managed houses—**Casa Alegria, Casa Canela, La Canelita,** and **Santa Benita**—with rentals varying from individual rooms to whole houses (P.O. Box 277, Zihuatanejo, Guerrero 40880, tel. 755/553-2800, fax 755/553-2807, casacanela@yahoo.com, www.troncones.com.mx/alegria, from $35 to $150); **Casa del Delfin Sonriente** (Smiling Dolphin) bed and breakfast (tel. 755/553-2803, U.S. tel. 831/688-6578, enovey@cruzio.com, $65 and up); **Casa Colorida** deluxe suites (U.S. tel. (Colorado) 303/400-5442, fax 303/680-9685, annmerritt@aol.com, www.casacolorida.com, $185–265); **Casa de Helen,** luxurious three-bedroom house (tel. 755/553-2800, tronconeshelen@yahoo.com, www.tronconeshelen.com, $225). For information on more rentals, visit websites www.troncones.com.mx and www.zihuatanejo.net.

For camping or RV parking spots, turn south (left) at the beach and follow the road half a mile past several likely spots to pull off and camp. At the far southern end, a lagoon spreads beside a pristine coral-sand beach, which curls around a low hill toward a picture-perfect little bay. Stores back by the entrance road can supplement your food and water supplies. El Burro Borracho may also let you park your RV in their lot out front for a fee.

Sports and Recreation
Lately, Dewey McMillin (tel. 755/553-2812, casadelatortuga@yahoo.com) of Casa de la Tortuga has taken the lead in providing local ecoadventure tours. These have included bird-watching and wildlife-viewing walks; a not-for-the-faint-of-heart jungle canopy tour along a cable hitched to the treetops; an exploration into nearby Majahua limestone cave, replete with rocky gardens of stalagmites and stalactites.

Michael Bensal at the Inn at Manzanillo Bay arranges sealife-viewing tours and fully equipped launches for four hours of fishing for 2–4 people for about $135.

Surfing has become a major Troncones recreation. The most popular spot is the palm-tufted inlet, locally known as Manzanillo Bay, location of both the Inn at Manzanillo Bay and Eden Beach Hacienda. Lately, a pair of enterprising lovers of the tropics, Michael and Ann Linn of San Luis Obispo, California, operating as **ISA (Instructional Surf Adventures) Mexico** (cell 755/558-3821, locally dial 044-755/558-3821, U.S. tel. (California) 514/563-6944, surf@isamexico.com, www.isamexico.com), have been offering both local day instruction and extended surfing packages during the fall–winter (Nov.–Apr.) season. Classes are small and all equipment and deluxe beachfront lodging is customarily included in packages, which run about $1,000 per person, double occupancy.

Shopping and Services
Michael Bensal maintains a shop, offering fine wines, Taxco silver, Cuban cigars, and surfboards new and used, at his Inn at Manzanillo Bay. Eva Robbins, at Eden Beach Hacienda, also has a shop, with a charming collection mostly of Guerrero country crafts: baskets, toys, silver jewelry, silk scarves, and much more.

The **Boutique** at the Tropic of Cancer Beach Club (from the Zihuatanejo entry road, turn left and continue about two blocks, to the Beach Club on the right) offers some decorative handicrafts, beachwear, a lending library, and some drugs and medications.

Local resident and certified massage therapist **Karolyn McCall** (in Troncones, cell 044-755/553-4512, karolyn_mccall@ yahoo.com) offers massage by appointment.

Folks interested in rentals or buying property in Troncones should contact Dewey Mc-Millin (tel. 755/553-2812, casadelatortuga@ yahoo.com).

A few local stores provide drinking water and groceries. For example, on the Zihuatanejo entrance road, on the right as you enter the village, **Gaby's** (tel. 755/553-2891 or 755/553-2892) offers some produce, basic groceries, and a long-distance telephone.

Getting to Troncones

Follow the signed paved turnoff to Playa Troncones from Highway 200, around Km 30, about 18 miles north of Zihuatanejo; or about 42 miles (73 km) south of the Río Balsas dam. Continue 2.2 miles to the Playa Troncones beachfront *ramadas.* Turn left for the camping spots, the main part of the beach, and El Burro Borracho; turn right for the other described lodgings, beginning with Casa Ki, about a mile farther along the beachfront forest road. From there, the car-negotiable gravel road continues about 1.5 miles along the beach to Playa Majahua.

MAJAHUA

Here you can enjoy a slice of this beautiful coast as it was before tourism bloomed at Troncones nearby. Instead of cell phones and the Internet, Majahua folks still enjoy plenty of palmy shade, stick-and-wattle houses, and lots of the fresh seafood that they serve in about half a dozen hammock-equipped *ramadas* scattered along the beach. One of the *ramadas* is competently run by a friendly family who calls it **Restaurant de Los Angeles.** Another of the best choices is *palapa* **Restaurant Las Brisas,** next door. A third good choice, for both lodging and food, is **Restaurant Doñna Martha** with plenty of lovingly prepared fresh fish, shrimp, and sometimes lobster, and **Bungalows La Majahua,** a pair of affordable ($30–50) bungalows with parking, right on the beach.

Camping, moreover, is safe and welcomed by local folks (although space, especially for RVs, is limited). Water is available, but campers should bring water or purifying tablets and food.

The beach curves from a rocky southeast point, past the lagoon of Río Lagunillas, and stretches miles northwest past shoreline palm and acacia forest. The sand is soft and dusky yellow, with mounds of driftwood but only seasonal shells. Waves break far out and roll in gradually, with little undertow. Fine left-breaking surf rises off the southern point. Boats are easily launchable (several *pangas* lie along the beach) during normal good weather.

To get to Playa Majahua directly, follow the signed turnoff from Hwy. 200 at Km 33, 20 miles northwest of Zihuatanejo (just south of the Río Lagunillas bridge), or 44 miles (70 km) southeast of the Río Balsas dam. Continue 2.9 miles (4.7 km) to the beach.

BEYOND TRONCONES

This northwest corner of the Acapulco region hides a few small havens for those who yearn for their fill of fresh seafood, uncrowded beach camping, and plenty of swimming, surfing, fishing, and beachcombing. And finally, those who venture to Guerrero's extreme northwest edge can encounter the great Río Balsas, the Mexican Pacific's mightiest river, whose drainage basin extends over five states: Jalisco, Morelos, Michoacán, Guerrero, and Oaxaca.

La Saladita

At La Saladita (The Little Salty Lagoon), the day used to climax when the oyster divers would bring in their afternoon catches. Now, however, the oysters are all fished out. While the oysters recover, divers go for octopus and lobster which, broiled and served with fixings, sell for about $10 for a one-pounder. You can also do your own fishing via rentable (offer $15/hour) beach *pangas,* which go out daily and routinely return with three or four 20-pound fish.

The beach itself is level far out, with rolling waves fine for surfing, swimming, boogie boarding, and bodysurfing. There are enough driftwood and shells for a season of beach-combing. The beach spreads for hundreds of yards on both sides of the road's end. Permanent *palapa* restaurants supply shade, drinks, and seafood.

Beach camping is customary, especially during the Christmas and Easter holidays. Other times, you may have the whole place to yourself. Bring your own food and water; the small stores at the highway village may help add to your supplies.

Although it's popular, camping is no longer necessary to stay overnight at La Saladita. **Indio's Bar and Grill** offers beachfront bungalow rentals, past the gate at the beach.

To get to La Saladita, at Km 40, 25 miles (40 km) northwest of Zihuatanejo and 39 miles (63 km) southeast of the Río Balsas, turn off at the village of Los Llanos. At 0.2 mile, turn right at the church and continue another 3.1 miles (5.1 km) to the beach, where a left fork leads you to Indio's, and a right leads you to the "Embarcadero" sector of the beach and Paco's and Ibañez *palapa* restaurants.

Atracadero

A few miles farther northwest, Atracadero is less frequented than La Saladita. Except for the fishing family's house down the beach, you probably would have the entire place to yourself most of the time. The beach *palapa* restaurant appears to operate only seasonally. Crowds must gather sometimes, however: the main *palapa* has, over time, accumulated a five-foot pile of oyster shells.

The beach sand itself is soft and yellow-gray. The waves, with good surfing breaks, roll in from far out, arriving gently on the sand. Boat launching would be easy during calm weather. Little undertow menaces casual swimmers, bodysurfers, or boogie boarders. Lots of driftwood and shells—clams, limpets, snails—cover the sand. The beach extends for at least three miles past palm groves on the northwest. A fenced grove and house occupy the southeast. A grassy lot on the northwest side could accommodate some tents and RVs. Bring your own food and water.

To get to Playa Atracadero, turn off at Highway 200 Km 64, near the hamlet of Joluta, 40 miles (64 km) northwest from Zihuatanejo and 24 miles (39 km) southeast from the Río Balsas. Bear left all the way, 2.1 miles (3.3 km) to the beach.

The Río Balsas

It's hard to remain unimpressed as you follow Highway 200 over the Río Balsas Dam for the first time. The dam, which marks the Michoacán–Guerrero state boundary, is huge and hulking. Behind it a grand lake mirrors the Sierra Madre, while on the opposite, downstream side, Mexico's greatest river spurts from the turbine exit gates hundreds of feet below. The river's power, converted into enough electric energy for a million Mexican families, courses up great looping transmission wires, while the spent river meanders toward the sea.

LÁZARO CÁRDENAS

The newish industrial port city of Lázaro Cárdenas, named for the Michoacán-born president famous for expropriating American oil companies, is an important transportation and service hub for the northwest Acapulco region. For tourists it's useful as a stopover only for services and bus connections, northwest with the Michoacán coast, Manzanillo and Puerto Vallarta, or north with the upland Michoacán destinations of Uruapan, Pátzcuaro, and Morelia. Most of its services, including banks, bus stations, post office, hospitals, hotels, and restaurants, are clustered along north–south Avenida Lázaro Cárdenas, the main ingress boulevard, about three miles from its Highway 200 intersection.

Accommodations and Food

Take a break from the sun beneath the shady streetfront awning of the **Restaurant Las Sombrillas** (8 A.M.–8 P.M. daily), across from Banamex. (Don't be afraid to ask the staff to turn the TV off or at least lower the volume.)

For cheaper but wholesome country cooking, check out the *fondas* (foodstalls) on side street Constitución de 1814, adjacent to the

IXTAPA AND ZIHUATANEJO

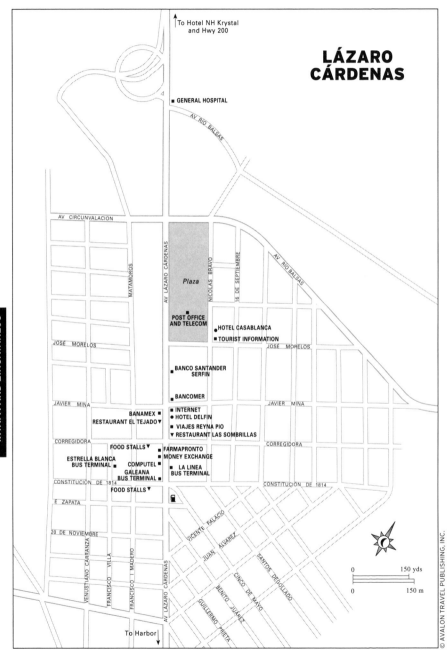

To Hotel NH Krystal and Hwy 200

LÁZARO CÁRDENAS

■ GENERAL HOSPITAL

AV RIO BALSAS

AV CIRCUNVALACION

MATAMOROS

AV LAZARO CARDENAS

Plaza

NICOLAS BRAVO

16 DE SEPTIEMBRE

AV RIO BALSAS

■ POST OFFICE AND TELECOM

● HOTEL CASABLANCA
■ TOURIST INFORMATION

JOSÉ MORELOS

JOSÉ MORELOS

■ BANCO SANTANDER SERFIN

■ BANCOMER

JAVIER MINA

JAVIER MINA

BANAMEX ■
RESTAURANT EL TEJADO ▼

■ INTERNET
● HOTEL DELFIN
■ VIAJES REYNA PIO
▼ RESTAURANT LAS SOMBRILLAS

CORREGIDORA

CORREGIDORA

FOOD STALLS ▼

■ FARMAPRONTO
■ MONEY EXCHANGE

ESTRELLA BLANCA
BUS TERMINAL ■
COMPUTEL ■
GALEANA
BUS TERMINAL ■

■ LA LINEA
BUS TERMINAL

CONSTITUCIÓN DE 1814

CONSTITUCIÓN DE 1814

FOOD STALLS ▼

E ZAPATA

20 DE NOVIEMBRE

VENUSTIANO CARRANZA

FRANCISCO VILLA

FRANCISCO I MADERO

AV LAZARO CARDENAS

VICENTE PALACIO

JUAN ALVAREZ

SANTOS DEGOLLADO

CINCO DE MAYO

BENITO JUAREZ

GUILLERMO PRIETO

0   150 yds
0   150 m

To Harbor

© AVALON TRAVEL PUBLISHING, INC.

Galeana bus station lot, and on side street Corregidora, the next block north.

If you decide to stay overnight, a number of nearby hotels offer reasonably priced lodging. The most centrally located is the **Hotel Delfín** (Av. L. Cárdenas 1633, Lázaro Cárdenas, Michoacán 60950, tel. 753/532-1418, fax 753/532-1419), across the street from the Galeana bus station. The approximately 20 rooms with baths, in three stories, cluster around an inner pool and patio. Rates run about $22 d, fan only, $32 with air-conditioning, with hot water, TV, and telephone.

For more class, go to the high-rise [C] **Hotel Casablanca** (on Bravo, tel. 753/537-3480, 753/537-3481, 753/537-3482, 753/537-3483, or 753/537-3484, fax 753/532-4036), a block east from Lázaro Cárdenas, visible behind Bancomer. It offers about six floors of light and comfortable modern-standard deluxe rooms with panoramic, private balcony views. Downstairs, past the lobby, a restaurant overlooks an inviting rear pool and patio. Rooms cost $36 s, $55 d, with air-conditioning, TV, and parking.

An even fancier hotel option is the **NH Krystal Express** (Av. Circuito de las Universidades 60, Lázaro Cárdenas, Michoacán 60950, tel. 753/533-2900 or 753/533-2941, toll-free U.S. tel. 888/726-0528 or Can. tel. 866/299-7096, nhlazarocardenas@nh-hotels.com, www.nh-hotels.com), on the west side of the ingress boulevard, Avenida Lázaro Cárdenas, about a quarter mile from the town center. It offers 120 deluxe rooms for about $85 d, with continental breakfast, restaurant, exercise gym, and whirlpool tub.

Tourist Information Office

For information and a selection of excellent maps and brochures, stop by the local branch of Michoacán state tourism (N. Bravo 475, 9 A.M.–6 P.M. Mon.–Fri., 10 A.M.–2 P.M. Sat.–Sun.), in front of Hotel Casablanca.

Travel Agents

A competent and conveniently situated travel agency (and possible information source) is **Viajes Reyna Pio** (Av. L. Cárdenas, tel.

753/532-3868 or 753/532-3935, fax 753/532-0723), right across from the Galeana bus station and Banamex. Alternatively, try **Chinameca Viajes** (on N. Bravo, tel. 753/537-0253), one block east from Avenida Lázaro Cárdenas and two blocks north of the Hotel Casablanca. Both are open approximately 9 A.M.–2 P.M. and 5–8 P.M. Monday through Saturday.

Money Exchange

Change your money at one of three banks, all with ATMs, clustered nearby. **Banamex** (Av. L. Cárdenas 1646, tel. 753/532-2020, 9 A.M.–4 P.M. Mon.–Fri., 10 A.M.–2 P.M. Sat.). If it's too crowded, try **Bancomer** (Av. L. Cárdenas 1555, tel. 753/532-3888, 9 A.M.–4 P.M. Mon.–Fri., 10 A.M.–2 P.M. Sat.), a block north and across the street; or **Banco Santander Serfén** (Av. L. Cárdenas 1681, tel. 753/532-0032, 9 A.M.–4 P.M. Mon.–Fri., 10 A.M.–2 P.M. Sat.), on the same side half a block farther north.

Communications

The *correo* (tel. 753/537-2387) is in the middle of the big grassy town plaza; look for it on the left as you arrive at the town center, two long blocks after the big traffic circle.

Telecomunicaciones, with telegraph, money orders, telephone, and public fax 753/532-0273, is next door to the post office. For telephone, plenty of public street phones accept widely available Ladatel telephone cards. More expensive, but with long hours, is the computer-assisted long-distance telephone and fax agency **Computel** (Av. L. Cárdenas 1810, tel./fax 753/532-4806, fax 753/532-4807, 7:30 A.M.–10 P.M. daily), next to the Galeana bus station at the corner of Constitución de 1814.

Connect to the Internet at the small store **Internet Sin Limite** (tel. 753/532-1480, 9 A.M.–10 P.M. Mon.–Sat.), corner of Javier Mina, across the street and south of Bancomer.

Health

The **General Hospital** (tel. 753/532-0900, 753/532-0901, 753/532-0902, 753/532-0903, or 753/532-0904), known locally as "Seguro

Social," is on the boulevard into town, left side, corner of H. Escuela Naval, a block before the big right-side traffic circle. Alternatively, visit highly recommended **Dr. Gustavo Cejos Pérez** (Melchor Ocampo 475, tel. 753/532-3902). For routine medicines and drugs, go to conveniently situated **Farmacia Pronto** (tel. 753/537-5002, 8 A.M.–10 P.M. daily), a few doors north of the Galeana bus station; or **Droguería Moderna** (tel. 753/532-0246, 7:30 A.M.–9 P.M. daily) on the main street across from the Galeana bus station.

Getting There and Away

By car or RV, the options to and from Lázaro Cárdenas are virtually the same as those for Ixtapa and Zihuatanejo. Simply add or subtract the 50 miles (80 km) or 1.25-hour travel difference between Ixtapa or Zihuatanejo and Lázaro Cárdenas.

By bus, a trio of long-distance bus terminals serves Lázaro Cárdenas travelers. From the Galeana (officially, Lineas Unidas del Sur) terminal (Av. L. Cárdenas 1810, tel. 753/532-0262 or 753/537-3868), **Ruta Paraíso** first-and second-class local-departure buses connect daily north with Apatzingán, Uruapan, Pátzcuaro, and Morelia. Very frequent local departures connect northeast along the coast with La Mira, Playa Azul, and Caleta de Campos. Additionally, several more first- and second-class departures connect northwest with Manzanillo and intermediate points. In an adjacent booth, agents (tel. 753/532-3006) sell tickets

for **Parhikuni** luxury-class buses (with a/c waiting lounge), connecting north with Michoacán destinations of Nueva Italia, Uruapan, Pátzcuaro, and Morelia.

Directly across the street, **La Linea** (tel. 753/537-1850) and associated lines maintains a small streetfront station. It offers four types of departures: executive class "Plus," connecting northeast with Guadalajara via Tecomán and Colima; first-class Autobuses de Jalisco, connecting north, then west, with Uruapan, Zamora, and Guadalajara; first-class Via 2000 buses, connecting north, then east, via Uruapan, Morelia, and Toluca, with Mexico City; and second-class Autobuses Sur de Jalisco connecting northwest with Manzanillo and also with Guadalajara, via Colima and Ciudad Guzmán.

The big **Estrella Blanca** terminal (tel. 753/532-1171) is two short blocks away, directly behind the Galeana terminal, on Francisco Villa between Constitución de 1814 and Corregidora. From there, one or two daily first-class local departures connect north with Michoacán destinations of Uruapan, Pátzcuaro, and Morelia. Three first-class buses stop, en route southeast to Zihuatanejo, Acapulco, and the Oaxaca coast, and northwest to Manzanillo, Puerto Vallarta, Mazatlán, and the U.S. border. In the opposite direction southeast, many first and second-class local departures connect with Zihuatanejo, Acapulco, and intermediate points, in addition to three Futura first-class departures that connect daily with Mexico City.

GUERRERO UPCOUNTRY

A treasury of surprises await travelers who venture out into Acapulco's pine-tufted sierra hinterland. The discoveries begin in Chilpancingo, Mexico's Home of the Brave, which basks in a banana-belt upland valley, ringed by mighty, cloud-tipped mountains.

From Chilpancingo as a base, explore upcountry Acapulco's River Country, and enjoy swimming, kayaking, rafting, and camping beside clear, spring-fed rivers and investigating stalactite-draped limestone caves.

Continue deeper into the sierra, to Acapulco's renowned Handicraft Country of Chilapa and Olinalá. Select from a treasury of soft palm baskets and sombreros, bright pottery, exotic masks, charmingly rustic furniture, and exquisite lacquerware.

Continue north to Iguala, both Independence memorial and Shrine to the Flag. Wonder at Iguala's surrealistically large Mexican flag and later take a bonus side trip to a duo of fascinating ancient indigenous ruins.

And finally, be sure to visit Taxco, the silver-rich colonial jewel of the highlands. After exploring its winding lanes and its museums and baroque monuments, visit Taxco's trio of nearby gems—the monumental limestone Grutas de Cacahuamilpa, the legendary ruined city of Xochicalco, and Ixcateopan, believed to be the final resting place of the heroic "Descending Eagle," Cuauhtémoc, the Aztecs' last emperor.

PLANNING YOUR TIME

A minimum of a week would be needed to enjoy the Guerrero Upcountry highlights; visitors with more leisure could easily stretch

© BRUCE WHIPPERMAN

HIGHLIGHTS

◖ **Chilpancingo Zócalo:** In Chilpancingo's historic center, enjoy exploring the monuments to Mexico's Independence and the Templo de Santa María de la Asuncón, where much of this history was actually made (page 176).

◖ **Headwaters of the Río Azul:** It seems a miracle that every minute, year-round, and especially on hot, dust-dry May afternoons, thousands of gallons of deliciously pure and cool water, enough to form a whole river, should well up from beneath the ground (page 194).

◖ **Chilapa Sunday Handicrafts Market:** Every Sunday, indigenous folks from all over central Guerrero bring their finest crafts to Chilapa for a day of bargaining and selling (page 198).

◖ **Templo de San Francisco:** Olinalá lacquerware artisans have gone all out to decorate the interior of their town church with their art. The result in the finely detailed traditional floral and animal designs that embellish the altar, the columns, the walls and the ceiling and more is attractively unique (page 202).

◖ **Hilltop Memorial Flag:** Climax your Iguala visit atop the hillside south of town to witness Mexico's largest flag, weighing a quarter ton and requiring a platoon of men to raise it at sunrise and lower it at sunset each day (page 212).

◖ **Santa Prisca:** First stop around the Taxco zócalo should be the celebrated baroque-style church built with the wealth extracted from Taxco's silver mines (page 223).

◖ **Grutas de Cacahuamilpa:** Few, if any, cave systems in the world are as grand, lovely,

and easily accessible as the Grutas de Cacahuamilpa (page 228).

◖ **Xochicalco:** Besides the site's world-class museum, be sure to visit the Pyramid of Quetzalcoatl, so named by modern-day archaeologists for its powerful stylized bas-relief design of Quetzalcoatl, Mexico's renowned and feared Plumed Serpent (page 228).

LOOK FOR ◖ TO FIND RECOMMENDED SIGHTS, ACTIVITIES, DINING, AND LODGING.

this out to a month. If, however, you only have three or four days, you should probably enjoy them all in and around Taxco, Mexico's silver capital. Spend a day strolling the winding hillside lanes, visiting the best of the best silver jewelry shops, the Museo Guillermo Spratling, the incomparably baroque **Santa Prisca** church, and the fascinating indigenous market. The next day, ride the stunningly scary *teleférico* (cableway) for a hike, golf, or tennis and lunch or a picnic at mountaintop Hotel Monte Taxco. On a subsequent day or days, make certain to visit the spectacular limestone **Grutas de Cacahuamilpa** (Caves of Cacahuamilpa) and, if you go early enough, continue by tour or car, to the storied ruined city, now world-class museum and archaeological site, of **Xochicalco.**

With three or four days more, you could add Guerrero Upcountry's River and Handicrafts Country to your itinerary. The first day, from Acapulco, go by tour, bus, or car for about 30 miles (48 km) for a rafting adventure on the Río Papagayo. Continue north for an overnight in either Chilpancingo or more conveniently, Colotlipa. The next day, head out for an adventure tour through the fascinatingly exquisite limestone Grutas de Juxtlahuaca and in the afternoon, continue to the nearby Río Azul for swimming, inner-tubing, and plenty of general frolicking in the cool, crystal-blue water. Continue back to Chilpancingo for overnight.

Head out early the next day (which must be a Sunday) and bargain for treasures at the fascinating **Chilapa Sunday Handicrafts Market.** Continue in the afternoon or the next day to the remote mountain town of Olinalá and spend at least an afternoon visiting home factory shops filled with the town's renowned glistening lacquerware.

With a day or two more, you could add Iguala, north of Chilpancingo, south of Taxco, to your itinerary. En route from Chilpancingo, you might include a three-hour side trip to an ancient lost city, now La Organera Xochipala Archaeological Zone. In the afternoon,

© BRUCE WHIPPERMAN

Locally made pottery, bark paintings, costume jewelry, leather, and much more are available at the small courtyard market in Taxco.

To Puerto
Escondido and
Oaxaca

Tlapa
Azoyu
Atlamajalcingo
del Monte
Xalpatláhuac
Acatlán
Axoxuco
Malinaltepec
Marquelia
Tlatlauquitepec
Cerro Tequilatemic
8,700m
Zapotitlán
Tabias
Tlacuapa
Cerro El
Maguey
2,750m
Atlistac
Cuautla
Caves of Pantitlán
Santa Cruz
Epazote
Acatlán
Cruz Grande
Zitlala
Xochitempa
Caves of
Juxtlahuaca
Chilapa
Atzacualoya
Colotlipa
Ayutla
**SUNDAY
HANDICRAFTS MARKET**
San Ángel
Santa
Fe
Cuauhtenango
Zotolitlán
**HEADWATERS OF
THE RÍO AZUL**
Tecuanapa
Quechultenango
Tixtla
Mochitlán
Atliaca
El Terreno
Petaquillas
Acahuizotla
El Ocotito
San Marcos
Chichihualco
Zumpango
del Río
CHILPANCINGO ZÓCALO
Chilpancingo
Tierra
Colorado
Lomas de
Chapultepec
Cerro Grande
2,850m
Tlahuizopa
Plan de
Lima
Filo de
Caballos
Corral
de Bravo
Jaleaca de
Catalán
Río Papagayo
PUEBLO BRAVO
Xaltianguis
Lomas
San
Juan
Laguna Tres
Palos
Río Grande
Yextla
Pie de la
Cuesta
Puerto Marques
Acapulco
Cerro
Teotepec
3,705m
Puerto
del Gallito
Río Coyuca
Coyuca
Bajos del
Ejido
Laguna
Coyuca

PACIFIC OCEAN

Costa Chica
Laguna
Chautengo
Laguna
Tecomate
Río Marquelia
Río Copala
Río Malinaltepec
Río Tecuilapa
Río Grande
Río Azul
Río Omitlán
Río
Papagayo

Costa Grande

To Ixtapa and
Zihuatanejo

10 mi
10 km

© AVALON TRAVEL PUBLISHING, INC.

in Iguala, a virtual shrine to the Mexican national flag, be sure to stroll around the three pleasantly shady downtown central plazas, and visit the **Museo y Santuario a la Bandera.** An hour before sunset, ride a taxi or *colectivo* to the hillside south of town to witness what must be Mexico's (if not the world's) most awesomely large national flag, powerfully rumbling and snapping, with mini–sonic booms, in the breeze.

Chilpancingo

The formal name of the Guerrero state capital, Chilpancingo de los Bravo (Chilpancingo of the Brave), reflects Mexico's kinship with the United States, "The Home of the Free and Land of the Brave." Historically, in both cases, "the Brave" was more than a mere patriotic turn of phrase. Like the Continental Congress that began meeting in Philadelphia in 1774, the members of the 1813 revolutionary Congress of Anahuac in Chilpancingo did so at the constant risk of their lives.

Chilpancingo, besides being the Guerrero state capital and the cradle of Mexican liberty, is also closely associated with Vicente Guerrero, the Mexican hero most comparable to the United States' George Washington. Probably more than any other, Guerrero, Mexico's second president, battled to win Mexico's 1821 independence and continued the struggle to ensure Mexico's 1824 constitution and resulting republican government.

Nevertheless, it's still priest-general José María Morelos who holds the hearts of Mexicans, eight generations after his death. It was Morelos who convened Mexico's first revolutionary legislature, the Congress of Anahuac, in Chilpancingo on September 14, 1813.

Morelos had earlier expressed his libertarian ideas, in the celebrated Sentimientos de la Nación, which, with as much force as the ideas of Thomas Jefferson a generation earlier, gave direction to the Congress of Anahuac's work. On November 6, 1813, the Congress declared a manifesto of principles, which notably included the idea that "sovereignty proceeds immediately from the people" and that Mexico should therefore "be free and independent."

It's interesting to note that the Mexican Act of Independence, 37 years after the American Declaration of Independence, took freedom a step farther. Among its principles, the Congress of Anahuac declared that "slavery be prohibited forever," a principle that required 52 more years and a terrible civil war to be established in the United States.

Arrival and Orientation

Judging from its narrow downtown streets, Chilpancingo (pop. 200,000, elev. 4,000 feet, 1,300 meters) is a little town that grew big. Traveling the 62 miles (100 km) by *cuota* (toll) expressway from Acapulco (or 83 miles, 133 km by old Highway 95), arrivees must make an effort not to miss the downtown. Both first-class buses and the south–north thruway Avenida Vicente Guerrero bypass the town center completely.

Buses deposit passengers at the Camionera Central (a mile north of the central plaza; taxi or ride a *colectivo* from there).

Drivers, watch carefully for turnoff signs. If you're fortunate, you'll get on to main south-end ingress Avenida Lázaro Cárdenas, which begins at the Ciudad Universitaria right turnoff. About half a mile (0.8 km) from the turnoff, bear right at a big traffic circle and follow the boulevard, which becomes Bulevar Juan Álvarez and passes, via a one-block tunnel, beneath the Chilpancingo *zócalo*.

SIGHTS
◖ Chilpancingo Zócalo

Traffic having been diverted from it and the surrounding streets, the Chilpancingo *zócalo* (central plaza) makes an enjoyable strolling ground.

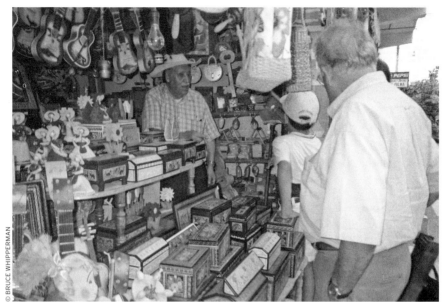

Chilpancingo's Diego Rico handicrafts store is chock-full of old-fashioned Mexican trinkets.

The best vantage point is the front steps of the tall Guerrero **Biblioteca Del Estado** (formerly the Palacio de Gobierno, statehouse). Face (or imagine you're facing) the plaza, officially the "Plaza of the First Congress of Anahuac," and you're looking east. North is on your left, south on your right. East across the plaza rises the classical facade of the Museo Regional de Chilpancingo, and to the left of that, the twin white bell towers of the Templo de Santa María de la Asunción, where the Act of Independence from Spain was declared on November 6, 1813.

Note the noble gilded statue of José María Morelos, at the plaza's northeast corner, below and in front of the church. It memorializes his Sentimientos de la Nación, with the pivotal quotation "No nation has the right to prevent another from the free use of its sovereignty."

At the adjacent, southeast plaza corner, below and in front of the museum, see the grand plaque, placed on September 13, 1985, that honors the 175th anniversary of the opening of the Congress of Anahuac. Its inscription, quoting Morelos, commemorates the end of the long period of Spanish dominion from August 12, 1521, until September 14, 1813: "On that day the chains of our servitude to Mexico-Tenochtitlán were broken forever in the brave town of Chilpancingo."

Through art, antiques, artifacts, and displays, the **Museo Regional de Chilpancingo** (tel. 747/472-8088, 10 A.M.–6 P.M. Tues.–Sun., $2) illustrates Guerrero geology, flora, fauna, archaeology, history, and folkways. A major attraction is the now-faded but epic historical mural by Roberto Cueva del Río and Luis Arenal that wraps around the entire inner patio. The mural begins at the patio's northeast (across the patio, left as you enter) corner and continues clockwise. The first panel shows the infant future emperor Cuauhtémoc (notice his birth sign, the descending eagle above the infant). Continue to the panel of the encounter of Cuauhtémoc with Cortés, then to the first corner, where another panel depicts the burial of the remains of Cuauhtémoc in Ixcateopan, near Taxco. Farther on, panels represent the independence heroes Morelos, Guerrero, and

CHILPANCINGO

To Tixtla, Chilapa, and Olinalá

93

DE LEÓN

FAIRGROUND, CHRISTMAS-NEW YEAR FAIR

HEROÍNAS DEL SUR

Barranca Petumpa

VICENTE LOMBARDO

AV. DE LOS GOBERNADORES

DAMIAN   VARGAS

LAURELES

5 DE FEBRERO

IGNACIO ZARAGOZA

AV. DEL SUR

AV. JUAN N. ÁLVAREZ SUR

SEGURO SOCIAL

AV. MIGUEL ALEMAN

UPN BUS STOP

IGNACIO RAMIREZ

HOSPITAL ANAHUAC

JUAN RUIZ DE ALARCÓN

HOTEL JACARANDAS

SEGURO SOCIAL CLINIC

AV. RUFFO FIGUEROA

To Río Azul, Río Papagayo Canyon, and Acapulco

Río Huacapa

100% NATURAL

HOTEL OMBU

HOTEL SAN CARLOS

AV. LÁZARO CÁRDENAS

CIUDAD UNIVERSITARIA

AUISPA CHILDREN'S MUSEUM ★

95   95D

BLVD. VICENTE GUERRERO (EXPRESSWAY)

VICENTE GUERRERO

CALLE 1

CALLE 3

CALLE 5

AV. JACARANDAS

Green Area

DE FEBRERO

28

450 yds

450 m

0

0

GUERRERO UPCOUNTRY

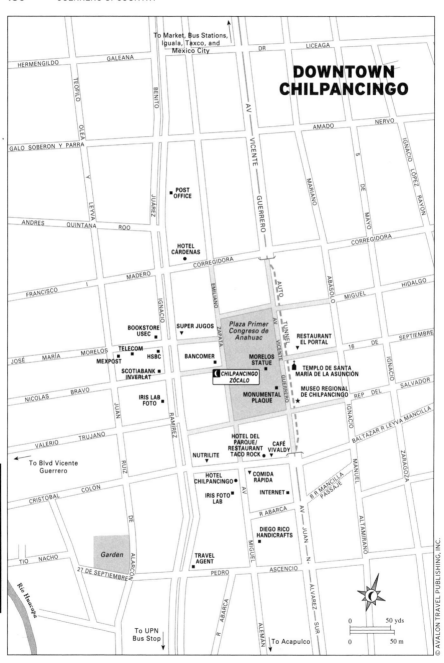

DOWNTOWN CHILPANCINGO

To Market, Bus Stations, Iguala, Taxco, and Mexico City

GUERRERO UPCOUNTRY

Hermanegildo Galeana (see sidebars "José María Morelos: Champion of Mexican Independence" and "Vicente Guerrero: Father of the Mexican Republic" in this chapter and "Hermanegildo Galeana: Gentleman Rebel" in *The Costa Grande* chapter), the Revolution of 1910, and, finally, the latter-day development of Guerrero state.

Step next door to the church, Templo de Santa María de la Asunción, the site revered in Mexico, not unlike Independence Hall in Philadelphia, as the place where Mexico's independence was declared. Note the polished, hand-carved church doors, with reliefs of Mexico's independence heroes: Morelos, first president Nicolás Bravo, Guerrero, and the magnificent eagle and serpent national symbol.

Sights Out of Downtown

Children will most certainly enjoy the small Chilpancingo **zoo** (tel. 747/472-5906, approx. 9 A.M.–5 P.M. Tues.–Sun., admission $2) near the corner of Moises Guevara and Arturo M. Adame, about half a mile northeast of the *zócalo*. The entrance is on the north side of a large park, with plenty of room to run around and spread a picnic.

Another good place for kids is the **Museo La Avispa** (tel. 747/471-2422 or 747/471-5444, www.museolaavispa.com.mx, 10 A.M.–3 P.M. daily, closed major holidays, admission $2) south of town, a block west of the corner of Bulevar Vicente Guerrero and Avenida Rulfo Figueroa. The museum's mission is to introduce technology with a host of hands-on, child-friendly (ages 4–12) activities.

ACCOMMODATIONS

Considering its many visitors on government or commercial business, Chilpancingo has relatively few hotels. Be certain to reserve at least a day (better a week) in advance. Some, but not all, Chilpancingo hotels accept credit cards. All hotel rates fall in the under $50 category. Most are compact, business-style hotels, with one exception: the restful, resort-style but moderately priced Hotel Jacarandas, in the southern suburb, convenient for drivers.

By location, starting downtown, the best city-center lodging choice is the busy business-style **C Hotel del Parque** (Colón 5, Chilpancingo, Guerrero 39000, tel. 747/472-3491 or 747/472-1364, fax 747/472-2547, alarcoma@prodigy.net.mx, $38 s, $48 d), a block south of the *zócalo*. Its 28 very clean rooms rise in four floors (but with no elevator) around a small inner lobby-patio. Inside, the rooms are comfortable, modern semideluxe, with hot-water shower baths, TV, phone, fans, and a good restaurant downstairs, but no pool. Parking nearby is extra, about $5.

In the same bustling south-of-*zócalo* neighborhood, but more economical, is the skillfully managed **Hotel Chilpancingo** (Miguel Alemán 8, Chilpancingo, Guerrero 39000, tel./fax 747/472-2446). The 40 clean, invitingly decorated, compactly arranged rooms connected by a maze of blue-tiled passageways offer many options. They range from the most basic and dark, to spacious light rooms with one to three double beds. The cheapest begin at about $10 d, and range upwards to about $50 for up to six people. All include private shower baths, carpet, flowery bedspreads and comfortable mattresses, fans, some TV, some air-conditioning, and credit cards accepted.

Even more downscale but still recommendable is the homey **Hotel Cárdenas** (Madero 11, Chilpancingo, Guerrero 39000, tel. 747/471-6153), a block north of the *zócalo*. Rooms in this converted old family home open on to an interior patio with chairs and shade umbrellas for relaxing. The plain but clean enough (I saw only one cockroach, and it was dying) bare-bulb rooms rent for about 14 s, $28 d, and $42 t, with hot-water shower baths.

Outside of the immediate downtown, visitors have a number of decent hotel choices. About a mile south of the *zócalo*, check out the newish **Hotel Ombu** (Av. L. Cárdenas 28, Chilpancingo, Guerrero 39000, tel. 747/472-5382 or 747/494-7910, fax 747/474-9911). Above the small lobby, three floors of 33 walk-up rooms rise around a spartan-chic inner atrium. Rooms themselves are simply but attractively decorated in tile, natural wood, and earth-tone

JOSÉ MARÍA MORELOS: CHAMPION OF MEXICAN INDEPENDENCE

As did his famous predecessor, George Washington, Mexican Independence General José María Morelos y Pavón convened his nation's first constitutional convention. The First Congress of Anahuac, an assemblage of leaders from all over Mexico, convened in Chilpancingo on September 14, 1813. It was virtually three years to the day after martyr-priest Miguel Hidalgo had ignited revolution from the balcony in Dolores, Guanajuato. Later, Morelos remembered: "On that day the chains of our servitude to Mexico-Tenochtitlán (Mexico City) were broken forever."

Those early days of revolution were heady times for a poor priest of such obscure origin. José María Morelos y Pavón was born in Valladolid (now Morelia, named in his honor), Michoacán, on September 30, 1765. Among experts, opinion is divided on Morelos's possible African-Mexican ancestry. Most historians go along with the major evidence: Morelos's swarthy, dark-eyed complexion and the well-known old legal document certifying that one of his grandmothers was a *"mujer libre,"* a standard legal phrase for a free, nonslave woman of African descent.

Young José no doubt was a devout Catholic. Early on, he wanted to study for the priesthood. While waiting to be admitted to seminary, he supported himself by working as a mule driver until he was admitted to the Valladolid Colegio San Nicolas in the mid-1780s.

While a student, José came under the influence of Father Miguel Hidalgo, who was the rector at San Nicolas. Hidalgo was not the usual role model for a budding acolyte. He was ambitious and much more interested in politics than in his priestly duties. Hidalgo's inner circle, which quickly included Morelos,

debated the ideas of the French Enlightenment philosophers Jean-Jacques Rousseau (*The Social Contract*) and Count Montesquieu (*The Spirit of the Laws*), who had strongly influenced the founding fathers of the brand-new United States of America.

Hidalgo, always seeking advancement, got an assignment to a rich Guanajuato parish, while José went west and served in a poor isolated corner of Michoacán.

After igniting revolution on September 15, 1810, Hidalgo led his raggedy peasant army, which grew rapidly to about 100,000 at its peak. Inspired, Morelos offered his services to Hidalgo, who told him to go south, raise an army, and capture Acapulco and the riches of the Manila galleon.

Morelos returned to his Michoacán homeland, raised a scruffy platoon of volunteers, and marched toward the coast. Along the way, Morelos recruited droves of volunteers, many of them African Mexican. They passed Zacatula and followed the coast east to Acapulco, arriving as an eager but ill-equipped 3,000-man guerrilla brigade.

In Acapulco, the only point of resistance (albeit stiff resistance) was the old Fuerte San Diego, where Morelos, after weeks of besieging the fort, divided his force. He left half surrounding the fort and led the remainder north to Chilpancingo, which he captured with the help of Hermanegildo Galeana and Nicolas Bravo.

Next, Morelos marched west, capturing Chilapa. Then, with a buoyantly robust force of 4,000, he continued north to Cuautla, in the present state of Morelos. Although besieged for 73 days by a superior royalist division, Morelos broke out with most of his men and marched southeast, where he captured Oaxaca, the prize of the south.

At Oaxaca, his radical egalitarian views, source of his popularity with his troops, surfaced:

> We must eliminate the outdated classifications separating us into black, mulatto, mestizo, and criollo... and call ourselves Americans for our origin as do the English, the French, and that other European country that is oppressing us.

The time was mid-1813, and Morelos was riding his crest of success. At 48, he was at his prime, cutting a dashing figure, topped by a colorful bandanna that wrapped his balding head. Napoleon Bonaparte is said to have paid Morelos the ultimate compliment: "With three such men as José Morelos, I could conquer the world."

Although a priest, Morelos, like his mentor Miguel Hidalgo, rejected sexual abstinence. He fathered several children by his indigenous common-law wife, Brigida Almonte, of Necupétaro, Michoacán.

One of Morelos's sons, Juan Almonte, born in 1803, gained fame, paradoxically working for the Mexican conservative cause. He served as President Bustamante's Minister of War during the 1830s, under General Santa Anna at the Alamo in Texas, later as ambassador to the United States and Britain, and finally in Emperor Maximilian's cabinet during the 1860s.

Morelos's signal achievement was the Congress of Anahuac, Mexico's first constitutional convention, which Morelos convened in Chilpancingo on September 14, 1813. Although subsequently driven from Chilpancingo by royalist forces, the Congress reconvened in Apatzingan, Michoacán, where it promulgated Mexico's first constitution on October 22, 1814.

Continually pressed by royalist troops, Morelos fought desperately for the remainder of his days protecting the Congress, which amounted to Mexico's first republican government. Finally, royalist troops captured him and spirited him to Mexico City on November 22, 1815. After a month-long trial during which Morelos argued eloquently for the justice of the *insurgente* cause, he was defrocked and taken to the city of San Cristóbal Ecatepec, where he was executed for treason by firing squad on December 27, 1815.

statue of José María Morelos, on the Chilpancingo *zócalo*

© BRUCE WHIPPERMAN

GUERRERO UPCOUNTRY

bedspreads and curtains. Tariffs run about $31 s, $35 d for a smallish, double-bed room and $49 for up to four in larger rooms with two double beds; all rooms come with good cable TV, phone, portable fan available, restaurant downstairs, and parking in the basement.

Farther south, about 1.5 miles (2.5 km) south of the town center is Chilpancingo's best: the government resort-style 【 **Hotel Jacarandas** (Av. Jacarandas, Chilpancingo, Guerrero 39300, tel. 747/472-4444, fax 747/472-4987). Guests enjoy a choice of about 50 rooms in a big, curving white jacaranda-decorated hillside block. Inside, rooms are clean, spacious, light, comfortable and open to airy private balconies overlooking a big blue pool-patio and tropical garden. For such amenities, rates run a reasonable $40 s, $49 d, $63 t, with cable TV, fan, phone, private hot-water shower baths, good restaurant, parking, and credit cards accepted. Reserve early; this place is often booked completely by conferences.

On the other hand, car travelers interested in an immaculate, well-managed lodging might like the **Parador del Marquez** (Km 276, Carretera Mexico–Acapulco, Chilpancingo, Guerrero 39000, tel. 747/472-6773, fax 747/472-9532) at the far south country edge of town. The hotel's location, about two miles (3 km) south of the town center, makes it likely to have a room when no other hotel in town does. The 20-odd rooms, in an inviting leafy garden, are immaculate and impeccably maintained in traditional Mexican tile, stucco, and brick decor. Choose from one king-size bed or two doubles. Rates run about $35 s or d in one bed; $49 d, t, or q in two beds, with cable TV, phone, parking, and good breakfast/lunch restaurant, but no pool.

On the north side of town, bus or car travelers might appreciate the convenience of the newish **Hotel Paraíso** (Chilpancingo, Guerrero 39010, tel. 474/471-1122 or 474/472-8863, fax 474/471-4691) on thruway Bulevar Vicente Guerrero, across from the bus station. Find it about a mile north of the *zócalo,* at the corner of 21 de Marzo. The 40-odd rooms enclose an inner parking-patio. Inside, they're comfortable and immaculate, with all-white semi-deluxe decor and hot-water shower baths. Rooms begin at about $45 d, with cable TV, phone, exercise gym, business center, restaurant/bar, air-conditioning, and parking.

FOOD

For snacks, try one of the many very clean streetfront *jugerías* and *loncherías* around the *zócalo*. For example, for good pizza and hamburgers, try **Comida Rápida** on Alemán, two blocks south of the plaza, at the corner of Colón. Alternatively, a few blocks north on the *zócalo's* northwest side, an excellent all-around choice is **Super Jugos,** with plenty of fresh *aguas,* juices, and hot *tortas* and *hamburguesas* (about $2).

As for restaurants, downtown's best choice for healthy goodies is 【 **Nutrilite** (Coló 11, tel. 747/494-1932, 7 A.M.–7 P.M. Mon.–Sat., 9 A.M.–7 P.M. Sun.), a block south of the *zócalo*, a few doors west of the corner of Alemán. Here, you can choose from a long list of breakfasts (whole wheat pancakes $2, eggs any style $2.50, fruit plate $2), or afternoon four-course *comida corrida* (with entrées such as stuffed cactus leaves or meatballs in chipotle sauce $3), plus a delicious harvest of fruit drinks ($2).

A few more sit-down restaurants provide good food in restful settings near the plaza. High marks go to refined 【 **Restaurant El Portal** (tel. 747/472-4668, 8:30 A.M.–10 P.M. daily) just off the *zócalo*, on the north side of the church, at the corner of Guerrero and Hidalgo. With open-air seating in view of the dramatic bust of Morelos across the street, El Portal is ideal for a relaxing snack or meal all day. In addition to a very recognizable menu of professionally prepared and served breakfasts, salads, soups, pastas, poultry, and meats ($2–6), it offers a bountiful three-course *comida corrida* ($3.50), 1–5 P.M. daily.

The **Restaurant Taco Rock** (Colón 5, tel. 747/472-3012 or 747/472-1285, 8 A.M.–midnight daily) in the Hotel del Parque, around the block south of the *zócalo*, is a very popular breakfast and lunch stop for business and professional people. At night it becomes a TV bar and nightclub, featuring Latin "taco rock" music. Entrées ($5–10) from a long Mexican-style coffee-shop menu are professionally prepared and presented.

Right next to Taco Rock is the contrastingly traditional and refined class-act **(** **Café Vivaldy** (Cristóbal Colón 3, tel. 747/472-2767, 8:30 A.M.–10 P.M. Mon.–Sat.), which serves up a deliciously unusual menu of breakfasts ($4–6), salads ($4–5), Mexican plates ($3–5), meats ($6–8), and baguette sandwiches ($3–4), plus a dozen gourmet coffees ($1–3). For dessert, sample one of their exquisite cakes (such as chocolate with pecans or strawberry cheesecake, about $2), all savored with Vivaldi's *Four Seasons* recorded music concerto singing lightly in the background.

Although it's not strictly vegetarian or macrobiotic, the menu of **100% Natural** (Av. L. Cárdenas 12, tel. 747/472-5457, 9 A.M.–9 P.M. daily), half a mile south of downtown, features plenty of healthy and tasty food. Choose from fruits and fruit *licuados,* granola, pancakes, eggs, yogurt, avocado, cheese, soya and meat burgers, french fries, and much more, in many styles, from scrumptious sandwiches to hearty entrée plates ($3–8). Service, by a dedicated squad of 20-somethings in white, beneath an open-air *palapa,* is exemplary.

EVENTS

Chilpancingo people unwind during the big year-end fair, **Feria de San Mateo, la Navidad, y el Año Nuevo,** December 24–January 8. The festivities kick off with the *teopancolaquio,* a ritual honoring the birth of God on Earth. Offerings include riots of flowers and regional dances, including Los Tlacololeros, Pescados (Fish), Diablos (Devils), and Manueles. Concurrent with all this is a grand commercial and agricultural fair, bullfights, carnival, fireworks, cockfights, and plenty of hearty Guerrero country food.

In nearby Tixtla (see *Excursions from Chilpancingo*), folks whoop it up during a couple of unique local fiestas. They celebrate the birthday of their most famous native son, Vicente

DANCE OF LOS TLACOLOLEROS

The noise and excitement of the Chilpancingo regional dance Los Tlacololeros remains a favorite of campesinos, who crowd in at fiesta time. The name refers to *tlacolol,* the Aztec word meaning "preparing the fields for planting" by the age-old slash and burn method, still widely used in the Sierra Madre backcountry.

The compelling drama centers on the whips, which the hilariously masked, cotton-and-sombrero-clothed men snap loudly on each others' padded arms, supposedly to imitate the crackle of the burning brush fire. In one version of the dance a she-dog called *la maravilla* makes a madcap chase after a *tigre* that threatens the campesinos.

All of a sudden, without warning, the fire mysteriously goes out while the dumbfounded dancers flail each other with increased desperation, trying frantically to find the culprit for the fire's failure. Soon, however, all is well that ends well as the loud rattling of chains simulates the fire's return, driving the *tigre* from the campesinos' midst.

Guerrero, on August 9, with a feast of cultural events, including music and favorite regional dances. Three weeks later, September 1–8, the Tixtla plaza is awash with celebrants for the **Fiesta de la Natividad de María.** Indigenous folks flood into town for the parade of floats, the carnival, fireworks, *jaripeo* bull roping and riding, and favorite traditional dances Los Manueles, Moros, Diablos, Tigres, and Tlacololeros. This is probably the most colorful time all year to visit the Tixtla Sunday market, known for its loads of for-sale native handicrafts.

SHOPPING

The best supermarket-department store in town is **Comercial Mexicana** (Calle Baltazar Leyva, tel. 747/472-6355, 8 A.M.–10 P.M. daily), recognizable by the tall orange and white pelican emblem-sign, by thruway Bulevar Vicente Guerrero (and McDonald's), about a mile north of downtown.

Although a few vendors sell handicrafts in the municipal market on Insurgentes, corner of Gardenias, about 1.5 miles north of the *zócalo,* the best source is the big Sunday *tianguis* (native market) in Tixtla.

One downtown store, however, does offer handicrafts. A couple blocks south of the plaza, check out **Artesanías Michacán** (Ramírez 17B, 9 A.M.–8 P.M. daily) of grandfatherly Diego Rico. Although he does hail from the state of Michocán, Diego offers curios from all over Mexico, made mostly of wood, leather, and pottery. They include a treasury of precious doodads, such as whirling *maltracas* noisemakers, sturdy *huaraches,* guitars both large and small, wriggling snakes, and bright lacquerware boxes.

For film and photo supplies and services, go to **Iris Lab** (tel. 747/472-6067, 9 A.M.–9 P.M. Mon.–Sat.), a block west of the plaza, on the west side of Ramírez between Trujano and Bravo. They stock many point-and-shoot cameras, both film and digital; camcorders; batteries; and accessories. They also develop and print color and black and white, and provide many digital services.

The scarcity of printed matter in Chilpancingo makes the collection of the mostly Spanish-language bookstore **Librería de la U.S.E.C.** (tel. 747/472-3656, 9 A.M.–9 P.M. Mon.–Sat.), at the corner of Juárez and Morelos, one block west of the plaza, all the more precious. Even if you don't buy anything, perusing the piles of many hundreds of volumes, covering myriad subjects from Don Quixote and the history of handicrafts to Faust and French-Spanish dictionaries, can provide a relaxing diversion for book lovers.

SERVICES
Banks

A number of bank branches, all with ATMs, cluster around the downtown plaza. The best bet is long-hours **HSBC** (Juárez 2, tel. 747/471-

2636, 8 A.M.–7 P.M. Mon.–Sat.), a block north and a block west of the plaza's northwest corner. Alternatively, go to **Bancomer** (tel. 747/472-2020, 8:30 A.M.–4 P.M. Mon.–Fri.), on the plaza's west side, corner of Bravo; or **Scotiabank Inverlat** (9 A.M.–5 P.M. Mon.–Fri.), one block west of the plaza at the corner of Bravo and Juárez.

Communications

Buy stamps and mail letters at the downtown *correo* (Vicente Guerrero 215, tel. 747/477-2275, 8 A.M.–3 P.M. Mon.–Fri., 9 A.M.–1 P.M. Sat.), a block and a half north of the *zócalo*'s northeast corner.

For secure mail, go to reformed government mail service **Mexpost** (Teofilio Olea y Leyva 1, tel. 747/471-0847), corner of Bravo, two blocks west of the *zócalo*. For telephone, fax, and money orders, go to **Telecom** (on Morelos, tel. 747/472-1154 or 747/472-2017, 8 A.M.–7:30 P.M. Mon.–Fri., 8 A.M.–12:30 P.M. Sat.–Sun.), two blocks west of the *zócalo*. If you need a telephone only, buy a widely available Ladatel card and use one of the many street phones scattered around the downtown.

Internet connections are commonly available in Chilpancingo. For example, try one of the pair of small Internet stores, **Centrinet** (tel. 747/491-6583) and **Cybertel** (tel. 747/471-6159), open approximately 9 A.M.–9 P.M. daily, both on the east side of Álvarez between Colón and Abarca, a block and a half south of the *zócalo*'s southeast corner.

Travel Agent

For airline and first-class bus tickets and hotel reservations, go to **Viajes Chilpancingo** (tel. 474/471-1389, tel./fax 474/472-9394, viajesleyva17@hotmail.com), at the corner of Ascencio and Ramírez, one block west and three blocks south of the *zócalo*'s southwest corner.

Health and Emergencies

Chilpancingo has up-to-date medical facilities. If you get sick, follow your hotel's recommendation. Otherwise, hail a taxi to whisk you to the very highly recommended private **Hospital Anahuac** (on Ignacio Ramírez, tel. 747/472-9505), about seven blocks south of the downtown *zócalo*. Alternatively, go to the 24-hour public **Centro de Salud** (Vicente Guerrero 45, tel. 747/474-7077), about 4 blocks north of the downtown *zócalo*, east side of the street. For fire emergencies, call the *bomberos* (tel. 474/472-2280). For police, call the *policia municipal* at emergency number 066.

GETTING THERE AND AWAY
By Bus
The main long-distance bus station, **Estrella Blanca,** is on side street 21 de Marzo, between thruway Vicente Guerrero and the municipal market, about 1.5 miles north of downtown.

Out front, a platoon of taxis, local buses, and *colectivos* ferry passengers to dozens of nearby destinations. Ladatel card-operated street telephones are available for calls.

Inside the smallish terminal, agents (tel. 474/472-0680) sell long-distance bus tickets. Both first- and second-class direct departures (including intermediate points) connect with Mexico City, Acapulco, Morelia, Guadalajara, Acapulco, Zihuatanejo, Puerto Vallarta, Iguala, Chilapa, Olinalá, Tlapa de Comonfort, Taxco, and the U.S. border at Nogales and Tijuana.

Outside, a few stands sell snacks, drinks, tacos, and sandwiches. For fresh items, stock up at the market, a block uphill.

Across the street, first-class **Estrella de Oro** (tel. 747/472-2130) buses connect north and south with Acapulco, Iguala, Taxco, and Mexico City.

By Car
Good roads make connections with Chilpancingo easy. To or from Acapulco, follow the *cuota* (toll) expressway a quick 62 miles (100 km, toll a steep $20) in about an hour and a quarter. *Libre* (toll-free) Highway 95 (83 miles, 133 km) connects with Acapulco in about twice the time, with much more than twice the hazard and wear and tear.

In the opposite direction, the *cuota* expressway connects Chilpancingo with Mexico City in 148 miles (239 km, auto toll about $30), but worth it, in about 3.5 hours. Make sure you arrive in Mexico City on a permitted day. The old Highway 95 connection, via Iguala and Taxco, with Mexico City, adds at least two hours to this under the best of conditions.

Connect north with Iguala in 67 miles (108 km, two hours), via old Highway 95; continue to Taxco in another 24 miles (38 km, one hour), for a total of 91 miles (145 km) and three hours.

For details on the east–west connection with Chilapa, Olinalá, and Tlapa de Comonfort, see *Getting There and Away* for both Chilapa and Olinalá in the *Handicrafts Country* section.

EXCURSIONS FROM CHILPANCINGO
Roads fan out from Chilpancingo to a number of spots worth visiting. These include Tixtla de Guerrero, the historic and colorful birthplace of Vicente Guerrero; the fascinatingly exotic La Organera Xochipala Archaeological Zone; and the easily accessible great outdoors of the Río Papagayo and canyon.

Tixtla de Guerrero
The trip to Tixtla (pop. 20,000) is part of the fun of going there. Although it's only eight miles (12 km), Tixtla is over a mountain, whose summit breezes are refreshing and the view beautiful. The first glimpse of Tixtla is its green patchwork of orchards and fields framed by high, pine-tufted ridges.

The place to arrive is the town-center *zócalo*. Bus riders, get off at the adjacent Tixtla market, at the end of the line. Drivers, turn left on to the main north–south town street, several blocks after entering the town. Let the church's bell tower be your guide to the central *zócalo*.

The *zócalo* focuses around the **Monument to Vicente Guerrero,** a bronze likeness of the great general in a heroic cape.

Next, head across the street, south from the

zócalo, to the house where Vicente Guerrero lived and directed Mexico's rebellion against Spain. Although it has been the Tixtla *presidencia municipal* since 1978, the house is a virtual shrine to Vicente Guerrero, not unlike Mount Vernon is for George Washington. The house's main attraction is a mural by Jaime A. Gómez de Payan that dramatically portrays major events and players in Mexican history. Moving clockwise: *insurgente* General Ignacio M. Altamirano (also born in Tixtla) with his hand on a jaguar's head; Benito Juárez surrounded by his contemporaries; José María Morelos passing the flame of liberty to Vicente Guerrero, who completes the struggle for independence; Emperor Cuauhtémoc, tortured for resisting Cortés.

From the *zócalo*, head west (away from the church) to an open ceremonial *zócalo*, fringed by market stalls and with a line of busts of eight of Tixtla's favorite sons and daughters.

VICENTE GUERRERO: FATHER OF THE MEXICAN REPUBLIC

The 1849 proposal for a new Mexican state to be carved from the states of Mexico, Puebla, and Michoacán would seem improbable, except that the proposed state was to be named Guerrero in honor of Mexico's famously popular independence hero and second president, Vicente Ramón Saldana Guerrero.

Vicente Guerrero, Mexico's first African-Mexican president, was born of working-class parents in the village of Tixtla, near Chilpancingo, on August 10, 1782. In 1811, Vicente was working successfully as a gunsmith when, inspired by Father Miguel Hidalgo's *insurgente* cause, he joined with priest-general José María Morelos's ragtag southern rebel forces.

Vicente's valor in battle and natural leadership ability led to his swift promotion. By 1815, however, with most of its original leaders, including Morelos, dead, the *insurgente* cause had lost momentum. Nevertheless, Guerrero grabbed the rebel banner in the south and rallied his men. Guerrero and his *compadre* commanders, Juan Álvarez and Pedro Ascencio, kept royalist brigadier Agustín de Itúrbide's troops in frustrated disarray, chasing the ragtag rebel bands throughout the southern Sierra Madre.

Vicente Guerrero was confronted by a crucial test in 1819. When offered amnesty, the exhausted Guerrero was tempted to give up. Even his father pleaded with him to surrender. But Guerrero remained resolute. In front of his men, Guerrero answered with the now-hallowed words, "Father, to me your voice is sacred... [but] the voice of my country comes first."

In 1821, Mexican royalists, faced with a new unfriendly liberal Spanish government, swallowed hard and joined Guerrero and the rebels. Under the flag (for which Guerrero had personally chosen the colors: red, white, and green) of "Three Guarantees" – independence, Catholicism, equality – Guerrero and Itúrbide rode victoriously into Mexico City.

But quickly, Itúrbide vaulted himself to glory as Emperor Agustín I of Mexico. As could be expected, Guerrero soon revolted, defeating Itúrbide's forces in battle on January 23, 1823, forcing Itúrbide to abdicate on March 19 and later to exile in May.

Mexican republicans took over and put together a national constitution in 1824. An election elevated liberal Guadalupe Victoria to president and conservative Nícolas Bravo to vice president. Although the restless Bravo revolted in 1827, the breach was temporarily resealed with the election of Vicente Guerrero as Mexico's second president in 1828.

Guerrero, although an able general and enormously popular war hero, was ill at ease among Mexico City's blue bloods. Guerrero left most of the salon politicking to his war minister, Leonardo Zavala (who had organized a popular revolt to get Guerrero elected), and Joel Poinsett, U.S. President Andrew Jackson's savvy ambassador to Mexico.

In the last analysis, although Guerrero's

All of the busts are looking west to the adjacent monument, dedicated jointly to Vicente Guerrero and Ignacio M. Altamirano. A large tablet records the words of Tixtla's most famous sons, which translate thus:

Before friendship, stands the homeland! Before sentiment, stands the idea! Before compassion, stands justice!
-Ignacio M. Altamirano

Your voice, father, is sacred to me; But the voice of my homeland comes first.
-Vicente Guerrero

From the Guerrero-Altamirano monument, walk south along Calle Federico Encarnación about four blocks. Turn right (west) and walk three blocks to the small park, the **Cuna (Cradle) de Vicente Guerrero.** Guerrero was born in the modest house (occupied) at the rear of the park on August 9, 1782.

egalitarian views were bad news to Mexico's powerful conservative chosen few, his untutored working-class and mixed-race background was the clincher. He simply didn't fit into Mexico City's upper crust. As it turned out, others were more than willing to take Guerrero's place.

One of those was Antonio López de Santa Anna, who became the darling of Mexican conservatives when his regiment batted down a half-hearted Spanish invasion on the Gulf Coast in July 1829. With Santa Anna's backing, conservative General Anastasio Bustamante mounted a revolt, forcing Guerrero to step down from the presidency in December 1829.

Guerrero again retreated to his southern home territory and drummed up yet another guerrilla revolt against the Mexico City *politicos*. As usual, Guerrero was master on his own ground. His irregulars outwitted government troops for a year.

Bustamante decided that trickery was the only way to defeat Guerrero. His agents got Guerrero to board the ship *Colombo*, in Acapulco, by bribing the ship's Genoese captain, archvillain Francisco Pichaluga. He took Guerrero, under custody, to Huatulco and handed him over to Bustamante's operatives on January 20, 1831.

Guerrero was next taken to the Valley of Oaxaca; after a bogus trial, he was executed by firing squad at the old Cuilapan basilica on February 14, 1831.

Sadly, the old warrior was gone. But his cause was not lost. Others – Juan Álvarez, Benito Juárez, Emiliano Zapata, Alvaro Obregón, Lázaro Cárdenas – and many more would carry Guerrero's banner for generations to come.

A monument memorializes Vicente Guerrero's immortal words.

GUERRERO UPCOUNTRY

If you get hungry during your Tixtla visit, a few clean plaza-front *torta* and taco *loncherías* supply wholesome snacks. For a further treat, hire a taxi to whisk you to the nearby **Centro Recreativo Tixtla** for a swim in the big spring-fed pool (and kiddie pool) and a picnic in the shade beneath a grove of big trees.

Although any day is good, Sunday is the best day to arrive in Tixtla, for the big *tianguis* (native market, tee-AHN-geese), when *campesinos* troop in to town loaded with handicrafts. These include soft palm *tenates* (tumpline baskets), sombreros, leather belts and huaraches, and colorfully embroidered *huipiles,* blouses, and skirts.

From Chilpancingo, get to Tixtla by mini-bus from the corner of Avenida Insurgentes and 17 de Octubre (near the market) about 10 blocks (0.6 mile, 1 km) north of the *zócalo.*

Drivers, get to Tixtla from downtown Chilpancingo's Avenida Juan Álvarez, about eight blocks south of the *zócalo.* Head east, uphill, along Laureles. After two blocks, turn left on Zaragoza; continue three blocks to Heronias del Sur and turn right, uphill. Continue east, going uphill at every intersection, until you arrive at the Tixtla *libramento* highway, where you turn right and follow the traffic.

La Organera Xochipala Archaeological Zone

The half-day (60 miles, 100 km) trip to La Organera Xochipala (named for the zone's giant organ cactuses) is typical of other sites

LA ORGANERA XOCHIPALA ARCHAEOLOGICAL ZONE

TOMB II

TEMPLE OF THE LIGHTS

NORTH PLAZA

WHITE PALACE

BANQUET ROOM

PALACE OF THE THREE PILARS

TOMB I

NORTH PLAZA

PALACE OF THE WALLS

PALACE OF THE FOUR PILLARS

PATIO OF THE ORGAN CACTUS

PLAZA OF THE CISTERN

PATIO OF THE MEZCAL

PATIO OF THE HIDDEN TOMB

TEMPLE OF SUNSET

SOUTH PATIO

BURNED PALACE

CIRCULAR EDIFICE

ALTAR

0   50 yds

0   50 m

of the Mezcala culture, which influenced the west and central inland areas of the present state of Guerrero for more than 1,000 years, until about A.D. 1400. Xochipala, which means "the flower that paints red" in the Aztec language, comprised an urban ceremonial center and defensive refuge, for a community that probably lived and farmed in an adjacent river valley.

At the present, expertly restored site, archaeologists have partially rebuilt more than two dozen significant constructions, including colonnaded palaces, false-arched passageways, plazas, patios, temples, rooms, tombs, basements, and a ball court. Its forest of towering organ cactuses adds to La Organera Xochipala's invitingly exotic ambience.

Archaeologists have uncovered five stages in La Organera Xochipala's history. The oldest, now covered over by more recent construction, started with walls of cemented blocks, associated with pottery fragments identifiable with the Mexican classic period, A.D. 200–350. During the second stage of construction, around 200 years later, the builders added false arches, one of which formed the dome of a tomb of an adolescent. Most of the visible construction was completed during the third epoch, centering around A.D. 800. Builders completed columned, circular structures that supported flat roofs. The site declined during the fourth, "decadent," stage, in which old buildings were either abandoned or merely maintained. The site was completely abandoned during the fifth stage, around A.D. 1400.

Important clues have been discovered in the trash dumps left by the inhabitants: much pottery, similar to that used today, stone hatchets, metates, tiles, polishing stones, arrow- and spearheads, leather, copper greenstone beads, and much more. All this, added to the evidence of trade in cotton, fruit, salt, seeds, and medicinal plants recorded at the time of the conquest, surely indicates a vibrant agricultural and commercial culture, with busy trade ties with both neighboring and distant communities.

From the main Chilpancingo bus station, get to La Organera Xochipala by second-class Tlacotepec-bound bus or *colectivo*. Ask the driver to let you off at the signed Zona Arqueológica side road on the left before Xochipala. The site is another two miles on foot.

Drivers, head north from Chilpancingo on old Highway 95 about 20 miles (33 km) to the signed Filo de Caballo paved secondary road. Turn left and continue uphill six miles (10 km) to the signed Zona Arqueológica dirt side road on the left. Continue two miles (3 km) to the signed gate on the right.

La Organera Xochipala Archaeological Zone is open approximately 9 A.M.–5 P.M. daily except holidays. Few facilities, except a toilet, are available. Bring drinks, food for a picnic, sturdy walking shoes, and a hat.

River Country

Chilpancingo serves as a convenient jumping-off point to enjoy this trio of uniquely lovely natural attractions, set like gems beneath the pine-tufted Sierra Madre del Sur.

Closest to Chilpancingo is the Río Azul, a popular Sunday picnic route, decorated along the way by a winding, intimate canyon; a lush green farm valley; and colorful, petite market towns, climaxed by an azure ribbon of crystalline springs.

Although all that would be quite enough, a marvelous natural treat hides at the end of the 31-mile road: the Grutas de Juxtlahuaca, a pristine wonderland grotto of varicolored limestone formations, underground rivers, prehistoric burial remains and wall paintings, all culminating in a wondrous garden of flowery, snow-white aragonite (calcium carbonate) crystals.

South of Chilpancingo, the clear green Río Papagayo and its rocky canyon provide plenty of opportunities for swimming, kayaking, rafting, hiking, and camping.

THE RÍO AZUL
Heading Out

By bus, this trip could be done from Chilpancingo in one very long day. Start out at dawn, via a Colitlipa-bound bus, from the Universidad Pedagogical Nacional (UPN, oo-pay-ENay) streetfront bus terminal at the corner of Ignacio Ramírez and Niños Héroes, about five blocks south of the Chilpancingo main *zócalo*.

For more leisure, hire a taxi for the day (figure about $50), or stay overnight, camping or staying in a *cabaña* at Balneario Santa Fe or in the Casa de Huépedes Citlalí in Colotlipa.

Travelers by car could likewise do this 74-mile (119-km) round-trip in a long day. Start off around 7 A.M., drive to the Grutas de Juxtlahuaca and explore until around 1 P.M. On the return, stop for a leisurely lunch and swim at the Balneario Santa Fe. In Chilpancingo, fill up with gasoline before you leave; other-wise, gasoline is customarily available en route at the Quechultenango *gasolinera*.

Along the Way: Petaquillas, Mochitlán, and Quechultenango

Drivers, follow old Highway 95 (not the expressway) south from Chilpancingo seven miles (11 km) to the signed Petaquillas–Quechultenango crossroad. Mark your odometer and turn left, east.

Immediately pass through **Petaquillas** (pop. 5,000, stores, local-style restaurants, town plaza, post office), known for its Balneario Bugambilias water slide, pool, and restaurant, a block from the town plaza. During the week before August 27, folks will also be celebrating their patronal **Fiesta de San Agustín** with bullfights, plenty of food, a carnival, and regional dances, including the Tlacololeros, Moros, Pastoras (Shepherdesses), and Diablos (Devils).

Continue east, winding through the narrow, precipitous canyon of the Río Azul. Although the riverbed will probably be dry during the winter and spring, don't worry; year-round springs keep the downstream delightfully crystal blue (except perhaps during some muddy summer rainy season floods).

At Mile 6 (Km 10) arrive at **Mochitlán** (pop. 4,000, *centro de salud,* post office, street market, taco shops, and stores), presiding over its lush irrigated riverbottom fields. If you have an extra few minutes, take a look inside the town's venerable barrel-nave church. It's the focus of the July 26 **Fiesta de Santa Ana,** when the townsfolk stage a float parade, carnival, fireworks, and enjoy regional dances, including the Tlacololeros, Santiagueros, Diablos, and Huexquitxles.

Continue east to **Quechultenango** (pop. 4,000), the dominant town of the upper Río Azul Valley, at Mile 17 (Km 27). As if proclaiming the town's importance, the brilliantly decorated church presides over the east side of the plaza. Enter and pass the flowery

EXPLORING THE GRUTAS DE JUXTLAHUACA

Although the Juxtlahuaca limestone cave complex, 30 miles (50 km) east of Chilpancingo, is not the world's largest, the treasures that it hides are exquisite and unique.

The cave complex, used as a burial ground and sacred site, probably by 400 B.C., was explored by latter-day investigators in 1926 and later more thoroughly by Andrés Ortega Covarrubias during the 1950s. Ortega uncovered a then-unknown entrance and eight underground branches, extending a total of about four miles (6 km).

As in all limestone caves, Juxtlahuaca's extensive stalagmites, stalactites, columns, and curtains result from the slight solubility of limestone (calcium carbonate) in water. Thus groundwater, over eons, gradually dissolved the limestone, forming hollow chambers.

The process continues with water droplets falling from the ceiling, leaving a small wet spot above and a similar wet spot below, which dry and deposit some limestone at top and bottom. The dripping continues, gradually building the deposits into long, massive formations that, after many thousands of years, often merge to form grand columns. Water dribbling down the cave walls can deposit limestone similarly, forming magnificent curtains, lovely enough for a maharaja's palace.

Moreover, variations in mineral content, especially iron, causes color variations in the deposits, from pure white to cream, dusty rose, and sienna. Explorers have named many of the formations thus created, such as the Enchanted Fountain, the Cathedral, the Salon of the Ghost, and the Tiger.

Bats and insects make up the bulk of the cave's permanent living inhabitants. Thousands of bats roost on the ceilings not far from the entrance; on the cave floor, cockroaches scurry, feasting on the bats' droppings.

Deep in the cave, humans have left their signs on the cave's walls and floors. Several burial sites, including complete petrified skeletons; much pottery; and *El Chaman, El Serpiente,* and *El Jaguar,* a trio of magnificent cave paintings; attest to the human presence that continues to the present day.

© BRUCE WHIPPERMAN

crystalline aragonite as delicate as snowflakes on the cave wall and ceiling at the Grutas de Juxtlahuaca

GUERRERO UPCOUNTRY

retablo behind the Virgin of Guadalupe on the left. Overhead, paintings of the Stations of the Cross decorate the ceiling, while up front, behind the altar, Santiago, mounted on a silver horse, brandishes a sword while trampling a hapless band of defeated Moors.

Community celebration focuses yearly at that very altar during the eight-day **Fiesta of Santiago,** combined with the unique indigenous rite of **Ocozuchil,** all of which culminates on the Santiago Feast Day of July 25. People flock in from neighboring communities, among them men decked out in red leather with machetes in hand, to perform the traditional dance Los Santiagueros. Representing Christian warriors, their machetes clash menacingly and repeatedly with the swords of the Moors, whom the Santiagueros finally vanquish and force to accept baptism.

Concurrently during the Santiago fiesta, other folks journey to the sierra to collect *ocozuchil,* an aromatic wild herb. When cut, the herb oozes a strong medicinal odor, thought to be curative. They walk to Quechultenango with the *ocozuchil* branches draped over their bodies and crowd into the church atrium. Inside, a chosen group of penitents pass one by one in front of the image of Santiago, with an *ocozuchil* branch in each hand. Afterward, they dance, whirling to the mesmerizing beat of the pre-Hispanic *teponaxtli* drum.

🄲 Headwaters of the Río Azul

The series of *manantiales* (springs) near Coxcamila, one mile farther east of Quechultenango, at Mile 18, are the marvelous main source of the Río Azul. At the Coxcamila village center, go right, south, on to the dirt side road to the springs, called locally El Borbollón. Follow the pedestrian file along the dirt entrance driveway about a quarter mile to a grove of giant old trees, from beneath whose gnarled roots cool crystal-clear water wells, free for everyone to enjoy.

On Sunday, dozens of cars loaded with picnickers arrive and eventually fill a big parking lot, where vendors sell corn on the cob, tamales, and soft drinks from wheelbarrows,

© BRUCE WHIPPERMAN

The headwaters of the Río Azul flow blue and crystalline.

cows stand around, men fill buckets for washing their trucks, and women do laundry and bathe their children, while everyone else seems to be frolicking in the water.

That this is the source is certain. Walk upstream 100 yards, and the river is a mere trickle during the dry season. But downstream, many tens of thousands of gallons a minute of clear water, delightfully cool on a warm day, flow constantly.

Camping in your own tent by the riverbank or self-contained RV in the parking lot is customary at El Borbollón. Police patrols assure night-time security.

Río Azul Balnearios

Farther downstream, activity focuses at three *balnearios* (bathing spots) on the Río Azul. These include **Los Manantiales** (several attractive swimming pools and restaurant at Mile 19, Km 31); **Los Sauces** (at Mile 22, Km 35, but apparently abandoned); and by far the most popular, **Balneario Santa Fe,** reachable by the signed paved side road, right at mile

19.4 (Km 31.2), about half a mile after Los Manantiales.

For Balneario Santa Fe, continue along the side road two miles (3 km), passing through the small but prosperous Santa Fe town, to the river overlook, then downhill the last quarter mile to the river.

A dozen shady *palapa* restaurants line the clear, two-foot-deep flowing stream, a welcome marvel, especially during the dry and oft-hot winter and spring.

Besides ready food for eating and hammocks for resting, old-fashioned water sports abound. After taking your fill of swimming, inner-tubing, and rafting, cross the river suspension bridge to the other side to the best of all possible swimming holes, complete with rope to swing out and plunge into the cool water.

If you decide to linger, the walk-in **Campamento Santa Fe,** also across the suspension bridge, offers some options. Choose one of the cramped (but probably fun for kids) *cabañas* ($8 for up to four people, $16 for up to eight). For a better choice, if you're equipped, set up your tent in one of the roomy camping spaces, $1.50 per person. Toilets are in shared lavatories. For a bath, jump in the river (or the swimming pool, if it's operating).

RV campers (with medium to small rigs) can park in a large riverside lot that is accessible by turning left from the downhill entrance road a couple hundred yards before the river at the driveway marked by a big tree on the left.

GRUTAS DE JUXTLAHUACA

The lightly touristed but wondrous Grutas de Juxtlahuaca takes its name from its neighboring village, Juxtlahuaca (hooks-tlah-WAH-kah). The small town of Colotlipa, four miles before the cave, is the jumping-off point for guides, food, and services.

Get to the Grutas de Juxtlahuaca from Colotlipa most conveniently by taxi (about $10). By car, drive to the eastern edge of town, where a Grutas sign directs you left on to a paved secondary road. After three miles, pass a sugar cane–pressing mill on the left, which squeezes out juice for sweet *tepache* or for fermentation

Curtains of stone embellish the wall of the Juxtlahuaca cave.

© BRUCE WHIPPERMAN

into fiery *aguardiente*. After four miles, arrive at the cave parking lot. Facilities consist only of a toilet and a *palapa* restaurant that is sometimes open.

Colotlipa

The town of Colotlipa (pop. 4,000) is not far past the Río Azul *balnearios,* 23 miles (37 km) east of old Highway 95. If you arrive during the February 18–26 **Fiesta del Señor de las Misericordias** (Lord of Mercy) festival, the plaza might be filled with celebrants who, at dawn on February 26, climax the festivities by saluting their *patrón* with jingle bells and *mañanitas.*

Besides having the usual services such as local-style restaurants, market fruits and vegetables, grocery stores, *centro de salud,* post office, and street telephones, Colotlipa is the place to hire your guide.

A right-side sign, on east–west plaza-front Calle Guerrero, marks the cave guides' at-home office (tel. 756/474-7006, 756/474-7034, or 756/474-7047). Up until the late

1990s, the main guide was Profesor Andrés Ortega Casarrubias, who during the 1950s was first to explore the cave thoroughly. Andrés, known famously as El Chivo, passed away in 2004. Now Andrés's son Andrés; his widow, Brenda; and his second son, Enrique; continue his mission as Chivo II, Chivo III, and Chivo IV, respectively.

The Chivo guides have inherited the exclusive Grutas de Juxtlahuaca guide franchise, awarded to Andrés by the governor of Guerrero in 1958. They lead individuals and small groups for about $20 per person, $10 per person in a larger group of four to eight. Call at least a day in advance for a reservation.

Their complete tour (in Spanish), which lasts two to three hours and stretches about two underground miles round-trip, is fascinating, but moderately difficult. If at all possible, try not to miss the climactic conclusion, which requires wading along a knee-to-waist-deep underground river, then crawling 100 feet along a cramped, damp passageway. You'll get wet, but at the end of the road a marvelous garden of flowery aragonite crystals will reward your effort. Be sure to take along a pair of tennis shoes for wading and a small backpack or camera holster and watertight bag to keep your camera dry and undamaged.

For a Colotlipa overnight, you can stay at **Casa de Huépedes Citlalí** (Calle Neri 21, no phone), run by friendly Xochi (SOH-chee) Ortega, two blocks east and half a block south of the Colotlipa *zócalo*. She offers clean rooms, with two double beds and shared toilet and hot-water shower, for $10 per room for up to four people. Make reservations through the Chivo guides, above. Besides managing her guesthouse, Xochi also runs a brisk business selling tacos on the curb in front of her house at night.

Hearty home-cooked food is also available in Colotlipa, at home restaurant **El Latino,** half a block south of the southeast corner of the town plaza. The hard-working owner serves country-style Mexican breakfasts around 8 A.M. ($2–4), an afternoon *comida* (such as beef stew, or chiles rellenos, $3–5), and snacks for supper (tacos, quesadillas, or eggs, $2–4) until around 7 P.M. (Don't be put off by the trucks parked adjacent to the restaurant tables. Besides providing meals for dozens of daily satisfied customers, the friendly, hardworking owner also rents garage space.)

THE RÍO PAPAGAYO

Only about 30 miles (50 km) south of Chilpancingo, both the old Highway 95 and the new *cuota* expressway 95D cross the free-flowing, wild Río Papagayo. Its cool waters and rocky canyon provide adventurers with plenty of swimming, rafting, canoeing, kayaking, hiking, rock-climbing, and informal camping opportunities. The best time for enjoying Río Papagayo outdoor activities is during the dry low-water months of October–January, when the river is an invitingly clear emerald-green color. High water during the rainy months of July, August, and sometimes September colors the river a muddy brown and possible flooding could put a damper on river adventure options.

Get to the Río Papagayo by second-class bus either from the Chilpancingo Estrella Blanca bus station or the Acapulco Estrella Blanca Ejido station. After an approximate hour and half trip from either city, ask the bus driver to let you off at the Bravo Town riverfront headquarters, marked by a prominent roadside arch near Km 322, a fraction of a mile north of the old Highway 95 Río Papagayo bridge.

By car, drive about 30 miles (50 km) or 45 minutes south from Chilpancingo (or the same north from Acapulco) via the Highway 95D *cuota* expressway to the Tierra Colorada exit and old Highway 95. For Bravo Town, exit at the Tierra Colorada interchange and head west under the expressway, along old Highway 95, about four downhill miles southwest to Bravo Town, or a fraction of a mile farther to the old Highway 95 bridge, where dirt roads lead downhill to the river.

(If you have an extra hour and enjoy handicrafts, stop by **Acahuizotla,** two miles off the Acapulco expressway, about 17 miles (28 km) south of Chilpancingo. Folks make and sell fetching curios carved from the rose-colored wood of the *palo de morado* tree.)

Bravo Town Ecoadventuring

The Río Papagayo outdoor adventure sports site, Bravo Town (Pueblo Bravo), is about 45 minutes by *cuota* expressway south of Chilpancingo (and about the same distance north of Acapulco). Bravo Town is a subsidiary branch of the popular Acapulco-based Shotover Jet boat excursion company (Shotover is the name of the New Zealand inventor of their jet boats) that used to operate out of the Bravo Town river site, but now offers jet boat rides in mangrove Laguna Dos Palos east of Acapulco.

At Bravo Town (tel. 744/484-1155, fax 744/484-2648, ventas@shotoverjet.com.mx, www.shotoverjet-acapulco.com, open year-round), you can enjoy many attractive, modestly priced features that include, for starters, a good snack restaurant, a blue pool, riverfront shade trees for picnicking, and space for tenting and RV parking ($5). Bravo Town's adventure tour offerings include river rafting, kayaking, hiking, camping, caving, rappelling, and climbing. For example, their half-day rafting excursion runs $50 per person from Bravo Town (or $60, including transportation, from their Acapulco headquarters at the Plaza Marbella on the Costera, beach side of the Diana circle). A more extensive adventure option is a two-day (Class 3 and 4) rafting expedition that includes rappelling and riverside overnight camping, for $300 per adult, kids cheaper, everything included. They also offer leisurely family-oriented trips that, besides gentle rafting, include exploring a natural riverside "museum" of fantastic rock formations, hiking, animal-watching, camping, and more.

Independent Adventures

Prepared and equipped lovers of the outdoors can also organize their own Río Papagayo adventures. Besides availing themselves of Bravo Town's snack restaurant, pool, and RV parking and tenting space (tent and air mattresses available for rent), plenty of sandy riverfront is also available for independent RV parking and tent camping below the Río Papagayo bridge (at old Highway 95 Km 322). Moreover, hearty country-style meals are obtainable at nearby restaurants such as **Bello I** (tel. 744/102-3305, 8 A.M.–9 P.M. daily), on Highway 95 about half a mile uphill from Bravo Town. Groceries, drinking water, and supplies are available at stores in Tierra Colorada town, along Highway 95, a fraction of a mile east of the Highways 95–95D toll expressway interchange.

Handicrafts Country

The renowned handicrafts of upcountry mountain towns **Chilapa** and **Olinalá** draw a steady stream of buyers and visitors. Be sure to arrive in Chilapa, only an hour's travel east of Chilpancingo, early for the Sunday *tianguis* (native market), where craftspeople from all over the Guerrero Sierra Madre bring their best for sale.

Afterward, travel a few hours farther east to Olinalá and visit the workshops of the masters of a preconquest lacquerware tradition whose intriguingly mysterious origins are lost in time.

CHILAPA

Presiding over its rich spring-fed mountain valley, Chilapa de Álvarez (pop. 20,000, elev. 4,300 feet, 1,310 meters) was named in honor of the liberal hero General Juan Álvarez (1810–1867).

History

The other part of the town's name comes from Chilapan, a description that comes from the Aztec—from *chili* (red), *atl* (water), and *pan* (on or above). It translates roughly as "on the red water," or simply, "red river."

An early historical reference to Chilapan comes from the time of Emperor Moctezuma I (Moctezuma Ilhuacamina), who, around A.D. 1450, was expanding his domain. He ordered his subordinate officer, Texcolo Tecutlique, to establish an outpost beneath the mountain Chilapantépetl, which eventually became the town of Chilapan.

In 1522, the Spanish, in the person of Hernán Cortés's lieutenant, conquistador Gonzalo Sandoval, conquered the local people.

Soon, Augustinian missionaries arrived and began converting the natives and building a church and convent, which they dedicated to Saint Augustine on October 5, 1533.

The Augustinian friars encouraged the Chilapa people to expand their long-established weaving tradition. For many centuries before the conquest, their elaborately crafted blankets, *huipiles,* and skirts had been traded all over southern Mexico. Under the guidance of the Augustinians, they broadened their skills, eventually crafting the wide variety of baskets, hats, napkins, and pottery that make up the rich Chilapa handicrafts tradition that continues to the present day.

Getting Oriented and Getting Around

The prime orientation point upon Chilapa arrival is the main highway crossing by the crafts market, marked by the permanent stalls behind the fence just east of the crossing. If you arrive on a Sunday, park your car or get off the bus and head for the crafts market. Later, from the crossing, you can reach the downtown plaza either on foot (about half a mile south), *bici-taxi* (bicycle rickshaw, BEE-see), taxi, or your own wheels.

◖ Chilapa Sunday Handicrafts Market

Beginning Saturday afternoon, country folks loaded with handmade goods begin arriving for the renowned Sunday handicrafts market. Their wealth of offerings customarily include an array of materials—leather bags, belts, coin purses, wallets, shoes, huaraches; shell and horn bracelets, combs, ashtrays, desk sets, lampshades; iron machetes, hatchets, daggers, swords, knives; many handpainted or embroidered textiles such as *ixtle* (agave fiber) bags, *rebozos* (shawls), napkins, tablecloths, *huipiles;* basketry such as palm sombreros, mats, and baskets and reed baskets; and wooden miniature castles and bulls, human tiger-masked figures, pine furniture, musical instruments, and animal figurines.

flowers at the Chilapa Sunday Handicrafts Market

castillos, wooden frames festooned with fireworks, on sale at the Chilapa market

Many crafts come from outside Chilapa—for example, shawls from Tenancingo; silver from Taxco; huaraches from Iguala and Tixtla; fireworks from Ayahualulco; lacquerware and tiger masks from Olinalá; papier-mâché from Mezcala; bright earth-red pottery from Atzcualoya; *amate* (painted bark paper) from Amayaltepec; animal figures from Temalacatzingo; and embroidered blouses and skirts from Acatlán.

You might also stroll through the colorful **main market,** adjacent, east of the crafts market. Here, the double meaning of *tianguis,* the native name for both awning and market, becomes abundantly clear in the seeming acres of colorful awnings. The excitement begins on the market-front steps, where women sell small piles of produce (radishes, corn, small pumpkins, squash, mangoes in the March–July season, beans, and mountain herbs).

(*Note:* Although unusual anywhere in Guerrero, some pickpockets unfortunately seem to be operating at the Chilapa Sunday *tianguis.* Their technique, which I experienced, was distraction by jostling. Be aware, and keep your unmissable items in a secure front waist belt. Moreover, women, zip your purses, and men, keep your wallet in your front pocket with a hand on it.)

Downtown Plaza and Cathedral

For more sights, head south to the downtown plaza and towering neo-Gothic cathedral, dedicated to St. Francis and seat of the local bishop. One of the cathedral's main attractions occurs every Sunday at noon, when the miraculous roses of the Virgin of Guadalupe are revealed to mechanical figures of Don Diego and Archbishop Zumárraga at the door on the right bell tower. Inside the cool nave, spectacularly large stained glass windows, each one donated by a Guerrero locality, add daytime cheer to the cavernous interior. Up front, contemplate the image of mother Mary above the altar being lifted to heaven by a band of angels.

Back outside the church, a fleet of **bici-taxis,** looking every bit like bicycle rickshaws

GUERRERO UPCOUNTRY

© BRUCE WHIPPERMAN

Chilapa's central plaza is spacious, shady, and usually tranquil.

from the Indian subcontinent, stop and pick up passengers at curbside.

Before leaving the Chilapa plaza, be sure to stop for a drink or snack and admire the marvelous mask collection at the plaza-front Casa Pilla restaurant.

Accommodations and Food

Chilapa visitors enjoy a pair of recommendable hotels. About three blocks north of the plaza is **Hotel María Hilda** (Av. Revolución 229, Chilapa, Guerrero, tel. 756/475-1840). The hotel's 36 rooms occupy two stairway-accessible floors above street level. Rooms are cool, clean, light, and sparely but comfortably furnished with bedspreads, curtains, and tiled hot-water shower baths. They have no reading lamps, however. Most rooms have one, two, or three double beds. A few rooms have king-size beds. Rates run $16 s, $19 d (one bed); $25 s or d in king; $25 d (two beds); $28 t (two beds); and $33 t (three beds), with cable TV and parking, but no fans or air-conditioning.

"Cleanliness Is Our Rule" at **Hotel Las**

Brisas (Prolongacion Av. Revolución 2, Chilapa, Guerrero, tel. 756/475-0769) at the Chilpancingo highway intersection. Here you get to choose from 36 clean rooms, comfortably furnished with double beds, shiny wood furniture, bright bedspreads, and small but tiled hot-water shower baths. Some rooms have bedside reading lamps. Expect to pay about $15 s or d (one bed); $26 d, t, or q (two beds); $35 for 3–6 in three beds, with cable TV, parking, fans, and air-conditioning. Reserve the quietest rooms (with least highway noise): 5, 6, or 7 on the second and third floors.

Some of Chilapa's best budget food is available at the several permanent *jugerías* (with juices, *tortas,* and *hamburguesas,* $1–3) and *fondas* (serving stews, soups, tacos, *chiles rellenos,* and enchiladas, $2–4), at the rear of the main market floor at the highway crossing north of downtown. One of the best is *fonda* **Doña Lilia** (7:30 A.M.–7 P.M. daily), which specializes in savory chicken or pork *pozole* and steaming *guisado de res* (beef stew).

Chilapa's best plaza-front eatery is restaurant-bakery **Casa Pilla** (tel. 756/475-0263, 8 A.M.–8 P.M. Mon.–Sat., 8 A.M.–7 P.M. Sun.) at the northeast downtown plaza corner. If not for the food, Casa Pilla is unforgettable for the spectacular mask collection that adorns its airy dining room. The menu is nevertheless both recognizable and appetizing for breakfast (pastries, fruit, omelettes, pancakes, $2–5) and lunch and dinner (hamburgers, spaghetti, pork chops, seafood, and *pozole,* $3–7).

Events

Chilapa takes time out for a pair of colorful yearly fiestas. First comes the **Fiesta de San Juan** around June 24, when folks crowd the plaza to watch a parade of floats, listen to the oompah of country bands, watch fireworks, and enjoy their favorite regional dances, including the Pescados (Fish) and Moros y Cristianos (Moors and Christians).

Those who didn't get a chance to celebrate earlier get another opportunity when townsfolk parade their patron at the August 15 **Fiesta de la Virgen de la Asunción.**

Services

A number of essential services are available near the Chilapa *zócalo*.

Find at least two banks with 24-hour ATMs. Best bet is long-hours **HSBC** (tel. 756/475-2396, 8 A.M.–7 P.M. Mon.–Fri., 8 A.M.–3 P.M. Sat.), walk a block north to Constitución from the plaza's northwest corner, turn left (west) and continue a block to the bank. Alternatively, go to **Banamex** (tel. 756/465-0010, 9 A.M.–4 P.M. Mon.–Fri.) on the east side of the plaza.

The *correo* (post office) (Calle 5 Oriente 394, tel. 756/475-0066, 8 A.M.–3 P.M. Mon.–Fri.) is on the south side of the plaza on Calle 5 Oriente (East); walk south from the plaza's southeast corner. At Calle 5 Oriente (just past the south end of the church), go left about three doors. For telephone, either buy a Ladatel phone card and use one of the plaza-front street telephones, or go to **Telecom** (9 A.M.–3 P.M. Mon.–Fri., 9 A.M.–noon Sat.–Sun.) on Calle 3 Poniente (West) for public telephone, fax, and money orders. From the southwest (church-front) plaza corner, walk south a block to Calle 3 Poniente. Turn right and continue three blocks past the Centro de Salud. Internet access is available at **Pese P Internet** store (tel. 756/475-2400, chelisinc@hotmail.com, 9 A.M.–9 P.M. daily), at the northeast plaza corner.

For medical attention, let your hotel desk clerk call a doctor for you. Alternatively, go to the **Centro de Salud** (Calle 3 Poniente 703, tel. 756/475-0077), with a doctor on call 24 hours a block east of the Telecom.

Getting There and Away

By Bus: From Chilpancingo, connect with Chilapa via a first- or second-class departure from the **Estrella Blanca** main bus station. From Acapulco, Chilapa connections are available from the Estrella Blanca Ejido terminal.

For Chilapa bus departure, go by taxi or *bici-taxi* to the local **Estrella Blanca terminal** (Av. Municipio Libre 1804, tel. 756/475-0032). To find it go about a block east of the market to Municipio Libre, then right (south) about a mile. From the terminal, a number of first- and second-class buses connect daily with Chilpancingo, Acapulco, and Mexico City. One bus per day connects with Olinalá, and several with Tlapa de Comonfort, where connections are available with Puebla and Oaxaca destinations.

Frequent *colectivo* connections are also available between about 5 A.M. and 7 P.M. at a pair of terminals across Highway 93 from the Chilapa main market, at the corner of Calle Municipio Libre. **Transportes Guerrerenses** vans connect west several times per day with Chilpancingo and all intermediate points. Next door, **Ruta Chilapa-Olinala** vans provide similar connections west with Olinalá and all intermediate points.

By Car: The good, super-scenic, all-paved but winding Highway 93 connects Chilpancingo with Chilapa in 34 miles (54 km), about an hour). In the opposite direction, Highway 93 connects Chilapa with Tlapa de Comonfort over three 7,000-foot ridges, in about 75 miles (121 km) of smooth, scenic, but winding highway, in about three hours. In all cases, fill up with gasoline at the Chilapa station on the highway.

Reach Olinalá by starting out driving east toward Tlapa. After about 57 miles (92 km, 2.5 hrs), turn left (north) from Highway 93 at the signed Olinalá junction. Continue north about 25 smooth miles (40 km, 1 hr) to Olinalá, for a total of about three and a half hours from Chilapa.

OLINALÁ

Reigning over its fertile, mountain-rimmed valley on the edge of the sunny basin of the Río Balsas, Olinalá is famous not only for its lacquerware, but also for its masks and furniture. Most Olinalá families are involved in lacquerware, and a number of artisans welcome visitors into their home factory-stores.

Arrival and Orientation

Olinalá (Place of Earthquakes, pop. 5,000, elev. 4,000 feet, 1,300 meters) is basically a large, easy-to-explore village. As in most Mexican towns, Olinalá's streets run north–south and east–west.

Incoming bus travelers arrive at the Olinalá street-corner bus terminal, uphill, about five blocks south of town. Continue on foot or take a taxi ($1) to the town plaza. Drivers, turn left (west) on to Olinalá main street Ibarra, a block after the ingress highway bridge. Within about three uphill blocks, you'll arrive at the main town plaza.

Orient yourself by the *presidencia municipal* portals on the plaza's west side, and the church on the opposite (east) side. Olinala's two main streets, Ramón Ibarra and Vicente Guerrero, run east–west along the south and north sides of the plaza, respectively.

◖ Templo de San Francisco

For a revealing preview of the finest of all possible Olinalá lacquerware, head first to the town showplace Templo de San Francisco, one of Mexico's most unique churches, on the plaza's east side.

Inside, a riot of lacquerware, known locally as *linaoe* (lee-nah-OH-ay), dominates the decorations. Although many local artisans have contributed to the decorations, some features stand out. The nave columns, in contrasting cream and maroon, are the work of the acknowledged Olinalá master *artesano* Francisco Coronel.

Also, don't miss the right front side chapel, dedicated to the Virgin of Guadalupe. And before you leave, be sure to look at the mural by the front door, featuring a unique Trinity.

Its deity-trio, all of whom resemble Jesus, rain avenging angels down upon devils and sinners in hell.

Handicrafts Shopping

Next, go to the source, the workshop-store of *maestro* **Francisco "Don Chico" Coronel** (Juan Aldama 12, tel. 756/473-0084). He welcomes visitors during the day. From the plaza's southwest corner, walk west, uphill, along Ibarra, a few blocks to Aldama, turn right, and continue a few doors to Coronel's house on the right. Inside, if you're lucky, you'll get to watch him applying the finishing touches to a fine piece of work. The masterfully crafted and detailed treasury—*bateas* (trays), *cajas* (boxes), *arcas* (chests), *calabazas* (gourds)—that decorates his workshop represents the pinnacle of Olinalá craftsmanship. Collectively, the pieces represent the essence of many centuries of experience and practice. Individually, each piece is the prized product of hours of meticulous work, gathering and processing the natural raw materials, sanding, painting, burnishing, engraving, and finally the fine finish painting that *maestro* Francisco applies. The prices that he asks, typically $40–60 for small-to-medium pieces, are modest indeed.

Several other Olinalá master artisans welcome visitors. Back at the plaza's southeast corner, walk downhill (east) along Ibarra one block. Turn right at Matamoros and continue a few doors to the shop of **Adolfo Escudero**

Mejia (Matomoros 5, tel. 756/473-0075). He specializes in beautiful, meticulously designed and adorned boxes, chests, chairs, and trays, many of innovative decoration.

Continue east, downhill, along Ibarra a long block to the corner of Comonfort, where you'll find **Artesanías Olinalá** (tel. 756/473-0022, 9 A.M.–8 P.M. Mon.–Sat.), the shop of personable Edilberto Jiménez Barrera. Inside, admire his treasury of mostly boxes and chests, but also many unusual-motif (for example, for lawyers, rancheros, and cockfighters) clocks.

Walk a few doors south on Comonfort, to find, on the left, Cajita Linaloe, the shop of *artesana* **Audelia Rendón Franco** (Comonfort 3, tel. 756/473-0029). Her factory store and workshop (visitors welcome), in the rear, is the ongoing result of more than 200 years of family tradition. It abounds with a myriad of lacquerware: mirrors, boxes large and small, *calabazas,* picture frames, jaguar masks, and much more.

For something quite different, continue two blocks east, across the bridge and uphill,

to the bouganvillea-draped house and garden of portrait artist **Bernardo Rosendo** (Comonfort 13, tel. 756/473-0019 or 756/473-1108) on the left side of the street. He specializes in ink, charcoal, and Olinaláa lacquer portraits of famous personages. Order a portrait of one of your Mexican heroes, or your favorite movie star, or ask him to make a portrait of you or someone you know. He has many examples of the rich and famous, but he'll need at least a photo of people he doesn't know. Call him for an appointment.

For yet more fine lacquerware, masks, and much more, visit the even more remote village of **Temalacatcingo** (pop. 2,000), 17 miles (27 km) by bus or *colectivo* via the gravel road north from Olinalá. After about 13 miles (20 km), turn right at the fork to Ahuacatlán, and continue past Ahuacatlán for about two miles.

Accommodations and Food

Olinalá accommodates visitors with at least two acceptable hotels. If you can tolerate roosters crowing at 6 in the morning, the best choice

© BRUCE WHIPPERMAN

Olinalá town square has a good snack restaurant beneath the plaza kiosk.

THE ART OF DON CHICO CORONEL

Olinalá's native son Francisco "Don Chico" Coronel is the nationally acknowledged master of the style of lacquerware that has made Olinalá famous. Born in 1941, young Francisco was apprenticed into the traditional craft of lacquerware as it had been learned by nameless generations of Olinalá youths before him.

Originally, Olinalá craftspeople had made an art of lacquer-decorated gourds. Demand extended the original craft to trinket and jewel boxes, then trays and chests, tables and chairs, and more.

But regardless of size and variety, the method has remained constant. First, the wood is collected, cut, carved to shape, and hand-sanded. A base coat of *chia* seed oil, colored with a locally gathered and ground natural mineral pigment, is applied and left to dry. The piece is then burnished to a shine with a smooth stone, and the whole process is repeated many times over. After the last coat of oil has been applied, the piece is left to dry for a month.

Craftspeople next lay out designs that are engraved into the piece, traditionally with a natural agave needle. Vivid colors are painted into the engraving to create a harmonious animal or floral design.

During the 1970s, Don Chico began adding gold to his colors, creating rich and lovely gilded flowers, birds, rabbits, and much more, in his designs.

Some Olinalá craftspeople, impatient with the time-consuming traditional materials and processes, are using commercial pigments and oils and faster machine methods. In some cases quality has suffered.

But that's not true of Don Chico's art. He continues to work by the traditional methods and materials. He's become so famous that presidents have commissioned him to make gifts representative of Mexican craftsmanship. Don Chico responded by making a magnificent tray for Queen Elizabeth II of Great Britain. And when Pope John Paul came to Mexico in July 2002 to canonize the first Latin American indigenous saint, President Vicente Fox presented John Paul a regal chest made by Francisco "Don Chico" Coronel of Olinalá.

© BRUCE WHIPPERMAN

Acknowledged Olinalá laquerware maestro Francisco "Don Chico" Coronel finishes a fine laquerware box.

is **Hotel Cindy** (Guerrero 46, tel. 756/473-0114, Olinalá, Guerrero, $12 s, $16 d), two blocks east of the plaza. I arrived the first time at night and nearly missed the place, because its illuminated sign says "Corona Hotel" (for Corona Beer, which installed the sign). This loosely run family establishment offers about 15 rooms (not all in operating condition as of this writing) in three exterior-corridor floors overlooking a parking lot-garden. If you make your way past the storefront-desk and the stashes of semitrash along hallways and in corners, you'll find the rooms decently clean and attractive, with pink bedspreads and tiled baths. With the added pluses of hot water, ceiling fan (make sure yours works), TV, parking, and airy upstairs restaurant, you'll have a deal.

Second choice goes to four-floor **Hotel Coral** (Ramón Ibarra s/n, tel. 747/473-0826, Olinalá, Guerrero) half a block east of the plaza. A popular stopping place for truck drivers, the Coral offers about 30 plain but clean bare-bulb rooms with colorful tile, fluffy bedspreads, curtains, and hot-water showers. For privacy and a minimum of noise, take a room on the top floor, away from the street. Rates run $12 s or d (in one double bed), $18 d (two double beds), with fan and TV; street parking only.

As for food, economy meals (soups, stews, tacos, enchiladas, *pozole,* and more) are the specialties of the several **fondas** (food stalls) that set up daily (and nightly) on the north side of the plaza.

For sit-down breakfast, lunch, and supper, the best choice in town is the charming **C Pozolería La Cabaña** (on Ibarra, 8 A.M.–10 P.M. Mon.–Sat., 8 A.M.–3 P.M. Sun.), half a block east of the plaza. Savvy owners have turned a rustic, massive-beamed old house into a restaurant that fits its name perfectly. Part of the fun of La Cabaña is the eclectic old-time collection—masks, *cazuelas* (stewing crocks), gourds, wooden spoons, longhorn cattle skulls, and a yellowed portrait of Emiliano Zapata—that decorates the walls. Although La Cabaña's specialty is savory, country-style *pozole,* your choices are more varied. For breakfast, choose among juice, Nescafé, fruits, eggs, and potatoes ($2–5); for lunch, order either à la carte or a three-course set *comida corrida,* with choice of seafood, stew, or chicken ($3–4); for supper, go for *pozole, chiles rellenos,* tacos, or enchiladas ($2–5).

Alternatively, go to friendly **Cocina Economica La Guadalupana** (8 A.M.–6 P.M. daily), on Ibarra across from the plaza, for breakfast ($2–3), a hearty *comida* ($3.50) for lunch, or early supper. Friendly, hard-working owner-chef Oralia Garcia specializes in wild game, such as rabbit or turkey.

Evenings after 9 P.M., when everything else in town is closed, you can often get a tasty snack, such as a hamburger or *torta* and juice, at the *jugería* beneath the town plaza elevated *kiosko* (bandstand) nightly until 10 or 11 P.M.

Events

If you like old-Mexico color and don't mind crowds, time your visit to coincide with either of Olinalá's big festivals, the **Fiesta de Pascua** (Passover) during the week before Easter Sunday, or the patronal **Fiesta de San Francisco de Asis,** October 2–5.

During the Easter festival, the highlight, besides plenty of food, handicrafts for sale, fireworks, cockfights, and carnival, is the procession of the Stations of the Cross that reenacts the Passion of Jesus.

Later, the San Francisco festival features much of the same, plus a big for-sale handicrafts exposition, *mojigangos* (giant dancing effigies), and favorite traditional dances, including Los Tigres, Los Tecuanes, and the French courtship Danza de los Doce Pares. (Make your hotel reservation early.)

Services

Olinalá provides some essential services within a block of the plaza.

For ATMs and money exchange, first try **HSBC** (tel. 756/473-0601, 8 A.M.–4 P.M. Mon.–Sat.) on Guerrero, a block west of the plaza. Alternatively, go to **Bancomer** (tel. 756/473-0332, 8:30 A.M.–4 P.M. Mon.–Fri.), on Ibarra across from the southeast corner of the plaza.

Find the *correo* (8 A.M.–3 P.M. Mon.–Fri.) and **Telecom** (tel. 756/473-0259, 9 A.M.–3 P.M. Mon.–Fri., 9 A.M.–noon Sat.) beneath the *presidencia municipal* portal, west of the plaza. Longer hours for public telephone and fax are available at the Farmacia Discuento.

Internet access is available at **Café@Internet** (Ibarra 27 Poniente, tel. 756/473-1039, 10 A.M.–10 P.M. daily), a block and a half west of the plaza.

Olinalá provides a number of medical options. For simple medications and advice, try **Farmacia Discuento** (tel. 756/473-0346, 8 A.M.–3 P.M. and 4–10 P.M. Mon.–Sat., 8 A.M.–3 P.M. Sun.), with Dr. Pardo Guzmán in charge, on the north side of Ibarra a block west of the plaza, corner of H. Colegio Militar. If you need a doctor, drop in to the 24-hour **Centro de Salud** (tel. 756/473-0040), across the street from Farmacia Discuento. Of Olinalá's private physicians, **Dr. Cipriano López Hernandéz** (Guerrero 105) is highly recommended, about four blocks downhill, east of the plaza. Alternatively, visit **Dr. Marizela Jiménez** (tel. 756/473-0990), also on Guerrero, half a block east of the plaza.

In an emergency, contact the *policias* (tel. 756/473-0006 or 756/473-0007), in the *presidencia municipal,* on the west side of the plaza.

Getting There and Away

By Bus: To reach Olinalá, bus travelers can connect via Estrella Blanca buses from western locations of Acapulco (via Chilpancingo) and Chilapa. From eastern locations in Puebla and Oaxaca you can reach Olinalá via Tlapa de Comonfort.

In Olinalá, a ticket agent (tel. 756/473-1050) on Ibarra, across from the plaza, sells tickets for all Estrella Blanca local bus connections, including Chilapa, Chilpancingo, Cuernavaca, Mexico City, and most intermediate destinations. Catch the bus at the hilltop terminal, about five blocks south of town, most conveniently reached by taxi.

From the same uphill bus station, Sur provides two second-class departures per day, connecting with northern and eastern destinations including Mexico City and the states of Puebla (via Izucar de Matamoros), Morelos (via Cuautla), and Oaxaca (transfer at Tlapa de Comonfort).

Also from the same uphill station, vans provide connections east, with Tlapa de Comonfort, and west with Chilapa and Chilpancingo, many times per day.

By Car: To or from Chilpancingo via Chilapa, drivers can connect with Olinalá, via Highway 93. Westbound, about 57 miles (92 km, 2.5 hrs) after Chilapa, head left (north) from Highway 93 at the signed Olinalá junction. Continue north about 25 smooth miles (40 km, 1 hr) to Olinalá, for a total of about three and a half hours from Chilapa (or 116 miles, 187 km, about five hours, from Chilpancingo).

To or from the north and east (Mexico City and the states of Morelos, Puebla, and Oaxaca), connect via Highway 190 via Izucar de Matamoros, Puebla; or Huajuapan de León, Oaxaca; at the Highway 190 junction with Highway 92 37 miles (59 km) southeast of Izucar, or 57 miles (92 km) northwest of Huajuapan. Head south 78 miles (126 km) to the Olinalá junction at Huamuxtitlán. Continue via west-bound secondary road another 17 miles (27 km) via Cuauhlote, Cualac, and Xhiacingo, to Olinalá. For this trip, figure a total of about four hours from Izucar, five from Huajuapan.

Iguala

Only a tiny fraction of the vacationers hurrying south to Acapulco bother to stop in Iguala (pop. 100,000, elev. 2,430 feet, 740 meters). Consequently, Iguala is nearly tourist-free. This is remarkable, since the town's official name, Iguala de la Independencia, is much more than a slogan. Iguala is a major patriotic-historic center of Mexico and cradle of Agustín de Itúrbide's Plan de Iguala, which spelled out Mexican independence, and his Bandera de las Trigarantías (Flag of the Three Guarantees), the red, white, and green tricolor beneath which Itúrbide finally rode triumphantly into Mexico City on September 27, 1821.

Local folks don't seem to mind the lack of tourist hullabaloo, however. They go about their business, living well from the agricultural bounty—fruit, corn, cattle—of their fertile, spring-fed valley.

They also love their pedestrian-friendly downtown, with a number of good restaurants and not one but three shady plazas, sprinkled with juice- and snackstands and cafés.

All this would be easily worth an overnight, but Iguala offers much more: a whole complex of many dozens of shops selling gold jewelry, the fascinating Museo y Santuario a la Bandera, and, not to be missed atop a breezy view hillside, a spectacularly large Mexican flag billowing gracefully above a monument to the Heroes of the Independence.

Excursions nearby lead to Lake Tuxpan, for possible boating and camping, and adjacent lovely Quinta "Happy" bathing resort. Farther afield, ruins enthusiasts can visit Teopantecuantlán and Cuetlajuchitlán, a pair of fascinating partly restored pre-Columbian ceremonial centers.

HISTORY

The name Iguala comes from the town's former Aztec-language label, Yohualtépetl, which means, very appropriately, "basin surrounded by mountains." After the conquest, the local Spanish missionaries shifted the name to the more pronounceable Yohuala, and finally, Iguala.

Chontal-speaking people at least as early as A.D. 800 founded the town, which was originally known as Motlacehuatl, an Iguala district still called "old town." During the Aztec expansions of the 1400s, warriors under direction of Emperor Izcoatl conquered Motlacehuatl and erected a temple. Aztec colonists arrived and prospered on the labor of their Chontal-speaking slaves and servants.

The Spanish arrived in 1522 and replaced the Aztec temple, warriors, and settlers with their own church, soldiers, and colonists. They prospered for nearly 300 years until the surrounding region, ignited by Miguel Hidalgo's 1810 cry for independence and led by Generals José María Morelos and Vicente Guerrero, became a focus of anti-Spanish rebellion.

From 1811 to 1821 Spanish troops fought an aggressive but losing campaign, battling rebel guerrillas from the cool, pine-tufted high sierra to Acapulco's summery shoreline. Finally, the independence drama climaxed in Iguala on February 24, 1821, when Agustín de Itúrbide, former royalist general turned rebel, joined forces with Guerrero.

Their agreement was based on the Plan de Iguala, an independence strategy based on more than two dozen points. The Plan de Iguala was essentially a moderate compromise that both the conservative white elite that Itúrbide represented and Guerrero's indigenous and mestizo campesinos could agree upon. It called for an independent Mexico with a parliament presided over by a constitutional Spanish monarchy, much as the 19th-century English monarchs presided over the Dominion of Canada. The Plan de Iguala even invited King Ferdinand VII of Spain to agree to all of this, which he never did.

The core of the plan that lasted were the Trigarantías (Three Guarantees): independence, Catholicism, and equality amongst all Mexicans (men only, however).

Later, on October 27, 1849, Iguala was chosen as the first capital of the new state of Guerrero, with General Juan Álvarez as governor. Soon, in early 1850, the first state legislature met in Iguala. Later, the capital shifted to Tixtla, and finally Chilpancingo by the end of the 19th century.

SIGHTS
Arrival and Orientation

Most bus passengers arrive at the Estrella Blanca bus station, north side of the main market, corner of Galeana and Salazar. For the center of town, walk or taxi the seven blocks north along Galeana (to the right as you exit the terminal), or ride a *colectivo* to the zócalo.

(If, however, you arrive at the east-side Estrella de Oro bus station, on Highway 95, do the same by either taxi or *colectivo* or by walking eight blocks west, away from the highway, along Bandera Nacional to the *zócalo*.)

Drivers arriving via Highway 95 from Taxco heading south, or from Chilpancingo heading north, follow Centro or Zócalo highway signs west after passing the *periférico* (peripheral boulevard)—heading south, turn right; heading north, turn left. Continue about eight blocks west to the *zócalo*.

At the Iguala town center you'll find a trio of inviting plazas: from east to west, first comes the **Plaza de Trigarantías,** bordered by Avenida Vicente Guerrero on the north and

© AVALON TRAVEL PUBLISHING, INC.

Avenida Bandera Nacional on the south. Move diagonally southwest, across the corner of Bandera Nacional and north–south Calle Altamirano, to find the broad garden **Plaza y Monumento a la Bandera,** bordered on the south by Calle Aldama.

Finally, move diagonally northwest, across the corner of Calle Juan Álvarez and Avenida Bandera Nacional, to the *zócalo,* the very heart of the town. Its bordering streets are one-block Constitución, on its north side; Juárez, on the west side; Reforma, on the south side; and Álvarez, on the east side. Note the landmarks: the Museo y Santuario a la Bandera on the Juárez (west) side and the Hotel María Isabel on its Constitución (north) side.

The Zócalo

The downtown *zócalo,* one of the most pleasant in Guerrero, is a relaxing people-watching sight all in itself. Pause for a refreshment at one of the juice bars and enjoy the shade beneath the 32 leafy tamarind trees, planted in 1832, thanks to General Don Luis Gonzaga Vieyra.

Museo y Santuario a la Bandera

From the *zócalo,* walk west across Juárez to the Museo y Santuario a la Bandera (tel. 733/333-6765, 9 A.M.–6 P.M. Tues.–Sat., 9 A.M.–3 P.M. Sun.). The museum has three main *salas* (exhibition halls), all worth a visit.

The **Sala de las Banderas** exhibits about two dozen historic Mexican flags, led off by the

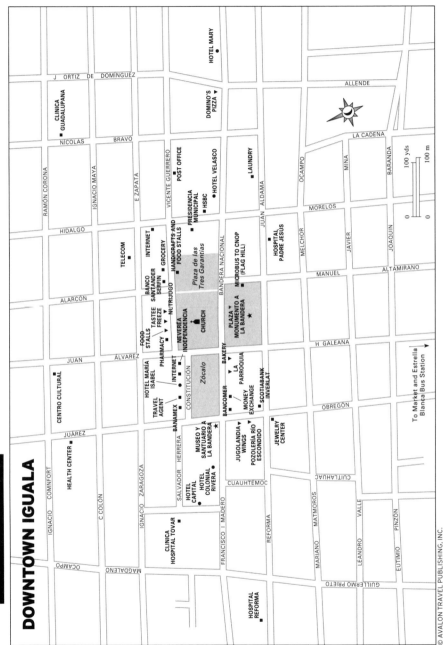

DOWNTOWN IGUALA

GUERRERO UPCOUNTRY

HOTEL MARY

J ORTIZ DE DOMÍNGUEZ

ALLENDE

CLINICA
GUADALUPANA

DOMINO'S
PIZZA

NICOLÁS   BRAVO

LA CADENA

RAMÓN CORONA

IGNACIO MAYA

E ZAPATA

VICENTE GUERRERO

POST OFFICE

HOTEL VELASCO

LAUNDRY

OCAMPO

MINA

BARANDA

100 yds

100 m

HIDALGO

PRESIDENCIA
MUNICIPAL

HSBC

JUAN ALDAMA

MORELOS

TELECOM

INTERNET

GROCERY

HANDCRAFTS AND
FOOD STALLS

Plaza de las
Tres Garantías

HOSPITAL
PADRE JESÚS

JAVIER

JOAQUÍN

ALARCÓN

BANCO
SANTANDER
SERFIN

NUTRIJUGO

Plaza de las
Tres Garantías

BANDERA NACIONAL

MICROBUS TO CNOP
(FLAG HILL)

MELCHOR

ALTAMIRANO

MANUEL

FOOD
STALLS

TASTEE
FREEZE

NEVERÍA
INDEPENDENCIA

CHURCH

PLAZA
MONUMENTO A
LA BANDERA

H. GALEANA

CENTRO CULTURAL

JUAN   ÁLVAREZ

HOTEL MARÍA
ISABEL

PHARMACY

INTERNET

Zócalo

BAKERY

LA
PARROQUIA

SCOTIABANK
INVERLAT

HEALTH CENTER

JUÁREZ

TRAVEL
AGENT

BANAMEX

CONSTITUCIÓN

BANCOMER

MONEY
EXCHANGE

OBREGÓN

CUITLÁHUAC

SALVADOR HERRERA

MUSEO Y
SANTUARIO A
LA BANDERA

JUGOLANDIA
WINGS

POZOLERIA RÍO
ESCONDIDO

JEWELRY
CENTER

To Market and Estrella
Blanca Bus Station

IGNACIO ZARAGOZA

HOTEL
CAPITAL

HOTEL
COLONIAL
RIVERA

CUAUHTÉMOC

REFORMA

MARIANO MATMOROS

VALLE

PINZÓN

CLINICA
HOSPITAL TOVAR

FRANCISCO I MADERO

LEANDRO

EUTIMIO

IGNACIO COMNFORT

C COLON

OCAMPO

MAGDALENO

HOSPITAL
REFORMA

GUILLERMO PRIETO

© AVALON TRAVEL PUBLISHING, INC.

celebrated tricolor Bandera de las Trigarantías, with its diagonal white, green, and red stripes. The stripes represent the Plan de Iguala's Three Guarantees: pure white for the Catholic religion, green for independence, and red representing equality for all the races of Mexico.

Also notable is the eagle-and-serpent Aztec "flag," from the Aztec historical document the *cronica Mexcáyotl,* as preserved in the postconquest record, the *Codex Duran.*

The 20-odd remaining flags are remarkable partly for their evolutionary linkages to the present Mexican national flag, adopted in 1952, at the end of the hall.

Continue to the **Sala Plan de Iguala,** which exhibits, besides the words of the Mexican national anthem, a copy of the original Plan de Iguala signed by Agustín de Itúrbide on February 24, 1821, and a more readable modern copy. The Plan de Iguala is interesting, partly for its comparison with the revolutionary-period documents of the United States. While the Mexican document effectively declares Catholicism to be the religion of the land and all races to be equal, its U.S. counterparts, such as the Declaration of Independence and the Bill of Rights, say nothing about equality of the races and next to nothing about religion, except the freedom to worship (or not to worship) thereof.

The third hall is the **Santuario a la Bandera,** with a grand, illuminated Mexican flag at one end of a hushed and darkened room.

More Downtown Sights

From the museum, head due east to the *zócalo*'s southeast corner. Diagonally southeast, across the corner of Álvarez and Bandera Nacional, spreads the **Plaza y Monumento a la Bandera.** The plaza's grand central memorial, dedicated in 1942 by then-President Manuel Ávila Camacho, reflects the Socialist Realism style of the day. It depicts an abnormally husky native couple, the woman with torch in hand, guarding the flag. On the monument itself, an inscription translates as: ". . . the city of Iguala, cradle of Mexican Independence, the consummation proclaimed here, on February 24, 1821." Before moving on, you might stroll over to the plaza's northeast (church side)

The Monumento a la Bandera decorates one of Iguala's three downtown plazas.

corner for a look at the bronze bust memorializing Francisco Gonzales Bocanegra, author of the words for the Mexican national anthem.

The **Centro Joyero de Iguala** (Jewelry Center, tel. 733/333-3778, 9 A.M.–7 P.M. daily) is both a sight and a shopping ground. Find it at the corner of Reforma and Obregón, just one block south of the *zócalo*'s southeast corner. Inside, a swarm of shops sell seemingly everything possible that can be made of gold.

The **Museo Ferrocarríl** (Rail Station Museum), in the process of being finished during the past few years, may be open for visitors by the time you read this. Find it at the west end of downtown: Taxi or walk (about a mile) beginning along Reforma, a block south of the *zócalo*. Go four blocks and turn left at the dead end (at the library), at Mariano Herrera. Continue one short block and turn right (west) at the fire station, corner of 18 de Marzo. Continue two short blocks to diagonal street Calzada del Ferrocarríl; follow it about two blocks to the old rail station, across the railroad track.

◖ Hilltop Memorial Flag

Although initially I didn't plan to go to the hilltop west of town for a close-up view of Iguala's big Mexican flag atop its summit, I changed my mind when one day I glanced west across town and noticed the flag for the first time. It was so fantastically huge that it dwarfed every tall building and tree (which were much closer) in the town foreground.

The hilltop where the giant flag was first raised in 1998, known as C.N.O.P. (pronounced say-enay-oh-pay), is officially the site of the **Monumento a los Héroes de la Independencia** (Monument to the Heroes of the Independence) featuring a shrine inside a summit building (9 A.M.–5 P.M. daily), which had closed by the time I arrived around 5:30 P.M. Nevertheless, it was fortunate that I had arrived during one of Iguala's oft-breezy late afternoons. The noise alone from the flag's graceful, slow-motion rippling was surprisingly powerful, like the repeated rumble and snap of a chorus of mini-sonic booms (which they in

© BRUCE WHIPPERMAN

Notice the tiny figure at the base of the pole, like an ant in comparison to the 200-foot length of Iguala's hilltop memorial flag.

fact are). The flagpole, a monumental stack of welded steel, about eight feet in diameter at the base, is a wonder in itself.

A small platoon of 25 men is required to carry and fold the 550-pound (250-kg) flag, which is brought down daily before sunset and raised around sunrise. To view the spectacle, arrive before approximately 5:30 A.M. or 5:30 P.M. in summer, 6:00 A.M. or 5:00 P.M. in winter.

Get to the flag by either taxi ($4 round-trip) from near the *zócalo* or *colectivo* ($0.50 one way) from the east (Av. Altimirano) side of the Plaza y Monumento a la Bandera.

By car, drive to the south leg of the *periférico* (peripheral boulevard). Head east until you see a chapel on the right, a block before the old Highway 95 underpass. Turn right and pass in front of the chapel, uphill. Continue up the all-paved grade, following the red, white, and green signs to the top.

ACCOMMODATIONS

All recommendable Iguala hotels fall in the moderate Under $50 category. During Iguala's very hot and dry spring months of April, May, and June, air-conditioning, if not essential, is certainly a desirable option if you can afford the extra expense (about $7). These listings start at the *zócalo* and move outward.

Start with Iguala's best all-around hotel, the ◖ **Hotel María Isabel** (Portal Constitución 5, Iguala, Guerrero 40000, tel. 733/333-3233 or 733/333-3242, fax 733/333-3240). Once Iguala's pride, now a bit worn but still worthy, the hotel offers about 40 clean (but less than immaculate), conservatively but thoughtfully decorated, dark-wood-paneled rooms with bath. The best and quietest are the upper rear rooms, with small balconies overlooking the tree-shaded pool-patio. Rentals cost $38 s, $47 d, $54 t with air-conditioning (simply a must for one's comfort in the hot spring months); $33, $38, and $43 with fan only, all with TV, fan, phone, large pool, parking, and convenient sidewalk restaurant downstairs. Credit cards are accepted.

Walk west of the *zócalo* for two more recommendable hostelries. On the short north–south street a block due west of the *zócalo*, find new **Hotel Capital** (José A. Ocampo 1, Iguala, Guerrero 40000, tel. 733/333-7121). Here, guests have the advantage of a quiet side-street location a mere block from the downtown action. Many of the 30-odd smallish rooms in three floors are dark, but invitingly decorated in color-coordinated shades of blue, with hot-water shower baths, tile floors, and attractive wooden furniture. Rentals (with one double bed only) cost $20 s, $23 d fan only; $27 s, $30 d with air-conditioning. Two beds cost $25 d, $30 t fan only, and $35 d and $40 t with air-conditioning; all include TV, parking, and small pool and patio.

A block south and a block and a half farther west is the classier old-standby hostelry, **Hotel Colonial Rivera** (Madero 3, Iguala, Guerrero 40000, tel./fax 733/333-3464, 733/333-2587, or 733/333-2547). The hotel's builders have packed a lot of hotel into a small space. Most of the two floors of 49 rooms line an invitingly leafy but narrow interior patio-garden. Unfortunately, most rooms are dark, with only one window (which must be covered for privacy) facing the exterior corridor. A few lighter, more private rooms face the street but are consequently noisier. The good news is that the rooms are immaculate and have attractive neo-colonial decor and some even have up-to-date noiseless air-conditioning. Rates, furthermore, are very moderate, at $23 s, $27 d, in a one-double-bed room, fan only; $33 and $38 with air-conditioning. Rooms with two double beds cost $32 d and $37 t fan only, $40 d and $45 t with air-conditioning; all have TV, phone, security box, and parking. There's a restaurant but no pool. Credit cards are accepted.

On the opposite, east side of the *zócalo* are a pair of good economy hotel choices, well managed by the same savvy owners. Two blocks east of the *zócalo*, find **Hotel Velasco** (Bandera Nacional 3, tel. 733/332-0566 or 733/332-8120, fax 733/332-5714). Clever design has placed the 30 rooms in two floors *above* (rather than beside) the noisy parking patio. Another attractive feature is an airy front breezeway, with tables and soft couches for relaxing. Corridors also have the same. Furthermore, rather than charging for power-hungry air-conditioning, owners have equipped a number of rooms with environmentally friendlier 1940s-genre "desert coolers" (with a fan blowing air through dripping water). One-double-bed rentals run a modest $16 s, $18 d, fan only; $19 s, $22 d, with desert cooler, also with ceiling fans. For two double beds, rates are $20 d fan only, $23 d with desert cooler, and $23 t fan only, $26 t with desert cooler. All rooms have hot-water shower baths, phones, cable TV, and parking. If you must have a room with air-conditioning, add about 20 percent to the fan-only prices above.

Two blocks farther east, find the **Hotel Mary** (at Bandera Nacional 39A, Iguala, Guerrero 40000, tel. 733/332-5020 or 733/332-5320, fax 733/332-5714). The three-floor Mary has modest prices and savvy amenities similar to its brother, the Velasco: breezeways with soft chairs for relaxing; clean, well-maintained rooms, ranging from $18 to 28 d, with hot-water shower baths; and a choice of room with fan, desert cooler, or air-conditioning. The Mary has the advantage of an enclosed bottom-floor garage, but the disadvantage of some noisier street-front rooms. Reserve a quieter room in the upper rear.

Additional nearby lodging choices are in Tuxpan (see *Excursions from Iguala*), either RV parking and/or tenting on the Laguna Tuxpan shoreline or at the inviting family resort, Quinta Happy.

FOOD
Snacks, Bakeries, and Food Stalls
Snacks and bakeries are plentiful downtown. For example, on one of Iguala's frequent warm afternoons, beat the heat with a *licuado* (ice, fruit, milk, and sugar, whipped to a milkshake-like froth but minus the calories) at one of the *jugerías* that dot the *zócalo* area. If you want more, they usually always serve fresh fruit, hot dogs, *hamburguesas,* and *tortas.*

For example, on the west side, pull up a stool at **Jugolandia Wings** (6 A.M.–11 P.M. daily), diagonally across from the *zócalo*'s southwest corner, across Madero from the

Museo y Santuario a la Bandera. On the *zócalo*'s east side, enjoy about the same tasty options at **Nutrijugo** on Vicente Guerrero, across (north) from the church.

For plenty of pastries, muffins, and doughnuts, visit **Panadería San Francisco** (8 A.M.–9 P.M. Mon.–Sat., 9 A.M.–3 P.M. Sun.) at the corner of Reforma and Galeana diagonally across from the southwest corner of the Plaza y Monumento a la Bandera.

Hearty budget country-style specialties (tacos, tostadas, *tortas, sincronizadas, pinguinos, quemeyes, alambre*) and more are offered by the platoon of *fondas* (food stalls) in the **Market San Francisco Plaza** on Guerrero, a block and a half east of the *zócalo,* past the church, across from the Plaza de Trigarantías.

Finally, enjoy an ice cream for dessert at one of Iguala's quaintest and most venerable institutions, the **Neveréa Independencia** (tel. 733/333-3169, 10 A.M.–9 P.M. daily) on the *zócalo*'s north side, a few doors east of the Hotel María Isabel. Here, the star of the show is an

Big rounds of white cheese are piled high in the Iguala city market.

© BRUCE WHIPPERMAN

antique ice-cream freezer, complete with a 1930s-era belt-drive compressor, open for everyone to admire. The ice cream, which is excellent (the house specialty is vanilla, in a dozen variations), seems an afterthought after witnessing the old machine that made it in action.

Cafés and Restaurants

Of the lineup of sidewalk cafés along the *zócalo's* north side, best is probably **Restaurant Bambino** (if you don't mind their TV; if so, ask them to turn down the volume) (tel. 733/333-6389, 8 a.m.–midnight daily) at the front of the Hotel María Isabel. Here you can get your day started right, with a choice of fruit, good espresso coffee, *panes dulces,* eggs any style, hotcakes, and much more ($2–5). For lunch and dinner, choose among plenty of sandwiches, salads, and meat, pasta, and poultry platters ($3–9).

Many downtown restaurants accommodate the crowds of Iguala locals who have the money to eat out. One of the town center's best is **❰ La Parroquia** (tel. 733/333-3400, 7 a.m.–midnight daily), which lives up to its name, made famous by the many good likenamed restaurants all over Mexico. Here, breakfasts are the main event. Choose from six, from the simple "American" (actually continental) breakfast to the hearty "Campesino" breakfast ($3–6). The lunch specialty is a four-course *comida corrida* (about $4). Otherwise order from a long all-day list of fruit, eggs, poultry, soups, salads, *antojitos,* and elaborate house specialties, such as Molcajete La Parroquia (roasted meats, cactus leaves, fondue, and much more), served in a stone grinding bowl ($3–13). Find La Parroquia, in the small Plaza San Ángel complex, near the *zócalo's* southeast corner.

Second restaurant choice goes to class-act mod **❰ Tastee Freeze-La Vaca Negra** (tel. 733/332-0177, 8 a.m.–11 p.m. daily), on Guerrero half a block east of the *zócalo,* across from the church. Although its name sounds like that of a fast-food joint, it's actually a refined coffee shop trying to appeal to the middle- and upper-class young at heart. It does it quite well

with a tasty, professionally prepared and served breakfast, lunch, and dinner menu ($4–10).

A number of town-center restaurants also serve folk hungering for country fare the way *abuelita hacia* (grandma used to make). The best example is **❰ Pozolería Río Escondido** (tel. 733/333-3362, 11 a.m.–11 p.m. daily), the place for you to learn even more if you think you already know Mexican food. Start out with appetizer *pata de puerco,* continue with *tacos de longaniza,* then *tostadas de tinga,* all about $2. If, on the other hand, you hanker for something familiar, go for the house specialty *pozole con todo* (with all the fixin's). Find it on Obregón, half a block south of the southwest *zócalo* corner.

If you want a spell away from old Mexico, go to **Domino's Pizza** (tel. 733/332-4567, 9 a.m.–midnight daily, $5–15), four blocks east of the *zócalo* at the corner of Ortiz de Domínguez and Bandera Nacional. Enter the cool white dining room and choose from the lineup of a dozen styles of the usual pizzas plus half a dozen local favorites you haven't heard of.

Finally, three blocks farther east, on Guerrero across from CMI hospital, in a relaxing open-air setting, try **Restaurant El Campanario** (tel. 733/110-2832, or 733/333-1258, 9 a.m.–11 p.m. daily), Iguala's source of fine Argentine cooking. Besides a bountiful selection of soups, salads, and Mexican plates ($4–8), they offer a hearty selection of tender beef, including rib-eye steak, *arrachera,* and prime rib ($8–12).

ENTERTAINMENT AND EVENTS

For child's play, Iguala has both the kid-friendly west-side park and playground **Parque Infantil del D.I.F.** (Integral Family Development) and its neighboring **CICI Parque Aquatico** water-slide park. Find them on the eastern extension of Vicente Guerrero, on opposite sides of the street a few hundred yards east of old Highway 95, by the *lienzo charro* (rodeo ring). Parque Infantil is a kiddie playground, open during daylight hours. The water slide park has two or three pools,

THE FLOWER OF CHRISTMAS

Mexican people tell a story of the lovely red poinsettia flower, which they know as the Flower of Christmas:

Once upon a time, on Nochebuena (Christmas Eve) in a village of southern Mexico, a poor girl named Angelita stood outside the village church sadly watching the faithful carrying rich offerings of fruit, candy, and flowers for the infant Jesus. Angelita was weeping, because she had nothing to offer.

At that moment an angel, shining with a brilliant light, appeared and told Angelita to pick some wild plants beside the road. Angelita did this and returned with a large but humble bunch of weeds. Inside, as she approached the altar, Angelita's weeds miraculously transformed themselves into lovely scarlet flowers.

At the same time, the Virgin above the altar lowered her arm in a gesture of love, and gold stars on her blue cape showered the faithful in the nave. Simultaneously, outside in the black night sky a single star glowed a brilliant white over the little pueblo.

From that time forward, Angelita's brilliant red flowers have blossomed all over southern Mexico just before Christmas. For that reason, people have named that gorgeous bloom the *flor de Nochebuena* and always offer bunches of them to the baby Jesus on December 24.

water slides, and a restaurant that's open daily 10 A.M.–6 P.M. Admission is $3.

Sunday afternoons (around 5 P.M., check with your hotel desk for times) at the *lienzo charro,* riders practice the art of *jaripeo* (bull riding and roping) and show off their skills of horsemanship. Sometimes young women in colorful *ropa típica* compete in a daredevil *escaramuza charra* in which they race sidesaddle, with abandon, around the ring. A frequent local treat is the noisy "oompah" wind instrument bands, known locally as the Bandas de Chile Frito. (Get to the *lienzo charro,* on the eastern prolongation of Bandera Nacional, past old Highway 95, about nine blocks east of the *zócalo,* by taxi.)

Iguala **Semana Santa** celebrations, in addition to the usual processions, *mañanitas,* stations of the cross, food, and carnival games, also feature a procession of dozens of *penitencias* who may be flaying themselves or crawling on hands and knees to the downtown church altar to ask for forgiveness.

The big patronal **Fiesta de San Francisco** features an October 4 parade of *locos* throwing water and eggs and whatever else in honor of St. Francis of Assisi, who's famous for his sense of humor.

The **Day of the Dead,** celebrated November 1 and 2, is big in Iguala. Families go to cemeteries and clean up the grave sites of their loved ones. They rebuild the "houses" of the dead and bring the favorite foods of the departed, thus tempting their relatives to leave the land of the dead and be with the family once again.

If you're in Iguala around the time of Carnaval (the week before Ash Wednesday), consider visiting the important town of Teloloapan (pop. 20,000), about 17 miles (27 km) along the Altamirano highway west of Iguala. The Teloloapan Carnaval (Mardi Gras), locally called the **Paseo de los Agullis,** is unique. Beginning a week before Ash Wednesday, usually in early February, celebrants dance through the streets to the rhythm of drum and tamborine and splash themselves with paint. On Tuesday before Ash Wednesday they climax it all with a dangerous competition, climbing a high tree for valuable prizes in its limbs. The merrymaking continues during the subsequent week, in the **El Segundo Viernes de Cuaresma** (Fiesta of the Second Friday of Lent), a weeklong (Mon.–Sun. after Ash Wednesday) celebration, including a daily round of traditional dances, a big handicrafts fair, and fireworks.

SHOPPING

Iguala's prime general shopping ground is the main town market, at the corner of Salazar and

Galeana six blocks south of the *zócalo*. Everything—from shoes and clothes to produce and hot food—seems to be on sale. Even if you don't buy anything, the market is an interesting place for wandering and enjoying the displays, especially the festoons of old-fashioned goods: flowers, mounds of spices, dried flower petals, cinnamon bark, *cal* (limestone), *panela* (rough brown sugar), and mountain-gathered herbs and remedies.

Iguala's handicrafts vendors cluster on the Plaza de Trigarantías, two blocks east of the *zócalo,* behind the church. Customarily about a dozen stands offer a large variety, including soft palm-leaf *tenates* (tumpline baskets) and *petates* (mats), wooden bowls and utensils, colorful pottery, masks, and much more.

Iguala is famous for its gold market, the **Centro Joyero de Iguala** (tel. 733/333-3778, 9 A.M.–7 P.M. daily), Mexico's third gold merchandising center after Taxco and Guadalajara. Find its many dozens of shops under one roof at the corner of Obregón and Reforma, a block south of the *zócalo*'s southwest corner. Inside is a budget jewelry lover's paradise, where the gold and silver is genuine, but most of the apparent rubies, diamonds, and emeralds are not. (Nevertheless, a few stores, such as Orovel's, downstairs, and Jeisha, upstairs, do carry genuine low-to-medium-quality gemstones.) If you want to check on the reasonableness of a price, ask the prospective seller to weigh it. Ordinary sterling silver pieces customarily sell reasonably for about $1 per gram, 12–22 karat (50–90 percent) gold for about $8–15 per gram.

SERVICES
Banks

Banks with ATMs are plentiful near the *zócalo.* Find **Banamex** (9 A.M.–4:30 P.M.) at the *zócalo*'s northwest corner; **Bancomer** (tel. 733/333-3401, 8:30 A.M.–4 P.M.) across the *zócalo* at the southwest corner; and **Banco Santander Serfén** (9 A.M.–4 P.M. Mon.–Fri., 9 A.M.–2 P.M. Sat.), one block east of the *zócalo*'s northeast corner, at the Guerrero and Alarcón corner. Find somewhat more flexible hours at the *casa de cambio* (money-exchange office) **Dimex** (tel. 733/333-6581, 8 A.M.–5 P.M. Mon.–Fri., 9 A.M.–2 P.M. Sat.–Sun.), on the *zócalo*'s southwest side.

Communications

Find the *correo* (9 A.M.–5 P.M. Mon.–Fri.) on the south side of Guerrero, two and a half blocks west of the *zócalo*. For telephone, buy a Ladatel card and use one of the many street telephones. Otherwise, go to **Telecom** (9 A.M.–8 P.M. Mon.–Fri.), northeast of the *zócalo* on Zapata between Alarcón and Hidalgo, for fax and money orders.

Connect to the Internet at **Arroba Internet** (tel. 733/332-4331, 9 A.M.–9 P.M. Mon.–Sat., 9 A.M.–5 P.M. Sun.), northeast of the *zócalo* on Hidalgo, half a block north of Guerrero. Alternatively, go to the hole-in-the-wall Internet shop (tel. 733/334-0741, 9 A.M.–9 P.M. Mon.–Sat., 10 A.M.–2 P.M. Sun.) at the northeast corner of the *zócalo*.

Health and Emergencies

For routine medications and remedies, try one of the many downtown pharmacies, such as **Farmacia Pronto** (on Guerrero, tel. 733/333-6855, 8 A.M.–midnight daily), half a block east of the *zócalo*'s northeast corner. They provide 24-hour prescription delivery (tel. 733/333-8475).

If you need a doctor, ask your hotel desk to call one for you. Otherwise, a handily situated internist, **Dr. Raoul Tovar** (Jose O. Ocampo 8, tel. 733/333-3624, 10 A.M.–4 P.M. and 6–8 P.M. Mon.–Fri.) is available for consultations at Clinica Tovar, his lovely garden-patio hospital-home, a block west of the *zócalo*'s northeast corner. His personable English-speaking wife, Ana, runs the reception.

Also in an emergency, a number of good hospitals provide round-the-clock services in the downtown area. Hire a taxi to take you to one of the following: **Hospital Reforma** (Reforma 54, tel. 733/333-5892 or 733/333-4539), **Sanatorio Padre Jesús** (Aldama 24, tel. 733/332-0801), or **Hospital Cristina** (Prolongación Álvarez 153, tel. 733/333-2514 or 733/333-7386).

For police, call 733/332-8005. In case of fire, contact the *bomberos* by emergency tel. 066.

Travel Agents

Often willing sources of information, find them in the downtown area. For example, try **Agencia de Viajes María Isabel** (tel./fax 733/333-0506, agencia_maria-isabel@hotmail.com, 9 A.M.–8 P.M. Mon.–Fri., 9 A.M.–3 P.M. Sat.–Sun.), next to the Hotel María Isabel.

Laundry

Get your clothes washed at **Lavandería Easy** (tel. 733/332-6189, 10 A.M.–8 P.M. Mon.–Sat., closed Sun.). From the *zócalo*'s southeast corner, walk one block south to Aldama, turn left and walk two and a half blocks west.

GETTING THERE AND AWAY
By Bus

The main bus station, **Central Camionera Estrella Blanca** (tel. 733/332-3473), is at Galeana and Salazar, six blocks south of the *zócalo*'s southeast corner.

The terminal has many services, including kept luggage ($1 for 3 hours, $7/day), long-distance telephone and fax office, air-conditioned first-class waiting room, cafeteria, and money exchange. Buy fresh fruits, vegetables, groceries, and handicrafts at the market across the street.

First- and second-class buses connect with many destinations in all directions, both long-distance and semilocal.

One first-class **Elite** departure connects daily northwest with the U.S. border at Mexicali and Tijuana, via Cuernavaca, Toluca, Guadalajara, Tepic, and Mazatlán, along the Pacific Coast.

One first-class **Futura** or **Turistar** departure connects daily north with the U.S. border at Nueveo Laredo, via Cuernavaca, Toluca, San Luis Potosí, Saltillo, and Monterrey.

Many first- and second-class buses connect (hourly during the day) north with Mexico City and south with Chilpancingo and Acapulco. Others connect northeast with Puebla via Izucar de Matamoros, where connections southeast with Oaxaca may be made.

Many second-class buses connect east with Altamirano and north with Toluca via Taxco.

A swarm of second-class **Flecha Roja** buses connect with dozens of small regional Guerrero and Morelos destinations, such as Huitzuco, Taxco, Zacapalco, Jojutla, Casahuatlán, and Cuautla.

First-class bus connections, north with Taxco, Cuernavaca, and Mexico City, and south with Chilpancingo and Acapulco, are also available at the alternative **Estrella de Oro** bus terminal (tel. 733/332-1029), on Highway 95 north, corner of Bandera Nacional, about eight blocks east of the *zócalo*.

By Car

Connect north 22 miles (36 km) with Taxco via old nontoll Highway 95 in about an hour. Alternatively connect north directly with Mexico City via Cuernavaca by *cuota* expressway Highway 95. (Find the expressway entrance along old Highway 95, on the southeast, Acapulco, end of town.) Allow about 2.5 hours for this 80-mile (129-km) trip. Make sure you arrive in Mexico City on a permitted driving day.

Connect south with Chilpancingo via old Highway 95, about 64 miles (103 km) in about two hours. Continue to Acapulco via the toll expressway 95D, an additional 62 miles (100 km), in another hour and a quarter.

Connect west with Altamirano from the *periférico*'s northwest side, via winding but scenic Highway 51, 114 miles (184 km) in about 3.5 hours.

EXCURSIONS FROM IGUALA
Tuxpan

Nearby Laguna Tuxpan makes an interesting excursion, if not for the lake itself, at least for the country views and the palmy Quinta "Happy" family resort.

Along the two-mile road to Tuxpan, the source of Iguala's prosperity becomes immediately apparent. Irrigation has been the key, turning the Iguala valley into an oasis of lush cornfields and a grand orchard of mango trees like the ones you see overhanging the Tuxpan road.

Soon, on the right, pass the refined restaurant *campestre* (country-style) **Villa Los Ocampo,** with plenty of shade and lots of room for kids to run around. The menu includes shrimp tacos, fish fillets, and brochettes, and also breakfast ($4–8).

Continue through the Tuxpan village (with a few small groceries, a post office, and a pharmacy or two) to the restaurants on the north Laguna Tuxpan shore. Two of the most inviting are **El Muelle,** with a pier to walk out on; and farther on, **Restaurant El Arbolito,** shaded by *tabachín* trees (which burst out with lovely red blossoms in season). Both restaurants offer good fish and shrimp dinners beneath airy lakeview *palapas.*

The lake itself is large, about a mile across, and spring-fed. Despite continual withdrawing of irrigation water, the lake level remains virtually constant year-round. When I was there, during the dry spring season, the lake was not very inviting. Local folks were dirtying it up washing clothes on the shoreline. Furthermore, people told me that the lake bass were small because fisherfolk are so poor that they take anything, regardless of size.

Nevertheless, the lake is cleaner and more appealing on the far west side, accessible by the lakeshore dirt road after the restaurants. Amenities include some shade trees, plenty of room for RV parking or tent camping (customary and allowed any time), and easy boat and kayak-launching access.

Much more inviting is the family-friendly ◖ **Balneario Quinta Happy** (tel. 733/332-3562); from the Tuxpan ingress road, follow the signed Quinta Happy fork to the right. This is a gorgeous spot for at least a picnic and at most a one-week stay. Amenities include five blue, palm-shaded swimming pools, three kiddie pools, restaurants, basketball, mini-market, tennis, volleyball and squash courts, and a soccer field, all surrounded by a beautiful orchard of palm, orange, *limón,* and mango trees. The Quinta Happy (*Alegre* in Spanish) accommodations are no less than you would expect: about 20 clean, semideluxe rooms around an inviting pool-patio, separated from the oft-noisy day-use area. Room decor is invitingly rustic, embellished with interior brick and hand-hewn wood furnishings. Rates run, for adults, about $30 s or d, $35 t or q; add $5 per kid, with TV, air-conditioning, and parking. For more peace and quiet, reserve a weekday stay.

Get to Tuxpan by local bus or *colectivo* from the Estrella Blanca bus station, seven blocks south of the *zócalo.* By car from the *zócalo,* via Bandera Nacional, after seven blocks turn right (south) at Highway 95. Continue under the *periférico* overpass. Approximately half a mile after the overpass, at the Rotary Internacional sign on the left, fork left on to the Tuxpan road. Continue to the signed Quinta Alegre fork on the right or straight ahead for Tuxpan village and lakeshore after another mile.

Cuetlajuchitlán Archaeological Site

Adventurous ruins enthusiasts might enjoy a day exploring at least one of a pair of important, partially restored archaeological sites, the closest about an hour by car, two hours by bus, east of Iguala.

Closest is Cuetlajuchitlán (kooay-tlah-hoo-chee-TLAHN), near the small town of Paso Morelos, just off the Mexico City–Acapulco *cuota autopista.* Cuetlajuchitlán, an Aztec (Náhuatl) label, has two possible contrasting translations: either "place of red flowers" or "shriveled place."

Engineers saved the site from destruction by building the 95D expressway tunnel, Los Querendes, under the archaeological zone, which covers about 90 acres (35 hectares). Investigators believe that Cuetlajuchitlán was occupied as early as 600 B.C. and reached its cultural and economic zenith around 200 B.C. Although little is known of the ethnic identity of its founders, archaeologists believe that Cuetlajuchitlán influenced a wide region, stretching north to the valley of Morelos state, south to the Pacific Coast, and east and west along the Río Balsas basin. The reason is that the cylindrical stone monoliths found extensively at Cuetlajuchitlán are also widespread in so many far-flung regions centering on Cuetlajuchitlán.

GUERRERO UPCOUNTRY

Consequently, archaeologists have begun to associate Cuetlajuchitlán with what they call the "Culture of the Cylinders."

The most fascinating part of the zone is the **Recinto Ceremonial,** a 100- by 60-foot enclosure at the heart of the ruins complex, with both a number of the stone cylinders and *tinas ceremoniales* (ceremonial baths), presumably for purification rituals.

Also of great interest, about 100 feet south of the Recinto Ceremonial, is the *taller de cantería* (stonework factory) with a number of the great cylindrical monoliths lying about, apparently finished but unused.

Two **Complejos Habitacionales** (Habitational Complexes), apparently for nobles and priests, can be explored about 100 feet northeast and about 300 feet west of the Recinto respectively.

Get to Cuetlajuchitlán by bus, via Huitzuco, an hour southeast from the Iguala main bus station. From Huitzuco, continue by bus or local minivan east to Paso Morelos, just past (east of) the Mexico City–Acapulco expressway. Continue by taxi or on foot (ask local directions) to the nearby archaeological site.

By car from Iguala, drive south along Highway 95 about six miles (9 km) to the left, eastbound turnoff road to Huitzuco. Continue another 14 miles (23 km) to Huitzuco and another 10 miles (16 km) to the expressway and Paso Morelos, just east of it. In Paso Morelos, ask directions to the site, nearby.

Teopantecuantlán Archaeological Site

Equally fascinating, but an hour and a half more remote, is Teopantecuantlán (tay-oh-pahn-tay-kooan-TLAHN), in the valley about 30 miles east of Cuetlajuchitlán. The entire archaeological zone, including both the ceremonial center and surrounding former agricultural village, occupies nearly a square mile (about 500 acres or 200 hectares).

The site is especially interesting because of the antiquity of its two main pieces of Olmec-style monumental art, heavy with jaguar symbolism, dating from around 1400 B.C. As a result, archaeologists have inferred connections between Teopantecuantlán and the similar Olmec-style art found in the cave paintings at Juxtlahuaca, 100 miles to the south.

Archaeologists believe Teopantecuantlán reached its zenith around 900 B.C., with irrigation that in turn led to bumper crops, rising population, economic specialization, wealth, and architectural innovation. Massive stone walls were raised, culminating in a pair of grand platforms and arched passageways leading to noble tombs.

Exploration of the site reveals partly restored remains of Teopantecuantlán's grandeur: pyramidal platforms, palaces, plazas, tombs, two ball courts, and an irrigation channel.

To get to Teopantecuantlán, follow the directions from Iguala to Cuetlajuchitlán in the previous listing. From Paso Morelos, by car or local minivan or bus, continue 22 miles (36 km) southeast to Atenango del Río, and another seven miles (12 km) to the right (south) turnoff to Copalillo village. After two more miles, at Copalillo, ask for local directions to the site, about 10 miles (16 km) farther by auto-accessible gravel road.

Taxco

As Acapulco thrives on what's new, Taxco (pop. 150,000) luxuriates in what's old. Nestling beneath forest-crowned mountains and decorated with monuments of its silver-rich past, Taxco now enjoys an equally rich flood of visitors, many of whom who stop en route to or from Acapulco. They come to enjoy its fiestas and clear, pine-scented air and to stroll the cobbled hillside lanes and bargain for world-renowned silver jewelry.

And despite the acclaim, Taxco preserves its diminutive colonial charm *because* of its visitors, who come to enjoy what Taxco offers. They stay in venerable, family-owned lodgings, walk to the colorful little *zócalo* where they admire the famous baroque cathedral, and wander among the awning-festooned market lanes just downhill.

But Taxco offers even more. Travel an hour north to wander within the colossal limestone fairyland of the renowned Grutas de Cacahua-

Silver crucifixes are a Taxco specialty.

milpa. On the same day, continue another hour north to marvel at the exquisite, untouristed remains of Xochicalco, ruined pre-Columbian capital and internationally acclaimed United Nations World Heritage site.

On yet another day, travel west an hour to Ixcateopan village and visit the revered resting place of Cuauhtémoc, the last Aztec emperor who, at the eventual cost of his life, rallied his people against the Spanish conquest.

HISTORY

The traditional hieroglyph representing Taxco shows athletes in a court competing in a game of *tlatchtli* (still locally played) with a solid *hule* (natural rubber) ball. "Tlachco," the Náhuatl name representing the place that had become a small Aztec garrison settlement by the eve of the conquest, literally translates as "Place of the Ball Game." The Spanish, more interested in simplicity than in linguistic details, shifted the name to the more pronounceable Taxco.

Colonization

In 1524, Hernán Cortés, looking for tin to alloy with copper to make bronze cannon, heard that people around Taxco were using bits of metal for money. Prospectors hurried out, and within a few years they struck rich silver veins in Tetelcingo, now known as Taxco Viejo (Old Taxco), seven miles downhill from present-day Taxco. The Spanish crown appropriated the mines and worked them with generations of forced native labor.

Eighteenth-century enlightenment came to Taxco in the person of José Borda, who, arriving from Spain in 1716, modernized the mine franchise his brother had been operating. Borda improved conditions and began paying the miners, thereby increasing productivity and profits. In contrast to past operators, Borda returned the proceeds to Taxco, building the monuments that still grace the town. His fortune built streets, bridges, fountains, arches, and his masterpiece, the church

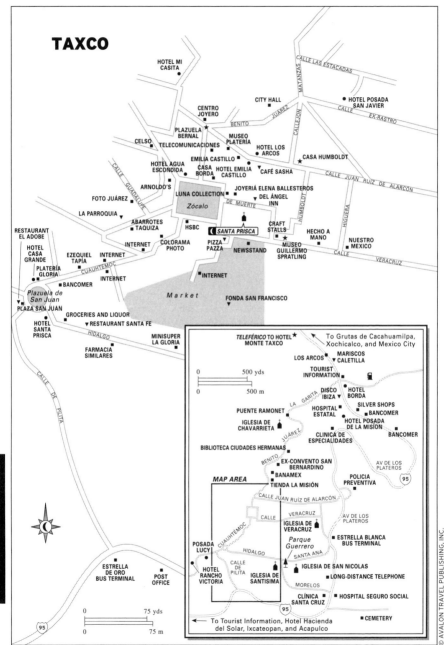

TAXCO

HOTEL MI CASITA

CITY HALL

CALLE LAS ESTACADAS

MATANZAS

HOTEL POSADA SAN JAVIER

CALLE EX-RASTRO

CALLEJÓN

JUÁREZ

BENITO

CENTRO JOYERO

PLAZUELA BERNAL

MUSEO PLATERÍA

CELSO

TELECOMUNICACIONES

HOTEL LOS ARCOS

CASA HUMBOLDT

EMILIA CASTILLO

HOTEL AGUA ESCONDIDA

CASA BORDA

HOTEL EMILIA CASTILLO

CAFÉ SASHA

CALLE JUAN RUIZ DE ALARCÓN

CALLE GUADALUPE

ARNOLDO'S

JOYERÍA ELENA BALLESTEROS

FOTO JUÁREZ

LUNA COLLECTION

Zócalo

DEL ÁNGEL INN

HUMBOLDT

HIGUERA

LA PARROQUIA

DE MUERTE

ABARROTES TAQUIZA

HSBC

SANTA PRISCA

CRAFT STALLS

HECHO A MANO

NUESTRO MEXICO

RESTAURANT EL ADOBE

INTERNET

COLORAMA PHOTO

PIZZA PAZZA

MUSEO GUILLERMO SPRATLING

CALLE

VERACRUZ

HOTEL CASA GRANDE

EZEQUIEL TAPÍA

INTERNET

NEWSSTAND

PLATERÍA GLORIA

CUAUHTÉMOC

INTERNET

INTERNET

BANCOMER

Market

FONDA SAN FRANCISCO

Plazuela de San Juan

PLAZA SAN JUAN

GROCERIES AND LIQUOR

RESTAURANT SANTA FE

HOTEL SANTA PRISCA

HIDALGO

MINISUPER LA GLORIA

FARMACIA SIMILARES

CALLE DE PILITA

ESTRELLA DE ORO BUS TERMINAL

POST OFFICE

| 0 | 75 yds |

| 0 | 75 m |

95

TELEFÉRICO TO HOTEL MONTE TAXCO

To Grutas de Cacahuamilpa, Xochicalco, and Mexico City

LOS ARCOS

MARISCOS CALETILLA

TOURIST INFORMATION

| 0 | 500 yds |

| 0 | 500 m |

DISCO IBIZA

HOTEL BORDA

SILVER SHOPS

LA GARITA

BANCOMER

PUENTE RAMONET

HOSPITAL ESTATAL

HOTEL POSADA DE LA MISIÓN

IGLESIA DE CHAVARRIETA

JUÁREZ

CLÍNICA DE ESPECIALIDADES

BANCOMER

BIBLIOTECA CIUDADES HERMANAS

BENITO

EX-CONVENTO SAN BERNARDINO

AV DE LOS PLATEROS

MAP AREA

BANAMEX

TIENDA LA MISIÓN

POLICIA PREVENTIVA

95

CALLE JUAN RUIZ DE ALARCÓN

CALLE

VERACRUZ

AV DE LOS PLATEROS

CUAUHTÉMOC

IGLESIA DE VERACRUZ

Parque Guerrero

ESTRELLA BLANCA BUS TERMINAL

POSADA LUCY

HIDALGO

SANTA ANA

IGLESIA DE SAN NICOLAS

HOTEL RANCHO VICTORIA

CALLE DE PILITA

IGLESIA DE SANTISIMA

LONG-DISTANCE TELEPHONE

MORELOS

CLÍNICA SANTA CRUZ

HOSPITAL SEGURO SOCIAL

95

CEMETERY

To Tourist Information, Hotel Hacienda del Solar, Ixcateopan, and Acapulco of Santa Prisca, which included a special chapel for the miners, who before had not been allowed to enter the church.

Independence and Modern Times

The 1810–1821 War of Independence and the subsequent civil strife reduced the mines to but a memory within a generation. They were nearly forgotten when William Spratling, an American artist and architect, moved to Taxco in 1929 and began reviving Taxco's ancient but moribund silversmithing tradition. Working with local artisans, Spratling opened the first cooperative shop, Las Delicias.

Spurred by the trickle of tourists along the new Acapulco highway, more shops opened, increasing the demand for silver, which in turn led to the reopening of the mines. Soon silver demand outpaced the supply. Silver began streaming in from other parts of Mexico to the workbenches of thousands of artisans in hundreds of cooperatively and family-owned shops dotting the still-quaint hillsides of a new, prosperous Taxco.

SIGHTS
Getting Oriented

Although the present city (elev. 5,850 feet, 1,780 meters) spreads much farther, the center of town encompasses the city's original seven hills, wrinkles in the slope of a towering mountain.

For most visitors, the downhill town limit is the *carretera,* the local stretch of old National Highway 95, now named Avenida de los Plateros, after the Taxco *plateros* (silversmiths) who put Taxco on Mexico's tourism map. The highway contours along the hillside from Los Arcos (The Arches) on the north end of town about two miles, passing the Calle Pilita intersection on the south edge of town. Along the *carretera,* immediately accessible to a steady stream of tour buses, lie the town's plusher hotels and many silver shops.

The rest of the town is fortunately insulated from tour buses by its narrow winding streets. From the *carretera,* the most important of them climb and converge, like bent spokes of a wheel, to the *zócalo.* Beginning with the

most northerly, the main streets (and the directions they run) are La Garita (uphill), Alarcón (downhill), Veracruz (downhill), Santa Ana (downhill), Salubridad (uphill), Morelos (downhill), and Pilita (downhill).

Getting Around

Although walking is Taxco's most common mode of transport, taxis go anywhere within the city limits for about $2. White *combi* collective vans (fare about $0.30) follow designated routes, marked on the windshields. Simply tell your specific destination to the driver. For side trips to nearby towns and villages, a fleet of Flecha Roja second-class local buses and *colectivos* leave frequently from their *carretera* terminal near the corner of Veracruz.

◖ Santa Prisca

All roads in Taxco begin and end on the *zócalo* at Santa Prisca church. French architect D. Diego Durán designed and built the church between 1751 and 1758 with money

© BRUCE WHIPPERMAN

Santa Prisca's baroque embellishments resemble the designs on fine silverplate.

from the fortune of silver king Don José Borda. The facade, decorated with saints on pedestals, arches, and spiraled columns, follows the baroque churrigueresque style (after Jose Churriguera, 1665–1725, the "Spanish Michelangelo"). Interior furnishings include an elegant pipe organ, brought from Germany via boat to Veracruz, thence overland by muleback in 1751, and several gilded side altars. The riot of interior elaboration climaxes in the towering gold-leaf main altar, which seems to drip with ornamentation in tribute to Santa Prisca, the Virgin of Guadalupe, and the Virgin of the Rosary, who piously preside above all. Dreamy Bible-story paintings by Miguel Cabrera decorate a chamber behind

TLATCHTLI: THE BALL GAME

Basketball fever is probably a mild affliction compared to the enthusiasm pre-Columbian crowds felt for *tlatchtli,* the ball game that was played throughout Mesoamerica and is still played in some places. Contemporary accounts and latter-day scholarship have led to a partial picture of *tlatchtli* as it was played centuries ago. Although details varied locally, the game centered around a hard, natural-rubber ball called a *tlatchtli,* which players batted back and forth across a center dividing line with leg-, arm-, and torso-blows.

Play and scoring was vaguely similar to tennis. Opponents, either individuals or small teams, tried to smash the ball past their opponents into scoring niches at the opposite ends of an I-shaped, sunken court. Players also could garner points by forcing their opponents to make wild shots that bounced beyond the court's retaining walls.

Courts were often equipped with a pair of stone rings fixed above opposing ends of the center dividing line. One scoring variation awarded immediate victory to the team who could manage to bat the *tlatchtli* through the ring.

Like tennis, players became very adept at batting the ball at high speed. Unlike tennis, the ball was solid and perhaps as heavy as two or three baseballs. Although protected by helmets and leather, players were usually bloodied, often injured, and sometimes even killed from opponents' punishing *tlatchtli*-inflicted blows. Matches were sometimes decided like a boxing match, with victory going to the opponent left standing on the court.

As with everything in Mesoamerica, tradition and ritual ruled *tlatchtli.* Master teachers subjected initiates to rigorous training, prescribed ritual, and discipline not unlike the ascetic lifestyle of a medieval monastic brotherhood.

Potential rewards were enormous, however. Stakes varied in proportion to a contest's ritual significance and the rank of the players and their patrons. Champion players could win fortunes in gold, feathers, or precious stones. Exceptional games could result in riches and honor for the winner and death for the loser, whose heart, ripped from his chest on the centerline stone, became food for the gods.

© BRUCE WHIPPERMAN

The stone ring at Xochicalco's northern ball court remains as it was discovered.

the main altar, while in a room to the right portraits of Pope Benedict IV, who sanctioned all this; and Manuel Borda, Santa Prisca's first priest; hang among a solemn gallery of subsequent *padres.*

Outside, landmarks around the plaza include the **Casa Borda** (10 A.M.–8 P.M. daily except Mon.), visible (as you face away from the church facade) on the right side of the *zócalo.* This former Borda family townhouse, built concurrently with the church in typical baroque colonial style, now serves as the Taxco Casa de Cultura, featuring exhibitions by local artists and artisans.

Downhill

Heading out and down the church steps, you can continue downhill in either of two interesting ways. If you walk left immediately downhill from the church, you reach the lane Calle Los Arcos, running alongside and below the church. From there, reach the **market** by heading right before the quaint archway over the street, down the winding staircase-lane, where you'll soon be in a warren of awning-covered stalls.

If, however, you head right from the church steps, another immediate right leads you beside the church along legendary **Calle de Muerte** (Street of Death), so named because of the former cemetery where the workers who died constructing the church were buried. (Note the skeleton on the church-front corner facing Calle de Muerte.)

Museo Guillermo Spratling

Continuing downhill, you'll find Museo Guillermo Spratling (tel. 762/622-1660, 9 A.M.–6 P.M. Tues.–Sat., 9 A.M.–3 P.M. Sun., hours may vary seasonally, admission $3) fronting the little plaza behind the church. On the main and upper floors, the National Institute of Archaeology displays intriguing carvings and ceramics (including unusual phallic examples), such as a ball-game ring, animal masks, and a priestly statuette with knife in one hand, human heart in the other. Basement-floor

Calle Los Arcos is one of Taxco's busiest streets since it leads directly to the market.

displays interestingly detail local history from the Aztecs through William Spratling.

Casa Humboldt

Back outside, one block down Alarcón (the downhill extension of Calle de Muerte), stands the Casa Humboldt (tel. 762/622-5501, 10 A.M.–5 P.M. Tues.–Sat., 10 A.M.–4 P.M. Sun., winter hours may be shorter, admission $3), named after the celebrated geographer (who is said to have stayed only one night, however). Now the state maintains it as the Museum of Viceregal (read colonial) Art. Displays feature a permanent collection of historical artifacts, including an exhibit about the Manila galleon, colonial technology, and colonial religious sculpture and painting.

Museo Platería

Nearby, the Museo Platería (Alarcón 4, third floor, 10 A.M.–6 P.M. daily), next door to the Hotel Emilia Castillo, illustrates a history of Taxco silvercraft and displays outstanding pieces by local artisans. (Alternately, you may

Taxco's Casa Humboldt preserves a treasury of colonial religious art.

enter the museum through the *zócalo*-front shopping patio of Las Artesanías, next to the Casa Borda.)

Other In-Town Sights

A short ride coupled with a walk circling back to the *zócalo* provides the basis for an interesting half-day exploration. Taxi or ride a *combi* to the Hotel Posada de la Misión, where the **Cuauhtémoc Mural** glitters on a wall near the pool. Executed by renowned muralist Juan O'Gorman with a riot of pre-Columbian symbols—yellow sun, pearly rabbit-in-the-moon, snarling jaguar, writhing serpents, fluttering eagle—the mural glorifies Cuauhtémoc, the last Aztec emperor. Cuauhtémoc, unlike his uncle Moctezuma, tenaciously resisted the conquest, but was captured and later executed by Cortés in 1525. His remains were discovered not long ago in Ixcateopan, about 24 miles west by local bus or car.

Continue your walk a few hundred yards north along the *carretera* (Mexico City direction) from the Hotel Posada de la Misión.

There, a driveway leading right just before the gas station heads to the Hotel Borda grounds. Turn left on the road just after the gate and you'll come to an antique brick smelter chimney and cable-hung derrick. These mark an inactive **mineshaft** descending to the mine-tunnel honeycomb thousands of feet beneath the town. The mines are still being worked from another entrance, but mostly for lead rather than silver. You can see the present-day works from the hilltop of the Hotel Hacienda del Solar on the south edge of town.

Now, return to the *carretera*, cross over and stroll the **Calle la Garita** about a mile back to the *zócalo*. Of special interest, besides a number of crafts stores and stalls, are the **Iglesia de Chavarrieta,** the **Biblioteca Taxco-Canoga Park** (library, with many English-language novels and reference books, 10 A.M.–7 P.M. Mon.–Fri., 10 A.M.–1 P.M. Sat.), and the former **Convento San Bernardino.**

Farther on, a block before the *zócalo,* pause to decipher the colored stone mosaic of the **Taxco Hieroglyph,** which decorates the

a large representation of a traditional hieroglyph in front of the Taxco Presidencia Municipal pavement in front of the Presidencia Municipal (City Hall). Inside, climb the stairs for a balcony-front view of the hieroglyph and the wall mural for a graphic review of Mexican history. See the main actors, from left to right: stolid Benito Juárez ("Respect for the rights of all is peace"); elderly General Porfirio Díaz gives away church and communal land to foreigners; banderilla-laden Emiliano Zapata declares his Plan de Ayala; President Lázaro Cárdenas in overalls expropriates foreign oil companies; and Aldolfo López Mateos declares free school textbooks, while Juárez, Kennedy, Kissinger, de Gaulle, and Nehru look on.

Teleférico to Hotel Monte Taxco

On the north side of town, where the *carretera* passes beneath Los Arcos, a cableway above the highway lifts passengers to soaring vistas of the town on one side and ponderous, pine-studded mesas on the other. It's open 7:30 A.M.–7:30 P.M. daily; round-trip tickets cost about $4, and kids are half price. The ride ends at the Hotel Monte Taxco, where you can make

a day of it golfing, horseback riding, playing tennis, eating lunch, and sunning on the panoramic-view pool deck. Return by taxi if you miss the last car.

Cristo del Monte

Above the west side of town, about two miles uphill from the *zócalo,* stands the colossal stone statue of Jesus, where folks enjoy an airy panoramic town view framed by lush, green looming mountains. Get there on foot (if you relish a 1,500-foot climb, wear a hat and carry water) or by taxi (about $2.50), *colectivo* (to Casahuates village), or car, west from the *zócalo* via Calle Cuauhtémoc, past the Hotel Victoria. On foot, after about two miles (3 km) fork right at the Huixteco sign and continue past Casahuates village about 200 yards, where a dirt driveway leads right to the Cristo del Monte park.

In-Town Vistas

You needn't go as far afield as the Hotel Monte Taxco or the Cristo del Monte to get a good

Panoramic views seem to appear around every Taxco corner.

© BRUCE WHIPPERMAN

GUERRERO UPCOUNTRY

© BRUCE WHIPPERMAN

the Cristo del Monte high above Taxco

view of the city streets and houses carpeting the mountainside. Vistas depend not only on vantage point but time of day, since the best viewing sunshine (which frees you from squinting) should come generally from *behind*. Consequently, spots along the highway (more or less east of town), such as the patios of the Hotel Posada de la Misión and the *mirador* atop the Hotel Borda, provide good morning views, while afternoon views are best from points west of town, such as the restaurant balcony or the hilltop of the Hotel Rancho Taxco Victoria.

EXCURSIONS FROM TAXCO

The monumental duo of the Grutas de Cacahuamilpa and the ruins of ancient Xochicalco makes for a long but fascinating day trip. Start early; the caves are about 20 miles (32 km) north of town (towards Mexico City) and Xochicalco is about 29 miles (47 km) farther. On another day, travel west for about 20 miles (32 km) to Ixcateopan to visit the final resting place of the Aztecs' last emperor.

◀ Grutas de Cacahuamilpa

These caves are well worth the effort. The Grutas de Cacahuamilpa (kah-kah-ooah-MEEL-pah) are one of the world's great cavern complexes. Forests of stalagmites and stalactites, in myriad shapes—Pluto the Pup, the Holy Family, a desert caravan, asparagus stalks, cauliflower heads—festoon a series of gigantic limestone chambers. The finale is a grand, 30-story hall that meanders for half a mile, like a fairyland in stone. The caves are open daily; hourly three-mile, two-hour walking tours in Spanish are included in the $5 admission fee and begin at 10 A.M. A few gift shops sell souvenirs; snack bars and *fonda*-style restaurants supply home-style food.

Colectivos leave hourly for the caves, beginning at 8:30 A.M., from just north of the Estrella Blanca bus station on the *carretera*. Watch for the word Grutas written on the windshields; expect to pay about $4 for a one-way fare. By car, get to the caves via Highway 95 north from Taxco; after 10 miles (16 km) from the northside Pemex station, fork left onto Highway 55 toward Toluca. Continue five more miles (8 km) and turn right at the signed Grutas de Cacahuamilpa junction. After a few hundred yards, turn right again into the entrance driveway.

◀ Xochicalco

Grand Xochicalco (soh-shee-KAHL-koh), an hour farther north from Cacahuamilpa, although lightly touristed, is a fountainhead of Mesoamerican legend. The archaeological zone, officially designated as a UNESCO World Heritage site, spreads over a half dozen terraced pyramid hilltops above a natural lake-valley that at one time sustained a large population. Xochicalco flowered during the late classic period around A.D. 800, partly filling the vacuum left by the decline of Teotihuacán, the previously dominant Mesoamerican classic city-state. Some archaeologists speculate that Xochicalco at its apex was the great center of learning, known in legend as Tamanchoan, where astronomer-priests derived and maintained calendars and where the Quetzalcoatl legend was born.

Your first stop should be the world-class **museum,** via the signed driveway east of the archaeological site. A grand entrance hall leads to six masterfully executed showrooms that illustrate the main currents of Xochicalco civilization: Earthly Gifts (flora, fauna, and trade); Warlords and Priests (don't miss the headless Lord in Red sun god); Xochicalco, Guardian of the People (centered around a pair of calendar-glyph stelae that undoubtedly records a historic Xochicalco event); Creators and Artists (don't miss the sensitively executed jaguar and coyote pieces); World of the Gods (dramatic illustration of the ball court and ring found on the site); and Daily Spaces (replica of a typical house, family altars and utensils, and realistic "Lord of Xochicalco").

Leave at least two hours to cover the site highlights. (The mandatory visitor exit time is 5:45 P.M. daily.) After visiting the excellent bookstore (that closes 5 P.M.), your first stop should be the unmissable **Pyramid of Quetzalcoatl** on the site's north side. From the parking lot, head south uphill for about 100 yards, where a wide path forks right, uphill. After approximately another 100 yards, when you reach level ground again, turn right and pass the beautifully reconstructed **eastern ball court** on your right. Continue another 50 yards or so until, on the wall about 200 feet your left, you see some stairs that you should climb, to the next upper level where the platform-like Pyramid of Quetzalcoatl (The Plumed Serpent) rises on the hilltop.

Vermilion paint remnants hint at the Pyramid's original appearance, which was perhaps as brilliant as a giant birthday cake. In bas-relief around the entire base a serpent writhes, intertwined with personages, probably representing chiefs or great priests. Above these are warriors, identified by their helmets and *atlatl,* or lance-throwers.

Most notable, however, is one of Mesoamerica's most remarkable bas-reliefs, flanking the

© BRUCE WHIPPERMAN

Xochicalco, a UNESCO World Heritage site, is both a fountainhead of Mesoamerican legend and one of Mexico's most regally restored ancient cities.

XOCHICALCO

To Tetlama

P

NORTHERN BALL COURT

OBSERVATORY

ACROPOLIS

PYRAMID OF QUETZALCOATL

EASTERN BALL COURT

CEREMONIAL PLAZA

TEMPLE OF THE STELES

TWO GLYPH STELA

RAMP OF THE ANIMALS

ENTRY WALKWAY

SOUTHERN BALL COURT

MAIN PLAZA

LA MALINCHE

CAUSEWAY

PALACE

CAUSEWAY

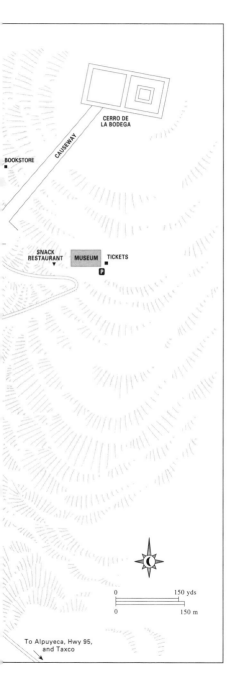

BOOKSTORE

CAUSEWAY

CERRO DE
LA BODEGA

SNACK
RESTAURANT MUSEUM TICKETS

0   150 yds

0   150 m

To Alpuyeca, Hwy 95,
and Taxco

staircase. It shows the 11th-week sign, *ozom-atli* (monkey), being pulled by a hand (via a rope) to join with the 5th-week sign, *calli* (house). Latter-day scholars generally interpret this as describing a calendar correction that resulted from a grand conclave of chiefs and sages from all over Mesoamerica, probably at this very spot.

About 100 yards south of the Pyramid of Quetzalcoatl rises the **Temple of the Stelae,** so named for three large stone tablets found beneath the floor. They narrate the events of the Quetzalcoatl legend, wherein Quetzalcoatl (discoverer of corn and the calendar) was transformed into the morning star (the planet Venus); he continues to rule the heavens as the brightest star and the Lord of Time.

About 100 yards farther south, the **Main Plaza** was accessible to the common people via roads from below. This is in contrast to the sacrosanct **Ceremonial Plaza** by the Eastern Ball Court nearby. South of the Ceremonial Plaza, the **Ramp of the Animals** (named for the carved animal-motif stones found along its length) slopes upward from east to west.

On the south end of the zone, a faintly visible causeway once connected the La Malinche pyramid, 200 yards to the southwest, with the Ceremonial Plaza.

That causeway passed the **Southern Ball Court,** which is strikingly similar to ball courts as far away as Toltec Tula in the north and Maya Copan in Honduras, far to the south. On the opposite side of the causeway from the Ball Court lies the **Palace,** a complex marked by many rooms with luxury features such as toilet drainage, fireplaces, and steam baths.

On the far northwest side of the complex is the **Observatory,** a room hollowed into the hill, stuccoed and fitted with a viewing shaft for timing the sun and star transits essential for an accurate calendar.

Misión Tours (at Hotel Posada de la Misión, tel. 762/622-1125 or 762/622-0063) offers tours to the ruins. To get to Xochicalco on your own, taxi or drive by continuing past the Grutas de Cacahuamilpa driveway entrance (mark your odometer). The route is straightforward, continuing by a single main road generally northeast, through Coatlá del Río (12 miles, 19 km), Mazatepec (20 miles, 33 km) and finally Miacatlán (23 miles, 37 km). There you bear right (east) at a fork (watch for Xochicalco signs) and continue past Rodeo hamlet (and lake on the right) to the Xochicalco signed road on the left that leads a mile or two uphill to the archaeological site, a total of 29 miles (46 km) and about an hour from Cacahuamilpa, or 48 miles (77 km) in two hours from Taxco.

The ruins are open 9 A.M.–6 P.M. daily (last visitor entry at 5 P.M., however). Admission (get tickets at the museum) runs about $5. Since caretakers shoo all visitors out by 5:45 P.M., arrive early enough to allow a couple of hours to explore the ruins. Although there is a restau-

CUAUHTÉMOC: THE LAST AZTEC EMPEROR

Cuauhtémoc (koo-ah-oo-TAY-mok) is more than just a national hero; he's the celebrated Aztec leader who said no to the Spanish conquistadores and, spitting on the spineless example of his uncle Moctezuma before him, did something about it. Faced with the disastrous reality that most of imperial Tenochtitlán's population of 250,000 was either dead or sick with smallpox, Cuauhtémoc rallied his people to hold out for 75 days against Spanish cannons and their 100,000-strong army of native allies.

That the story of Cuauhtémoc was more than a legend became clear when, on September 26, 1949, official investigators announced the discovery of Cuauhtémoc's long-missing remains, in the small municipality of Ixcateopan, not far from the famous Acapulco-region silver town of Taxco, Guerrero.

Cuauhtémoc was born into the comfort and privilege of the Mexican imperial family on February 23, 1501. His father, Ahuitzotl, was the son of the eighth Aztec emperor, also Ahuitzotl. His mother, princess Cuayautitalli, was the daughter of the lord of Zompancuahuitl (now Ixcateopan, Guerrero).

His given name, Cuauhtémoc, translates from the Aztec language as "descending eagle." Cuauhtémoc's traditional hieroglyph is thus marked by a stylized diving eagle.

Orphaned by his father when still an infant, Cuauhtémoc was brought up by his mother. At the age of 15 he entered Calmécac academy for sons of noble military officers and priests. His formal education initiated him into the secrets of the gods and the sciences of astronomy and the calendar.

After completing his schooling, Cuauhtémoc followed his uncle, Moctezuma II, in his infamous "War of the Flowers" conquests. During this time he proved his valor and skill, gaining the high rank of *tlacetechutli,* the command equivalent of a modern colonel.

Moctezuma II, upon returning home in glory with thousands of captives, presided over the elevation of his nephew, Cuauhtémoc, as governor of the important Tlatelolco and Teotecuhtli districts of the capital Tenochtitlán.

The good times didn't last, however, for soon Hernán Cortés and his small but determined band of armored soldiers and cavalry was entering the gates of Tenochtitlán. Cuauhtémoc's uncle, frozen by fear that Cortés might be the returned god Quetzalcoatl, quickly surrendered himself and all of his golden treasure to the wily Cortés. On July 1, 1520, angered by Spanish brutality and their emperor's fearful acquiescence, the Tenochtitlán populace rebelled, killing Moctezuma II and forcing the Spanish into their disastrous Noche Triste (Sad Night) retreat, at the end of which an exhausted Cortés sat down and cried for the loss of half of his men.

The Aztecs' triumph was short-lived, however. Although they had rid themselves of the Spanish, smallpox, the Spaniards' deadly legacy, began spreading among the people. When the Spanish, returned to Tenochtitlán in late May 1521 reinforced by a vast corps of native allies, Cuauhtémoc, by contrast, ruled a city decimated by smallpox. Nevertheless, with herculean resolve, he united his people, exhorting those who could care for the wounded, gather rocks, or help pile bricks for a barricade.

rant by the museum, you should probably be prepared with some food and drinks, and be sure to come with a hat, water, and comfortable walking shoes.

Ixcateopan

The picturesque little furniture-making town of Ixcateopan (eeks-kah-tay-OH-pan, Land of Cotton) has become famous for the remains

(now controversial) of the last Aztec emperor, Cuauhtémoc, which archaeologists uncovered there on September 26, 1949.

The renown has been beneficial. The town streets and plaza are smartly cobbled with the local white marble, and houses and shops are neatly painted and whitewashed. At the center of all this stands Cuauhtémoc's resting place, the venerable **Iglesia de Santa María de la**

After a bloody siege two and a half months long, Cortés resorted to leveling the capital to capture it. On August 13, 1521, Cuauhtémoc, desperate for reinforcements, set out to find them, but he was captured and brought before Cortés and his translator-mistress, Malinche. Cuauhtémoc pointed to the dagger that Cortés held in his belt and said to Malinche, "Malintzin, since I've resisted you in the defense of my city and my people, and come by coercion and in chains before you, take that dagger and kill me with it."

Cortés, however, didn't allow Cuauhtémoc such an honorable death. Perhaps hoping that he could convince him to be his puppet emperor, Cortés kept him in captivity for another four years. He even took Cuauhtémoc and a retinue of Aztec nobles along on his ill-fated expedition to Honduras in 1523–1525. Tortured with foreboding that Cuauhtémoc and his compatriots were plotting against him, Cortés had Cuauhtémoc hanged on February 28, 1525.

Cuauhtémoc's grisly remains were still suspended in the hanging tree when Cuauhtémoc's warrior companion, Tzilactzín, rescued them. Afraid that vandals would desecrate

the body, he took down Cuauhtémoc's corpse and wrapped it in aromatic leaves. He and a band of about 30 companions, all deserters of Cortés's expedition, carried the remains for 40 days and nights and buried them secretly at Ixcateopan, the home of Cuauhtémoc's mother. There, 424 years later, Cuauhtémoc's lineal descendant, Salvador Rodrigo Juárez, and historian and Professor Eulalia Guzmán announced the discovery of Cuauhtémoc's remains. They are on public display before the altar of Ixcateopan town church, Santa María de la Asunción, in a glass casket above the spot where they were found.

The remains of Cuauhtémoc, the Mexicans' last emperor, lie in Santa María de la Asunción church, in Ixcateopan.

Asunción, at the south side of the town plaza. Inside, Jairo Rodríguez, son of the codiscoverer of what he believes are Cuauhtémoc's remains and lineal descendant of Cuauhtémoc himself, devotes his life to maintaining the sanctuary and its small adjoining museum. Cuauhtémoc's supposed relics themselves, which were subjected to careful investigation when they were unearthed, lie in a glass case directly over the spot where they were buried beneath the altar stones centuries ago.

(*Note:* Some experts recently have disputed the authenticity of the remains. Controversy and bickering erupted and in 2005 led the town mayor to strip Jairo Rodriguéz of his official title as keeper of the remains. Time only can tell how this will all wash out.)

The **museum** next door to the remains details the story of Cuauhtémoc's heroic defense of the Aztec capital, Tenochtitlán, and his capture, torture, and subsequent execution by Cortés on February 28, 1525. Copies of pictograms, known as codices, such as the *Codex Vatican-Ríos* (1528), displayed in the museum, represent Cuauhtémoc (literally, The Descending Eagle) with an inverted, stylized eagle above his head. The sanctuary and museum hours are 9 A.M.–3 P.M. and 4–5 P.M. Monday–Saturday, 9 A.M.–3 P.M. Sunday. Jairo sells an excellent booklet ($3) in Spanish that details the fascinating story of the discovery and authentication of what he believes are his ancestor's remains.

Outside, be sure to take a look at the town **archaeological site** (10 A.M.–5 P.M. Wed.–Sun.), about three blocks downhill past the church, on main street Calle V. Guerrero. The main remains, called the "Temple of Cotton," echoing the name Ixcateopan, reveal a ceremonial complex, including a pair of pedestals, royal rooms, and a former spring leading through what appear to have been wash basins (presumably for the cotton the high priests may have ritually processed there).

Farther afield, you might be able to find a guide to show you the limestone caves, **Grutas de San Miguel,** near neighboring San Miguel village (about an hour by high-clearance Jeep, SUV, or truck); off the highway back to Taxco, fork right at the dirt road, at some houses, about seven miles from Ixcateopan.

Customarily sleepy Ixcateopan wakes up for three annual fiestas. The fun kicks off in February, when folks celebrate their indigenous roots with a weeklong party of daily flower processions, indigenous dances, and fireworks, all climaxing around the February 23 birthday of Cuauhtémoc.

The customary arrival of the governor of Guerrero, the Acapulco Symphony, and maybe even the president of Mexico, on September 26, the discovery date of Cuauhtémoc's remains, culminates another week of celebrating.

Finally, townsfolk bring in the New Year in grand style with a combined Christmas-carnival-New Year celebration of their patron Santo Niño de Atocha.

Besides its historic interest, Ixcateopan and its environs—the rustic old church and garden, the tranquil plaza, the surrounding lush oak-forested hills—invite lingering. Moreover, the amiable, frankly curious townsfolk—who are definitely not overwhelmed by tourists—are ready for visitors. They operate some pretty fair plaza-front country restaurants and a homey local hotel, the **Posada del Rey** (Calle V. Guerrero 14, Ixcateopan, Guerrero, tel. 736/366-2368, $18 s, $24 d), a block past the plaza, across the street from the church. The family managers offer eight clean rooms around a tranquil inner patio, furnished with attractive, locally crafted wood furniture and homespun bedspreads. Rooms have private hot-water shower baths.

Get to Ixcateopan via a *colectivo* labeled Ixcateopan. Catch it in front of the Estrella Blanca bus station in Taxco, or at any point on the *carretera* before the south-side, signed turn-off road to Ixcateopan. Expect to pay about $2 per person, one-way.

Drivers, follow the signed fork west (turn right if traveling south) from the *carretera,* past the Pemex *gasolinera* about a mile south of town. Mark your odometer. Continue about an hour along the very scenic (a pair of waterfalls, good for picnicking and splashing, at Mile 4.5/Km 7.2 and Mile 11/Km 17.7), sometimes potholed, paved road for 23 miles (37 km) to the town plaza.

ACCOMMODATIONS

Taxco's dry, temperate climate relegates air-conditioning, ceiling fans, and central heating to frills offered only in the most expensive hotels. All of the hotel recommendations below have hot water and private baths, however.

Taxco's low-end hotels (under $50, but nevertheless comfortable) cluster in the colorful *zócalo* neighborhood, while the midrange and high-end ($50 and up) lodgings are scattered mostly along the *carretera*.

Under $50

Walk west of the *zócalo* half a block past Plazuela de San Juan to the **Posada Lucy** (Carlos J. Nibbi 8, Taxco, Guerrero 40200, tel./fax 762/622-1780) on the left. Here, owners offer 32 budget rooms in a rambling complex, fortuitously isolated below and away from street noise. Airy patios with chairs and tables invite quiet relaxation. Inside, rooms are simply but attractively decorated with color-coordinated curtains, bedspreads, and handmade wooden furniture. Prices run a reasonable $18 s or $23 d in one bed; $46 for 3 or 4 people in two double beds.

Five blocks northwest of the *zócalo,* find the inviting ◖ **Hotel Posada San Javier** (Estacas 32, Taxco, Guerrero 40200, tel. 762/622-3177, tel./fax 762/622-2351, posadasanjavier@hotmail.com). Although it's a climb to the *zócalo,* this very popular hotel, built around a tranquil inner garden, offers about 40 immaculate rooms, a lovely pool-patio framed in lush verdure, and airy verandas for relaxing. All this for only $35 s, $38 d, 40 t; very large junior suites run $55 d. All with parking, and an inviting reading room with lots of books. Reserve a week in advance.

Back by the *zócalo,* on Alarcón just downhill west of the *zócalo,* a pair of former colonial mansions, now popular hotels, face each other across the street. First choice goes to the spacious, refined ◖ **Hotel Los Arcos** (J. Ruiz de Alarcón 4, Taxco, Guerrero 40200, tel. 762/622-1813, fax 762/622-7982, hotelosarcostaxco@ yahoo.com, www.hotellosarcos.net, $34 s, $40 d). The 24 rooms rise in three vine-draped tiers around an inner patio, replete with reminders of old Mexico. The rooms feature thoughtfully selected handmade polished wooden furniture, tile floors, rustic wall art, and immaculate hand-painted cobalt-on-white tile bathrooms.

Across the street, the **Hotel Emilia Castillo** (J. Ruiz de Alarcón 7, Taxco, Guerrero 40200, tel./fax 762/622-1396, hotelemilia@ hotmail.com or reservations1@hotelemilia-castillo.com, www.hotelemiliacastillo.com) is small and intimate, with plants, carved wood, paintings, and sculptures gracing every wall and corner. Rooms, in neocolonial decor, are clean and comfortable. The owners also run an adjacent silver boutique, whose displays decorate the downstairs lobby. The 14 rooms rent for about $35 s, $40 d, $45 t, junior suite $58; credit cards are accepted.

Head uphill, past the opposite (west) side of the plaza, and follow Cuauhtémoc to the Plazuela de San Juan and the adjacent **Hotel Santa Prisca** (Cena Obscura 1, P.O. Box 42, Taxco, Guerrero 40200, tel. 762/622-0080 or 762/622-0980, fax 762/622-2938, htl_staprisca@yahoo.com). This tranquil, dignified old hostelry surrounds an oft-fragrant garden of orange trees; its off-lobby dining room shines with graceful details, such as beveled glass, a fireplace, blue-white stoneware and ivy-hung portals. Its tile-decorated rooms, in two floors around the garden just outside, are clean and comfortable. Standard rooms go for about $32 s, $45 d, $50 t; larger superior-grade rooms $35 s, $50 d, $55 t, all with private baths and parking. Credit cards accepted.

Continue two blocks west of the *zócalo,* uphill past the end of Cuauhtémoc, to the **Hotel Victoria** (Carlos J. Nibbi 5 and 7, Taxco, Guerrero 40200, tel. 762/622-1014 or 762/622-0004, fax 762/622-0010, info@ victoriataxco.com, www.victoriataxco.com), which rambles along its view hillside in a picturesque state of decay. Built sometime back in the 1930s, the hotel usually slumbers on weekdays, reviving on weekends and holidays. (Actually, it's two hotels in one—the Victoria uphill and the former Rancho Taxco, neglected and returning to the earth across the road, downhill.) The Victoria, which at this writing was suffering from considerable deferred maintenance, nevertheless retains much of its original charm, including hand-hewn furniture, whitewashed stucco walls, riots of bougainvillea, a spreading top-level view garden, plus a big pool downhill and a relaxed lobby-level restaurant and bar where guests enjoy the best afternoon vista in town. Some of the spacious, comfortable rooms have luxurious view balconies. If you prefer peace and quiet, ask for one of the rooms away from the road, Nos. 22–28, off the upper *terraza mirador* (view patio) where, summer nights, you can enjoy the singing of the tree frogs and watch the lightning flicker in the clouds far away. Standard-grade rooms run about $45 s or d, higher during weekends and holidays and festivals. Semideluxe junior suites cost about $65. All with parking; credit cards accepted.

$50-100

Picturesquely tucked on an uphill lane, just two blocks north of the *zócalo,* find 🄲 **Hotel Mi Casita** (Altos de Redondo #1, Taxco, Guerrero 40200, tel./fax 762/627-1777, reservations@hotelmicasita.com, www.hotelmicasita.com). A charmingly rustic retreat for a cadre of savvy lovers of Mexico, the Hotel Mi Casita blooms with a treasury of delightful Mexicana. Its 12 rooms and suites, most with panoramic balcony views of the surrounding city and cloud-tipped mountains, are individually decorated with fetching designer lamps, hand-painted wall art, and colorful Talavera-tiled bathrooms. Rentals, some quaintly petite, ordinarily begin at about $50 s or d and range upward to about $80 for the largest suites. Add about 25 percent during holidays.

Taxco's only *zócalo*-front hostelry, the **Hotel Agua Escondida** (Calle Guillermo Spratling 4, Taxco, Guerrero 40200, tel. 762/622-0726 or 762/622-1166, fax 762/622-1306, hotelaguaesc@prodigy.net.mx, www.aguaescondida.com), stands on the diagonally opposite corner from the church. A multilevel maze of

hidden patios, rooftop sundecks, and dazzling city views, the Agua Escondida has dozens of clean, comfortable rooms. The name, which translates as "Hidden Water," must refer to its big swimming pool, which is tucked away in a far rooftop corner. Rooms vary; if you have the choice, look at several. Try to avoid the traffic-noisy streetfront rooms. If you don't mind climbing, some of the upper-floor rooms have airy, penthouse views. The 76 rooms run about $40 s, $64 d, $76 t weekends and holidays, with 15 percent midweek discount, all with parking. Credit cards accepted.

Thanks to new owners, the formerly neglected **Hotel Borda** (Cerro de Pedregal, P.O. Box 483, Taxco, Guerrero 40200, tel. 762/622-0225, fax 762/622-0617, info@hotelborda.com, www.hotelborda.com) is being restored to approximate the luxury hotel it once was. This is fortunate, for the hotel's magnificent assets—grand vistas, spacious garden, and luxurious blue pool and patio—remain as attractive as ever. The 110 clean, comfortable, and invitingly decorated rooms rent for about $70 s or d Sunday–Thursday, $80 s or d Friday and Saturday, with restaurant, bar, fans, and parking. Credit cards accepted.

Over $100

The luxuriously tranquil **Hotel Hacienda del Solar** (P.O. Box 96, Taxco, Guerrero 40200, tel./fax 762/622-0857, hdadelsolar@prodigy.net.mx) spreads over a hilltop forest garden on the southern edge of town. Guests in many of the 22 airy and spacious rooms enjoy private patios, fireplaces, and panoramic valley and mountain views. Rooms, in deluxe and junior suite versions, vary individually but are all artfully furnished with appointments including hand-woven rugs, colorful tile, paintings, and folk art. Some rooms share a spacious living area near the lovely view pool and patio; junior suites have huge beds and deep tile bathtubs. Other amenities include a view restaurant called the Ventana (Window) de Taxco and a cocktail lounge. Rooms for two go for about $110 deluxe and $140 junior suite. (*Note:* The Hotel Hacienda del Solar seems to be all but empty during the summer. When I arrived in September, it had no guests, no light in the rooms, and the pool was murky green. The staff fixed everything up, however, because I booked four nights, which turned out to be very pleasant.)

Resort-style 🌙 **Hotel Monte Taxco** (Lomas de Taxco, Taxco, Guerrero 40200, tel. 762/622-1300 or 762/622-1301, fax 762/622-1428, reservaciones@montetaxco.com.mx, www.montetaxco.com) stands atop a towering mesa accessible by either a steep road or *teleférico* (cableway) from the highway just north of town. On weekends, the hotel is often packed with well-heeled families from Mexico City, whose kids play organized games while their parents enjoy the panoramic poolside view or play golf and tennis. The 156 deluxe rooms, most with view balconies, rent from about $140 s or d (Sun.–Thurs. $110), with air-conditioning, phones, cable TV; credit cards accepted. Facilities include restaurants, shops, a piano bar, disco, weekend live music, parking, a gym, pool, sauna, and spa. The adjacent country club offers a nine-hole golf course, tennis courts, and horseback riding.

If you'd like to stay atop Monte Taxco, a good alternative to the hotel would be to rent one of the neocolonial-style apartments of the **Villas Monte Taxco** (tel. 762/622-2305, fax 762/622-5609) adjacent to the golf course, 100 yards outside the Hotel Monte Taxco front door. For about $110 per night (four nights $270) you get a deluxe, one-bedroom mountain-view apartment with kitchenette, living room, dining room, use of the pool, and access to the golf course, tennis courts, horseback riding, mountain trails, and the Hotel Monte Taxco's facilities next door.

Back down on the highway in town, the **Hotel Posada de la Misión** (Cerro de la Misión 32, Taxco, Guerrero 40200, tel. 762/622-0063 or 762/622-0533, fax 762/622-2198, hpm-reserva@posadamision.com, www.posadamision.com) spreads over a view hillside. Its guests, many on group tours, enjoy cool, quiet patios, green gardens, plant-lined corridors, a sunny pool and deck, a view restaurant, and parking. Many of the semideluxe rooms have panoramic city views; some have fireplaces. All rooms have color TV and phones. Standard rooms rent for about $140 d Sunday–Thursday, $160 Friday and Saturday, including breakfast, with credit cards accepted. Kids under 12 stay free in parents' room, with half off on meals. Christmas and New Year's prices are higher. Some readers have complained about unkempt rooms; make sure everything's in order before moving in. Find it just off the *carretera,* uphill side, 200 yards south of the Pemex gas station.

FOOD
Stalls and Snacks

The numerous *fondas* upstairs on the top floors above the *artesanías* section of the market are Taxco's prime source of wholesome country-style food. For just about the best of all of the *fondas,* check out Fonda San Francisco. The quality of *fonda* fare is a matter of honor for the proprietors, since among their local patrons word of a little bad food goes a long way. It's very hard to go wrong, moreover, if your selections are steaming hot and made fresh before your own eyes (in contrast, by the way, to most restaurant and hotel fare).

You can choose from a potpourri that might include steaming bowls of *menudo* or *pozole,* ($3) plates of pork or chicken *mole* ($4), or *molcajetes* filled with steaming meat and broth and draped with hot *nopales* ($5).

Stalls offering other variations appear evenings on the *zócalo.* Some families sell hot dogs and hamburgers, others tacos, others *pozole,* while another, which labels itself La Poblana, sometimes arrives in a truck and offers french-fried bananas, *churros,* and potato chips fried on the spot until about 10:30 P.M. next to the church.

Restaurants

Although its restaurants are not what draws Taxco's visitors, Taxco nevertheless offers some recommendable dining options. Of the *zócalo* restaurant choices, the upstairs **La Parroquia** (tel. 762/622-3096, 9 A.M.–11 P.M. daily), a half block from the church steps, ranks among the best; credit cards are accepted. The front balcony tables are ideal perches for watching the people parade below while enjoying a good breakfast, lunch, or dinner ($4–8).

Another good bet on the *zócalo* is **Pizza Pazza** (tel. 762/622-5500, noon–midnight daily), upstairs at the corner, right-hand side of the cathedral. Although the menu offers a little bit of everything, the specialty is good pizza, in about 15 varieties ($5–10). Extras include relaxed ambience, professional service, checkered tablecloths, and airy, plaza-view balcony tables. If the TV bothers you, the staff won't mind turning it down to low volume, if asked.

Arguably Taxco's best restaurant, **Ⅽ Café Sasha** (tel. 762/627-6464, 8 A.M.–midnight daily) is on Alarcón downhill one block from the *zócalo*, next to the Hotel Emilia Castillo. Here, in a retro-era Bohemian atmosphere, the hardworking American-Mexican owner-couple puts out a steady stream of savory coffee and healthy specialties of the house, including delicious omelettes ($5), whole wheat bread, crepes ($4), veggie burritos ($3), and Thai chicken ($6).

At least recommendable for its refined old-world ambience, the restaurant **Ⅽ Del Ángel Inn** (Celso Muñoz 4, 2nd floor, tel. 762/622-5525, 7 A.M.–10 P.M. daily), a few steps down from the *zócalo* churchfront, left corner, adds an airy view and good food to the reasons for going there. Inside, rustic old-adobe walls, regal stone columns, and baroque statuary enhance the pleasing effect. As for food, choose from a very recognizable, tasty menu of appetizers, soups, salads, pasta, Mexican specialties, meats, and more. Figure about $10–15, plus drinks, per person.

A block from the *zócalo,* along Calle Cuauhtémoc overlooking Plazuela de San Juan, try Mexican-style **Restaurant El Adobe** (Plazuela de San Juan 13, tel. 762/622-1416, 8 A.M.–11 P.M. daily). For breakfast, you can enjoy juice, eggs, and hotcakes; for lunch, hamburgers, tacos, and enchiladas; for dinner, steak Adobe-style and shrimp brochette ($5–12).

Of the restaurant options, the best for old-Mexico ambience is the local favorite **Restaurant Santa Fe** (tel. 762/622-1170, 8 A.M.–10 P.M. daily), on the left a few doors downhill from Plazuela de San Juan. Tasty,

professionally prepared and served country fare keeps a battalion of faithful patrons happy. Although the long à la carte menu varies from *pozole* and soup to chicken and fish, the main event is the daily four-course *comida* of soup (try *crema de zanahoria*, cream of carrot), spaghetti, main dish (try *chiles rellenos*), and dessert, about $5. It's good for breakfast, too ($3–5).

You're likely to enjoy the **Hotel Rancho Victoria** restaurant (7:30 A.M.–8 P.M. daily), especially for lunch and dinner. Although the food ($6–12) is quite good, the main attraction is the best afternoon view in town. The restaurant is uphill a block past the Plazuela de San Juan; from the *zócalo,* walk west along Cuauhtémoc and continue two blocks past Plazuela de San Juan. Credit cards are accepted.

A classy spot where you can enjoy the view, a swim, and lunch after seeing the Cuauhtémoc Mural is the adjacent **Restaurant El Mural** at the Hotel Posada La Misión on the *carretera,* open daily for breakfast 7–9:30 A.M. ($5–10), lunch 1–3:30 P.M. ($5–12), and dinner 7–11 P.M. ($7–20). If the place is packed with tour groups, have a drink, enjoy the mural, and go somewhere else.

ENTERTAINMENT AND EVENTS

Taxco people mostly entertain each other. Such spontaneous diversions are most likely around the *zócalo,* which often seems like an impromptu festival of typical Mexican scenes. Around the outside stand the monuments of the colonial past, while on the sidewalks sit the native people who come in from the hills to sell their onions, tamales, and pottery. Kids run between them, their parents and grandparents watching, while young men and women flirt, giggle, and jostle one another until late in the evening.

Three restaurant/bars on the side adjacent to the church provide good perches for viewing the hubbub. Visitors can either join the locals at **Bar Berta,** on the church corner, or take a balcony seat and enjoy the bouncy music with the mostly tourist crowd at **Bar Paco** next door. For more tranquillity, head upstairs to **Restaurant La Parroquia** a few steps farther on.

Later, or on another day, continue your Taxco party via the recorded music pouring out of the speakers (live rock 'n' roll on Sat.) at the restaurant/bar **Concha Nostra,** upstairs at Hotel Casa Grande, at Plazuela de San Juan.

Local discomaniacs flock to **Disco Ibiza** on the *carretera,* a few doors from Hotel Posada Misión, beginning around 10 P.M. most nights and especially weekends.

For more melodies for dancing, the **Hotel Monte Taxco** (tel. 762/622-1300 or 762/622-1301), always offers a piano bar and discotheque Windows and a trio weekends and seasonally. At the **Hotel Posada de la Misión** (tel. 762/622-0063 or 762/622-0533), patrons usually can enjoy a roving trio for lunch and a piano bar nightly. Programs vary; call the hotels to confirm.

Festivals

An abundance of local fiestas provide the excuses for folks to celebrate, starting on January 17 and 18 with the **Festival of Santa Prisca.** On the initial day, kids and adults bring their pet animals for blessing at the church. At dawn the next day, pilgrims arrive at the *zócalo* for *mañanitas* in honor of the saint, then head for folk dancing inside the church.

During the year Taxco's many neighborhood churches celebrate their saints' days (such as Chavarrieta, March 4; Veracruz, the four weeks before Easter; San Bernardino, May 20; Santísima Trinidad, June 13; Santa Ana, July 26; Asunción, August 15; San Nicolas, September 10; San Miguel, September 19; San Francisco, October 4; and Guadalupe, December 12) with food, fireworks, music, and dancing.

Religious fiestas climax during Semana Santa (Easter week), when, on the Thursday and Good Friday before Easter, cloaked penitents file through the city, carrying gilded images and bearing crowns of thorns.

On the Monday after the November 2 Día de los Muertos (Day of the Dead), Taxco people head to pine-shaded **Parque Huixteco**

(PAR-kay weesh-TAY-koh) atop the Cerro Huixteco behind town to celebrate their unique **Fiesta de los Jumiles.** In a ritual whose roots are lost in pre-Columbian legend, people collect and feast on *jumiles* (small crickets)—raw or roasted—along with music and plenty of beer and fixings. Since so many people go, transportation is easy. Drive or ride a *colectivo* (marked Huixteco on windshield) along the west-side road (westward extension of Cuauhtémoc from the *zócalo*) uphill about two miles. Fork right at the Huixteco sign. Continue for several miles to the mountaintop Parque Huixteco.

SPORTS AND RECREATION

Stay in shape as local folks do by walking Taxco's winding, picturesque side streets and uphill lanes. And, since all roads return to the *zócalo,* getting lost is rarely a problem.

For more formal sports, the **Monte Taxco Country Club** has horses ready for riding ($15/hour), three good tennis courts ($14/hour), and a nine-hole golf course available for use by non-guests for $50 per person. Contact the country club sports desk, in the little house about 50 yards away from the Hotel Monte Taxco's front entrance, or call the hotel (762/622-1300). Informal *sendas* (hiking paths; ask directions from the horse-rental attendant) branch from the horse paths to the surrounding luscious pine- and cedar-forested mesa country. Take sturdy shoes, water, and a hat.

SHOPPING
Market

Taxco's big market day is Sunday, when the town is loaded with people from outlying villages selling produce and live pigs, chickens, and ducks. The market is just downhill from Los Arcos, the lane that runs below the right side of the *zócalo* church (as you face the church). From the lane, head right before the arch and down the staircase. Soon you'll be descending through a warren of market stalls. Pass the small Baptist church on Sunday and hear the congregation singing like angels floating above the market. Don't miss the spice stall, **Yerbería Castillo,** piled with the

For a Taxco dog, any sunny spot seems a good place for a snooze.

intriguing wild remedies collected by owner Elvira Castillo and her son Teodoro.

Farther on you'll pass mostly scruffy meat stalls but also some clean juice stands, such as **Liquados Memo** (7 A.M.–6 P.M. daily), where you can rest with a delicious fresh *zanahoria* (carrot), *toronja* (grapefruit), or *sandía* (watermelon) juice.

Before leaving the market, be sure to ask for *jumiles* (hoo-MEE-lays), live crickets that are sold in bags for about a penny apiece, ready for folks to pop into their mouths.

If *jumiles* don't suit your taste, you may want to drop in for lunch at one of the *fondas* upstairs, above the market's *artesanías* section.

Taxco Handicrafts

Before visiting the individual private handicrafts shops, you might look around the submarket **Mercado de Artesanías** (watch for the sign above the main Taxco market downhill staircase) stalls that offer an abundance of priced-to-sell mini-treasures, such as silver chains, necklaces, earrings, belts, huaraches, and wallets. Furthermore, if you're in town on Saturday, you might also taxi down to the Estrella Blanca bus station on the highway and browse around the **Saturday Silver Market** that spreads along the street out front of the station.

And furthermore, while in town, be sure not to miss the common but colorful handicrafts, such as the host of charming ceramic cats, turtles, doves, fish, and other figurines that local vendors sell very cheaply. Find them everywhere—in the market, on street corners, and especially in front of the Museo Spratling. If you buy, bargain—but not too hard, for the people are poor and have often traveled far.

Taxco abounds in private handicrafts shops, most of them specializing in silver but a number of others specializing in Guerrero and Oaxaca masks, woodcrafts, pottery, and much more. Taxco's picturesque maze of up-and-downhill lanes makes handicrafts shopping both taxing and enjoyable at the same time.

I have arranged my list of favorite handicrafts stores so that, without too much backtracking, you can get a good look at lots of lovely handicrafts in an afternoon's (mostly downhill) stroll around town. Save your energy by taxiing uphill to the first shop on the list.

Lacquered pottery can be found on many Taxco curbsides.

Start uphill right above the *zócalo* at **Arnoldo** (Palma 1, tel. 762/622-1272, 9 A.M.–8:30 P.M. Mon.–Sat., 10 A.M.–5:30 P.M. Sun.), upstairs across the uphill lane next to Hotel Agua Escondida, where the friendly proprietors, Arnoldo Jacobo and his son Raoul, are more than willing and able to explain every detail about their fascinating array of merchandise. Masks are the prime attraction, and hundreds of masks from all over Guerrero—stone and wood, antique and new—line the walls like a museum. All of the many motifs, varying from blue-eyed sea goddesses and black men puffing cigarettes to inscrutable Aztec gods in onyx and grotesque lizard-humanoids, are priced to sell.

Other shops nearby have similar offerings, such as Arnoldo's neighbor, **Celso** (Palma 4, tel. 762/622-2848, 10 A.M.–2 P.M. and 4–8 P.M. Mon.–Tues. and Thurs.–Sat., 10 A.M.–4 P.M. Sun., closed Wed.), a stone's throw away just uphill.

Taxco handicrafts

© BRUCE WHIPPERMAN

Next, head back downhill to the Hotel Agua Escondida curbfront, and bear right along the *zócalo's* uphill sidewalk (across the *zócalo* from the church), then continue west along Calle Cuauhtémoc past the parade of small silver shops. Continue two blocks to the **Platería Gloria** (Plazuela de San Juan 7, tel. 762/622-2047 or 762/622-0410, fax 762/622-6498, 9 A.M.–7 P.M. Mon.–Sat., 11 A.M.–4 P.M. Sun.), on the uphill side of the little roundabout plaza, Plazuela de San Juan. For sheer volume and selection of everything lovely, this is the place, with literally thousands of charming silver necklaces, bracelets, rings, place settings, pendants, candlesticks: You name it, they have it, in myriad sizes, styles, and prices.

For a very carefully selected general Mexico handicrafts assortment—Puebla Talavera ceramics, Tonalá papier-mâché, metalwork, pewter—take a look inside the shop beneath Restaurant Adobe, signed Plaza San Juan, also on the west side of Plazuela de San Juan (tel. 762/622-1683, 10 A.M.–8 P.M. Mon.–Sat., 10 A.M.–3 P.M. Sun.).

Return east along Cuauhtémoc back to the *zócalo's* right, downhill side. Just after the Santa Prisca churchfront, turn right at Calle de Muerte, and immediately on the left, find what must be Taxco's most elegantly extravagant silver shop, the **Joyería Elena Ballesteros** (Calle de Muerte 4, tel. 762/622-3767, fax 762/622-3907, silver@ballesteros.com, www.ballesteros.com). More than just a labor of love, this is a virtual shrine to silver, beginning with the simply exquisite, moving to dining-room tables loaded with enough plate for a maharaja's banquet, to gleaming, 10-pound $50,000 crucifixes, and a huge gold tree of life.

Return uphill, to the *zócalo* corner, then turn right for a look around the grotto-like interior of **Luna Collection** (tel. 762/622-6447, 9 A.M.–8 P.M. daily) in the *zócalo*-front complex Patio de las Artesanías, on the right before the Casa Borda. Inside you'll find showrooms decorated with pendulous plaster stalacites hanging above faux stalagmites, seemingly dripping with fine silver jewelry (all of which, owners say, with a smile, was the model for the Grutas de Cacahuamilpa complex).

Continue, passing the Casa Borda. At the corner, just before the Hotel Agua Escondida, head right steeply downhill a block to the petite Plazuela Bernal and the **Centro Joyero** (tel. 762/622-7504, 10 A.M.–7 P.M. Mon.–Sat.,

© BRUCE WHIPPERMAN

Reproduction masks decorate a Taxco handicrafts store.

11 A.M.–5 P.M. Sun.) on the left side of the plazuela. Inside, find a number of small shops with many fine, priced-to-sell pieces.

Continue downhill a block along Alarcón to one of Taxco's most venerable institutions, the family-owned shop of **Emilia Castillo** (J. R. Alarcón 7, tel. 762/622-3471, emilia@emiliacastillojewelry.com, www.emiliacastillojewelry.com, 10 A.M.–7 P.M. Mon.–Sat., 10 A.M.–4 P.M. Sun.), adjacent to the lobby of the Hotel Emilia Castillo on the right side of the street. Run by a branch of the industrious and prolific Castillo clan, the shop offers all in-house work, specializing in porcelain and silver, at reasonable prices. Here, unlike at many shops, you can bargain a bit.

Continue east along Alarcón passing Casa Humboldt; after two short blocks, turn right at Calle Higuera, arriving after one block at **Nuestro Mexico** (Veracruz 8, tel. 762/622-0976, nuestromexico@hotmail.com, 10:30 A.M.–8 P.M. daily except Thurs.) on the left, at the corner of Veracruz. Inside, enjoy a look around at their interesting all-Guerrero clutter of wood and ceramic reproduction

masks, soaring angels, ceramic coffee cups, silver, and much more.

A few doors uphill back toward the *zócalo* along Veracruz, find elegant **Hecho a Mano** (Hand-Made, Veracruz 4), of master silversmith Manuel Porcayo. If originality is what you prefer, he can provide you with a treasury of one-of-a-kind necklaces, bracelets, rings, collars, pendants, and much more.

Finally, continue uphill a block to Humboldt lane, on the right, in the small plaza in front of the Museo Spratling. Here, choose your favorites among a trove of priced-to-sell indigenous handicrafts: fetching painted pottery animals, cheerful Father Suns, colorful *amate* (fig-tree-bark) placemats, emerald-hued beads, cool sombreros, polished wooden bowls, and much, much more.

Photo and Grocery Stores

The small **Colorama** (Cuauhtémoc 7, tel. 762/622-3394, 10 A.M.–8 P.M. Mon.–Sat.) photo shop, half a block west of the *zócalo,* offers a modest stock of merchandise such as batteries, point-and-shoot cameras, popular print film (100–1600 ASA), and slide film.

Better-stocked **Tienda la Misión** (Benito Juárez 215, tel. 762/622-0116, 10 A.M.–8 P.M. Mon.–Sat., 10 A.M.–2 P.M. Sun.), a few blocks past the *presidencia municipal* next to Banamex, offers some cameras and accessories and Kodak film, including Tri-X Pan, Plus-X, and Ektachrome. It also does photocopying, including enlargement and reduction.

Petite grocery store **La Plazuela** (Guadalupe 2, tel. 762/622-0633, 9 A.M.–10 P.M. daily), uphill (west) from the *zócalo,* has a little bit of everything.

Alternatively, go to **Minisuper La Gloria** (tel. 762/622-3878, 8 A.M.–10 P.M. daily), on Hidalgo a long block downhill from Plazuela de San Juan.

INFORMATION AND SERVICES
Tourist Information Offices, Guides, and Travel Agents

Taxco has a pair of tourist information offices, both beside the highway at opposite ends of town, open approximately 9 A.M.–8 P.M. daily.

The knowledgeable and English-speaking officers readily answer questions and furnish whatever maps and literature they may have. The north office (tel. 762/622-0798) is next to the north-end Pemex gas station; the south office (tel. 762/621-1136) is about a quarter mile south of the south-end Pemex station.

Personable, veteran Mexico guide **Benito Flores Batalla** (tel./fax 762/622-0542), who staffs the north-side tourist information office, offers his services as a guide. For starters, he offers a 3.5-hour city tour for $30, if you supply the car; $60 if he supplies the car. Longer trips might include the Grutas de Cacahuamilpa, Xochicalco, and Ixcateopan.

The same is approximately true for **Enrique Viveros** (tel. 762/621-1136, cell 01-762/623-3238 long distance in Mexico, dial 044-762/623-3238 within Taxco), who staffs the south-end information office.

One of the most reliable travel agents in town is **Turismo Misión** (tel. 762/622-1125 or 762/622-0063, 9 A.M.–2 P.M. and 5–7 P.M. Mon.–Fri., 9 A.M.–3 P.M. Sat.), on the *carretera* at the Hotel Posada de la Misión.

Publications

English-language books and newspapers are hard to find in Taxco. Nevertheless, the bookstore **Agente de Publicaciones Raoul Domínguez** (tel. 762/622-0794, 9 A.M.–2 P.M. and 4:30–8 P.M. daily), on the Los Arcos lane adjacent to and below the church, has used English-language paperbacks. If it doesn't have what you want, try **Casa Domínguez** newsstand (Los Arcos 7, tel. 762/622-0133, 10:30 A.M.–2:30 P.M. and 4–7:30 P.M. Mon.–Sat., 10 A.M.–2:30 P.M. Sun.), a few doors downhill.

The scarcity of English reading matter makes the collection at the small library **Biblioteca Ciudades Hermanas** (Sister Cities Library, 9 A.M.–1 P.M. and 3–7 P.M. Mon.–Fri., 9 A.M.–1 P.M. Sat.) even more precious. You'll find several shelves of English-language novels, nonfiction, magazines, and reference books. Most of the collection was donated by volunteers from Taxco's sister city, Canoga Park, California. The library is a five-minute walk downhill from the city hall on the alley off Juárez, on the right half a block past Banamex.

Money Exchange

Banks near the *zócalo* and their ATMs are Taxco's cheapest source of pesos. The good longest-hours option is **HSBC** (tel. 762/622-7300 or 762/622-7506, 8 A.M.–7 P.M. Mon.–Sat.), to the right (west) of the churchfront. Alternatively, a couple blocks along Cuauhtémoc from the *zócalo,* try **BBVA Bancomer** (tel. 762/622-2674 or 762/622-4966, 8:30 A.M.–4 P.M. Mon.–Fri.).

Communications

The town-center *correo* (8 A.M.–5 P.M. Mon.–Fri., 9 A.M.–1 P.M. Sat.) is in the *presidencia municipal* on Juárez, downhill (east) from the *zócalo*. The highway branch (8 A.M.–3 P.M. Mon.–Fri.), downhill, is half a block north of the Estrella de Oro bus station. **Telecomunicaciones** (tel. 762/622-4885, fax 762/622-0001, 9 A.M.–3 P.M. Mon.–Fri.), off the *zócalo* behind the Casa Borda, downhill, offers telex, money orders, and public fax services.

Public street telephones all over the town center allow cheap, easy long-distance direct dialing with widely available Ladatel telephone cards. Get them everywhere, especially at pharmacies and liquor and grocery stores.

Internet access is available at **Interplaza** computer center (9 A.M.–9 P.M. Mon.–Sat., 9 A.M.–5 P.M. Sun.) in the town market, 200 feet down the steps below the right (west) side of the church. If Interplaza is closed, go to the hole-in-the-wall Internet store (11 A.M.–11 P.M. daily) on Cuauhtémoc, half a block west of the *zócalo.*

Health and Emergencies

Taxco has a pair of respected private hospitals, both on the *carretera*. The **Clínica de Especialidades** (Av. de los Plateros 33, tel. 762/622-1111 or 762/622-4500), has a 24-hour emergency room, X-rays, a laboratory, a 24-hour pharmacy, and many specialists on call. The **Clínica Santa Cruz** (tel. 762/622-3012), offers similar services, also on Avenida de los Plateros, at the corner of Morelos, across from the government Seguro Social hospital.

For routine medicines and remedies, go to one of the several good local pharmacies, such as **Farmacia Similares** (on Hidalgo, one block downhill from Plazuela de San Juan, tel. 762/627-2214, 8 A.M.–9 P.M. Mon.–Sat., 8 A.M.–9 P.M. Sun.). Alternatively, go to the good 24-hour pharmacy at the Clínica de Especialidades, on the *carretera*.

For police emergencies, contact the *policía*, either on duty on the *zócalo*, at the *presidencia municipal* two blocks downhill (Juárez 6, tel. 762/622-0007), or at the substation on the side street Calle Fundaciones, one block below the *carretera* near the corner of Alarcón.

GETTING THERE AND AWAY
By Car or RV
National Highway 95 provides the main connection south with Acapulco in a total of about 148 miles (238 km) of easy driving via Iguala, accessible in 22 miles (36 km) via winding, old Highway 95. From there, continue south via Highway 95 to Chilpancingo (for a total of about 86 miles, 138 km). For Acapulco, continue another 62 miles (100 km) via the *cuota autopista*. Allow about four and a half hours' driving time for the entire Taxco–Acapulco trip, either direction.

Alternatively, you can save about an hour to Acapulco by following *cuota autopistas* the whole way, by first heading north (towards Cuernavaca and Mexico City) out of town. Follow the Mexico City *cuota* signs about 25 miles (40 km) to the Mexico 95D *cuota autopista,* where you fork south towards Chilpancingo and Acapulco. Allow about three and a half hours for this longer but quicker 192-mile (310-km) Taxco–Acapulco route.

Highway 95 also connects Taxco north via Cuernavaca with Mexico City, a total of about 106 miles (170 km). The new leg of the Taxco–Mexico City *cuota autopista* splits off

from old Highway 95 about two miles north of town. For those in a hurry, it cuts about half an hour off the driving time. Otherwise, follow the scenic, curving old Highway 95 about 20 miles (32 km) to its intersection with Highway 95 *cuota autopista.* Congestion around Mexico City may lengthen the driving time to about three hours in either direction. (*Note:* Authorities limit driving your car in Mexico City according to the last digit of your license plate.)

Highway 55 (junction at Cacahuamilpa) gives Michoacán- and Jalisco-bound drivers the desirable option of avoiding Mexico City by connecting Taxco directly with Toluca (and thence the fast east–west *cuota autopista* 15D, five hours to Guadalajara). The two-lane Highway 55 is paved and in good condition for its entire 74 miles (119 km). Fortunately, a faster, safer *cuota autopista* along the northern half of Highway 55 shortens the Taxco–Toluca driving time by at least an hour over the old winding, nontoll highway. Northbound, figure about 2.5 hours driving time to Toluca; southbound, allow about two hours.

By Bus
Competing lines **Estrella Blanca** (tel. 762/622-0131) and **Estrella de Oro** (tel. 762/622-0648) operate separate stations a few blocks apart on the downhill *carretera*. Both offer several luxury- and first-class connections north with Mexico City via Cuernavaca and south with Acapulco via Iguala and Chilpancingo.

Additionally, Estrella Blanca offers connections with Puebla, and the very useful option for northwest-bound travelers of bypassing Mexico City via the super-scenic Highway 55 route via Ixtapan del Sal (an interesting spa town) to Toluca. In Toluca, you can connect via Pátzcuaro, Michoacán; or Guadalajara, Jalisco; to the palmy Pacific beach destinations of Troncones, Ixtapa, Zihuatanejo, Playa Azul, Manzanillo, Puerto Vallarta, San Blas, and Mazatlán.

THE COSTA CHICA

In reality the Costa Chica, the "Little Coast," which traditionally includes the coast of Guerrero east of Acapulco and the adjoining coast of Oaxaca, isn't so little after all. Highway 200, heading out of the Acapulco hubbub, requires 150 miles to traverse the scattered groves, forests, fields, and villages to the Mixtec and Amusgo indigenous country around Pinotepa Nacional, Oaxaca.

To many thousands of Costa Chica indigenous peoples, Spanish is a foreign language. Many of them live in remote foothill villages, subsisting as they always have on corn and beans, without telephones, sewers, schools, or roads. Those who live near towns often speak the Spanish they have learned by coming to market. In the Costa Chica town markets of Ometepec, Xochistlahuaca, and Pinotepa Nacional you will brush shoulders with them—

mostly Mixtecs, Amusgos, and Chatinos—men sometimes in pure-white cottons and women in colorful embroidered *huipiles* over wrapped hand-woven skirts.

Besides the indigenous people, you will often see African Mexicans—*morenos* (brown ones)—also known as *costeños* because their settlements cluster near the coast. Descendants of African slaves imported hundreds of years ago, the *costeños* subsist on the produce from their village gardens and the fish they catch.

Costa Chica *indígenas* and *costeños* have a reputation for being unfriendly and suspicious. If true in the past (it's certainly less so in the present), they have had good reason to be suspicious of outsiders, who in their view have been trying to take away their land, gods, and lives for 400 years.

HIGHLIGHTS

Playa Las Peñitas: "Precious" is the best word to describe this rocky nook on a breezy strand. The main attraction, besides tasty seafood and comfortable hotels, is a sacred, tidepool-enfolded sea rock that folks visit en masse on May 3, the Día de la Cruz (page 252).

Parroquia de Santiago: Ometepec folks are so proud of their magnificent parish church that, evenings, they illuminate its lovely baby blue and white facade and the rooftop statue of the avenging Santiago for all to see (page 254).

Ometepec Sunday Market: In Ometepec, the handicrafts action centers around the downtown plaza, while across town at the formal market a mountain of old-fashioned goods, draws a big crowd of traditionally costumed Amusgo- and Mixtec-speaking country folks (page 254).

Xochistlahuaca: Every week, thousands of Amusgo-speaking indigenous people put on their Sunday-best *traje* and converge on the awning-festooned center *tianguis* of Xochistlahuaca to bargain, gossip, and flirt (page 259).

Pinotepa Nacional Market: Pinotepa Nacional, an important market town of the Oaxaca Costa Chica, is a magnet for indigenous coastal Mixtec-speaking people (page 263).

Huaxpáltepec Pre-Easter Fair: You will not be able to avoid this best-of-all-possible indigenous market experiences if your arrival coincides with this important fair during the local festival of Jesus the Nazarene, four days preceding the fourth Friday before Easter Sunday (page 268).

LOOK FOR **(** TO FIND RECOMMENDED SIGHTS, ACTIVITIES, DINING, AND LODGING.

Communication is nevertheless possible. For the residents of a little mountain or shoreline end-of-road village, your arrival might be the event of the day. People are going to wonder why you came. Smile and say hello. Buy a soda at the store or *palapa*. If kids gather around, don't be shy. Draw a picture in your notebook. If a child offers to do likewise, you've succeeded.

PLANNING YOUR TIME

Although you can traverse the Costa Chica in less than a day, try to save some time to linger a few days to stop to soak in the local color of the market towns and enjoy the natural diversions along the way. For example, kayakers and wildlife-viewers might enjoy a whole day exploring the mangrove-laced wildlife-rich wetland

© BRUCE WHIPPERMAN

Indigenous Costa Chica men often wear traditional white cottons.

Laguna Chautengo. If so, you might want to linger even longer for tenting, beachcombing, fishing, and surfing in or near the cross-lagoon breezy barrier-beach village, San José de la Barra.

On the other hand, most anyone could easily enjoy an overnight or two at each of the petite south-seas beach resorts of Playa Ventura and Playa Las Peñitas. At Playa Ventura, you can choose among several beachfront hotels, especially the top-pick but modest Hotel Villa Tortuga, whose savvy but kindly owner also welcomes tenters and invites guests to participate in his sea-turtle rescue project during the August–October turtle season. Also at Playa Ventura, RVers and tenters could linger for a day, a week, or a season enjoying the miles-long wild Playa Ventura strand, ripe for surf fishing, camping, and beachcombing.

In contrast, **Playa Las Peñitas,** a scenically petite golden strand, offers three good beachfront hotels (two with inviting pools), a unique natural tidepool bathing spa, a luscious child-friendly lagoon, and a lineup of rustic beachfront *palapa* restaurants.

Farther east, Ometepec, the capital of the indigenous Costa Chica Guerrero hinterland, deserves at least two days, one of which should be Sunday. That will give you time to visit both the fascinating Xochistlahuaca *tianguis* and the big **Ometepec Sunday Market** back in town on the same day. Stay overnight in the relaxing top-pick Hotel Bello Nido with pool.

Moving farther east, toward the Oaxaca border, be sure to stop in Cuajinicuilapa and visit the unique Museo de las Culturas Afromestizos. With another day or two you could explore the nearby African-Mexican coastal country hinterland around the breezy beach fishing hamlet of Puerto Maldonado. There, you can overnight by parking your RV or setting up your tent near the beachfront Las Brisas *palapa* restaurant or stay overnight at the modest guesthouse Casa de Huéspedes Valle Encantado nearby.

Continue east into Oaxaca and explore the coastal Amusgo- and Mixtec- speaking country around Pinotepa Nacional. Spend at least one Pinotepa Nacional overnight at the Hotel Carmona with pool; visit the big **Pinotepa Nacional Market** and maybe make a handicrafts side trip to one or two nearby upcountry towns, such as north to Pinotepa Don Luis (for *pozohuanco* wraparound skirts, masks) or San Pedro Amusgos (for *huipiles*); or east to Huazolotitlán (for masks) or maybe Huaxpaltepec, which hosts a sprawling, fascinatingly indigenous **Pre-Easter Fair** that virtually blocks Highway 200 ten miles east of Pinotepa.

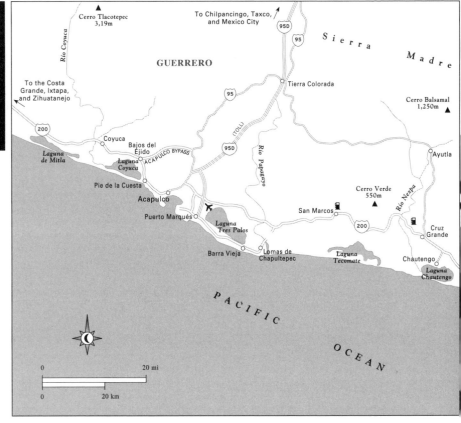

Along the Road to Ometepec

If you're going by bus, ride one of the several daily first-class or second-class buses from the Estrella Blanca (Avenida Ejido) terminal in Acapulco. Let the highway kilometer markers (both at roadside and on the asphalt itself) lead you to your chosen destination. A minute ahead of time, let the driver know where to let you off.

If driving from Acapulco, mark your odometer at the traffic circle where Highways 95 and 200 intersect over the hill north from Acapulco. If, on the other hand, you bypass that congested point via the Acapulco airport road, set your odometer to zero at the east-side interchange near Puerto Marqués where the airport highway continues along the overpass, but where you either exit to the right before the overpass, and follow the Highway 200 Pinotepa Nacional sign north; or continue on the overpass, straight ahead another couple of miles, to pick up the new *cuota autopista*, on the left, which will whisk you to the Highway 200 turnoff in less than 10 minutes. Mileages and kilometer markers along the road are

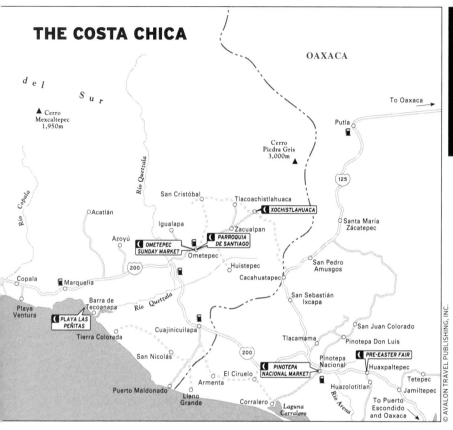

THE COSTA CHICA

OAXACA

© AVALON TRAVEL PUBLISHING, INC.

sometimes the only locators of side road turn-offs to hidden villages and beaches.

Fill up the car with gas in Acapulco before starting out. After that, gas is at least available at Cruz Grande (56 miles, 91 km), Marquelia (91 miles, 146 km), Ometepec (110 miles, 177 km), Pinotepa Nacional (157 miles, 253 km), Jamiltepec (175 miles, 283 km), and Puerto Escondido (247 miles, 398 km).

SAN MARCOS

San Marcos (pop. 10,000), 36 miles (58 km) east of Acapulco, is a frequent first stop for essential services along the Costa Chica. It has a **Banamex** with 24-hour ATM (tel. 745/453-0036, 9 A.M.–3 P.M. Mon.–Fri.);

Centro de Salud on the highway; a pharmacy, **Farmapronto** (tel. 745/453-1697); a doctor (Mauricio Ibarra); streetfront Ladatel card-operated telephones; and a *correo* and *teleco-municaciones* (tel. 745/453-0130, 9 A.M.–3 P.M. Mon.–Fri., 9 A.M.–noon Sat.). Find the pharmacy, bank, doctor and more on the town *jardín,* on main street Hidalgo, about 0.3 mile (0.5 km) north of the highway.

Accommodations and Food

San Marcos's best hotel, **Le Carma** (tel. 745/453-0037, $20 d) on the highway, south side, is recommendable for an overnight. Although the hotel's loose management leaves something to be desired, guests enjoy a major plus: cooling off in the hotel's inviting blue pool. The approximately 20 clean rooms have fans and hot-water shower baths.

For food, try **Restaurant Ruth** (approx. 8 A.M.–9 P.M. daily) on the highway, on the same south side and about a block east of the hotel. Although the restaurant is less than spotless, its food is plentiful and tasty and the dogs and roosters in the back add a homey touch. Ruth provides country-style food, such as *huevos a la Mexicana* ($3) for breakfast, perhaps chicken in mole sauce ($4) for afternoon *comida,* and *antojitos* such as tacos and quesadillas ($2-3) for supper. If that's not your style, check out Restaurant Edith across the highway.

LAGUNA CHAUTENGO AND PLAYA VENTURA

These laid-back havens are attractive for different reasons: Playa Ventura is for those who enjoy civilized south-seas delights, while the broad Laguna Chautengo estuary attracts folks hankering for wild things, such as troves of wildlife for viewing and photographing, pristine beaches for camping, and swarms of good-eating *lisa* (mullet), *sierra* (mackerel), and *robalo* (snook), just for the catching.

Laguna Chautengo

Follow the good turnoff road four miles (about 6 km) east of Cruz Grande (43 miles, 69 km east of Acapulco). Continue 3.7 miles (6 km) to the boat landing. Here, the big mangrove lagoon spreads about eight miles in both directions along the coast and four miles across to the barrier sandbar. Most of the year Laguna Chautgengo is a freshwater reservoir of the Ríos Nexpa, Jalapa, and Copala. But during the rainy season the lagoon breaks through the sandbar, slicing a channel at the beachfront hamlet of Pico de Monte that beckons far across the lagoon.

Boatmen customarily charge $10 one way per person or $20 per boat (of up to 10 passengers) for the cross-lagoon round-trip, which includes waiting for the passengers to enjoy a fish dinner at one of the several beachfront *palapas.* If you're going to camp overnight on the beach, let your boatman know when to return and pick you up.

Although road's-end facilities amount to no more than a dock and a snack restaurant, alternatives exist. Rent a boat and captain (figure $10–20 per hour) and mount your own fishing trip. Or do the same with your own boat or kayak. Launching appears easily doable from the calm, gently sloping shoreline.

Playa Ventura

Three miles east of the small town of Copala, 77 miles (123 km) from Acapulco, a roadside sign points toward Playa Ventura. Four miles down a paved road, which a truck-bus from Copala traverses regularly, you arrive at pavement's-end at Ventura village. From there, a miles-long golden-sand beach arcs gently east. Past a lighthouse, the beach leads to a point, topped by a picturesque stack of granite rocks known locally as Casa de Piedra (House of Stone).

Playa Ventura can provide nearly everything for a restful day or week in the sun. Although development is gradually crowding them out, good tent or RV (maneuverable medium rigs, vans, or campers) spots still sprinkle the inviting, outcropping-dotted shoreline, especially on the east side, past Casa de Piedra. Shady *palapas* set up by former campers stand ready for rehabilitation and reuse by new arrivals.

Surf fishing (with net-caught bait fish) is fine from the beach, while *pangas* go out for deep-sea catches. Good surfing breaks angle in from the points, and, during the rainy season, the behind-the-beach lagoon is good for fishing, shrimping, and wildlife-viewing. (Bring your kayak or inflatable raft.)

The palm-lined beach stretches southeast for miles. Past the Casa de Piedra outcropping, an intimate *palapa-* and *panga*-lined sandy cove curves invitingly to yet another palmy point, Pico del Monte. Past that lies still another, even more pristine, cove and beach.

Accommodations and Food

Besides the village stores, space for tenting and RV parking and food is available at a number of family-run *loncherías* and beach *palapa* restaurants, the most visible of which is which is beachfront **Restaurant and Ramada Pérez.** If anyone dispels the rumor that *costeño* folks are unfriendly, it's the hospitable Pérez family team (father Bulmaro, mother Virginia, sons Luis, Reyes, and Arturo, and daughter Reina), who have put together the modest beginnings of a little resort. The Pérez's invite visitors to park RVs in their small lot, where they offer a friendly word, showers, a homemade swimming pool, kiddie pool, and a bit of shade for a reasonable $6 per party per day. For tenters, they rent spaces beneath their shady beachfront *ramada* for the same price. Furthermore, besides the Perez's main oceanfront restaurant, son Luis has added a breezy rooftop *palapa* hamburger restaurant, and his brother Arturo has created his life dream of a petite but elegant Discoteca Pérez.

Others have followed the Pérez example. From the Pérez compound, move east along the beach to find plumy **Las Palmeras,** which offers a shady, spacious grove for tenting and RV parking. Continue next door to beachfront restaurant and campground **Doña Maura,** with plenty of space for small-to-medium self-contained RVs and tents beneath shady palm-frond *ramadas.* Next come a couple of inviting restaurants, first **El Faro,** with a working lighthouse, and finally the thatched **Jay** restaurant.

Most, if not all, of Playa Ventura's hotels are on Playa Ventura's west side. At least three of them are recommendable. Heading west, first find beachfront **Hotel Doña Celsa** (tel. 741/411-5891), with about 20 clean, modern but smallish rooms on two floors around a parking patio. Rentals run about $25 d with fans, $40 with air-conditioning ($40 and $55 holidays), all with tiled baths and tepid-water showers, pool, restaurant, and small grocery.

Alternatively, continue west about a 100 yards to restaurant and **Hotel Tomy** (tel. 741/501-8172), also right on the beach, with about 20 rooms, some with airy ocean views, encircling a parking-pool-patio. Prices for the clean, sparely furnished but comfortable furnished tiled rooms, are certainly right at about $20 d, $30 holidays, with private baths.

For the best hotel choice, continue another quarter mile west to █ **Hotel Villa Tortuga** (tel. 741/411-5863), life project of dedicated environmentalist René A. Cuevas Brito, who maintains his own turtle hatchery right on the beach beside his hotel. For lodging, he offers 14 immaculate, attractively decorated, comfortable rooms with private baths for about $25 d, $35 t or q, with fans, a shady oceanfront palm grove, and restaurant. Moreover, René invites his guest to join his turtle saving effort for the potential reward (around October) of seeing thousands (13,000 total in October 2005) of baby turtles return safely to the sea. He also invites tenters to camp in the shade of his palm grove for $5 a day.

The increasing popularity of Playa Ventura as a beach destination has led to a growing colony of beachfront homes. A number of the original Playa Ventura families are getting rich selling lots. Luis Pérez tells me that the going price is currently about $10,000 for a 60-foot by 60-foot beachfront lot. Before putting your money down, be sure to research the legal details of owning property in Mexico. Go through a reputable real estate agent, such as Century 21 and others (see *Long-Term Rentals* and the sidebar "Owning Paradise" in the *Acapulco* chapter).

MARQUELIA

The small market town of Marquelia (pop. 10,000, 91 miles, 146 km, east of Acapulco) offers a number of services and is a jumping-off point for the charming beachfront haven of Playa Las Peñitas and the hardscrabble end-of-the-road fishing village of Barra de Tecoanapa. You can't miss Marquelia, since its market stalls crowd the highway.

THE COSTA CHICA

The owner of the Hotel Villa Tortuga invites his guests to rescue turtle eggs and bury them for incubation in his fenced enclosure.

Especially worthy is the refined country-style, open-air **⟨ Restaurant Don Pinito** (tel. 741/416-0028, 7:30 A.M.–9 P.M. daily), on the eastern side of downtown, north side of the highway.

⟨ PLAYA LAS PEÑITAS

Just east of Marquelia, turn south (if not driving, catch a truck ride) on the signed Playa Las Peñitas turnoff road. After 3.5 miles (5.7 km) go right at the signed driveway 50 yards to the beach. The main attraction, popular with local holiday vacationers and Sunday picnicking families, is the long, steep, yellow-sand beach, lined with seafood *palapas* and Las Peñitas (the Little Rocks), a family of sandstone rocks picturesquely perched on the shoreline.

At high tide, one of Las Peñitas becomes a small islet, where folks have set a pilgrimage cross around which the faithful congregate for devotions on the May 3 (Día de la Cruz) holiday. It provides a perfect playground for kids

scampering and splashing in the waves that curl gently around the islet. Moreover, families frolic in a bathtublike tidepool on one side of the islet, dunking themselves in the gentle waves that fill its foamy basin.

Small inviting hotels embellish the lovely Las Peñitas picture. Most accessible right on the beach is the former **Hotel Puerto Palisada,** which has been taken over by new owners (who have yet to re-name it). They offer four sparely but comfortably furnished detached bungalows with baths and fans in a shady beachfront palm grove, for about $40 for up to four people, $60 holidays, with a lovely blue pool and patio. For information and reservations (in Spanish) contact owner-manager Teresita Andrea Bautista, who lives in Mexico City, at 55/5590-9568, or her parents, David Bautista Priegro and Enerina Arizmendi, at their *ferretería* (hardware store, tel. 741/416-0012) in Marquelia, on the west-end street bordering the river, a short block off the highway, south side.

Las Peñitas ("Little Rocks")

BARRA DE TECOANAPA

Continue 1.5 miles by car (or, if without wheels, by truck; offer to pay), ford a shallow river, immediately pass a store, then bear left, passing through Guadalupe village. Continue another 4.5 miles (7.2 km) to road's end at Barra de Tecoanapa (pop. 1,000).

The village spreads for about a mile along the sandbar of the Río Quetzala, which empties into the sea from its lagoon-estuary about a quarter mile east of town. You can continue (drivers, be careful of soft sand) along the beach track to the embarcadero, decorated with a few dozen fishing *lanchas* pulled up on the lagoon-front. The river channel through the sandbar allows ocean fish (*sierra, robalo, lisa*) to populate the lagoon.

The village appears to owe its existence to fishing and the holiday and weekend visitors who enjoy fresh seafood at its scattering of humble beachfront *palapa* restaurants. Terns and pelicans diving into onshore waves signal ideal conditions for surf fishing.

Although life on the Barra de Tecoanapa is simple and ruled by the unhurried rhythms of sun and tide, local folks, whose houses are primarily of stick and thatch, do enjoy a few 21st-century amenities, including a basketball court, two or three small stores, a kindergarten, a primary school, and a potable water system.

All this might spell heaven for experienced visitors equipped to enjoy country beachfront living. If you don't mind a few curious townsfolk, plenty of space is available for beachfront tenting and RV parking, especially west of town. Rent a boat or float your own either at the lagoon or right on the beachfront. Waves, which break gradually about 100 yards out, recede with only slight undertow, fine for wading, splashing, and boogie boarding. Although the waves I saw appeared too mild for surfing, stronger swells, a likely seasonal possibility, might produce ideal surfing conditions.

Ometepec and Vicinity

Ometepec (pop. 15,000) is the capital of the Guerrero coastal indigenous heartland. In Ometepec's foothill backcountry, Spanish is a foreign language. About half of the Ometepec *municipio* (pop. 50,000) people are native Amusgo-speaking people. In more remote *municipios,* such as Xochistlahuaca (soh-chees-tlah-WAH-kah), more than three-quarters speak native tongues.

Bright markets with their piles of fruit and flowers, old-fashioned handmade goods, and crowds of folks in colorful native dress are the reward for visitors who venture uphill to spend time exploring these vibrant towns.

ORIENTATION

Ometepec is readily accessible via a 10-mile paved road that branches off Highway 200 at a big signed intersection 110 miles (177 km) east of Acapulco. Besides being an important market and service center that draws crowds of native peoples, notably Amusgos and Mixtecs, from outlying villages to its big Sunday market, Ometepec (elev. 1,000 feet) enjoys a cooler climate. Reflecting its upland location, the town's name, from the Náhuatl (Aztec) language, combines *ome* (two) and *tepec* (hill) to mean "land between two hills."

Ometepec orients itself along a single street, Avenida Cuauhtémoc. Entering town eastbound, via the ingress highway from the coast, you pass under a big entrance arch. The main market is immediately on the right.

Avenida Cuauhtémoc continues east past the main (Estrella Blanca) long-distance bus station. After about half a mile, the thoroughfare angles right (southeast), through the business district, passing a parade of shops, restaurants, hotels, and banks. Finally, at the petite *zócalo* on the left, Cuauhtémoc bends due south and ends within a block in front of the main church, dedicated to Santiago (St. James).

Ometepec's pride and joy is its church, dedicated to Santiago (St. James).

SIGHTS

◖ Parroquia de Santiago

Ometepec's church, although not old (it was built during the 1960s), is both popular and handsome. Evenings, spotlights keep its lovely blue and white facade shining long after dark. During the day, the faithful crowd through its gates and approach the facade, populated with its choir of white-shining saints and angels. Atop this all presides a sculpture of a mounted, sword-brandishing Santiago. Approach even closer and admire the church's grand polished wooden doors, climaxed in the center by yet another Santiago, this time with his horse's hooves trampling the defeated Moors. Inside, swallows swoop beneath the airy nave's ceiling and perch and chirp in the chandeliers. Above the altar rises a grand dome whose paintings depict a vista of heaven so pleasing that it seems as pretty as the view must be through the pearly gates themselves.

◖ Ometepec Sunday Market

Ometepec's other famous attraction, the Sunday *tianguis,* operates in two sections: one on the west side, just inside the town entrance

arch, and the other around the downtown *zócalo.* At the *zócalo* are most of the handicrafts, including embroidered *huipiles,* huaraches, and sombreros. In the west-side section you'll find a small mountain of everything else: forest-gathered herbs, seeds, and spices, *chiles,* homemade brooms, fruits (mangoes, grapes, and bananas), vegetables (radishes, sweet potatoes, tomatoes), tobacco (in aromatic bunches of big dried leaves), and mounds of dried fish, all in one spreading, semiorganized five-acre area. (For more market sights, see *Xochistlahuaca* in this chapter.)

ACCOMMODATIONS

Ometepec has several hotels, all of which accept cash only. They do a brisk business, accommodating the town's many market, business, and festival visitors.

The **Hotel Venus II** (Crucero de Talapa, Ometepec, Guerrero 41700, tel. 741/412-2349, hotel_venus@hotmail.com) stands prominently to the left of the arch as you enter Ometepec. The hotel, at the uncongested edge of town and with a secure gated parking lot, is convenient for visitors with cars. Past the reception, the

To Estrella Blanca Bus Station, Town Entrance Arch, Hotel Venus II, Hwy 200, Acapulco, and Oaxaca

OMETEPEC

To Xochistlahuaca

GALEANA

HOTEL BELLO NIDO

HOTEL LOS ALMENDROS

N BRAVO

AV. CUAUHTÉMOC

HOTEL MONTERO MAYREN

VICENTE GUERRERO

HOTEL RIVERA LÓPEZ

HSBC ■

BANCO SANTANDER SERFIN ■

■ MINIVANS TO XOCHISTLAHUACA

● HOTEL GUADALUPE

SUNDAY CRAFT STALLS ■

■ BANAMEX

Zócalo

■ SUNDAY CRAFT STALLS

AMPARITO ▼

J G JIMENEZ

■ HUARACHES
■ SOMBREROS
■ PHARMACY/INTERNET

PANIFICADORA OMETEPEC ■

RESTAURANT LAS DELICIAS ▼

SUNDAY ■ CRAFT STALLS

POST OFFICE ■ TELECOM ■ PRESIDENCIA MUNICIPAL ■

Atrium

Plaza Constitución

PARROQUIA DE SANTIAGO

0   100 yds
0   100 m

place is modern and clean, with guests in many rooms enjoying balcony vistas (of the parking lot below and hills beyond). The hotel's 20-odd rooms cost about $17 d with fan, $25 with air-conditioning, all with private hot-water shower baths, good cable TV, and a one-block walk to the west-side market. The **Hotel Venus I** (tel. 741/415-8026 or 741/415-8027, hotel_venus@ hotmail.com), the Venus II's sister hostelry, stands prominently at the Highway 200–Ometepec intersection, 10 miles downhill.

The remainder of Ometepec's hotels is downtown. Move southwest to first find comfortable **(Hotel Bello Nido** (Cuauhtémoc 50, Ometepec, Guerrero 41700, tel. 741/412-0141 or 741/412-0234), about three blocks from the *zócalo*. Past the small but inviting lobby, the hotel rises in three motel-style floors around an appealing pool-patio. Rooms are clean and furnished with dark bedspreads, drapes, and tiled shower baths, but with no bedside reading lamps. Rentals run about $15 s, $17 d in one double bed, $25 d, t, or q in two double beds, with TV, fans, and parking. Add about $10 for air-conditioning. For more tranquillity, light, and privacy, reserve a room on an upper floor room in the back, away from the busy streetfront.

Across the street from Hotel Bello Nido is the worthy new business-style **Hotel Los Almendros** (Cuauhtémoc 52, Ometepec, Guerrero 41706, tel. 741/412-2691). It offers 18 clean, attractively tiled, tan-motif rooms with shiny modern-standard hot-water bathrooms. Rentals run $17 s, $20 d, $31 t with fans, $24 s, $26 d, $35 t with air-conditioning, cable TV and parking.

A few cheaper hotel options cluster in the middle of the downtown action, about a block farther east. Best of the bunch is downscale **Hotel Rivera López** (Cuauhtémoc 22, Om-

THE AMUSGO PEOPLE

If not the most numerous, the Amusgos are the most visible of the Acapulco region's indigenous groups. On Sunday, crowds of Amusgo-speaking people flock to easily accessible market towns in the Costa Chica foothills about 100 miles east of Acapulco.

The Amusgo homeland comprises an approximately 30- by 40-mile territory straddling the Oaxaca–Guerrero border. About a third of the 30,000 Amusgo speakers live in Oaxaca, around the small centers of Cacahuatepec and San Pedro Amusgos, while the remaining majority lives on the Guerrero side, near the centers of Ometepec, Xochistlahuaca, and Tlacoachistlahuaca.

Linguists reckon that the Amusgo language, a member of the Mixtec language subfamily, separated from Mixtec between 2000 and 1000 B.C. Around A.D. 1000 the Amusgos came under the domination of the strong coastal Oaxaca Mixtec kingdom of Tututepec. In A.D. 1457 they were conquered by the Aztecs and, not long after, by the Spanish in the 1520s. Decimation of the Amusgo population by disease during the 16th century led to the importation of African slave labor, whose descendants, known locally as *negros* or *costeños*, live along the Guerrero-Oaxaca coastline.

The Amusgo population eventually recovered; many of the old colonial-era haciendas remained intact until modern times and continued to employ Amusgo people as laborers. The Amusgos, isolated from the mainstream of modern Mexican life, retain their age-old corn-bean-squash subsistence farming tradition. Moreover, they have received little atten-tion from anthropologists or archaeologists, although several intriguing archaeological mounds exist near Amusgo villages.

Amusgo women are nevertheless famous for their hand-embroidered *huipiles*, whose colorful floral and animal designs fetch willing customers in the Acapulco region and Oaxaca tourist centers. Even better, Amusgo women often wear their *huipiles*, appearing as heavenly visions of spring on dusty small-town side streets.

At Xochistlahuaca's Sunday Market virtually all bargaining is conducted in the indigenous Amusgo language.

© BRUCE WHIPPERMAN

Ometepec's Sunday Market

etepec, Guerrero 41700, tel. 741/412-0028). Choose from 33 sparely furnished rooms in three floors around an inner parking patio. Rooms cost about $15 s or $17 d in one double bed; $19 d, $24 t or q in two double beds, with TV, fans, parking, and hot-water shower bath. Add about $8 for air-conditioning.

Finally, half a block from the *zócalo,* lovers of old Mexico might appreciate the **Hotel Guadalupe** (Cuauhtémoc 20, Ometepec, Guerrero 41700, tel. 741/412-2228). The approximately 20 plain but clean rooms surround a leafy interior garden patio. They rent for about $12 s or d, with room-temperature-water private shower baths, and no fans.

FOOD

Most eating out in Ometepec occurs in one of two locales. The busiest of these is the west-side main market, where *fondas* offer country-style offerings of savory *guisado* (stews of chicken, pork, beef), piles of *antojitos* (*chiles rellenos, pozole,* tamales, tacos), and much more. (Permanent market *fondas* depend on repeat customers and therefore serve whole-

some food. If in doubt, remember that cooked food, if it's steaming, will also be safe.)

The remainder of the eateries concentrate downtown, scattered along Cuauhtémoc and near the *zócalo.* Probably the best choice is ◖ **Restaurant Las Delicias,** at the end of Cuauhtémoc, in view of the churchfront. Although basically a taco shop after 6 P.M., Las Delicias serves breakfasts (pancakes, omelettes, french toast $2–3) and *comida,* a set four-course lunch ($3–4, noon–6 P.M.). Evenings until midnight, the main offerings are tacos *al pastor* (barbecued beef and pork, $2) in a dozen tasty options, with a mound of stuffings served on a plate along with a bottomless supply of hot tortillas. Yum.

Moreover, Restaurant Las Delicias offers more than food. After the busy supper crowd mostly clears out around 8 or 9, the restaurant becomes a relaxing spot to spend a balmy hour or two, enjoying the lovely illuminated church-front view (and if you're lucky the full moon rising behind and above it).

The Ometepec downtown restaurant that everyone seems to recommend is **Amparito** (Juan Garcia Jiménez 11, tel. 741/412-2044, 7:30 A.M.–9 P.M. daily), past Bana-mex, downhill two blocks east of the *zócalo.* Amparito, named after the grandmotherly owner, although specializing in seafood plates (shrimp, octopus, whole fish, fillets, $4–8), does offer nonseafood specials. These might include *codorniz* (quail, $8) or *guisado de res* (beef stew, $6). For breakfasts ($3–5), it can serve anything from eggs any style and French toast to pancakes or the good, local *pan dulce* with fresh fruit. If the TV noise bothers you, ask the staff to please lower the volume (*favor de moderar el volumen*—fah-VOR day moh-day-RAHR AYL vo-LOO-mayn).

For dessert, sample the fresh baked goods of **Panificadora Ometepec** (Cuauhtémoc 9, 7 A.M.–9 P.M. daily), a few doors north of Restaurant Las Delicias. On the other hand, if you're hankering for something sweet after the bakery closes, listen for someone whistling along Cuauhtémoc near the *zócalo.* Most likely it will be the *platano frito* (sweet fried banana) vendor with his cart.

ENTERTAINMENT AND EVENTS

Ometepec is known for a number of festivals, notably the Easter-week **Semana Santa,** which includes, besides the usual religious Masses and processions, cattle, agricultural, and handicrafts expositions, *jaripeo* (bull riding and roping), and a carnival. Festivities climax with regional folk dance performances, including the favorite, Los Chilenos, said to have originated in Ometepec.

If you arrive in town on certain dates, join the festivities—May 3: Fiesta del Día de la Santa Cruz (Holy Cross); July 24–26: Fiesta de Santiago; September 9–11: Fiesta de San Nicolás Tolentino; September 15–16: Fiestas Patrias, including the 11 P.M. reenactment of Father Miguel Hidalgo's Grito de Dolores at the *presidencia municipal,* and the dances of El Mulo y La Tortuga (Mule and the Turtle) and El Macho.

The region's most popular festival is the **Fiesta del Señor del Perdón** at Igualapa (pop. 3,000), half an hour northwest of Ometepec. It may be worthwhile to make a special trip for this important indigenous fiesta, which local folks throw yearly on the third Friday of Lent (two weeks, two days after Ash Wednesday).

The main event is a pilgrimage to pay respects to the Señor del Perdón (Lord of Pardon), visited by thousands, arriving on all fours, on their knees, by foot, or by car or bus. They arrive to ask, at least, for small favors and, at most, for miracles. And judging from the Señor del Perdón's popularity, the wishes are often granted.

Miracles nothwithstanding, merrymaking abounds, especially among the swarm of campesinos—mostly speaking dialects of Amusgo, Mixtec, and Tlapanec languages—decked out in their Sunday-best *traje.* For a feast of scents, sounds, and sights, simply walk among the dozens of stalls around the Igualapa pilgrimage church, the Santuario del Señor del Perdón. Before departing, make sure to enjoy the whirl and flash of regional dances performed by a number of brightly costumed troupes.

From Ometepec, get to Igualapa either via taxi or *colectivo* from the west-side market or by car. Follow the west exit road toward Highway 200. About a mile from the west edge of town, turn right at the Igualapa turnoff road; continue about 7 miles (11 km) to Igualapa.

SHOPPING

Handicrafts are mostly sold downtown on Sunday at *zócalo*-front stores and stalls. Get huaraches and sombreros at a pair of stores on the *zócalo*'s east side. Women also sell embroidery and embroidered *huipiles* on the *zócalo,* mostly at temporary north-side stalls, on Sunday.

Foto Alfa (tel. 741/412-1245, 8 A.M.–8 P.M. Mon.–Sat., 9 A.M.–2 P.M. Sun.), on Cuauhtémoc a block northwest of the *zócalo,* offers developing, popular film varieties, some supplies, and point-and-shoot cameras.

The best spot for groceries and fresh fruits and vegetables in town is the main market, at the west end of Cuauhtémoc.

SERVICES

Many establishments offer essential services near the downtown *zócalo.* (*Note:* At the *zócalo,* orient yourself by the church, which is *south* of the *zócalo.*)

Banks, all with ATMs, include **Banamex** (tel. 741/412-0880 or 741/412-1354, 9 A.M.–4 P.M. Mon.–Fri.), at the *zócalo*'s northeast corner; long-hours **HSBC** (Cuauhtémoc 52, tel. 741/412-2878 and 741/412-2879, 8 A.M.–7 P.M. Mon.–Fri., 8 A.M.–3 P.M. Sat.), a couple of blocks northwest of the *zócalo;* and neighboring **Banco Santander Serfén** (tel. 741/412-0113, 9 A.M.–4 P.M. Mon.–Fri.).

Mail letters at the *correo* (9 A.M.–1:30 P.M. Mon.–Fri.) at Plaza Constitución in the *presidencia municipal,* two short blocks south of the *zócalo.* Money orders and public fax are available at neighboring **Telecom** (tel. 741/412-0386, 9 A.M.–2:30 P.M. Mon.–Fri., 9 A.M.–noon Sat.), also at the *presidencia municipal.* For local and long-distance calls, use

Ladatel card-operated streetfront phones. Internet access and copies are available at **Super Farmacia Mexicana** (tel. 741/412-0657, 8:30 A.M.–9:30 P.M. daily) on the southeast *zócalo* corner.

If you get sick, consult with highly recommended **Dr. Alfredo Yañez Lobato** (tel. 741/412-0224). If he's not available, ask a taxi to take you to the private **Hospital de la Amistad** (tel. 741/412-0985 or **Hospital Seguro Social** (tel. 741/412-0392).

GETTING THERE AND AWAY

Estrella Blanca (tel. 741/412-0035) provides a number of bus connections, most in the morning, with Acapulco and intermediate Costa Chica points, from its station on Cuauhtémoc, just west of its bend toward the *zócalo*.

Although few, if any, long-distance buses from Ometepec connect directly with the very interesting easterly Costa Chica destinations of Cuajinicuilapa and Pinotepa Nacional in Oaxaca, alternatives exist. You can get an early taxi or *colectivo* downhill to the Highway 200 intersection. There, continue by *colectivo*, or wait for an Estrella Blanca (Elite, Gacela, Flecha Roja) eastbound bus. (*Note:* The Ometepec Estrella Blanca agent may be able to tell you the bus connection times at the Highway 200 intersection.)

Driving to and from Ometepec is easy. To or from westerly Costa Chica destinations, simply follow Highway 200: one hour to/from Marquelia–Playa Las Peñitas, 33 miles (53 km); 1.5 hours to/from Copala–Playa Ventura, 48 miles (72 km); and 4.5 hours to/from Acapulco, 120 miles (194 km).

Similar good (but winding) road conditions prevail in the easterly direction: three-quarters of an hour to/from Cuajinicuilapa, 25 miles (41 km); and two hours, 58 miles (93 km) to/from Pinotepa Nacional, Oaxaca.

◖ XOCHISTLAHUACA

Plan your Ometepec visit for a Friday or Saturday arrival (reserve your hotel room a week early) so you can visit the colorful indigenous Sunday markets at both Ometepec and Xo-chistlahuaca (pop. 3,000), about 17 miles (27 km) northeast. On the other hand, the things you find along the road to Xochi (SOH-chee), as Xochistlahuaca is known locally, may persuade you to linger.

The name Xochistlahuaca, which in the Náhuatl (Aztec) language means "plain of flowers," is apt, especially during the summer rains, when wildflowers bloom all over the town's foothill *municipio* (township). Although an interesting destination all on its own, Xochi is a jumping-off point for even more remote Amusgo towns such as Chacalapa, Huistepec, and others with even less pronounceable names, such as Tlacoachistlahuaca.

Although the name Xochistlahuaca is of Aztec origin, the town is virturally all Amusgo speaking, and you can be certain that the Xochi folks have their own name for their town. At the Xochi Sunday market you may have to search around for someone who can translate Spanish into Amusgo well enough to help you bargain for one of the prized embroidered *huipiles* for which Amusgo women are renowned.

Although most Xochi young folks learn Spanish in school, and outside vendors descend to sell plastic dishes and transistor radios every Sunday, Xochistlahuaca and its surrounding *municipio* is a domain firmly rooted in tradition. Here, *curanderos* still do much of the healing, women often recuperate from childbirth in a *temascal* (ritual heat bath), and campesinos in their *milpas* still thank the earth spirits and the Lord of the Mountain for their harvests.

Along the Road to Xochistlahuaca

Get to Xochi by *colectivo* from the Ometepec downtown corner of Cuauhtémoc and Vicente Guerrero, a block north of the *zócalo*. If you have only one Sunday to visit, leave early for Xochi to allow time upon return to see the Ometepec market by 1 or 2 in the afternoon. Drivers, mark your odometer as you head northeast along Guerrero, from the same corner in Ometepec. Along the 17-mile (27-km)

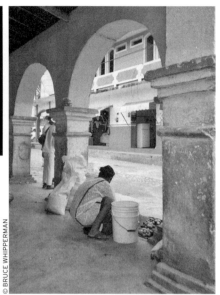

© BRUCE WHIPPERMAN

A woman rests in one of Xochistlahuaca's few quiet corners on market Sunday.

cession of swimming holes decorated by giant, friendly, water-sculptured rocks. (During the June–Sept. rainy season, however, the river may be a yucky muddy brown, but it will clear to an inviting jade-green as the rains abate by October.) Although swimming holes near the bridge are sometimes crowded with noisy local teens, spots upstream, via the hikeable (or 4WD-navigable) riverside trail, would probably be cleaner, more tranquil, and possible for overnight tenting.

Strolling Xochistlahuaca

Follow the crowd to the Xochi *tianguis* that spreads over the middle of town from the intersection of Calles Morelos and Reforma. Along Reforma, a block uphill from the corner, stands the **Museo Comunitario** (10 A.M.– 5 P.M. Mon.–Fri.), on the right. The museum's collection includes donated prehistoric artifacts and historical papers. Plans include adding a handicrafts store in the near future. Although the museum is not ordinarily open on Sunday, someone (try Ireneo Santana Guerrero, tel. 741/415-2149) may be available to open it up for you.

As in many backcountry areas, some men and most women wear *traje* unique to their home towns. Xochi women distiguish themselves with a creamy white, embroidered cotton *huipil* decorated with a pair of crimson over-the-shoulder ribbons, both front and back.

Women dominate both buying and selling. Buyers bustle about, concentrating mostly on staples (fruit and vegetables and housewares), perhaps pausing to pick out a bit of ribbon or jewelry as a treat. Sellers wait patiently behind their piles of offerings, which vary from flowers and metates to mangoes and mameys.

Sometime during your Xochi visit you might enjoy taking a look inside the attractive, blue-and-white-decorated main church, atop the hill in the middle of town. Although the present (1930) structure is not old, the church it replaced, also dedicated to archangel St. Michael, dated back a good three hundred years. The cool, blue-and-white interior features San Miguel, sword in hand, presiding above the

route are a number of interesting stops that you may want to visit on a later day.

After about three miles, pass **Balneario Camino Real** (9 A.M.–6 P.M. daily), with a big blue swimming pool, kiddie pool, restaurant, and shade for picnicking.

At Mile 3.5 (Km 5.6), arrive at San José village, marked by a gas station and then a road fork. (The right fork, worth exploring on its own, heads down into the lush Río Catarina valley, crosses the river, and continues uphill to indigenous Huistepec village and beyond.)

For Xochi, follow the left fork and continue about nine miles (15 km) from Ometepec, where the road splits. The left fork heads five miles (8 km) to **Tlacoachistlahuaca,** an interesting indigenous market town and *municipio,* comparable to Xochi.

For Xochi, bear right at the fork and continue straight ahead. Pass through Zacualpan village at around Mile 11 (Km 17). Continue to the Río San Pedro bridge at about Mile 15 (Km 24). Feast your eyes on the luscious pro-

© BRUCE WHIPPERMAN

At the Xochistlahuaca Sunday Market, the tomatoes are as fresh as the bargaining is sharp.

altar, between and above (and larger than) the Virgin Mary and Jesus.

For a rest and a good lunch, head to airy **Comedor Velé** (vay-LAY, 9 A.M.–10 P.M. daily), Xochi's best eatery, on Morelos, half a block west of Reforma. Take a seat in the shade and choose from a very recognizable list of *tortas, hamburguesas,* enchiladas, tacos ($2–4), and fresh seafood ($3–5). Friendly, hardworking owner-chef Aquileo Morales López is *a su servicio* (at your service).

CUAJINICUILAPA

Astride Highway 200, a few miles before the Oaxaca border, Cuajinicuilapa (kwah-hee-nee-kwee-LAH-pah) (pop. 10,000) is the major market town and cultural center for the dozen-odd eastern Guerrero *costeño* communities. These include farming villages Los Hoyos, Montecillos, San Nicolas, and the airy, laid-back local fishing port, Puerto Maldonado.

In Cuajinicuilapa, known locally as Cuaji (koo-AH-hee), 125 miles (199 km) east of Aca-

pulco, the market hubbub crowds both the east and west ends of town. The clutter clears, however, at the town center, marked by a big covered basketball court.

Museo de las Culturas Afromestizos

Behind the basketball court stands the **Museo de las Culturas Afromestizos** (10 A.M.–2 P.M. and 5–7 P.M. daily except Mon.). The museum is unmissable, being one of the very few Mexican museums dedicated to African Mexican history and culture. Inside, it offers several excellent, professionally prepared displays, plus a library, and dance, theater, guitar, and crafts workshops.

Accommodations and Services

A pair of town-center hotels offer comfortable lodgings. Best is the 30-room 🅒 **Hotel Marin** (tel. 741/414-0021), a few doors east of the basketball court. It's built along a shady corridor interspersed with lush green tropical mini-patios. The comfortable, invitingly decorated rooms run $16 s, $17 d with fan, $20 s or d with air-conditioning.

Second choice goes to the more basic **Hotel Alejim** (tel. 741/414-0310), on the west side of town. The plainly decorated rooms go for $17 s, $21 d with fan, $24 s, $28 d with air-conditioning.

Cuaji has a **Banamex** (9 A.M.–4 P.M. Mon.–Fri.); a Centro de Salud (no phone, open 24 hours); a pharmacy, **Farmapronto** (tel. 741/414-1074, 7 A.M.–2 P.M. and 4–8 P.M. Mon.–Sat., 7 A.M.–2 P.M. Sun.); *correo* (8 A.M.–3 P.M. Mon.–Fri.); Ladatel-operated street telephones, and **Telecomunicaciones** (tel. 741/414-0337, 9 A.M.–3 P.M. Mon.–Fri., 9 A.M.–noon Sat.–Sun.) for money orders and public fax.

PUERTO MALDONADO

This country coastal fishing village (pop. 1,000), about 20 miles (32 km) south of Cuajinicuilapa, appeared on the map initially because of its lighthouse. A reassuring beacon, the lighthouse perches atop the tip of the point of land called Punta Maldonado, crowning the 100-foot-high bluff that lines this remote coast.

The lighthouse adds a picturesque aspect to the entire scene: a long, breeze-swept beach curving east, while west of the Punta (Point) a few fisherfolks' homes, a couple of stores, a small guesthouse, and a sprinkling of fishing *lanchas* decorate the strand.

Here, life goes on quietly and easily. You can stroll the beach, picking up a bit of driftwood and a shell or two, joke with the locals, play with the kids, watch the fishermen mend their nets, or rent a boat and mount your own fishing excursion.

Along the Road to Puerto Maldonado

Get to Puerto Maldonado by minibus from the middle of Cuaji, by the basketball court. Drivers, head east from the town. After only a mile, turn right (south) on to the signed Puerto Maldonado road near Km 201. Mark your odometer.

After about 10 miles (16 km) pass through Montecillos village (pop. about 2,000), a mixed mestizo African-Mexican community. Farther along, at around 15 miles (24 km), at Tejastruda village, notice the apparently evangelistic church, decorated with both a Christian cross and what appears to be the Star of David. Finally, arrive at Puerto Maldonado just after 19 miles (31 km) from Highway 200.

Sights and Recreation

Get oriented at the rustic **Las Brisas Palapa,** perched on the scenic Punta Maldonado beach-tip. From beneath the *palapa,* drink in the gorgeous panorama as the waves curl around the Punta and swish and disappear into the coral-dotted golden sand of the point's west-side beach.

Use the existing posts in front of the *palapa* for a volleyball game (bring your own ball and net), explore the tidepools, or launch your own boat from the beach. Surfing on the waves that swell inshore past the point and break diagonally along the beach line is a regular pastime here.

Accommodations and Food

You can park your self-contained RV or set up your tent beneath the point's small but sheltering palm grove. A few village stores can supply essential groceries and water.

Travelers can also stay at the guesthouse **Casa de Huéspedes Valle Encantado,** in the beach fishing village about a quarter mile west of the point. The three plain but clean rooms rent for about $10 s or d, with private bath (but room-temperature water only). For reservations, leave a message with the *caseta* operator at long-distance radio tel. 01-200/126-2552 or 01-200/126-2551.

For prepared food, visit either the beachfront *palapa* or the airy, oceanview *comedor* that the friendly guesthouse owner also operates, just above the beach. If you need medical attention, visit the Centro de Salud on the bluff above the beach.

Pinotepa Nacional and Vicinity

In Oaxaca, Pinotepa Nacional (pop. about 50,000; 157 miles, 253 km, east of Acapulco; 90 miles, 145 km, west of Puerto Escondido) and its neighboring communities comprise the hub of an important coastal indigenous region. Mixtec, Amusgo, Chatino, and other peoples stream into town for markets and fiestas in their *traje,* ready to combine business with pleasure. They sell their produce and crafts—pottery, masks, handmade clothes—at the market, then later get tipsy, flirt, and dance.

So many people had asked the meaning of their city's name that the town fathers wrote the explanation on a wall next to Highway 200 on the west side of town. Pinotepa comes from the Aztec words *pinolli* (crumbling) and *tepetl* (mountain)—thus "Crumbling Mountain." The second part of the name came about because during colonial times the town was called Pinotepa Real (Royal). This wouldn't do after independence, so the name became Pinotepa Nacional, reflecting the national consciousness that emerged during the 1810–1821 struggle for independence.

The Mixtecs, the dominant regional group, disagree with all this, however. To them, Pinotepa has always been Ñií Yo-oko (Little Place). Only within the town limits do the Mexicans (mestizos), who own most of the town businesses, outnumber the Mixtecs. The farther from town you get, the more likely you are to hear people conversing in the Mixtec language, a complex tongue that uses a number of subtle tones to make meanings clear.

GETTING ORIENTED

On Pinotepa's west side, Highway 200 splits into the town's two major arteries, which rejoin on the east side. The north, west-bound branch is called Aguirre Palancares; the south, east-bound branch, the more bustling of the two branches, passes between the town-center *zócalo* and church and is called Avenida Porfirio Díaz on the west side and Avenida Benito Juárez on the east. The main north–south street, Avenida Pérez Gasga, runs past both the churchfront and the *presidencia municipal,* which faces east, toward the *zócalo.*

◖ PINOTEPA NACIONAL MARKET

Highway 200 passes a block north of the main town market, by the big, fenced-in secondary school, on the west side, about a mile west of the *zócalo.* Despite the Pinotepa market's oft-exotic goods—snakes, iguanas, wild mountain fruits, forest herbs, and spices—its people, nearly entirely Mixtec, are its main attraction, especially on the big Wednesday and Sunday market days. Men wear pure white loose cottons, topped by woven palm-leaf hats. Women wrap themselves in their lovely striped purple, violet, red, and navy blue *pozahuancos.* Many women carry atop their heads a polished

POZAHUANCOS

To a coastal Mixtec woman, her *pozahuanco* is a lifetime investment symbolizing her maturity and social status, something that she expects to pass on to her daughters. Heirloom *pozahuancos* are wraparound, horizontally striped skirts of hand-spun thread. Women dye the thread by hand, always including a pair of necessary colors: cotton dyed a light purple (*morada*) from secretions of tidepool-harvested snails, *Purpura patula pansa;* and silk dyed scarlet red with cochineal, a dye extracted from the beetle *Dactylopius coccus,* cultivated in the Valley of Oaxaca. Increasingly, women are weaving *pozahuancos* with synthetic thread, which has a slippery feel compared to the hand-spun cotton. Consider yourself lucky if you can get a traditionally made *pozahuanco* for as little as $100. If someone offers you a look-alike for $20, you know it's an imitation.

tan *jicara* (gourd bowl), which, although it's not supposed to, looks like a whimsical hat. Older women (and younger ones with babies at their breasts) go bare-breasted with only their white *huipiles* draped over their chests as a concession to mestizo custom. Others wear an easily removable *mandil,* a light cotton apron-halter above their *pozahuancos.* A few women can ordinarily be found offering colorful *pozahuancos* made with cheaper synthetic thread for about $20. The women told me that traditional all-handmade *pozahuancos* (hand-spun, hand-sewn, and hand-dyed with naturally gathered pigments) are more commonly available in outlying market towns, notably Pinotepa Don Luis.

FESTIVALS

Although the Pinotepa market days are big, they don't compare to the week before Easter (Semana Santa). People get ready for the finale with processions, carrying the dead Christ through town to the church each of the seven Fridays before Easter. The climax comes on Good Friday (Viernes Santa), when a platoon of young Mixtec men paint their bodies white to portray Jews, and while intoning ancient Mixtec chants shoot arrows at Christ on the cross. On Saturday, the people mournfully take the Savior down from the cross and bury him, and on Sunday gleefully celebrate his resurrection with a riot of fireworks, food, and folk dancing.

Although not as spectacular as Semana Santa, there's plenty of merrymaking, food, dancing, and processions around the Pinotepa *zócalo* church on July 25, the day of Pinotepa's patron, Santiago (St. James).

ACCOMMODATIONS

The motel-style 🄲 **Hotel Carmona** (Av. Porfirio Díaz 127, Pinotepa Nacional, Oaxaca 71600, tel. 954/543-2322), about three blocks west of the *zócalo,* offers three stories of clean, not fancy but comfortable rooms and a big backyard garden with pool and sundeck. For festival dates, make reservations. The 50 rooms run about $16 s, $22

d, $28 t, with fan only; $24, $33, and $40, with air-conditioning.

If the Carmona is full, check the two high-profile newer hotels, Pepe's and Las Gaviotas, beside the highway on the west side of town. Of the two, **Pepe's** (Carretera Pinotepa Nacional-Acapulco Km 1, Pinotepa Nacional, Oaxaca 71600, tel. 954/543-4347, fax 954/543-3602), is the much better choice. It offers 35 spacious, semideluxe rooms for a reasonable $10 s, $14 d fan only, $20 and $26 with air-conditioning, with good TV, hot water, restaurant, and parking. Rooms at only-stay-in-an-emergency **Hotel Las Gaviotas** (tel. 954/543-2838, fax 954/543-2056) rent for $14 d with fan, $18 with air-conditioning.

Third choice goes to clean **Hotel Marisa** (Av. Juárez 134, tel. 954/543-2101 or 954/543-3190), downtown on the north side of the highway. Rooms are $10 s or d, $16 t with fan; $20 s or d, $30 t with air-conditioning, all with parking.

Campers enjoy a tranquil spot (best during the dry, calm, clear-water late fall-winter-spring season) on the Río Arena about two miles east of Pinotepa. Eastbound, turn left just after the big river bridge. Continue a few hundred yards, past a pumphouse on the left, to a track that forks down to the riverbank. Notice the waterfall cascading down the rocky cliff across the river. You will sometimes find neighbors—in RVs or tents, and poor but friendly sand collectors—set up on the riverside beneath the abandoned Restaurant La Roca (now just a rock-wall ruin) a few hundred yards up the smooth stream, excellent for kayaking (if you have some way of returning back upstream). *Note:* Lately the sand collectors have preempted much of the east bank space. You might find more room to spread out on the opposite river bank. Get there just west of the bridge, by following the dirt track downhill along the southwest riverbank.

FOOD

For a light lunch or supper, try the very clean, family-run 🄲 **Burger Bonny** (11 A.M.– 10 P.M. daily), at the southeast corner of the *zócalo.* Besides six varieties of good hamburgers,

Burger Bonny offers *tortas,* tacos, french fries, hot dogs, microwave popcorn, fruit juices, and *refrescos* at very reasonable prices.

Also worthy is traditional-style **🍷 Fonda Toñita** (7 A.M.–9 P.M. Mon.–Sat.), a block north of the churchfront at the corner of Aguirre Palancares. Local folks flock here for the hearty afternoon *comida* (pick the entrée, and you get rice and tortillas thrown in free); it's also good for breakfast.

Third restaurant choice goes to **Tacos Orientales** (6–11 P.M. daily), with 15 styles of tacos, from fish to *carnitas* (three for $2.50). Find it on Pérez Gasga, half a block north of the churchfront.

On the other hand, consider *marisquería* **Peñitas** (8 A.M.–midnight daily) next door, which specializes in fresh seafood however you like it: fried, baked, breaded, *al mojo,* and more.

For a quick and convenient on-the-road breakfast, lunch, or dinner, stop by the restaurant of high-profile **Pepe's Hotel** (8 A.M.–10 P.M. daily) west of town.

SHOPPING AND SERVICES

Visit the market on Wednesday and Sunday. For film and film-processing, step to the Konica **photo shop** next door on the south side of the *zócalo.*

Exchange money over the counter or use the ATM at any Pinotepa bank. Try **Bancomer** (tel. 954/543-3022 or 954/543-3190, 8:30 A.M.–4 P.M. Mon.–Fri.), corner of Porfirio Díaz and Progreso, two blocks west of the *zócalo;* or **Banamex** (9 A.M.–4 P.M. Mon.–Fri.), across the street. Alternatively, try the long-hours **HSBC** (tel. 954/543-3949 or 954/543-3969, approx. 8 A.M.–7 P.M. Mon.–Fri., 8 A.M.–3 P.M. Sat.), also on Avenida Progreso, but across Porfirio Díaz and uphill a block from Bancomer.

The *correo* (tel. 954/543-2264, 8 A.M.–7 P.M. Mon.–Fri.) is about half a mile west of downtown, a block past Hotel Pepe's and across the street. Find the *Telecomunicaciones* (on Av. Pérez Gasga, 8 A.M.–7:30 P.M. Mon.–Fri., 9 A.M.–noon Sat.–Sun.), one block north of the *zócalo* church, for money orders, public

telephone, and fax. For telephone, use Ladatel card-operated street telephones, or go to the long-hours *larga distancia* Lada Central telephone and fax office on the south side of the *zócalo.*

For a doctor, go to the **Clínica Rodriguez** (Aguirre Palancares 503, tel. 954/543-2330), one block north, two blocks west of the *zócalo* churchfront. Get routine medications at one of several town pharmacies, such as the 24-hour **Super Farmacia** on Porfirio Díaz, a block west of the *zócalo* churchfront.

GETTING THERE AND AWAY

For travelers by car or RV, Highway 200 connects west to Acapulco (160 miles, 258 km) in an easy 4.5 hours driving time. The 89-mile (143-km) eastward connection to Puerto Escondido can be done safely in about 2.5 hours. Additionally, the 239-mile (385-km) Highway 125–Highway 190 route connects Pinotepa Nacional to Oaxaca, via Putla de Guerrero and Tlaxiaco (136 miles, 219 km). Although winding most of the way and potholed at times, the road is generally uncongested. It's safely driveable in a passenger car from Pinotepa to Oaxaca (near Oaxaca, turn off and follow the *cuota autopista*) in about eight hours (under dry conditions), and seven hours in the reverse, downhill, direction from Oaxaca.

For bus travelers, at the new **Camionera Central** about half a mile west of downtown, several long-distance bus lines connect Pinotepa Nacional with destinations north, northwest, east, and west. Dominant line **Estrella Blanca** (tel. 954/543-3194), via subsidiaries Turistar, Elite, Cuautémoc, Gacela, and Flecha Roja, offers several daily first- and second-class *salidas de paso* (departures buses passing through): west to Acapulco, Zihuatanejo, Lázaro Cárdenas, and Mexico City; and east to Puerto Escondido, Pochutla (Puerto Ángel), Bahías de Huatulco, and Salina Cruz.

Other independent, mostly second-class lines also operate out of the same terminal. **Fletes y Pasajes** (tel. 954/543-6016) connects with inland points Tlaxiaco and

Teposcolula, via Putla de Guerrero, along Highway 125, continuing along Highway 190 via Nochixtlán, to Oaxaca. **Estrella del Valle** (tel. 954/543-5476) also connects with Oaxaca, but in the opposite direction, via Highway 200 east to Puerto Escondido and Pochutla (Puerto Ángel), thence north along Highway 175, via San José del Pacifico and Miahuatlán, to Oaxaca. On the other hand **Estrella Roja del del Sureste** (tel. 954/543-6017) connects by yet another route with Oaxaca: along Highway 200 east to Puerto Escondido, thence north along Highway 131, via El Vidrio (Juquila) and Sola de Vega.

A welter of local buses connect with dozens of nearby towns and villages from a streetside terminal (tel. 954/543-2697) downtown, north side of Aguirre Plancaes, half a block north and half a block east of the *zócalo* churchfront. Destinations include Jamiltepec, Huazolotitlán, Pinotepa Don Luis, San Juan Colorado, Cacahuatepec, San Pedro Amusgos, and many more.

EXCURSIONS NORTH OF PINOTEPA

The local patronal festival year begins early, on January 20, with the uniquely Mixtec festival of San Sebastián at **Pinotepa Don Luis** (pop. 5,000), about 15 miles, by back roads, northeast of Pinotepa Nacional. Village bands blare, fireworks pop and hiss, and penitents crawl until the finale, when dancers whirl the local favorite dance, Las Chilenas.

Yet another exciting time around Pinotepa Nacional is during Carnaval, when nearby communities put on big extravaganzas. Pinotepa Don Luis, sometimes known as Pinotepa Chica (Little Pinotepa), is famous for wooden masks the people make for their big Carnaval festival. The celebration usually climaxes on the Sunday before Ash Wednesday, when everyone seems to be in costume and a corps of performers gyrates in the traditional dances: Paloma (Dove), Tigre (Jaguar), Culebra (Snake), and Tejón (Badger).

Pinotepa Don Luis bubbles over again with excitement during Semana Santa, when the faithful carry fruit- and flower-decorated trees to the church on Good Friday, explode Judas effigies on Saturday, and celebrate by dancing most of Easter Sunday.

San Juan Colorado, a few miles north of Pinotepa Don Luis, usually appears as just another dusty little town until Carnaval, when its festival rivals that of its neighbors. Subsequently, on November 29, droves of Mixtec people come into town to honor their patron, San Andres. After the serious part at the church, they celebrate with a cast of favorite dancing characters such as Malinche, Tigre, Tortuga, and Charros (Cowboys).

Oaxaca Amusgo Country

Cacahuatepec (pop. about 5,000; on Hwy. 125 about 25 miles north of Pinotepa Nacional) and its neighboring community San Pedro Amusgos are important centers of the Amusgo people. Approximately 20,000 Amusgos live in a roughly 30-mile-square region straddling the Guerrero–Oaxaca state border. Their homeland includes, besides Cacahuatepec and San Pedro Amusgos, Ometepec, Xochistlahuaca, Zacoalpán, and Tlacoachistlahuaca on the Guerrero side.

The Amusgo language is linguistically related to Mixtec, although it's unintelligible to Mixtec speakers. Before the conquest, the Amusgos were subject to the numerically superior Mixtec kingdoms until the Amusgos were conquered by the Aztecs in A.D. 1457, and later by the Spanish.

Now, most Amusgos live as subsistence farmers, supplementing their diet with occasional fowl or small game. Amusgos are best known to the outside world for their lovely animal-, plant-, and human-motif *huipiles,* which Amusgo women always seem to be hand-embroidering on their doorsteps.

Although Cacahuatepec enjoys a big market each Sunday, that doesn't diminish the importance of its big Easter weekend festival; the day of Todos Santos (All Saints' Day), November 1; and Day of the Dead, November 2, when, at the cemetery, people welcome their ancestors to rejoin the family.

THE MIXTECS

Sometime during the 1980s, the Mixtecs regained their preconquest population of about 350,000. Of that total, around one-third speaks only their own language. Their villages and communal fields spread over tens of thousands of square miles of remote mountain valleys north and west of Oaxaca and east of Acapulco. Their homeland, the Mixteca, is divided into three distinct regions: Mixteca Alta, Mixteca Baja, and the Mixteca Costera.

The **Mixteca Alta** centers in the mountains about 100 road miles due west of Oaxaca city, in the high, cool, roof of Oaxaca, centering on the market towns of Tlaxiaco and Juxtlahuaca.

Mixteca Baja communities, such as San Miguel Tequistepec, Tonalá, and Juxtlajuaca, dot the dry northwestern Oaxaca–eastern Guerrero mountains and valleys, centering roughly on Huajuapan de León on Highway 190.

In the **Mixteca Costera**, important Mixtec communities exist in or near Pinotepa Nacional, Huaxpaltepec, and Jamiltepec, all along Highway 200 in southwestern Oaxaca and southeastern Guerrero.

The Aztec-origin name Mixtecos (People of the Clouds) was translated directly from the Mixtecs' name for their own homeland: Aunyuma (Land of the Clouds). The Mixtecs' name

for themselves, however, is Nyu-u Sabi (People of the Rain).

When the conquistadores arrived, the Mixtecs were under the thumb of the Aztecs, who, after a long, bitter struggle, had wrested control of Oaxaca from combined Mixtec-Zapotec armies in 1486. The Mixtecs naturally resented the Aztecs, whose domination was transferred to the Spanish during the colonial period, and, in turn, to the mestizos during modern times. The Mixtecs still defer to the town Mexicans, but they don't like it. Consequently, many rural Mixtecs, with little state or national consciousness, have scant interest in becoming Mexicanized.

In isolated Mixtec communities, traditions still rule. Village elders hold final authority, parents arrange marriages through go-betweens, and land is owned communally. Catholic saints are thinly disguised incarnations of old gods such as Tabayukí, ruler of nature, or the capricious and powerful *tono* spirits that lurk everywhere.

In many communities, Mixtec women exercise considerable personal freedom. At home and in villages, they often still work barebreasted. And while their men get drunk and carry on during festivals, women dance and often do a bit of their own carousing. Whom they do it with is their own business.

San Pedro Amusgos celebrations are among the most popular regional fiestas. On June 29, the day of San Pedro, people participate in religious processions, and costumed participants dressed as Moors and Christians, bulls, jaguars, and mules dance before crowds of men in traditional whites and women in beautiful heirloom *huipiles.* Later, on the first Sunday of October, folks crowd into town to enjoy the traditional processions, dances, and sweet treats of the fiesta of the Virgen de la Rosario (Virgin of the Rosary).

Even if you miss the festivals, San Pedro Amusgos is worth a visit to buy *huipiles* alone. Three or four shops sell them along the main

street through town. Look for the sign of **Trajes Regionales Elia** (tel. 954/582-08697), the little store run by Elia Guzmán when she's not in Oaxaca City. Besides dozens of beautiful embroidered garments, she stocks a few Amusgo books and offers friendly words of advice and local information.

EXCURSIONS EAST OF PINOTEPA

For 30 or 40 miles east of Pinotepa Nacional, where road kilometer markers begin at zero again near the central plaza, Highway 200 stretches through the coastal Mixtec heartland. It's intriguing to explore, especially during festival times.

C Huaxpáltepec Pre-Easter Fair

The population of San Andres Huaxpáltepec (oo-wash-PAHL-tay-payk), about 10 miles east of Pinotepa, sometimes swells from about 4,000 to 20,000 or more during the three or four days before the day of Jesus the Nazarene, on the fourth Friday of Lent (or in other words, the fourth Friday after Ash Wednesday). The entire town spreads into a warren of shady stalls offering everything from TVs to stone metates. (Purchase of a corn-grinding metate, which sells for about $25, including *mano*—stone roller, is as important to a Mixtec family as a refrigerator is to an American. Mixtec husband and wife usually examine several of the concave stones, deliberating the pros and cons of each before deciding.)

The Huaxpáltepec fair is typical of the larger Oaxaca country expositions. Even the highway becomes a lineup of stalls; whole native clans camp under the trees; and mules, cows, and horses wait patiently around the edges of a grassy trading lot as men discuss prices. (The fun begins when a sale is made, and the new owner tries to rope and harness his bargain steed.)

Huazolotitlán

At nearby Santa María Huazolotitlán (ooah-shoh-loh-teet-LAN, pop. 3,000), several resident woodcarvers craft excellent masks. Local favorites are jaguars, lions, rabbits, bulls, and human faces. Given a photograph (or a sitting), one of them might even carve your likeness for a reasonable fee (figure perhaps $40–60). Near the town plaza, ask for José Luna, Lázaro Gómez, or the master Idineo Gómez, all of whom are related and live in *barrio* Ñií Yucagua.

Textiles are also locally important. Look for the colorfully embroidered animal and floral motif *huipiles, manteles,* and *servilletas* (native smocks, tablecloths, and napkins). You might also be able to bargain for a genuine heirloom *pozahuanco* for a reasonable price.

Besides all the handicrafts, Huazolotitlán people celebrate the important local **Fiesta de**

low-fired pottery at the Nazarene pre-Easter fair in Huaxpáltepec

© BRUCE WHIPPERMAN

la Virgen de la Asunción around August 13–16. The celebrations customarily climax with a number of favorite traditional dances, in which you can see why masks are locally important, especially in the dance of the Tigre and Tortuga. The finale comes a day later, celebrated with the ritual dance of the Chareos, dedicated to the Virgin.

Get to Huazolotitlán in about two miles along the paved (but oft-potholed) road that forks south uphill from Highway 200 in Huaxpaltepec. Drive, hitchhike (with caution), ride the local bus, or hire a taxi for about $3.

Jamiltepec

About 18 miles (at Km 30) east of Pinotepa Nacional is the hilltop town formally known as Santiago Jamiltepec (hah-meel-teh-PAYK). Two-thirds of its 20,000 inhabitants are Mixtec. A grieving Mixtec king named the town in memory of his infant son, Jamilly, who was carried off by an eagle from this very hilltop.

The market, while busy most any day, is biggest and most colorful on Thursday. The town's main fixed-date festivals are celebrated on September 1, January 1, and February 15. In addition, Jamiltepec celebrates its famous pre-Easter (week following Domingo de Ramos, or Palm Sunday) festival, featuring neighborhood candlelight processions accompanied by 18th-century music. Hundreds of the faithful bear elaborate wreaths and palm decorations to the foot of their church altars.

Jamiltepec is well worth a stop if only to visit Santiago de la Cruz Velasco's handicrafts shops **Yu-uku Cha-kuaa** (Hill of Darkness). The personable Santiago runs both his home shop and a better-stocked one at the Jamiltepec plaza market because the government cluster of shops (Centro Artesanal de la Costa, on the highway) was closed down, victim of a dispute over control.

Some of the crafts—masks, *huipiles,* carvings, hats—occupy the shelves and racks in Santiago's shop in the market, signed Artesanía Yu-uku Cha-kuaa, by the north entrance (ask for Santiago by name). He stays open until about 4 P.M. If you don't want to miss him, write Santiago a letter at his home shop (Av. Principal, esquina Fco. Madero, Barrio Grande, Sec. 5, Jamiltepec, Oaxaca 71700).

If you want to stay overnight, Jamiltepec has a couple of recommendable hotels. Down on the highway, west side of town, check out the **Hotel Mirador,** with about 20 comfortable, albeit dark, rooms for about $20 d with fans, $25 with air-conditioning. Also worthy downtown on the north side of the market is **Hotel Dáaz** (tel. 954/582-8050), with about 10 clean but a bit worn upstairs patio rooms for around $10 d, with fans.

BACKGROUND

Land and Sea

A look at the map of North America reveals that Acapulco lies very far south, at the 17th parallel of latitude, which, as seen from the north pole, places Acapulco four-fifths of the way to the equator. Furthermore, Acapulco's longitude, smack on the 100th parallel, places it both far east and far west, depending on your point of view. From Washington, D.C., Acapulco is a far 1,400 miles west; from San Francisco, Acapulco is a far 1,400 miles east. And from both, it is a far 1,400 miles south, well into the tropical land of perpetual summer: a plumy paradise, where frost never bites.

Yes, a paradise; and that dream continues to propel Acapulco to the stars among the world's renowned tropical resorts while at the same time making it Mexico's most popular beach destination.

Acapulco's popularity is well deserved. The many faces of Acapulco—its curving blue bay, framed by crystalline golden beaches and steep, green-forested ridges; the shade-dappled old town plaza; the fine food; the continuous entertainments; and the hotels, both modest and luxurious, continue to draw millions of yearly visitors from all over the world.

THE ACAPULCO REGION

Locally, Acapulco's influence extends far beyond its city limits into the entire Acapulco region, an ethnically and geographically diverse domain that encompasses, broadly, the entire Mexican state of Guerrero.

The deep-south state of Guerrero (pop. 3,200,000, area 25,000 square miles, 65,000 square km) is about the same size as the U.S. state of West Virginia (or the European country of Austria). It stretches about 250 miles (400 km) along Mexico's south Pacific coast and extends about 150 miles (250 km) inland. In contrast to West Virginia and Austria, however, the Acapulco region covers a vastly diverse, ruggedly corrugated landscape of coastal plain, foothills, and high sierra, interspersed with a number of large and small upland valleys, many of which drain into the basin of the grand Río Balsas, Mexico's mightiest river.

COSTA CHICA AND COSTA GRANDE

Mountains notwithstanding, Acapulco's influence extends most strongly along the coast, and the Acapulco region has enough coastline for a pair of subregions that Acapulco people call the Costa Chica (Little Coast) and the Costa Grande (Big Coast). Labels aside, both coasts are big: the Costa Chica spreads 100 miles (160 km) east from Acapulco, to the state of Oaxaca border, while the Costa Grande spreads 150 miles (250 km) northwest, past Ixtapa and Zihuatanejo to the great Río Balsas, which forms the border with the state of Michoacán.

LAGOONS, BAYS, COVES, AND BEACHES
Lagoons and Barrier Beaches

The landforms that define the entire Acapulco region spread north, east, and west from Acapulco Bay's sun-drenched shoreline. For example, arrivees can enjoy from their airplane windows an aerial view of one such feature, the blue expanse of a mangrove-lined lagoon, Laguna Tres Palos, a minute before airport touchdown. This is only the beginning of a procession of such *lagunas* that dot the

Acapulco region coastline: to the east along the Costa Chica, after Laguna Tres Palos, are Laguna Tecomate and Laguna Chautengo; to the west, along the Costa Grande, first Laguna Coyuca, then Laguna Mitla, Estero Valentín, and Laguna Potosí.

Although all of the lagoons are accessible, Laguna Coyuca at Pie de la Cuesta, a few miles west of Acapulco, is most accessible and also very typical. All the Acapulco region's *lagunas* result from the opposing forces of surging water: the ocean waves and currents pushing sand shoreward against the flow of the rivers, coursing down from the sierra, depositing many millions of gallons of fresh water at the shoreline.

It's a see-saw struggle that the rivers temporarily win, if only during the summer–early fall wet season. Freshwater floods accumulated in the lagoons break though the shoreline sandbars and open channels to the ocean. Pacific waves rush in, carrying with them a bounty of sea creatures and nutrients, and for a spell

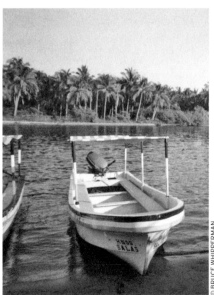

© BRUCE WHIPPERMAN

Laguna Coyuca provides manifold recreational opportunities.

Flocks of birds nest, preen, splash, and flap in the Acapulco region's many coastal mangrove lagoons, such as at Isla Presidio, at Laguna Coyuca, shown.

during the summer the lagoons become slightly salty (brackish).

However, when the river flood abates in the early fall, the persistent ocean waves and currents deposit their burden of sand, closing the channels through the *barras* (sandbars). Soon, the lagoons again become fresh, sweet, and clear.

On the ocean side of the lagoons lie the Acapulco region's hidden barrier beaches, with plenty of fine yellow sand, an abundance of fresh breezes, and seasonal driftwood, seashells, and sometimes even *palapa* restaurants and reusable shady palm-frond *ramadas* awaiting new occupants. All are accessible, some easily, such as Playa Revolcadero and Barra Vieja, by road about 10 miles east of Acapulco; or farther afield east, San José de la Barra, by launch from Laguna Chautengo. To the west, find Playa Pie de La Cuesta (by road) a few miles from Acapulco; the beach of Laguna de Mitla (by road); Playa Paraíso (by short launch trip); and Playa Boca Chica (by launch or road).

Bays and Coves

Gorgeous beaches also decorate many of the Acapulco region's plumy bays and coves. Besides the famous golden resort strands of Acapulco, Zihuatanejo, and Ixtapa, many other breeze-swept sandy coasts and small bays and coves hide lovely beaches. East along the Costa Chica and especially worth exploring are the petite resort beaches of Playa Ventura, Playa Las Peñitas, and Punta Maldonado. West along the Costa Grande, likewise gorgeous are El Carrizal, Playa Tlalcoyunque, Playa Escondida, Playa Ojo de Agua, Playa Barra de Potosí, and the coral-strewn gem, Playa Troncones.

COASTAL PLAIN, FOOTHILLS, AND SIERRA

The Acapulco region's coastal plain, source of a major fraction of the region's agricultural wealth, concentrates along a relatively narrow strip. It begins at the lagoons' inland edges and, crossed by many south-flowing rivers, extends inland, only about 15 miles in the west along the Costa Grande, and broadening to about twice that at the eastern, Oaxaca end of the Costa Chica.

North of the coastal strip, the cooler, lush, forested foothills, about equal in width to the coastal plain, gradually rise, from an elevation of about 1,000 feet to 3,000 feet (300 to 900 meters). Several tradition-rich foothill market towns, such as Petatlán and Atoyac on the Costa Grande, and Ayutla, Acatlán, and Ometepec on the Costa Chica, are equally rich centers of lumber, produce (mangoes, papayas, tamarind, coffee, honey), and handicrafts.

The Sierra Madre del Sur

The foothills sharply give way to the Acapulco region's great mother of ranges, the Sierra Madre del Sur, a succession of gigantic, cloud-tipped mountains extending in an unbroken east–west line. Many of their jagged summits top 10,000 feet (3,000 meters). The line of rugged sentinels extends from Cerro Tejamil (10,460 feet, 3,190 meters) northeast of Zihuatanejo, all the way east to Cerro San Marcos (10,170 feet, 3,100 meters) by the Oaxaca border. In the middle, tallest of all the Acapulco region's summits, is mighty Cerro Teotepec, rising to 11,647 feet (3,550 meters), only 43 miles (70 km) as the crow flies northwest of Acapulco.

The Río Balsas and Other Rivers

As precipitously as the sierra rises in the south, it drops in the north, into the basin of the Río Balsas, which drains a gigantic realm, including parts of five states—Jalisco, Michoacán, Morelos, Puebla, Oaxaca—and most of the Acapulco region.

The people of the Río Balsas basin are both victims and benefactors of the Sierra Madre and their Río Balsas. The mighty sierra forms a great rain shadow, blocking Pacific breeze–borne moisture and turning their homeland into the notorious Tierra Caliente: hot and desert-like most of the year. But the people, by their own ingenuity and with a little government help, benefit from the waters of the river. Aided by dams and irrigation, they have created rich

oases of corn, cattle, cotton, mangoes, melons, bananas, and alfalfa by the riverbank.

Despite the dominance of the Río Balsas, many other rivers contribute to the Acapulco region. Without exception, from the Río San Cristóbal in the west, to the Río Quetzala in the east, they flow southward across the coastal plain, nurturing groves and fields and replenishing the wildlife-rich lagoons along the coast.

Most important of all these is the Río Papagayo, in the Acapulco region's center, which, joining its lovely spring-fed tributary, the Río Azul, winds southward through its precipitous, scenic canyon to the sea, at Lomas de Chapultepec village, only 15 miles (25 km) east of Acapulco.

CLIMATE

Nature has graced the Acapulco region with a microclimate tapestry. Although rainfall, offshore breezes, and vegetation introduce refreshing local variations, elevation provides the broad brush. The entire coastal strip (including the mountain slopes and plateaus up to 4,000 or 5,000 feet) luxuriates in the tropics.

The seashore is a land of perpetual summer. Winter days are typically warm and rainless, peaking at 80–85°F (27–30°C) and dropping to 60–70°F (16–21°C) by midnight.

Increasing elevation gradually decreases both temperature and humidity. In Chilpancingo (elev. 4,000 feet) you can expect warm, dry winter days at 75–80°F (24–27°C) and cooler nights around 55–65°F (14–18°C).

Similar but sometimes cooler winter weather prevails in higher, 5,800-foot (1,800-meter) Taxco. Days will usually be balmy and spring-like, climbing to around 75°F (24°C) by early afternoon, with nights dropping to a temperate 45–55°F (8–15°C).

On the other hand, Iguala, in the sunny and dry Río Balsas basin, will be at least warm year-round. In the winter expect 80–85°F (27–30°C) days and 65–70°F (19–21°C) nights.

The sunny, dry spring months of April and May are customarily the Acapulco region's warmest months. By mid-June, cooling rains arrive, moderating summer temperatures.

Summer days on the beaches are warm, humid, and sometimes rainy. July, August, and September forenoons are typically bright, warming to the high 80s or low 90s (around 33°C). By afternoon, however, clouds often gather and bring short, sometimes heavy, showers. By late afternoon, the clouds part, the sun dries the pavements, and the tropical breeze is just right for enjoying a sparkling sunset.

Chilpancingo and Taxco summers are delightful. Afternoon temperatures rise to the 80s (27–32°C) and cool to the balmy 70s (21–26°C), perfect for strolling, during the evenings. In Iguala, however, late spring and summer temperatures are often hot, typically 85–95°F (30–36°C) during the dry April and May, but cooling a few degrees during the June–September rains.

Flora and Fauna

Abundant sun and summer rains nurture the vegetation of the Acapulco region. At some roadside spots, spiny bromeliads, pendulous passion fruits, and giant candelabra cactuses luxuriate, beckoning to admirers. Now and then visitors may stop, attracted by something remarkable, such as a riot of flowers blooming from apparently dead branches or what looks like grapefruit sprouting from the trunk of a roadside tree. More often, travelers pass by the long stretches of thickets, jungles, marshes, and dry uplands without stopping; however, a little knowledge of what to expect can blossom into recognition and discovery, transforming the humdrum into the extraordinary.

VEGETATION ZONES

Mexico's diverse landscape and fickle rainfall have sculpted its wide range of plant forms. Botanists recognize at least 14 major Mexican vegetation zones, seven of which occur in the Acapulco region.

Directly along the coastal highway travelers often pass long sections of three of these zones: savanna, thorn forest, and tropical deciduous forest.

Savanna

Great swaths of pasturelike savanna stretch along Highway 200 between Acapulco and Zihuatanejo. In its natural state, savanna often appears as a palm-dotted sea of grass—green and marshy during the rainy summer, dry and brown by late winter.

Although grass rules the savanna, palms give it character. Most familiar is the **coconut,** the *cocotero* (*Cocos nucifera*)—the world's most useful tree—used for everything from lumber to candy. Coconut palms line the beaches and climb the hillsides—drooping, slanting, rustling, and swaying in the breeze like troupes of hula dancers. Less familiar, but with as much personality, is the Mexican **fan palm,** or *palma real* (*Sabal mexicana*), festooned with black fruit and spread flat like a señorita's fan.

The savanna's list goes on: the grapefruitlike fruit on the trunk and branches identify the **gourd tree,** or *calabaza* (*Crescentia alata*). The mature gourds, brown and hard, are famously useful, in a dozen ways, from making music and drinking hot chocolate to carrying water and scooping corn for tortillas.

Orange-sized, pumpkinlike gourds mark the **sand box tree,** or *jabillo* (*Hura polyandra*), so named because they once served as desktop boxes full of sand for drying ink. The Aztecs, however, called it the exploding tree, because the ripe gourds burst their seeds forth with a bang like a firecracker.

The waterlogged seaward edge of the savanna nurtures lagoon-front forests of the **red mangrove,** or *mangle colorado* (*Rhizophora mangle*), short trees that seem to stand in the water on stilts. Their new roots grow downward from above; a time-lapse photo would show them marching, as if on stilts, into the lagoon.

© BRUCE WHIPPERMAN

Large stretches of Acapulco savanna are home to flocks of cattle egrets, migrants from Africa that arrived in Mexico around 1900.

Thorn Forest

Lower rainfall leads to the hardier growth of the thorn forest—domain of the pea family— the legumes marked in late winter and spring by bursts of red, yellow, pink, and white flowers. Look closely at the blossoms and you will see they resemble the familiar wild sweet pea of North America. Even when the blossoms are gone, you can identify them by seed pods that hang from the branches. Local folks call them by many names. These include the *tabachín*, the scarlet Mexican bird of paradise; and its close relative the *flamboyán*, or **royal poinciana**, an import from Africa, where it's called the "flame tree."

Other spectacular members of the pea family (called "shower trees" in Hawaii) include the bright yellow **abejón**, which blooms nearly year-round; and the **coapinol**, marked by hosts of white blooms (March–July) and large, dark-brown pods. Not only colorful but useful is the **fishfuddle**, with pink flowers and long pods, from which fisherfolk derive a fish-stunning poison.

More abundant (although not so noticeable) are the legumes' cousins, the **acacias** and **mimosas**. Long swaths of thorn forest sometimes grow right to the coastal highway and side-road pavements, so that the road appears tunnel-like through a tangle of brushy acacia trees. Pull completely off the road for a look and you will spot the small yellow flower balls, ferny leaves, and long, narrow pods of the **boat spine acacia,** or *quisache tempamo* (*Acacia cochliacantha*). Take care, however, around the acacias; some of the long-thorned varieties harbor nectar-feeding, biting ants.

Perhaps the most dramatic member of the thorn community is the **morning glory tree,** or *palo blanco* (*Ipomoea aborescens*), which announces the winter dry season by a festoon of white trumpets atop its crown of seemingly dead branches.

The Mexican penchant for making fun of death shows in the alternate name for *palo del muerto,* or the tree of the dead. It is also called *palo bobo* (fool tree) in some locales because

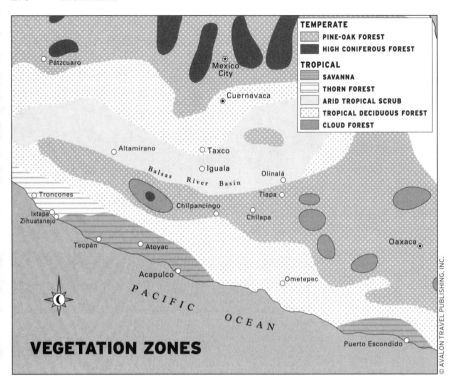

TEMPERATE
- PINE-OAK FOREST
- HIGH CONIFEROUS FOREST

TROPICAL
- SAVANNA
- THORN FOREST
- ARID TROPICAL SCRUB
- TROPICAL DECIDUOUS FOREST
- CLOUD FOREST

VEGETATION ZONES

© AVALON TRAVEL PUBLISHING, INC.

folks believe if you take a drink from a stream near its foot, you will go crazy.

Tropical Deciduous Forest

In rainier areas, the thorn forest grades into tropical deciduous forest. This is the "friendly" or "short-tree" forest, blanketed by a tangle of summer-green leaves that fall in the dry winter to reveal thickets of branches. Some trees show bright fall reds and yellows, later blossoming with brilliant flowers—spider lily, cardinal sage, pink trumpet, poppylike yellowsilk (*pomposhuti*), and mouse-killer (*mala ratón*), which swirl in the spring wind like cherry-blossom blizzards.

The tropical deciduous forest makes up the lush jungle coat that swathes much of the Acapulco region's coastal foothills. It is especially lush during the rainy summer, in the uplands along Highway 193, above Atoyac de Álva-

rez, northwest of Acapulco. Here, vine-strewn thickets overhang the road, like the edges of a lost prehistoric world, where at any moment you expect a dinosaur to rear.

The biological realities here are nearly as exotic. A four-foot-long green iguana, looking every bit as primitive as a dinosaur, slithers across the pavement. Beside the road, a spreading, solitary **strangler fig** (*Ficus padifolia*) stands, draped with hairy, hanging air roots (which, in time, plant themselves in the ground and support the branches). Its Mexican name, *matapalo* (killer tree), is gruesomely accurate, for strangler figs often entwine themselves in death embraces with less aggressive tree-victims.

Much more benign is the gentle giant of the Acapulco region's tropical deciduous forest, the **Mexican elm,** or *olmo* (*Chaetoptelea mexicana*). Probably Mexico's tallest tree, the *olmo* reaches a height of at least 285 feet (87 meters); the world's tallest, the California redwood, reaches 364 feet. It closely resembles its near relative, the American elm, notably in the shape of its serrated leaves and its hair-fringed fruit. Its tough, heavy wood, ideal for floors and door sills, makes it one of the Acapulco region's most valuable lumber trees.

Well-watered zones of the tropical deciduous forest have become home to a platoon of useful **introduced plants.** These include the common India-native **mango,** "king of fruit" (April–July), and Africa-native *platano* (banana). Also introduced and common, but not so recognizable, is the **coffee shrub,** or locally *cafeto* (*Coffea arabica*). Coffee is widely grown in the Acapulco region, notably in the foothill forests, upcountry from Atoyac de Álvarez. Coffee shrubs grow unobtrusively, often in an apparent wild "jungle" right next to the highway, beneath the shady canopy of taller trees. Farmers limit them to about five feet in height. They're recognizable by their camellia-bush appearance, with shiny, dark-green leaves, star-shaped white flowers, and red berries, in season.

Excursions by Jeep or foot along shaded, off-highway tracks through the tropical deciduous forest can bestow delightful jungle scenes; however, unwary travelers must watch out for the poison-oaklike *mala mujer,* the "evil woman" tree. The oil on its large five-fingered leaves can cause an itchy rash.

Pine-Oak Forest

Along the upland highways (notably on the higher reaches of north–south Highway 95 and the Chilpancingo–Chilapa–Olinalá Highway

POINSETTIA

Although this lovely red flowering plant only became known and appreciated by the wider world during the 1800s, the people of Mexico have enjoyed the poinsettia for millennia. It grows in gorgeous wild profusion in semitropical mountain zones of southwestern Mexico, especially in the Acapulco region and the neighboring states of Michoacán, Morelos, Oaxaca, and Chiapas.

The Aztecs, who called the poinsettia *cuetlaxochitle*, used its sap to control fevers and its crimson red petals (actually not petals, but colored leaves, called bracts) for dye. The emperor Moctezuma II (1466–1520) especially adored the *cuetlaxochitle*. He ordered caravans of them brought to his capital at Tenochtitlán to honor an Aztec goddess who was said to have died of a broken heart. The *cuetlaxochitle*, a legend recounted, had been born from one drop of the goddess's blood.

Most present-day Mexican folks know the poinsettia as the *flor de Nochebuena* (flower of Christmas Eve). It blooms during the late autumn and early winter, just in time for people to give birthday bouquets to the baby Jesus at churches all over Mexico on December 24.

An eminent German botanist, Karl Lugwig Wilenow, was among the first outsiders to study the poinsettia, from cuttings brought to him from central America. In 1800, recognizing it as a member of the grand Euphorbia family, Wilenow christened it *Euphorbiaceae pulcherrima*, meaning "most beautiful of the Euphorbias."

Although apt, this name has been largely forgotten because of the work of Joel Robert Poinsett, amateur botanist and U.S. ambassador to Mexico during the 1820s. Poinsett, keenly interested in identifying new species wherever he traveled in Mexico, noticed the spectacularly red plant growing beside the road. He brought specimens back to the United States and nurtured them in his South Carolina greenhouse. This led to the plant's spread and ultimate immense popularity all over North and South America, Europe, and most parts of the world.

In 1836, a group of Scottish botanists proposed to honor Poinsett's work by renaming his find *Poinsettia pulcherrima*. The name stuck, and now people everywhere enjoy holiday festoons of the charmingly divine plant known simply as the poinsettia.

© BRUCE WHIPPERMAN

The fleshy cabbage agave, shown here near Chilapa, is a well-known resident of Guerrero inland mountainsides.

93) the tropical forest gives way to temperate pine-oak forest. Here, many of Mexico's 112 oak and 39 pine species thrive. Oval two-inch cones and foot-long drooping needles (three to a cluster) make the **pino triste,** or sad pine (*Pinus lumholtzii*), appear in severe need of water. Unlike many of Mexico's pines, it produces neither good lumber nor much turpentine, although it *is* prized by guitar makers for its wood.

Much more regal in bearing and commercially important are the tall pines, including the **Mexican white pine** (*Pinus ayacahuite*), known locally as the *pinabete.* It grows to about 100 feet when mature and resembles the white pine of northern regions, with long, bluish-green needles, five to a bunch and pendulous, scaly 4- to 6-inch often reddish-brown cones that shed winged seeds. Equally notable is the **Montezuma pine** (*Pinus montezumae*), or the *ocote macho.* It likewise grows long (but gray) cones and needles, five to a bunch, but is distinguishable by its interesting, drooping needles.

Pines often grow in stands, mixed at lower elevations with **oaks,** which occur in two

broad classifications—*encino* (evergreen, small-leafed) and *roble* (deciduous, large-leafed)—both much like the live oaks that dot California hills and valleys. Clustered on their branches and scattered in the shade, *bellota* (acorns) distinctly mark them as oaks.

Arid Tropical Scrub

This desertlike vegetation zone coincides with the semiarid Río Balsas basin, which sprawls for hundreds of miles east–west (reachable both along Highway 51 and north–south Highway 95) between Chilpancingo and Taxco. Although superficially appearing like the temperate deserts of the southwest United States and northern Mexico, the arid tropical scrub zone nurtures a botanic treasury of tropical, frost-sensitive plants, sculpted by extreme heat and drought.

The signature king of all these hardy plants is the spectacular **candelabra cactus,** *Lemaireocereus weberi* or *candelabro.* Mature specimens, as wide and high as a four-story building, with a dozen or more 10-ribbed vertical columns, resemble a giant dining-table candelabra.

The candelabra's look-alike cousin is the

organ-pipe cactus, *Marginatocereus margin-atus* or *órgano.* Distinguish it by its smaller but still formidable size (10–20 feet in height) and its five to seven ribs per vertical column.

At some spots, great forests of tall, pole-straight *tetetzo* cactuses, *Pachycereus ruficeps,* inhabit the arid tropical scrubland. Up to 50 feet tall, they can collectively resemble a grand army of cactus sentinels, guarding the rocky landscape.

Although not cactuses, many of the 300-odd members of the agave family thrive in dryer areas of the Acapulco region. Although some are cultivated (for beverages, fiber, soap, and more), others grow wild. One such is the charming **cabbage agave,** *Agave perryi,* which grows in families of neat, round, cabbagelike plants, up to three feet in diameter, with bluish-green, broad, spined leaves.

Cloud Forest and High Coniferous Forest

The Acapulco region's rarest and most exotic vegetation zones are removed from the coastal tourist centers. Adventurers who travel to certain high, dewy mountainsides, beginning around 5,000 feet, can explore the plant and wildlife community of the cloud forest. One such example lies along Highway 196, about 30 miles (50 km) uphill from Atoyac de Álvarez, past the village of El Paraíso. There, abundant cool fog nourishes a Pleistocene remnant forest of dripping tree ferns, liquid amber maples, lichen-draped pines and oaks, above a mossy carpet of orchids, bromeliads, and begonias.

About 20 miles (32 km) farther uphill along the same route, the Acapulco region's least accessible vegetation zone, the high coniferous forest, swathes the 9,000- to 11,000-foot slopes of Cerro Teotepec. This pristine alpine island, accessible only on horseback or by foot, nurtures stands of pines, spruce, and fir interspersed with grassy meadows, similar to the Rocky Mountain slopes in the United States and Canada. Here, besides the white and Montezuma pines, find hardy stands of **sacred fir,** *Abies religiosa* or *oyamel;* **Mexican cypress,** *Cupressa lusitanica;* and the high-altitude **alder,** *Alnus firmifolia.* (*Note:* Do not attempt the cloud forest and high

coniferous forest explorations alone. Inquire at the Atoyac de Álvarez *presidencia municipal* for an experienced guide.)

For a wealth of details, consult M. Walter Pesman's delightful *Meet Flora Mexicana* (which is out of print, but major libraries often have a copy). Also informative is the popular paperback *Handbook of Mexican Roadside Flora,* by Charles T. Mason Jr. and Patricia B. Mason.

WILDLIFE

Despite continued habitat destruction—forests are logged, wetlands filled, and savannas plowed—great swaths of the Acapulco region still abound with wildlife. Common in the temperate pine-oak forest highlands are mammals familiar to U.S. residents such as the mountain lion (*puma*), coyote, fox (*zorro*), rabbit (*conejo*), and quail (*codorniz*).

However, the tropical coastal forests and savannas are home to fascinating species seen only in zoos north of the border. The reality of this dawns on travelers when they glimpse something exotic, such as raucous, screeching swarms of small green parrots rising from the roadside, or an armadillo or coati nosing in

A number of small parrots make their home in Acapulco's forests and wetlands.

© BRUCE WHIPPERMAN

the sand just a few feet away from them at the forested edge of an isolated beach.

Population pressures have nevertheless decreased wild habitats, endangering many previously abundant animal species. If you are lucky, you may find a tracker who can lead you to a band of now-rare reddish-brown **spider monkeys** (*monos*) raiding a wild fruit tree. And deep in the mountain fastness, you may be led to a view of the endangered striped cat, the **ocelot** (*ocelotl*) or its smaller cousins, the **margay** (*tigrillo*) and the tan **jaguarundi** (*onza, leoncillo*). On such an excursion, if you are really fortunate, you may hear the "chesty" roar or catch a glimpse of a jaguar, the fabled *tigre*.

El Tigre

Each hill has its own *tigre,* a Mexican proverb says. With black spots spread over a yellow-tan coat, stretching five feet (1.5 meters) and weighing 200 pounds (90 kg), the typical jaguar resembles a muscular spotted leopard. Although hunted since prehistory, and now endangered, the jaguar lives on in the Acapulco region, where it hunts along thickly forested stream bottoms and foothills. Unlike the mountain lion, the jaguar will eat any game. Jaguars have even been known to wait patiently for fish in rivers and to stalk beaches for turtle and egg dinners. If they have a favorite food, it is probably the piglike wild peccary, *jabalí.* Experienced hunters agree that no two jaguars will have the same prey in their stomachs.

© BRUCE WHIPPERMAN

the wild piglike *jabalí*

Although humans have died of wounds inflicted by cornered jaguars, there is little or no hard evidence that they eat humans, despite legends to the contrary.

Armadillos, Coatis, and Bats

Armadillos are cat-sized mammals that act and look like opossums but carry reptilianlike shells. If you see one, remain still, and it may walk right up and sniff your foot before it recognizes you and scuttles back into the woods.

A common inhabitant of the tropics is the raccoonlike coati (*tejón, pisote*). In the wild, coatis like shady stream banks, often congregating in large troops of 15–30 individuals. They are identified by their short brown or tan fur, small round ears, long nose, and straight, vertically held tail. With their endearing and inquisitive nature, coatis are often kept as pets; the first coati you see may be one on a string offered for sale at a local market.

Mexican bats (*murciélagos*) are widespread, with at least 126 species compared to 37 in the United States. In Mexico, as everywhere, bats are feared and misunderstood. As sunset approaches, many species come out of their hiding places and flit through the air in search of insects. Most people, sitting outside enjoying the early evening, will mistake their darting silhouettes for those of birds, who, except for owls, do not generally fly at night.

Bats are often locally called *vampiros,* even though only three relatively rare Mexican species actually feed on the blood of mammals—nearly always cattle—and of birds.

The many nonvampire Mexican bats carry their vampire cousins' odious reputation with forbearance. They go about their good works, pollinating flowers, clearing the air of pesky gnats and mosquitoes, ridding cornfields of mice, and dropping seeds, thereby restoring forests. Limestone caves, such as the Grutas de Juxtlahuaca, are the best places to see bats.

BIRDS

The coastal lagoons of the Acapulco region lie astride the Pacific Flyway, one of the Americas' major north–south paths for migrating

© BRUCE WHIPPERMAN

a forest of angular sea rocks, tidepools, foaming surf, and perching pelicans

waterfowl. Many of the familiar American and Canadian species, including pintail, gadwall, baldpate, shoveler, redhead, and scaup, arrive October–January, when their numbers will have swollen into the millions. They settle near food and cover—even at the borders of cornfields, to the frustration of farmers.

Besides the migrants, swarms of resident species—**herons** and **egrets** (*garzas*), cormorantlike **anhingas, lily-walkers** (*jacanas*), and hundreds more—stalk, nest, and preen in the same lagoons.

Few spots are better for observing seabirds than the beaches of the Acapulco region. **Brown pelicans** and black-and-white **frigate birds** are among the prime actors. When a flock of pelicans spots a school of favorite fish, they go about their routine deliberately. Singly or in pairs, they circle and plummet into the waves to come up, more often than not, with fish in their gullets. Each bird then bobs and floats over the swells for a minute or two, seeming to wait for its dozen or so fellow pelicans to take their turns. This continues until they've bagged a dinner of 10–15 fish apiece.

Frigate birds, the scavengers par excellence of the Mexican Pacific coast, often profit by the labor of the teams of fisherfolk who haul in nets of fish on Acapulco-region beaches. After they auction off the choice morsels of perch, tuna, red snapper, octopus, or shrimp to merchants, and the local villagers have scavenged everything else edible, the motley residue of small fish, sea snakes, skates, squid, slugs, and sharks is thrown to a screeching flock of frigate birds.

The wild blue mangrove lagoons of the Costa Chica and Costa Grande, east and west of Acapulco, nurture a trove of wildlife, especially birds, ripe for viewing on foot or by boat tours.

For more details on Mexico's mammals and birds in general, check out Les Baletsky's *Tropical Mexico: The Ecotraveler's Wildlife Guide* and other works cited in *Suggested Reading*.

REPTILES AND AMPHIBIANS
Snakes, Gila Monsters, and Crocodiles

Mexico has 460-odd snake species, the vast

majority shy and nonpoisonous; they will get out of your way if you give plenty of warning. In the Acapulco region poisonous snakes have been largely eradicated in city and tourist areas. In brush or jungle areas, carry a stick or a machete and beat the bushes ahead of you while watching where you put your feet. When hiking or rock-climbing in the country, don't put your hand in niches you can't see.

You might even see a snake underwater while swimming offshore at an isolated Acapulco region beach. The **yellow-bellied sea snake,** *Pelamis platurus* (to about two feet), although rare and shy, can inflict fatal bites. If you see a yellow-and-black snake underwater, get away, pronto.

Some eels, which resemble snakes but have gills like fish and inhabit rocky crevices, can inflict nonpoisonous bites and should also be avoided.

The Mexican land counterpart of the *Pelamis platurus* is the **coral snake** (*coralillo*), which occurs as about two dozen species, all with multicolored bright bands that always include red. Although relatively rare, small, and shy, coral snakes occasionally inflict serious, sometimes fatal, bites.

More aggressive and generally more dangerous is the Mexican **rattlesnake** (*cascabel*) and its viper relative, the **fer-de-lance** (*Bothrops atrox*). About the same in size (to six feet) and appearance as the rattlesnake, the fer-de-lance is known by various local names, such as *nauyaca, cuatro narices, palanca,* and *barba amarilla.* It is potentially more hazardous than the rattlesnake because it lacks a warning rattle.

The Gila monster (confined in Mexico to northern Sonora) and its southern tropical relative, the yellow-spotted, black **escorpión** (*Heloderma horridum*), are the world's only poisonous lizards. Despite its beaded skin and menacing, fleshy appearance, the *escorpión* only bites when severely provoked; and, even then, its venom is rarely, if ever, fatal.

The **crocodile** (*cocodrilo, caimán*), once prized for its meat and hide, came close to vanishing in Mexican Pacific lagoons until the government took steps to ensure its survival; it's now officially protected. A few isolated breeding populations live on in the wild, while government and private hatcheries are breeding more for the eventual repopulation of lagoons where crocodiles once were common.

Two crocodile species occur in the Acapulco region. The true crocodile, *Crocodilus acutus,* has a narrower snout than its local cousin, *Caiman crocodilus fuscus,* a type of alligator (*lagarto*). Although past individuals have been recorded at up to 15 feet long, wild native crocodiles and alligators are usually young and only three feet or less in length.

Sea Turtles

The story of Mexican sea turtles is similar: they once swarmed ashore on Acapulco regional beaches to lay their eggs. Prized for their meat, eggs, hide, and shell, the turtles were severely devastated. Now officially protected, sea turtles are coming ashore in growing numbers at some isolated locations. Of the four locally occurring species, the **olive Ridley turtle** (*tortuga golfina*) and the **green turtle** (*tortuga negra* or *caguama*) are the most common. The green and olive Ridley, although officially endangered, have stabilized because of persistent government and volunteer efforts. The two other, relatively rare, locally occurring sea turtles are the **hawksbill** (*carey*) and the **leatherback** (*tortuga de cuero*). (For many more sea turtle details, see the sidebar "Saving Turtles" in the *Costa Grande* chapter.)

FISH AND MARINE MAMMALS

Shoals of fish abound in Acapulco's waters. Four billfish species are found in deep-sea grounds several miles offshore: **swordfish, sailfish,** and **blue** and **black marlin.** All are spirited fighters, though the sailfish and marlin are generally the toughest to bring in. The blue marlin is the biggest of the four; in the past, 10-foot specimens weighing more than 1,000 pounds were brought in at Pacific-coast marinas. Lately, four feet and 200 pounds for a marlin, and 100 pounds for a sailfish, are more typical. Progressive captains now encourage victorious anglers to return these magnificent "tigers of the sea" (especially the sinewy sailfish and blue marlin, which make for poor eating) to the deep after they've won the battle.

Billfish are not the only prizes of the sea, however. Serious fish lovers also seek varieties of tunalike **jack,** such as **yellowtail, Pacific amberjack, pompano, jack crevalle,** and the tenacious **roosterfish,** named for the "comb" atop its head. These, and the **yellowfin tuna, mackerel,** and *dorado,* which Hawaiians call mahimahi, are among the delicacies sought in Acapulco waters.

Accessible from small boats offshore and by casting from shoreline rocks are varieties of **snapper** (*huachinango, pargo*) and **sea bass** (*cabrilla*). Closer to shore, **croaker, mullet,** and **groupers** can be found foraging along sandy bottoms and in rocky crevices.

Sharks and **rays** inhabit nearly all depths, with smaller fry venturing into beach shallows and lagoons. Huge **Pacific manta rays** appear to be frolicking, their great wings flapping like birds, not far off Acapulco shores. Just beyond the waves, local fisherfolk bring in **hammerhead, thresher,** and **leopard sharks.**

Also common is the **stingray,** which can inflict a painful wound with its barbed tail. Experienced swimmers and waders avoid injury by both shuffling (rather than stepping) and watching their feet in shallow waters with sandy bottoms. (For more fish talk and a chart of species encountered in Acapulco waters, turn ahead to *Sports and Recreation.*)

Dolphins and Whales
The playful antics of the once-numerous **Pacific bottlenosed dolphin** are nevertheless sometimes observable from Acapulco region–based tour and fishing boats, and sometimes even from beaches. (Sadly, dolphins often get caught and drown in fishing trawlers' nets.)

Although the **California gray whale** has a migration pattern extending only to the southern tip of Baja California, occasional pods stray farther south, where deep-sea fishermen and cruise- and tour-boat passengers see them in deep waters offshore.

Larger whale (*ballena*) species, such as the **humpback** and **blue** whale, appear to enjoy tropical waters even more, ranging the north Pacific tropics from the southwest Mexican Pacific shore west to Hawaii and beyond.

History

Once upon a time, maybe as long as 30,000 years ago, the first bands of hunters, perhaps following great game herds, crossed from Siberia to the American continent. They drifted southward, many of them eventually settling in the lush upland valleys and coastlines of present-day Mexico.

Much later, perhaps around 5000 B.C., these early people began gathering and grinding the seeds of a hardy grass that required only the summer rains to thrive. After generations of selective breeding, this grain, called *teocentli,* the sacred seed (which we call maize or corn), led to prosperity.

EARLY CIVILIZATIONS
With abundant food, villages grew into towns, and towns evolved into small cities. Leisure classes arose—artists, architects, warriors, and ruler-priests—who had time to think and create. With a calendar, they harnessed the constant wheel of the firmament to life on earth, defining the days to plant, harvest, feast, travel, and trade.

Of Mexico's early urban peoples, the Olmecs were foremost. Around 1500 B.C. they were establishing large ceremonial centers along the Gulf of Mexico Coast. At La Venta, in present-day Tabasco state, archaeologists have uncovered the Olmecs' most spectacular remains: giant stone heads, up to nine feet in height, with decidedly negroid features and football helmet–like caps. Other sculptures, many of lovely jade, show a strong jaguar cult influence, in the form of half-human, half-jaguar masklike faces.

The Olmec influence arrived early in the present-day Acapulco region. Olmec-style jaguar-motif art has been uncovered at Teopantecuantlán, an upland ceremonial center dating from around 1000 B.C. Moreover, Olmec-style wall paintings decorate caves, notably the Grutas de Juxtlahuaca and Oxtotitlán, in lush highland valleys about 100 miles north of Acapulco.

Monte Albán, Teotihuacán, and Xochicalco

After the decline of the Olmecs, around 500 B.C., other civilizations rose. Monte Albán, in Oaxaca, which was flourishing around the time of Jesus, is thought by many experts to be Mexico's first true city. Later, Teotihuacán, north of present-day Mexico City, grew into one of the world's great metropolises, with a population of about 250,000, by A.D. 500.

Teotihuacán's epic monuments still stand: the towering Pyramid of the Sun, at the terminal of a grand avenue, faces a great Pyramid of the Moon. Along the avenue sprawls a monumental temple-court, surrounded by scowling effigies of Quetzalcoatl, the feathered serpent god of gods.

Eventually both Monte Albán and Teotihuacán crumbled; they were all but abandoned by A.D. 700, leaving a host of former vassal city-states to tussle among themselves. In the Acapulco region, first among these was Xochicalco, near Taxco, 150 miles (250 km) north of present-day Acapulco.

The Living Quetzalcoatl

Xochicalco's wise men tutored a young noble who was to become a living legend. In A.D. 947, Topiltzín (literally, Our Prince) was

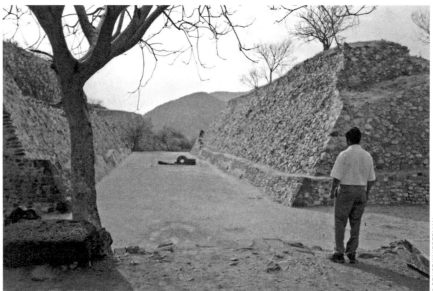

The Northern Ball Court at Xochicalco (note the half-buried stone ball) undoubtedly hosted many grand high-stakes ceremonial contests.

born. Records recite Topiltzín's achievements. He advanced astronomy, agriculture, and architecture and founded the city-state of Tula in A.D. 968, north of old Teotihuacán. Contrary to the times, Topiltzín opposed human sacrifice. He ruled benignly for two decades, becoming so revered that his people knew him as the living Quetzalcoatl, the plumed serpent god incarnate.

Bloodthirsty local priests, lusting for human victims, tricked him with alcohol, however; Topiltzín awoke groggily one morning, in bed with his sister. Devastated with shame, Quetzalcoatl banished himself. He headed east from Tula with a band of retainers in A.D. 987, vowing that he would return during the anniversary of his birth year, Ce Acatl. Legends say he sailed across the eastern sea and rose to heaven as the morning star.

The Aztecs

The civilization that Topiltzín founded, known to historians as the Toltec (People of Tula), was eventually eclipsed by others. These included the Aztecs, a collection of seven aggressive immigrant subtribes. Migrating around during the 11th century A.D., from a mysterious western land of Aztlán (Place of the Herons) into the lake-filled valley that Mexico City now occupies, the Aztecs survived by being forced to fight for every piece of ground they occupied.

Around the same time, another Aztec subtribe was migrating into the present-day Acapulco region. As did their Valley of Mexico cousins, they competed fiercely with the original inhabitants and finally rose to dominance by war and intermarriage over their defeated vassals. By A.D. 1100, their Náhuatl (Aztec-language) kingdom, called Coixcaltlapan, sprawled over both the central valleys and the Río Balsas basin and parts of the western coast, around Zacatula and Atoyac.

Meanwhile, to the north, the Valley of Mexico Aztecs, who called themselves the México, had also clawed their way to dominion. In A.D. 1325 they founded their capital, Tenochtitlán, on an island in the middle of the valley-lake.

From there, Aztec armies, not unlike Roman legions, marched out and subdued faraway kingdoms and returned with booty of gold, brilliant feathers, precious jewels, and captives, whom they enslaved and sacrificed by the thousands as food for their gods.

Among those gods they feared was Quetzalcoatl, who, legends said, was bearded and fair-skinned. It was a remarkable coincidence, therefore, that the bearded, fair-skinned Castilian Hernán Cortés landed on Mexico's eastern coast on April 22, 1519, during the year of Ce Acatl, exactly when Topiltzín, the living Quetzalcoatl, had vowed he would return.

THE CONQUEST

Although a generation had elapsed since Christopher Columbus founded Spain's West Indian colonies, returns had been meager. Moreover, Columbus's original goal of reaching China by sailing west had eluded the Spanish explorers. Geographers and navigators realized that, instead of China, Columbus had discovered a new continent. Perhaps, explorers hoped, China lay only a bit farther west, tantalizingly just beyond the setting sun.

Hernán Cortés, a poor Spanish nobleman, then only 34, promoted an expedition of 11 small ships and 550 men and sailed westward from Cuba in February 1519. Upon landing near present-day Veracruz, he was in trouble. His men, mostly soldiers of fortune, hearing stories of a powerful Aztec empire west beyond the mountains, had realized the impossible odds they faced and became restive.

Cortés, however, cut short any thoughts of mutiny by burning his ships. As he led his grumbling but resigned band of adventurers toward the Aztec capital of Tenochtitlán, Cortés played Quetzalcoatl to the hilt, awing local chiefs. Coaxed by Doña Marina, Cortés's native translator-mistress, local chiefs began to add their warrior-armies to Cortés's march against their Aztec overlords.

Moctezuma, Lord of Tenochtitlán

Once inside the walls of Tenochtitlán, the

MALINCHE AND CORTÉS

If it hadn't been for Doña Marina (received as a gift from a local chief), Hernán Cortés may have become a mere historical footnote. Doña Marina, speaking both Spanish and native tongues, soon became Cortés's interpreter, go-between, and negotiator. She persuaded a number of important chiefs to ally themselves with Cortés against the Aztecs. Clever and opportunistic, Doña Marina was a crucial strategist in Cortés's deadly game of divide and conquer. She eventually bore Cortés a son and lived in honor and riches for many years, profiting greatly from the Spaniards' exploitation of the Mexicans.

Latter-day Mexicans do not honor her by the gentle title of Doña Marina, however. They call her Malinche, after the volcano – the ugly, treacherous scar on the Mexican landscape – and curse her as the female Judas who betrayed her country to the Spanish. *Malinchismo* has become known as the tendency to love things foreign and hate things Mexican.

Aztecs' Venicelike island-city, the Spaniards were dazzled by gardens of animals, gold and palaces, and a great pyramid-enclosed square where tens of thousands of people bartered goods gathered from all over the empire.

However, Moctezuma, the lord of that empire, was frozen by fear and foreboding, unsure if these figures truly represented the return of Quetzalcoatl. He quickly found himself hostage to Cortés and then died a few months later during a riot against Spanish greed and brutality. On July 1, 1520, on what came to be called *noche triste* (the sad night), the besieged Cortés and his men broke out, fleeing for their lives along the lake causeway from Tenochtitlán, carrying Moctezuma's treasure. Many of them drowned beneath their burdens of gold booty, while the survivors hacked a bloody retreat through thousands of screaming Aztec warriors to safety on the lakeshore.

Aztec Defeat and Spanish Victory

Despite his grievous setback, Cortés regrouped and reinforced his small army with an armed sailboat fleet and 100,000 Indian warrior-allies and invaded Tenochtitlán a year later. The defenders, led by Cuauhtémoc, Moctezuma's nephew, refused to surrender, forcing Cortés to destroy the city to take it. Tenochtitlán fell on August 13, 1521.

After his triumph, Cortés took former Emperor Cuauhtémoc captive. He forced Cuauhtémoc and his retainers to march with him on an ill-fated expedition to Honduras in 1523–1525. Tortured with foreboding that Cuauhtémoc and his compatriots were plotting against him, Cortés had Cuauhtémoc hanged on February 28, 1525.

But, unknown to Cortés, Cuauhtémoc's followers secretly took his remains hundreds of miles north and may have buried them at Ixcateopan, the home of Cuauhtémoc's mother, near present-day Taxco. There, 424 years later, on September 26, 1949, remains believed by many to be Cuauhtémoc's were discovered and remain there in state to this very day.

New Spain

With the Valley of Mexico firmly in his grip, Cortés sent his lieutenants south, north, and west to explore and extend the limits of his domain, which eventually expanded to more than a dozenfold the size of old Spain. In a letter to his king, Charles V, Cortés christened his empire New Spain of the Ocean Sea, a label that remained Mexico's official name for 300 years.

THE SEARCH FOR CHINA

Even during his struggle with the Aztecs, Cortés continued to dream Columbus's old dream. Somewhere west lay China, and he was determined to find it. As early as 1520 Cortés began sending his lieutenants to Mexico's southern Pacific coast to look for safe, timber-rich harbors, where he would build the ships to China.

First on the Pacific shore was Gonzalo de Uribe, who, in 1520, arrived at Zacatula, at the mouth of the Río Balsas, west of Zihuatanejo. Besides bringing back gold samples, he told Cortés of a good harbor and plenty of big trees for building ships.

Discovery of Acapulco Bay

In 1522, conquistador Pedro de Alvarado founded the Acapulco region's first town, at Acatlán on the Costa Chica. Around the same time, Rodriguez de Villafuerte sailed into Acapulco Bay, which he named Bahía de Santa Lucia, a label that persisted on maps for generations.

After reporting to Cortés of the bay's calm anchorage and abundance of shoreline trees, Villafuerte returned, and by 1530 had built two ships, the *San Miguel* and *San Marcos,* on the shore of Acapulco Bay. For his efforts, Villafuerte was awarded *encomienda* rights (taxes and labor of an indigenous district) over Acapulco and a big slice of the present Acapulco region.

Among the dozen-odd early Pacific expeditions (several of which were personally financed by Cortés), five set out from Acapulco. In 1532, Diego Hurtado de Mendoza sailed for China via the north Pacific and never returned. Another expedition, loaded with supplies for conquistador Pizarro in Peru, sailed in 1535; in the same year, Cortés himself sailed out, searching for treasure in Baja California. Then, in 1539, Cortés sent Francisco de Ulloa northwest to search for the fabled golden Seven Cities of Cibola, but he was never heard from again. Finally, in 1540, Domingo de Castillo set out to map Mexico's Pacific coast. He returned with detailed charts and tantalizing hints of the location of Cibola.

Cortés's Monument

Disheartened by his failure to find China (or, at least, more golden cities), and discouraged with interference by his king's Mexican representatives, Cortés returned to Spain to reassert his authority at court. But mired down by lawsuits, a small war, and his daughter's marital troubles, he fell ill and died in Spain on December 2, 1547. Cortés's remains, according to his will, were eventually laid to rest in a vault at the Hospital de Jesús, which he had founded in Mexico City.

Since latter-day Mexican politics preclude memorials to the Spanish conquest, no monument anywhere in Mexico commemorates Cortés's remarkable achievements. His single monument, historians note, is Mexico itself.

The Manila Galleon

Although a handful of the early Spanish voyages of exploration did actually reach Asia, none had returned to Mexico until priest-navigator Andrés de Urdaneta discovered the north Pacific trade winds that pushed his ship *San Pedro* swiftly east back to America. He (together with the only other shipmate who had enough strength to do it) dropped anchor in Acapulco Bay on October 3, 1565, with a trove of Chinese treasures in his ship's hold.

Thus, more than three generations after Columbus and 40 years of failed trans-Pacific voyages from Mexico that lost dozens of ships and hundreds of lives, the western trade route to Asia was finally a reality.

Not long thereafter, authorities in Spain designated Acapulco as Mexico's sole Pacific trading port. Once a year, at least one silver-laden ship, known to the Spanish as the Nao de China, and to the English as the Manila galleon, set sail for the Spanish colony of Manila in the Philippines. It returned with an emperor's dream of rich silks, delicate porcelain, exquisite lacquerware, glittering gold, and rare spices.

For more than 250 years thereafter, merchants from all over Mexico and Peru gathered in Acapulco for a grand yearly trade fair. Bulging with bags of silver and a small mountain of trade goods, such as cochineal, cinnamon, jewels, and cacao, they camped out in Acapulco, eagerly awaiting the Manila galleon's return.

Pirate Threats

Attracted by the Manila galleon's treasures, Dutch, French, Portuguese, and English pirates, sometimes in squadrons of several heavily armed vessels, menaced the Mexican coast. The most famous was Francis Drake, known to the colonists as the feared El Draque. Drake raided a number of Spanish Pacific settlements during his 1578–1580 circumnavigation of the globe. After finishing with the South American colonies, Drake headed north, where he sacked Huatulco on April 13, 1579. He waited in vain for the Manila galleon outside of Acapulco, then continued northwest to California, then across the Pacific.

After a Dutch pirate fleet had attacked Acapulco in 1614, New Spain Viceroy Diego Fernandez de Córdoba decided to build a fort overlooking Acapulco Bay. It successfully deterred hostile attacks, until termites, hurricanes, old age, and finally an earthquake finished the old fort off in 1776. A bigger, stronger fort, the Fuerte San Diego, replaced it in 1783 and remains to the present day.

COLONIAL MEXICO
The Missionaries

Even while the conquistadores subjugated the Mexicans, missionaries began arriving to teach, heal, and baptize them. A dozen Franciscan brothers impressed natives and conquistadores alike by trekking the entire 300-mile stony path from Veracruz to Mexico City in 1523. Missionary authorities generally enjoyed a sympathetic ear from Charles V and his successors, who earnestly pursued Spain's Christian mission, especially when it coincided with its political and economic goals.

SIR FRANCIS DRAKE: THE PIRATE EL DRAQUE

The most renowned raider of the Spanish Main was Francis Drake, or the feared "El Draque," as the Spanish called him. The first European corsair to menace Spain's Pacific colonies, Drake left England in 1577 in command of five vessels and 166 men.

Supposedly headed on a trading mission to Africa, Drake's true purpose became clear when he ordered the attack and capture of a Portuguese merchant ship in the Eastern Atlantic. By the time he had crossed westward to South America, his disillusioned crew and merchant partners on board mutinied. Executing the leader of the mutineers, Drake abandoned two of his least-seaworthy ships. Next, rallying the remainder of his men, he changed the name of his ship from the stodgy *Pelican* to the proud *Golden Hind*.

In attempting the westward passage through the stormy Strait of Magellan, at the extreme southern tip of South America, he lost two of his remaining three ships. Undaunted, Drake sailed his *Golden Hind* up the west coast of South America, raiding and sacking every possible port – Valparaíso, Lima, Arica – and capturing the royal treasure ship the *Cacafuego*.

Contrary to the Spaniards' worst fears, Drake's approach to robbery was very courtly. No one, Spanish or native, was intentionally harmed. Treasure seemed to be Drake's sole objective. During his last attack on the Pacific Coast, at Huatulco, on April 13, 1579, he even stole the church bell.

The ultimate prize, however, was the Manila galleon. He lurked offshore at Acapulco for a time, but seeing no treasure ship, Drake skipped northwest and dropped anchor and resupplied at undefended Zihuatanejo. He continued northwest for months, searching doggedly for the Manila galleon.

Finally, Drake stopped to rest at a safe anchorage probably somewhere on the present-day northern California coast, at a place that he recorded had cliffs as fair as the white cliffs of Dover. He records in his log that he stayed for five weeks, traded with the native folks, repaired the *Golden Hind*, and erected his famous "plate of brass," yet to be found. On it he inscribed the claim, in the name of his queen, to the domain of "Nova Albion," now California.

The *Golden Hind* continued west across the Pacific, passing the Spice Islands and India and rounding the south Cape of Africa. Drake arrived in England on September 26, 1580, to a glorious welcome by Queen Elizabeth, having voyaged 35,000 miles and collected a booty of 50,000 pounds of silver.

The King Takes Control

Increasingly after 1525, the crown, through the Council of the Indies, began to wrest power away from Cortés and his conquistador lieutenants, many of whom had been granted rights of *encomienda:* taxes and labor of an indigenous district. From the king's point of view, tribute pesos collected by *encomenderos* from their native serfs reduced the gold that would otherwise flow to the crown. Moreover, many *encomenderos* callously enslaved and sold their native wards for quick profit. Such abuses, coupled with European-introduced diseases, began to reduce the Native Mexican population at an alarming rate.

The king and his councillors, realizing that without their local labor force, New Spain would vanish, acted decisively, instituting new laws and a powerful viceroy, Don Antonio de Mendoza, to enforce them.

In 1542, the Council of the Indies, through Viceroy Mendoza, promulgated its liberal New Laws of the Indies. They rested on high moral ground: The only Christian justification for New Spain was the souls and welfare of the Native Mexicans. Slavery was outlawed and the colonists' *encomienda* rights over land and the Indians were to eventually revert to the crown.

Despite near-rebellion by the colonists, Mendoza and his successors kept the lid on New Spain. Although some *encomenderos* held their privileges into the 18th century, chattel slavery of Native Mexicans was abolished in New Spain 300 years before Lincoln's Emancipation Proclamation.

Peace reigned in Mexico for 10 generations. Viceroys came, served, and went; settlers put down roots; friars built country churches; and the conquistadores' rich heirs played while the natives worked.

In the port of Acapulco, as the Manila galleon departed and returned safely nearly every year, a small colony of merchants took up residence, built comfortable homes, and got fat on the labor of their native servants and the profits of the Manila galleon's increasingly rich trove of silks, spices, porcelain, lacquerware, and gold.

The Church

Apart from the missionaries, whose authority flowed directly from the pope in Rome, Mexican parish churches (*parroquias*), most of which remain to the present day, were founded and controlled by local bishops. As did the missionaries, parish churches generally moderated the Native Mexicans' toil. On feast days, the natives would dress up, parade their patron saint, drink *pulque,* and ooh and aah at the fireworks.

The church nevertheless profited from the status quo. The biblical tithe—one-tenth of everything earned—filled clerical coffers. By 1800, the church owned half of Mexico.

Moreover, both the clergy and the military were doubly privileged. They enjoyed the right of *fuero* (exemption from civil law) and could be prosecuted only by ecclesiastical or military courts.

Trade and Commerce

In trade and commerce, New Spain existed for the benefit of the mother country. For nearly the entire colonial era, exterior trade was funneled through only Veracruz on the Gulf and Acapulco on the Pacific. Trade was allowed only with Spain and certain Spanish colonies. As a result, colonists had to pay dearly for often-shoddy Spanish manufactures. The Casa de Contratación (the royal trade regulators) always ensured the colony's yearly payment deficit would be made up by bullion shipments from Mexican mines, from which the crown raked 10 percent off the top.

Despite its faults, New Spain, by most contemporary measures, was prospering in 1800. The native labor force was both docile and growing, and the galleons carried increasing tonnages of silver and gold to Spain. The authorities, however, failed to recognize that Mexico had changed in 300 years.

Criollos – The New Mexicans

Nearly three centuries of colonial rule gave rise to a burgeoning population of more than a million *criollos*—Mexican-born, pure European descendants of Spanish colonists, many rich and educated—to whom power was denied.

POPULATION CHANGES IN NEW SPAIN

	Early Colonial (1570)	Late Colonial (1810)
peninsulares	6,600	15,000
criollos	11,000	1,100,000
mestizos	2,400	704,000
indígenas	3,340,000	3,700,000
negros	22,000	630,000

High government, church, and military office always had been the preserve of a tiny minority of *peninsulares*—whites born in Spain. *Criollos* could only watch in disgust as unlettered, unskilled *peninsulares,* derisively called *gachupines* (wearers of spurs), were boosted to authority over them.

Mestizos, Indígenas, and African Mexicans

Upper-class luxury existed by virtue of the sweat of Mexico's mestizo, *indígena* (indigenous), and *negro* laborers and servants. African slaves were imported in large numbers during the 17th century after typhus, smallpox, and measles epidemics had wiped out most of the *indígena* population. Although the African Mexicans, whose communities are still concentrated around Veracruz and the Costa Chica east of Acapulco, contributed significantly (crafts, healing arts, dance, music, drums, and marimba), they had arrived last and experienced discrimination from everyone.

INDEPENDENCE

Although the *criollos* stood high above the *mestizo, indígena,* and *negro* underclasses, that seemed little compensation for the false smiles, deep bows, and costly bribes that *gachupines* demanded.

The chance for change came during the aftermath of the French invasion of Spain in 1808, when Napoléon Bonaparte replaced King Ferdinand VII with his brother Joseph on the Spanish throne. Most *peninsulares* backed the king; most *criollos,* however, inspired by the example of the recent American and French revolutions, talked and dreamed of independence. One such group, urged by a firebrand parish priest, acted.

El Grito de Dolores

"¡Viva México! Death to the gachupines!" Father Miguel Hidalgo cried passionately from the church balcony in the Guanajuato town of Dolores on September 16, 1810, igniting action. A mostly *indígena,* machete-wielding army of 20,000 coalesced around Hidalgo and his compatriots, Ignacio Allende and Juan Aldama. Their ragtag force raged out of control through central Mexico, massacring hated *gachupines* and pillaging their homes.

Hidalgo advanced on Mexico City but, unnerved by stiff royalist resistance, retreated and regrouped around Guadalajara. His rebels, whose numbers had swollen to 80,000, were no match for a disciplined, 6,000-strong royalist force. On January 17, 1811, Hidalgo (now "Generalisimo") fled north toward the United States but was soon apprehended, defrocked, and executed. His head and those of his comrades hung from the walls of the Guanajuato granary for 10 years in compensation for the slaughter of 138 *gachupines* by Hidalgo's army.

The 10-Year Struggle

Others carried on, however. Hidalgo's heroic efforts had immediately found crucial support in the Acapulco region. An African-Mexican former student of Hidalgo, José María Morelos, journeyed south from central Mexico and recruited an entire rebel brigade in the countryside west and north of Acapulco. Attracted by the riches of the Manila galleon deposited at the port, the rebel army laid siege to Acapulco. Morelos avoided getting bogged down by the siege by splitting his force. He took half of his troops north, where he achieved signal victories, capturing Chilpancingo, Tixtla, and Chilapa in the upcountry Acapulco region.

where Mexicans declared independence from Spain in November 1813

was amazed at Itúrbide's proposal: that Mexico should become an independent constitutional monarchy, headed by the king of Spain, and based on "Three Guarantees"—the renowned Trigarantias: independence, Catholicism, and equality—that their army would enforce.

Mexico Wins Independence

On February 24, 1821, in the Acapulco-region town of Iguala, Guerrero and Itúrbide announced their proposal, which became known, famously, as the Plan de Iguala. The plan immediately gained wide support, and on September 21, 1821, Itúrbide rode triumphantly into Mexico City at the head of his Army of Trigarantias. Mexico was independent at last.

Independence, however, solved little except to expel the *peninsulares.* With an illiterate populace and no experience in self-government, Mexicans began a tragic 40-year love affair with a fantasy: the general on the white horse, the gold-braided hero who could save them from themselves.

The Rise and Fall of Agustín I

After the king of Spain refused titular reign over an independent Mexico, Itúrbide was crowned Emperor Agustín I by the bishop of Guadalajara on July 21, 1822. He soon lost his charisma, however. In a pattern that became sadly predictable for generations of topsy-turvy Mexican politics, an ambitious garrison commander issued a *pronunciamiento,* or declaration of rebellion, against him; old revolutionary heroes endorsed a plan to install a republic. Itúrbide, his braid tattered and brass tarnished, abdicated in February 1823.

The Disastrous Era of Santa Anna

The new Mexican republic, founded in 1824, teetered along, changing hands between conservative and liberal control, for nine chaotic years. But, by 1833, the government was bankrupt; mobs demanded the ouster of conservative President Anastasio Bustamante, who had executed the rebellious old revolutionary hero, Vicente Guerrero.

Antonio López de Santa Anna, the ambitious

Buoyed by success, Morelos focused the independence movement in Chilpancingo, organizing the Congress of Anahuac that declared Mexican independence from Spain on November 6, 1813. Continuously threatened by Spanish counterattacks, Morelos successfully kept the Congress of Anahuac intact by moving the delegates, one step ahead of the Spanish troops, to a number of southern Mexico locations. Tragically, Morelos did not live to realize the fruits of his struggle; he was captured and executed by the Spanish in December 1815.

After Morelos's death, his compatriot, Vicente Guerrero, also of African-Mexican descent, continued their hit-and-run war of attrition for five years. In 1821, a new liberal government (which included a new constitutional monarchy) in Spain pulled the rug out from beneath Mexican royalist conservatives, who began to defect to the cause of Mexican independence. The royalist commander in the south, Brigadier Agustín de Itúrbide, asked for a meeting with Guerrero. Guerrero military commander whose troops had defeated an abortive Spanish counterrevolution in Veracruz, issued a *pronunciamiento* against Bustamante; Congress obliged, elevating Santa Anna to "Liberator of the Republic" and naming him president in March 1833.

Santa Anna would pop in and out of the presidency like a jack-in-the-box 10 more times before 1855. First, he foolishly lost Texas to rebellious Anglo settlers in 1836; then he lost his leg (which was buried with full military honors) fighting the emperor of France.

Santa Anna's greatest debacle, however, was to declare war on the United States with just 1,839 pesos in the treasury. With his forces poised to defend Mexico City against a relatively small 10,000-man American invasion force, Santa Anna inexplicably withdrew and the United States Marines surged into the "Halls of Montezuma," Chapultepec Castle, where Mexico's six beloved Niños Héroes cadets fell in the losing cause on September 13, 1847.

In the subsequent treaty of Guadalupe Hidalgo, Mexico lost nearly half of its territory—the present states of New Mexico, Arizona, California, Nevada, Utah, and Colorado—to the United States.

Finally, Mexican leaders decided enough was enough. General Juan Álvarez (the first governor of the new state of Guerrero, founded in 1849) and Ignacio Comonfort denounced Santa Anna; in 1854, in Ayutla, on the Costa Chica, they proposed the Plan de Ayutla to get rid of him. With virtually all of his support eroded, Santa Anna fled into permanent exile in 1855.

REFORM, CIVIL WAR, AND INTERVENTION

While conservatives searched for a king to replace Santa Anna, liberals, led by Supreme Court Chief Justice Benito Juárez, plunged ahead with three controversial reform laws: the Ley Juárez, Ley Lerdo, and Ley Iglesias. These *reformas,* augmented by a new Constitution of 1857, directly attacked the privilege and power of Mexico's landlords, clergy, and generals. They abolished *fueros* (the separate military and church courts), reduced huge landed estates, and stripped the church of its excess property and power.

Conservative generals, priests, *hacendados* (landholders), and their mestizo and *indígena* followers revolted. The resulting War of the Reform (not unlike the U.S. Civil War) ravaged the countryside for three long years. The balance in Guerrero was tilted toward the liberal side by forces of General Juan Álvarez, whose brigades eventually won out over conservative General Miguel Miramón. Finally, the victorious army paraded triumphantly in Mexico City on New Year's Day 1861.

Later that year, at the urging of President Benito Juárez, the federal congress bestowed Mexico's highest honor, of "Benemérito de la Patria," on the old liberal soldier, Juan Álvarez.

Juárez and Maximilian

Benito Juárez, the leading *reformista,* had won the day. Like his contemporary Abraham Lincoln, Juárez, of pure Zapotec native blood, overcame his humble origins to become a lawyer, a champion of justice, and the president who held his country together during a terrible civil war. Like Lincoln, Juárez had little time to savor his triumph.

Imperial France invaded Mexico in January 1862, initiating the bloody five-year imperialist struggle known infamously as the French Intervention. After two costly years, the French pushed Juárez's liberal army into the hills and installed the king that Mexican conservatives thought the country needed. Austrian Archduke Maximilian and his wife, Carlota, the very models of modern Catholic monarchs, were crowned emperor and empress of Mexico in June 1864.

The naive Emperor Maximilian I was surprised that some of his subjects resented his presence. Meanwhile, Juárez refused to yield, stubbornly performing his constitutional duties in a somber black carriage one jump ahead of the French occupying army. The climax came in May 1867, when the liberal forces besieged and defeated Maximilian's army at Querétaro. Juárez, giving no quarter, sternly ordered Maximilian's execution by firing squad on June 19, 1867.

RECONSTRUCTION AND THE PORFIRIATO

Juárez worked day and night at the double task of reconstruction and reform. He won reelection but died, exhausted, in 1872.

The death of Juárez, the stoic partisan of reform, signaled hope to Mexico's conservatives. They soon got their wish: General Don Porfirio Díaz, the "Coming Man," was elected president in 1876.

Pax Porfiriana

Don Porfirio is often remembered wistfully, as old Italians remember Mussolini: "He was a bit rough, but, dammit, at least he made the trains run on time."

Although Porfirio Díaz's humble Oaxaca mestizo origins were not unlike Juárez's, Díaz was not a democrat: When he was a general, his officers took no captives; when he was president, his country police, the *rurales,* shot prisoners in the act of "trying to escape."

Order and Progress, in that sequence, ruled Mexico for 34 years. Foreign investment flowed into the country; new railroads brought the products of shiny factories, mines, and farms to modernized Gulf and Pacific ports. Mexico balanced its budget, repaid foreign debt, and became a respected member of the family of nations.

The human price was high. Don Porfirio allowed more than one hundred million acres—one-fifth of Mexico's land area (including most of the arable land)—to fall into the hands of his friends and foreigners. Poor Mexicans suffered the most. By 1910, 90 percent of the *indígenas* had lost their traditional communal land. In the spring of 1910, a smug, now-cultured and elderly Don Porfirio anticipated with relish the centennial of Hidalgo's Grito de Dolores.

REVOLUTION AND STABILIZATION
¡No Reelección!

Porfirio Díaz himself had first campaigned on the slogan *No Reelección,* which expresses the idea that the president should step down after one term. Although Díaz had stepped down once in 1880, he had gotten himself reelected for 26 consecutive years. In 1910, Francisco I. Madero, a short, squeaky-voiced son of rich landowners, opposed Díaz under the same banner.

Although Díaz had jailed him before the election, Madero refused to quit campaigning. From a safe platform in the United States, he called for a revolution to begin on November 20, 1910.

Villa and Zapata

Not much happened, but soon the millions of poor Mexicans who had been going to bed hungry began to stir. In Chihuahua, followers of Francisco (Pancho) Villa, an erstwhile ranch hand, miner, peddler, and cattle rustler, began attacking the *rurales,* dynamiting railroads, and raiding towns. Meanwhile, in the south, horse trader, farmer, and minor official Emiliano Zapata and his *indígena* guerrillas were terrorizing rich *hacendados* and forcibly recovering stolen ancestral village lands. Zapata's movement gained steam and by May had taken the Morelos state capital, Cuernavaca. Meanwhile, Madero crossed the Río Grande and joined with Villa's forces, who took Ciudad Juárez.

The *federales* (government army troops) began deserting in droves, and on May 25, 1911, Díaz submitted his resignation.

As Madero's deputy, General Victoriano Huerta, put Díaz on his ship of exile in Veracruz, Díaz confided, "Madero has unleashed a tiger. Now let's see if he can control it."

The Fighting Continues

Emiliano Zapata, it turned out, was the tiger Madero had unleashed. Meeting with Madero in Mexico City, Zapata fumed over Madero's go-slow approach to the "agrarian problem," as Madero termed it. By November, Zapata had denounced Madero. "*¡Tierra y Libertad!*" ("Land and Liberty!") the Zapatistas cried, as Madero's support faded. The army in Mexico City rebelled; Huerta forced Madero to resign on February 18, 1913, and then murdered him four days later.

The rum-swilling Huerta ruled like a Chicago mobster; general rebellion, led by the "Big Four"—Villa, Alvaro Obregón, and Venustiano Carranza in the north, and Zapata in the south—soon broke out. Pressed by the rebels and refused U.S. recognition, Huerta fled into exile in July 1914.

Fighting sputtered on for three years as authority see-sawed between revolutionary factions. Finally Carranza, whose forces ended up controlling most of the country by 1917, got a convention together in Querétaro to formulate political and social goals. The resulting Constitution of 1917, while restating most ideas of the Reformistas' 1857 constitution, additionally prescribed a single four-year presidential term, labor reform, and subordinated private ownership to public interest. Every village had a right to communal *ejido* land, and subsoil wealth could never be sold away to the highest bidder.

The Constitution of 1917 was a revolutionary expression of national aspirations and, in retrospect, represented a social and political agenda for the entire 20th century. In modified form, it has lasted to the present day.

Obregón Stabilizes Mexico

On December 1, 1920, General Alvaro Obregón legally assumed the presidency of a Mexico still bleeding from 10 years of civil war. Although a seasoned revolutionary, Obregón was also a pragmatist who recognized peace was necessary to implement the goals of the revolution. In four years, his government pacified local uprisings, disarmed a swarm of warlords, executed hundreds of *bandidos,* obtained U.S. diplomatic recognition, assuaged the worst fears of the clergy and landowners, and began land reform.

All this set the stage for the work of Plutarco Elías Calles, Obregón's Minister of Gobernación (Interior) and handpicked successor, who won the 1924 election. Aided by peace, Mexico returned to a semblance of prosperity. Calles brought the army under civilian control, balanced the budget, and shifted Mexico's so-

cial revolution into high gear. New clinics vaccinated millions against smallpox, new dams irrigated thousands of previously dry acres, and campesinos received millions of acres of redistributed land.

By single-mindedly enforcing the pro-agrarian, pro-labor, and anti-clerical articles of the 1917 constitution, Calles made many influential enemies. Infuriated by the government's confiscation of church property, closing of monasteries, and deportation of hundreds of foreign priests and nuns, the clergy refused to perform marriages, baptisms, and last rites. As members of the Cristero movement, militant Catholics crying *"¡Viva Cristo Rey!"* armed themselves, torching public schools and government property and murdering hundreds of innocent bystanders.

Simultaneously, Calles threatened foreign oil companies, demanding they exchange their titles for 50-year leases. A moderate Mexican supreme court decision over the oil issue and the skillful arbitration of American ambassador Dwight Morrow smoothed over both the oil and church troubles by the end of Calles's term.

Calles, who started out brimming with revolutionary fervor and populist zeal, became increasingly conservative and dictatorial. Although he bowed out peaceably in favor of Obregón (the constitution had been amended to allow one six-year nonsuccessive term), Obregón was assassinated two weeks after his election in 1928. Calles continued to rule for six more years through three puppet-presidents: Emilio Portes Gil (1928–1930), Pascual Ortíz Rubio (1930–1932), and Abelardo Rodríguez (1932–1934).

For the 14 years since 1920, the revolution had first waxed, then waned. With a cash surplus in 1930, Mexico skidded into debt as the Great Depression deepened and Calles and his cronies lined their pockets. In blessing his minister of war, General Lázaro Cárdenas, for the 1934 presidential election, Calles expected more of the same.

Lázaro Cárdenas, President of the People

The 40-year-old Cárdenas, former governor of

Michoacán, immediately set his own agenda, however. He worked tirelessly to fulfill the social prescriptions of the revolution. As morning-coated diplomats fretted, waiting in his outer office, Cárdenas ushered in delegations of campesinos and factory workers and sympathetically listened to their petitions.

In his six years of rule, Cárdenas moved public education and health forward on a broad front, supported strong labor unions, and redistributed 49 million acres of farmland, more than any president before or since.

Cárdenas's resolute enforcement of the constitution's Artículo 123 brought him the most renown. Under this pro-labor law, the government turned over a host of private companies to employee ownership and, on March 18, 1938, expropriated all foreign oil corporations.

In retrospect the oil corporations, most of which were British, were not blameless. They had sorely neglected the wages, health, and welfare of their workers while ruthlessly taking the law into their own hands with private police forces. Although Standard Oil cried foul, U.S. President Franklin Roosevelt did not intervene. Through negotiation and due process, the U.S. companies eventually were compensated with $24 million, plus interest. In the wake of the expropriation, President Cárdenas created Petróleos Mexicanos (Pemex), the national oil corporation that continues to run all Mexican oil and gas operations.

Manuel Avila Camacho

Manuel Avila Camacho, elected in 1940, was the last general to be president of Mexico. His administration ushered in a gradual shift of Mexican politics, government, and foreign policy as Mexico allied itself with the U.S. cause during World War II. Foreign tourism, initially promoted by the Cárdenas administration, ballooned. Good feelings surged as Franklin Roosevelt became the first U.S. president to officially cross the Río Grande when he met with Camacho in Monterrey in April 1943.

In both word and deed, moderation and evolution guided President Camacho's policies. *"Soy creente"* ("I am a believer"), he declared to the Catholics of Mexico as he worked earnestly to bridge Mexico's serious church–state schism. Land-policy emphasis shifted from redistribution to utilization as new dams and canals irrigated hundreds of thousands of previously arid acres. On one hand, Camacho established IMSS (Instituto Mexicano de Seguro Social) and on the other, trimmed the power of labor unions.

As World War II moved toward its 1945 conclusion, both the United States and Mexico were enjoying the benefits of four years of governmental and military cooperation and mutual trade in the form of a mountain of strategic minerals that had moved north in exchange for a similar mountain of U.S. manufactures that moved south.

CONTEMPORARY MEXICO
The Mature Revolution

During the decades after World War II, beginning with moderate President Miguel Alemán (1946–1952), Mexican politicians gradually honed their skills of consensus and compromise as their middle-aged revolution bubbled along under liberal presidents and sputtered haltingly under conservatives. Doctrine required of all politicians, regardless of stripe, that they be "revolutionary" enough to be included beneath the banner of the PRI (Partido Revolucionario Institucional), Mexico's dominant political party.

Mexico's revolution hasn't been very revolutionary about women's rights, however. The PRI didn't get around to giving Mexican women, millions of whom fought and died during the revolution, the right to vote until 1953.

Adolfo Ruíz Cortínes, Alemán's secretary of the interior, was elected overwhelmingly in 1952. He fought the corruption that had crept into government under his predecessor, continued land reform, increased agricultural production, constructed new ports, eradicated malaria, and built a number of automobile assembly plants.

Women, voting for the first time in a national election, kept the PRI in power by electing

The Ayuntamiento Municipal, also known as the Presidencia Municipal, is the Mexican equivalent of a city or town hall in the U.S. and Canada.

liberal Adolfo López Mateos in 1958. Resembling Lázaro Cárdenas in social policy, López Mateos redistributed 40 million acres of farmland, forced automakers to use 60 percent domestic components, built thousands of new schools, and distributed hundreds of millions of new textbooks. *"La electricidad es nuestra"* ("Electricity is ours"), Mateos declared as he nationalized foreign power companies in 1962.

Despite his left-leaning social agenda, unions were restive under López Mateos. Protesting inflation, workers struck; the government retaliated, arresting Demetrios Vallejo, the railway union head, and renowned muralist David Siqueiros, former communist party secretary.

Troubles notwithstanding, López Mateos climaxed his presidency gracefully in 1964 as he opened the celebrated National Museum of Anthropology, appropriately located in Chapultepec Park, where the Aztecs had first settled 20 generations earlier.

In 1964, as several times before, the outgoing president's interior secretary succeeded his former chief. Dour, conservative Gustavo Díaz Ordaz immediately clashed with liberals, labor, and students. The pot boiled over just before the 1968 Mexico City Olympics. Reacting to a student rebellion, the army occupied the National University; shortly afterward, on October 2, government forces opened fire with machine guns on a downtown protest, killing and wounding hundreds of demonstrators.

Maquiladoras

Despite its serious internal troubles, Mexico's relations with the United States were cordial. President Lyndon Johnson visited and unveiled a statue of Abraham Lincoln in Mexico City. Later, Díaz Ordaz met with President Richard Nixon in Acapulco.

Meanwhile, bilateral negotiations produced the Border Industrialization Program. Within a 12-mile strip south of the U.S.–Mexico border, foreign companies could assemble duty-free parts into finished goods and export them without any duties on either side. Within a

© BRUCE WHIPPERMAN

dozen years, a swarm of such plants, called maquiladoras, were humming as hundreds of thousands of Mexican workers assembled and exported billions of dollars worth of shiny consumer goods—electronics, clothes, furniture, pharmaceuticals, and toys—worldwide.

Concurrently, in Mexico's interior, Díaz Ordaz pushed Mexico's industrialization ahead full steam. Foreign money financed hundreds of new plants and factories. Primary among these was the giant Las Truchas steel plant at the new industrial port and town of Lázaro Cárdenas at the Pacific mouth of the Río Balsas, at the western border of the Acapulco region.

Discovery, in 1974, of gigantic new oil and gas reserves along Mexico's Gulf coast added fuel to Mexico's already rapid industrial expansion. During the late 1970s and early 1980s billions in foreign investment, lured by Mexico's oil earnings, financed other major developments—factories, hotels, power plants, roads, airports—all over the country.

Economic Trouble of the 1980s

The negative side to these expensive projects was the huge dollar debt required to finance them. President Luis Echeverría Alvarez (1970–1976), diverted by his interest in international affairs, passed Mexico's burgeoning financial deficit to his successor, José López Portillo. As feared by some experts, a world petroleum glut during the early 1980s burst Mexico's ballooning oil bubble and plunged the country into financial crisis. When the 1982 interest came due on its foreign debt, Mexico's largest holding company couldn't pay the $2.3 billion owed. The peso plummeted more than fivefold, to 150 per U.S. dollar. At the same time, prices doubled every year.

But by the mid-1980s, President Miguel de la Madrid (1982–1988) was straining to get Mexico's economic house in order. He sliced government and raised taxes, asking rich and poor alike to tighten their belts. Despite getting foreign bankers to reschedule Mexico's debt, de la Madrid couldn't stop inflation. Prices skyrocketed as the peso deflated to 2,500 per U.S.

dollar, becoming one of the world's most devalued currencies by 1988.

Salinas de Gortari and NAFTA

Public disgust led to significant opposition during the 1988 presidential election. Billionaire PAN (National Action Party) candidate Michael Clothier and liberal National Democratic Front candidate Cuauhtémoc Cárdenas ran against the PRI's Harvard-educated technocrat Carlos Salinas de Gortari. The vote was split so evenly that all three candidates claimed victory. Although Salinas eventually won the election, his showing, barely half of the vote, was the worst ever for a PRI president.

Salinas nevertheless climaxed his presidency by negotiating the North American Free Trade Agreement (NAFTA) with U.S. President George Bush and Canadian Prime Minister Brian Mulrooney in 1992.

But, on the very day in early January 1994 that NAFTA took effect, rebellion broke out in the poor, remote state of Chiapas. A small but well-disciplined campesino force, calling itself Ejército Zapatista Liberación Nacional (Zapatista National Liberation Army or EZLN), or "Zapatistas," captured a number of provincial towns and held the former governor of Chiapas hostage.

To further complicate matters, while Salinas de Gortari's chief negotiator, Manuel Camacho Solís, was attempting to iron out a settlement with the Zapatista rebels, Luis Donaldo Colosio, Salinas's handpicked successor, was gunned down just months before the August balloting. However, instead of disintegrating, the nation united in grief; opposition candidates eulogized their fallen former opponent and later earnestly welcomed his replacement, stolid technocrat Ernesto Zedillo, in Mexico's first presidential election debate.

In a closely watched election relatively unmarred by irregularities, Zedillo piled up a solid plurality against his PAN and PRD opponents. By perpetuating the PRI's 65-year hold on the presidency, the electorate had again opted for the PRI's familiar although imperfect middle-aged revolution.

New Crisis, New Recovery

Zedillo, however, had little time to savor his victory. The peso, after having been pumped up a thousand-fold by Salinas's free and easy monetary policies, crashed, losing half of its value in the few months around Christmas 1994. Mexican financial institutions were in danger of defaulting on their obligations to international investors. To stave off a worldwide financial panic, U.S. President Clinton, in February 1995, secured an unprecedented multi-billion dollar loan package for Mexico.

Although disaster was temporarily averted, the cure for the country's ills was another painful round of inflation and belt-tightening for poor Mexicans. During 1995, inflation soared, wages dropped, and malnutrition soared sixfold, while Third-World diseases, such as cholera and dengue fever, resurged in the countryside.

Meanwhile, as negotiations with the rebel Zapatistas sputtered on and off in Chiapas, popular discontent erupted in Guerrero, leading to the massacre of 17 unarmed campesinos at Aguas Blancas, in the hills west of Acapulco, by state police in June 1995. One year later, at a demonstration protesting the massacre, a new, well-armed revolutionary group, Ejército Popular Revolucionario (People's Revolutionary Army, or EPR), appeared. A few months later, EPR guerrillas killed two dozen police and soldiers at several locations, mostly in southwestern Mexico. Although President Zedillo's immediate reaction was moderate, platoons of soldiers were soon scouring rural Guerrero, Oaxaca, Michoacán, and other states, searching homes and arresting suspected dissidents. Public response was mostly negative, though some locals felt that they were far better off in the hands of the army than those of state or federal police.

Mexican democracy got a much-needed boost when notorious Guerrero governor Ruben Figueroa, who had tried to cover up the Aguas Blancas massacre with a bogus video-tape, was forced from office. At the same time, the Zedillo government gained momentum in addressing the Zapatistas' grievances in Chiapas, even as it decreased federal military presence, built new rural electrification networks, and refurbished health clinics.

Moreover, Mexico's economy began to improve. By mid-1996, inflation had slowed to a 20 percent annual rate, investment dollars were flowing back into Mexico, the peso had stabilized at about 7.5 to the U.S. dollar, and Mexico had paid back half the borrowed U.S. bailout money.

Economic Recovery and Political Reforms

The best news for which the Zedillo administration could justly claim credit was the dramatically improving national economy. By mid-1998, annual inflation had dropped below 15 percent, investment dollars continued to pour into Mexico, the peso was stable at about 8 to the U.S. dollar, and Mexico had paid back every penny of the money from the 1995 U.S. bailout.

Moreover, in the political arena, although the justice system generally left much to be desired, a pair of unprecedented events signaled an increasingly open political system. In the 1997 congressional elections, voters elected a host of opposition candidates, depriving the PRI of an absolute congressional majority for the first time since 1929. A year later, in early 1998, Mexicans were participating in their country's first primary elections—in which voters, instead of politicians, chose party candidates.

Although President Zedillo had had a rough ride, he entered the twilight of his 1994–2000 term able to take credit for an improved economy, some genuine political reforms, and relative peace in the countryside. The election of 2000 revealed, however, that the Mexican people were not satisfied.

End of an Era: Vicente Fox Unseats the PRI

During 1998 and 1999 the focal point of

opposition to the PRI's three-generation rule had been shifting from lackluster left-of-center Cuauhtémoc Cárdenas to relative newcomer Vicente Fox, former president of Coca-Cola Mexico and clean former PAN governor of Guanajuato.

Fox, who had announced his candidacy for president two years before the election, seemed an unlikely challenger. After all, the minority PAN had always been the party of wealthy businessmen and the conservative Catholic right. But blunt-talking, six-foot-five Fox, who sometimes campaigned in cowboy boots and a ten-gallon hat, preached populist themes of coalition building and "inclusion." He backed up his talk by carrying his campaign to hard-scrabble city *barrios,* dirt-poor country villages, and traditional outsider groups, such as Jews.

Meanwhile, as the campaign heated up in early 2000, PRI candidate Francisco Labastida, ex–Interior Secretary and governor of the drug-plagued state of Sinaloa, sounded the usual PRI themes to gatherings of party loyalists. At the same time, dour PRD liberal Cuauhtémoc Cárdenas, resigning from a mediocre term as mayor of Mexico City, faded to a weak third place.

In a closely monitored election on July 2, 2000, Fox decisively defeated Labastida, 42 percent to 38 percent, while Cárdenas received only 17 percent. Fox's win also swept a PAN plurality (223/209/57) into the 500-seat Chamber of Deputies lower house (although the Senate remained PRI-dominated).

Nevertheless, in removing the PRI from the all-powerful presidency after 71 consecutive years of domination, Fox had ushered Mexico into a new, much more Democratic era.

Despite stinging criticism from his own ranks, President Zedillo, who historians were already judging as the real hero behind the new democratic era, made an unprecedented, early appeal, less than a week after the election, for all Mexicans to unite behind Fox.

On the eve of his December 1 inauguration, Mexicans awaited Fox's speech with hopeful anticipation. He did not disappoint them.

Although acknowledging that he couldn't reverse 71 years of PRI entrenchment in one six-year term, he vowed to ride the crest of reform, revamp the tax system, and reduce poverty by 30 percent, by creating a million new jobs a year through new private investment in electricity and oil production and by forming a new common market with Latin America, the United States, and Canada.

He promised, moreover, to secure Mexican democracy by a much-needed reform of police, the federal attorney general, and the army. Perhaps most difficult of all, Fox called for the formation of an unprecedented "Transparency Commission" to investigate a generation of past grievances, including the 1968 massacre of student demonstrators and assassinations of, among others, a Roman Catholic cardinal in 1993 and a presidential candidate in 1994.

Vicente Fox, President of Mexico

Wasting little time getting started, President Fox first headed to Chiapas to confer with indigenous community leaders. Along the way, he shut down Chiapas military bases and removed dozens of military roadblocks. Back in Mexico City, he sent the long-delayed peace plan, including the indigenous bill of rights, to Congress. Zapatista rebels responded by journeying en masse from Chiapas to Mexico City, where, in their black masks, they addressed Congress, arguing for indigenous rights. Although by mid-2001, Congress had passed a modified version of the negotiated settlement, and the majority of states had ratified the required constitutional amendment, indigenous leaders condemned the legislation plan as watered down and unacceptable, while proponents claimed it was the best possible compromise between the Zapatistas' demands and the existing Mexican constitution.

On the positive side, by mid-2002, Vicente Fox could claim credit for cracking down on corruption and putting drug lords in jail, negotiating a key immigration agreement with the United States, keeping the peso stable, clamping down on inflation, and attracting a record pile of foreign investment dollars.

Furthermore, Fox continued to pry open the door to democracy in Mexico. In May 2002, he signed Mexico's first freedom of information act, entitling citizens to timely copies of all public documents from federal agencies. Moreover, Fox's long-promised "Transparency Commission" was taking shape. In July 2002, federal attorneys were taking unprecedented action. They were questioning a list of 74 former government officials, including ex-President Luis Echeverría, about their roles in government transgressions, notably political murders and the University of Mexico massacres during the 1960s and 1970s.

But, Mexico's economy, reflecting the U.S. economic slowdown, began to sour in 2001, losing half a million jobs and cutting annual growth to 2.5 percent, down from the 4.5 percent that the government had predicted. Furthermore, a so-called "Towelgate" furor (in which aides had purchased dozens of $400 towels for the presidential mansion) weakened Fox's squeaky-clean image.

In the July 7, 2003, congressional elections, voters took their frustrations out on the PAN and gave its plurality in the Chamber of Deputies to the PRI. When the dust settled, the PRI total had risen to 225 seats, while the PAN had slipped to 153. The biggest winner, however, was the PRD, which gained more than 40 seats, to a total of about 100.

Fortunately, however, by 2004 the Mexican economy, reflecting that of the United States, was beginning to turn around. Exports to the United States soared to record levels in the spring of 2004.

In early 2005, reflecting Vicente Fox's victory in 2000, democracy got a big boost in Guerrero as voters broke the PRI's 76-year lock-grip on the governorship and state legislature. On February 6, 2005, voters swept the liberal populist PRD African-Mexican former mayor of Acapulco, Carlos Zeferino Torreblanca, into the governor's office. In doing so, voters have expressed high hopes that can-do Zeferino will lead Guerrero into a fresh new era of good government.

By late 2005, despite only modest gains and with his term nearly spent, critics were increasingly claiming that Vicente Fox was a lame-duck president who had run out of time to accomplish what he promised. But Fox, despite a hostile congress that almost continuously blocked his legislative proposals, could claim some significant accomplishments. During his first five years, he had pushed through significant gains in indigenous rights, national reconciliation and government transparency, drug enforcement, U.S.–Mexico immigration policy, social security reform, housing, and education. Moreover, in addition to nurturing a recovering economy, no one could deny that Fox had kept exports robust, the peso strong against the dollar, and had clamped the lid on inflation.

So, by early 2006, although many Mexican men and women in the street had mostly given up on Fox's promises to re-make the economy and political system, most still believed that unseating the PRI was good for Mexico, and acknowledged that even Fox couldn't be expected to completely undo in six years what 71 years of PRI dominance had created.

Economy and Government

THE MEXICAN AND GUERRERO ECONOMIES
Post-Revolutionary Gains

By many measures, Mexico's 20th-century revolution appears to have succeeded. Since 1910, illiteracy has plunged tenfold from 80 to 8 percent, life expectancy has risen from 30 years to more than 70, infant mortality has dropped from a whopping 40 percent to about 2 percent, and, in terms of caloric intake, Mexicans are eating about twice as much as their forebears at the turn of the 20th century.

Decades of steady economic growth account for rising Mexican living standards. The Mexican economy has repeatedly rebounded from recessions by virtue of its plentiful natural resources, notably oil and metals; diversified manufacturing, such as cars, electronics, and petrochemicals; steadily increasing tourism; exports of fruits, vegetables, and cattle; and its large, willing, low-wage workforce.

Recent Mexican governments, moreover, have skillfully exploited Mexico's economic strengths. The Border Industrialization Program has led to millions of jobs in thousands of border maquiladora factories, from Tijuana and the mouth of the Río Grande, now spreading to interior centers such as Monterrey, Guadalajara, and Mexico City. The increased manufacturing output has produced manifold economic benefits, including reduced dependency on oil exports, burgeoning job growth and foreign trade as Mexico joined in the General Agreement on Tariffs and Trade (GATT) in 1986 and NAFTA in 1994. Consequently, Mexico has become a net exporter of goods and services to the United States, its largest trading partner. Although Mexico suffered a peso collapse of about 70 percent (in relation to the U.S. dollar) during the mid-1990s, the Zedillo administration acted quickly. Belt-tightening measures brought inflation down to 10 percent per year and restored the flow of foreign investment back into Mexico by the late 1990s.

In 2000, the new Fox administration continued its predecessor's prudent economic course, which has further reduced inflation to a healthy low of about 4 percent during 2004

Whole chickens cost about $6 in Mexico.

© BRUCE WHIPPERMAN

and 2005 and stabilized the peso at between 10 and 11 per dollar for the entire five-year (2000–2005) period. And despite the 2001–2003 U.S.–Mexican economic slowdown that decreased demand for Mexican products (and consequently wiped out many hundreds of thousands of Mexican jobs), the economy had recovered to a healthy 4 percent growth rate and (consequent robust job growth) during 2004 and 2005.

Guerrero Economic Challenges

Many of Mexico's latter 20th-century economic gains have bypassed Mexico's poor southern states of Chiapas, Oaxaca, and Guerrero. Of the three, Guerrero perennially ranks low in most indicators of quality of life, such as income, infant mortality, malnutrition, and illiteracy.

Although rich in sunshine, mountainous Guerrero lacks arable land and needs more water and capital to irrigate what arable land exists. Under the right conditions, bountiful crops of sesame, corn, tomatoes, citrus, mangoes, peanuts, alfalfa, soy, and *chiles* sprout quickly from bottomland fields.

A potentially valuable crop in Guerrero is coffee, now cultivated by thousands of farmers in the vine-draped lower slopes of the coastal mountains. However, as all over the developing world, growing a crop is the easiest part of trying to make a living from it. Isolation, quality control, and access to markets have kept Guerrero coffee farmers poor. To make matters even worse, the bottom has fallen out of worldwide coffee prices during recent years. It seems patently unjust that farmers can get only about $0.50 per pound for the same coffee that, after transport and roasting, sells in United States and European grocery stores for $6 or $7 per pound.

The bright part of the Guerrero economy is tourism, which accounts, both directly and indirectly, for most of the earnings of half of Guerrero families. If it weren't for the resorts of Acapulco, Ixtapa, Zihuatanejo, and Taxco, most Guerrero people would be even poorer than they are now.

© BRUCE WHIPPERMAN

A skilled laborer, such as this mason, makes about US$10 per day.

But, reason for hope exists. In 2000 the Mexican government launched a renewable six-year investment strategy, Development Plan for the Mexican South, which provides money for irrigation, education, roads, utilities, telecommunications, and more, with an eye toward lifting the economies of Guerrero and its poor neighboring states closer to those of the rest of Mexico.

Long-Term Economic Challenges

Despite huge gains, Mexico's Revolution of 1910 is nevertheless incomplete. Improved public health, education, income, and opportunity have barely outdistanced Mexico's population, which has increased nearly sevenfold—from 15 million to 106 million—between 1910 and 2005. For example, although the illiteracy rate has decreased, the actual number of Mexican people who can't read, about 10 million, has remained about constant since 1910.

Moreover, the land reform program, once thought to be a Mexican cure-all, has long been a disappointment. The *ejidos* of which Emiliano Zapata dreamed have become mostly symbolic. The fields are typically small and unirrigated. Furthermore, *ejido* land, being communal, is not easily accepted by banks as loan collateral. Capital for irrigation networks, fertilizers, and harvesting machines is consequently lacking. Communal farms are typically inefficient; the average Mexican field produces about *one-quarter* as much corn per acre as a U.S. farm. Mexico must accordingly use its precious oil-dollar surplus to import millions of tons of corn—originally indigenous to Mexico—annually.

The triple scourge of overpopulation, lack of arable land, and low farm income has driven millions of campesino families to seek better lives in Mexico's cities and the United States. Since 1910, Mexico has evolved from a largely rural country, where 70 percent of the population lived on farms, to an urban nation where 70 percent of the population lives in cities. Fully one-fifth of Mexico's people now live in Mexico City.

Nevertheless, the future appears bright for many privately owned and managed Mexican farms, concentrated largely in the northern border states. Exceptionally productive, they typically work hundreds or thousands of irrigated acres of crops, such as tomatoes, lettuce, *chiles,* wheat, corn, tobacco, cotton, fruits, alfalfa, chickens, hogs, and cattle, just like their counterparts across the border in California, New Mexico, Arizona, and Texas.

Staples—wheat for bread, corn for tortillas, milk, and cooking oil—are all imported and consequently expensive for the typical working-class Mexican family, which must spend half or more of its income (typically $400 per month) for food. Recent inflation has compounded the problem, particularly for the millions of families on the bottom half of Mexico's economic ladder.

Although average gross domestic product figures for Mexico—about $10,000 per capita (much less for Guerrero) compared to about $40,000 for the United States—place it above nearly all other developing countries, averages, when applied to Mexico, mean little. A primary socioeconomic reality of Mexican history

remains: the richest one-fifth of Mexican families earns about 10 times the income of the poorest one-fifth. A relative handful of people own a large hunk of Mexico, and they don't seem inclined to share much of it with the less fortunate. As for the poor, the typical Mexican family in the bottom one-third income bracket often owns neither car nor refrigerator, and the children typically do not finish elementary school.

GOVERNMENT AND POLITICS
The Constitution of 1917

Mexico's governmental system is rooted in the Constitution of 1917, which incorporated many of the features of its reformist predecessor of 1857. The 1917 document, with amendments, remains in force. Although drafted at the behest of conservative revolutionary Venustiano Carranza by his handpicked Querétaro "Constitucionalista" congress, it was greatly influenced by liberal Álvaro Obregón and generally ignored by Carranza during his subsequent three-year presidential term.

Although many articles resemble those of its U.S. model, the Constitution of 1917 contains provisions that stem directly from Mexican experience. Article 27 addresses the question of land. Private property rights are qualified by societal need; subsoil rights are public property, and foreigners and corporations are severely restricted in land ownership. Although the 1917 constitution declared *ejido* land inviolate, 1994 amendments allow, under certain circumstances, the sale or use of communal land as loan security.

Article 23 severely restricts church powers. In declaring that "places of worship are the property of the nation," it stripped churches of all title to real estate, without compensation. Article 5 and Article 130 banned religious missionary orders, expelled foreign clergy, and denied priests and ministers all political rights, including voting, holding office, and even criticizing the government.

Article 123 establishes the rights of labor: to organize, bargain collectively, strike, work a maximum eight-hour day, and receive a minimum wage. Women are to receive equal pay for equal work and be given a month's paid leave for childbearing. Article 123 also establishes social security plans for sickness, unemployment, pensions, and death.

On paper, Mexico's constitutional government structures appear much like their U.S. prototypes: a federal presidency, a two-house Congress, and a Supreme Court, with their counterparts in each of the 32 states. Political parties field candidates, and all citizens vote by secret ballot.

Mexico's presidents, however, have traditionally enjoyed greater powers than their U.S. counterparts. They need not seek legislative approval for many cabinet appointments, can suspend constitutional rights under a state of siege, can initiate legislation, veto all or parts of bills, refuse to execute laws, and replace state officers. The federal government, moreover, retains nearly all taxing authority, relegating the states to a role of merely administering federal programs.

Although ideally providing for separation of powers, the Constitution of 1917 subordinates both the legislative and judicial branches, with the courts being the weakest of all. The Supreme Court, for example, can only, with repeated deliberation, decide upon the constitutionality of legislation. Five separate individuals must file successful petitions for writs *amparo* (protection) on a single point of law to affect constitutional precedent.

Democratizing Mexican and Guerrero Politics

Reforms in Mexico's stable but top-heavy "Institutional Revolution" came only gradually. Characteristically, street protests were brutally put down at first, with officials only later working to address grievances. Generations of dominance by the PRI, the "Institutional Revolutionary Party," led to widespread cynicism and citizen apathy. Regardless of who gets elected, the typical person on the street used to say, the officeholder was bound to retire with his or her pockets full.

Nevertheless, by 1985, movement toward more justice and pluralism seemed be in store for Mexico. During the subsequent dozen years, minority parties increasingly elected candidates to state and federal office. Although none captured a majority of any state legislature, the strongest non-PRI parties, such as the conservative pro-Catholic Partido Acción Nacional (PAN, National Action Party) and the liberal-left Partido Revolucionario Democratico (PRD), elected governors. In 1986, minority parties were given federal legislative seats, up to a maximum of 20, for winning a minimum of 2.5 percent of the national presidential vote. In the 1994 election, minority parties received public campaign financing, depending upon their fraction of the vote.

After his 1994 inaugural address, in which he called loudly and clearly for more reforms, President Ernesto Zedillo quickly began to produce results. He immediately appointed a respected member of the PAN opposition party as attorney general—the first non-PRI cabinet appointment in Mexican history. Other Zedillo firsts were federal Senate confirmation of both Supreme Court nominees and the attorney general, multiparty participation in the Chiapas peace negotiations, and congressional approval of the 1995 financial assistance package received from the United States. Zedillo, moreover, organized a series of precedent-setting meetings with opposition leaders that led to a written pact for political reform and the establishment of permanent working groups to discuss political and economic questions.

Perhaps most important was Zedillo's campaign and inaugural vow to separate both his government and himself from PRI decision-making. He kept his promise, becoming the first Mexican president, in as long as anyone could remember, who did not choose his successor.

A New Mexican Revolution

Finally, in 2000, like a Mexican Gorbachev, Ernesto Zedillo, the man responsible for many of Mexico's earlier democratic reforms, watched as PAN opposition reformer Vicente Fox swept Zedillo's PRI from the presidency after a 71-year rule. Moreover, despite severe criticism from his own party, Zedillo quickly called for the country to close ranks behind Fox. Millions of Mexicans, still dazed but buoyed by Zedillo's statesmanship and Fox's epoch-making victory, eagerly awaited Fox's inauguration address on December 1, 2000.

He promised nothing less than a new revolution for Mexico and backed it up with concrete proposals: reduce poverty by 30 percent with a million new jobs a year from revitalized new electricity and oil production, a Mexican Silicon Valley, and free trade between Mexico, all of Latin America, and the United States and Canada. He promised justice for all, through a reformed police, army, and the judiciary. He promised conciliation and an agreement with the Zapatista rebel movement in the south, including a bill of rights for Mexico's native peoples.

But five years later, in early 2006, with his grand vision only fractionally fulfilled, no one can fairly say that Vicente Fox didn't try. Like few, if any, Mexican presidents before him, he remained true to his belief in a democratic presidency: negotiating, haranguing, cajoling, and compromising with a cadre of legislators who stubbornly blocked nearly all of his reform proposals.

Time and again Vicente Fox admitted the messiness and difficulty of the Democratic process. But he also remained convinced and committed to the belief that there could be no turning from the democratic path for Mexico. In a 2004 interview, he pointed out that, at least, he had ended "Presidencialismo," the decades-old Mexican habit of bowing to a strong, even sometimes ruthless, president. And perhaps that is how historians will remember Vicente Fox. Maybe they will remember him as the president who with courage and honesty truly did begin a New Mexican Revolution, by earnestly leading his country along the difficult but true path to a more just and prosperous future for all Mexicans.

People

Let a broad wooden chopping block represent Mexico; imagine hacking it with a sharp cleaver until it is grooved and pocked. That fractured surface resembles Mexico's central highlands, where most Mexicans, divided from each other by high mountains and yawning *barrancas,* have lived since before history.

The Mexicans' deep divisions, in large measure, led to their downfall at the hands of the Spanish conquistadores. The Aztec empire that Hernán Cortés conquered was a vast but fragmented collection of tribes. Speaking more than 100 mutually alien languages, those original Mexicans viewed each other suspiciously, as barely human barbarians from strange lands beyond the mountains. And even today the lines Mexicans draw between themselves—of caste, class, race, wealth—are the result, to a significant degree, of the realities of their mutual isolation.

POPULATION

The Spanish colonial government and the Roman Catholic religion provided the glue that through 400 years has welded Mexico's fragmented people into a burgeoning nation-state. Mexico's population, nearly 100 million by the year 2000, increased during the previous decade, but at a rate diminished to about half that of previous decades. Increased birth control and emigration largely account for the slowdown.

Mexico's population has not always been increasing. Historians estimate that European diseases, largely measles and smallpox, wiped out as many as 25 million—perhaps 95 percent—of the *indígena* population within a few generations after Cortés stepped ashore in 1519. The Mexican population dwindled from an estimated 20 million at the eve of the conquest to a mere one million inhabitants by 1600. It wasn't until 1950, four centuries after Cortés, that Mexico's population recovered to its preconquest level of about 20 million.

Mestizos, Indígenas, Criollos, and African Mexicans

Although by 1950 Mexico's population had recovered, it was completely transformed. The mestizo, a Spanish-speaking person of mixed blood, had replaced the pure Native Mexican, the *indígena* (een-DEE-hay-nah), as the typical Mexican.

The trend continues. Perhaps three of four Mexicans would identify themselves as mestizo, that class whose part-European blood elevates them, in the Mexican mind, to the level of *gente de razón* (people of "reason" or "right"). And there's the rub. The *indígenas* (or, mistakenly but much more commonly, Indians), by the usual measurements of income, health, or education, squat at the bottom of the Mexican social ladder.

The typical *indígena* family lives in a small adobe house in a remote valley, subsisting on corn, beans, and vegetables from its small, unirrigated *milpa*. They usually have chickens, a few pigs, and sometimes a cow, but no electricity; their few hundred dollars a year in cash income isn't enough to buy even a small refrigerator, much less a truck.

The usual *mestizo* family, on the other hand, enjoys most of the benefits of the 21st century. They typically own a modest concrete house in town. Their furnishings, simple by developed-world standards, will often include an electric refrigerator, washing machine, propane stove, television, and car or truck. The children go to school every day, and the eldest son sometimes looks forward to college.

MEXICAN NAMES

Foreign visitors, confounded by long handles such as Doña Juana María López de Díaz, wonder how Mexican names got so complicated.

The preceding Doña Juana example is especially complicated because it's a typical women's name, and women's names are generally more complex than typical men's names.

So, let's explain a man's name first. Take the national hero, Vicente Ramón Guerrero Saldaña. Vicente is his first given name; Ramón, the second given name, corresponding to the "middle" name in the United States. The third, Guerrero, is customarily the father's first surname, and the last, Saldaña, his mother's first surname. Only on formal occasions are men referred to with all four of their names. Simply Vicente Guerrero would do most of the time.

Now, back to Doña Juana. I threw a curve at you by introducing "Doña." It's an honorific, used as "Dame," for a distinguished woman. ("Don" is the corresponding honorific for Spanish men.)

So, skipping the honorific, women's names start out like men's: first given name, Juana; second given name, María, and father's first surname, López.

Now, things get more complicated. For unmarried women, the naming is the same as for men. But when a woman gets married, she customarily replaces her second surname with her husband's first surname, preceded by "de," meaning "of." So in the example, Juana is evidently a married woman, who has substituted "de Díaz" (her husband's first surname being Díaz) for her second surname, all adding up to "Juana María López de Díaz."

Thankfully, however, informal names for women also are simplified. Juana, above, would ordinary shorten her name to her first given name, followed by her husband's first surname: simply Juana Díaz.

All of the above notwithstanding, many Mexican women do not go along with this male-dominated system at all and simply use their maiden names as they were known before they were married.

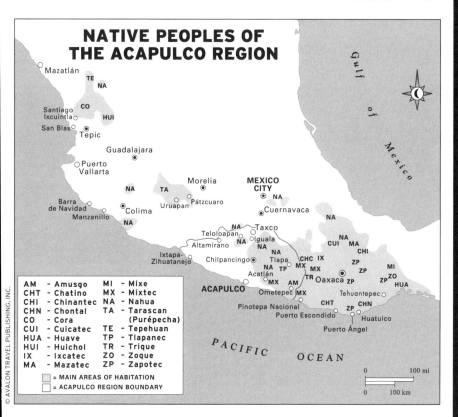

NATIVE PEOPLES OF THE ACAPULCO REGION

AM	– Amusgo	MI	– Mixe
CHT	– Chatino	MX	– Mixtec
CHI	– Chinantec	NA	– Nahua
CHN	– Chontal	TA	– Tarascan
CO	– Cora		(Purépecha)
CUI	– Cuicatec	TE	– Tepehuan
HUA	– Huave	TP	– Tlapanec
HUI	– Huichol	TR	– Trique
IX	– Ixcatec	ZO	– Zoque
MA	– Mazatec	ZP	– Zapotec

☐ = MAIN AREAS OF HABITATION
☐ = ACAPULCO REGION BOUNDARY

© AVALON TRAVEL PUBLISHING, INC.

Sizable *negro* communities, descendants of 18th-century African slaves, live in the Gulf states and along the Guerrero–Oaxaca Pacific coastline. Last to arrive, the *negros* experience discrimination at the hands of everyone else and are integrating very slowly into the mestizo mainstream.

Above the *mestizos,* a small *criollo* (Mexican-born white) minority, a few percent of the total population, inherits the privileges—wealth, education, and political power—of its colonial Spanish ancestors.

THE *INDÍGENAS*

Although anthropologists and census takers classify them according to language groups (such as Náhuatl, Mixtec, and Zapotec), *indígenas* generally identify themselves as residents of a particular locality rather than by language or ethnic grouping. And although, as a group they are referred to as *indígenas* (native, or aboriginal), individuals are generally uncomfortable at being labeled as such.

While the *mestizos* are the emergent self-conscious majority class, the *indígenas,* as during colonial times, remain the invisible people of Mexico. They are politically conservative, socially traditional, and tied to the land. On market day, the typical *indígena* family might make the trip into town. They bag tomatoes, squash, or peppers, and tie up a few chickens or a pig. The rickety country bus will often be full and the *mestizo* driver may wave them away, giving preference to his friends, leaving them to trudge stoically along the road. Indigenous people from all over Mexico, especially the southeast states of Michoacan, Guerrero, and Oaxaca, come to the Acapulco region to sell their crafts.

Their lot, nevertheless, has been slowly improving. *Indígena* families now almost always have access to a local school and a clinic. Improved health has led to a large increase in their population. Official census figures, however, are probably low. *Indígenas* are traditionally suspicious of government people, and census takers, however conscientious, seldom speak the local language.

Recent figures, however, indicate at least 8 percent of Mexicans are *indígenas*—that is, they speak one of Mexico's 50-odd native languages. Of these, one-quarter speak no Spanish at all. These fractions are changing only slowly. Many *indígenas* prefer the old ways. If present trends continue, the year 2019, 500 years after the Spanish arrival, will mark the return of the Mexican indigenous population to the preconquest level of 20 million.

Indígena Language Groups

The Maya speakers of Yucatán and the aggregate of the Náhuatl (Aztec language) speakers of the central plateau are Mexico's most numerous *indígena* groups, totaling three million (one million Maya, two million Nahua).

Official figures, which show that the Acapulco region's indigenous population amounts to about 370,000, or about 14 percent of the region's total population, may be misleading. Official counts often do not measure the droves of transient folks—migrants and new arrivals—who sleep in vehicles, shantytowns, behind their crafts stalls, and with friends and relatives. Although they are officially invisible, you will see them in Acapulco, Ixtapa, and Zihuatanejo, walking along the beach, for example, laden with their for-sale fruit or handicrafts—men in sombreros and scruffy jeans, women in homemade full-skirted dresses with

aprons much like your great-great-grandmother may have worn.

Immigrants in their own country, indigenous people flock to cities and tourist resorts from hardscrabble rural areas. Although of pure native blood, they will not acknowledge it or will even be insulted if you ask them if they are *indígenas*. It would be more polite to ask them where they're from. If from Michoacán, they'll usually speak Tarasco (more courteously, say Purépecha: poo-RAY-pay-chah); if from Oaxaca, the answer will probably be Zapateco, Mixteco, or Chatino; or from Guerrero, the answer will probably be Náhuatl, Tlapaneco, Mixteco, or Amusgo.

As immigrants always have, they come seeking opportunity. If you're interested in what they're selling, bargain with humor. And if you err, let it be on the generous side. They are proud, honorable people who prefer to walk away from a sale rather than to lose their dignity.

Dress

Country markets are where you're most likely to see people in traditional dress. There, some elderly men still wear the white cottons that blend Spanish and native styles. Absolutely necessary for men is the Spanish-origin straw sombrero (literally, shade-maker) on their heads, loose white cotton shirt and pants, and leather huaraches on their feet.

Women's dress, by contrast, is more colorful. It can include a *huipil* (long, embroidered dress) embroidered in bright floral and animal motifs and a handwoven *enredo* (wraparound skirt that identifies the wearer with a locality, also called a *pozahuanco*). A *faja* (waist sash) and, in winter, a *quechquémitl* (shoulder cape) complete the ensemble.

RELIGION

"God and Gold" was the two-pronged mission of the conquistadores. Most of them concentrated on gold, while missionaries tried to shift the emphasis to God. They were famously successful; more than 90 percent of Mexicans profess to be Catholics.

Catholicism, spreading its doctrine of equality of all people before God and incorporating native gods into the church rituals, eventually brought the *indígenas* into the fold. Within 100 years, nearly all Native Mexicans had accepted the new religion, which raised the universal God of humankind over local tribal deities.

The Virgin of Guadalupe

Conversion of the *indígenas* was sparked by the vision of Juan Diego, a humble farmer. In 1531, on the hill of Tepayac north of Mexico City, Juan Diego saw a brown-skinned version of the Virgin Mary enclosed in a dazzling aura of light. She told him to build a shrine in her memory on that spot, where the Aztecs had long worshipped their "earth mother," Tonantzín. Juan Diego's brown virgin told him

to go to the cathedral and relay her instruction to Archbishop Zumárraga.

The archbishop, as expected, turned his nose up at Juan Diego's story. The vision returned, however, and this time Juan Diego's brown virgin realized that a miracle was necessary. She ordered him to pick some roses at the spot where she had first appeared to him (a true miracle, since roses had been previously unknown in the vicinity) and take them to the archbishop. Juan Diego wrapped the roses in his rude fiber cape, returned to the cathedral, and placed the wrapped roses at the archbishop's feet. When he opened the offering, Zumárraga gasped: Imprinted on the cape was an image of the brown virgin herself—proof positive of a genuine miracle.

In the centuries since Juan Diego, the brown virgin—La Virgen Morena, or Nuestra

DUENDES: SPIRITS OF MEXICO

Once upon a time, most everyone believed that the world was full of spirits that inhabited every object in creation: trees, rocks, animals, mountains, even the wind and the stars. World mythology is replete with examples, from the leprechauns of Ireland and the fairies of Mount Tirich Mir in Pakistan to the spirits who haunt old Hawaiian *heiaus* (temples) and the *duendes* of Mexico.

Eventually many a campesino will take his children to his mountainside cornfield to introduce them to the *duendes*, the elfin beings that folks sometimes glimpse in the shadowed thickets where they hide from mortals.

At the upper end of his field, the campesino father addresses the *duendes:* "With your permission we clear your brush and use your water because it is necessary to nourish our corn and beans. Please allow us, for otherwise, we would starve."

Modernized city Mexicans, generations removed from country village life, often scoff at such antique beliefs. That is, until the family

doctor fails to cure their weakened spouses or sick children. Then they often run to a *curandero* or *curandera* (folk healer).

"Enduendado" (affliction by an angry *duende*), the curandero sometimes diagnoses. Often the cure is simple and savvy: teas and poultices of forest-gathered herbs; other times it is mystical, such as "purifying" by passing an egg all over the afflicted one's body to draw out the illness, and then breaking the egg into a bowl. The shape the broken yolk takes, maybe of a snake, might determine the treatment, which could be long and intricate: massage with lotions of herbs and oils, followed by a *temazcal* (sweat bath) rubdown with rough maguey fibers, all consummated by intense prayers to the Virgin of Guadalupe to force the *duende* to cease the affliction.

Many times the folk cure fails; other times, however, it succeeds, and with enough frequency to convince millions of Mexicans of the power of the village folk healer to purge a *duende*'s poisonous spell.

Señora La Virgen de Guadalupe—has blended native and Catholic elements into something uniquely Mexican. In doing so, she has become the virtual patroness of Mexico, the beloved symbol of Mexico for *indígenas, mestizos, negros,* and *criollos* alike.

In the summer of 2002, Pope John Paul journeyed to Mexico to perform a historic gesture. Before millions of joyous faithful, on July 31, 2002, the frail aging pontiff elevated Juan Diego to sainthood, thus making him Latin America's first indigenous person to be so honored.

With few exceptions, every Acapulco regional town and village celebrates the cherished memory of its Virgin of Guadalupe on December 12. This celebration, however joyful, is but one of the many fiestas that Mexicans, especially the *indígenas,* live for. Each village holds its local fiesta in honor of its patron saint, who is often a thinly veiled sit-in for a local preconquest deity. Themes appear Spanish—Christian vs. Moors, devils vs. priests—but the native element is strong, sometimes dominant.

The inscription over church doors welcomes each entrant with *"Paz y Bien."* (Peace and Well Being).

Sports and Recreation

BEACHES

Their soft sand, gentle waves, and south-seas ambience have made the golden shores of Acapulco, Ixtapa, and Zihuatanejo a magnet for a generation of seekers of paradise. And while those brilliant strands are justly renowned, travelers are increasingly discovering the many small beach hideaways, such as Pie de la Cuesta, Troncones, Barra de Potosí, Playa Escondida, El Carrizal, Playa Ventura, and Playa Las Peñitas, that beckon beyond the famous resorts.

Other travelers take adventure a step further and set up camp to enjoy the solitude and the rich wildlife of even more pristine shorelines. They explore beaches that vary from pristine driftwood-strewn barrier dunes and wildlife-rich jungle lagoons to foamy tidepools and sand of seemingly innumerable colors and consistencies.

Sand makes the beach—and the Acapulco region has plenty—from warm golden quartz to cool, velvety white coral. Some beaches drop steeply to turbulent, close-in surf, fine for fishing. Others are level, with gentle, rolling breakers, made for surfing and swimming.

Beaches are fascinating for the surprises they yield. The Acapulco region's beaches, especially the hidden strands near resorts and the dozens of miles of wilderness beaches and tidepools, yield troves of shells and treasures of flotsam and jetsam for those who enjoy looking for them. Beachcombing is more rewarding during the summer–fall storm season, when big waves deposit acres of fresh shells—among them conch, scallop, clams, combs of Venus, whelks, limpets, olives, cowries, starfish, and sand dollars.

During the summer rainy season, beaches near river mouths are often fantastic outdoor galleries of wind- and water-sculpted snags and giant logs deposited by the downstream flood.

Viewing Wildlife

Wildlife-watchers should keep quiet and always be on the alert. Animal survival depends on their seeing you first. Occasional spectacular offshore sights, such as whales, porpoises, and manta rays, or an onshore giant constrictor, beached giant squid or Pacific octopus, crocodile, or even a jaguar looking for turtle eggs are the reward of those prepared to recognize them. Don't forget your binoculars and Steve Howell's *Bird-Finding Guide to Mexico.*

WATER SPORTS

Swimming, surfing, sailboarding, snorkeling, scuba diving, kayaking, sailing, and personal watercraft riding are the Acapulco region's water sports of choice.

Safety First

Viewed from Acapulco region beaches, the Pacific Ocean usually lives up to its name. Many protected inlets, safe for child's play, dot the coastline. Unsheltered shorelines, on the other hand, can be deceiving. Smooth water in the calm forenoon often changes to choppy in the afternoon; calm ripples that lap the shore in March can grow to hurricane-driven walls of water in November. Such storms can wash away sand, temporarily changing a wide, gently sloping beach into a steep one plagued by turbulent waves and treacherous currents.

Undertow, whirlpools, cross-currents, and occasional oversized waves can make ocean swimming a fast-lane adventure. Getting unexpectedly swept out to sea or hammered onto the beach bottom by a surprise breaker are potential hazards.

Never attempt serious swimming when tipsy or full of food; never swim alone where someone can't see you. Always swim beyond big breakers (which come in sets of several, climaxed by a huge one, which breaks highest and farthest from the beach). If you happen to get caught in the path of such a wave, avoid it by *diving directly toward and under it,* letting it roll harmlessly over you. If you are unavoidably swept up in a whirling, crashing breaker, try to roll and tumble with it, as football players tumble, to avoid injury.

Look out for other irritations and hazards. Now and then swimmers get a nettlelike (but usually harmless) jellyfish sting. Be careful around coral reefs and beds of sea urchins; corals can sting (like jellyfish) and you can additionally get infections from coral cuts and sea-urchin spines. *Shuffle* your feet along sandy bottoms to scare away stingrays before stepping on one. If you're unlucky, its venomous tail-spines may inflict a painful wound.

Snorkeling and Scuba Diving

A number of exciting clear-water sites, especially around Ixtapa and Zihuatanejo, and offshore Isla Roqueta in Acapulco, await both beginner and expert scuba divers. Veteran divers usually arrive during the dry winter and early spring when river outflows are mere trickles, leaving offshore waters clear. In Acapulco, Ixtapa, and Zihuatanejo, professional dive shops rent equipment, provide lessons and guides, and transport divers to choice sites.

While convenient, rented equipment is often less than satisfactory. To be sure, serious divers bring their own gear. This should probably include wetsuits in the winter, when many swimmers begin to feel cold after an unprotected half-hour in the water.

Surfing, Sailing, Sailboarding, and Kayaking

Although Acapulco Bay itself seldom if ever offers any good surfing opportunities, nearby Playa Revolcadero does. Moreover, a few good surfing spots sprinkle the Ixtapa-Zihuatanejo area. Farther afield, a number of crystalline strands, such as Troncones, Piedra Tlalcoyunque, Playa Escondida, Playa

Cayaquitos, Playa El Calvario, Playa Ventura, and Punta Maldonado, offer good seasonal surfing breaks.

The surf everywhere is highest and best during the July–November hurricane season, when big swells from storms far out at sea attract platoons of surfers to favored beaches.

Sailboarders, sailboaters, and kayakers—who, by contrast, require more tranquil waters—do best in the Acapulco region's winter or spring. Aquatics shops rent sailboarding outfits, sailboats, and kayaks at a number of resort hotel beaches on both Acapulco and Zihuatanejo Bays and Ixtapa's main beach.

The Acapulco region's many coastal lagoons offer fine sailboating and kayaking opportunities. Very accessible examples are Laguna Coyuca at Pie de la Cuesta, just northwest of Acapulco, and Laguna Barra de Potosí, just southeast of Zihuatanejo. (Bring your own equipment, however; few if any rentals are available.)

While beginners can have fun with the equipment available from rental shops, serious surfers, sailboarders, sailboaters, and kayakers should pack their own gear.

POWER SPORTS

Acapulco, and to a lesser extent Ixtapa, have long been centers for motorboating, water-skiing, parasailing, and personal watercraft riding. Crowded conditions on Acapulco Bay have fortunately pushed most water-skiing to spacious Laguna Coyuca (at Playa Pie de la Cuesta) east of town. There, a few well-equipped providers offer equipment and lessons for about $100 per hour.

In parasailing, a motorboat pulls while a parachute lifts you, like a soaring gull, high over the ocean. After five or 10 minutes the driver deposits you—usually gently—back on the sand.

Personal watercraft (such as Waverunners) are like snowmobiles except that they operate on water, where, with a little practice, beginners can quickly learn to whiz over the waves.

Although Acapulco and Ixtapa resort hotels' aquatic shops generally provide experienced power-sports crews and equipment, crowded conditions increase the hazard to both participants and swimmers. You, as the patron, are paying plenty for the privilege; you have a right to expect that your providers and crew are well-equipped, sober, and cautious.

Beach Buggies and ATVs

Some visitors enjoy racing along the beach and rolling over dunes in beach buggies and ATVs (all-terrain vehicles—*motos* in Mexico), balloon-tired, three-wheeled motor scooters. While certain resort rental agencies cater to the growing use of such vehicles, limits are in order. Of all the proliferating high-horsepower beach pastimes, these are the most intrusive. Noise, exhaust, and gasoline pollution, injuries to operators and bystanders, scattering of wildlife and destruction of their habitats have led (and I hope will continue to lead) to the restriction of dune buggies and ATVs on beaches.

TENNIS AND GOLF

Most Mexicans are working too hard to be playing much tennis and golf. Consequently, nearly all courses and courts are private. Acapulco golfers enjoy one public *campo de golf* (golf course) and at least two plush private ones. In Ixtapa, one public and one private course serve golfers.

As for tennis, plenty of private courts are available in both Acapulco and Ixtapa. If you are planning on a lot of golf and tennis, check into (or inquire about court rental at) one of the many hotels with these facilities. Use of hotel tennis courts is often, but not always, included in your hotel tariff. If not, fees will run about $10 per hour. Golf greens fees, which begin at about $50 for 18 holes, are always extra.

FISHING

Experts agree: The Acapulco region (and increasingly Zihuatanejo) is a world-class deep-sea and surf fishing ground. Sportspeople routinely bring in dozens of species from among the hundreds that have been hooked in Acapulco region waters.

FISH

A bounty of fish darts, swarms, jumps, and wriggles in the Acapulco region's surf, reefs, lagoons, and offshore depths. While many make delicious dinners (albacore, *dorado*, pompano, red snapper, roosterfish), others are tough (sailfish), bony (bonefish), and even poisonous (puffers). Some grow to half-ton giants (marlin, grouper), while others are diminutive reef-grazers (parrot fish, damselfish, angelfish) whose bright colors delight snorkelers and divers. Here's a sampling of what you might find underwater or on your dinner plate:

albacore (*albacora, atún*): 2-4 feet in size; blue; deep waters; excellent taste

angelfish (*ángel*): one foot; yellow, orange, blue; reef fish*

barracuda (*barracuda, picuda*): two feet; brown; deep waters; good taste

black marlin (*marlin negro*): six feet; blue-black; deep waters; good taste

blue marlin (*marlin azul*): eight feet; blue; deep waters; poor taste

bobo (*barbudo*): one foot; blue, yellow; surf; fair taste

bonefish (*macabi*): one foot; blue or silver; inshore; poor taste

bonito (*bonito*): two feet; black; deep waters; good taste

butterfly fish (*muñeca*): six inches; black, yellow; reef fish*

chub (*chopa*): one foot; gray; reef fish; good taste

croaker (*corvina*): two feet; brownish; inshore bottoms; rare and protected

damselfish (*castañeta*): four inches; brown, blue, orange; reef fish*

dolphinfish, mahi mahi (*dorado*): three feet; green, gold; deep waters; good taste

grouper (*garropa*): three feet; brown, rust; offshore and in reefs; good taste

grunt (*burro*): eight inches; black, gray; rocks, reefs*

jack (*toro*): 1-2 feet; bluish-gray; offshore; good taste

mackerel (*sierra*): two feet; gray with gold spots; offshore; good taste

mullet (*lisa*): two feet; gray; sandy bays; good taste

needlefish (*agujón*): three feet; blue-black; deep waters; good taste

Pacific porgy (*pez de pluma*): 1-2 feet; tan; sandy shores; good taste

parrot fish (*perico, pez loro*): one foot; green, pink, blue, orange; reef fish*

pompano (*pómpano*): one foot; gray; inshore bottoms; excellent taste

puffer (*botete*): eight inches; brown; inshore; poisonous

red snapper (*huachinango, pargo*): 1-2 feet; reddish pink; deep waters; excellent taste

roosterfish (*pez gallo*): three feet; black, blue; deep waters; excellent taste

sailfish (*pez vela*): five feet; blue-black; deep waters; poor taste

sardine (*sardina*): eight inches; blue-black; offshore; good taste

sea bass (*cabrilla*): 1-2 feet; brown, ruddy; reef and rock crevices; good taste

shark (*tiburón*): 2-10 feet; black to blue; in- and offshore; good taste

snook (*robalo*): 2-3 feet; black-brown; brackish lagoons; excellent taste

spadefish (*chambo*): one foot; black-silver; sandy bottoms; reef fish*

swordfish (*pez espada*): five feet; black to blue; deep waters; good taste

triggerfish (*pez puerco*): 1-2 feet; blue, rust, brown, black; reef fish; excellent taste

wahoo (*peto, guahu*): 2-5 feet; green to blue; deep waters; excellent taste

yellowfin tuna (*atún amarilla*): 2-5 feet; blue, yellow; deep waters; excellent taste

yellowtail (*jurel*): 2-4 feet; blue, yellow; offshore; excellent taste

*generally too small to be considered edible

Surf Fishing

Most good fishing beaches away from the immediate resort areas will typically have only a few locals (mostly with nets) and fewer visitors. Mexicans typically do little sportfishing. Most either make their living from fishing, or they do none at all. Consequently, few shops sell sportfishing equipment in the Acapulco region; plan to bring your own surf-fishing equipment, including hooks, lures, line, and weights.

Your best general information source before you leave home is a good local bait-and-tackle shop. Tell the folks there where you're going, and they'll often know the best lures and bait to use and what fish you can expect to catch with them.

In any case, the cleaner the water, the more interesting your catch. On a good day, your reward might be *sierras, cabrillas,* porgies, or pompanos pulled from the Acapulco region surf.

You can't have everything, however. Foreigners cannot legally take Mexican abalone, coral, lobster, clams, rock bass, sea fans, shrimp, turtles, or seashells. Neither are they supposed to buy them directly from fishermen.

Deep-Sea Fishing

Zihuatanejo and Acapulco have long been world-class sportfishing grounds. A deep-sea boat charter generally includes the boat and crew for a full or half day, plus equipment and bait for two to six people, not including food or drinks. The full-day price depends upon the season. Around Christmas and New Year's and before Easter (when reservations will be mandatory) a boat can run $400 and up at Acapulco and Zihuatanejo. During low season, however, you might be able to bargain a captain down to as low as $200.

Renting an entire big boat is not the only choice. Winter sportfishing is sometimes so brisk at Acapulco and Zihuatanejo that travel agencies can make reservations for individuals for about $70 per person per day.

Pangas, seating 2–6 passengers, are available for as little as $50, depending on the season. Once, six of my friends hired a *panga* for $50, had a great time, and came back with a boat-load of big tuna, jack, and mackerel. A restaurant cooked them as a banquet for a dozen of us in exchange for the extra fish, and I discovered for the first time how heavenly fresh *sierra veracruzana* can taste.

Bringing Your Own Boat

If you're going to do lots of fishing, your own boat may be your most flexible and economical option. One big advantage is that you can go to the many excellent fishing grounds the charter boats do not frequent. Keep your equipment simple, scout around the dock, and keep your eyes peeled and ears open for local regulations and customs, plus tide, wind, and fish-edibility information.

Fishing Licenses and Boat Permits

Anyone 16 or older who is either fishing or riding in a fishing boat in Mexico is required to have a fishing license. Although Mexican fishing licenses are obtainable from certain travel and insurance agents or at government fishing offices everywhere along the coast, save yourself time and trouble by getting both your fishing licenses and boat permits by mail ahead of time from the Mexican Department of Fisheries. Call at least a month before departure (tel. 619/233-4324, fax 619/233-0344) and ask for (preferably faxed) applications and the fees (which are reasonable but depend upon the period of validity and the fluctuating exchange rate). On the application, fill in the names (exactly as they appear on passports) of the people requesting licenses. Include a cashier's check or a money order for the exact amount, along with a stamped, self-addressed envelope. Address the application to the Mexican Department of Fisheries (Oficina de Pesca), 2550 5th Avenue, Suite 15, San Diego, CA 92103-6622.

BULLFIGHTING

It is said there are two occasions for which Mexicans arrive on time: funerals and bullfights.

Bullfighting is a recreation, not a sport. The bull is outnumbered seven to one and the outcome is never in doubt. Even if the matador (literally, killer) fails in his duty, his assistants will entice the bull away and slaughter it in private beneath the stands.

La Corrida de Toros

Moreover, Mexicans don't call it a "bullfight"; it's the *corrida de toros,* during which six bulls are customarily slaughtered, beginning at around 5 P.M. After the beginning parade, featuring the matador and his helpers, the picadores and the banderilleros, the first bull rushes into the ring in a cloud of dust. Clockwork *tercios* (thirds) define the ritual: the first, the *puyazos* (stabs), requires that two picadores on horseback thrust lances into the bull's shoulders, weakening it. During the second *tercio,* the banderilleros dodge the bull's horns to stick three long, streamered darts into its shoulders.

Trumpets announce the third *tercio* and the appearance of the matador. The bull—weak, confused, and angry—is ready for the finish. The matador struts, holding the red cape, daring the bull to charge. Form now becomes everything. The expert matador takes complete control of the bull, which rushes at the cape, past its ramrod-erect opponent. For charge after charge, the matador works the bull to exactly the right spot in the ring—in front of the judges, a lovely señorita, or perhaps the governor—where the matador mercifully delivers the precision *estocada* (killing sword thrust) deep into the drooping neck of the defeated bull.

Most sizable Acapulco region towns, including Zihuatanejo, Taxco, Chilpancingo, Iguala, and Ometepec, stage *corridos de toros.*

In Acapulco, *corridos de toros* are staged Sunday at 5:30 P.M. seasonally, usually January–March, at the arena (here called a *frontón*) near west-side Playa Caletilla.

Festivals and Events

Mexicans love a party. Urban families watch the calendar for midweek national holidays that create a *puente* (bridge) to the weekend and allow them to squeeze in a three- to five-day mini-vacation. Visitors should likewise watch the calendar. Such holidays (especially Christmas and Semana Santa, pre-Easter week) mean packed buses, roads, and hotels, especially around the Acapulco region's beach resorts.

Country people, on the other hand, await their local saint's or holy day. The name of the locality often provides the clue. For example, in San Marcos, on the Costa Chica, 30 miles west of Acapulco, expect a celebration in late April, around April 25, the feast day of St. Mark. People dress up in their traditional best, sell their wares and produce in a street fair, join a procession, get tipsy, and dance in the plaza.

FIESTAS

The following calendar lists national and notable Acapulco region holidays and festivals. Dates may vary. If you want to attend a specific local fiesta, contact a local travel agent or tourism bureau for information. (But, if you happen to be where one of these is going on, get out of your car or bus and join in!)

Jan. 1: **¡Feliz Año Nuevo!** (New Year's Day); national holiday.

Jan. 6: **Día de los Reyes** (Day of the Kings); traditional gift exchange.

Jan. 17–18: **Fiesta de Santa Prisca** in Taxco; families bring their pet animals for blessing at the church. The next day, pilgrims arrive at the *zócalo* for *mañanitas* in honor of the saint, then head for folk dancing inside the church.

Jan. 20–21: **Fiesta de San Sebastián;** townsfolk honor the saint martyred in Rome in A.D. 288.

Jan. 23–Feb. 2: **Fiesta de la Virgen de la Salud;** processions, dancing, food, and fireworks.

Feb. 2: **Día de Candelaria;** plants, seeds, and candles blessed; processions and bullfights.

February: During the four days before *Miercoles de Ceniza* (Ash Wednesday, 46 days before Easter Sunday), usually in late February, many towns and villages stage **Carnaval** (Mardi Gras) extravaganzas; especially in Teloloapan, near Iguala.

March 10–17: **Fiesta de San Patricio** (St. Patrick's Day festival).

Fifth Friday before Easter Sunday: **Fiesta del Señor del Perdón;** grand pilgrimage festival, in Igualapa, near Ometepec.

Fourth Friday before Easter Sunday: **Fiesta de Jesús el Nazareno** in Huaxpáltepec; traditional Dance of the Conquest, big native country fair.

March 19: **Día de San José** (Day of St. Joseph).

March 21: **Birthday of Benito Juárez,** the "Hero of the Americas;" national holiday.

April 1–7: **Feria de Café** (Coffee Fair) in Atoyac de Álvarez; coffee farmers sell their best; also plenty of horse trading, handicrafts, country food, and bull riding and roping.

April 1–19: **Fiesta de Ramos** (Palm Sunday); local area crafts fair, food, dancing, mariachis; especially in Jamiltepec.

April: **Good Friday,** two days before Easter Sunday.

April: **Semana Santa** (pre-Easter Holy Week culminating in Domingo Gloria, Easter Sunday, a national holiday) especially in Taxco, Pinotepa Nacional, Teloloapan, Petatlán, Ometepec, Iguala, Olinalá, and Jamiltepec.

May 1: **Fiesta del Primer de Mayo** in Atliaca, near Tixtla; age-old indigenous rite; sacrifices, praying for rain, and traditional dances at the sacred site Sótano (Sinkhole) de Oztotempa.

May 1: **Labor Day;** national holiday.

May 3: **Fiesta del Día de la Santa Cruz** (Holy

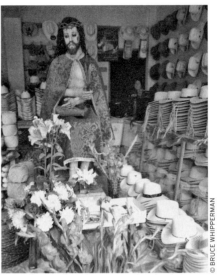

A sombrero store becomes a lovely shrine during Chilapa's fiesta days.

Cross); processions to hilltops and sacred sites; many towns, but especially in Ometepec.

May 3–15: **Fiesta of St. Isador the Farmer;** blessing of seeds, animals, and water; agricultural displays, competitions, and dancing.

May 5: **Cinco de Mayo;** celebrates the defeat of the French at Puebla in 1862; national holiday.

May 10: **Mother's Day;** national holiday.

June 24: **Fiesta de San Juan Bautista** (Festival of St. John the Baptist); fairs and religious festivals, playful dunking of people in water, especially in Chilapa.

June 29: **Día de San Pablo y San Pedro** (Day of St. Peter and St. Paul).

July 20–30: **Fiesta de Santiago Apóstol** (Festival of St. James the Apostle) in many locations, but especially in Pinotepa Nacional, Quechultenango, and Ometepec.

Aug. 6–7: **Fiesta del Padre Jesús;** grand pilgrimage celebration of Petatlán's beloved *patrón,* accompanied by plenty of merrymaking, traditional dances, country food, and fireworks.

Aug. 9: **Fiesta de Vicente Guerrero** in Tixtla; folks celebrate with cultural events, music, and traditional dances the birthday of their famous native son, Vicente Guerrero.

Aug. 14–15: **Fiesta de la Virgen de la Asunción** (Festival of the Virgin of the Assumption); the celebration of the ascension of Mother Mary into heaven, especially in Chilapa.

Sept. 1–8: **Fiesta de la Natividad de María;** indigenous folks flood into Tixtla to sell handicrafts, get tipsy, and watch their favorite traditional dances.

Sept. 9–11: **Fiesta de San Nicolás Tolentino** in Ometepec.

Sept. 14: **Charro Day** (Cowboy Day) all over Mexico; rodeos.

Sept. 15–16: **Dias Patrias** (Patriotic Days); national holiday; mayors everywhere reenact Father Hidalgo's 1810 Grito de Dolores from city hall balconies at 11 P.M. on the night of 15 September, especially in Teloloapan and Ometepec.

Sept. 27–Oct. 2: **Fiesta de San Miguel;** often with the Danza de los Cristianos y Moros (Dance of the Christians and Moors).

Oct. 4: **Día de San Francisco** (Day of St. Francis of Assisi), especially in Iguala and Olinalá.

Oct. 12: **Día de la Raza** (Day of the Race); national holiday that commemorates the union of the races.

Nov. 1: **Día de Todos Santos** (All Souls' Day); in honor of the souls of children; the departed descend from heaven to eat sugar skeletons, skulls, and treats on family altars.

Nov. 2: **Día de los Muertos** (Day of the Dead); in honor of ancestors; families visit cemeteries and decorate graves with flowers and favorite food of the deceased; especially colorful in Iguala and Taxco.

Monday after the Day of the Dead: **Fiesta de los Jumiles** in Taxco; folks collect and feast on raw or roasted *jumiles* (small crickets) and enjoy music and plenty of fixings.

Nov. 7–30: **Feria de la Nao de China** in Acapulco; fair celebrating the galleon trade that linked colonial Acapulco with China via the Philippines.

Nov. 20: **Revolution Day;** anniversary of the Revolution of 1910–1917; national holiday.

Nov. 28–Dec. 5: **National Silver Fair** in Taxco; Mexico's most skilled silversmiths compete for prizes amid a whirl of concerts, dances, and fireworks.

Dec. 1: **Inauguration Day;** national government changes hands every six years: 2006, 2012, 2018 . . .

Dec. 8: **Día de la Purísima Concepción** (Day of the Immaculate Conception).

Dec. 12: **Día de Nuestra Señora de Guadalupe** (Festival of the Virgin of Guadalupe, patroness of Mexico); processions, music, and dancing nationwide, especially around the Acapulco *zócalo* and the adjacent Pozo de la Nación neighborhood.

Dec. 16–24: **Christmas Week;** week of *posadas* and piñatas; midnight Mass on Christmas Eve.

Dec. 24–Jan. 8: **Feria de San Mateo, la Navidad, y el Año Nuevo** in Chilpancingo; the festivities kick off with the *teopancolaquio,* a ritual honoring the birth of God on Earth. Subsequently folks celebrate with favorite traditional dances, bullfights, carnival, fireworks, cockfights, and plenty of food.

Dec. 25: **¡Feliz Navidad!** (Christmas Day); Christmas trees and gift exchange; national holiday.

Dec. 31: **New Year's Eve.**

Arts and Crafts

Mexico is so stuffed with lovely, reasonably priced handicrafts (*artesanías,* ar-tay-sah-NEE-ahs) that many crafts devotees, if given the option, might choose Mexico over heaven. A sizable fraction of Acapulco-region families still depend upon homespun items—clothing, utensils, furniture, native herbal remedies, religious offerings, adornments, toys, musical instruments—which either they or their neighbors craft at home. Many such traditions reach back thousands of years, to the beginnings of Mexican civilization. The accumulated knowledge of manifold generations of artisans has, in many instances, resulted in finery so prized that whole villages devote themselves to the manufacture of a certain class of goods.

In the Acapulco region, handicrafts shoppers who venture away from the coastal resorts to the source towns and villages will most likely benefit from lower prices, wider choices,

and, most important, the privilege of encountering the artisans themselves.

The Acapulco region's three prime handicrafts source towns are **Taxco,** renowned for silver jewelry; **Olinalá,** for fine lacquerware, furniture, and jaguar masks; and **Chilapa,** for the trove of charming handicrafts that folks bring in from outlying villages and sell at the Sunday crafts market. In Chilapa you might be able to buy items made of **horn** (*cuerno*): mescal bottles, combs, pen holders, ash trays, and lampshades; **ironwork** (*hierro*): hachets, daggers, swords, and knives; **maguey fiber** (*ixtle*): hand-painted bags and purses; **embroidery** (*bordado*): napkins, tablecloths, and shawls (*rebozos*); **basketry and woven fiber** (*cestería*): palm sombreros, reed baskets, purses, mats (*petates*), and palm baskets (*tenates*); **wood** (*madera*): masks, lacquerware, miniature human and animal figurines, furniture; **leather** (*cuero*): purses, belts, wallets; and **pottery** (*alfarería*).

BASKETRY AND WOVEN CRAFTS

Weaving straw, leaves, palm fronds, and reeds is among the oldest of Mexican crafts traditions. Mat and basketweaving methods and designs 5,000 years old survive to the present day. In the dry sierra and Río Balsas basin of northeastern Guerrero, people weave *petates* (straw mats) upon which vacationers stretch out on the beach and which local folks use for everything, from keeping tortillas warm to shielding babies from the sun. Palm-leaf weaving is a near-universal occupation. The craft spills over to Acapulco and the Costa Chica, where you might see a person waiting for a bus or even walking down the street while weaving creamy white palm leaf strands into a coiled basket. (Despite appearances, the product, if made of palm leaf, is not strictly a basket—*canasta* in Spanish—which is made of reeds, but instead a *tenate,* which has no handle like a basket does, but a woven tumpline

© BRUCE WHIPPERMAN

Palm-leaf mats are big sellers at the Chilapa Sunday Handicrafts Market.

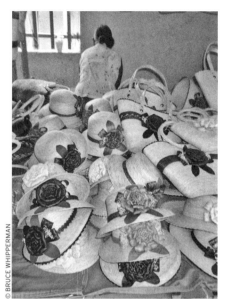

Ingenuity and hard work turn palm leaves into lovely Mexican-style sun bonnets.

that folks loop over their foreheads when carrying a load.)

Not unlike the origami paper-folders of Japan, folks who live around Lago Pátzcuaro in neighboring Michoacán have taken basketweaving to its ultimate by crafting virtually everything—from toy turtles and Christmas bells to butterfly mobiles and serving spoons—from the reeds they gather along the lakeshore.

Hatmaking has likewise attained high refinement in Mexico. Many of the same Guerrero palm-leaf weavers who craft *petates* and *tenates* also craft sombreros. Also, in Sahuayo, Michoacán (near the southeast shore of Lago Chapala), and due east across Mexico, in Becal, Campeche, workers also craft so-called Panama hats, or *jipis* (HEE-pees), of palm leaf. The measure of a fine palm leaf hat is its softness and flexibility—so pliable that you can stuff one into your purse or pants pocket without damage.

CLOTHING AND EMBROIDERY

Although **traje** (traditional indigenous dress) has nearly vanished in urban Mexico, signifi-cant numbers of Mexican women, especially in remote districts of Michoacán, Guerrero, Oaxaca, Chiapas, and Yucatán, make and wear *traje*. Most common is the *huipil*, a full, square-shouldered, short- to midsleeved dress, often hand-embroidered with animal and floral designs. Notable *huipil* designs come from Xochistlahuaca, Guerrero, and San Pedro de Amusgos, Oaxaca (Amusgo tribe: white cotton, often embroidered with abstract colored animal and floral motifs; San Andrés Chicahuaxtla, Oaxaca (Trique tribe: white cotton, richly embroidered red stripes, interwoven with green, blue, and yellow, and hung with colored ribbons); Tehuántepec, Oaxaca (Zapotec tribe: white cotton, with bright multicolored flowers embroidered along two or four vertical seams). Beyond the Pacific coast, Yucatán Maya *huipiles* are among the most prized. They are of white cotton and embellished with big, brilliant machine-embroidered flowers around the neck and shoulders.

Shoppers sometimes can buy other, less common types of *traje,* such as a *quechquémitl* (shoulder cape), often made of wool and worn as an overgarment in winter. The *enredo,* a full-length skirt, wraps around the waist and legs like a Hawaiian sarong. Mixtec women on the Guerrero–Oaxaca border around Pinotepa Nacional commonly wear the *enredo,* known locally as the *pozahuanco* (poh-sah-oo-AHN-koh) below the waist and, when at home, go bare-breasted. When wearing their *pozahuancos* in public, they usually tie a *mandil,* a wide calico apron, around their front side. Women weave the best *pozahuancos* using cotton thread dyed a light purple with secretions of tidepool-harvested snails, *Purpura patula pansa,* and silk dyed deep red with cochineal, extracted from the dried bodies of a locally cultivated scale insect, *Dactylopius coccus.* On a typical day, two or three women will be selling handmade *pozahuancos* at the Pinotepa Nacional market.

Colonial-era Spanish styles have blended with native *traje,* producing a wider class of dress, known generally as **ropa típica.** Lovely embroidered *blusas* (blouses), *rebozos* (shawls), and *vestidos* (dresses) fill boutique racks and market stalls all over the Acapulco region. Among the most popular is the so-called Oaxaca wedding dress, made of cotton with a crochet-trimmed riot of diminutive flowers hand-stitched about the neck and yoke. Some of the finest examples are made in San Antonino Castillo, just north of Ocotlán in the Valley of Oaxaca.

In contrast to women, only a small fraction of Mexican men—members of remote groups, such as Amusgos in Xochistlahuaca, Guerrero; Huichol, Cora, and Tarahumara in northwest Mexico; and Maya and Lacandón in the southeast—wear *traje.* Nevertheless, shops offer some fine men's *ropa típica,* such as wool jackets and serapes for northern or highland winter wear, and *guayaberas,* hip-length, pleated dress shirts.

Fine *bordado* (embroidery) embellishes much traditional Mexican clothing, as well as *manteles* (tablecloths) and *servilletas* (napkins). As everywhere, women define the art of embroidery. Although some still work by hand at home, cheaper machine-made factory lace and needlework is more commonly available in shops.

LEATHER

Acapulco region shops offer an abundance of leather goods, which, if not manufactured locally, are shipped from the renowned leather centers. These include Guadalajara, Mazatlán, and Oaxaca (sandals and huaraches), and León (shoes, boots, and saddles). For unique and custom-designed articles you'll probably have to confine your shopping to the expensive tourist resort shops. For more usual though still attractive leather items such as purses, wallets, belts, coats, and boots, veteran shoppers go to local city markets.

FURNITURE

Although furniture is usually too bulky to carry back home with your airline luggage, low Mexican prices allow you to ship your purchases home and enjoy beautiful, unusual pieces for a fraction of what you would pay—if you could find them—at home.

A number of classes of furniture (*muebles,*

moo-AY-blays) are crafted in villages near the sources of raw materials—either wood, leather, reeds, bamboo, or wrought iron.

Sometimes it seems as if every house in Mexico is furnished with wood **colonial-style furniture.** The basic design of much of it dates at least back to the Middle Ages. Although variations exist, most colonial-style furniture is heavily built. Table and chair legs are massive, often lathe-turned; chair backs are usually straight and vertical. Although usually varnished, colonial-style tables, chairs, and chests sometimes shine with inlaid wood or tile, or animal and flower designs. Family shops turn out good furniture, usually in the highlands, where suitable wood is available. Among the best known places to find these products is Guadalajara's Tonalá and Tlaquepaque villages, Lago Pátzcuaro (especially Tzintzuntzan), Ixcateopan, and Olinalá.

A second, very distinctive class of Mexican furniture is **equipal,** usually roundish tables, chairs, and sofas, made of brown pigskin or cowhide stretched over wooden frames. Factories are mostly in Guadalajara, Zacoalco, Tlaquepaque, and Tonalá.

It is intriguing that **lacquered furniture,** in both process and design, has much in common with lacquerware produced half a world away in China. Moreover, Mexican lacquerware tradition both predated the conquest and was originally practiced only on the Pacific, where legends persist of preconquest contact with Chinese traders. Consequently, a number of experts believe that the Mexicans learned the craft of lacquerware from Chinese artists, centuries before Columbus.

Today, artisan families in and around Pátzcuaro, Michoacán, and Olinalá carry on the tradition. The process, which at its finest resembles cloisonné manufacture, involves carving and painting intricate floral and animal designs, followed by repeated layerings of lacquer, clay, and sometimes gold and silver to produce satiny, jewel-like surfaces.

A few villages produce furniture made of plant fiber, such as reeds, raffia, and bamboo. In some cases, entire communities, such as Ihuatzio (near Pátzcuaro), and Villa Victoria (in Mexico state, west of Toluca), have long harvested the bounty of local lakes and marshes as the basis for their products.

Wrought iron, produced and worked according to Spanish tradition, is used to produce tables, chairs, and benches. Ruggedly fashioned in a riot of baroque scrollwork, pieces often decorate garden, patio, and park settings. Many colonial cities, notably San Miguel de Allende, Toluca, Guanajuato, Guadalajara, and Oaxaca are wrought-iron manufacturing centers.

GLASS AND STONEWORK

Glass manufacture, unknown in pre-Columbian times, was introduced by the Spanish. Today, factories scattered all over the country turn out mountains of *burbuja* (boor-BOO-hah) bubbled glass tumblers, goblets, plates, and pitchers, usually in blue, green, or red. Finer glass is manufactured around Guadalajara; especially in suburban Tlaquepaque and Tonalá villages, you can watch artisans blow glass into a number of shapes, notably, paper-thin balls in red, green, or blue.

Artisans usually work stone near sources of supply. Puebla, Mexico's main source of onyx (*onix,* OH-neeks), is the manufacturing center for the galaxy of mostly rough-hewn, cream-colored items, from animal charms and chess pieces to beads and desk sets, that crowd curio-shop shelves throughout the country. *Cantera,* a volcanic tufa stone occurring in pastel shades from pink to green, is used similarly.

For a keepsake from a truly ancient Mexican tradition, don't forget the hollowed-out stone metate (may-TAH-tay), a corn-grinding basin, and the three-legged *molcajete* (mohl-kah-HAY-tay), a mortar for grinding *chiles.*

HUICHOL ART

Growing demand, especially around Guadalajara and Puerto Vallarta, has greatly stimulated the supply of Huichol art. Originally produced by shamans for ritual purposes, pieces such as beaded masks, *cuadras* (rectangular yarn paintings), gourd rattles, arrows, and yarn *cicuri* (God's eyes) have a ritual symbolism. Eerie beaded masks of wood often represent the Huichols' earth mother, Tatei Urianaka. The larger *cuadras,* of colored acrylic yarn painstakingly glued in intermeshing patterns to a plywood base, customarily depict the drama of life being played out between the main actors of the Huichol pantheon. For example, as Tayau (Father Sun) radiates over the land, alive with stylized cactus, flowers, peyote buds, snakes, and birds, antlered "Brother Deer" Kauyumari heroically battles the evil sorcerer Kieri, while nearby, Tatei Urianaka gives birth.

JEWELRY

Gold and silver were once the basis for Mexico's wealth. Her Spanish conquerors plundered a mountain of gold—religious offerings, necklaces, pendants, rings, bracelets—masterfully crafted by a legion of native metalsmiths and jewelers. Unfortunately, much of that indigenous tradition was lost because for generations the Spanish denied the Mexicans access to precious metals while they introduced Spanish methods. Nevertheless, a small goldworking tradition survived the dislocations of the 1810–1821 War of Independence and the 1910–1917 revolution. Silvercrafting, moribund during the 1800s, was revived in the Acapulco region in Taxco, principally through the joint efforts of architect-artist William Spratling and the local community.

Today, spurred by the tourist boom, jewelry-making is thriving in Mexico. Taxco, where a swarm of local families, guilds, and cooperatives produce sparkling silver and gold adornments, is the acknowledged center. Scores of Taxco shops display the results—shimmering ornamental butterflies, birds, jaguars, serpents, turtles, and fish from ancient native tradition. Pieces, mostly in silver, vary from humble but attractive trinkets to glittering necklaces, silver candelabras, and place settings for a dozen, sometimes embellished with precious stones.

Additionally, Iguala, not far south of Taxco, and Petatlán, a short drive southeast of Zihuatanejo, are thriving market centers of affordable 14-carat gold rings, necklaces, chains, bracelets, and pendants.

WOODCARVING AND MUSICAL INSTRUMENTS

Masks

Spanish and Native Mexican traditions have blended to produce a multitude of masks—some strange, some lovely, some scary, some endearing, all interesting. The tradition flourishes in the strongly indigenous southern Pacific states of Michoacán, Guerrero (especially in Chilapa and Olinalá), and Oaxaca (especially in Pinotepa Don Luis and Huazolotitlá), where campesinos gear up all year for the village festivals. These include Semana Santa (Easter week), Carnaval (Mardi Gras, usually in February), early December (Virgin of Guadalupe), and the festival of the local patron, whether it be San José, San Pedro, San Pablo, Santa María, Santa Barbara, or one of a host of others. Every local fair has its favored dances, such as the Dance of the Conquest, the Christians and Moors, the Old Men, or the Jaguar, in which masked villagers act out age-old allegories of fidelity, sacrifice, faith, struggle, sin, and redemption. For a singularly fascinating display of Acapulco region masks, be sure to visit the Casa de la Máscara (House of Masks) in Acapulco.

Although masks are made of many materials—from stone and ebony to coconut husks and paper—wood, where available, is the medium of choice. For the entire year, village master-carvers cut, shave, sand, and paint to ensure that each participant will be properly disguised for the festival.

The popularity of masks has led to an entire made-for-tourist mask industry of mass-produced duplicates, many cleverly antiqued. Many shops in Taxco, Acapulco, and Zihuatanejo sell attractive reproductions. Examine the goods carefully; if the price is high, don't buy unless you're convinced it's a real antique.

Alebrijes

Tourist demand has made *alebrijes* (zany wooden animals) a Oaxaca growth industry. Virtually every family in certain Valley of Oaxaca villages—notably Arrazola and San Martin Tilcajete—runs a factory studio. There, piles of *copal* wood, which men carve and women finish and intricately paint, become whimsical giraffes, dogs, cats, iguanas, gargoyles, dragons, and most of the possible permutations in between. The farther from the source you get, the higher the *alebrije* price becomes; what costs $5 in Arrazola will probably run about $10 in the Acapulco region and $30 in the United States or Canada.

Others commonly available are the charming colorfully painted wooden fish carved mainly in Guerrero, and the burnished, dark hardwood animal and fish sculptures of desert ironwood from the state of Sonora.

Musical Instruments

The great majority of Mexico's guitars and other stringed instruments are made in Paracho in Michoacán. There, scores of cottage factories turn out guitars, violins, mandolins, *viruelas,* ukuleles, and a dozen more variations every day. They vary widely in quality, so look carefully before you buy. Make sure that the wood is well cured and dry; damp, unripe wood instruments are more susceptible to warping and cracking.

METALWORK

Bright copper, brass, and tinware, sturdy ironwork, and razor-sharp knives and machetes are made in a number of regional centers. Copperware, from jugs, cups, and plates to candlesticks—and even the town lampposts and bandstand—all comes from Santa Clara del Cobre, a few miles south of Pátzcuaro, Michoacán.

Although not the source of brass itself, Tonalá, in the Guadalajara eastern suburb, is the place where brass is most abundant and beautiful, appearing as menageries of brilliant, fetching birds and animals, sometimes embellished with shiny nickel highlights.

A number of Oaxaca family factories turn out fine cutlery—swords, knives, machetes—scrolled cast-iron grillwork, and a swarm of bright tinware or *hojalata* mirror frames, masks, and glittering Christmas decorations.

Be sure not to miss the miniature *milagros,*

an unusual decorative iron chest

one of Mexico's most charming forms of metalwork. Usually of brass, they are of homely shapes—a horse, dog, or baby, or an arm, head, or foot—and, accompanied by a prayer, are pinned by the faithful to the garment of their favorite saint who they hope will intercede to cure an ailment or fulfill a wish.

PAPER AND PAPIER-MÂCHÉ

Papier-mâché has become a high art in Tonalá, Jalisco, where a swarm of birds, cats, frogs, giraffes, and other animal figurines are meticulously crafted by building up repeated layers of glued paper. The result—sanded, brilliantly varnished, and polished—resembles fine sculpture rather than the humble newspaper from which it was fashioned.

Other paper goods you shouldn't overlook include piñatas (durable, inexpensive, and as Mexican as you can get), available in every town market; colorful decorative cutout-banners (string overhead at your home fiesta) from San Salvador Huixcolotla, Puebla; and **amate,** wild fig tree bark paintings in animal and flower motifs, from Xalitla and Ameyaltepec, Guerrero.

POTTERY AND CERAMICS

Although Mexican pottery tradition is as diverse as the country itself, some varieties stand out. Among the most prized is the so-called Talavera (or Majolica), the best of which is made by a few family-run shops in Puebla. The labels Talavera and Majolica derive from Talavera, the Spanish town from which the tradition migrated to Mexico; before that it originated on the Spanish Mediterranean island of Mayorca (thus Majolica), from a combination of still older Arabic, Chinese, and African ceramic styles. Shapes include plates, bowls, jugs, and pitchers, hand-painted and hard-fired in intricate bright yellow, orange, blue, and green floral designs. So few shops make true Talavera these days that other, cheaper, look-alike grades, made around Guanajuato, are more common, selling for as little as one-tenth of the price of the genuine article.

More practical and nearly as prized is the hand-painted, high-fired stoneware from Tonalá in Guadalajara's eastern suburbs. Although made in many shapes and sizes, such stoneware is often sold as complete dinner place settings. Decorations are usually in abstract floral and animal designs, hand-painted over a reddish clay base.

From the same tradition come the famous *bruñido* pottery animals of Tonalá. Round, smooth, and cuddly as ceramic can be, the Tonalá animals—very commonly doves and ducks, but also cats and dogs and sometimes even armadillos, frogs, and snakes—seem to embody the essence of their species.

Some of the most charming Mexican pottery, made from a ruddy low-fired clay and crafted following pre-Columbian traditions, comes from western Mexico, especially Colima. Charming figurines in timeless human poses—flute-playing musicians, dozing grandmothers, fidgeting babies, loving couples—and animals, especially Colima's famous playful dogs, decorate the shelves of a sprinkling of shops.

The Acapulco region also sustains a vibrant pottery tradition. In crafts shops everywhere you'll find the humble but very attractive unglazed brightly painted animals—cats, ducks,

Votive figurines decorate a Taxco street display.

air) method of firing, which removes oxygen from the clay's red (ferric) iron oxide, converting it to black ferrous oxide.

Although most latter-day Mexican potters have become aware of the health dangers of lead pigments, some for-sale pottery may still contain lead. The hazard comes from low-fired pottery in which the lead has not been firmly melted into the glaze. Acids in foods such as lemons, vinegar, and tomatoes dissolve the lead pigments, which, when ingested, eventually result in lead poisoning. In general, the hardest, shiniest pottery, which has been twice fired—such as the high-quality Tonalá stoneware used for dishes—is the safest.

fish, and many others—that folks bring to resort centers from their village family workshops.

Much more acclaimed are certain types of pottery from the valley surrounding the city of Oaxaca. The village of Atzompa is famous for its tan, green-glazed clay pots, dishes, and bowls. Nearby San Bártolo Coyotepec village has acquired equal renown for its black pottery, sold all over the world. Doña Rosa, now deceased, pioneered the crafting of big round pots without using a potter's wheel. Now made in many more shapes by Doña Rosa's descendants, the pottery's exquisite silvery black sheen is produced by the reduction (reduced

WOOLEN WOVEN GOODS

Mexico's finest wool weavings come from Teotitlán del Valle, in the Valley of Oaxaca, less than an hour's drive east of Oaxaca city. The weaving tradition, carried on by Teotitlán's Zapotec-speaking families, dates back at least 2,000 years. Many families still carry on the arduous process, making everything from scratch. They gather the dyes from wild plants and the bodies of insects and sea snails. They hand-wash, card, spin, and dye the wool and even travel to remote mountain springs to gather water. The results, they say, *vale la pena* (are worth the pain): intensely colored, tightly woven carpets, rugs, and wall hangings that retain their brilliance for generations.

Rougher, more loosely woven blankets, jackets, and serapes come from other parts, notably mountain regions, especially around San Cristóbal Las Casas, in Chiapas, and Lago Pátzcuaro in Michoacán.

ESSENTIALS

Accommodations

The Acapulco region has many hundreds of lodgings to suit every style and pocketbook: world-class resorts, small beachside hotels, homey *casas de huéspedes* (guesthouses), palm-shaded trailer parks, and many dozens of miles of pristine beaches, ripe for camping.

HIGH AND LOW SEASONS

Acapulco region high seasons depend on whether the visitors are international or domestic: international visitors, mostly from the United States, Canada, and Europe, begin arriving in droves around December 20 and remain in significant numbers through Easter. Mexican vacationers, on the other hand, concentrate in the resorts during holidays, especially Christmas–New Year's and Semana Santa (pre-Easter week), and weekends, especially during *puentes* (long weekends) around national holidays, and July and August.

As for resort preferences, the new-town district of Acapulco is most popular with most international visitors; both the old town and the new town with Mexicans. Ixtapa and Zihuatanejo are mostly popular with international visitors, less so with Mexicans. Taxco, on the

© BRUCE WHIPPERMAN

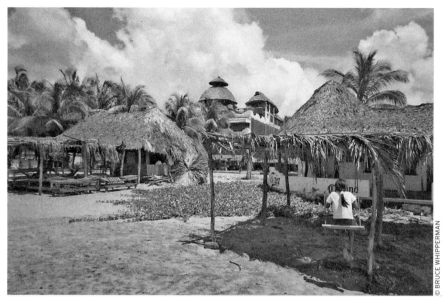

El Carrizal, on the Costa Grande

other hand, is mostly popular with Mexico City Mexicans, especially during holidays and weekends.

So, make sure you arrive with reservations in Acapulco, Ixtapa, and Zihuatanejo during the winter–spring season and Taxco during Christmas–New Year's, pre-Easter week, weekends, and July and August.

PICKING A HOTEL

The hundreds of accommodations described in this book are positive recommendations—checked out in detail—good choices, from which you can pick according to your taste and purse.

Hotel Rates

The rates listed in the destination chapters are U.S. dollar equivalents of peso prices, 15 percent IVA (Value Added) taxes included, as quoted by the hotel management at the time of writing. Where many hotels are available—Acapulco, Ixtapa, Zihuatanejo, and Taxco—hotels are listed in ascending order of high-season, double-occupancy rate. Both low- and high-season rates are quoted whenever possible and are intended as a general guide only. Since rates fluctuate sharply according to local demand, quoted figures will probably only approximate the asking rate when you arrive. (Some readers, unfortunately, try to bargain by telling desk clerks that, for example, the rate should be $30 because they read it in this book. This is unwise, because it makes hotel managers and clerks reluctant to quote rates for fear readers might hold their hotels responsible for such quotes years later.)

In the Acapulco region, hotel rates depend strongly upon inflation and season. To cancel the effect of relatively steep Mexican inflation, rates are reported in U.S. dollars. However, when settling your hotel bill, *you should always pay in pesos.*

Saving Money

The hotel prices quoted in this book are rack rates: the maximum tariff, exclusive of packages and promotions, that you would pay if you walked in and rented an unreserved room for a night. Savvy travelers seldom pay the maximum. Always inquire if there are any discounts or packages (*descuentos o paquetes,* des-koo-AYN-tohs OH pah-KAY-tays). At most times other than the super-high Christmas to New Year's and Easter weeks, you can usually get at least one or two free days for a one-week stay. Promotional packages available during slack seasons may include free extras such as breakfast, a car rental, a boat tour, or a sports rental. A travel agent or travel website can be of great help in shopping around for such bargains.

You nearly always save additional money if you deal in pesos only. Insist on both booking your lodging for an agreed price in pesos and paying the resulting hotel bill in the same pesos, rather than dollars. The reason is that dollar rates quoted by hotels are often based on the hotel desk exchange rate, which is customarily about 5 percent, or even as much as 15 percent, less than bank rates. For example, if the clerk tells you your hotel bill is $1,000, instead of handing over the dollars, or having him mark $1,000 on your credit card slip, ask him how much it is in pesos. Using the desk conversion rate, he might say something like 10,000 pesos (considerably less than the 11,000 pesos that the bank might give for your $1,000). Pay the 10,000 pesos in cash or make sure the clerk marks 10,000 pesos on your credit card slip, and save yourself $100.

For stays of more than two weeks, you'll most likely save money and add comfort with an apartment or condominium rental. Monthly rates range $500–1,500 (less than half the comparable hotel per diem rate) for comfortable one-bedroom furnished kitchenette units, often including resort amenities such as pool and sundeck, beach club, and private view balcony.

Airlines regularly offer air/hotel packages, which, by combining your hotel and air fees, may save you lots of pesos. Accommodations are usually, but not exclusively, in luxury resorts. See a travel website or travel agent or contact the airlines directly.

GUESTHOUSES AND LOCAL HOTELS

As did most of the celebrated Mexican Pacific coast resorts, both Acapulco and Zihuatanejo began with an old town, which expanded to a new *zona hotelera* (hotel strip) where big hostelries rise along a golden strand. In the old town, near the piquant smells, sights, and sounds of traditional Mexico, are the *casas de huéspedes* and smaller local hotels where rooms are often arranged around a plant-decorated patio.

Such lodgings vary from scruffy to spic-and-span, and humble to semideluxe. At minimum, you can expect a plain room, a shared toilet and hot-water shower, and plenty of atmosphere for your money. High-season rates, depending on the resort and amenities, are typically between $15 and $40 for two. Discounts are often available for long-term stays. *Casas de huéspedes* will rarely be near the beach, unlike many of the medium-to-high-end local hotels.

Medium-to-High-End Local Hotels

Locally owned and operated hotels make up most of the recommendations of this book.

Hotel Los Arcos in Taxco

Many veteran travelers find it hard to understand why people come to Mexico and spend $200–400 a day for a hotel room when good alternatives run between $40 and $100, high season, depending upon the resort.

Many locally run hostelries are right on the beach, sharing the same velvety sand and golden sunsets as their much more expensive international-class neighbors. Local hotels, which depend as much on Mexican tourists as foreigners, generally have clean, spacious rooms, often with private view balconies, ceiling fans, and toilet and hot-water bath or shower. What they often lack are the plush extras—air-conditioning, cable TV, phones, tennis courts, exercise gyms, and golf courses—of the luxury resort hotels.

Booking these hotels is straightforward. All can be dialed direct (from the United States, dial 011-52, then the local area code and number) for information and reservations; like the big resorts, many have websites and email addresses, and some even have U.S. and Canada toll-free phone numbers. Always ask about money-saving packages (*paquetes*) and promotions (*promociones*) when reserving.

INTERNATIONAL-CLASS RESORTS

The Acapulco region has many beautiful, well-managed international-class resort hotels. They spread along the pearly strands of Acapulco Bay, Zihuatanejo, and Ixtapa. Their super-deluxe amenities, moreover, need not be overly expensive. During the right time of year you can vacation at many of the big-name spots, such as Barceló (formerly Sheraton), Fairmont, Melia, Las Brisas, Hyatt, Fiesta Americana, NH Krystal, Best Western—for surprisingly little. While high-season room tariffs ordinarily run $150–350, low-season (May–Nov., and to a lesser degree, Jan.–Feb.) packages and promotions can cut these prices to as low as $100. Shop around for savings via your Sunday newspaper travel section, travel agents, and by contacting the hotels directly through their toll-free phone numbers or websites.

APARTMENTS, BUNGALOWS, CONDOMINIUMS, AND VILLAS

For longer stays, many visitors prefer the convenience and economy of an apartment or condominium or the luxurious comfort of a villa vacation rental. Choices vary, from spartan studios to deluxe beachfront suites and rambling view homes big enough for entire extended families. Prices depend strongly upon season and amenities, from $500 per month for the cheapest to at least 10 times that for the most luxurious.

A Mexican variation on the apartment style of accommodation is called a bungalow, although, in contrast to English-language usage, it does not usually imply a detached dwelling. Common in Zihuatanejo, a bungalow accommodation generally means a kitchenette-suite with less service, but with more space and beds. For families or for long stays by the beach, where you want to save money by cooking your own meals, such an accommodation might be ideal.

At the low end, you can expect a clean, furnished apartment within a block or two of the beach, with kitchen and regular maid service. More luxurious condos, very common in Acapulco and Ixtapa and which usually rent for $500 per week and up, are typically high-rise ocean-view suites with hotel-style desk services and resort amenities, such as a pool, whirlpool tub, sundeck, and beach-level restaurant.

Higher up the scale, villas and houses vary from moderately luxurious homes to sky's-the-limit beach-view mansions, blooming with built-in designer luxuries, private pools and beaches, tennis courts, and gardeners, cooks, and maids.

Shopping Around

You'll generally find the most economical apartment, condo, and house rental deals through on-the-spot local contacts, such as the tourist newspaper want ad section, neighborhood For Rent signs, or local listing agents.

If you prefer making rental arrangements before arrival, you can usually write, fax, email, or telephone managers—many of whom speak English—directly, using the numbers given in the destination chapters of this book.

Many additional rentals are available through agents who will make long-distance rental agreements. Moreover, such rentals are becoming increasingly available through the Internet.

Yet another fertile vacation rental source is the Sunday travel section of a major metropolitan daily, such as the *Los Angeles Times* or the *San Francisco Chronicle*, which routinely list Acapulco-region vacation rentals. Also, local real estate agents such as Century 21, which specializes in nationwide and foreign contacts, sometimes list (or know someone who does list) Acapulco region vacation rentals.

Home Exchange and Renting Out Your Own House

You may also want to consider using the services of a home exchange agency/website whereby you swap homes with someone in the Acapulco region for an agreed-upon time. For a list of agencies, see the Internet Resources at the back of this book, or simply enter "home exchange" into an Internet search engine.

On the other hand, it may be easier to rent or lease your own house and use the income to rent a house or apartment in the Acapulco region. (Although some people—including myself—have found this strategy successful, talk to someone who's done it to find out if it's your cup of tea.)

CAMPING AND TRAILER PARKS
Beach Camping

Informal beach camping is popular among middle-class Mexican families, especially during the Christmas–New Year's week and during Semana Santa. The crowds even overflow on to the resort beaches of Acapulco, Zihuatanejo Bay, and Ixtapa, where folks set up tents or simply sleep under the stars.

On nearly all other Acapulco-region beaches

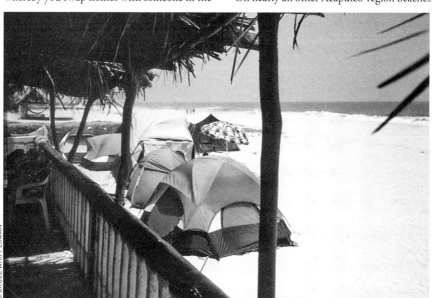

© BRUCE WHIPPERMAN

Beach camping right next to *palapa* restaurants is enjoyed by many local vacationers on Costa Grande (here, at El Carrizal) and Costa Chica beaches.

plenty of camping space is always available. The choice spots, such as Playa Ventura, Playa Las Peñitas, and Playa Puerto Maldonado on the Costa Chica; and Playa El Carrizal, Playa Paraíso, the Laguna de Mitla beach, Playa Escondida, Playa La Barrita, and Playa Ojo de Agua on the Costa Grande, typically have a shady palm grove for camping and at least one *palapa* restaurant that serves drinks and fresh seafood. (Heads up for falling coconuts, especially when it's windy.) Cost for parking and tenting is often minimal, typically only the price of food at the restaurant.

Days are often perfect for swimming, strolling, and fishing, and nights are balmy—too warm for a sleeping bag, but fine for a hammock (which allows the air circulation that a tent does not). However, good tents keep out mosquitoes and other pesties, which may be further discouraged by a good bug repellent. Tents can get hot, requiring only a sheet or very light blanket for sleeping cover.

As for the safety of camping on isolated beaches, opinions vary from dire warnings of *bandidos* to bland assurances that all is peaceful along the coast. The truth is somewhere in between. Trouble is most likely to occur in the vicinity of resort towns, where a few local thugs sometimes harass isolated campers.

When scouting out an isolated beach for camping, a good rule is to arrive early enough in the day to get a feel for the place. Buy a soda at the *palapa* or store and take a stroll along the beach. Say *"Buenos días"* to the people along the way; ask if the fishing is good (*"¿Pesca buena?"*). Above all, use your common sense and intuition. If the people seem friendly, ask if it's *seguro* (safe). If so, ask permission: *"¿Es bueno acampar acá?"* ("Is it okay to camp around here?"). You'll rarely be refused.

Camping Upcountry

Scenic river canyons provide some of the most inviting camping opportunities in the Acapulco region's vast upcountry hinterland. Two of the best are at Campamento Santa Fe and El Borbollón on the spring-fed Río Azul (Blue River) about 20 miles east of Chilpancingo. Other promising spots are on the Río Papagayo at Pueblo Bravo (on old Highway 95, about 30 miles south of Chilpancingo), and the Río San Pedro, near Xochistlahuaca.

You can enjoy one of the most informative and entertaining discussions of camping in Mexico in *The People's Guide to Mexico.*

Trailer Parks

Campers who prefer company to isolation usually stay in trailer parks. Unfortunately, development has squeezed out many Acapulco-region trailer parks. Nevertheless, two good trailer parks remain, on breezy Playa Pie de la Cuesta a few miles northwest of Acapulco. Two marginal trailer parks (one very small and another with virtually no facilities) are also available in Zihuatanejo.

Food and Drink

Some travel to the Acapulco region for the food. True Mexican food is old-fashioned, home-style fare requiring many hours of loving preparation. Such food is short on meat and long on corn, beans, rice, tomatoes, onions, eggs, and cheese.

Mexican food is the unique product of thousands of years of native tradition. It is based on corn—*teocentli,* the Aztec "holy food"—called *maíz* (mah-EES) by present-day Mexicans. In the past, a Mexican woman spent much of her time grinding and preparing corn: soaking the grain in lime water, which swells the kernels and removes the tough seed-coat, and grinding the bloated seeds into meal on a stone metate. Finally, she patted the meal into tortillas and cooked them on a hot, baked mud griddle.

Sages (men, no doubt) wistfully imagined that gentle pat-pat-pat of women all over Mexico to be the heartbeat of Mexico, which they feared would cease when women stopped making tortillas.

Fewer women these days make tortillas by hand. The gentle pat-pat-pat has been replaced by the whir and rattle of the automatic tortilla-making machine in myriad *tortillerías,* where women and girls line up for their family's daily kilo-stack of tortillas.

Tortillas are to the Mexicans as rice is to the Chinese and bread to the French. Mexican food is invariably some mixture of sauce, meat, beans, cheese, and vegetables wrapped in a tortilla, which becomes the culinary be-all: the food, the dish, and the utensil wrapped into one.

If a Mexican man has nothing to wrap in his lunchtime tortilla, he will content himself by rolling a thin filling of salsa (*chile* sauce) in it.

HOT OR NOT?

Much food served in Mexico is not "Mexican." Eating habits, as most other customs, depend upon social class. Upwardly mobile Mexicans typically shun the corn-based *indígena* fare in favor of the European-style food of the Spanish colonial elite: chops, steaks, cutlets, fish, clams, omelets, soups, pasta, rice, and potatoes.

Such fare is often as bland as Des Moines on a summer Sunday afternoon. *No picante*— not spicy—is how the Mexicans describe bland food. *Caliente,* the Spanish adjective for "hot"

CATCH OF THE DAY

Ceviche (say-VEE-chay): A chopped raw fish appetizer as popular on Acapulco region beaches as sushi is on Tokyo side-streets. Although it can contain anything from conch to octopus, the best ceviche consists of diced *tiburón* (young shark) or *sierra* (mackerel) fillet and plenty of fresh tomatoes, onions, garlic, and *chiles,* all doused with lime juice.

Filete de pescado: A fish fillet, sautéed *al mojo* (ahl MOH-hoh) – with butter and garlic.

Pescado frito: Fish, pan-fried whole; if you don't specify that it be cooked *a medio* (lightly), the fish may arrive well done, like a big, crunchy french fry.

Pescado veracruzana: A favorite everywhere. Best with *huachinango* (red snapper), smothered in a savory tomato, onion, *chile,* and garlic sauce. *Pargo* (snapper), *mero* (grouper), and *cabrilla* (sea bass) are also popularly used in this and other specialties.

Shellfish: These are abundant and include *ostiones* (oysters) and *almejas* (clams) by the dozen; *langosta* (lobster) and *langostina* (crayfish) *asado* (broiled), *al vapor* (steamed), or fried. Pots of fresh-boiled *camarones* (shrimp) are sold on the street by the kilo; cafés will make them into *cóctel,* or prepare them *en gabardinas* (breaded) at your request.

(as in hot water), does not, in contrast to English usage, imply spicy, or *picante.*

VEGETARIAN FOOD

Although the availability of healthy food is increasing, strictly vegetarian and vegan cooking is the exception in Mexico, as are macrobiotic restaurants, health-food stores, and organic produce. Meat is such a delicacy for most Mexicans that they can't understand why people would give it up voluntarily. If, as a vegetable-lover, you can manage with corn, beans, cheese, eggs, *legumbres* (vegetables), and fruit, Mexican cooking will suit you fine.

SEAFOOD

Early chroniclers wrote that Aztec Emperor Moctezuma employed a platoon of runners to bring fresh fish 300 miles every day from the sea to his court. In the Acapulco region, fresh seafood is fortunately much more available from many dozens of shoreline establishments, varying from thatched beach *palapas* to five-star hotel restaurants.

Despite the plenty, Acapulco region seafood prices reflect high worldwide demand, even at the humblest seaside *palapa.* The freshness and variety, however, make even the typical dishes seem bargains at any price.

MEXICAN FOOD

On most Mexican-style menus, diners will find variations on a number of basic themes:

Carnes (meats): **Carne asada** is grilled beef, usually chewy and well-done. Something similar you might see on a menu is *cecina* (say-SEE-nah), dried salted beef grilled to a shoeleather-like consistency. Much more appetizing is **birria**, a Guadalajara specialty. Traditional *birrias* are of lamb or goat, often wrapped and pit-roasted in maguey leaves, with which it is served, for authenticity. In addition to *asada*, meat cooking styles are manifold, including *guisado* (stewed), *al pastor* (spit barbecue), and *barbacoa* (grill barbecued). Cuts include *lomo* (loin), *chuleta* (chop), *milanesa* (cutlet), and *albóndigas* (meatballs).

Chiles rellenos: Fresh roasted green chiles, usually stuffed with cheese but sometimes with fish or meat, coated with batter, and fried. They provide a piquant, tantalizing contrast to tortillas.

Enchiladas and **tostadas:** variations on the filled-tortilla theme. Enchiladas are stuffed with meat, cheese, olives, or beans and covered with sauce and baked, while tostadas consist of toppings served on crisp, open-faced tortillas.

Guacamole: This luscious avocado, onion, tomato, lime, and salsa mixture remains the delight it must have seemed to its Aztec inventors centuries ago. In nontourist Mexico,

it's served sparingly as a garnish, rather than in appetizer bowls as is common in the U.S. Southwest (and Mexican resorts catering to North Americans). (Similarly, in nontourist Mexico, burritos and fajitas, both stateside inventions, seldom if ever appear on menus.)

Moles (MOH-lays): uniquely Mexican specialties. *Mole poblano,* a spicy-sweet mixture of chocolate, *chiles*, and a dozen other ingredients, is cooked to a smooth sauce, then baked with chicken (or turkey, a combination called *mole de pavo*). So *típica* it's widely regarded as the national dish.

Quesadillas: made from soft flour tortillas, rather than corn, quesadillas resemble tostadas and always contain melted cheese.

Sopas: Soups consist of vegetables in a savory chicken broth, and are an important part of both *comida* (afternoon) and *cena* (evening) Mexican meals. *Pozole,* a rich steaming stew of hominy, vegetables, and pork or chicken, often constitutes the prime evening offering of small side street shops. *Sopa de taco*, an ever-popular country favorite, is a medium-spicy cheese-topped thick *chile* broth served with crisp corn tortillas.

Tacos or **taquitos:** tortillas served open or wrapped around any ingredient.

Tamales: as Mexican as apple pie is American. This savory mixture of meat and sauce imbedded in a shell of corn dough and baked

FRUITS AND JUICES

Squeezed vegetable and fruit juices (*jugos,* HOO-gohs) are among the widely available delights of the Acapulco region. Among the many establishments—restaurants, cafés, and *loncherías*—willing to supply you with your favorite *jugo,* the *jugerías* (juice bars) are often the most fun. Colorful fruit piles usually mark *jugerías.* If you don't immediately spot your favorite fruit, ask anyway; it might be hidden in the refrigerator.

Besides your choice of pure juices, a *jugería* will often serve *licuados.* Into the juice, they whip powdered milk, your favorite fruit, and sugar to taste for a creamy afternoon pick-me-up or evening dessert. One big favorite is a cool banana-chocolate *licuado,* which comes out tasting like a milkshake minus the calories.

ALCOHOLIC DRINKS

The Aztecs sacrificed anyone caught drinking alcohol without permission. The later, more lenient, Spanish attitude toward getting *borracho* (soused) has led to a thriving Mexican renaissance of native alcoholic beverages: tequila, mescal, Kahlúa, pulque, and *aguardiente.* Tequila and mescal, distilled from the fermented juice of the maguey, originated in Oaxaca,

---

in a wrapping of corn husks is rarely known by the singular, however. They're so yummy that one tamale invariably leads to more tamales.

Tortas: the Mexican sandwich, usually hot meat with fresh tomato and avocado, stuffed between two halves of a crisp *bolillo* (boh-LEE-yoh) or Mexican bun.

Tortillas y frijoles refritos: cooked brown or black beans, mashed and fried in pork fat, and rolled into tortillas with a dash of vitamin-C-rich salsa to form a near-complete combination of carbohydrate, fat, and balanced protein.

BEYOND THE BASICS

Mexican food combinations seem endless. Mexican corn itself has more than 500 recognized culinary variations, all from indigenous tradition. This has led to a myriad of permutations on the taco, such as *sopes* (with small and thick tortillas), *garnacho* (flat taco), *chilaquile* (shredded taco), *chalupa* (like a tostada), and *gorditas* (thick corn tortillas).

Taking a lesson from California nouveau cuisine, avante-garde Mexican chefs are returning to traditional ingredients. They're beginning to use more and more *chiles* – habanero, poblano, jalapeño, and more – prepared with many variations, such as chipotle, ancho, *piquín,* and *mulato. Flor de calabaza* (squash flowers) and *nopal* (cactus) leaves are increasingly finding their way into soups and salads.

More often chefs are serving the wild game – *venado* (venison), *conejo* (rabbit), *guajalote* (turkey), *codorniz* (quail), *armadillo,* and *iguana* – that country Mexicans have always depended upon. As part of the same trend, *cuitlacoche* (corn mushroom fungus), *chapulines* (french-fried small grasshoppers), and *gusanos de maguey* (maguey worms) are being increasingly added as ingredients in fancy restaurants.

gorditas

where the best are still made. Quality tequila (named after the Guadalajara-area distillery town) and mescal come 76 proof (38 percent alcohol) and up. A small white worm, endemic to the maguey, is customarily added to each bottle of factory mescal for authenticity.

Pulque, although also made from the sap of the maguey, is locally brewed to a modest alcohol content between that of beer and wine. The brewing houses are sacrosanct preserves, circumscribed by traditions that exclude women and outsiders. The brew, said to be rich in nutrients, is sold to local *pulquerías* and drunk immediately. If you are ever invited into a *pulquería,* it is an honor you cannot refuse.

Aguardiente, by contrast, is the notorious fiery Mexican "white lightning," a locally distilled, dirt-cheap ticket to oblivion for poor Mexican men.

While pulque comes from age-old indigenous tradition, beer (introduced by 19th-century German brewers) is the beverage of modern mestizo Mexico. More full-bodied than "light" U.S. counterparts, Mexican beer enjoys an enviable reputation.

Those visitors who indulge usually know their favorite among the many brands, from light to dark: Superior, Corona, Pacífico, Tecate, Carta Blanca, Modelo, Dos Equis, Bohemia, Tres Equis, and Negro Modelo. Nochebuena, a hearty dark brew, becomes available only around Christmas.

Mexicans have yet to develop much of a taste for *vino tinto* or *vino blanco* (red or white table wine), although some domestic wines (such as the Baja California labels Cetto and Domecq and the boutique Monte Xanic) are at least very drinkable and at best excellent.

BREAD AND PASTRIES
Wonderful locally baked bread is a delightful surprise to many first-time visitors to the Acapulco region. Small bakeries everywhere put out trays of hot, crispy-crusted *bolillos* (rolls)

© BRUCE WHIPPERMAN

Delicious *panes dulce* (sweet bread) is for many first-time visitors a surprise delight of a Mexico vacation.

A TROVE OF FRUITS AND NUTS

Besides carrying the usual temperate fruits, *jugerías* and especially markets are seasonal sources of a number of exotic (followed by an *) varieties.

avocado (*aguacate* – ah-wah-KAH-tay): Aztec aphrodisiac

banana (*platano*): many kinds – big and small, red and yellow

chirimoya* (*chirimoya*): green scales, white pulp, sometimes called an *anona*

ciruela*: looks like (but tastes better than) a small yellow-to-red plum

coconut (*coco*): coconut "milk," called *agua coco,* is a wonderful and healthy thirst quencher

grapes (*uvas*): August–November season

guanabana*: looks, but doesn't taste, like a green mango

guava (*guava*): delicious juice, widely available canned

lemon (*lima real* – LEE-mah ray-AHL): uncommon and expensive; use lime instead

lime (*limón* – lee-MOHN): abundant and cheap; douse salads with it

mamey* (*mamey* – mah-MAY): yellow, juicy fruit; excellent for jellies and preserves

mango (*mango*): king of fruit, in a 100 varieties April–September

orange (*naranja* – nah-RAHN-ha): greenish skin but sweet and juicy

papaya (*papaya*): said to aid digestion and healing

peach (*durazno* – doo-RAHS-noh): delicious and widely available as canned juice

peanut (*cacahuate* – kah-kah-WAH-tay): home roasted and cheap

pear (*pera*): fall season

pecan (*nuez*): for a treat, try freshly ground pecan butter

*piña anona** looks like a thin ear of corn without the husk; tastes like pineapple

pineapple (*piña*): huge, luscious, and cheap

strawberry (*fresa* – FRAY-sah): local favorite

tangerine (*mandarina*): common around Christmas

watermelon (*sandía* – sahn-DEE-ah): perfect on a hot day

yaca* (YAH-kah): a relative of the Asian jackfruit, with pebbly green skin, round and as large as a football; yummy mild taste

*zapote** (sah-POH-tay): yellow, fleshy fruit, said to induce sleep

*zapote colorado**: brown skin, red, puckery fruit, like persimmon; commonly, but incorrectly, called *mamey*

© BRUCE WHIPPERMAN

oven-fresh peanuts, pecans, pistachios, and sunflower seeds

and *panes dulces* (sweet bread). The pastries vary from simple cakes, muffins, cookies, and doughnuts to fancy fruit-filled turnovers and puffs. Half the fun occurs before the eating: grab a tray and tongs, peruse the goodies, and pick out the most scrumptious. With your favorite dozen or so finally selected, you take your tray to the cashier, who deftly bags everything up and collects a few pesos (two or three dollars) for your entire mouthwatering selection.

Shopping

WHAT TO BUY
Although bargains abound in Mexico, savvy shoppers are selective. Steep import and luxury taxes drive up the prices of foreign-made goods such as cameras, computers, sports equipment, and English-language books. Instead, concentrate your shopping on locally made items: leather, jewelry, cotton resort wear, Mexican-made designer clothes, and the galaxy of handicrafts for which Mexico is renowned.

HANDICRAFTS
The upcountry towns of Chilapa, Olinalá, and Taxco are the Acapulco region's renowned sources of handicrafts. And, although most crafts are not made in the resorts of Acapulco, Ixtapa, and Zihuatanejo, each has dozens of good private handicrafts stores and several crafts markets where local folks maintain stalls stuffed with their homemade crafts. Moreover, the rich cornucopia of crafts from other Mexican centers, such as Oaxaca, around Guadalajara, and the Lago Pátzcuaro region of Michoacán, spills over to the Acapulco region.

BARGAINING
Bargaining will stretch your money even further. It comes with the territory in Mexico and needn't be a hassle. On the contrary, if done with humor and moderation, bargaining can be an enjoyable way to meet Mexican people and gain their respect, even friendship.

The local crafts market is where bargaining is most intense. For starters, try offering half the asking price. From there on, it's all psychology: you have to content yourself with not having to have the item. Otherwise, you're sunk; the vendor will probably sense your need and stand fast. After a few minutes of good-humored bantering, ask for *el último precio* (the final price), in which, if it's close, you may have a bargain.

BUYING SILVER AND GOLD JEWELRY
Silver jewelry, the finest of which is crafted in Taxco, fills dozens of shops there and a number of shops in Acapulco, Ixtapa, and Zihuatanejo.

© BRUCE WHIPPERMAN

A little lacquer and lots of ingenuity turns coconut shells into lovely decorations.

Moreover, Iguala, half an hour's drive south of Taxco, is a center of gold jewelry.

One hundred percent pure silver is rarely sold because it's too soft. Silver (sent from processing mills in the north of Mexico to be worked in Taxco shops) is nearly always alloyed with 7.5 percent copper to increase its durability. Such pieces, identical in composition to sterling silver, should have ".925," together with the initials of the manufacturer, stamped on their back sides. Other, less common grades, such as "800 fine" (80 percent silver), should also be stamped.

If silver is not stamped with the degree of purity, it probably contains no silver at all and is an alloy of copper, zinc, and nickel, known by the generic label "alpaca," or "German" silver. Once, after haggling over the purity and prices of his offerings, a street vendor handed me a shiny handful and said, "Go to a jeweler and have them tested. If they're not real, keep them." Calling his bluff, I took them to a jeweler, who applied a dab of hydrochloric acid to each piece. Tiny, tell-tale bubbles of hydrogen revealed the cheapness of the merchandise, which I returned the next day to the vendor.

Some shops price sterling silver jewelry simply by weighing, which typically translates to about $1 per gram. If you want to find out if the price is fair, ask the shopkeeper to weigh it for you.

Iguala, an hour's drive south of Taxco, is a center of gold jewelry. People prize pure gold, partly because, unlike silver, it does not tarnish. Gold, nevertheless, is rarely sold pure (24 karat); for durability, it is alloyed with copper. Typical purities, such as 18 karat (75 percent) or 14 karat (58 percent), should be stamped on the pieces. If not, chances are they contain no gold at all.

Getting There

BY AIR
From the United States and Canada

The vast majority of travelers reach the Acapulco region by air. Flights are frequent and reasonably priced. Competition sometimes shaves prices down as low as $400 for an Acapulco or Ixtapa-Zihuatanejo round-trip.

Air travelers can save lots of money by shopping around. Don't be bashful about asking for the cheapest price. Make it clear to the airline or travel agent you're interested in a bargain. Ask the right questions: are there special-incentive, advance-payment, night, midweek, tour package, or charter fares? Peruse the ads in the Sunday newspaper travel section for bargain-oriented travel agencies. Check airline and bargain-oriented Internet travel sites, such as **www.orbitz.com, www.expedia.com,** and **www.travelocity.com.**

Although some agents charge booking fees and don't like discounted tickets because their fee depends on a percentage of ticket price, many will nevertheless work hard to get you a bargain, especially if you book an entire air/hotel package with them.

Although few airlines fly directly to the Acapulco region from the northern United States and Canada, many charters do. In locales near Vancouver, Calgary, Ottawa, Toronto, Montreal, Minneapolis, Chicago, Detroit, Cleveland, and New York, consult a travel agent or website for charter flight options. Be aware that charter reservations, which often require fixed departure and return dates and provide minimal cancellation refunds, decrease your flexibility. If available charter choices are unsatisfactory, then you might choose to begin your vacation with a connecting flight to one of the Acapulco-region gateways, such as Seattle, San Francisco, Los Angeles, Phoenix, Dallas, Houston, or Chicago.

You may be able to save money by booking an air/hotel package through one of the

AIRLINES TO THE ACAPULCO REGION

A number of airlines offer direct flights to Acapulco (AC) or Ixtapa-Zihuatanejo (IX), or Mexico City (MX), where quick air or bus connections with Acapulco and Ixtapa-Zihuatanejo may be made. The airlines with the most flights, in approximate descending order of activity, are **Mexicana, Aeroméxico, American, Delta, Aviacsa, Continental, America West, Alaska,** and **Air Canada.** Others offering flights are Azteca, Aerocalifornia, Allegro, and Canadian World of Vacations charter. Some flights may be seasonal (usually winter–spring) only.

AIRLINE	ORIGIN	DESTINATIONS
Mexicana	Los Angeles	MX
tel. 800/531-7921	San Francisco	MX
www.mexicana.com	San Jose	MX
	Las Vegas	MX
	Portland	MX
	Tijuana	MX
	Denver	MX
	San Antonio	MX
	Chicago	AC, MX
	New York	MX
	Miami	MX
	Toronto	MX
	Montreal	MX
	Vancouver	MX
	Baltimore/Washington	MX
Aeroméxico	Los Angeles	MX
tel. 800/237-6639	San Diego	MX
www.aeromexico.com	Ontario	MX
	Tijuana	MX
	Phoenix	MX
	Houston	MX
	Dallas	MX
	Chicago	MX
	New York	MX
	Miami	MX
	Atlanta	MX
American	Dallas	AC, MX
tel. 800/433-7300	Chicago	MX
www.aa.com	Miami	MX

AIRLINE	ORIGIN	DESTINATIONS
Delta	Los Angeles	MX
tel. 800/221-1212	Dallas	MX
www.delta.com	Atlanta	MX
	New York	MX
Aviacsa	Los Angeles	MX
tel. 800/758-2188	Las Vegas	MX
www.aviacsa.com	Houston	MX
	Miami	MX
	Tijuana	AC
	Chicago	MX
Continental	Houston	AC, IX, MX
tel. 800/231-0856	Newark	MX
www.continental.com		
America West	Phoenix	IX, AC, MX
tel. 800/363-2597		
www.americawest.com		
Alaska Airlines	Los Angeles	IX
tel. 800/426-0333	San Francisco	IX
www.alaskaair.com		
Air Canada	Toronto	MX
tel. 888/247-2262	Calgary	IX
www.aircanada.com		
Azteca	Dallas	MX
agent tel. 305/446-9820	Laredo	MX
www.azteca.com.mx	El Paso	MX
Aerocalifornia	Los Angeles	MX
tel. 800/237-6225	Tijuana	MX
www.aerocalifornia-usa.com		

airlines that routinely offer them from their Acapulco region gateway cities:

- **Aeroméxico:** tel. 800/245-8585
- **Alaska:** tel. 800/468-2248
- **American:** tel. 800/321-2121
- **America West:** tel. 800/356-6611
- **Continental:** tel. 800/634-5555
- **Delta:** tel. 800/872-7786
- **Mexicana:** tel. 866/281-3047

From Europe, Latin America, and Australasia

A few airlines fly across the Atlantic directly to Mexico City. These include **Lufthansa,** which connects directly from Frankfurt, and **Aeroméxico,** which connects directly from Paris and Madrid. In Mexico City, several connections with the Acapulco region are available, mostly via Mexicana and Aeroméxico airlines.

From Latin America, **Aeroméxico** connects directly with Mexico City from São Paulo, Brazil; Santiago, Chile; and Lima, Peru. A number of other Latin American flag carriers also fly directly to Mexico City.

Very few flights cross the Pacific directly to Mexico, except for **Japan Airlines,** which connects Tokyo-Osaka to Mexico City via Vancouver. More commonly, travelers from Australasia routinely transfer at San Francisco, Los Angeles, or Phoenix for the Acapulco region.

Baggage, Insurance, "Bumping," and In-Flight Meals

The tropical Acapulco region makes it easy to pack light. Use my packing checklist at the last minute to make certain that you're not leaving something important behind. Veteran tropical travelers condense their luggage to carry-ons only. Airlines routinely allow one carry-on (not exceeding 45 inches in combined length, width, and girth), a small book bag, and a purse. Thus relieved of heavy burdens, your trip will become much simpler.

Even if you can't avoid checking luggage, loss of it needn't ruin your vacation. *Always carry your irreplaceable items in the cabin with you.* These should include all money, credit cards, traveler's checks, keys, tickets, cameras, passport, prescription drugs, and eyeglasses.

At the X-ray security check, insist that your film and cameras be hand-inspected. Regardless of what attendants claim, repeated X-ray scanning will fog any undeveloped film, especially the sensitive ASA 400, 800, and 1600 high-speed varieties.

Travelers packing lots of expensive baggage, or who (because of illness, for example) may have to cancel a nonrefundable flight or tour, might consider buying travel insurance. Travel agents routinely sell packages that include baggage, trip cancellation, and default insurance. Baggage insurance covers you beyond the (typically $1,000 domestic, $500 international, check with your carrier) airlines' liability limits.

Trip cancellation insurance pays if you must cancel your prepaid trip, while default insurance protects you if your carrier or tour agent does not perform as agreed. Travel insurance, however, can be expensive. Traveler's Insurance Company, for example, offers $1,000 of baggage insurance per person for two weeks for about $50. (For more information, see the *Internet Resources* or call a travel agent.) Weigh your options and the cost against benefits carefully before putting your money down.

It's wise to reconfirm both departure and return flight reservations, especially during the busy Christmas and Easter seasons. This is a useful strategy, as is prompt arrival at check-in, against getting "bumped" (losing your seat) by the tendency of airlines to overbook the rush of high-season vacationers. For further protection, always try to get your seat assignment and boarding pass included with your ticket.

Airlines generally try hard to accommodate travelers with dietary or other special needs. When booking your flight, inform your travel agent or carrier of the necessity of a low-sodium, low-cholesterol, vegetarian, or lactose-reduced meal, or other requirements.

BY BUS

As air travel rules in the United States, bus travel rules in Mexico. Hundreds of gleaming luxury- and first-class buses with names such as Elite, Turistar, Futura, Omnibus de Mexico, Primera Plus, Transportes Pacífico, and Estrella Blanca (White Star) depart the border daily, headed for the Acapulco region.

Since North American bus lines ordinarily terminate just north of the Mexican border, you must usually disembark and walk to the Mexican *migración* (immigration) office just across the border. After having completed the necessary but very simple paperwork, proceed to the nearby *sitio taxi* (taxi stand) and hire a taxi (agree upon the price before getting in) to take you the few miles to the *camionera central* (central bus station).

First- and luxury-class bus service in Mexico is much cheaper and more frequent than in the United States. Tickets for comparable trips in Mexico cost a fraction of what you'd pay in the United States (as little as $50 for a 1,000-mile trip, compared to $150 in the United States).

Nevertheless, in Mexico, as on U.S. buses, you often have to take it as you find it. *Asientos reservados* (seat reservations), *boletos* (tickets), and information must generally be obtained in person at the bus station, and credit cards and traveler's checks are not often accepted. Neither are reserved bus tickets typically refundable, so don't miss the bus. On the other hand, plenty of buses roll south almost continually.

From California and the West

Cross the border to Tijuana, Mexicali, or Nogales, where you can ride one of several bus lines south along the Mexican Pacific coast route (National Highway 15): Estrella Blanca subsidiaries first-class Elite (which connects the whole way to Ixtapa, Zihuatanejo, and Acapulco), deluxe-class Turistar, second-class Transportes Norte de Sonora; or first-class independent Transportes del Pacífico.

At Mazatlán or Tepic, depending on the line, you transfer or continue on the same bus, west via Guadalajara, or south via Puerto Vallarta (the longer but more scenic option). If you choose Guadalajara, you have a pair of options: If your first destination is Zihuatanejo, transfer there to the Estrella Blanca–affiliate bus south

via Uruapan (in Michocáan) to the coast at Zihuatanejo. If, however, your first destination is Acapulco, take the Estrella Blanca–affiliate bus that bypasses Mexico City, via Toluca, thence south via expressway 95D to Acapulco.

If however, you choose to go via Puerto Vallarta, from Tepic, continue south through Manzanillo, along the gorgeously scenic Michoacán coast, to Ixtapa, Zihuatanejo, or Acapulco. Allow a minimum of two full 24-hour days for either option. Carry liquids and food (which might only be minimally available en route) with you.

Instead of doing the trip in one big bite, you might stop overnight or more for a rest in Guadalajara (go to semideluxe Hotel La Serena adjacent to the bus station, tel. 33/3600-0910, fax 33/3600-1974, $35 d) or in Puerto Vallarta (Hotel Rosita on the beach, tel. 322/223-2177, tel./fax 322/223-2000, $45) en route.

From the U.S. Midwest, South, and East

From the U.S. Midwest, cross the border from El Paso to Ciudad Juárez and ride one of the Estrella Blanca subsidiaries (luxury-class Turistar or Transportes Chihuahuenses) via Chihuahua and Torreón to either Mexico City Norte (North), or preferably, the Mexico City Sur (South) bus terminal.

From the Sur (sometimes known as Taxqueña) terminal, many buses connect directly with Taxco (Futura, Estrella de Oro), Acapulco via Chilpancingo (independent Estrella de Oro, or Estrella Blanca deluxe-class affiliates Turistar or Futura and second-class Transportes Cuauhtémoc), and Zihuatanejo. If you go from the Norte terminal, ride Estrella Blanca affiliates Turistar or Futura, or independent Estrella de Oro to Acapulco, Ixtapa, or Zihuatanejo. For the entire trip, allow at least two full days to Acapulco, a few hours longer for Ixtapa or Zihuatanejo.

From southern and eastern parts of the United States (and alternatively from the Midwest), cross the border at Laredo, Texas, to Nuevo Laredo and ride one of Estrella Blanca deluxe-class subsidiaries Turistar, Elite, or Futura to the Mexico

City Norte (or possibly Sur) terminal. Continue south, exactly as described above. Allow a minimum of a day and a half (36 hours) for the trip to Acapulco.

BY CAR OR RV

If you're adventurous and like going to out-of-the-way places, but still want to have all the comforts of home, you may enjoy driving your car or RV to the Acapulco region. On the other hand, consideration of cost, risk, wear on both you and your vehicle, and the congestion hassles in towns may change your mind.

Mexican Car Insurance

Mexico does not recognize foreign insurance. When you drive into Mexico, Mexican auto insurance is at least as important as your passport. At the busier crossings, you can get it at insurance "drive-ins" just north of the border. The many Mexican auto insurance companies are government-regulated; their numbers keep prices and services competitive.

Many Mexico insurance agents' long-hours offices line the border just north of the big crossings, especially at Tijuana, Mexicali, Nogales, Ciudad Juárez, Nuevo Laredo, and Matamoros. Although these are convenient, it may be wiser and even more convenient to get your car insurance ahead of time.

Sanborn's Mexico Insurance (tel. 956/682-6677, toll-free tel. 800/222-0158, info@sanbornsinsurance.com, www.sanbornsinsurance.com), one of the best-known agencies, certainly seems to be trying hardest. Besides insurance, Sanborn's offers a number of books and services, including the *Recreational Guide to Mexico,* a good all-Mexico road map, "smile-by-mile" *Travelog* guide to "every highway in Mexico," hotel discounts, and more. Much of the above is available to members of Sanborn's "Sombrero" Club.

Alternatively, look into **Vagabundos del Mar** (toll-free tel. 800/474-2252, www.vagabundos.com), an RV-oriented Mexico fishing and travel club that offers memberships that include a newsletter, caravaning opportunities, discounts, insurance, and much more.

Mexican car insurance runs from a bare-bones rate of about $6 a day for minimal $10,000/$50,000 (property damage/medical payments) coverage to a more typical $12 a day for more complete $20,000/$100,000 coverage. On the same scale, insurance for a $50,000 RV and equipment runs about $30 a day. These daily rates decrease sharply for six-month or one-year policies, which run from about $200 for the minimum to $400–1,600 for complete, high-end coverage.

If you get coverage for broken glass, personal effects, and legal expenses with these rates, you're lucky. Mexican policies don't usually cover them.

You should get something for your money, however. The deductibles should be no more than $300–500, the property damage/medical payments should be about double the legal minimum of $10,000/$25,000, and you should be able to get your car fixed in the United States and receive payment in U.S. dollars for losses. If not, shop around.

A Sinaloa Note of Caution

Although *bandidos* no longer menace Mexican roads (but loose burros, horses, and cattle still do), be cautious in the infamous marijuana- and opium-growing region of Sinaloa state north of Mazatlán. It's best not to stray from Highway 15 between Culiacán and Mazatlán or from Highway 40 between Mazatlán and Durango. Curious tourists have been assaulted in the hinterlands adjacent to these roads.

The Green Angels

The Green Angels have answered many motoring tourists' prayers in Mexico. Bilingual teams of two, trained in auto repair and first aid, help distressed tourists along main highways. They patrol fixed stretches of road at least twice daily by truck. To make sure they stop to help, pull completely off the highway and raise your hood. You may want to hail a passing motorist or trucker with a Mexican cell phone to call emergency direct tel. 078, the Mexico Tourism–Green Angels hotline, for you.

If, for some reason, you have to leave your

DRIVING DISTANCES TO THE ACAPULCO REGION

NOTE: DISTANCES ARE SHOWN AS MILES/KILOMETERS.
APPROXIMATE DRIVING TIMES ARE SHOWN AS HOURS:MINUTES.

— MAIN ROAD   — EXPRESSWAY

© AVALON TRAVEL PUBLISHING, INC.

ROAD SAFETY

Hundreds of thousands of visitors enjoy safe Mexican auto vacations every year. Their success is due in large part to their frame of mind: Drive defensively, anticipate and adjust to danger before it happens, and watch everything – side roads, shoulders, the car in front, and cars far down the road. The following tips will help ensure a safe and enjoyable trip.

- **Don't drive at night.** Range animals, unmarked sand piles, pedestrians, one-lane bridges, cars without lights, and drunken drivers are doubly hazardous at night.

- **Don't exceed the speed limit.** Although speed limits are rarely, it's still smart to follow them. Mexican country roads are often narrow and shoulderless. Poor markings and macho drivers who pass on curves are best faced at a speed of 40 mph (64 kph) rather than 75 mph (120 kph).

- **Don't drive on sand.** Even with four-wheel-drive, you'll eventually get stuck if you drive often or casually on beaches. When the tide comes in, who'll pull your car out?

- **Slow down** at the *topes* (speed bumps) at the edges of towns and for *vados* (dips), which can be dangerously bumpy and full of water.

- **Extend courtesy of the road.** This goes hand-in-hand with safe driving. Both courtesy and machismo are more infectious in Mexico; on the highway, it's much safer to spread the former than the latter.

- **Use *cuota autopistas*.** When convenient for your destination, these toll expressways allow for maximum speed and safety.

- **Call the Green Angels.** If you do have car trouble, the Green Angels can help. Call (or ask a passing motorist to call) them at emergency tel. 078, during daytime hours.

vehicle on the roadside, don't leave it unattended. Hire a local teenager or adult to watch it for you. Unattended vehicles on Mexican highways are quickly stricken by a mysterious disease, the symptom of which is rapid loss of vital parts.

Mexican Gasoline

Pemex, short for Petroleos Mexicanos, the government oil monopoly, markets diesel fuel and two grades of unleaded gasoline: 92-octane *premio* (PRAY-mee-oh) and 87-octane magna (MAHG-nah). Magna is good gas, yielding performance similar to that of U.S.-style regular unleaded gasoline. (My original car, whose manufacturer recommended 91-octane, ran well on Magna.) It runs about $0.60 per liter (or about $2.30 per gallon). On main highways, Pemex makes sure that major stations (typically spaced about 30 miles apart in the countryside) stock Magna.

Gas Station Thievery

Although the problem has abated considerably in recent years (by the hiring of female attendants), boys who hang around gas stations to wash windows are notoriously light-fingered. When stopping at the *gasolinera,* make sure that your cameras, purses, and other moveable items are out of reach. Also, make sure that your car has a lockable gas cap. If not, insist on pumping the gas yourself, or be super-watchful as you pull up to the gas pump to make certain that the pump reads zero before the attendant pumps the gas.

A Healthy Car

Preventive measures spell good health for both you and your car. Get that tune-up (or that long-delayed overhaul) *before,* rather than after, you leave.

Carry a stock of spare parts, which will be more difficult to get and more expensive in Mexico than at home. Carry an extra tire or two, a few cans of motor oil and octane enhancer, oil and gas filters, fan belts, spark plugs, tune-up kit, ignition points, and fuses. Be prepared with basic tools and supplies, such

MEXICO CITY DRIVING RESTRICTIONS

To reduce smog and traffic gridlock, authorities have limited which cars can drive on which days in Mexico City, depending upon the last digit of their license plates. If you violate these rules, you risk getting an expensive ticket. On Monday, no vehicle may be driven with final digits 5 or 6; Tuesday, 7 or 8; Wednesday, 3 or 4; Thursday, 1 or 2; Friday, 9 or 0. Weekends, all vehicles may be driven.

as screwdrivers, pliers including Vice-Grip, lug wrench, jack, adjustable wrenches, tire pump and patches, tire pressure gauge, steel wire, and electrical tape. For breakdowns and emergencies, carry a folding shovel, a husky rope or chain, a gasoline can, and flares.

Car Repairs in Mexico

The American big three—General Motors, Ford, and Chrysler—as well as Nissan and Volkswagen are represented by extensive dealer networks in Mexico. Latecomers Toyota and Honda are also represented, although to a much lesser extent. Getting your car or truck serviced at such agencies is straightforward. While parts will probably be higher in price, shop rates run about half U.S. prices, so repairs will generally come out cheaper than back home.

The same is not true for repairing other makes, however. Mexico has few, if any, other car or truck dealers; consequently, officially certified mechanics for other Japanese, British, and European makes are hard to find.

Nevertheless, many clever Mexican independent mechanics can fix any car that comes their way. Their humble *talleres mecánicos* (repair shops, tah-YER-ays may-KAH-nee-kohs) dot town and village roadsides everywhere.

Although most mechanics are honest, beware of unscrupulous operators who try to col-

lect double or triple their original estimate. If you don't speak Spanish, find someone who can assist you in negotiations. *Always* get a cost estimate, including needed parts and labor, in writing, even if you have to write it yourself. Make sure the mechanic understands, then ask him to sign it before he starts work. Although this may be a hassle, it might save you a much nastier hassle later. Shop labor at small, independent repair shops should run $10–20 per hour. For much more information, and for entertaining anecdotes of car and RV travel in Mexico, consult Carl Franz's *The People's Guide to Mexico.*

Bribes (*Mordidas*)

The usual meeting ground of the visitor and Mexican police is in the visitor's car on a highway or downtown street. To the tourists, such an encounter may seem mild harassment by the police, accompanied by vague threats of going to the police station or impounding the car for such-and-such a violation. The tourist often goes on to say, "It was all right, though… we

An Acapulco oil change runs about $3 for labor. Bring your own oil.

© BRUCE WHIPPERMAN

paid him $20 and he went away. … Mexican cops sure are crooked, aren't they?"

And, I suppose, if people want to go bribing their way through Mexico, that's their business. But calling Mexican cops crooked isn't exactly fair. Police, like most everyone else in Mexico, have to scratch for a living, and they have found that many tourists are willing to slip them a $20 bill for nothing. Rather than crooked, I would call them hungry and opportunistic.

Instead of paying a bribe, do what I've done a dozen times: remain cool, and if you're really guilty of an infraction, calmly say *"Boleto, por favor"* ("Ticket, please"). After a minute or two of stalling, and no cash appearing, the officer most likely will not bother with a ticket, but will wave you on with only a warning. If, on the other hand, the officer does write you a ticket, he will probably keep your driver's license, which you will be able to retrieve at the *presidencia municipal* the next day in exchange for paying your fine.

Crossing the Border

Squeezing through the border traffic bottlenecks during peak holidays and rush hours can be time-consuming. Avoid crossing 7–9 A.M. and 4:30–6:30 P.M.

Highway Routes from the United States

If you decide to drive to the Acapulco region, you have your choice of three general routes. Maximize comfort and safety by following the broad *cuota* expressways that often parallel the old narrow *libre* routes. Despite the increased cost (about $150 total to Acapulco for a car, double or triple that for a motorhome) the *cuota* expressways will save you at least a day, probably two (including the extra food and hotel tariffs) and wear and tear on both your vehicle and your nerves. Most folks in passenger cars should allow at least three (more likely four or five, depending on the route) full south-of-the-border driving days to Acapulco, Ixtapa, or Zihuatanejo. Larger RVs and motorhomes should allow at least a day or two more.

From the U.S. Pacific Coast and West, fol-low National Highway 15 (called 15D as the toll expressway) from the border at Nogales, Sonora, an easy hour's drive south via I-19 from Tucson, Arizona. (California drivers, unless you have some special reason for doing so, *do not cross the border farther west at Tijuana or Mexicali;* access by U.S. Interstate Highways 8 and/or 10 to Nogales and Highway 15 via Tucson is half a day quicker than the corresponding two-lane south-of-the-border route.)

From Nogales, Highway 15D continues southward smoothly, leading you through cactus-studded mountains and valleys that turn into lush farmland and tropical coastal plain and forest by the time you arrive at Mazatlán. Watch for the peripheral bypasses (*periféricos*) and truck routes that guide you past the congested downtowns of Hermosillo, Guaymas, Ciudad Obregón, Los Mochis, and Culiacán. Between these centers, you speed along, via the *cuota* expressway, all the way to Mazatlán. If you prefer not to pay the high tolls (about $60 Nogales–Mazatlán for a car, much more for motorhome), stick to the old *libre* highway. Hazards, bumps, and slow going might force you to reconsider, however.

From Mazatlán, continue along the narrow (but soon to be replaced) two-lane route to Tepic. There, you can either fork left (east) along Highways 15 or 15D east to Guadalajara, or fork right (south) along Highway 200 to Puerto Vallarta.

If you opt for the Guadalajara route, continue east past Tepic along the easy *cuota autopista* 15D to Guadalajara. There, you link eastward, via crosstown expressway (watch for signs) Avenida Lázaro Cárdenas to Mexico City–bound expressway 15D on the east side of town. Continue east on 15D past Morelia to Toluca, where you *do not continue ahead for Mexico City.* Instead, connect, on the southeast side of town, with Highway 55 (Boulevard José M. Pino Suárez to Metepec) that, after continuing several miles southeast, connects directly with southbound *cuota autopista* 55D to spa resort Ixtapan del Sal. Continue south on Highway 55 and connect directly with either old Highway 95 to Taxco and Iguala, or expressway 95D south, via Chilpancingo, to Acapulco (total about 1,700 miles, 2,730 km, minimum 36 hours at the wheel to Acapulco, 40 hours to Ixtapa or Zihuatanejo).

Although slower, the Puerto Vallarta route to the Acapulco region is more scenic and easier to follow. From Tepic, simply continue south, via two-lane Highway 200, through the palmy coastal resorts of Puerto Vallarta, Manzanillo, and the spectacularly scenic Michoacán coast, to Ixtapa, Zihuatanejo, and Acapulco (total about 1,600 miles, 2,580 km, minimum 40 hours at the wheel to Acapulco, 36 hours to Zihuatanejo).

Although choosing between the Puerto Vallarta and Guadalajara options appears to be a toss-up, the Guadalajara route, via expressway nearly all the way, allows for safer driving more hours per day. In effect, this might amount to as little as four days of south-of-the border traveling, in comparison to about five or six days via Puerto Vallarta. However, the extra day or two required by the Puerto Vallarta option might be well worth the scenery and the opportunity to stop in beautiful ocean-front spots along the way. But never mind, you can have it both ways: go one way coming and the other way going.

From the U.S. Midwest, South, and East, a number of routes are possible. Probably fastest and most direct is via the southern Texas Laredo–Nuevo Laredo border crossing. Continue south via *cuota autopistas* 85D, 40D, and 57D to Mexico City, thence to Acapulco via *cuota autopista* 95D. Along the way, keep an eye out for the Mexico (meaning Mexico City) signs that mark suburban bypasses (commonly labeled *libramiento* or *periférico*): before Monterrey (*periférico* Highway 40 or 40D); before Saltillo (*libramiento* Highway 57 or 57D); before San Luis Potosí (Highway 57 or 57D); before Querétaro (Highway 57D).

At the Mexico City northern outskirt, bypass the congested Mexico City downtown the same way by following the right fork Cuernavaca- or Acapulco-direction *periférico*; after several miles also fork right along Boulevard Avila Camacho *periférico,* until finally

you see the sign for *cuota* Cuernavaca/Acapulco Highway 95D. From there, you can breeze all the way to Acapulco either direct or via the smooth, wide, and scenic two-lane Taxco–Iguala Highway 95 toll cutoff.

Also, make sure that you're not in Mexico City on your forbidden day, determined by the last digit of your car license.

BY FERRY

An alternative, but much longer, route to the Acapulco region is by ferry from the southern tip of Baja California. Bus travelers should cross the border at Tijuana or Mexicali and ride Autobuses Blanca Coordinados (ABC) through the long desert to La Paz (about 20 hours). Car travelers also cross at Tijuana or Mexicali and follow good, two-lane Mexico National Highway 1 (900 miles, 1,500 km) south to La Paz.

At La Paz (a pleasant Mexican town during the winter, although often very hot during the late spring, summer, and most of the fall), your choice is **Baja Ferries** (tel. 612/125-7443, fax 612/123-0504, within Mexico toll-free tel. 800/122-1414, www.bajaferries.com). They take passengers (about $65 per adult, kids $35) and vehicles (motorcycle $55, car $100, motorhomes about $450) across to Topolobambo, near Los Mochis, in northern Sinaloa, swiftly in about six hours. The boat, the big, shiny *California Star,* which accommodates about 200 vehicles and 1,000 passengers, departs La Paz daily around 3 P.M. Reservations are strongly recommended, especially during Christmas and Easter holidays, when commercial vehicles may "bump" passenger vehicles.

During recent years, ferry service has been in a state of flux and subject to change. Be sure to check through the contact numbers and/or websites for the newest ferry information before making the long desert trip south to La Paz.

BY TOUR, CRUISE, AND SAILBOAT

For travelers on a tight time budget, prearranged tour packages can provide a hassle-free route for sampling the attractions of Acapulco-region coastal resorts and upcountry towns and cities. If, however, you prefer a self-paced vacation, or desire thrift over convenience, you should probably defer tour arrangements until after arrival. Many Acapulco-region travel and tour agencies are as close as your hotel telephone or front-lobby tour desk and can customize a tour for you. Options vary from city highlight tours and bay snorkeling adventures to shopping in inland colonial cities and sightseeing overnights to boat adventures through wildlife-rich mangrove jungle hinterlands.

By Cruise or Sailboat

Travel agents and websites advertise many cruises that include Acapulco and/or Ixtapa and Zihuatanejo on their itineraries. Vacationers who enjoy being pampered with lots of food and ready-made entertainment (and who don't mind paying for it) can have great fun on cruises. Accommodations on a typical 10-day winter tour or cruise (which would include several days in Ixpata and Zihuatanejo and/or Acapulco) can run as little as $100 per day per person, double occupancy, to as much as $1,000 or more.

If, however, you want to get to know Mexico and the local people, a cruise is not for you. Included lodging, food, and entertainment are the main events of a cruise; shore sightseeing excursions, which generally cost plenty extra, are a sideshow.

Sailboats, on the other hand, offer an entirely different kind of sea route to the Acapulco region. **Ocean Voyages** (1709 Bridgeway, Sausalito, CA 94965, tel. 415/332-4681 or 800/299-4444, fax 415/332-7460, sail@ocean-voyages.com, www.oceanvoyages.com), a California-based agency, arranges passage on a number of sail and motor vessels that regularly depart to Ixtapa, Zihuatanejo, and Acapulco from ports such as San Diego, Los Angeles, San Francisco, Seattle, and Vancouver, British Columbia. It offers customized itineraries and flexible arrangements that can vary from complete round-trip voyages to weeklong coastal idylls between Acapulco-region ports of call. Some captains allow passengers to save money by signing on as crew.

Getting Around

BY BUS

The bus is the king of the Mexican road. Dozens of lines connect virtually every town in the Acapulco region. Three distinct levels of service—deluxe, first-class, and second-class—are generally available. **Deluxe-class** (called Turistar, Futura, Diamante, and Primera Plus, depending upon the line) express coaches speed between major towns, seldom stopping en route. In exchange for relatively high fares (about $30 Acapulco–Zihuatanejo or $40 Acapulco–Taxco, for example), passengers often enjoy rapid passage and airline-style amenities: plush reclining seats, air-conditioning, an onboard toilet, video, and aisle attendant.

Although less luxurious, for about half the price **first-class** service is frequent and always includes reserved seating. Additionally, passengers enjoy soft reclining seats and air-conditioning (if it is working). Besides their regular stops at or near most towns and villages en route, first-class bus drivers, if requested, will usually stop and let you off anywhere along the road.

Second-class bus seating is unreserved. In outlying parts of the Acapulco region, there is even a class of bus beneath second-class, but given the condition of many second-class buses, it seems as if third-class buses wouldn't run at all. Such buses are the stuff of travelers' legends: the recycled old GMC, Ford, and Dodge schoolbuses that stop everywhere and carry everyone and everything to even the smallest villages tucked away in the far mountains. As long as there is any kind of a road, the bus will most likely go there.

Now and then you'll read a newspaper story of a country bus that went over a cliff somewhere in Mexico, killing the driver and a dozen unfortunate souls. The same newspapers, however, never bother to mention the half million safe passengers for whom the same bus provided trips during its 15 years of service before the accident.

Second-class buses are not for travelers with weak knees or stomachs. Often, you will initially have to stand, cramped in the aisle, in a crowd of campesinos. They are warm-hearted but poor people, so don't tempt them with open, dangling purses or wallets bulging in back pockets. Stow your money safely away. After a while, you will be able to sit down. Such privilege, however, comes with obligation, such as holding an old woman's bulging bag of carrots or a toddler on your lap. But if you accept your burden with humor and equanimity, who knows what favors and blessings may flow to you in return.

Tickets, Seating, and Baggage

Mexican bus lines do not usually publish schedules or fares. You have to ask someone who knows (such as your hotel desk clerk), or call the bus station. Not many travel agents bother handling bus tickets. If you don't want to spend the time to get a reserved ticket yourself, hire someone trustworthy to do it for you. Another option is to get to the bus station early enough on your traveling day to ensure that you'll get a bus to your destination.

Although some lines accept credit cards and issue computer-printed tickets at their major stations, most reserved bus tickets are sold for cash and handwritten, with a *número de asiento* (specific seat number) on the back. If you miss the bus, you lose your money. Furthermore, airlines-style automated reservations systems have not yet arrived at many Mexican bus stations. Consequently, you can generally buy reserved tickets only at the *salida local* (local

departure) station. (An agent in Puerto Vallarta, for example, cannot ordinarily reserve you a ticket on a bus that originates in Tepic, 100 miles up the road.)

Request a reserved seat, if possible, with numbers 1–25 in the *delante* (front) to *medio* (middle) of the bus. The rear seats are often occupied by smokers, drunks, and rowdies. At night, you will sleep better on the *lado derecho* (right side), away from the glare of oncoming traffic lights.

Baggage is generally secure on Mexican buses. Label it, however. Overhead racks are generally too cramped to accommodate airline-sized carry-ons. Carry a small bag with your money and irreplaceables on your person; pack clothes and less-essentials in your checked luggage. For peace of mind, watch the handler put your checked baggage on the bus and watch to make sure it is not mistakenly taken off the bus at intermediate stops.

If your baggage gets misplaced, remain calm. Bus employees are generally competent and conscientious. If you are patient, recovering your luggage will become a matter of honor for many of them. Baggage handlers are at the bottom of the pay scale; a tip for their mostly thankless job is very much appreciated.

On long trips, carry food, beverages, and toilet paper. Station food may be dubious, and the sanitary facilities may be ill-maintained.

If you are waiting for a first-class bus at an intermediate *salida de paso* (passing departure), you have to trust to luck that there will be an empty seat. If not, your best option may be to ride a more frequent second-class bus.

BY CAR OR RV
Rental Car

Car and Jeep rentals are an increasingly popular transportation option for Acapulco-region travelers. They offer mobility and independence for local sightseeing and beach excursions. In the resorts, most of the gang's there: Hertz, Avis, Alamo, and Budget, plus several local outfits. They generally require drivers to have a valid driver's license, passport, a major

To Guadalajara

Morelia

Pátzcuaro

Uruapan

Zitácuaro

Nueva
Italia

Altamirano

Arcelia

To Manzanillo

Lázaro
Cárdenas

Zihuatanejo

Ixtapa

Petatlán

Puerto del
Gallo

Atoyac de Álvarez

La Venta

Acapulco

Costa Grande

PACIFIC

OCEAN

140/225
3:00

91/146
2:30

60/97
1:30

30/50
0:45

30/51
0:40

6/10
0:15

42/69
1:00

130/210
4:00

83/133
2:15

32/52
1:00

127/204
4:00

143/230
3:00

49/79
1:15

22/35
0:30

9/15
0:15

78/126
2:30

81/130
2:00

79/127
2:30

50/80
1:30

30/48
0:45

13/21
0:20

13/20
0:20

15D

15

14D

37

37D

37D

37

134

51

134

200

200

196

0 ———— 25 mi
0 ———— 25 km

NOTE: DISTANCES ARE SHOWN AS MILES/KILOMETERS.
APPROXIMATE DRIVING TIMES ARE SHOWN AS HOURS:MINUTES.

DRIVING DISTANCES WITHIN THE ACAPULCO REGION

To Queretaro

57D

Mexico City

78/126
2:00

150
D
(TOLL)

Tlaxcala

30/48
0:45

95D (TOLL)

55/89
1:30

Toluca

74/119
2:15
550

(TOLL)

Cuernavaca

29/47
1:00

Cuautla

42/67
1:00

Puebla

76/123
1:30

(TOLL)

55

64/105
1:45

22/36
0:30

39/61
1:00

160

190

Izucar de
Matamoros

150

131
D

Tehuacán

Taxco

51/82
1:30

(TOLL)

39/63
1:00

Iguala

95

950

65/105
1:45

95/153
1:45

89/143
2:30

93

57/91
2:00

125

135

131
D

(TOLL)

Olinalá

22/35
1:00

Huajuapan
de León

40/64
1:15

190

Chilapa

35/57
1:15

71/115
2:30

Tlapa

Chilpancingo

32/51
0:35

37/60
1:00

171/275
6:00

125

To Oaxaca

95
950

Tierra Colorada

29/46
0:40

54/87
2:00

Ayutla

20/33
0:45

63/102
2:00

Cruz Grande

10/16
0:20

Ometepec

16/26
0:30

48/78
1:30

200

Cuajinicuilapa

32/52
1:00

Pinotepa
Nacional

Costa

Chica

200

To Puerto
Escondido

credit card, and may require a minimum age of 25. Some local companies do not accept credit cards, but offer lower rates in return.

Base prices of international agencies such as Hertz and Avis are not cheap. With a 17 percent value-added tax and mandatory insurance, rentals run more than in the United States. The cheapest possible rental car, usually a used, stick-shift VW Beetle, runs $40–60 per day or $250–450 per week, depending on location and season. Prices are highest during Christmas and pre-Easter weeks. Before departure, use the international agencies' toll-free numbers and websites for availability, prices, and reservations. During nonpeak seasons, you may save lots of pesos by waiting until arrival and renting a car through a local agency. Shop around, starting with the agent in your hotel lobby or with the local Yellow Pages (under *"Automoviles, renta de"*).

Car insurance that covers property damage, public liability, and medical payments is an absolute must with your rental car. If you get into an accident without insurance, you will be in deep trouble, and probably sent to jail. Narrow, rough roads and animals grazing at roadside make driving in Mexico more hazardous than back home. (For important car safety and insurance information, see *By Car or RV* under *Getting There* earlier in this chapter.)

BY TAXI, LOCAL TOUR, AND HITCHHIKING
Taxis

The high prices of rental cars make taxis a viable option for local excursions. Cars are luxuries, not necessities, for most Mexican families. Travelers might profit from the Mexican money-saving practice of piling everyone in a taxi for a Sunday outing. You may find that an all-day taxi and driver, who, besides relieving you of driving, will become your impromptu guide, will cost no more than a rental car.

The magic word for saving money by taxi is *colectivo:* a taxi you share with other travelers. The first place you'll practice getting a taxi will

be at either the Acapulco or Ixtapa-Zihuatanejo airport, where *colectivo* tickets are routinely sold from booths at the terminal door.

If, however, you want your own private taxi, ask for a *taxi especial,* which will run about three or four times the individual tariff for a *colectivo.*

Your airport experience will prepare you for in-town taxis, which rarely, if ever, have meters. You must establish the price before getting in. Bargaining comes with the territory in Mexico, so don't shrink from it, even though it seems a hassle. If you get into a taxi without an agreed-upon price, you are letting yourself in for a more serious and potentially nasty hassle later. If your driver's price is too high, he'll probably come to his senses as soon as you hail another taxi.

After a few days, getting taxis around town will be a cinch. You'll find that you don't have to take the more expensive taxis lined up in your hotel driveway. If the price isn't right, walk toward the street and hail a regular taxi.

In town, if you can't find a taxi, it may be because taxis are waiting for riders at the local stand, called a taxi *sitio.* Ask someone to direct you to it: *"Disculpe. ¿Dónde está el sitio taxi, por favor?"* ("Excuse me. Where is the taxi stand, please?").

Local Tours and Guides

For many Acapulco-region travelers, locally arranged tours offer a hassle-free alternative to sightseeing by rental car or taxi. Hotels and travel agencies, many of whom maintain front-lobby travel and tour desks, offer a bounty of sightseeing, water sports, bay cruise, fishing, and wildlife-viewing tour opportunities.

Hitchhiking

Most everyone agrees hitchhiking is not the safest mode of transport. If you're unsure, don't do it. Hitchhiking doesn't make for a healthy steady travel diet, nor should you hitchhike at night.

The recipe for trouble-free hitchhiking requires equal measures of luck, savvy, and technique. The best places to catch rides are where people are arriving and leaving anyway, such as bus stops, highway intersections, gas stations, and on the highway out of town.

Male/female hitchhiking partnerships seem to net the most rides (although it is techni-cally illegal for women to ride in commercial trucks). The more gear you and your partner have, the fewer rides you will get. Pickup and flatbed truck owners often pick up passengers for pay. Before hopping onto the truck bed, ask how much the ride will cost.

Information and Services

PASSPORTS, TOURIST CARDS, AND VISAS

The Mexican government welcomes visitors into their country. Certain rules do apply, however. If you require more information than the guidelines presented below, you can contact the Mexico Tourism Board hotline at toll-free U.S./Can. tel. 800/44-MEXICO (800/446-3942) or visit www.visitmexico.com. For more detailed help, you can contact either your closest office of the Mexico Tourism Board (see the sidebar "Mexico Tourism Board Offices") or contact one of the many North American Mexico consulates or embassies (for a list of Mexican consulates, visit www.mex-online.com/consulate.htm).

Your Passport

Your passport (or birth or naturalization cer-tificate) is your positive proof of national identity; without it, your status in any foreign country is in doubt. Don't leave home with-out one. U.S. citizens may obtain passports (allow four to six weeks) at local post offices. For-fee private passport agencies can speed this process and get you a passport within a week, maybe less.

Entry into Mexico

For U.S. and Canadian citizens, entry by air into Mexico for a few weeks could hardly be easier. Airline attendants hand out *tarjetas turísticas* (tourist cards) en route and officers make them official by glancing at passports and stamping the cards at the immigration gate. Business-travel permits for 30 days or fewer are handled by the same simple proce-dures.

At your south-of-the-border port of entry, Mexican border immigration officials require that all entering U.S. citizens 15 years old or over must present proper identification—either a valid U.S. passport, original or a notarized copy of your birth certificate, military ID, or state driver's license, while naturalized citizens must show naturalization papers (or a laminated naturalization card) or valid U.S. passport.

Canadian citizens must show a valid pass-port or original birth certificate. Nationals of other countries (especially those such as Hong Kong, which issue more than one type of pass-port) may be subject to different or additional regulations. For advice, consult your local Mexican consulate.

More Options

For more complicated cases, get your tourist card early enough to allow you to consider the options. Tourist cards can be issued for mul-tiple entries and a maximum validity of 180 days; photos are sometimes required. If you don't request multiple entry or the maximum time, your card will probably be stamped sin-gle entry, valid for some shorter period, such as 90 days. If you are not sure how long you'll stay in Mexico, request the maximum (180 days is the absolute maximum for a tourist card; long-term foreign residents routinely make semiannual "border runs" for new tour-ist cards).

MEXICO TOURISM BOARD OFFICES

More than a dozen Mexico Tourism Board *(Consejo de Promoción Turístico de Mexico)* offices and scores of Mexican government consulates operate in the United States, Canada, Europe, and South America. Consulates generally handle questions of Mexican nationals abroad, while Mexico Tourism Boards serve travelers heading for Mexico.

For straightforward questions and Mexico regional information brochures, call toll-free U.S./Can. tel. 800/44-MEXICO (800/446-3942) or Europe tel. 800/111-2266, or visit www.visitmexico.com. If you need more detailed information and can read a bit of Spanish, visit www.cptm.com.mx. Otherwise, contact one of the North American, European, or South American Mexico Tourism Board offices for guidance:

IN NORTH AMERICA

Los Angeles:
1880 Century Park East
Suite 511
Los Angeles, CA 90067
tel. 310/282-9112
fax 3103/282-9116
losangeles@visitmexico.com
from Arizona, California, Colorado, Hawaii, Idaho, Montana, Nevada, New Mexico, and Utah

Vancouver:
999 West Hastings Street
Suite 1110
Vancouver, British Columbia V6C 2W2
tel. 604/669-2845
fax 604/669-3498
mgto@telus.net.
from Alaska, Washington, Oregon, Idaho, Wyoming, and Montana and the Canadian provinces of British Columbia, Alberta, Yukon, Northwest Territories, and Saskatchewan

Houston:
4507 San Jacinto
Suite 308
Houston TX 77004
tel. 713/772-2581
fax 713/772-6058
houston@visitmexico.com
from Texas, Oklahoma, and Louisiana

Miami:
5975 Sunset Drive #305
Miami, FL 33143
tel. 786/621-2909
fax 786/621-2907
miami@visitmexico.com
from Alabama, Arkansas, Florida, Georgia, Mississippi, Tennessee, North Carolina, and South Carolina

Chicago:
225 North Michigan Avenue
18th Floor, Suite 1850
Chicago, IL 60601
tel. 312/228-0517
fax 312/225-0515
chicago@visitmexico.com
from Illinois, Indiana, Iowa, Kansas, Michigan, Minnesota, Missouri, Nebraska, North Dakota, Ohio, South Dakota, and Wisconsin

New York:
100 Madison Avenue
Suite 11C
New York, NY 10152
tel. 212/308-2110
fax 212/308-9060
newyork@visitmexico.com
from Connecticut, Delaware, Kentucky, Maine, Maryland, Massachusetts, New Hampshire, New Jersey, New York, Pennsylvania, Rhode Island, Vermont, Virginia, Washington, D.C., and West Virginia

Toronto:
2 Bloor Street West
Suite 1502
Toronto, Ontario M4W 3E2
tel. 416/925-0704
fax 416/925-6061
toronto@visitmexico.com
from Ontario and Manitoba

Montreal:
1 Place Ville Marie
Suite 1931
Montreal, Quebec H3B2C3
tel. 514/871-1052 or 514/871-1103
fax 514/871-3825
montreal@visitmexico.com.
from New Brunswick, Newfoundland, Nova
Scotia, Prince Edward Island, and Quebec,

IN EUROPE

In Europe, travelers may use the tourism
information number, all-Europe toll-free
Mex. tel. 800/11-2266, visit the website
www.visitmexico.com, or contact the local
offices directly.

London:
Wakefield House
41 Trinity Square
London EC3N 4DT, England, UK
tel. 207/488-9392
fax 207/265-0704
uk@visitmexico.com.

Frankfurt:
Taunusanlage 21
60325 Frankfurt-am-Main, Deutschland
tel. 697/103-3383
fax 697/103-3895
germany@visitmexico.com.

Paris:
4, Rue Notre-Dame des Victoires
75002 Paris, France
tel. 1/428-69612, 1/428-69613
fax 1/428-60580
france@visitmexico.com.

Madrid:
Calle Velázquez 126
28006 Madrid, España
tel. 91/561-3520, 91/561-1827
fax 91/411-0759
spain@visitmexico.com.

Rome:
Via Barbarini 3
piso 7, 00187 Roma, Italia
tel. 06/487-4698
fax 06/487-3630 or 06/420-4293
italy@visitmexico.com

IN SOUTH AMERICA

Contact the Mexico Tourism Board in
either Argentina or Brazil:

Buenos Aires:
Avenida Santa Fe 920
1054 Buenos Aires, Argentina
tel. 1/4393-7070 or 1/4393-6235
fax 1/4393-6607
argentina@visitmexico.com.

São Paulo:
Alameda Administrativo
Rocha Azevedo 882, Conjunto 31
Tercer Andar, São Paulo, Brazil, 01410-002
tel. 3088-2129 or 3082-5005
fax 3083-5005
brasil@visitmexico.com.

IN JAPAN

Contact the Mexico Tourism Board at
the Mexican Embassy in Tokyo:
Third Floor Annex
2-15-1-3F, Nagata-Cho, 2-chome
Chiyoda-ku, Tokyo 100-0014, Japan
tel. 335/030-290
fax 335-643
japan@visitmexico.com.

Student and Business Visas

A visa is a notation stamped and signed on your passport showing the number of days and entries allowable for your trip. Apply for a student visa at the Mexican consulate nearest your home well in advance of your departure; the same is true if you require a business visa of longer than 30 days. One-year renewable student visas are available (sometimes with considerable red tape). An ordinary 180-day tourist card may be the easiest option, if you can manage it.

Entry for Children

Children under 15 can be included on their parents' tourist cards, but complications occur if the children (by reason of illness, for example) cannot leave Mexico with both parents. Parents can avoid such red tape by getting a passport and a Mexican tourist card for each of their children.

In addition to passport or birth certificate, minors (under age 18) entering Mexico without parents or legal guardians must present a notarized letter of permission signed by both parents or legal guardians. Even if accompanied by one parent, a notarized letter from the other must be presented. Divorce or death certificates must also be presented, when applicable. Airlines will require the name, address, and telephone number of the person meeting unaccompanied minors upon arrival in Mexico.

Acapulco-region travelers should hurdle all such possible delays far ahead of time in the cool calm of their local Mexican consulate rather than the hot, hurried atmosphere of a border or airport immigration office.

Entry for Pets

A pile of red tape can delay the entry of dogs, cats, and other pets into Mexico. Be prepared with veterinary-stamped health and rabies certificates for each animal. For more information contact your local Mexico consulate or regional Mexico Tourism Board.

Don't Lose Your Tourist Card

If you do, be prepared with a copy of the original, which you should present to the nearest federal Migración (Immigration) office (on duty long hours at the Acapulco and Ixtapa-Zihuatanejo international airports) and ask for a duplicate tourist permit. Lacking this, you might present some alternate proof of your date of arrival in Mexico, such as a stamped passport or airline ticket. Savvy travelers carry copies of their tourist cards with them, while leaving the originals safe in their hotel rooms or hotel desk safes.

Car Permits

If you drive to Mexico, you will need a permit for your car. Upon entry into Mexico, be ready with originals and copies of your proof-of-ownership or registration papers (state title certificate, registration, or notarized bill of sale), current license plates, and current driver's license. The auto permit fee runs about $30, payable only by non-Mexican bank MasterCard, Visa, or American Express credit cards. (The credit-card-only requirement discourages those who sell or give away U.S.-registered cars in Mexico without paying customs duties.) Credit cards must bear the same name as the vehicle proof-of-ownership papers.

The resulting car permit becomes part of the owner's tourist card and receives the same length of validity. Vehicles registered in the name of an organization or person other than the driver must be accompanied by a notarized affidavit authorizing the driver to use the car in Mexico for a specific time.

Border officials generally allow you to carry or tow additional motorized vehicles (motorcycle, another car, large boat) into Mexico but will probably require separate documentation and fee for each vehicle. If a Mexican official desires to inspect your trailer or RV, go through it with him or her.

Accessories, such as a small trailer, boat shorter than six feet, CB radio, or outboard motor, may be noted on the car permit and must leave Mexico with the car.

For more details on motor vehicle entry and what you may bring in your baggage to Mexico, consult the AAA (American Automobile Association) *Mexico TravelBook.*

Since Mexico does not recognize foreign automobile insurance, you must buy Mexican automobile insurance.

Crossing the Border and Returning Home

Squeezing through border bottlenecks during peak holidays and rush hours can be time-consuming. Avoid crossing 7–9 A.M. and 4:30–6:30 P.M.

Just before returning across the border with your car, park and have an *aduana* (customs) official *remove and cancel the holographic identity sticker that you received on entry.* If possible, get a *recibo* (receipt) or some kind of verification that it's been *cancelado* (canceled). Tourists have been fined hundreds of dollars for inadvertently carrying uncanceled car entry stickers on their windshields.

At the same time, return all other Mexican permits, such as tourist cards and hunting and fishing licenses. Also, be prepared for Mexico exit inspection, especially for cultural artifacts and works of art, which may require exit permits. Certain religious and pre-Columbian artifacts, legally the property of the Mexican government, cannot be taken from the country.

If you entered Mexico with your car, you cannot legally leave without it except by permission from local customs authorities, usually the Aduana (Customs House) or the Oficina Federal de Hacienda (Federal Treasury Office).

All returnees are subject to U.S. immigration and customs inspection. These inspections have become much more time-consuming since September 11, 2001. On a good day, the wait amounts to about an hour. The worst bottlenecks are at busy border crossings, especially Tijuana and, to a lesser extent, Mexicali, Nogales, Ciudad Juárez, Laredo, and Brownsville, all of which should be avoided during peak hours.

U.S. law allows a fixed value (at present $400) of duty-free goods per returnee. This may include no more than one liter of alcoholic spirits, 200 cigarettes, and 100 cigars. A flat 10

percent duty will be applied to the first $1,000 (fair retail value, save your receipts) in excess of your $400 exemption. You may, however, mail packages (up to $50 value each) of gifts duty-free to friends and relatives in the United States. Make sure to clearly write "unsolicited gift" and a list of the value and contents on the outside of the package. Perfumes (over $5), alcoholic beverages, and tobacco may not be included in such packages.

Improve the security of such mailed packages by sending them by Mexpost class, similar to U.S. Express Mail service. Even better (but much more expensive), send them by Federal Express or DHL, which maintain offices in Acapulco, Ixtapa, and Zihuatanejo.

For more information on U.S. customs regulations important to travelers abroad, request a copy of the useful pamphlet *Know Before You Go* from the U.S. Customs Service (1300 Pennsylvania Avenue, Washington, DC 20229, tel. 202/354-1000, www.customs.ustreas.gov).

Additional U.S. rules prohibit importation of certain fruits, vegetables, and domestic animal and endangered wildlife products. Certain live animal species, such as parrots, may be brought into the United States, subject to 30-day agricultural quarantine upon arrival, at the owner's expense. For more details on agricultural product and live animal importation, request the free booklet *Travelers' Tips* from the U.S. Department of Agriculture (Washington, D.C. 20250, tel. 202/720-2791, www.usda.gov).

For more information on the importation of endangered wildlife products, contact the Fish and Wildlife Service (1849 C Street NW, Washington, DC 20240, tel. 202/208-4717, www.fws.gov).

MONEY
The Peso: Down and Up

Overnight in early 1993, the Mexican government shifted its monetary decimal point three places and created the "new" peso, which now trades at around 11 per U.S. dollar. Since the peso value sometimes changes rapidly, U.S. dollars have become a much more stable indicator of Mexican prices; for this reason they are used in this book to report prices. You should, nevertheless, always use pesos to pay for everything in Mexico.

Since the introduction of the new peso, the centavo (one-hundredth of a new peso) has reappeared, in coins of 5, 10, 20, and 50 centavos. Incidentally, the dollar sign, "$," also marks Mexican pesos. Peso coins (*monedas*) in denominations of 1, 2, 5, 10, and 20 pesos, and bills, in denominations of 20, 50, 100, 200, and 500 pesos, are common. Since banks like to exchange your travelers checks for a few crisp large bills rather than the often-tattered smaller denominations, ask for some of your change in 50- and 100-peso notes. A 500-peso note, while common at the bank, may look awfully big to a small shopkeeper, who might be hard-pressed to change it.

Banks, ATMs, and Money Exchange Offices

Mexican banks, like their North American counterparts, have lengthened their business hours. Your best choice is usually a branch of the Hong Kong-Shanghai Banking Corporation (HSBC) bank, which maintains very long hours: often Monday–Saturday 8 A.M.–7 P.M. Banamex (Banco Nacional de Mexico), generally the most popular with local people, usually posts the best in-town dollar exchange rate in its lobbies; for example: *Tipo de cambio: venta 10.615, compra 10.720,* which means the bank will sell pesos to you at the rate of 10.615 per dollar and buy them back for 10.720 per dollar.

ATMs (automated teller machines), called *Cajeros Automáticos,* kah-HAY-rohs ahoo-toh-MAH-tee-kohs, are rapidly becoming the money source of choice in Mexico. Virtually every bank has a 24-hour ATM, accessible (with proper PIN identification code) by a swarm of U.S. and Canadian credit and ATM cards. *Note:* Some Mexican bank ATMs may "eat" your ATM card if you don't retrieve it within about 15 seconds of completing your transaction. Retrieve your card *immediately* after getting your cash.

Although bank charges, typically about $2, for ATM cash remain small, the pesos you can usually get from a single card is limited to about $300 or less per day. Since the ATM charge is generally a fixed fee, regardless of the amount you withdraw, you will save money by withdrawing the maximum available in a single transaction.

Even without an ATM card, you don't have to go to the trouble of waiting in long bank service lines. Opt for a less-crowded bank, such as Bancomer, Banco Serfín, HSBC, or a private *casa de cambio* (money-exchange office). Often most convenient, such offices often offer long hours and faster service than the banks for a fee (as little as $0.50 or as much as $3 per $100).

Keeping Your Money Safe

Travelers checks, the traditional prescription for safe money abroad, are widely accepted in the Acapulco region. Even if you plan to use your ATM card, buy some U.S.-dollar travelers checks (of a well-known brand such as American Express or Visa) as an emergency reserve. Canadian travelers checks and currency are not as widely accepted as U.S. travelers checks, European and Asian even less. Unless you like signing your name or paying lots of per-check commissions, buy denominations of $100 or more.

In the Acapulco region, as everywhere, thieves circulate among the tourists. Keep valuables in your hotel *caja de seguridad* (security box). If you don't particularly trust the desk clerk, carry what you cannot afford to lose in a money belt. Pickpockets love crowded markets, buses, and airport terminals where they can slip a wallet out of a back pocket or dangling purse in a blink. Guard against this by carrying your wallet in your front pocket, and your purse, waist pouch, and daypack (which clever crooks can sometimes slit open) on your front side.

Don't attract thieves by displaying wads of money or flashy jewelry. Don't get sloppy drunk; if so, you may become a pushover for a determined thief.

Don't leave valuables unattended on the

beach; share security duties with trustworthy-looking neighbors, or leave a secure bag with a shopkeeper nearby.

Tipping

Without their droves of visitors, Mexican people would be even poorer. Deflation of the peso, while it makes prices low for outsiders, makes it rough for Mexican families to get by. The help at your hotel typically get paid only a few dollars a day. They depend on tips to make the difference between dire and bearable poverty. Give the *camarista* (chambermaid) and floor attendant 20 pesos every day or two. And whenever uncertain of what to tip, it will probably mean a lot to someone—maybe a whole family—if you err on the generous side.

In restaurants and bars, Mexican tipping customs are similar to those in the United States: tip waiters, waitresses, and bartenders about 15 percent for satisfactory service.

Credit Cards

Credit cards, such as Visa, MasterCard, and, to a lesser extent, American Express and Discover, are generally honored in the hotels, restaurants, handicrafts shops, and boutiques that cater to foreign tourists. You will generally get better bargains, however, in shops that depend on local trade and do not so readily accept credit cards. Such shops sometimes offer discounts for cash sales.

Whatever the circumstance, your travel money will usually go much further in Acapulco region than back home. Despite the national 15 percent ("value added" IVA) sales tax, local lodging, food, and transportation prices will often seem like bargains compared to the developed world. Outside of the pricey high-rise beachfront strips, pleasant, palmy hotel room rates often run $40 or less.

COMMUNICATIONS
Using Mexican Telephones

Although Mexican phone service has improved in the last decade, it's still sometimes hit-or-miss. If a number doesn't get through, you may have to redial it more than once. When someone answers (usually *"Bueno"*) be especially courteous. If your Spanish is rusty, say, *"¿Por favor, habla inglés?"* (POR fah-VOR, AH-blah een-GLAYS). If you want to speak to a particular person (such as María), ask, *"¿María se encuentra?"* (mah-REE-ah SAY ayn-koo-AYN-trah).

Since November 2001, when telephone numbers were standardized, Mexican phones operate pretty much the same as in the United States and Canada. In Acapulco, for example, a complete telephone number is generally written like this: 744/485-4709. As in the United States, the 744 denotes the telephone *lada* (LAH-dah, area code) and the 485-4709 is the number that you dial locally. If you want to dial this number *larga distancia* (long-distance), first dial 01 (like 1 in the United States), then 744/485-4709. All Mexican telephone numbers, with only three exceptions, begin with a three-digit *lada,* followed by a seven-digit local number. (The exceptions are Monterrey, Guadalajara, and Mexico City, which have

Street telephones are operable with readily purchasable "Ladatel" phone cards.

© BRUCE WHIPPERMAN

two-digit *ladas* and eight-digit local numbers. The Mexico City *lada* is 55; Guadalajara's is 33, Monterrey's is 81. (For example, a complete Guadalajara phone number would read 33/6897-2253.)

In Acapulco-region towns and cities, direct long-distance dialing is the rule—from hotels, public phone booths, and efficient private *larga distancia* telephone offices. The cheapest, often most convenient way to call is by buying and using a public-telephone Ladatel card. Buy them in 20-, 30-, 50-, and 100-peso denominations at the many outlets—such as mini-markets, pharmacies, liquor stores—that display the blue and yellow Ladatel sign.

Calling Mexico and Calling Home

To call Mexico direct from the United States, first dial 011 (for international access), then 52 (for Mexico), followed by the Mexican area code and local number.

For station-to-station calls to the United States from Mexico, dial 001 plus the area code and the local number. For calls to other countries, ask your hotel desk clerk or see the easy-to-follow directions in the local Mexican telephone directory.

Another convenient way (although a much more expensive one) to call home is via your personal telephone credit card. Contact your U.S. long-distance operator by dialing 001-800/462-4240 for AT&T, 001-800/674-7000 for MCI, or 001-800/877-8000 for Sprint.

Yet another (although very expensive) way of calling home is collect. You can do this in one of two ways: Simply dial 09 for the local English-speaking international operator, or dial one of the AT&T, MCI, and Sprint numbers listed above.

Note: Beware of certain private "To Call Long Distance to the U.S.A. Collect and Credit Card" telephones installed prominently in airports, tourist hotels, and shops. Tariffs on these phones often run as high as $10 per minute (with a three-minute minimum), for a total of $30, whether you talk three minutes or not. Always ask the operator for the rate, and if it's too high, buy a $3 Ladatel card that

will give you about six minutes to the United States or Canada.

In smaller towns, you must often do your long-distance phoning in the *larga distancia* (local phone office). Typically staffed by a young woman and often connected to a café, the *larga distancia* becomes an informal community social center as people pass the time waiting for their phone connections.

Post, Telegraph, and Internet Access

Mexican *correos* operate similarly, but more slowly and less securely, than their counterparts in the developed world. Mail services usually include *lista de correo* (general delivery, address letters *a/c lista de correo),* *por avión* (airmail), and Mexpost secure and fast delivery service (like U.S. Express Mail), usually from separate Mexpost offices. *Correos* also provide *servicios filatelicas* (philatelic services) and *giros* (postal money orders).

Mexican ordinary mail is sadly unreliable and pathetically slow. If, for mailings within

Mexican regular mail is slow and unreliable.

Mexico, you must have security, use the efficient, reformed government Mexpost service. For international mailings, check the local yellow pages for widely available DHL or Federal Express courier service.

Telégrafos (telegraph offices), usually near the post office, send and receive *telegramas* (telegrams) and *giros.* Telecomunicaciones (Telecom), the new high-tech telegraph offices, add telephone and public fax to the available services.

Internet service, including personal email access, has arrived in the Acapulco region's cities and larger towns. Internet cafés are becoming increasingly common, especially in Acapulco, Ixtapa, Zihuatanejo, Chilpancingo, Iguala, and Taxco. Online rates run about $1–2 per hour.

Electricity and Time

Mexican electric power is supplied at U.S.-standard 110 volts, 60 cycles. Plugs and sockets are generally two-pronged, nonpolar (like the pre-1970s U.S. ones). Bring adapters if you're going to use appliances with polar two-pronged or three-pronged plugs. (A two-pronged polar plug has different-sized prongs, one of which is too large to plug into an old-fashioned nonpolar socket.)

The Acapulco region operates on central time, just like Mexico City and most of the rest of the country, except for the northwest states of Sinaloa, Nayarit, and Sonora, which operate on mountain time, and Baja California Norte, which operates on Pacific time.

SPECIALTY TRAVEL
Bringing the Kids

Children are treasured like gifts from heaven in Mexico. Traveling with kids will ensure your welcome most everywhere. On the beach, take extra precautions to make sure they are protected from the sun.

A sick child is no fun for anyone. Fortunately, clinics and good doctors are available even in small towns. When in need, ask a storekeeper or a pharmacist, *"¿Dónde hay un doctor, por favor?"* (DOHN-day eye oon doc-TOHR por fah-VOHR). In most cases, within five

minutes you will be in the waiting room of the local physician or hospital.

Children who do not favor typical Mexican fare can easily be fed always available eggs, cheese, *hamburguesas,* milk, oatmeal, corn flakes, bananas, cakes, and cookies.

Your children will generally have more fun if they have a little previous knowledge of Mexico and a stake in the trip. For example, help them select some library picture books and magazines so they'll know where they're going and what to expect, or give them responsibility for packing and carrying their own small travel bag.

Be sure to mention your children's ages when making air reservations; child discounts of 50 percent or more are often available. Also, if you can arrange to go on an uncrowded flight, you can stretch out and rest on the empty seats.

Travel for People with Disabilities

Mexican airlines and hotels are becoming increasingly aware of the needs of travelers with disabilities. Open, street-level lobbies and large, wheelchair-accessible elevators and rooms are available in most Acapulco-region resort hotels.

United States law forbids travel discrimination against otherwise qualified people with disabilities. As long as your disability is stable and not liable to deteriorate during passage, you can expect to be treated like any passenger with special needs.

Make reservations far ahead of departure and ask your agent to inform your airline of your needs, such as boarding wheelchair or in-flight oxygen. Be early at the gate to take advantage of the pre-boarding call.

For many helpful details to smooth your trip, get a copy of *Survival Strategies for Going Abroad* by Laura Hershey, published in 2005 by Mobility International USA (P.O. Box 10767, Eugene, OR 97440, tel. 541/343-1284 voice/TDD, fax 541/343-6812, www.miusa.org). Mobility International is a valuable resource for many lovers of Mexico with disabilities, for it encourages travelers with a goldmine of information and literature and can provide them with valuable Mexico connections. A

$35 membership gets you a regular newsletter and referrals for international exchanges and homestays.

Similarly, **Partners of the Americas** (1424 K St. NW, Suite 700, Washington, DC 20005, tel. 202/628-3300 or 800/322-7844, fax 202/628-3306, info@partners.net, www.partners.net), with chapters in 45 U.S. states, works to improve understanding of disabilities and facilities in Mexico and Latin America. It maintains communications with local organizations and individuals whom travelers with disabilities may contact at their destinations.

Gay and Lesbian Travel

The great majority of visitors find Acapulco people both gracious and tolerant. This extends from racial color-blindness to being broad-minded about sexual preference. As long as gay and lesbian visitors don't flaunt their own preference, they will find acceptance most anywhere in the Acapulco region.

As a result, both Acapulco and to a smaller extent, Zihuatanejo, have acquired a growing cadre of gay- and lesbian-friendly hotels, bars, and entertainments. For example, for Acapulco and Zihuatanejo hotel details, visit the gay-and lesbian-oriented travel websites www.purpleroofs.com/mexico and www.gayjourney.com/hotels/mexico/htm.

Some gay- and lesbian-oriented Internet and print publishers also offer excellent travel guidebooks. One of the most experienced is **Damron Company** (tel. 415/255-0404 or 800/462-6654, www.damron.com), which publishes, both in print and by Internet subscription, the *Damron Women's Travel* and *Damron Men's Travel* guidebooks, that contain a wealth of gay and lesbian travel information, including some listings in the Acapulco region.

Also, **Purple Roofs** provides a plethora of gay and lesbian travel information that likewise includes the Acapulco region, through its website www.purpleroofs.com.

If you're interested in gay and lesbian travel advice and services, check out **Now Voyager** (tel. 415/626-1169 or 800/255-6951, www.nowvoyager.com), a reliable San Francisco,

California–based travel agency. They offer a multitude of services, from tours and air tickets to travel insurance and hotel reservations.

Travel for Senior Citizens

Age, according to Mark Twain, is a question of mind over matter: If you don't mind, it doesn't matter. Mexico is a country where whole extended families, from babies to great-grandparents, live together. Elderly travelers will benefit from the respect and understanding Mexicans accord to older people. Besides these encouragements, consider the number of retirees already in havens in Puerto Vallarta, Guadalajara, Lago Chapala, and other regional centers.

Certain organizations support senior travel. Leading the field is **Elderhostel** (11 Ave. de Lafayette, Boston, MA 02111-1746, tel. 877/426-8056, www.elderhostel.org). Elderhostel invites folks over 50 to join their extensive U.S. and international program of special tours, study, homestays, and people-to-people travel itineraries. Contact them for their free catalogs.

A number of newsletters publicize senior vacation and retirement opportunities. Among the best is the *Mexico File* (Simmonds Publications, 5580 La Jolla Blvd. #306, La Jolla, CA 92037, tel./fax 858/456-4419 or 800/563-9345 voice mail, mf@mexicofile.com, www.mexicofile.com) monthly newsletter that, besides featuring pithy stories by Mexico travelers and news updates, offers an opportunity-packed classified section of Mexico rentals, publications, services, and much more. Subscriptions are $39/year.

Some books publicize senior travel opportunities. One of the pithiest is *Unbelievably Good Deals and Great Adventures You Can't Have Unless You're Over 50,* by Joan Rattner Heilman (McGraw Hill, 2003). Its 200 pages are packed with details of how to get bargains on cruises, tours, car rentals, lodgings, and much, much more.

Seniors with Internet access (as close as your neighborhood library these days) will find a gold mine of senior-oriented travel information online: On the Google search engine (www.google.com), I typed in "Senior Travel" and netted more than 83 million responses. Near the top of the list was the **Transitions Abroad** site, www.transitionsabroad.com, which offers dozens upon dozens of articles and links about seniors living, working, and traveling abroad. Other top-pick sites that I netted at the same time included the super-informative www.elderhostel.com, www.independent-travel.com, and www.smartertravel.com.

Health and Safety

STAYING HEALTHY

In the Acapulco region, as everywhere, prevention is the best remedy for illness. For those visitors who confine their travel to the beaten path, a few basic common-sense precautions will ensure vacation enjoyment.

Resist the temptation to dive headlong into Mexico. It's no wonder that people get sick—broiling in the sun, gobbling peppery food, guzzling beer and margaritas, then discoing half the night—all in their first 24 hours. An alternative is to give your body time to adjust. Travelers often arrive tired and dehydrated from travel and heat. During the first few days, drink plenty of bottled water and juice, and take siestas.

Immunizations and Precautions

A good physician can recommend the proper preventatives for your Acapulco-region trip. If you are going to stay pretty much in town, your doctor will probably suggest little more than updating your basic typhoid, diphtheria-tetanus, hepatitis, and polio shots.

For camping or trekking in remote tropical areas—below 4,000 feet or 1,200 meters—doctors often recommend a gamma-globulin shot against hepatitis A and a schedule of chloroquine pills against malaria. While in backcountry areas, use other measures to discourage mosquitoes—and fleas, flies, ticks, no-see-ums, "kissing bugs", and other tropical pesties—from biting you. Common precautions include sleeping under mosquito netting, burning *espirales mosquito* (mosquito coils), and rubbing on plenty of pure DEET (n,n di-methyl-meta-toluamide) "jungle juice," mixed in equal parts with rubbing (70 percent iso-propyl) alcohol. Although super-effective, 100 percent DEET dries and irritates the skin.

Sunburn

For sunburn protection, use a good sunscreen with a sun protection factor (SPF) rated 15 or more, which will reduce burning rays to one-fifteenth or less of direct sunlight. Better still, take a shady siesta-break from the sun during the most hazardous midday hours. If you do get burned, applying your sunburn lotion (or one of the "caine" creams) after the fact usually decreases the pain and speeds healing.

Safe Water and Food

Although municipalities have made great strides in sanitation, food and water are still potential sources of germs in some parts of the Acapulco region. Although it's probably safe most everywhere, except in a few upcountry localities, it's still probably best to drink bottled water only. Hotels, whose success depends vitally on their customers' health, generally provide *agua purificada* (purified bottled water). If, for any reason, the available water is of doubtful quality, add a water purifier, such as Potable Aqua brand (get it at a camping goods stores before departure) or a few drops per quart of water of *blanqueador* (household chlorine bleach) or *yodo* (tincture of iodine) from the pharmacy.

Pure bottled water, soft drinks, beer, and fresh fruit juices are so widely available it is easy to avoid tap water, especially in restaurants. Ice and *paletas* (frozen juice-on-a-stick) may be risky, especially in small towns.

MEDICAL TAGS AND AIR EVACUATION

Travelers with special medical problems might consider wearing a medical identification tag. For a reasonable fee, **Medic Alert** (P.O. Box 1009, Turlock, CA 95381, tel. 209/668-3333 or 888/633-4298, www.medicalert.org), provides such tags. Additionally, they offer a multitude of travel-related medical services, such as an information hotline that will provide doctors with your vital medical background information, and much more.

For life-threatening emergencies, highly recommended **Aeromedevac** (Montgomery Field, 3550 Afton Rd. #200, San Diego, CA 92123, tel. 619/284-7910 or 800/462-0911, from Mexico 24-hr tel. 001-800/832-5087, www.aeromedevac.com) provides high-tech jet ambulance service from any Mexican locale to a U.S. hospital for roughly $20,000.

Alternatively, for similar services, consider Alabama-based **Medjet Assistance** (toll-free U.S. tel. 800/963-3538, www.medjetassist.com). In emergencies worldwide, call U.S. tel. 205/595-6626 collect.

Washing hands before eating in a restaurant is a time-honored Mexican ritual that visitors should religiously follow. The humblest Mexican eatery will generally provide a basin to *lavar las manos* (wash the hands). If it doesn't, don't eat there.

Hot, cooked food is generally safe, as are peeled fruits and vegetables. Milk and cheese these days in Mexico are generally processed under sanitary conditions and sold pasteurized (ask, *"¿Pasteurizado?"*) and are typically safe. Mexican ice cream used to be both bad-tasting and of dubious safety, but national brands available in supermarkets are so much improved that it's no longer necessary to resist ice cream while in town.

In recent years, much cleaner public water and increased hygiene awareness have made salads—once shunned by Mexico travelers—generally safe to eat in tourist-frequented Acapulco-region cafés and restaurants. Nevertheless, lettuce and cabbage, particularly in country villages, are more likely to be contaminated than tomatoes, carrots, cucumbers, onions, and green peppers. In any case, you can try dousing your salad in *vinagre* (vinegar) or plenty of sliced *limón* (lime) juice, the acidity of which kills some but not all bacteria.

First-Aid Kit

In the tropics, ordinary cuts and insect bites are more prone to infection and should receive immediate first aid. A first-aid kit with aspirin, rubbing alcohol, hydrogen peroxide, water-purifying tablets, household chlorine bleach or iodine for water purifying, swabs, bandages, gauze, adhesive tape, Ace bandage, chamomile (*manzanilla*) tea bags for upset stomachs, Pepto-Bismol, acidophilus tablets, antibiotic ointment, hydrocortisone cream, mosquito repellent, knife, and good tweezers is a good precaution for any traveler and mandatory for campers.

HEALTH PROBLEMS
Traveler's Diarrhea

Traveler's diarrhea (known in Southeast Asia as "Bali Belly" and in Mexico as *turista* or "Montezuma's Revenge") sometimes persists, even among prudent vacationers. You can suffer *turista* for a week after simply traveling from California to Philadelphia or New York. Doctors say the familiar symptoms of runny bowels, nausea, and sour stomach result from normal local bacterial strains to which newcomers' systems need time to adjust. Unfortunately, the dehydration and fatigue from heat and travel reduce your body's natural defenses and sometimes lead to a persistent cycle of sickness at a time when you least want it.

Time-tested protective measures can help your body either prevent or break this cycle. Many doctors and veteran travelers swear by Pepto-Bismol for soothing sore stomachs and stopping diarrhea. Acidophilus, the bacteria found in yogurt, is widely available in the United States in tablets and aids digestion.

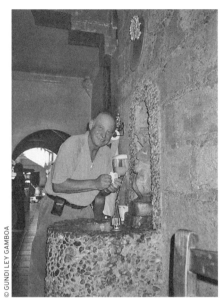

Washing your hands before meals is a time-honored Mexican custom.

Warm *manzanilla* (chamomile) tea, used widely in Mexico (and by Peter Rabbit's mother), provides liquid and calms upset stomachs. Temporarily avoid coffee and alcohol, drink plenty of *manzanilla* tea, and eat bananas and rice for a few meals until your tummy can take regular food.

Although powerful antibiotics and antidiarrhea medications such as Lomotil and Imodium are readily available over *farmacia* counters, they may involve serious side effects and should not be taken in the absence of medical advice. If in doubt, consult a doctor.

Chagas' Disease and Dengue Fever

Chagas' disease, spread by the "kissing" (or, more appropriately, "assassin") bug, is a potential hazard in the Mexican tropics. Known locally as a *vinchuca*, the triangular-headed, three-quarter-inch (two-centimeter) brown insect, identifiable by its yellow-striped abdomen, often drops upon its sleeping victims from the thatched ceiling of a rural house at night. Its bite is followed by swelling, fever, and weakness and can lead to heart failure if left untreated. Application of drugs at an early stage can, however, clear the patient of the trypanosome parasites that infect victims' bloodstreams and vital organs. See a doctor immediately if you believe you're infected.

Most of the precautions against malaria-bearing mosquitoes also apply to dengue fever, which does occur (although uncommonly) in outlying tropical areas of Mexico. The culprit here is a virus carried by the mosquito species *Aedes aegypti.* Symptoms are acute fever, with chills, sweating, and muscle aches. A red, diffuse rash frequently results, which may later peel. Symptoms abate after about five days, but fatigue may persist. A particularly serious, but fortunately rare, form, called dengue hemorrhagic fever, afflicts children and can be fatal. See a doctor immediately. Although no vaccines or preventatives, other than deterring mosquitoes, exist, you should nevertheless see a doctor immediately.

For more good tropical preventative information, get a copy of the excellent pamphlet distributed by the International Association of Medical Advice to Travelers (IAMAT).

Scorpions and Snakes

While camping or staying in a *palapa* or other rustic accommodation, watch for scorpions, especially in your shoes, which you should shake out every morning. Scorpion stings and snakebites are rarely fatal to an adult but are potentially very serious for a child. Get the victim to a doctor calmly but quickly.

Sea Creatures

While snorkeling or surfing, you may suffer a coral scratch or jellyfish sting. Experts advise you to wash the afflicted area with ocean water and pour alcohol (rubbing alcohol or tequila) over the wound, then apply hydrocortisone cream available from the *farmacia.*

Injuries from sea urchin spines and stingray barbs are painful and can be serious. Physicians recommend similar first aid for both: remove the spines or barbs by hand or with tweezers, then soak the injury in as-hot-as-possible fresh water to weaken the toxins and provide relief. Another method is to rinse the area with an antibacterial solution—rubbing alcohol, vinegar, wine, or ammonia diluted with water. If none are available, the same effect may be achieved with urine, either your own or someone else's. Get medical help immediately.

Tattoos

All health hazards don't come from the wild. A number of Mexico travelers have complained of complications from black henna tattoos. When enhanced by the chemical dye PPD, an itchy rash results that can lead to scarring. It's best to play it safe: If you must have a vacation tattoo, get it at an established, professional shop.

MEDICAL CARE

For medical advice and treatment, let your hotel (or if you're camping, the closest *farmacia*) refer you to a good doctor, clinic, or hospital. Mexican doctors, especially in medium-sized and small towns, practice like private doctors in the United States and Canada once did before health insurance, liability, and group practice. They will come to you if you request it; they often keep their doors open even after regular hours and charge reasonable fees.

You will receive generally good treatment at the many local hospitals in the Acapulco-region's tourist centers. If you must have an English-speaking, American-trained doctor, the International Association for Medical Assistance to Travelers (IAMAT, 1623 Military Road #279, Niagra Falls, NY 14304-1745, tel. 716/754-4883; in Canada at 40 Regal Road, Guelph, ON N1K 1B5, tel. 519/836-0102, or 1287 St. Clair Ave. West, Toronto, Ontario M6E 1B8, tel. 416/652-0137; info@iamat.org, www.iamat.org) publishes an updated booklet of qualified member physicians, some of whom practice in Acapulco, Ixtapa, and Zihuatanejo. IAMAT also distributes a very detailed *How to Protect Yourself Against Malaria* guide, together with worldwide malaria-risk and communicable-disease charts.

For more useful information on health and safety in Mexico, consult Drs. Robert H. Paige and Curtis P. Page's *Mexico: Health and Safety Travel Guide* (Tempe, AZ: Med to Go Books, 2004), or Dirk Schroeder's *Staying Healthy in Asia, Africa, and Latin America* (Emeryville, CA: Avalon Travel Publishing, 2000).

CONDUCT AND CUSTOMS
Safe Conduct

Mexico is an old-fashioned country where people value traditional ideals of honesty, fidelity, and piety. Crime rates are low; visitors are often safer in Mexico than in their home cities.

Even though four generations have elapsed since Pancho Villa raided the U.S. border, the image of a Mexico bristling with *bandidos* persists. And similarly for Mexicans: despite the century and a half since the *yanquis* invaded Mexico City and took half their country, the communal Mexican psyche still views gringos (and, by association, all white foreigners) with revulsion, jealousy, and wonder.

Fortunately, the Mexican love-hate affair with foreigners does not usually apply to individual visitors. Your friendly *"buenos dias"* ("good morning") or *"por favor"* ("please"), when appropriate, is always appreciated, whether in the market, the gas station, or the hotel. The shy smile you will most likely receive in return will be your small, but not insignificant, reward.

Women

Your own behavior, despite low crime statistics, largely determines your safety in Mexico. For women traveling solo, it is important to realize that the double standard is alive and well in Mexico. Dress and behave modestly and you will most likely avoid embarrassment. Whenever possible, stay in the company of friends or acquaintances; find companions for beach, sightseeing, and shopping excursions. Ignore strange men's solicitations and overtures. A Mexican man on the prowl will invent the sappiest romantic overtures to snare a gringa. He

MACHISMO

I once met an Acapulco man who wore five gold wristwatches and became angry when I quietly refused his repeated invitations to get drunk with him. Another time, on the beach near San Blas, two drunk campesinos nearly attacked me because I was helping my girlfriend cook a picnic dinner. Outside Taxco I once spent an endless hour in the seat behind a bus driver who insisted on speeding down the middle of the two-lane highway, honking aside oncoming automobiles.

Despite their ethnic and socioeconomic differences, all four men shared the common affliction of machismo, an affliction that seems to possess many Mexican men. Machismo is a sometimes-reckless obsession to prove one's masculinity, to show how macho you are. Men of many nationalities share the instinct to prove themselves. Japan's *bushido* samurai code is one example.

When confronted by a Mexican braggart, male visitors should remain careful and controlled. If your opponent is yelling, stay cool, speak softly, and withdraw as soon as possible. On the highway, be courteous and unprovoking – don't use your car to spar with a macho driver. Drinking often leads to problems. It's best to stay out of bars or cantinas unless you're prepared to deal with the macho consequences. Polite refusal of a drink may be taken as a challenge. If you visit a bar with Mexican friends or acquaintances, you may be heading for a no-win choice between a drunken all-night *borrachera* (binge) or an insult to the honor of your friends by refusing.

For women, machismo requires even more cautious behavior. In Mexico, women's liberation is long in coming. Although a handful of Mexican women have risen to positions of political or corporate power, they constitute a small minority.

Female visitors should keep a low profile and wear bathing suits and brief shorts only at the beach. They can follow the example of their Mexican sisters by making a habit of going out in the company of friends or acquaintances, especially at night. Many Mexican men believe an unaccompanied woman wants to be picked up. Ignore their offers; any response, even refusal, might be taken as an encouraging sign. If, on the other hand, there is a Mexican man whom you'd genuinely like to meet, the traditional way is an arranged introduction through family or friends.

Mexican families, as a source of protection and friendship, should not be overlooked – especially on the beach or in the park, where, among the gaggle of kids, grandparents, aunts, and cousins, there's room for one more.

will often interpret anything but a firm "no" as a "maybe," and a "maybe" as a yes.

Men

For male visitors, alcohol often leads to trouble. Avoid bars and cantinas; and if, given Mexico's excellent beers, you can't abstain completely, at least maintain soft-spoken self-control in the face of challenges from macho drunks.

The Law and Police

While Mexican authorities are tolerant of alcohol, they are decidedly intolerant of other substances such as marijuana, psychedelics, cocaine, and heroin. Getting caught with such drugs in Mexico usually leads to swift and severe results.

Equally swift is the punishment for nude sunbathing, which is both illegal in public and offensive to Mexicans. Confine your nudist behavior to very private locations.

Although with decreasing frequency lately, traffic police in Acapulco, Ixtapa, and Zihuatanejo sometimes seem to watch foreign cars with eagle eyes. Officers seem to inhabit busy intersections and one-way streets, waiting for confused tourists to make a wrong move. If they whistle you over, stop immediately or you will really get into hot water. If guilty, say *"Lo siento"* ("I'm sorry") and be cooperative. Although the officer probably won't mention it, he or she is usually hoping that you'll cough up a $20 *mordida* (bribe) for the privilege of driving away.

Don't do it. Although he may hint at confiscating your car, calmly ask for an official *boleto* (written traffic ticket) if you're guilty, in exchange for your driver's license (have a copy), which the officer will probably keep if he writes a ticket. If after a few minutes no money appears, the officer will most likely give you back your driver's license rather than go to the trouble of writing the ticket. If not, the worst that will usually happen is you will have to go to the *presidencia municipal* the next morning and pay the $20 to a clerk in exchange for your driver's license.

Pedestrian and Driving Hazards

Although the Acapulco region's potholed pavements and "holey" sidewalks won't land you in jail, one of them might send you to the hospital if you don't watch your step, especially at night. "Pedestrian beware" is especially good advice on Mexican streets, where it is rumored that some drivers speed up rather than slow down when they spot a tourist stepping off the curb. Falling coconuts, especially frequent on windy days, constitute an additional hazard to unwary campers and beachgoers.

Driving Mexican country roads, where slow trucks and carts block lanes; campesinos stroll the shoulders; and horses, burros, and cattle wander at will; is hazardous—doubly so at night.

Socially Responsible Travel

Latter-day jet travel has brought droves of vacationing tourists to developing countries largely unprepared for the consequences. As the visitors' numbers swell, power grids black out, sewers overflow, and roads crack under the strain of accommodating more and larger hotels, restaurants, cars, buses, and airports.

Worse yet, armies of vacationers drive up local prices and begin to change native customs. While visions of tourists as sources of fast money replace traditions of hospitality, television wipes out folk entertainments, Coke and Pepsi substitute for fruit drinks, and prostitution and drugs flourish.

Some travelers have said enough is enough and are forming organizations to encourage visitors to travel with increased sensitivity to native people and customs. They have developed travelers' codes of ethics and guidelines that encourage visitors to stay at local-style accommodations, use local transportation, and seek alternative vacations and tours, such as language-study and cultural programs and people-to-people work projects.

What to Take

"Men wear pants, ladies be beautiful" was once the dress code of one of the Mexican Pacific's classiest hotels. Men in the casual Acapulco region can get by easily without a jacket, women with simple skirts and blouses.

Loose-fitting, hand-washable, easy-to-dry clothes make for trouble-free tropical vacationing. Synthetic or cotton-synthetic-blend shirts, blouses, pants, socks, and underwear will fit the bill practically always on the Acapulco region's balmy coast. For breezy nights, bring a lightweight windbreaker. If you're going up-country (Chilpancingo, Iguala, Taxco), add a medium-weight jacket.

In all cases, leave showy, expensive clothes and jewelry at home. Stow items that you cannot lose

PACKING CHECKLIST

Use this list as a last-minute check to make sure that you've packed all of the items essential to your Mexico trip:

NECESSARY ITEMS
__ camera, film (expensive in Mexico)
__ comb
__ guidebook, reading books
__ inexpensive watch, clock
__ keys, tickets
__ lightweight clothes, hat for sun
__ money, ATM card, and/or travelers checks
__ mosquito repellent
__ prescription eyeglasses
__ prescription medicines and drugs
__ purse, waist-belt carrying pouch
__ sunglasses, sunscreen
__ swimsuit
__ toothbrush, toothpaste
__ tourist card, visa
__ windbreaker

USEFUL ITEMS
__ address book
__ birth control
__ checkbook, credit cards
__ contact lenses
__ dental floss
__ earplugs
__ first-aid kit
__ flashlight, batteries
__ immersion heater
__ lightweight binoculars
__ portable radio/cassette player
__ razor

__ travel booklight
__ vaccination certificate

NECESSARY ITEMS FOR CAMPERS
__ collapsible gallon plastic bottle
__ dish soap
__ first-aid kit
__ hammock (buy in Mexico)
__ insect repellent
__ lightweight hiking shoes
__ lightweight tent
__ matches in waterproof case
__ nylon cord
__ plastic bottle, quart
__ pot scrubber/sponge
__ sheet or light blanket
__ Sierra Club cup, fork, and spoon
__ single-burner stove with fuel
__ Swiss army knife
__ tarp
__ toilet paper
__ towel, soap
__ two nesting cooking pots
__ water-purifying tablets or iodine

USEFUL ITEMS FOR CAMPERS
__ compass
__ dishcloths
__ hot pad
__ instant coffee, tea, sugar, powdered milk
__ moleskin (Dr. Scholl's)
__ plastic plate
__ poncho
__ short (votive) candles
__ whistle

in your hotel safe or carry them with you in a sturdy zipped purse or a waist pouch on your front side.

Packing

What you pack depends on how mobile you want to be. If you're staying the whole time at a self-contained resort, you can take the two suitcases and one carry-on allowed by airlines. If, on the other hand, you're going to be moving around a lot, you'd do better to condense everything to one easily carried bag with wheels that doubles as luggage and soft backpack.

Experienced travelers accomplish this by packing prudently and tightly, choosing items that will do double or triple duty.

Campers will have to be super-careful to accomplish this. Fortunately, camping along the tropical coast requires no sleeping bag. Simply use a hammock (buy it in Mexico) or, if sleeping on the ground, a sleeping pad and a sheet for cover. In the winter, you may have to buy a light blanket at most. A compact tent that you and your partner can share is a must against bugs, as is mosquito repellent. A first-aid kit is absolutely necessary.

RESOURCES

Glossary

Many of the following words have a social-historical meaning; others you will not find in the usual English–Spanish dictionary.

abarrotes, abarrotería grocery, grocery store

agencia de viajes travel agent

alcalde mayor or municipal judge

alfarería pottery

alfarero, alfarera potter

andando walkway or strolling path

antojitos native Mexican snacks, such as tamales, *chiles rellenos*, tacos, and enchiladas

artesanías handicrafts, as distinguished from *artesano* or *artesana*, a person who makes handicrafts

audiencia one of the royal executive-judicial panels sent to rule Mexico during the 16th century

ayuntamiento either the town council or the building where it meets

bienes raices literally "good roots," but popularly, real estate

birria goat, pork, or lamb stew, in spiced tomato broth, especially typical of Jalisco

boleto ticket, boarding pass

caballero literally, "horseman," but popularly, gentleman

cabecera head town of a municipal district, or headquarters in general

cabrón literally a cuckold, but more commonly, bastard, rat, or S.O.B.; sometimes used affectionately

cacique chief or boss

calandria early 1800s-style horse-drawn carriage, common in Guadalajara

camionera bus station

campesino country person; farm worker

canasta basket of woven reeds, with handle

casa de huéspedes guesthouse, usually operated in a family home

caudillo dictator or political chief

centro de salud health center

charro, charra gentleman cowboy or cowgirl

chingar literally "to rape," but also the universal Spanish "f" word, the equivalent of "screw" in English

churrigueresque Spanish baroque architectural style incorporated into many Mexican colonial churches, named after José Churriguera (1665-1725)

ciclopista bike path

científicos literally, scientists, but applied to President Porfirio Díaz's technocratic advisers

codex An early Mexican colonial-era document of preconquest legends, history, and customs, dictated by reputable indigenous witnesses, under the direction of Spanish chroniclers. Many codices are preserved in European museums.

cofradía Catholic fraternal service association, either male or female, mainly in charge of financing and organizing religious festivals

colectivo a shared public taxi or minibus that picks up and deposits passengers along a designated route (also *taxi colectivo*)

colegio preparatory school or junior college

colonia suburban subdivision/satellite of a larger city

Conasupo government store that sells basic foods at subsidized prices

correo post office

criollo person of all-Spanish descent born in the New World

cuadra Huichol yarn painting, usually rectangular

cuota toll, as in *cuota autopista* (toll expressway)

Cuaresma Lent

curandero(a) indigenous medicine man or woman

damas ladies, as in "ladies room"

Domingo de Ramos Palm Sunday

ejido a constitutional, government-sponsored form of community, with shared land ownership and cooperative decision making

encomienda colonial award of tribute from a designated indigenous district

estación de ferrocarril railroad station

farmacia pharmacy or drugstore

finca farm

fonda foodstall or small restaurant, often in a traditional market complex

fraccionamiento city sector or subdivision

fuero the former right of clergy to be tried in separate ecclesiastical courts

gachupín "one who wear spurs"; a derogatory term for a Spanish-born colonial

gasolinera gasoline station

gente de razón "people of reason"; whites and mestizos in colonial Mexico

gringo once derogatory but now commonly used term for North American whites

grito impassioned cry, as in Hidalgo's Grito de Dolores

gruta limestone cavern

hacienda large landed estate; also the government treasury

hidalgo nobleman; called honorifically by "Don" or "Doña"

indígena indigenous or aboriginal inhabitant of all-native descent who speaks his or her native tongue. Commonly, but incorrectly, an Indian (*indio*).

jardín garden

jaripeo the hazardous art of bull riding and roping, a popular event during *charreadas* (known as rodeos in the southwest United States)

jejenes "no-see-um" biting gnats

judiciales the federal or state "judicial" or investigative police, best known to motorists for their highway checkpoint inspections

jugería stall or small restaurant providing a large array of squeezed vegetable and fruit *jugos* (juices)

juzgado the "hoosegow," or jail

larga distancia long-distance telephone service, or the *caseta* (booth) where it's provided

licenciado academic degree (abbrev. Lic.) approximately equivalent to a bachelor's degree

lonchería small lunch counter, usually serving juices, sandwiches, and *antojitos*

machismo; macho exaggerated sense of maleness; person who holds such a sense of himself

mañanitas early-morning Masses, usually in honor of a patron saint

mestizo person of mixed native/European descent

mescal alcoholic beverage distilled from the fermented hearts of maguey (century plant)

milpa native farm plot, usually of corn, squash, and beans

mojigango a comical, often giant effigy, usually performed by a costumed person on stilts as part of a fiesta celebration

molcajete a sturdy three-legged grinding bowl, often made of lava rock and traditionally used for grinding *chiles;* but in country-style restaurants, a savory stew of *nopales,* vegetables, broth, and meat, served in a *molcajete* and labeled as such on the menu

mordida slang for bribe; literally "little bite"

nopales edible cactus leaves

palapa thatched-roof structure, often open and shading a restaurant

panga outboard launch (*lancha*)

papier-mâché the craft of glued, multilayered paper sculpture, especially in Tonalá, Jalisco, where creations resemble fine pottery or lacquerware

Pasquas, Semana Santa, Domingo de Pasquas Easter, Easter week, Easter Sunday

Pemex acronym for Petróleos Mexicanos, the national oil corporation

peninsulares the Spanish-born ruling colonial elite

peón a poor wage-earner, usually a country native

petate a mat, traditionally woven of palm leaf

piñata papier-mâché decoration, usually in animal or human form, filled with treats and broken open during a fiesta

plan political manifesto, usually by a leader or group consolidating or seeking power

Porfiriato the 34-year (1876–1910) ruling period of President-dictator Porfirio Díaz

pozahuanco horizontally striped hand-woven wraparound skirt

pozole stew, of hominy in broth, usually topped by shredded pork, cabbage, and diced onion

preventiva municipal (or sometimes state) police

presidencia municipal the headquarters, like a U.S. city or county hall, of a Mexican *municipio* (county-like local governmental unit)

pronunciamiento declaration of rebellion by an insurgent leader

puente literally "bridge," but commonly a holiday weekend, when resort hotels often fill and reservations are highly recommended

puta a derogatory term for women

pueblo town or people

quinta a villa or country house

quinto the royal "one-fifth" tax on treasure and precious metals

retorno cul-de-sac

ropa típica traditional dress, derived from the Spanish colonial tradition (in contrast to *traje*, traditional indigenous dress)

rurales pre-1910 federal country police force created to fight *bandidos*

taxi especial private taxi, as distinguished from *taxi colectivo* (collective taxi)

telégrafo telegraph office, lately converting to high-tech *telecomunicaciones,* or *telecom*, offering telegraph, telephone, and public fax services

tenate soft, pliable basket, without handle, woven of palm leaf

tianguis native market, also an awning, pronounced tee-AHN-geese

traje traditional indigenous dress

vaquero cowboy

vecinidad neighborhood

vinchuca "kissing" or "assassin" bug

yanqui Yankee

zócalo town plaza or central square

ABBREVIATIONS

Av. *avenida* (avenue)

Blv. *bulevar* (boulevard)

Calz. *calzada* (thoroughfare, main road)

Fco. Francisco (proper name, as in "Fco. Villa")

Fracc. *Fraccionamiento* (subdivision)

Nte. *norte* (north)

Ote. *oriente* (east)

Pte. *poniente* (west)

s/n *sin número* (no street number)

Spanish Phrasebook

Your Mexico adventure will be more fun if you use a little Spanish. Mexican folks, although they may smile at your funny accent, will appreciate your halting efforts to break the ice and transform yourself from a foreigner to a potential friend.

Spanish commonly uses 30 letters—the familiar English 26, plus four straightforward additions: ch, ll, ñ, and rr, which are explained in "Consonants," below.

PRONUNCIATION

Once you learn them, Spanish pronunciation rules—in contrast to English—don't change. Spanish vowels generally sound softer than in English. (Note: The capitalized syllables below receive stronger accents.)

Vowels

a like ah, as in "hah": **agua** AH-gooah (water), **pan** PAHN (bread), and **casa** CAH-sah (house)

e like ay, as in "may:" **mesa** MAY-sah (table), **tela** TAY-lah (cloth), and **de** DAY (of, from)

i like ee, as in "need": **diez** dee-AYZ (ten), **comida** ko-MEE-dah (meal), and **fin** FEEN (end)

o like oh, as in "go": **peso** PAY-soh (weight), **ocho** OH-choh (eight), and **poco** POH-koh (a bit)

u like oo, as in "cool": **uno** OO-noh (one), **cuarto** KOOAHR-toh (room), and **usted** oos-TAYD (you); when it follows a "q" the **u** is silent; when it follows an "h" or has an umlaut, it's pronounced like "w"

Consonants

b, d, f, k, l, m, n, p, q, s, t, v, w, x, y, z, and ch pronounced almost as in English; **h** occurs, but is silent–not pronounced at all.

c like k as in "keep": **cuarto** KOOAR-toh (room), Tepic tay-PEEK (capital of Nayarit state); when it precedes "e" or "i," pronounce **c** like s, as in "sit": **cerveza** sayr-VAY-sah (beer), **encima** ayn-SEE-mah (atop).

g like g as in "gift" when it precedes "a," "o," "u," or a consonant: **gato** GAH-toh (cat), **hago** AH-goh (I do, make); otherwise, pronounce **g** like h as in "hat": **giro** HEE-roh (money order), **gente** HAYN-tay (people)

j like h, as in "has": **Jueves** HOOAY-vays (Thursday), **mejor** may-HOR (better)

ll like y, as in "yes": **toalla** toh-AH-yah (towel), **ellos** AY-yohs (they, them)

ñ like ny, as in "canyon": **año** AH-nyo (year), **señor** SAY-nyor (Mr., sir)

r is lightly trilled, with tongue at the roof of your mouth like a very light English d, as in "ready": **pero** PAY-doh (but), **tres** TDAYS (three), **cuatro** KOOAH-tdoh (four).

rr like a Spanish r, but with much more emphasis and trill. Let your tongue flap. Practice with **burro** (donkey), **carretera** (highway), and Carrillo (proper name), then really let go with **ferrocarril** (railroad).

Note: The single small but common exception to all of the above is the pronunciation of Spanish **y** when it's being used as the Spanish word for "and," as in "Ron y Kathy." In such case, pronounce it like the English ee, as in "keep": Ron "ee" Kathy (Ron and Kathy).

Accent

The rule for accent, the relative stress given to syllables within a given word, is straightforward. If a word ends in a vowel, an n, or an s, accent the next-to-last syllable; if not, accent the last syllable.

Pronounce **gracias** GRAH-seeahs (thank you), **orden** OHR-dayn (order), and **carretera** kah-ray-TAY-rah (highway) with stress on the next-to-last syllable.

Otherwise, accent the last syllable: **venir** vay-NEER (to come), **ferrocarril** fay-roh-cah-REEL (railroad), and **edad** ay-DAHD (age).

Exceptions to the accent rule are always marked with an accent sign: (á, é, í, ó, or ú), such as **teléfono** tay-LAY-foh-noh (telephone), **jabón** hah-BON (soap), and **rápido** RAH-pee-doh (rapid).

BASIC AND COURTEOUS EXPRESSIONS

Most Spanish-speaking people consider formalities important. Whenever approaching anyone for information or some other reason, do not forget the appropriate salutation—good morning, good evening, etc. Standing alone, the greeting *hola* (hello) can sound brusque.

Hello. *Hola.*
Good morning. *Buenos días.*
Good afternoon. *Buenas tardes.*
Good evening. *Buenas noches.*
How are you? *¿Cómo está usted?*
Very well, thank you. *Muy bien, gracias.*
Okay; good. *Bien.*
Not okay; bad. *Mal or feo.*
So-so. *Más o menos.*
And you? *¿Y usted?*
Thank you. *Gracias.*
Thank you very much. *Muchas gracias.*
You're very kind. *Muy amable.*
You're welcome. *De nada.*
Goodbye. *Adios.*
See you later. *Hasta luego.*
please *por favor*
yes *sí*
no *no*
I don't know. *No sé.*
Just a moment, please. *Momentito, por favor.*
Excuse me, please (when you're trying to get attention). *Disculpe or Con permiso.*
Excuse me (when you've made a boo-boo). *Lo siento.*
Pleased to meet you. *Mucho gusto.*
How do you say . . . in Spanish? *¿Cómo se dice... en español?*
What is your name? *¿Cómo se llama usted?*
Do you speak English? *¿Habla usted inglés?*
Is English spoken here? (Does anyone here speak English?) *¿Se habla inglés?*
I don't speak Spanish well. *No hablo bien el español.*
I don't understand. *No entiendo.*
How do you say... in Spanish? *¿Cómo se dice... en español?*
My name is... *Me llamo...*
Would you like... *¿Quisiera usted...*
Let's go to... *Vamos a...*

TERMS OF ADDRESS

When in doubt, use the formal *usted* (you) as a form of address.

I *yo*
you (formal) *usted*
you (familiar) *tu*
he/him *él*
she/her *ella*
we/us *nosotros*
you (plural) *ustedes*
they/them *ellos (all males or mixed gender); ellas (all females)*
Mr., sir *señor*
Mrs., madam *señora*
miss, young lady *señorita*
wife *esposa*
husband *esposo*
friend *amigo (male); amiga (female)*
sweetheart *novio (male); novia (female)*
son; daughter *hijo; hija*
brother; sister *hermano; hermana*
father; mother *padre; madre*
grandfather; grandmother *abuelo; abuela*

TRANSPORTATION

Where is... ? *¿Dónde está... ?*
How far is it to... ? *¿A cuánto está... ?<@P>*
from... to... *de... a...*
How many blocks? *¿Cuántas cuadras?*
Where (Which) is the way to... ? *¿Dónde está el camino a... ?*
the bus station *la terminal de autobuses*
the bus stop *la parada de autobuses*
Where is this bus going? *¿Adónde va este autobús?*
the taxi stand *la parada de taxis*
the train station *la estación de ferrocarril*
the boat *el barco*
the airport *el aeropuerto*
I'd like a ticket to... *Quisiera un boleto a...*
first (second) class *primera (segunda) clase*
roundtrip *ida y vuelta*

reservation *reservación*
baggage *equipaje*
Stop here, please. *Pare aquí, por favor.*
the entrance *la entrada*
the exit *la salida*
the ticket office *la oficina de boletos*
(very) near; far *(muy) cerca; lejos*
to; toward *a*
by; through *por*
from *de*
the right *la derecha*
the left *la izquierda*
straight ahead *derecho; directo*
in front *en frente*
beside *al lado*
behind *atrás*
the corner *la esquina*
the stoplight *la semáforo*
a turn *una vuelta*
right here *aquí*
somewhere around here *por acá*
right there *allí*
somewhere around there *por allá*
street; boulevard *calle; bulevar*
highway *carretera*
bridge; toll *puente; cuota*
address *dirección*
north; south *norte; sur*
east; west *oriente (este); poniente (oeste)*

ACCOMMODATIONS

hotel *hotel*
Is there a room? *¿Hay cuarto?*
May I (may we) see it? *¿Puedo (podemos) verlo?*
What is the rate? *¿Cuál es el precio?*
Is that your best rate? *¿Es su mejor precio?*
Is there something cheaper? *¿Hay algo más económico?*
a single room *un cuarto sencillo*
a double room *un cuarto doble*
double bed *cama matrimonial*
twin beds *camas gemelas*
with private bath *con baño*
hot water *agua caliente*
shower *ducha*
towels *toallas*

soap *jabón*
toilet paper *papel higiénico*
blanket *frazada; manta*
sheets *sábanas*
air-conditioned–*aire acondicionado*
fan *abanico; ventilador*
key *llave*
manager *gerente*

FOOD

I'm hungry *Tengo hambre.*
I'm thirsty. *Tengo sed.*
menu *lista; menú*
order *orden*
glass *vaso*
fork *tenedor*
knife *cuchillo*
spoon *cuchara*
napkin *servilleta*
soft drink *refresco*
coffee *café*
tea *té*
drinking water *agua pura; agua potable*
bottled carbonated water *agua mineral*
bottled uncarbonated water *agua sin gas*
beer *cerveza*
wine *vino*
milk *leche*
juice *jugo*
cream *crema*
sugar *azúcar*
cheese *queso*
snack *antojo; botana*
breakfast *desayuno*
lunch *almuerzo*
daily lunch special *comida corrida (or el menú del día depending on region)*
dinner *comida (often eaten in late afternoon); cena (a late-night snack)*
the check *la cuenta*
eggs *huevos*
bread *pan*
salad *ensalada*
fruit *fruta*
mango *mango*
watermelon *sandía*
papaya *papaya*

banana *plátano*
apple *manzana*
orange *naranja*
lime *limón*
fish *pescado*
shellfish *mariscos*
shrimp *camarones*
meat (without) *(sin) carne*
chicken *pollo*
pork *puerco*
beef; steak *res; bistec*
bacon; ham *tocino; jamón*
fried *frito*
roasted *asada*
barbecue; barbecued *barbacoa; al carbón*

SHOPPING

money *dinero*
money-exchange bureau *casa de cambio*
I would like to exchange traveler's checks. *Quisiera cambiar cheques de viajero.*
What is the exchange rate? *¿Cuál es el tipo de cambio?*
How much is the commission? *¿Cuánto cuesta la comisión?*
Do you accept credit cards? *¿Aceptan tarjetas de crédito?*
money order *giro*
How much does it cost? *¿Cuánto cuesta?*
What is your final price? *¿Cuál es su último precio?*
expensive *−caro*
cheap *barato; económico*
more *más*
less *menos*
a little *un poco*
too much *demasiado*

HEALTH

Help me please. *Ayúdeme por favor.*
I am ill. *Estoy enfermo.*
Call a doctor. *Llame un doctor.*
Take me to . . . *Lléveme a . . .*
hospital *hospital; sanatorio*
drugstore *farmacia*
pain *dolor*

fever *fiebre*
headache *dolor de cabeza*
stomach ache *dolor de estómago*
burn *quemadura*
cramp *calambre*
nausea *náusea*
vomiting *vomitar*
medicine *medicina*
antibiotic *antibiótico*
pill; tablet *pastilla*
aspirin *aspirina*
ointment; cream *pomada; crema*
bandage *venda*
cotton *algodón*
sanitary napkins *use brand name, e.g., Kotex*
birth control pills *pastillas anticonceptivas*
contraceptive foam *espuma anticonceptiva*
condoms *preservativos; condones*
toothbrush *cepilla dental*
dental floss *hilo dental*
toothpaste *crema dental*
dentist *dentista*
toothache *dolor de muelas*

POST OFFICE AND COMMUNICATIONS

long-distance telephone *teléfono larga distancia*
I would like to call . . . *Quisiera llamar a . . .*
collect *por cobrar*
station to station *a quien contesta*
person to person *persona a persona*
credit card *tarjeta de crédito*
post office *correo*
general delivery *lista de correo*
letter *carta*
stamp *estampilla, timbre*
postcard *tarjeta*
aerogram *aerograma*
air mail *correo aereo*
registered *registrado*
money order *giro*
package; box *paquete; caja*
string; tape *cuerda; cinta*

AT THE BORDER

border *frontera*

customs *aduana*
immigration *migración*
tourist card *tarjeta de turista*
inspection *inspección; revisión*
passport *pasaporte*
profession *profesión*
marital status *estado civil*
single *soltero*
married; divorced *casado; divorciado*
widowed *viudado*
insurance *seguros*
title *título*
driver's license *licencia de manejar*

AT THE GAS STATION
gas station *gasolinera*
gasoline *gasolina*
unleaded *sin plomo*
full, please *lleno, por favor*
tire *llanta*
tire repair shop *vulcanizadora*
air *aire*
water *agua*
oil (change) *aceite (cambio)*
grease *grasa*
My . . . doesn't work. *Mi . . . no sirve.*
battery *batería*
radiator *radiador*
alternator *alternador*
generator *generador*
tow truck *grúa*
repair shop *taller mecánico*
tune-up *afinación*
auto parts store *refaccionería*

VERBS
Verbs are the key to getting along in Spanish. They employ mostly predictable forms and come in three classes, which end in *ar*, *er*, and *ir*, respectively:

to buy *comprar*
I buy, you (he, she, it) buys *compro, compra*
we buy, you (they) buy *compramos, compran*

to eat *comer*
I eat, you (he, she, it) eats *como, come*
we eat, you (they) eat *comemos, comen*

to climb *subir*
I climb, you (he, she, it) climbs *subo, sube*
we climb, you (they) climb *subimos, suben*

Got the idea? Here are more (with irregularities marked in **bold**).

to do or make *hacer*
I do or make, you (he she, it) does or makes *hago, hace*
we do or make, you (they) do or make *hacemos, hacen*

to go *ir*
I go, you (he, she, it) goes *voy, va*
we go, you (they) go *vamos, van*

to go (walk) *andar*
to love *amar*
to work *trabajar*
to want *desear, querer*
to need *necesitar*
to read *leer*
to write *escribir*
to repair *reparar*
to stop *parar*
to get off (the bus) *bajar*
to arrive *llegar*
to stay (remain) *quedar*
to stay (lodge) *hospedar*
to leave *salir (regular except for salgo, I leave)*
to look at *mirar*
to look for *buscar*
to give *dar (regular except for doy, I give)*
to carry *llevar*
to have *tener (irregular but important: tengo, tiene, tenemos, tienen)*
to come *venir (similarly irregular: vengo, viene, venimos, vienen)*

Spanish has two forms of "to be." Use *estar* when speaking of location or a temporary state of being: "I am at home." *"Estoy en casa."* "I'm sick." *"Estoy enfermo."* Use *ser* for a permanent state of being: "I am a doctor." *"Soy doctora."*

Estar **is regular except for** *estoy,* **I am.** *Ser* **is very irregular:**

to be *ser*
I am, you (he, she, it) is *soy, es*
we are, you (they) are *somos, son*

NUMBERS

zero *cero*
one *uno*
two *dos*
three *tres*
four *cuatro*
five *cinco*
six *seis*
seven *siete*
eight *ocho*
nine *nueve*
10 *diez*
11 *once*
12 *doce*
13 *trece*
14 *catorce*
15 *quince*
16 *dieciseis*
17 *diecisiete*
18 *dieciocho*
19 *diecinueve*
20 *veinte*
21 *veinte y uno or veintiuno*
30 *treinta*
40 *cuarenta*
50 *cincuenta*
60 *sesenta*
70 *setenta*
80 *ochenta*
90 *noventa*
100 *ciento*
101 *ciento y uno or cientiuno*
200 *doscientos*
500 *quinientos*
1,000 *mil*
10,000 *diez mil*
100,000 *cien mil*
1,000,000 *millón*
one half *medio*
one third *un tercio*
one fourth *un cuarto*

TIME

What time is it? *¿Qué hora es?*
It's one o'clock. *Es la una.*
It's three in the afternoon. *Son las tres de la tarde.*
It's 4 A.M. *Son las cuatro de la mañana.*
six-thirty *seis y media*
a quarter till eleven *un cuarto para las once*
a quarter past five *las cinco y cuarto*
an hour *una hora*

DAYS AND MONTHS

Monday *lunes*
Tuesday *martes*
Wednesday *miércoles*
Thursday *jueves*
Friday *viernes*
Saturday *sábado*
Sunday *domingo*
today *hoy*
tomorrow *mañana*
yesterday *ayer*
January *enero*
February *febrero*
March *marzo*
April *abril*
May *mayo*
June *junio*
July *julio*
August *agosto*
September *septiembre*
October *octubre*
November *noviembre*
December *diciembre*
a week *una semana*
a month *un mes*
after *después*
before *antes*

Suggested Reading

Some of these books are informative, others are entertaining, and all of them will increase your understanding of Mexico. Some are easier to find in Mexico than at home, and vice versa. Take a few along on your trip. If you find others that are especially noteworthy, let us know. Happy reading.

HISTORY

Brunk, Samuel. *Emiliano Zapata, Revolution and Betrayal in Mexico.* Albuquerque: University of New Mexico Press, 1995. A detailed narrative of the renowned revolutionary's turbulent life, from his humble birth in Anenecuilco village in Morelos, through his de facto control of Mexico City in 1914–1915, to his final betrayal and assassination in 1919. The author authoritatively demonstrates that Zapata, neither complete hero nor complete villain, was simply an incredibly determined native leader who paid the ultimate price in his selfless struggle for land and liberty for the campesinos of southern Mexico.

Calderón de la Barca, Fanny. *Life in Mexico, with New Material from the Author's Journals.* New York: Doubleday, 1966. Edited by H. T. and M. H. Fisher. An update of the brilliant, humorous, and celebrated original 1913 book by the Scottish wife of the Spanish ambassador to Mexico.

Casasola, Gustavo. *Seis Siglos de Historia Gráfica de Mexico (Six Centuries of Mexican Graphic History).* Mexico City: Editorial Gustavo Casasola, 1978. Six fascinating volumes of Mexican history in pictures, from 1325 to the present.

Collis, Maurice. *Cortés and Montezuma.* New York: New Directions Publishing Corp., 1999. A reprint of a 1954 classic piece of well-researched storytelling. Collis traces Cortés's conquest of Mexico through the defeat of his chief opponent, Aztec Emperor Moctezuma.

He uses contemporary eyewitnesses—notably Bernal Díaz de Castillo—to revivify one of histories greatest dramas.

Cortés, Hernán. *Letters From Mexico.* Translated by Anthony Pagden. New Haven, CT: Yale University Press, 1986. Cortés's five long letters to his king, in which he describes contemporary Mexico in fascinating detail, including, notably, the remarkably sophisticated life of the Aztecs at the time of the conquest.

Davies, Nigel. *Ancient Kingdoms of Mexico.* London: Penguin Books, 1982. An authoritative history of the foundations of Mexican civilization. Clearly traces the evolution of Mexico's five successive worlds—Olmec, Teotihuacán, Toltec, Aztec, and finally Spanish—that set the stage for present-day Mexico.

Díaz del Castillo, Bernal. *The True Story of the Conquest of Mexico.* Translated by Albert Idell. Garden City: Doubleday, 1956. A soldier's still-fresh tale of the conquest from the Spanish viewpoint.

Fernández, Miguel Ángel. *The China Galleon.* Translated by Debra Nagao. Photographs by Michel Zabé. Monterrey, Mexico: Vitro Corporativo, S.A. de C.V., 2000. This authoritatively researched, masterfully translated, and gorgeously illustrated coffee-table volume traces the colorful history of the Manila galleon, and consequently Acapulco, from the fall of Constantinople in A.D. 1453 to the present day. The author shows how the allure of Asia's aromatic spices, glistening lacquerware, smooth silks, glittering gold and gems, and radiant porcelains propelled the Spanish to realize Columbus's old dream and transform the Pacific into the Spanish lake that it remained for 300 years.

Garfias, Luis. *The Mexican Revolution.* Mexico City: Panorama Editorial, 1985. A concise

Mexican version of the 1910–1917 Mexican revolution, the crucible of present-day Mexico.

Gugliotta, Bobette. *Women of Mexico.* Encino, CA: Floricanto Press, 1989. Lively legends, tales, and biographies of remarkable Mexican women, from Zapotec princesses to Independence heroines.

León-Portilla, Miguel. *The Broken Spears: The Aztec Account of the Conquest of Mexico.* New York: Beacon Press, 1962. Provides an interesting contrast to Díaz del Castillo's account.

Meyer, Michael, and William Sherman. *The Course of Mexican History.* New York: Oxford University Press, 1991. An insightful, 700-plus-page college textbook in paperback. A bargain, especially if you can get it used.

Novas, Himlice. *Everything You Need to Know About Latino History.* New York: Plume Books (Penguin Group), 1994. Chicanos, Latin rhythm, La Raza, the Treaty of Guadalupe Hidalgo, and much more, interpreted from an authoritative Latino point of view.

Reed, John. *Insurgent Mexico.* New York: International Publisher's Co., 1994. Republication of 1914 original. Fast-moving, but not unbiased, description of the 1910 Mexican revolution by the journalist famed for his reporting of the subsequent 1917 Russian revolution. Reed, memorialized by the Soviets, was resurrected in the 1981 film biography *Reds.*

Ridley, Jasper. *Maximilian and Juárez.* New York: Ticknor and Fields, 1999. This authoritative historical biography breathes new life into one of Mexico's great ironic tragedies, a drama that pitted the native Zapotec "Lincoln of Mexico" against the dreamy, idealistic Archduke Maximilian of Austria-Hungary. Despite their common liberal ideas, they were drawn into a bloody no-quarter struggle that set the Old World against the New, ending in Maximilian's execution, the insanity of his wife, and the emergence of the United States as a power to be reckoned with in world affairs.

Ruíz, Ramon Eduardo. *Triumphs and Tragedy: A History of the Mexican People.* New York: W.W. Norton, Inc., 1992. A pithy, anecdote-filled history of Mexico from an authoritative Mexican-American perspective.

Simpson, Lesley Bird. *Many Mexicos.* Berkeley: The University of California Press, 1962. A much-reprinted, fascinating broad-brush version of Mexican history.

UNIQUE GUIDEBOOKS AND TIP BOOKS

American Automobile Association. *Mexico TravelBook.* Heathrow, FL: American Automobile Association, 2002. Short, sweet summaries of major Mexican tourist destinations and sights. Also includes information on fiestas, accommodations, restaurants, and a wealth of information relevant to car travel in Mexico. Available in bookstores, or free to AAA members at affiliate offices.

Church, Mike and Terry Church. *Traveler's Guide to Mexican Camping.* Livingston, TX: Rolling Homes Press (161 Rainbow Drive, #6157, Livingston, TX 77399-1061). This is an unusually thorough guide to trailer parks all over Mexico, with much coverage of the Pacific Coast. Detailed maps guide you accurately to each trailer park cited, and clear descriptions tell you what to expect. The book also provides very helpful information on car travel in Mexico, including details of insurance, border crossing, highway safety, car repairs, and much more.

Franz, Carl. *The People's Guide to Mexico.* Emeryville, CA: Avalon Travel Publishing, 12th edition, 2002. An entertaining and insightful general A to Z guide to the joys and pitfalls of independent economy travel in Mexico.

Graham, Scott. *Handle With Care: Guide to Socially Responsible Travel in Developing Countries.* Chicago: The Noble Press, 1991. Should you accept a meal from a family who lives in a grass house? This insightful guide answers this and hundreds of other tough questions for people who want to travel responsibly in the third world.

Guilford, Judith. *The Packing Book.* Berkeley: Ten Speed Press, third edition, 1998. The secrets of the carry-on traveler, or how to make everything you carry do double and triple duty. All for the sake of convenience, mobility, economy, and comfort.

Luboff, Ken. *Living Abroad in Mexico.* Emeryville, CA: Avalon Travel Publishing, 2005. A handy package of traveler's tools for living like a local in Mexico. Provides much general background and some specific details on settling (and perhaps making a living) in one of a number of Mexico's prime expatriate living areas, such as Puerto Vallarta, Lago Chapala, Cuernavaca, San Miguel de Allende, Zihuatanejo, and Acapulco.

Jeffrey, Nan. *Adventuring with Children.* Ashland, MA: Avalon House Publishing, 1995. This unusually detailed book starts where most travel-with-children books end. It contains, besides a wealth of information and practical strategies for general travel with children, specific chapters on how you can adventure—trek, kayak, river-raft, camp, bicycle, and much more—successfully with the kids in tow.

Mader, Ron. *Adventures in Nature Mexico.* Emeryville, CA: Avalon Travel Publishing, 1998. An internationally acknowledged expert on ecotravel in Latin America details dozens of environmentally sensitive adventure tours in Mexico. Destinations vary widely, from scuba diving off Cozumel and exploring lost Maya cities to jeeping through the Copper Canyon and rescuing turtle eggs on Oaxaca beaches.

Simmonds, David, ed. *The Mexico File.* La Jolla, CA: Simmonds Publications (5580 La Jolla Blvd., #306, La Jolla, CA 92037, U.S. tel./fax 858/456-4419 or toll-free U.S. tel. 800/563-9345 voice mail, www.mexicofile.com).

A monthly newsletter that, besides featuring pithy stories by Mexico travelers and news updates, offers an opportunity-packed classified section of Mexico vacations rentals, publications, services and much more. Subscriptions are $39/year.

Weisbroth, Ericka, and Eric Ellman. *Bicycling Mexico.* New York: Hunter, 1990. These intrepid adventurers describe bike trips from Puerto Vallarta to Acapulco, coastal and highland Oaxaca, and highland Jalisco and Michoacán.

Werner, David. *Where There Is No Doctor.* Berkeley, CA: Hesperian Foundation (1919 Addison St., Berkeley, CA 94704, toll-free U.S. tel. 888/729-1796, www.hesperian.org). How to keep well in the tropical backcountry.

Whipperman, Bruce. *Moon Handbooks Pacific Mexico.* Emeryville, CA: Avalon Travel Publishing, seventh edition, 2005. A wealth of information for traveling the Pacific Coast route, through Mazatlán, Guadalajara, and Puerto Vallarta, Ixtapa, and Zihuatanejo, to Acapulco and beyond.

FICTION AND POETRY

Bowen, David, and Juan A. Ascencio. *Pyramids of Glass.* San Antonio, TX: Corona Publishing Co., 1994. Two dozen or so stories that lead the reader along a month-long journey through the bedrooms, the barracks, the cafés, and streets of present-day Mexico.

Boyle, T.C. *The Tortilla Curtain.* New York: Penguin-Putnam, 1996; paperback edition, Raincoast Books, 1996. A chance intersection of the lives of two couples, one affluent and liberal Southern Californians, the other poor homeless illegal immigrants, forces all to come to grips with the real price of the American Dream.

De la Cruz, Sor Juana Inez. *Poems, Protest, and a Dream.* New York: Penguin, 1997. Masterful translation of collection of love and religious poems by the celebrated pioneer Mexican nun and feminist (1651–1695).

Doerr, Harriet. *Consider This, Señor*. New York: Harcourt Brace, 1993. Four expatriates tough it out in a small Mexican town, adapting to the excesses—blazing sun, driving rain, vast, untrammeled landscapes—meanwhile interacting with the local folks while the local folks observe them, with a mixture of fascination and tolerance.

Fuentes, Carlos. *Where the Air Is Clear*. New York: Farrar, Straus and Giroux, 1971. The seminal work of Mexico's celebrated novelist.

Fuentes, Carlos. *The Years with Laura Díaz*. Translated by Alfred MacAdam. New York: Farrar, Straus, and Giroux, 2000. A panorama of Mexico from independence to the 21st century, through the eyes of one woman, Laura Díaz, and her great-grandson, the author. As one reviewer said, since she ". . . as a Mexican woman, would like to celebrate Carlos Fuentes; it is worthy of applause that a man who has seen, observed, analyzed and criticized the great occurrences of the century now has a woman, Laura Díaz, speak for him."

Jennings, Gary. *Aztec*. New York: Atheneum, 1980. Beautifully researched and written monumental tale of lust, compassion, love, and death in preconquest Mexico.

Nickles, Sara, ed. *Escape to Mexico*. San Francisco: Chronicle Books, 2002. A carefully selected anthology of 20-odd stories of Mexico by renowned authors, from Steven Crane and W. Somerset Maugham to Anais Nin and David Lida, who all found inspiration, refuge, adventure, and much more, in Mexico.

Peters, Daniel. *The Luck of Huemac*. New York: Random House, 1981. An Aztec noble family's tale—of war, famine, sorcery, heroism, treachery, love, and finally disaster and death—in the Valley of Mexico.

Porter, Katherine Ann. *The Collected Stories*. New York: Delacorte, 1970.

Rulfo, Juan. *The Burning Plain*. Austin: University of Texas Press, 1967. Stories of people torn between the old and new in Mexico.

Rulfo, Juan. *Pedro Paramo*. Rulfo's acknowledged masterpiece, published last in 1980, established his renown. The author, thinly disguised as the protagonist, Juan Preciado, fulfills his mother's dying request by returning to his shadowy Jalisco hometown, Comala, in search of this father. Although Preciado discovers that his father, Pedro Páramo (whose surname implies "wasteland"), is long dead, Preciado's search resurrects his father's restless spirit, which recounts its horrific life tale of massacre, rape, and incest.

Traven, B. *The Treasure of the Sierra Madre*. New York: Hill and Wang, 1967. Campesinos, *federales,* gringos, and *indígenas* all figure in this modern morality tale set in Mexico's rugged outback. The most famous of the mysterious author's many novels of oppression and justice set in Mexico's jungles.

Villaseñor, Victor. *Rain of Gold*. New York: Delta Books (Bantam, Doubleday, and Dell), 1991. The moving, best-selling epic of the author's family's gritty travails. From humble rural beginnings in the Copper Canyon, they flee revolution and certain death, struggling through parched northern deserts to sprawling border refugee camps. From there they migrate to relative safety and an eventual modicum of happiness in Southern California.

PEOPLE AND CULTURE

Berrin, Kathleen. *The Art of the Huichol Indians.* New York: Harry N. Abrams Publishing, 1978. Lovely, large photographs and text by a symposium of experts provide a good interpretive introduction to Huichol art and culture.

Castillo, Ana. *Goddess of the Americas.* New York: Riverhead Books, 1996. Here, a noted author has selected from the works of seven interpreters about Mesoameriacan female deities; and whose visions range as far and wide as Sex Goddess, the Broken-Hearted, the Subversive, and the Warrior Queen.

Lewis, Oscar. *Children of Sanchez.* New York: Random House, 1961. Poverty and strength in the Mexican underclass, sympathetically described and interpreted by renowned sociologist Lewis.

Medina, Sylvia López. *Cantora.* New York: Ballantine Books, 1992. Fascinated by the stories of her grandmother, aunt, and mother, the author seeks her own center by discovering a past that she thought she wanted to forget.

Meyerhoff, Barbara. *Peyote Hunt: The Sacred Journey of the Huichol Indians.* Ithaca, NY: Cornell University Press, 1974. A description and interpretation of the Huichol's religious use of mind-bending natural hallucinogens.

Palmer, Colin A. *Slaves of the White God.* Cambridge, MA: Harvard University Press, 1976. A scholarly study of why and how Spanish colonial authorities imported African slaves into America and how they were used afterward. Replete with poignant details, taken from Spanish and Mexican archives, describing how the Africans struggled from bondage to eventual freedom.

Riding, Alan. *Distant Neighbors: A Portrait of the Mexicans.* New York: Random House Vintage Books, 1985. Rare insights into Mexico and Mexicans.

Toor, Frances. *A Treasury of Mexican Folkways.* New York: Crown Books, 1947, reprinted by Bonanza, 1985. An illustrated encyclopedia of vanishing Mexicana—costumes, religion, fiestas, burial practices, customs, legends—compiled during the celebrated author's 35 years of residence in Mexico.

Wauchope, Robert, ed. *Handbook of Middle American Indians.* Vols. 7 and 8. Austin: University of Texas Press, 1969. Authoritative surveys of important Indian-speaking groups in northern and central (vol. 8) and southern (vol. 7) Mexico.

FLORA AND FAUNA

Goodson, Gar. *Fishes of the Pacific Coast.* Stanford, CA: Stanford University Press, 1988. More than 500 beautifully detailed color drawings highlight this pocket version of all you ever wanted to know about the ocean's fishes (including common Spanish names) from Alaska to Peru.

Howell, Steve N. G. *Bird-Finding Guide to Mexico.* Ithaca, NY: Cornell University Press, 1999. A unique portable guide for folks who really want to see birds in Mexico. Unlike other bird books, the author presents a unique and authoritative site guide, with dozens of clear maps and lists of birds seen at sites all over Mexico. Pacific sites include Mazatlán, San Blas, Puerto Vallarta, El Tuito, Manzanillo, Oaxaca, and many more. Use this book along with Howell and Webb's *A Guide to the Birds of Mexico and North America.*

Howell, Steve N. G., and Sophie Webb. *A Guide to the Birds of Mexico and Northern America.* Oxford: Oxford University Press, 1995. All the serious birder needs to know about Mexico's rich species treasury. Includes authoritative habitat maps and 70 excellent color plates that detail the male and females of about 1,500 species.

Leopold, Starker. *Wildlife of Mexico.* Berkeley: University of California Press, 1959. Classic, illustrated layperson's survey of common Mexican mammals and birds.

Mason Jr., Charles T., and Patricia B. Mason. *Handbook of Mexican Roadside Flora.* Tucson: University of Arizona Press, 1987. Authoritative identification guide, with line illustrations, of all the plants you're likely to see in the Acapulco region.

Morris, Percy A. *A Field Guide to Pacific Coast Shells.* Boston: Houghton Mifflin, 1974. The complete beachcomber's Pacific shell guide.

Pesman, M. Walter. *Meet Flora Mexicana.* Delightful anecdotes and illustrations of hundreds of common Mexican plants. Published around 1960, now out of print.

Peterson, Roger Tory, and Edward L. Chalif. *Field Guide to Mexican Birds.* Boston: Houghton Mifflin, 1999. With hundreds of Peterson's crisp color drawings, this is a must for serious birders and vacationers interested in the life that teems in the Acapulco region's beaches, forests, and lagoons.

Wright, N. Pelham. *A Guide to Mexican Mammals and Reptiles.* Mexico City: Minutiae Mexicana, 1989. Pocket-edition lore, history, descriptions, and pictures of commonly seen Mexican animals.

ART, ARCHITECTURE, AND CRAFTS

Baird, Joseph. *The Churches of Mexico.* Berkeley, CA: University of California Press, 1962. Mexican colonial architecture and art, illustrated and interpreted.

Cordrey, Donald, and Dorothy Cordrey. *Mexican Indian Costumes.* Austin: University of Texas Press, 1968. A lovingly photographed, written, and illustrated classic on Mexican Indians and their dress, emphasizing textiles.

Covarrubias, Miguel. *Indian Art of Mexico and Central America.* New York: Knopf, 1957. A timeless work by the renowned interpreter of *indígena* art and design.

Martínez Penaloza, Porfirio. *Popular Arts of Mexico.* Mexico City: Editorial Panorama, 1981. An excellent, authoritative, pocket-size exposition of Mexican art.

Morrill, Penny C., and Carol A. Berk. *Mexican Silver.* Atglen, PA: Shiffer Publishing Co. (4880 Lower Valley Road, Atglen, PA 19310), August 2001. Lovingly written and photographed exposition of the Mexican silvercraft of Taxco, Guerrero, revitalized through the initiative of Frederick Davis and William Spratling in the 1920s and 1930s. Color photos of many beautiful, museum-quality pieces supplement the text, which describes the history and work of a score of silversmithing families who developed the Taxco craft under Spratling's leadership. Greatly adds to the traveler's appreciation of the beautiful Taxco silvercrafts widely available in Taxco, Acapulco, Ixtapa, and Zihuatanejo.

Mullen, Robert James. *Architecture and Its Sculpture in Viceregal Mexico.* Austin: University of Texas Press, 1997. The essential work of Mexican colonial-era cathedrals and churches. In this lovingly written and illustrated life work, Mullen breathes new vitality into New Spain's preciously glorious colonial architectural legacy.

Sayer, Chloë. *Arts and Crafts of Mexico.* San Francisco: Chronicle Books, 1990. All you ever wanted to know about your favorite Mexican crafts, from papier-mâché to pottery and toys and Taxco silver. Beautifully illustrated by traditional etchings and David Lavender's crisp black-and-white and color photographs.

Internet Resources

A number of websites offer plenty of information to help prepare for your Acapulco-Ixtapa-Zihuatanejo adventure.

GENERAL TRAVEL

U.S. Department of State
www.state.gov/travel

The U.S. State Department's very complete information website. Lots of subheadings and links to a swarm of topics, including Mexican consular offices in the United States, U.S. consular offices in Mexico, travel advisories, and links to other government information, such as importation of food, plants, and animals; U.S. customs; health abroad; airlines; and exchange rates.

Travel Insurance Services
www.travelinsure.com

This site is good for worldwide travel insurance and other services.

World Travel Center
www.worldtravelcenter.com

Another good site for traveler's insurance.

Sanborns Insurance
www.sanbornsinsurance.com

Site of the long-time, very reliable Mexico auto insurance agency, with the only north-of-the-border adjustment procedure. Get your quote online, order their many useful publications, and find out about other insurance you many have forgotten.

SPECIALTY TRAVEL

Elderhostel, Inc.
www.elderhostel.org

This Boston-based nonprofit organization has a very sizable catalog of ongoing study tours, many in the Mexican Pacific states.

Mobility International
www.miusa.org

A wonderfully organized and complete site, with a flock of services for travelers with disabilities, including many people-to-people connections in Mexico.

Purple Roofs
www.purpleroofs.com

One of the best general gay travel websites, based in San Francisco. It offers details of about six gay and lesbian-friendly Acapulco and Zihuatanejo hotels, in addition to a wealth of gay-friendly travel-oriented links worldwide.

HOME EXCHANGE

International Home
Exchange Network
www.homexchange.com

Offers resources for temporarily trading your home with someone else in dozens of places in the world, including Acapulco, Ixtapa, and Zihuatanejo.

Intervac
www.intervacus.com

Another great resource for listing your home and browsing others for a temporary property swap.

HomeLink International
www.homelink.org

HomeLink offers property exchange listings in a variety of countries.

GENERAL MEXICO

Visit Mexico
www.visitmexico.com

The official website of the public-private Mexico Tourism Board; a good general site for official information, such as entry requirements. It has lots of summarily informative subheadings, not unlike an abbreviated guidebook. If you can't find what you want here, and you can read a bit of Spanish, visit www.cptm.com.mx, the more detailed Mexican version of the same website, or call the toll-free tel. 800/44-MEXICO (800/446-3942), or email contact@visitmexico.com.

Mexico Online
www.mexonline.com

Very extensive, well-organized site with many subheadings and links to Mexico's large and medium destinations, and even some to small destinations. For example, Ixtapa and Zihuatanejo is typical, with manifold links, including about many dozens of accommodations, from luxury hotels to modest bed-and-breakfasts. It's an excellent resource.

Mexconnect
www.mexconnect.com

An extensive Mexico site, with dozens upon dozens of subheadings and links, especially helpful for folks thinking of traveling, working, living, or retiring in Mexico.

Mexico Desconocido
www.mexicodesconocido.com.mx

The site of the excellent magazine *Mexico Desconocido* (Undiscovered Mexico) that mostly features unusual and off-the-beaten-track destinations, many in the Acapulco region. Accesses a large library of past articles, which are not unlike a Mexican version of *National Geographic Traveler.* Click the small "English" button at the top to translate. Excellent, hard-to-find information, with good English translation.

Planeta
www.planeta.com

Life project of Latin America's dean of ecotourism, Ron Mader, who furnishes a comprehensive clearinghouse of everything ecologically correct, from rescuing turtle eggs in Jalisco to preserving cloud forests in Peru. Contains dozens of subheadings competently linked for maximum speed. For example, check out the Mexico travel directory for ecojourneys, maps, information networks, parks, regional guides, and a mountain more.

HOTEL, CONDO, AND APARTMENT RENTALS

1st Choice Vacation Rentals
www.choice1.com

An excellent site for picking a vacation rental house, condo, or villa, with information and reservations links to individual owners. Prices vary from moderate to luxurious. Coverage extends to a number of Acapulco-region resorts, including Acapulco, Zihuatanejo, Ixtapa, Troncones, and Taxco.

Owner Direct Vacation Rentals
www.ownerdirect.com

An extensive vacation rental site with about half a dozen links to many Mexico destinations, including Acapulco, Ixtapa, and Zihuatanejo condo, house, and villa rentals.

Mexico Travel Net
www.mexicotravelnet.com

Good source of upscale hotel specials in Acapulco, Ixtapa, and Zihuatanejo.

Condo Villa Hotel World
www.villaworld.com

Lists several upscale condos and villas in Acapulco and Zihuatanejo.

DESTINATIONS

Acapulco Convention and Visitors Bureau
www.visitacapulco.com.mx

This site broadly covers the ground from sightseeing and shopping to hotels and transportation. The information is usually available via links to individual providers' websites, with quick email contact for services and hotel bookings.

Acapulco Heat
www.acabtu.com.mx

Website of the former tourist newspaper *Acapulco Heat* that now has gone electronic. It provides useful links (all in Spanish) to many mid-scale hotels, rental condos, houses, apartments, real estate agencies, restaurants, community events and organizations, travel activities, and entertainments.

Zihuatanejo.net
www.zihuatanejo.net

A top-notch, very complete, and well-maintained commercial site, listing nearly everywhere to stay (with reservation and email links) and dine, everything to do, and much more in Zihuatanejo, Ixtapa, Troncones, and Barra de Potosí. In English or Spanish. Excellent.

Zihua.net
www.zihua.net

Similar to, but smaller than, www.zihuatanejo.net, this site (along with its twin, www.ixtapa.net) nevertheless has lots of useful, mostly commercial, information and links.

Zihuantanejo Rentals
www.zihuatanejo-rentals.com

The site of savvy local resident Leigh Roth, who lists (with gorgeous photos) several high-end (and a few moderately priced) condo, apartment, and villa rental options, most near Playas La Madera and La Ropa. She also includes informative sections on restaurants, shopping, activities, personal anecdotes ("Who's Been to Huautla de Jiménez?"), and stories.

Ixtapa-Zihuatanejo.com
www.ixtapa-zihuatanejo.com

The official site of Ixtapa and Zihuatanejo government tourism bureaus, with listings (but sparse details) of many hotels, villas, bungalows, restaurants (by food category), tours, sports, and more. At this writing, however, a number of links lead to dead ends. Although it was not possible to book all hotel reservations directly, hotel email and web links to many hotel websites were available.

Troncones
www.troncones.com.mx

Good site, especially for hotels, with many links to Troncones's small beachfront hotels and bed-and-breakfasts. Also links to a number of restaurants, services, real estate, and much more.

Troncones.net
www.troncones.net

A good alternative to www.troncones.com.mx, also with several hotel, bed-and-breakfast, restaurant, and activities links.

Barra de Potosí
www.barra-potosi.com

A good site, with several links to Barra de Potosí bed-and-breakfasts, hotels, activities and services.

Index

ARCHAEOLOGICAL SITES

C

HANDICRAFTS

WILDLIFE-VIEWING

www.moon.com

For helpful advice on planning a trip, visit www.moon.com for the **TRAVEL PLANNER** and get access to useful travel strategies and valuable information about great places to visit. When you travel with Moon, expect an experience that is uncommon and truly unique.

MAP SYMBOLS

≈≈≈ Expressway	**◖** Highlight	✗ Airfield	⚲ Golf Course
Primary Road	○ City/Town	✈ Airport	**P** Parking Area
Secondary Road	◉ State Capital	▲ Mountain	⛢ Archaeological Site
- - - - Unpaved Road	⊛ National Capital	✚ Unique Natural Feature	⚱ Church
------- Trail	★ Point of Interest		⛽ Gas Station
·········· Ferry	● Accommodation	⚘ Waterfall	Glacier
─┼─┼─ Railroad	▾ Restaurant/Bar	▲ Park	Mangrove
≈≈≈ Pedestrian Walkway	▪ Other Location	⬛ Trailhead	Reef
▥ Stairs	Δ Campground	⛷ Skiing Area	Swamp

CONVERSION TABLES

°C = (°F - 32) / 1.8
°F = (°C x 1.8) + 32
1 inch = 2.54 centimeters (cm)
1 foot = 0.304 meters (m)
1 yard = 0.914 meters
1 mile = 1.6093 kilometers (km)
1 km = 0.6214 miles
1 fathom = 1.8288 m
1 chain = 20.1168 m
1 furlong = 201.168 m
1 acre = 0.4047 hectares
1 sq km = 100 hectares
1 sq mile = 2.59 square km
1 ounce = 28.35 grams
1 pound = 0.4536 kilograms
1 short ton = 0.90718 metric ton
1 short ton = 2,000 pounds
1 long ton = 1.016 metric tons
1 long ton = 2,240 pounds
1 metric ton = 1,000 kilograms
1 quart = 0.94635 liters
1 US gallon = 3.7854 liters
1 Imperial gallon = 4.5459 liters
1 nautical mile = 1.852 km

MOON ACAPULCO, IXTAPA & ZIHUATANEJO

AVALON
publishing group incorporated

Avalon Travel Publishing
An Imprint of
Avalon Publishing Group, Inc.

1400 65th Street, Suite 250
Emeryville, CA 94608, USA
www.moon.com

Editor: Elizabeth McCue
Series Manager: Kathryn Ettinger
Acquisitions Manager: Rebecca K. Browning
Copy Editor: Amy Scott
Graphics Coordinator: Elizabeth Jang
Production Coordinators: Elizabeth Jang,
 Darren Alessi
Cover & Interior Designer: Gerilyn Attebery
Map Editor: Kat Smith
Cartographers: Christine Markiewicz, Kat Bennett
Cartography Manager: Mike Morgenfeld
Indexer: Rachel Kuhn

ISBN-10: 1-56691-980-0
ISBN-13: 978-1-56691-980-7
ISSN: 1548-8012

Printing History
1st Edition – 2004
2nd Edition – October 2006
5 4 3 2 1

KEEPING CURRENT

If you have a favorite gem you'd like to see included in the next edition, or see anything
that needs updating, clarification, or correction, please drop us a line. Send your
comments via email to feedback@moon.com, or use the address above.